the WARS of
the ROSES

Hugh Bicheno was awarded a first class degree in History at Cambridge. He later joined SIS (MI6) and later still spent many years working as a kidnap and ransom negotiator, mainly in Latin America. His previous books include *Crescent and Cross: The Battle of Lepanto, 1571* (2003), *Razor's Edge: The Unofficial History of the Falklands War* (2006) and *Elizabeth's Sea Dogs* (2012).

Also by Hugh Bicheno:

Gettysburg

Midway

Crescent and Cross: The Battle of Lepanto, 1571

Rebels and Redcoats: The American Revolutionary War

Razor's Edge: The Unofficial History of the Falklands War

Vendetta: High Art and Low Cunning at the Birth of the Renaissance

Elizabeth's Sea Dogs: How the English Became the Scourge of the Seas

the WARS of the ROSES

THE BLOODY STRUGGLE FOR ENGLAND'S THRONE

HUGH BICHENO

HEAD of ZEUS

An Apollo Book

First published separately as *Battle Royal* (2015) and *Blood Royal* (2016)
This revised and updated edition first published in the UK
in 2019 by Apollo, an imprint of Head of Zeus Ltd

9 7 5 3 1 2 4 6 8

A catalogue record for this book is available from
the British Library.

ISBN (PB): 9781789544725
ISBN (E): 9781789544732

Printed and bound in Great Britain by
CPI Group (UK) Ltd, Croydon CR0 4YY

Head of Zeus Ltd
First Floor East
5–8 Hardwick Street
London EC1R 4RG

WWW.HEADOFZEUS.COM

To Jack and Isabella
Ruan, Sebastian and Tiago
with a grandfather's love

CONTENTS

PART II

APPENDICES

MAPS

──────────── TABLES ────────────

──────────── FAMILY TREES ────────────

PROTAGONISTS
AND MARRIAGES

PRECURSORS

Beauchamp, Richard (1382–1439), 13th Earl of Warwick. Dominant lord in south Wales and west Midlands. Married (1st) Elizabeth Berkeley and (both 2nd) Isabel Despenser.

Beauchamp, Richard (d.1422), 1st Earl of Worcester and 2nd Baron Bergavenny. Welsh Marcher lord. First husband of Isabel Despenser. Sole heir married Edward Neville (see Yorkists).

Beaufort, Henry (d.1447), Cardinal Archbishop of Winchester.

Beaufort, Joan (d.1440). Her marriage to Ralph Neville created much of the tinder for the Wars of the Roses.

Beaufort, John (1404–44), 1st Duke of Somerset. Married Margaret Beauchamp of Bletsoe.

Bedford, John (1389–1435), Duke of. Brother of Henry V. Heirless.

Gloucester, Humphrey (1390–1447), Duke of. Brother of Henry V. Heirless.

Montacute, Thomas (1388–1428), 4th Earl of Salisbury. Sole heir Alice married Richard Neville (see Yorkists).

Mowbray, John (1415–61), 3rd Duke of Norfolk, also Earl of Nottingham and Surrey. Nationwide landowner, main holdings in East Anglia diluted by the dower of his mother Katherine née Neville. Married Eleanor, sister of Henry, John, Thomas and William Bourchier.

Neville, Ralph (1364–1425), 1st Earl of Westmorland. His second marriage to Joan Beaufort created much of the tinder for the Wars of the Roses.

Pole, William de la (1396–1450), 1st Duke of Suffolk. East Anglian and, through marriage to Alice Chaucer, Oxfordshire lord. Chief minister of Henry VI until 1450.

Valois, Catherine de (1401–37), dowager queen. Henry VI's mother. Lover of Owen Tudor.

YORKISTS & LANCASTRIANS

Angus, Earl of – see Douglas, Black and Red.

Anjou, Marguerite d' (1430–82), Henry VI's queen, mother of Edward of Westminster and heroic leader of the Lancastrians.

Anjou, René d' (d.1480), Duke of. Failed claimant to kingdoms of Naples and Aragon, indifferent father of Marguerite.

Arundel, Earl of – see FitzAlan.

Audley, Lord – see Tuchet.

Austria, Archduke Maximilian of (d.1519), heir of Emperor Frederick III of Habsburg, married Duchess Marie of Burgundy.

Beauchamp, Anne (1426–92), 16th Countess of Warwick by right. Married Richard Neville, the Kingmaker. See Appendix F.

Beauchamp, Eleanor (1408–67). Daughter of Richard and Elizabeth Berkeley. Dowager Baroness Roos, mother of Thomas, 9th Baron Roos. Married (2nd) Edmund Beaufort. See Appendix F.

Beauchamp, Elizabeth (1415–48), 3rd Baroness Bergavenny by right. Sole heir of Richard and Isabel Despenser. Married Edward Neville. See Appendix F.

Beauchamp, Elizabeth (1417–80). Daughter of Richard and Elizabeth Berkeley. Married George, dubious Baron Latimer, son of Ralph Neville and Joan Beaufort. See Appendix F.

Beauchamp, Margaret (1404–67). Daughter of Richard and Elizabeth Berkeley. Married John Talbot, 1st Earl of Shrewsbury. See Appendix F.

Beauchamp of Bletsoe, Margaret (1405–82). Wealthy Bedfordshire, Wiltshire and Dorset landowner. Married (2nd) John Beaufort, by whom Margaret Beaufort, and (3rd) Lionel, 6th Baron Welles.

Beaufort, Edmund (1406–55), 2nd Duke of Somerset. Lieutenant of Normandy. Younger brother and heir of John. Added estates in Gloucestershire, Denbigh and Isle of Wight. Married Eleanor Beauchamp.

Beaufort, Edmund (d.1471), styled Duke of Somerset, Henry's younger brother.

Beaufort, Henry (1436–64), 3rd Duke of Somerset. Eldest son of Edmund and Eleanor Beauchamp. Devoted Lancastrian.

Beaufort, John (d.1471), styled Marquess of Dorset. Henry's youngest brother.

Beaufort, Margaret (1443–1509), daughter of John. Married (1) Edmund Tudor, Earl of Richmond, by whom mother of Henry VII; (2) Henry Stafford, younger son of the Duke of Buckingham; (3) Thomas, Baron Stanley.

Beaujeu, Anne of (d.1522), eldest daughter of Louis XI, regent for Charles VIII.

Beaumont, John (1410–60), 1st Viscount. East Midlands and East Anglian lord. Lifelong friend of Henry VI. Married (2nd) Katherine Neville, dowager Duchess of Norfolk.

Beaumont, William (d.1507), Viscount. Son of John's first marriage. Unjustly attainted Lancastrian.

Bedford, Duchess/Duke of – see Luxembourg, Jacquetta de/ Neville, George.

Bellingham, Henry (d.1484), one of the last Lancastrian knights to submit.

Bergavenny, Lord – see Neville.

Berkeley, William (d.1492), Lord Berkeley/Earl of Nottingham. Victor over Viscount Lisle at Nibley Green.

Berners, Lord – see Bourchier, John.

Berry, Charles (d.1472), Duke of. Troublesome younger brother of Louis XI.

Blount, Walter (d.1474), Lord Mountjoy. Married widow of 1st Duke of Buckingham.

Bonville, Cecily (d.1529), Baroness Bonville and Harington by right. Wealthiest heiress in England, married Thomas Grey, Marquess of Dorset.

Bonville, William (1392–1461), 1st Baron. West Country magnate. Married (1st) Margaret, sister of Edmund, Lord Grey of Ruthyn, and (2nd) Elizabeth Courtenay, daughter of the 3rd Earl of Devon. Initially Lancastrian, he became Yorkist through alliance with the Nevilles.

Bonville, William (d.1460), Eldest son of 1st Baron Bonville and Margaret Grey. Married Elizabeth, heir to the barony of Harington in Dorset.

Bonville, William (1442–60), 6th Baron Harington. Son of William Bonville and Elizabeth Harington. Married Katherine, daughter of Richard Neville and Alice Montacute.

Booth, Laurence (d.1480), Prince-Bishop of Durham, Lord Chancellor and Archbishop of York.

Booth, William (d.1464), Archbishop of York, older half-brother of Laurence.

Boteler, Lady Eleanor (d.1467), née Talbot, mistress of Edward IV.

Boteler, Ralph (1394–1473), 1st Baron Sudeley. Lord Treasurer 1443–6. Gloucestershire lord. Member of William de la Pole's affinity. His only son Thomas, who predeceased him, was married to Eleanor, daughter of John Talbot, 1st Earl of Shrewsbury, who was later betrothed to Edward IV.

Bourchier, Edward (d.1539), Lord FitzWarin.

Bourchier, Eleanor (d.1474), dowager Duchess of Norfolk, Henry's sister.

Bourchier, Henry (d.1483), 1st Viscount Bourchier, Earl of Essex, Lord Treasurer. Married Isabel, Richard of York's only sister. Uncle of Edward IV by marriage.

Bourchier, Humphrey (d.1471), Lord Cromwell, Henry's son.

Bourchier, Humphrey (d.1471), son of Lord Berners.

Bourchier, John (d.1474), 1st Baron Berners. Younger brother of Henry and William, older brother of Thomas and of Eleanor, Duchess of Norfolk.

Bourchier, John (d.1495), Lord Ferrers of Groby by marriage, Henry's son.

Bourchier, John (d.1539), Lord FitzWarin. Youthful supporter of Henry Tudor.

Bourchier, Thomas (d.1486), Cardinal Archbishop of Canterbury, Henry's younger brother.

Bourchier, William (d.1470), Lord FitzWarin by marriage, Henry's brother.

Bourchier, William (d.1480), Viscount Bourchier, Henry's heir, married Anne Woodville. Their son inherited the earldom of Essex.

Bracher, William (d.1485), Yeoman of the Crown. He betrayed his comrades.

Brackenbury, Robert (d.1485), Gloucester retainer, Constable of the Tower of London.

Bray, Reginald (d.1503), Confidential courier of Lady Margaret Beaufort, built Henry VII Chapel, Westminster Abbey.

Bromflete, Henry (1412–69), 1st Baron Vescy. Father-in-law of Thomas, 8th Baron Clifford.

Brooke, Edward (d.1464), 6th Baron Cobham. Kent lord. Married Elizabeth, daughter of James Tuchet.

Brooke, John (d.1512), Lord Cobham. Devoted Yorkist.

Brugge, Lodewijk van (d.1492), lord of Gruuthuse, made Earl of Winchester for helping Edward IV recover the throne.

Buckingham – see Stafford.

Burgh, Thomas (d.1496), lord of Gainsborough, Edward IV's Master of the Horse.

Butler, James (1420–61), 1st Earl of Wiltshire, later 5th Earl of Ormonde. Estates in the West Country, Gloucestershire, Staffordshire, Oxfordshire and Cambridgeshire. Close friend of Henry VI. Married Eleanor, daughter of Edmund Beaufort and Eleanor Beauchamp.

Butler, John (d.1478), Earl of Ormond in Ireland.

Catesby, William (d.1485), betrayer of Lord Hastings, close confederate of Richard III.

Chaucer, Alice (1404–75), dowager Duchess of Salisbury. East Anglian and Oxfordshire landowner. Married William de la Pole. Their son first betrothed to John Beaufort's daughter Margaret, later married Elizabeth, Richard of York's second daughter.

Clapham, John (d.1470), Midlands esquire of the body to the Kingmaker.

Clarence, George (d.1478), Duke of. Treacherous younger brother of Edward IV; married Isabel Neville, the Kingmaker's elder daughter.

Clifford, Thomas (1414–55), 8th Baron. Northern lord. Married Joan, daughter of 6th Baron Dacre.

Clifford, John (1435–61), 9th Baron. Married Margaret, sole heir of Lord Vescy.

Clinton, John (1410–64), 5th Baron. Northamptonshire and Staffordshire lord. Married Joan, daughter of 5th Baron Ferrers of Chartley.

Cobham – see Brooke.

Conyers, John (d.1489), steward of Middleham for the Kingmaker and Richard of Gloucester.

Cooke, Thomas (d.1478), London draper and alderman, Lord Mayor in 1462. Persecuted by Edward IV.

Corbet, Richard (d.1493), Shropshire knight, fought for Henry Tudor.

Courtenay of Bocconoc, Hugh (d.1471), cousin of the Earls of Devon. Lancastrian, son Edward fought for Henry Tudor and made Earl of Devon.

Courtenay of Powderham, brothers William, Walter and Humphrey. Opponents of their cousins the Earls of Devon, members of Clarence's affinity.

Courtenay, Elizabeth (d.1493), widow of James Luttrell and Humphrey Tuchet, both killed fighting for Lancaster, godmother to Clarence's son.

Courtenay, Henry (d.1469), heir to the attainted earldom of Devon. Judicially murdered.

Courtenay, John (d.1471), restored as Earl of Devon in 1470.

Courtenay, Peter (d.1492), Bishop of Exeter. Fought for Henry Tudor

Courtenay, Thomas (1414–58), 13th Earl of Devon. West Country magnate. Married Margaret, sister of John and Edmund Beaufort. Initially strongly Yorkist he became Lancastrian when York allied with the Nevilles, allies of his deadly rival William Bonville.

Courtenay, Thomas (1432–61), 14th Earl of Devon. West Country magnate. See entry for his namesake father under Yorkists. Married Marie of Anjou, illegitimate daughter of Charles, Count of Maine, Queen Marguerite's uncle.

Cromwell, Baron – see Bourchier.

Cromwell, Ralph (d.1456), 3rd Baron. Rapacious east Midlands lord.

Dacre – see Fiennes.

Dacre, Humphrey (d.1485), heir to attainted Dacre of the North barony, restored 1473.

Dacre of the North, Randolph (1412–1461), 1st Baron. Scots Marcher lord. Son of 6th Baron Dacre. Henry VI created new title for him after the barony went with his niece to Yorkist Richard Fiennes.

Daubeney, Giles (d.1508), leading 1483 rebel, later Lord Daubeney.

Devereux, Walter (1432–85), 7th Baron Ferrers of Chartley by marriage. Lands around Weobley, Herefordshire, and in Staffordshire, Leicestershire and Lincolnshire. York retainer. Lifelong Yorkist, supporter of Richard III.

Devon – see Stafford of Southwyck and Courtenay.

Dorset, Marquess of – see Beaufort and Grey.

Douglas, Archibald 'Bell the Cat' (d.1513), Red Earl of Angus.

Douglas, George (d.1463), Red Earl of Angus.

Douglas, James (d.1488), last Black Earl of Angus.

Dudley – see Sutton.

Duras, Gaillard (d.1481), lord of. Narbonnais exile, loyal Yorkist, Governor of Calais.

Dynham, John (d.1501), Lord, comrade-in-arms of Edward IV, Lord Treasurer.

Edward of Westminster (1453–71), Prince of Wales. Son of Henry VI and Marguerite d'Anjou.

Edward IV (1442–83), King of England, son of Richard of York and Cecily Neville, married Elizabeth Woodville. Formerly the Earl of March.

Edward V (d.1483), briefly King of England.

Edward of Middleham (d.1484), Prince of Wales, Richard III's son.

Edward of Westminster (d.1471), Prince of Wales, Henry VI's son, married Anne Neville.

Essex, Earl of – see Bourchier.

Exeter, Duke of – see Holland.

Fauconberg, Bastard of – see Neville.

Fauconberg, Lord – see Neville.

Ferrers of Chartley, Lord – see Devereux and Clinton.

Ferrers of Groby, Elizabeth (d.1483), Baroness by right, mother of Elizabeth Woodville's first husband John Grey, married (2) John Bourchier.

Fiennes, James (1390–1450), 1st Baron Saye and Sele. Kent lord. Close friend of Henry VI. Murdered 1450 during Cade's Rebellion. His son became a Yorkist.

Fiennes, Richard (d.1483), 7th Baron Dacre by marriage to Joan, granddaughter of the 6th Baron, initiating a feud with her Lancastrian uncle Humphrey Dacre.

Fiennes, William (d.1471), 2nd Baron Saye and Sele. Kent lord. Became Yorkist after his father was abandoned by Henry VI and murdered in 1450.

FitzAlan, Thomas (d.1524), Lord Maltravers, married Margaret Woodville.

FitzAlan, William (1417–87), 16th Earl of Arundel, married the Kingmaker's sister Joan. Prominent lord in south-east England.

FitzHugh, Henry (1472), 5th Baron. Yorkshire lord. Neville retainer. Kingmaker retainer, married his sister Anne.

Fitzwarin, Lord – see Bourchier.

Fogge, John (d.1490), household treasurer for Henry VI and Edward IV. Fought for Henry Tudor.

Fortescue, Dr John (d.1480), jurist, Marguerite d'Anjou's chancellor in exile.

Fortescue, John (d.1515), Hertfordshire knight, esquire of the body to Edward IV.

Fulford, Thomas (d.1490). Lancastrian West Country knight and outstandingly persistent troublemaker.

Gates, Geoffrey (d.1477), Marshal of Calais for the Kingmaker.

Gloucester, John of, illegitimate son of Richard III.

Gloucester, Richard, Duke of – see Richard III.

Grey of Codnor, Henry (d.1496), Lord. Disputatious Midlands magnate.

Grey of Groby, John (1432–61). Son of Elizabeth, 6th Baroness Ferrers of Groby by right, and Edward Grey. First husband of Elizabeth Woodville, later Edward IV's queen.

Grey of Powys, John (d.1497), created baron in 1482, a title claimed by his attainted father but not previously confirmed.

Grey of Ruthyn, Edmund (1416–90), 4th Baron. Welsh Marcher and Bedfordshire lord. Married Katherine, daughter of Henry Percy, 1st Earl of Northumberland, and Eleanor Neville.

Grey of Ruthyn, Henry (d.1490), Lord, later Earl of Kent. Eldest son married Eleanor Woodville, second son married Anne Woodville, widow of William, Viscount Bourchier.

Grey of Wilton, Reginald (d.1494), 7th Baron. Herefordshire lord. Married (1st) Tacinda, daughter of Owen Tudor and dowager Queen Catherine de Valois, and (2nd) Thomasine, illegitimate daughter of John Beaufort, Duke of Somerset.

Grey, Edward (d.1504), Viscount Lisle by marriage, Queen Elizabeth's brother-in-law from her first marriage. Richard III supporter.

Grey, Richard (d.1483), younger son of Elizabeth Woodville's first marriage, member of the Prince of Wales's Council.

Grey, Ralph (d.1464), Northumberland Yorkist turncoat.

Grey, Thomas (d.1501), Marquess of Dorset, elder son of Elizabeth Woodville's first marriage, married (1) Anne Holland, daughter of Anne of York; (2) Cecily Bonville.

Grey, William (d.1478), Bishop of Ely. papal appointee, Yorkist.

Greystoke, Ralph (1414–87), 5th Baron. Yorkshire Lord. Kingmaker retainer, married Henry FitzHugh's sister.

Gruuthuse, lord of – see Brugge.

Harcourt, Robert (d.1470), Midlands Kingmaker retainer.

Harrington, James (d.1485?), Gloucester retainer, feuded with Lord Stanley.

Hastings, Richard (d.1503), Lord Welles by marriage, son of William.

Hastings, William (d.1483), Lord, Edward IV's intimate friend and Lord Chamberlain. Mortal enemy of the Woodvilles, married the Kingmaker's sister Katherine.

Haute, Richard (d.1487), comptroller of the Prince of Wales's household, married Earl Rivers's sister Elizabeth.

Henry VI, King of England (1421–71) (r. 1422–61; 1470–71). Married Marguerite d'Anjou.

Henry VII (d.1509), King of England, married Elizabeth of York.

Herbert of Raglan, William (1423–69), Lord Herbert, later Earl of Pembroke. Lifelong Yorkist retainer. Held Wales for Edward IV, half-brother of the Vaughan brothers, married Anne, sister of Walter Devereux.

Herbert, Richard (d.1469), younger brother of the elder William.

Herbert, Walter (d.1507), younger brother of the younger William. Fought for Henry Tudor.

Herbert, William (d.1491), Lord Dunster/Earl of Pembroke/Earl of Huntingdon, married (1) Mary Woodville; (2) Katherine, bastard daughter of Richard III.

Hervey, Nicholas (d.1471), Bristol City Recorder, Lancastrian.

Hildyard, Robert (d.1485), rebel 'Robin of Holderness'.

Holland, Henry (d.1475), 3rd Duke of Exeter and Earl of Huntington. Hereditary Admiral of England, minor landowner. Married and divorced Edward IV's sister Anne of York.

Howard, John (d.1485), Lord, later Duke of Norfolk. Henchman of Edward IV, key player in Richard III's *coup d'état* and right-hand man.

Hungerford, Robert (d.1464), 2nd Baron, Lord Hungerford and Moleyns. Mainly West Country lord. Die-hard Lancastrian.

Hungerford, Thomas (d.1469), heir to the attainted barony.

Hungerford, Walter (d.1540), fought for Henry Tudor, barony restored.

Kemp, John, (1380–1454), Cardinal Archbishop of Canterbury.

Kendall, John (d.1485), Richard III's private secretary.

Kennedy, James (d.1465), Bishop of St Andrews. Opponent of regent Mary of Guelders.

Kent, Earl of – see Neville, William and Grey of Ruthyn, Edmund.

Kingmaker – see Richard Neville.

Langstrother, John (d.1471), Prior of St John's Hospital. Kingmaker henchman.

Latimer, Lord – see Neville.

Lincoln, Earl of – see Pole, de la.

Lisle – see Talbot.

Lovell, John (d.1465), 8th Baron, plus several other titles. Wealthy Midlands lord. Married Joan, daughter of John, 1st Viscount Beaumont.

Lovell, Francis (d.1488?), Lord and Viscount Lovell. Lifelong friend of Richard III.

Lumley, Thomas (d.1485), Lord. Neville then Richard of Gloucester retainer, died before Bosworth.

Luttrell family, attainted Somerset Lancastrian family, fought for Henry Tudor, restored.

Luxembourg, Jacquetta de (1416–72), Duchess of Bedford, Countess Rivers, Woodville matriarch. Lands in Normandy and Richmondshire. Married (2nd) Richard Woodville.

Luxembourg, Louis de (d.1475), Count of Saint-Pol, brother of Jacquetta. Perpetual schemer.

Mackerell, Dr Ralph, Jurist, colleague of John Morton, diehard Lancastrian.

Maltravers, Lord – see FitzAlan, Thomas.

March, Edward – see Edward IV.

Maredudd, Rhys ap (d.1510), Denbigh uplands clan chief, fought for Henry Tudor.

Markham, Dr John (d.1479), Chief Justice who defied Edward IV.

Moleyns, Lord – see Hungerford, Robert.

Montacute, Alice (1406–62), 5th Countess of Salisbury by right. Extensive estates in Warwickshire, the South West and around Bisham, Berkshire. Married Richard Neville.

Montagu – see Neville.

Montgomery, Thomas (d.1495), diplomat for Edward IV, fought for Henry Tudor.

More, Thomas (d.1535), Author of the Tudor 'black legend' of Richard III.

Morton, Dr John (d.1500), councillor to Marguerite d'Anjou in exile, made Bishop of Ely by Edward IV. Bitter opponent of Richard III.

Mountjoy, Lord – see Blount.

Mowbray, Anne (d.1481), Countess of Norfolk, married Richard, Duke of York.

Mowbray, John (1444–76), 4th Duke of Norfolk. Landownings diluted further by his mother's dower. Married Elizabeth, daughter of John Talbot, 1st Earl of Shrewsbury, and Margaret Beauchamp.

Neville, Anne (d.1485), the Kingmaker's younger daughter, married (1) Edward of Westminster; (2) Richard, Duke of Gloucester; later Richard III.

Neville, Cecily (1415–95), known as 'Proud Cis'. Youngest daughter of Ralph Neville and Joan Beaufort, sister to Richard, Earl of Salisbury and aunt to Richard, Earl of Warwick. Married Richard of York, matriarch of the Yorkist dynasty.

Neville, Edward (1407–76), 3rd Baron Bergavenny by marriage to Elizabeth Beauchamp. Youngest son of Ralph and Joan Beaufort. When his wife died he was dispossessed by his nephew Richard, Earl of Warwick, but remained a loyal Yorkist.

Neville, George (d.1469), Lord Latimer by marriage, the Kingmaker's uncle and ward.

Neville, George (d.1476), Bishop of Exeter, Archbishop of York, the Kingmaker's brother.

Neville, George (d.1483), Duke of Bedford, deprived 1478, son of John Neville.

Neville, Isabel (d.1476), the Kingmaker's elder daughter, married George, Duke of Clarence.

Neville, John (d.1461), 1st Baron. Northern lord. Brother of Ralph, 2nd Earl of Westmorland, acted as his guardian after he became demented.

Neville, John (d.1471), 1st Baron Montagu, Earl of Northumberland, Marquess Montagu, the Kingmaker's brother.

Neville, Katherine (d.1483), eldest daughter of Ralph and Joan Beaufort. Married (1st) John Mowbray, 3rd Duke of Norfolk, (2nd) Thomas Strangeways, (3rd) John, 1st Viscount Beaumont and (4th) John Woodville, forty-six years her junior.

Neville, Katherine (d.1504), the Kingmaker's sister, married (1) William Bonville, Baron Harington of Aldingham; (2) William, Lord Hastings.

Neville, Ralph (d.1499), Lord, later Earl of Westmorland, Gloucester retainer.

Neville, Richard (1400–60), 5th Earl of Salisbury by marriage to Alice Montacute, adding her lands to his dominant lordships in Yorkshire and Richmondshire. Eldest son of Ralph and Joan Beaufort.

Neville, Richard 'the Kingmaker' (d.1471), Earl of Warwick and Earl of Salisbury. Dominant lord in the east Midlands and south Wales by marriage to Anne Beauchamp.

Neville, Robert (1404–57), Bishop of Durham. Third son of Ralph and Joan Beaufort.

Neville, Thomas 'Bastard of Fauconberg' (d.1471), illegitimate son of William Neville.

Neville, William (d.1463), Lord Fauconberg by marriage, Earl of Kent, the Kingmaker's uncle. The most experienced Yorkist commander.

Noreys, William (d.1506), Lancastrian knight reconciled with Edward IV, fought for Henry Tudor.

Norfolk, Duke of – see Mowbray and Howard.

Northumberland – see Percy.

Ogle, Robert (d.1469), 1st Baron. Northumberland lord, experienced commander and lifelong Neville retainer. Rebel 'Robin of Redesdale'.

Oldhall, William (d.1460). Speaker of the Commons 1450–51. Much persecuted Yorkist retainer.

Ormonde – see Butler, James.

Oxford, Earl of – see Vere, John.

Parr of Kendal, William (d.1483), Lord. Westmorland Neville retainer, later Edward IV's household comptroller.

Paston, John, father (d.1466) and two namesake sons (d.1479, 1509), East Anglian gentry whose letters and papers are an invaluable source for the period 1422–1509.

Pembroke, Earl of – see Tudor and Herbert.

Percy of Scoton, Robert (d.1485), Lifelong Yorkist, Gloucester retainer.

Percy, Henry (1394–1455), 2nd Earl of Northumberland (attainted title restored 1416). Dominant lord in Northumberland, major landowner in Cumberland and Yorkshire. Married Eleanor, second daughter of Ralph Neville and Joan Beaufort.

Percy, Henry (1421–61), 3rd Earl of Northumberland. Through marriage to Eleanor, Baroness Poynings, acquired lands in Sussex and Kent.

Percy, Henry (d.1489), attainted Earl of Northumberland, restored 1470. Gloucester retainer.

Percy, Ralph (d.1464), uncle of Henry. Die-hard Lancastrian.

Pole, John de la (d.1487), Earl of Lincoln, married daughter of Thomas FitzAlan.

Pole, John de la (1442–92), Earl of Suffolk (father's dukedom forfeited in 1450). Infant betrothal to Margaret, daughter of John Beaufort, annulled. Married Elizabeth, Richard of York's second daughter.

Ratcliffe, Richard (d.1485), Richard III's right-hand man in the North.

Richard (d.1459), Duke of York, married Cecily Neville, patriarch of the Yorkist dynasty.

Richard (d.1483), Duke of York, Edward IV's second son, married Anne Mowbray.

Richard III (d.1485), King of England, Duke of Gloucester, married Anne Neville, the Kingmaker's younger daughter.

Richmond, Countess/Earl of – see Beaufort and Tudor.

Rivers, Earl – see Woodville and Richard.

Robin of Holderness – see Hildyard.

Robin of Redesdale – see Ogle.

Roos, Edmund (d.1504), exiled heir to attainted barony, restored 1485.

Roos, Thomas (1427–64), 9th Baron. East Midlands and Yorkshire lord. Son of Eleanor Beauchamp by her first marriage, half-brother to her sons by Edmund Beaufort. Married Philippa Tiptoft, sister of Yorkist John, 1st Earl of Worcester. Diehard Lancastrian.

Rougemont Grey, Thomas (d.1461), 1st Baron. Minor West Country lord. Brother of the Yorkist Edmund, Lord Grey of Ruthyn. Married Margaret, daughter of 5th Baron Ferrers of Groby.

Russell, John (d.1494), Bishop of Lincoln, Edward IV's Lord Privy Seal, Richard III's Lord Chancellor.

Rutland, Edmund (1443–60) Earl of. Richard of York's second son.

Salisbury, Earl of – see Montacute and Neville.

Salkeld, Richard (d.1501), Cumberland Neville retainer, Constable of Carlisle.

Savage, John (d.1492), Yorkist, Stanley retainer, fought for Henry Tudor.

Saye and Sele, Lord – see Fiennes.

Scales, Lord – see Woodville.

Scales, Thomas (d.1460), 7th Baron. Mainly Norfolk lord. Leading commander in Normandy. Godfather of Edward, Richard of York's eldest son. Sole heir Elizabeth married (2nd) Anthony Woodville.

Scrope of Bolton, John (1437–98), 5th Baron. Yorkshire Neville retainer, married Joan, sister of Henry FitzHugh.

Scrope of Masham, Thomas (d.1475), 5th Baron. Yorkshire lord. Neville retainer. Married Elizabeth, daughter of 5th Baron Greystoke.

Scrope of Masham, Thomas (d.1493), Lord. Yorkshire Neville retainer.

Shaw, Dr Ralph (d.1484), renowned preacher, brother of the Lord Mayor of London.

Shore, Jane (d.1527?), Edward IV's last mistress.

Shrewsbury, Earl of – see Talbot.

Somerset, Duke of – see Beaufort.

St Leger, Thomas (d.1483), second husband of Anne of York.

Stafford of Grafton, Humphrey (d.1486), Die-hard supporter of Richard III.

Stafford of Hooke, Humphrey (1439–69). Captured at Calais and defected to become one of Edward of March's closest companions.

Stafford of Southwyck (previously Hooke), Humphrey (d.1469), Lord, later Earl of Devon. Edward IV's comrade-in-arms and later his regime lock on the West Country.

Stafford, Humphrey (1402–60), 1st Duke of Buckingham. Nationwide landowner. Lieutenant of Calais. Married Anne, daughter of Ralph Neville and Joan Beaufort.

Stafford, Humphrey (1424–58), courtesy earldom of Stafford. Eldest son of the Duke of Buckingham whom he predeceased. Married Margaret, daughter of Edmund Beaufort and Eleanor Beauchamp.

Stafford, Henry (d.1471), uncle of the Duke of Buckingham, married Margaret Beaufort.

Stafford, Henry (d.1471). Younger son of the Duke of Buckingham. Second husband of Margaret, daughter of John Beaufort and Margaret Beauchamp of Bletsoe.

Stafford, Henry (d.1483), Duke of Buckingham. Key player in Richard of Gloucester's *coup d'état* who rebelled against him two months later, married Katherine Woodville.

Stafford, John (d.1473), Earl of Wiltshire, uncle of the Duke of Buckingham.

Stanley, George (d.1503), Lord Strange by marriage to niece of Elizabeth Woodville. Their son inherited the earldom of Derby.

Stanley, Thomas (d.1504), 2nd Baron, titular King of Mann and later Earl of Derby. Dominant lord in Lancashire. He betrayed, successively, Henry VI, Edward IV, Henry VI again, Edward V and Richard III. Married (1) the Kingmaker's sister Eleanor; (2) Margaret Beaufort.

Stanley, William (d.1495), younger brother of Thomas. North Wales March magnate and member of the Prince of Wales's Council, fought for Edward IV in 1461 and 1471 and for Henry Tudor in 1485. Totally loyal to the Yorkist cause.

Stewart, Bernard (d.1508), Seigneur d'Aubigny and commander of the *Garde Écossaise* who fought for Henry Tudor.

Stillington, Richard (d.1491), Bishop of Bath and Wells, Lord Chancellor to Edward IV. Instrumental in Richard III's *coup d'état*.

Stourton, John (1454–85), 3rd Baron. West Country lord.

Sudeley, Lord – see Boteler.

Suffolk, Duke of – see Pole, de la.

Sutton, John (1400–87), 1st Baron Dudley. Close friend of Henry VI, changed sides after being wounded at Blore Heath.

Sutton, William (d.1483), Bishop of Durham, son of John. Fought for Edward IV.

Tailboys, William (d.1464). East Midlands and Northumberland lord, Lancastrian thug.

Talbot, George (d.1538), Earl of Shrewsbury, Richard III's ward.

Talbot, Gilbert (d.1517), granduncle of George, leader of Talbot affinity for Henry Tudor.

Talbot, John (1384–1453), 1st Earl of Shrewsbury. Welsh Marcher lord. Outstanding commander in Normandy. Married (1st) Maud Nevill (*sic*), Baroness Furnivall, and (2nd) Margaret Beauchamp.

Talbot, John (1413–60), 2nd Earl of Shrewsbury. Eldest son of 1st Earl and Maud Nevill. Married Elizabeth, daughter of James Butler.

Talbot, John (d.1473), 3rd Earl of Shrewsbury. Cautious Lancastrian.

Talbot, Thomas (d.1470), 2nd Viscount Lisle. Killed by Lord Berkeley at Nibley Green. See Appendix F.

Thomas, Morgan and David ap, two eldest of three Lancastrian brothers.

Thomas, Rhys ap (d.1525), youngest of the Thomas brothers. Fought for Henry Tudor.

Tiptoft, John (d.1470), 1st Earl of Worcester. Fierce supporter of Edward IV. Welsh Marcher and Cambridgeshire lord. Married Cecily Neville, dowager Duchess of Warwick and daughter of Richard and Alice Montacute. Heartbroken when she died a year later on pilgrimage to the Holy Land and in Italy 1457–61.

Tresham, Thomas (d.1471), Speaker of the Commons, Lancastrian.

Trollope, Andrew (d.1461). Talbot and later Somerset retainer. Immensely experienced Normandy veteran.

Tuchet, James (1398–1459), 5th Baron Audley. East Midlands lord. Married (1st) Margaret, daughter of 6th Baron Roos, and (2nd) Eleanor, daughter of Edmund Holland, 4th Earl of Kent, and Constance of York.

Tuchet, John (d.1490), 6th Baron Audley. Father killed fighting for Lancaster at Blore Heath; comrade-in-arms of Edward IV. John changed sides after being captured at Calais and became one of Edward of March's closest companions.

Tuddenham, Thomas (d.1462). East Midlands lord, Lancastrian thug.

Tudor, Edmund (d.1456), 1st Earl of Richmond. Eldest son of Owen and Catherine de Valois. Married Margaret, daughter of John Beaufort and Margaret Beauchamp of Bletsoe.

Tudor, Henry – see Henry VII.

Tudor, Jasper (1431–95), 1st Earl of Pembroke, attainted then restored 1485. Second son of Owen and Catherine de Valois. Henry's uncle and companion in exile.

Tudor, Owen (1400–61), Lover of dowager Queen Catherine de Valois.

Tunstall, Richard (d.1492), twice-attainted Lancastrian knight, served Edward IV as an ambassador, made a garter knight by Richard III and a privy counsellor by Henry VII.

Tyrell, James (d.1502), Richard III's esquire of the body, entrusted with confidential tasks.

Vaughan, Roger of Tretower (d.1470), half-brother of William Herbert. Lifelong Yorkist retainer. Beheaded by Jasper Tudor.

Vaughan, Thomas of Hergest (d.1469), half-brother of William Herbert. Lifelong Yorkist retainer.

Vaughan, Thomas of Monmouth (d.1483), no relation to the others, Edward IV's household treasurer and member of the Prince of Wales's Council.

Vaughan, Thomas of Tretower (d.1486?), son of Roger. Probably killed leading rebellion against Henry VII.

Vaughan, Thomas (n.d.), son of Walter. Fanatical Yorkist.

Vaughan, Walter/Watkin (d.1456), of Bredwardine in Herefordshire. Lifelong Yorkist retainer. Eldest of the Vaughan brothers.

Vere, John (1408–62), 12th Earl of Oxford. Mainly Essex lord.

Vere, John (d.1513), attainted Earl of Oxford restored 1485, married the Kingmaker's sister Margaret.

Vescy – see Bromflete.

Warkworth, John (d.1500), author of one of the best sources for the early years of Edward IV's reign.

Warwick – see Beauchamp and Neville.

Welles, Lionel (1406–61), 6th Baron. Lincolnshire lord. Married (2nd) Margaret Beauchamp of Bletsoe.

Welles, Richard (1428–1470), 7th Baron Willoughby by marriage. Heir to Lionel. Attainted then restored 1468, attainted again 1470.

Welles, Robert (d.1470), son of Richard.

Wenlock, John (d.1471), 1st Baron, Speaker of the Commons and Lieutenant of Calais. Lancastrian suborned by Warwick.

Willoughby – see Welles.

Wiltshire – see Butler.

Woodville, Anne (d.1489), daughter of Richard and Jacquetta, mother of future Earls of Essex and of Kent.

Woodville, Anthony (d.1483), Lord Scales by marriage, Earl Rivers, eldest son of Richard and Jacquetta, head of the Prince of Wales's Council.

Woodville, Catherine (d.1497), daughter of Richard and Jacquetta, married (1) Henry Stafford, Duke of Buckingham, and mother of his heir; (2) Jasper Tudor.

Woodville, Edward (d.1488), son of Richard and Jacquetta. Fought for Henry Tudor.

Woodville, Eleanor (d.1512), daughter of Richard and Jacquetta, married Anthony, eldest son of Edmund Grey of Ruthyn.

Woodville, Elizabeth, daughter of Richard and Jacquetta, married (1) John Grey of Groby; (2) Edward IV.

Woodville, Jacquetta (d.1509), daughter of Richard and Jacquetta, married John, Lord Strange of Knockyn. Their daughter Baroness Strange by right married George Stanley.

Woodville, Joan (d.1462), sister of Richard, married Richard Haute.

Woodville, John (d.1469), son of Richard and Jacquetta, married dowager Duchess of Norfolk.

Woodville, Lionel (d.1484), Bishop of Salisbury, son of Richard and Jacquetta.

Woodville, Margaret (d.1490), daughter of Richard and Jacquetta, married Thomas FitzAlan, Lord Maltravers, mother of future Earl of Arundel.

Woodville, Mary (d.1481), daughter of Richard and Jacquetta, married William Herbert, Lord Dunster, Earl of Pembroke and Earl of Huntingdon, mother of his sole heiress.

Woodville, Richard (1405–69), 1st Baron Rivers. Woodville Patriarch. Minor Kent lord. Married Jacquetta of Luxembourg. Eldest child Elizabeth married (1st) John Grey of Groby and (2nd) Edward IV.

Woodville, Richard (d.1491), Earl Rivers, son of Richard and Jacquetta.

Worcester, Earl of – see Tiptoft, John.

Worcester, William of (d.1482?), author of *Annales Rerum Anglicarum*, an occasionally useful source for the period up to 1468.

York, Anne of (d.1476), Edward IV's older sister, married and divorced Henry Holland, then married her lover Thomas St Leger.

York, Cecily of (d.1507), third daughter of Edward IV, betrothed to the future James IV of Scotland, married to one of his retainers by Richard III.

York, Duke of – either Richard, Yorkist dynasty patriarch, or his namesake grandson.

York, Elizabeth of (d.1503), Edward IV's second sister, married John de la Pole, Duke of Suffolk, mother of his namesake heir, Earl of Lincoln.

York, Elizabeth of (d.1503), eldest daughter of Edward IV, married Henry VII.

York, Margaret of (d.1503), Edward IV's youngest sister, married Duke Charles of Burgundy.

York, Richard of (1411–60), 3rd Duke. Nationwide estates, main concentrations in the Welsh Marches and East Anglia. Lieutenant of Normandy and of Ireland. Married Cecily Neville.

Zouche, John (d.1526), Lord, strong supporter of Richard III, attainted 1485, restored 1495.

OTHER

Anjou, Marie d' (1404–63), aunt of Queen Marguerite. Married Charles VII of France.

Anjou, René (1409–80), Duke of. Father of Queen Marguerite. Married Isabelle of Lorraine.

Aragón, Yolande de (1384–1442), grandmother of Queen Marguerite.

Bresse, Phillipe of (d.1497), Prince of Savoy. Bitter enemy of Louis XI.

Brézé, Pierre de (d.1465). Seneschal of Normandy. Fiercely loyal to Yolande de Aragón, her daughter Isabelle and granddaughter Marguerite. Rose to high office in France thanks to the influence of Agnès Sorel.

Brittany, Frañsez (d.1488), Duke of. Erratic supporter of the Lancastrian cause.

Burgundy, Charles 'the Bold' (d.1477), Duke of, previously Count of Charolais, married (2) Margaret of York.

Burgundy, Marie (d.1482), Duchess of, only child of Charles 'the Bold', married Archduke Maximilian of Austria.

Burgundy, Philippe (d.1467), Duke of (r. 1419–67), married Isabella of Portugal, John of Gaunt's granddaughter.

Chandée, Philibert de, lord of Montfalcon, future Marshal of France. Commanded Henry Tudor's vanguard and rewarded with the earldom of Bristol.

Charolais, Count of – see Burgundy, Charles 'the Bold', Duke of.

Charles VII (1403–61), King of France (r. 1422–61). Married Marie d'Anjou.

Chastellain, Georges (d.1475), Chronicler, secretary to Pierre de Brézé, courtier of Charles 'the Bold'.

Commynes, Philippe de (d.1511), Chronicler, councillor to Charles 'the Bold' and Louis XI.

Crowland Continuator, Invaluable anonymous clerical chronicler.

Coppini, Francesco (d.1464). Papal Legate.

Dauphin – designation of French heir- apparent.

Frederick III (d.1493), first Habsburg Holy Roman Emperor.

Guelders, Mary of (d.1463), married James II of Scotland, regent mother of James III.

Hall, Edward (d.1547), Tudor chronicler.

Isabella (d.1504), Queen of Castille by right, rejected by Edward IV.

James I (1394–1437), King of Scotland (r. 1406–37). Married Joan Beaufort, John of Gaunt's daughter.

James II (1430–60), King of Scotland (r. 1437–60). Married Mary of Guelders, cousin of Philippe II of Burgundy.

James III (1451–88), King of Scotland (r. 1460–88), kidnapped by his nobles in 1480.

Landais, Pierre (d.1485), chief minister to Duke Frañsez of Brittany.

Lorraine, Isabelle (1400–53), Duchess of. Mother of Queen Marguerite.

Louis XI 'the Universal Spider' (1423–83), King of France (r. 1461–83).

Luxembourg, Jacques de (d.1487), lord of Richebourg, brother of Jacquetta of Luxembourg.

Luxembourg, Louis (1418–75), Count of Saint-Pol. Brother of Jacquetta of Luxembourg.

Maletta, Alberico (d.1466), Milanese ambassador to Louis XI.

Maine, Charles (1414–72), Count of. Uncle of Queen Marguerite. Married Isabelle of Luxembourg, sister of Jacquetta and Louis.

Mancini, Dominic, Observed and reported the events of 1483 in London for the French court.

Milan, Duke of – see Sforza.

Pius II (1405–64), Pope (r. 1458–64).

Portugal, Isabella of (d.1471), Duchess of Burgundy.

Richemont, Arthur de (1393–1458). Breton prince. As Charles VII's Constable of France he was the architect of France's first standing army and of the campaign that expelled the English from France. Duke of Brittany for one year in 1457–8.

Savoy, Bona of (d.1503), princess of Savoy, rejected by Edward IV, married Galeazzo Maria Sforza.

Saint-Pol, Count of – see Luxembourg.

Sforza, Francesco (d.1466), Duke of Milan.

Sforza, Galeazzo Maria (d.1476), Duke of Milan.

Sorel, Agnès (1422–50), Charles VII's official mistress.

Vergil, Polydore (d.1555), Tudor historian.

1. HISTORIC COUNTIES AND REGIONS OF ENGLAND & WALES

A   Anglesey
B   Bedfordshire
H   Huntingdonshire
Hx Hexhamshire
I   Isle of Ely
M   Middlesex
R   Rutland
Rch Richmondshire

Edinburgh

SCOTLAND

Northumberland

Cumberland

Hx

Durham

Westmorland

Rch

North

THE NORTH

Riding

East

West

Yorkshire

Riding

Isle of Man

Lancashire

Riding

York

A

Flint

Cheshire

Derbyshire

Nottinghamshire

Lincolnshire

Caernarvon

Denbigh

WALES

Merioneth

THE MARCHES

Shropshire

Staffordshire

MIDLANDS

Leicestershire

R

Norfolk

Norwich

Montgomery

Warwickshire

Northamptonshire

Cambridgeshire

EAST ANGLIA

Cardigan

Radnor

Herefordshire

H

Suffolk

Pembroke

Worcestershire

I

Brecknock

B

Carmarthen

Monmouth

Gloucestershire

Oxfordshire

Buckinghamshire

Hertfordshire

Essex

HOME

M

London

Glamorgan

SOUTH WEST

Berkshire

Surrey

COUNTIES

Kent

Bristol

Wiltshire

Somerset

Hampshire

Sussex

WEST COUNTRY

Dorset

Exeter

Devon

Cornwall

Isle of Wight

© Hugh Bicheno

xxxvii

2. PRINCIPAL ESTATES OF THE CROWN AND LEADING MAGNATES
c. 1455

A	Arundel (FitzAlan)
B	Buckingham (Stafford)
Bt	Beaumont
C	Clifford
Cr	Cromwell
D	Devon (Courtenay)
Da	Dacre
E	Essex (Bourchier)
G	Grey of Ruthyn
H	Hungerford
K	King (inc. Lancaster)
M	Norfolk (Mowbray)
N	Neville (Salisbury/Warwick)
n	Neville (Westmorland)
P	Percy (Northumberland)
Q	Queen's dower
Qp	Queen/Prince of Wales
R	Roos
S	Somerset (Beaufort)
St	Stanley
T	Talbot (Shrewsbury/Lisle)
V	Vere (Oxford)
W	Wiltshire (Ormonde)
Y	York (duchy)

The aim of this map is to illustrate the patchwork-quilt nature of landholdings.
Only named manors are shown, in approximately the correct location. A third of all
landholdings were ecclesiastical, but only the most important are marked with a cross.

© Hugh Bicheno

3. HALF-CONQUERED FRANCE
c. 1429

Calais
Flanders
B
St
P Artois
Brabant
E Picardy
Hainault
Luxembourg
Rouen
Normandy
Valois
Rethel
Reims
Île de
Alençon Perche France
Paris
Champagne
Bar
**Duchy of
Lorraine
(Anjou)**
Brittany
Maine
V **D**
Rennes
Anjou Blois Orléans Nemours
Touraine Nevers
Dijon
County of
Burgundy
S
Bourges
Poitou Berry Burgundy
La Marche Bourbon
Angoulême Limoges Forez
**Duchy of
Savoy**
Périgord Auvergne
Turenne
Bordeaux
Guyenne
Albret Rodez
Dauphiné
Bayonne
Gascony Armagnac
Béarn **M**
Papal
State
Bigorre Comminges Languedoc
Provence
Foix Narbonne

**Kingdom
of
Castilla**
Kingdom of Navarra
Kingdom of Aragón

SMALL
COUNTIES
B Boulogne
D Dunois
E Eu
M Mirande
P Ponthieu
S Sancerre
St Saint-Pol
V Vendôme

© *Hugh Bicheno*

―――――――― International frontiers
▪▪▪▪▪▪▪▪▪▪ Areas controlled by England, Burgundy and Brittany
·············· Burgundian and Breton patrimony

French royal demesne in italics
The Duke of Orléan's lands included Orléans, Valois, Blois, Dunois and Périgord
The Duke of Anjou's lands included Anjou, Maine, Provence and Bar
The Duke of Bourbon's lands included Bourbon, Auvergne, Forez and Vendôme
The Counts of Sancerre were a cadet branch of the House of Bourbon
The Duke of Alençon was also the Count of Perche
The Count of Burgundy-Nevers' lands inclued Nevers, Rethel and Eu
The Count of Armagnac's lands included Armagnac, Rodez and La Marche
The Counts of Nemours were a cadet branch of the House of Armagnac
The Count of Foix's lands included Béarn and Bigorre
The Lord of Albret's lands included Albret and Limoges

4. ROADS, RIVERS, SIEGES AND BATTLEFIELDS 1440–62

✘ Battle ⚔ Siege

Edinburgh

SCOTLAND

Berwick
Norham
Roxburgh
Bamburgh
Dunstanburgh
Alnwick

Hadrian's Wall Newcastle

Carlisle Naworth *Tyne*

Dere Street

Tees

Ure

Stamford Bridge ✘

York

✘ **Towton**

Wakefield ✘ ✘ **Ferrybridge**

Aire

Humber Street

Manchester

Caernarvon Denbigh Chester Lincoln

Trent

Blore Heath ✘

Fosse Way

Ermine Street

Shrewsbury Wroxeter Leicester Thetford Norwich

Watling Street High Cross Thorpe Waterville

Ludlow ✘ Coventry *Ouse*

Mortimer's Cross ✘ Godmanchester

Severn *Avon* **Northampton** ✘ *Ichfield Way*

Hereford

Carmarthen *Wye* Dunstable Colchester

Caerleon Gloucester *Akeman Street* **St Albans**

Cirencester *Thames* London

Bristol *Fosse Way* *Portway* *Watling Street* Dover

⚔ Taunton Southampton Chichester *Stane Street*

Exeter

Powderham

© *Hugh Bicheno*

xl

5. ROADS, RIVERS,
SIEGES AND
BATTLEFIELDS,
1462–85

Edinburgh

Berwick

SCOTLAND

MAP 29

Hadrian's Wall

Newcastle

Tyne

Carlisle

Dere Street

Tees

Ure

Aire

York

Humber Street

Manchester

Trent

Fosse Way

Lincoln

Caernarvon

Chester

Ermine Street

Watling Street

Shrewsbury

Wroxeter

Bosworth
X

Leicester

X **Losecote**

Thetford

Norwich

Ouse

MAP 32

Ludlow

Coventry

High Cross

Northampton

Godmanchester

Severn

Avon

X **Edgcote**

Icknield Way

Hereford

X **Tewkesbury**

Wye

Gloucester

Akeman Street

Dunstable

St Albans

Colchester

Carmarthen

Caerleon

Cirencester

Thames

Barnet X ● London

Bristol

Fosse Way

Portway

Watling Street

Dover

Stane Street

Southampton

Chichester

Exeter

© Hugh Bicheno

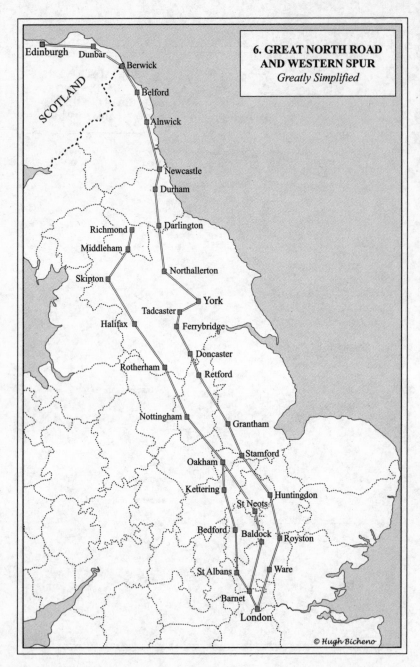

6. GREAT NORTH ROAD AND WESTERN SPUR
Greatly Simplified

Edinburgh Dunbar Berwick

SCOTLAND

Belford

Alnwick

Newcastle

Durham

Richmond Darlington

Middleham

Skipton Northallerton

York

Tadcaster

Halifax Ferrybridge

Doncaster

Rotherham Retford

Nottingham Grantham

Stamford

Oakham

Kettering Huntingdon

St Neots

Bedford Baldock Royston

St Albans Ware

Barnet

London

© Hugh Bicheno

the WARS of
the ROSES

PRINCES OF THE BLOOD

Henry III = Eleanor of Provence
(1207–72)   (d.1291)

Edmund 'Crouchback'
1st Earl of Leicester and Lancaster

Thomas
2nd Earl of Leicester
and Lancaster

Henry
3rd Earl of Leicester
and Lancaster

Matilda = William
Burgh
3rd Earl
of Ulster

Elizabeth
4th Countess

Joan = John
Mowbray
3rd Baron
Mowbray

*Mowbray
Clan*

Eleanor = Richard
FitzAlan
10th Earl
of Arundel

*FitzAlan
Clan*

Mary = Henry Percy
3rd Baron
Percy

*Percy
Clan*

Edmund = Isabella
of Langley   of Castille
Duke of York

Thomas of = Eleanor
Woodstock   Bohun
Duke of
Gloucester

Richard
of Conisburgh
3rd Earl of
Cambridge
House of York

Constance = Thomas
of York   Despenser
1st Earl of
Gloucester

Anne of = 1. Thomas Stafford
Gloucester   3rd Earl of Stafford

2. Edmund Stafford
5th Earl of Stafford

3. William Bourchier
1st Count of Eu

*House of
Stafford-Bouchier*

1. Richard = Isabel = 2. Richard
Beauchamp   Beauchamp
1st Earl of   13th Earl of
Worcester   Warwick

Elizabeth = Edward Neville
1st Baron
Bergavenny

Henry = Cecily
Beauchamp   Neville
1st Duke of
Warwick

Anne Beauchamp = Richard
16th Countess   Neville
of Warwick   *House of
Neville*

PREFACE

At an early stage of my research I found it necessary to create two reference lists of the English peers, by seniority (A and C) and alphabetically (B), and another of the senior clergy (D and E). Appendix F details the most violently divisive of all the many inheritance disputes.

The Protagonists and Marriages list and the family trees in the appropriate chapters illustrate networks of kinship too burdensome to stress sufficiently in the text. Genealogy defined status and title to property, and also the alliances and disputes that exploded into the Wars of the Roses. It really was a 'Cousins' War'. In Part II, the focus does shift towards individuals like Richard 'The Kingmaker' Neville (see Appendix H).

The French participle 'de' was still commonly used by the English nobility well into the fifteenth century, but for simplicity's sake I have omitted it while retaining the more distinctive 'de la'. I have anglicised most non-English titles, while retaining the participle for French names only when stated in full (thus Pierre de Brézé).

The pound sterling (£), the mark, and the *livre tournois* were not coins, but units of account. The mark was two-thirds of a pound sterling. The *livre tournois* to pound sterling exchange rate fluctuated from 6.6 = £1 in the 1420s to 11.3 = £1 in 1436–7, and then back down again. The continental gold crown was a coin worth one-fifth of a pound sterling.

To provide the modern standard of living equivalence given in [square brackets] after the sums in contemporary units, I averaged the figures from MeasuringWorth.com at ten-yearly intervals to arrive at a rough and ready rate of £1 = £636 for the period 1430–85. Had I used the 'economic status' equivalence instead, it would have been £1 = £18,166.

None of the contemporary or near-contemporary accounts are entirely dependable, and some are deliberately misleading. When even an accurate factual narrative is elusive, character and motive is almost entirely speculative. Modern facial reconstruction techniques can put flesh on skulls, but only imagination and empathy can suggest what went on inside them.

Their way of life was very different, but they were driven by the same appetites and passions as we. Although the religious dimension cannot be dismissed, we are on safer ground in assuming that the main driver of our story was dedication of all who lived above the subsistence level to the pursuit of sex, money and, above all, power.

PART I

PASSIONATE PRINCESSES

T HE ULTIMATE WINNERS OF THE WARS OF THE ROSES WERE the grandchildren of two enchanting women. The quality was so strong in one of them that she was accused of witchcraft in 1469 and again, *post mortem*, in 1484. The first, potentially lethal accusation was made at the instigation of Richard 'the Kingmaker' Neville, Earl of Warwick, following a *coup d'état* during which he murdered her husband and one of her sons.

The woman thus accused was Jacquetta (christened Jacqueline) de Luxembourg, widow of John, Duke of Bedford, the eldest surviving uncle of King Henry VI of England and at the time of their marriage the next in line for the throne. He was so taken with 17-year-old Jacquetta that in 1433 he married her with indecent haste five months after the death of his first wife Anne, the sister of the Duke Philippe of Burgundy, thereby deeply offending a crucial English ally in the endgame of the Hundred Years War.

After Bedford died two years later, childless Jacquetta was granted permission to enjoy her generous dower lands on condition she not remarry without a royal licence. This she omitted to obtain in 1437, when she secretly married the famously handsome 32-year-old Sir Richard Woodville, by whom she was pregnant. While she risked losing her dower, technically he committed treason by changing the legal status of a member of the royal family without the king's permission.

The couple were fortunate that 15-year-old King Henry VI was mourning the recent death of his mother Catherine, who had blazed a wide trail by cohabiting with her Welsh major-domo Owen Tudor without benefit of clergy. Catherine de Valois was the youngest daughter of King Charles VI of France and Isabeau of Bavaria. When Charles first lapsed into paranoid schizophrenia, Isabeau was forced to play a leading role in the uniformly disastrous subsequent events of her husband's reign.

Between 1407 and 1435 the Valois endured a 'Cousins' War' among the many branches of the French royal family that was far more threatening to the survival of the kingdom than the divisions among the English Plantagenets. Isabeau steered a pragmatically shifting course among the factions and was accused by her enemies of every vice imaginable, sometimes without cause.

Anarchy in France encouraged Henry V to assert his claim to the French throne after he became king of England in 1413. After his crushing victory at Agincourt two years later, he conquered Normandy, lost to the English crown over 200 years earlier. Rouen, the Norman capital, fell to the English in January 1419, and in September, after the Dauphin Charles had his cousin Duke Jean II of Burgundy treacherously assassinated, Jean's heir Philippe joined the assault on his Valois cousins' territories. The Anglo-Burgundian alliance became formal in May 1420, when Charles VI signed the Treaty of Troyes, a near total capitulation to Henry's demands.

The lynchpin of the treaty was Henry's marriage in June to Catherine, but Charles VI also disinherited his 17-year-old name-sake son (whom Isabeau said was not his at all) in favour of Henry. Disaffected French nobles rallied around the disowned dauphin and invoked alliances with Castille and with Scotland, whose uncrowned King James I, a captive in England since 1406, served with the English army in 1420–21. Spanish ships transported a Scots army led by the Earl of Buchan, son of the regent Duke of Albany, to the dauphin's capital at Bourges.

Catherine's eldest sister Isabelle, then 7 years old, had been married to Richard II of England in 1396. After Richard was overthrown and murdered by his cousin Henry IV (Bolingbroke) three years later, Isabelle bravely refused to marry Henry's namesake heir. Almost from the moment Catherine was born the two Henrys had seen her as a suitable dynastic alternative. When Henry V finally met the 17-year-old in the summer of 1419 he was so captivated by her that he abandoned his demand for a huge dowry in addition to the territorial concessions he and Duke Philippe won at Troyes.

After their marriage at Troyes Cathedral in June 1420 and a honeymoon spent on campaign, Henry and his bride crossed to England, where Catherine was crowned queen at Westminster Abbey in February 1421. The couple embarked on a royal progress through the kingdom, but a month later, at about the time Catherine became pregnant, shocking news from France interrupted their journey.

Henry's brother Thomas, Duke of Clarence, lieutenant in France during the king's absence, had been killed at Baugé in Anjou, leading a hot-headed charge by men-at-arms unsupported by archers against the elite Scots component of a larger Franco-Scots army.* Henry returned to France in June to retrieve the situation and never saw his namesake son, who was born on 6 December.

The king regained the initiative with two successful sieges, of Dreux in the late summer of 1421 and Meaux from October until May 1422, when Catherine joined him. It was not to be a happy reunion. Henry had contracted cholera and died at Vincennes, just outside Paris, on 31 August 1422, sixteen days short of his thirty-sixth birthday.

Four miles away and less than two months later his father-in-law Charles VI also died. In 1435, to justify breaking his alliance with England, Duke Philippe of Burgundy was to argue that the line of succession agreed at Troyes became void when Henry predeceased Charles.

---

* Buchan was killed and the Scots army annihilated by Bedford at Verneuil, the 'second Agincourt', in August 1424.

Both 9-month-old Henry VI and 19-year-old Charles VII were proclaimed kings of France. Neither was crowned until the visionary teenager Jeanne d'Arc shamed Charles out of his defeatist lethargy. In July 1429, following Jeanne's tide-turning victory over the English at Orléans in May, he was crowned at newly recovered Reims Cathedral, France's Westminster Abbey.

Henry was not even crowned king of England until four months later. Two years later he was crowned king of France at Nôtre-Dame Cathedral in Paris by his uncle Cardinal Henry Beaufort, Bishop of Winchester. The royal party had spent the previous eighteen months at Rouen, the capital of occupied Normandy. Also at Rouen was Jeanne d'Arc, captured in May 1430 and sold to the English by Jacquetta's uncle Jean, Count of Ligny. Despite having evaded the theological traps set for her, to the lasting shame of the House of Lancaster she was condemned for heresy by a French ecclesiastical court suborned by Bedford, with Cardinal Beaufort presiding. She was burned at the stake in Rouen marketplace on 30 May 1431.

When Henry V died there was no chance that his widow, a 21-year-old woman and sister to the rival claimant to the French throne, would be permitted to play any political role; nor was there any indication she wished to do so. Catherine was a devoted mother and gave no cause for concern until 1427, when she fell in love with the dashing Edmund Beaufort, six years her junior, who had been setting hearts aflutter ever since arriving at court.

Like the ruling House of Lancaster, the Beauforts were descendants of John of Gaunt, Edward III's third son. However, while the royal family were descended from his marriage to Blanche of Lancaster, the Beauforts were the product of his subsequent love affair with Katherine Swynford. Although the Beaufort children were legitimated by papal decree and royal charter after John and Katherine married in 1396, in 1407 Henry IV added the proviso *excepta regali dignitate*, barring his half-siblings and their descendants from inheriting the throne. Whether or not he had the right to alter what was supposed to be a fair copy of the original charter was a moot issue as long as the legitimate Lancastrian succession was assured.

The second generation of Beauforts were an attractive brood. The hostage King James I of Scotland fell in love with Edmund's sister Joan. Dowager Queen Catherine was dame of honour at the wedding. At his long-delayed coronation in 1424 James obliged the surly Scots nobles to swear allegiance to Joan as well as himself.

So, even before falling for Edmund, Catherine de Valois was well acquainted with the Beauforts and would have known that Edmund's older brother John, Earl of Somerset, had been taken prisoner after following his stepfather the Duke of Clarence to defeat at Baugé. Irrespective of Catherine's charms, Edmund must have regarded dalliance with the richest woman in England, who might influence the court to help ransom his brother, as practically a fraternal obligation, while the prospect of marriage was mouth-watering.

The possibility was far from appealing to Henry VI's uncle Humphrey, Duke of Gloucester, the youngest son of Henry IV and the senior member of the Council that governed England during the king's minority. Bedford, Gloucester's one-year-older brother, was regent in France. None of Henry V's brothers had legitimate issue and the survival of their dynasty was vested in the boy Henry VI. The prospect of a royal stepfather from the bastard Beaufort line was intolerable.

Bishop Henry Beaufort, by 1424 the last male survivor of the first generation of Beauforts, was the crown's principal creditor. He had been instrumental in denying Gloucester the regency in England and was his main rival in the Council. Their retainers came close to doing battle at London Bridge in October 1425, when Gloucester blocked what he believed was an attempt to take the infant king into the bishop's custody. At issue were not only influence and power, but also surety for the bishop's loans, on which the crown had defaulted.

Bedford was obliged to return from France to mediate during

1426. There were many strands to the compromise eventually reached, including the appointment of the neutral Richard Beauchamp, Earl of Warwick, to be the young king's governor. The core deal, however, was a partial financial settlement with Bishop Beaufort. In return the bishop resigned from the office of lord chancellor and the ruling Council.

Bedford also required Beaufort to travel back with him to France in March 1427. As regent, Bedford was empowered to grant Beaufort permission to accept promotion to cardinal, which Henry V had refused him when the pope first proposed it in 1419. Beaufort's career in papal service only briefly diverted his attention from English politics, but it gave Gloucester grounds to accuse him of divided loyalties when he resumed his place in the Council.

With the new cardinal out of the way, Gloucester dealt with the threat from Edmund by an Act of Parliament stating that if Catherine remarried without the king's consent, the husband would be stripped of his lands. The Act also specified that permission could only be granted by the king, then 6 years old, once he reached his majority. Finally, the Act also declared that any children of an unsanctioned marriage would still be members of the royal family, a proviso designed to give the royal uncles control over them. With his hopes thus dashed, Edmund departed for France to begin a long military career.

In rebellion, Catherine left the court and moved to Wallingford Castle in Oxfordshire, part of her dower. There she proceeded to raise a family with her servant Owen Tudor, a man with no lands to lose, furthermore without benefit of clergy, thus finessing the letter of Gloucester's act. Henry IV had deprived Welshmen of many civil rights during the last great Welsh revolt led by Owain Glyn Dŵr in 1400–12, but Owen Tudor had earned English rights by military service in France, even though his father was Glyn Dŵr's nephew.

The couple produced a child almost every year from about 1429. The first we can be sure of was named Edmund, which has led some to speculate that Beaufort might have been the true father.

A second son, Jasper, was to be a major player in the Wars of the Roses. Another son and two daughters followed them. It is possible a last daughter died in childbirth along with her 35-year-old mother in January 1437, although by then Catherine had retired to Bermondsey Abbey outside London, and in her will wrote of a 'grievous malady, in the which I have been long, and yet am, troubled and vexed'.

Catherine was buried in Westminster Abbey. Her painted wooden funeral effigy in the abbey museum is one of the oldest surviving life-like depictions of any member of the royal family. We cannot be sure the original of a much-copied portrait profile of Henry V was painted from life (his right profile was disfigured by a near-fatal arrow wound at the 1403 Battle of Shrewsbury), but it fits a contemporary description of an oval face, a long straight nose, straight dark hair and a ruddy complexion.

Apart from the nose his son fits this description barely at all, whereas the similarities between Catherine's effigy and another much-copied portrait of Henry VI when he was 19 years old are striking. Mother and son shared the same hair, complexion, cheekbones, jaw-line, chin, rosebud mouth and arching eyebrows. More remarkably, a portrait of Catherine's Tudor great-grandson Henry VIII at about the same age also shows a strong family likeness.

Did Henry VI inherit his maternal grandfather's schizophrenia? The condition commonly peaks between the ages of 15 and 25, with women experiencing a second peak between 25 and 35, and this may have been Catherine's 'grievous malady'. Even so, the heritability of schizophrenia from a single parent is low. It is much higher when both parents are afflicted, and Henry VI may also have inherited a predisposition to mental illness from his father, who had a messianic delusion that he could unite Christendom under his banner.

Following Catherine's death, Tudor took sanctuary at Westminster Abbey when summoned by Gloucester to appear before the Council. He was assured he could depart in safety, but was then arrested and locked up like a common criminal in Newgate prison. His confiscated worldly wealth was £137 10s. 4d, no small amount [about £87,500 in today's purchasing power], but minuscule in comparison with Catherine's dower.

In a manifest charade Tudor 'escaped' early in 1438, was allegedly recaptured by John, Baron Beaumont, one of the king's closest friends, taken to Windsor Castle and held there under the protection of none other than Catherine's former suitor Edmund Beaufort. Owen was later pardoned and his property restored, and he became a member of the king's household. Meanwhile his sons were placed in the care of the Abbess of Barking, sister of William de la Pole, Earl of Suffolk, the king's chief minister. Owen never married and many years later, on learning he was to be executed, his last words were 'that head shall lie on the stock that was wont to lie on Queen Catherine's lap'.

• ઼ •

Upon the death of the king's mother 20-year-old Jacquetta, dowager Duchess of Bedford, became the highest ranking lady in the royal family, with precedence over Gloucester's ambitious second wife Eleanor Cobham. Eleanor had previously been Gloucester's mistress when she was a lady-in-waiting to his first wife, Jacqueline d'Hainault, whom he brutally discarded in 1428. Consequently the duke was not in a position to adopt a high moral tone when a pregnant Jacquetta revealed she had married Richard Woodville not long after Catherine's death.

Also, Gloucester was once again struggling for influence with Cardinal Beaufort, who was delighted to see Gloucester's highly eligible sister-in-law Jacquetta take herself off the political chessboard. Better still, although Woodville was the son of one of the late Duke of Bedford's closest officials, and knighted by the duke himself, he had subsequently served under Suffolk – who began his service to the king as a protégé of the cardinal. Suffolk was also, by marriage, lord of the Woodville estate at Grafton in Northamptonshire.

We may presume the newly orphaned young king was inclined to leniency towards a young woman whose conduct mirrored his late mother's. It was in his gift to legitimate Jacquetta's marriage, and he did so. However, in contrast to Jacquetta's first visit to England after marrying Bedford, when she was inducted into the Order of the Garter, on this occasion the couple was not received at court and Woodville was fined £1,000 [£636,000].

Cardinal Beaufort put up the money, nominally in exchange for a few of her manors, but clearly to bind the couple to his interest. Their exclusion from court may have been at the suggestion of Gloucester, but it also resolved the problem of protocol posed by the gross imbalance of rank between Jacquetta and Richard Woodville.

If the noble councillors believed Richard had married Jacquetta for her money, they could not have been more wrong. Theirs was a lastingly passionate relationship, and she bore him fourteen children over the next twelve years. Given how dangerous childbirth was, that Jacquetta's dower was for her life only and how politically exposed he would become if she died, Richard would certainly have restrained his enthusiasm if cold calculation played any part in the marriage.

The couple returned to France, he to pursue his military career and she to attempt to secure her income from lands in Normandy that constituted a major part of her Bedford dower. With Burgundy now hostile, the English position in northern France was precarious, which kept Richard busy but would have made Jacquetta's task difficult even if she had not been almost constantly pregnant. She appears to have shuttled across the Channel to give birth at Grafton, leaving the babies in her father-in-law's household while she returned to France to pursue her claims – and get pregnant again.

It is to be expected that two such beautiful people as Jacquetta and Richard would produce stunningly good-looking offspring. Sadly, presumption is all we have, as no likenesses from life survive of either of the parents or any of their fourteen children – save one. Three copies survive of a lost original portrait of Elizabeth, their eldest child, painted after she married Edward IV. The least over-painted is at Queens' College, Cambridge – she and her ill-fated predecessor Marguerite d'Anjou being the founders for whom the college is named. Although crudely executed, the portrait conveys a luminous quality, which helps to explain why Elizabeth Woodville became the first commoner queen regnant of England.

The distinctive course taken by English history under Henry VIII may well have owed something to the mitochondrial DNA of Catherine and Jacquetta. Having acquired financial independence by fulfilling their dynastic duty as daughters, they found fulfilment with men who prized them as women above all. We know Owen Tudor's last thoughts were of long-dead Catherine, and we may safely assume Richard Woodville's were of Jacquetta in the grim hours before he, too, was beheaded.

Sometimes love does conquer all: despite having turned their backs on the game of power, Catherine and Jacquetta became the common ancestors of every English monarch since 1485. Before that could happen, all those with a superior claim to the throne had first to wipe each other out. This they did in what was in essence a decades-long, murderously sordid dispute over an inheritance within a deeply dysfunctional extended family. It became merciless not despite but *because* the combatants had so much in common, and projected their own darkest intentions onto each other.

This was something so humanly fascinating that the greatest author to adorn the English language wrote eight plays about it. Prudent sycophancy towards the dynasty under which he lived gave Shakespeare the unifying theme of his first historical series, three-part *Henry the Sixth* and *Richard the Third*, namely that divinely ordained order was overthrown by the deposition and murder of Richard II by his cousin Henry of Bolingbroke, Duke of Lancaster. Decades of strife ensued before the restoration of divine order under the Tudors.

The theme is absent from his subsequent, more accomplished series from *Richard the Second* through two-part *Henry the Fourth*, leading to the patriotic apotheosis of *Henry the Fifth*. The final chorus laments that after Henry V's early death, 'so many had the managing, that they lost France, and made his England bleed'. The plays have indelibly coloured popular perception of late medieval England, and historians cannot ignore them.

Nor should they: it was an extraordinary period in English history. Four of the six kings crowned between 1399 and 1485 were usurpers who killed their predecessors, undermining the concept of divine right as well as the prestige of the ruling class. A more mature appreciation of history and of human nature led Shakespeare to discount the role of divine judgement when he wrote the second, more psychologically penetrating series.

HOUSE OF LANCASTER

IN HIS *COMMENTARIES* POPE PIUS II DISMISSED HIS CON-temporary Henry VI of England as 'a man more timorous than a woman, utterly devoid of wit or spirit, who left everything in his wife's hand'. The verdict of history is equally implacable: he was one of the most ineffectual and divisive monarchs with which any nation has ever been cursed. The only open question is how many of the disasters that characterized his reign can be attributed to his wife or his proverbial 'evil councillors', and how many to personal initiatives.

Henry was at the younger end of the age bracket in which schizo-phrenia commonly declares itself when he assumed the full powers of personal kingship in November 1437. A portrait of him four years later shows the staring, vacant facial expression characteristic of the disease, and he ticked many other diagnostic boxes long before disabling symptoms became apparent. Chief among them were an inability to feel normal joy or pleasure (later portrayed as saintliness), extreme sensitivity to disagreement, inappropriate emotional responses to serious events (such as giggling at bad news), and no facility to weigh the likely consequences of his decisions, from which came a cavalier disregard for abiding by them.

The word 'childlike' was often applied to him, which explains why he commanded (often exasperated) affection from so many. Children, however, are often cruel, and on occasions Henry acted in a way that can only be described as sadistic. One such was his vindictive persecution in 1441 of Eleanor Cobham, wife of his uncle the Duke of Gloucester, for treasonable necromancy. Suffolk was behind the prosecution, but he would not have dared attack a prince of the blood without the king's support. Eleanor was paraded through the streets of London in her shift like a prostitute, and then imprisoned for life. Her alleged accomplices were first tortured to implicate her, and then cruelly executed.

It was not the first time a Lancastrian king employed an accusation of witchcraft against an inconvenient woman. Henry V used it against his stepmother Joan of Navarre, but spared her a trial after legally stealing much of her dower. She was under house arrest first at Pevensey Castle in Kent, where her youngest stepson Gloucester was a frequent visitor. In 1429 Joan gifted her chapel and its furnishings to Gloucester's wife Eleanor Cobham.

Although Gloucester was not implicated in his wife's supposed crimes and divorced her, his status as the king's heir presumptive was irrevocably compromised. He was forced into retirement, leaving the way clear for Suffolk and other members of the king's inner circle, to whom Henry began to grant the reversion of crown lands and offices held by the duke. For these to take effect Gloucester had to die. In 1447 he was arrested on a charge of treason and conveniently died in custody two days later. Suffolk was made a duke the following year.

In July 1447 a court presided over by Suffolk convicted the late duke's illegitimate son and eight others of plotting to kill the king and sentenced them to be drawn, hanged and quartered. Suffolk only appeared with a royal pardon after they had been dragged through the streets, cut down alive after hanging and stripped naked in preparation for ritual disembowelment. A visiting French delegation was disgusted by the charade, and reported that the people of London shared the sentiment.

The episode marked the start of the cult of 'Good Duke Humphrey' among the common people, and a corresponding hatred of Suffolk.

HOUSE OF LANCASTER

John of Gaunt = Blanche of Lancaster
(1340–99)   (d.1368)

Philippa = John I of   Elizabeth   **Henry IV** = Mary Bohun
(d.1415)   Portugal   (d.1426)   (Bolingbroke)   (d.1394)
                                        (1367–1413)

Isabella of Burgundy
(d.1471)

Henry V = Catherine   John   Blanche = Louis III
(1387–1422) de Valois   Duke of   (d.1409)   Elector
           (d.1437)   Bedford   Palatine
                          (d.1435)
                          no issue

Thomas   Humphrey   Eric,   = Philippa
Duke of   Duke of   King of   (d.1440)
Clarence   Gloucester   Denmark,
(d.1421)   (d.1447)   Sweden
no issue   no issue   and
                            Norway

Henry VI = Marguerite d'Anjou
(1421–71)   (1430–82)

Edward of Westminster
(1455–71)

It is an error to believe that, like many another chief minister before and after him, Suffolk was simply the lightning rod for growing popular discontent with the king. Although many others shared in the ill-gotten spoils from Gloucester's estate, Suffolk's greed was particularly flagrant.

Nonetheless, he undoubtedly did get blamed for the king's failings. The once canonical view of Henry as a well-meaning soul misled by self-seeking courtiers has been comprehensively demolished.* Contemporary French and other non-English sources reveal that the manner in which England lost its French empire, which destabilized Henry's reign, bears the imprint of the king's own dithering personality.

Seen through the lens of current understanding of schizophrenia this is not surprising. Henry was almost unsteerable by his councillors, evil or otherwise. They could, obviously, encourage him to pursue a certain policy, but only if it was in accordance with his inclinations. What they could not do was control its implementation, because his aversion to disagreement made it impossible to discuss the pros and cons of any particular decision.

Anyone who has acted as an adviser to powerful individuals knows how to frame a question so the preferred outcome appears to be the correct answer. Medieval courtiers were masters of the process of subtle manipulation recently dubbed 'nudge theory'. But in the end, and most acutely with regard to Henry VI, they had to be, above all, 'yes' men willing to greet every royal pronouncement as wise and insightful. 'Yes – but' men were compelled to walk a fine line with any monarch; in Henry's case that line simply did not exist.

A further contributing factor to Henry's psychology was growing up in the overpowering shadow of the legendary father he never knew, and being schooled to govern as he had. Yet Henry V had been a terrifyingly focused and above all immensely brave individual,

* Notably by Bertam Wolffe's exhaustively researched biography.

who came to the throne as a fully grown man and commanded respect and devotion not merely as king but also as a victorious leader of men in battle. Objectively his were shoes too big to fill: Henry VI did not even try.

On the plus side his father and grandfather had crushed domestic challenges arising from the 1399 usurpation, and Henry VI's absolute right to rule was fully accepted not only by the nobility but also by the country at large. The minority Council and the king's uncles preserved and extended Henry V's conquests, and sizeable assets reverted to the crown following the deaths of the dowager queens and his uncles. When Henry VI assumed personal kingship he was more politically and financially secure than his father had been, and disposed of considerably more patronage.

Feudalism – the holding of lands in exchange for service or labour – had long ago ceased to provide the basis of political power in England. In its place, the country was a patchwork of 'affinities' – networks of those deriving benefit from noble patronage and influence (known as 'good lordship'). Henry had a liveried retinue of over 300 knights and esquires, and the next largest personal following, a mere thirty-six of similar rank, wore the livery of the wealthy Humphrey Stafford, Duke of Buckingham, who owned manors in twenty-two counties. However, their *affinities* were an order of magnitude greater than their retinues.

In the king's case this was further multiplied by direct patronage. When Henry assumed personal kingship there were only 61 lay peerages, several of them multiple holdings by one peer – 3 dukedoms, 14 earldoms and 43 baronies. By 1450 he had created or recreated 36 more – 6 dukes, 2 Marcher lords, 2 marquesses, 8 earls, 2 viscounts and 16 barons. Even today, largely honorific life peerages are an important element of government patronage; in the fifteenth century, men would do almost anything to be granted the lands and legal privileges of hereditary nobility.

The king also had in his gift over a thousand royal offices. These were additional to those in his private estate, which included the principality of Wales (conjoined with the earldom of Chester), the dukedoms of Cornwall, Lancaster and Hereford, earldoms of Leicester, Lancaster, Derby and Northampton, the barony of Halton in Cheshire, the royal appanage of Richmondshire and the royal peculiar of Hexhamshire. Royal appointments were commonly devolved to the members of the king's household, but he could revoke them all at will.

· ∽ ·

Alongside these many advantages, however, Henry faced challenges in the form of changes to the deep political culture of the nation, which would expose his failings to a higher degree of public scrutiny. His reign saw the ruling house complete the transition from being a French family that governed England to being an English family struggling to retain its holdings in France. English only became the language of government under Henry V, the first monarch since the Norman Conquest to use it in his private correspondence.

The monarchy lost some of its majesty along with the element of mystery when the king's subjects could better understand how they were governed – although the genie of doubt about the natural order of things was already well out of the bottle. In the fourteenth century a diffuse proto-Protestant religious movement known as Lollardy followed the lead of the lay theologian John Wycliffe in rejecting the corruption of the Church. Papal authority had already been severely undermined by the French capture of the papacy from 1305 to 1378, followed by a vituperative schism between rival papacies at Avignon and Rome.

In the midst of all this, starting in 1348, repeated pandemics of bubonic, pneumonic and septicaemic plagues, known collectively as the Black Death, nearly halved the population. Unfortunately the best of the clergy took a deadly hit from the plague, which in its airborne, almost invariably fatal pneumonic form, struck down the most diligent among them as they tended to the dying. Meanwhile the bubonic plague wiped out even cloistered communities, whose grain stores were magnets for infected rats.

Secondary consequences included a sharp decline in rental income as the countryside became depopulated. Many landowners were compelled to enter into agreements with the reduced labour force, under which they assumed the capital costs and most of the risks in return for, typically, half the produce. The Church's relative income, however, increased steadily through donations. The massive transfer of wealth from secular to clerical hands eventually led to the clergy's expropriation and the Protestant Reformation – but long before that, outrage at the venality of the princes of the Church had reached boiling point.

Wycliffe produced the first partial translation of the Bible into English in 1382. In February 1395, 122 years before Martin Luther nailed his Ninety-Five Theses, in Latin, to the door of the castle church in Wittenberg, a group of Lollards nailed their Twelve Conclusions, in the vernacular, to the door of Westminster Hall, the heart of secular government in England.

Although Wycliffe and his followers had enjoyed the protection of John of Gaunt and other nobles who wished to get their hands on Church wealth, this ended after the 1381 Peasants' Revolt, which Wycliffe condemned but one of whose leaders, John Ball, preached Lollardy. Widespread unrest opened noble eyes (in particular Gaunt's, after his Savoy palace was sacked by the London mob) to the threat it posed to their own authority. After he seized power, John of Gaunt's son Henry IV forbade translation and private ownership of the Bible, and authorized the burning of heretics.

The name 'Peasants' Revolt' is, anyway, an historical solecism. It was more like a strike by agricultural workers empowered by their relative scarcity, led by minor officials and smallholders. The old historical consensus of medieval England as a peasant society where people were tied to the land by communal obligations, as in mainland Europe and Scotland, has long since been demolished. There is compelling evidence, as early as the thirteenth century, of a sizeable body of hired labour, and that land was a commodity owned by individuals – of either sex – who could buy, sell and bequeath it at will.*

As they did in their simultaneous conquest of Sicily, the Norman invaders of 1066 simply overlaid their authority on existing laws and customs. Anglo-Saxon property rights were refined by the contractual basis of feudalism, with the concept of binding contracts remaining after the link between land and service eroded. As a result England was a highly litigious society, which demanded at least a pretence of impartiality from state officials.

· ✑ ·

Impartiality was something that Henry VI's administration signally failed to provide. He certainly must have known Richard II's downfall was precipitated by his illegal seizure of entailed Lancastrian lands from his cousin, who overthrew him to become Henry IV. He did not appreciate, however, that the cumulative effect of many small abuses of power by royal household members and their affinities could have a similar effect. Even when not committed in his name, every unpunished arbitrary act by his household diminished his sovereign authority.

Although England had been governed for fifteen years without domestic disturbances by his minority Council, once he was free to do so Henry seldom stayed at the Palace of Westminster, preferring Windsor Castle, Sheen, Eltham, Kennington and, after 1447, Gloucester's opulent palace at Greenwich. He ruled through a small number of trusted ministers, in permanent attendance during his 'progresses' through the country. Apart from a two-year period in 1442–3, when he was fully taken up with a strategy he hoped would lead to peace in France, his tours averaged three months per year between 1437 and 1453.

* This evidence was unearthed by Alan Macfarlane in his groundbreaking *The Origins of English Individualism*.

In principle Henry's regular peregrinations should have enabled him to gain the trust of his kingdom. Unfortunately they sowed ill will instead, because his entourage did not pay the roaming court's bills to local suppliers. Also, he mainly stayed at royal palaces, within a growing cocoon of liveried retainers. Chief among those most constantly with him was Suffolk and his own close associate John Sutton, created Baron Dudley in 1440. Two who became part of Henry's inner circle thanks to Cardinal Beaufort's influence were the erudite Adam Moleyns, made Bishop of Chichester in 1445, and Reginald Boulers, made Abbot of Gloucester in 1437 and Bishop of Hereford in 1450.

Three others were Henry's bosom friends. The closest was the royal chaplain William Ayscough, appointed Bishop of Salisbury shortly after Henry assumed personal kingship, and subsequently the king's confessor. John, Baron Beaumont, had been the king's companion since infancy and was created the first ever viscount in the English peerage in 1432. Another royal friend was James Fiennes, created Baron Saye and Sele in 1447, who probably abused Henry's trust more than any other.

The young king's alienation of crown revenues through gifts to his favourites was similar to the behaviour of his ill-fated great-uncle Richard II. Ironically, the principal beneficiary of Richard's fecklessness had been his uncle John of Gaunt, who thereby built up the affinity that made it possible for his own son to seize the throne and found the Lancastrian dynasty. One of the few things Henry VI's grandfather and father agreed on was that none of their subjects should become as over-mighty as the founder of their dynasty had been.

At the same time pressure for territorial expansion and consolidation was growing, because landowners' incomes per acre declined in absolute terms from the middle of the fourteenth century. Land ownership was a zero-sum game and nobles could only expand their holdings through inheritance, marriage or royal gift. Among the most valuable forms of royal patronage were permission to marry and the assignment of wardships – the care and control of wealthy orphans during their minorities. In the case of orphan girls, their estates were generally captured by their guardians through marriage to their own sons.

A startling illustration of this involved the girl co-heirs of the wealthy Humphrey Bohun, Earl of Hereford, Essex and Northampton. After Eleanor, the elder, married Edward III's youngest son Thomas of Woodstock, they pressured Eleanor's sister Mary into becoming a nun, to give them sole possession of the Bohun inheritance. Thomas's older brother John of Gaunt abducted Mary from the convent and, following payment of a large fine to his nephew the king, married her to his own eldest son, the future Henry IV.

Not the least of Henry V's reasons for embarking on a career of conquest was to provide an outlet for the martial energy and the rapacity of his land-hungry nobles. The Norman Conquest of 1066 had established a unitary English state under a monarchy kept strong by ensuring that few nobles were ever permitted to accumulate the large contiguous holdings that enabled the great French lords to defy their king. The exceptions were the lords expected to police the borders (Marches) of Wales and Scotland. Unsurprisingly, they were historically the most troublesome of the king's subjects.

In 1326 Queen Isabella and her lover, the Welsh Marcher lord Roger, Baron Mortimer, overthrew and killed her husband Edward II. Four years later, by then Earl of March, Roger suffered a degrading death at the end of a rope, was attainted (see explanation below) and all his titles and lands declared forfeit by the young Edward III.

The Scots Marcher Henry, Baron Percy, helped overthrow Richard II and was created Earl of Northumberland by a grateful Henry IV. Although Percy's son Harry 'Hotspur' rebelled and was killed at the 1403 Battle of Shrewsbury, the father was spared retribution. He was attainted for another failed rebellion two years later, after which he fled to Scotland. Three years later his head ended up adorning London Bridge.

There was usually a third act to the cycle of treason and exemplary punishment. Attainder, also known as 'corruption of blood', declared the individual a non-person in a legal sense and so terminated rights of both patrilineal and matrilineal inheritance. Thus the attainted noble's forfeiture of hereditary titles and lands also deprived his family. Punishing the innocent sat ill with medieval concepts of kingship, however, and attainder was rarely sustained.

Thus the ancestral Mortimer lands and the earldom of March were restored to Roger's grandson in 1354, while Percy's attainder was revoked and the earldom restored to Hotspur's son in 1416. In part this was because of the strategic importance of the lands in question and the deep local roots of the Mortimer and Percy affinities; but it also illustrated how respectful of property rights even kings had to be.

There was another consideration. A subject permanently deprived of his family lands could only hope for redress by force of arms. He might claim to be rebelling only to recover his patrimony, as Henry Bolingbroke did in 1399, but in practice he could only be secure if the monarch was overthrown. Meanwhile, if the king kept the expropriated lands he was regarded as a thief, and if he awarded them to others he would experience the paradox of patronage succinctly summed up by the infamous Mayor James Curley of Boston: 'Every time you do a favour for a constituent, you make nine enemies and one ingrate'.

In sum, successful kingship was a balancing act requiring a wide range of political skills. The main reason why primogeniture became the sanctified mechanism of succession was to avoid a civil war every time a king died; but another reason to abide with one ruling family was that the heir could be expected to have learned the necessary skills by observing them exercised by his father. Henry VI was denied the opportunity to learn from his father and, bombarded by exhortation to live up to the idealized example of a man with whom he never formed a living bond, must have secretly resented his memory.

In practical terms the most burdensome part of Henry V's legacy was the war in France. His son was the antithesis of a warrior and regarded conquered Normandy as more trouble than it was worth – something his father's generation could never accept. However, in early 1447 the leading figures of the old guard departed the scene when Cardinal Beaufort died sixteen days after Humphrey of Gloucester. Their furious disagreements had caused their influence to decline once Henry VI assumed personal kingship and they had, anyway, fought each other to a standstill by 1440.

Uniquely for the period we have handsome contemporary likenesses of the two men: a crayon copy of an earlier drawing from life of Gloucester as a young man, and Van Eyck's portrait of the plainly dressed cardinal in his late fifties, the earliest naturalistic painting of any Englishman. Apart from the Lancaster nose, it is hard to discern a family likeness; but both project a strength of character sadly lacking in their young nephew and king.

For all their rancour they were princes of the blood devoted to their dynasty. Both shared Henry V's vision of Christendom united under a dual Lancastrian monarchy, and differed only on the means to pursue what was, objectively, an insane ambition. Gloucester could never bring himself to accept that his brother's legacy was unsustainable, but by the end of the 1430s the cardinal had reluctantly concluded that Henry VI was a broken reed.

Unfortunately Beaufort tried to salvage the Lancastrian dynasty's fortunes while simultaneously advancing the interests of his younger relatives. Although this was normal behaviour by senior prelates – the word 'nepotism' comes from the favours showered on their *nipoti* (nephews, often actually sons) by popes and princes of the Church – it was to have tragic consequences for his king, and for England.

HOUSE OF BEAUFORT

THE BEAUFORTS TOOK THEIR FAMILY NAME FROM THEIR birthplace, a castle in the Loire valley owned by their father John of Gaunt, 15 miles east of Angers, the capital of Anjou. The four Beaufort siblings, John, Henry, Thomas and Joan, were born illegitimate during the 1370s, but in 1396 John of Gaunt married their mother, Katherine Swynford. Church law viewed all the children of parents who married as legitimate, no matter when the marriage took place. Further legitimated by papal decree and royal charter, the Beauforts regarded themselves as – and the bordure of their coat of arms proclaimed them to be – the cadet branch of the Lancastrian dynasty.

English civil law was less accommodating with regard to inheritance, something emphasized by their half-brother Henry IV when he barred the Beauforts from the succession. Henry's policy was to keep them closely tied to his own family by curtailing any independent ambition they might entertain. Thus he revoked the senior titles and the lands awarded by Richard II to John, the eldest of the Beauforts. Instead, Henry gave him a revocable annuity of £1,000 [£636,000]. John retained the earldom of Somerset and the lands settled on him by their father, but these yielded only another £1,000.

Likewise, when Bishop Henry Beaufort resigned as Lord Chancellor following his appointment to the wealthy see of Winchester, Henry IV's attitude towards him changed. Even though the bishop performed his office admirably during the Percy rebellion and had undone a simultaneous French threat to Calais through skilled diplomacy, the king now began to view everything he did with suspicion. Perhaps with good reason, as the bishop was a key figure in Prince Henry's attempt to supplant his father's authority.

When, after distinguished military and diplomatic service, John Beaufort died in 1410, within four months his widow Margaret Holland, a wealthy woman in her own right, was betrothed to Thomas, Duke of Clarence, Henry IV's second son. Clarence claimed custody of John's heirs and took possession of the income from John's estate. This went plainly against John's will and was contested – with little success – by Bishop Henry, his brother and executor.

Only 9 miles north of Beaufort lay Baugé, scene of the disastrous battle in which the king's younger brother, the Duke of Clarence, met his death in 1421. The two eldest surviving sons of John Beaufort, who accompanied their stepfather on the Anjou campaign, were captured after the battle. The younger, 15-year-old Thomas, was released in 1427 through a prisoner exchange arranged by Cardinal Beaufort, but died four years later. Seventeen-year-old John Beaufort, Earl of Somerset, remained in French hands until 1438. John's captivity was prolonged because his mother refused to diminish the estates she administered in his name.

The rivalry between the Duke of Gloucester and Cardinal Beaufort also added to the young earl's misfortune, as the French first demanded an exchange for the Duke of Bourbon, captured at Agincourt. After Bourbon died in captivity they proposed an exchange for the Count of Angoulême, held as surety since 1412 for the Duke of Orléans's debt to Clarence, John's late stepfather. Gloucester prevented both exchanges.

After Henry VI assumed personal kingship he lent a sympathetic ear to the petition of Edmund, John's youngest brother, on his sibling's behalf. Agreement was reached for John's ransom to be offset by the payment due from Angoulême, plus the release of the Count

HOUSE OF BEAUFORT

k. = killed in battle   x. = executed

John of Gaunt = Katherine Swynford
(1340–99)   (d.1403)

John = Margaret = 2. Thomas   Henry
1st Earl of   Holland   1st Duke of   Cardinal Archbishop
Somerset   (d.1439)   Clarence   of Winchester
(d.1410)   (d.1447)

Henry   John = Margaret   Joan = James I
2nd Earl of   1st Duke of Beauchamp   (d.1445) of Scotland
Somerset   Somerset   (d.1482)   (d.1437)
(d.1418)   (d.1444)

                                      James II of Scotland
                                          (d.1460)

Margaret = Edmund Tudor   Eleanor = James Butler   Anne = William
(d.1509)   Earl of   (d.1501)   Earl of   (d.1496) Paston
            Pembroke   Wiltshire   (d.1496)
            (d.1456)   and
                                        Ormonde
                                        (x.1461)
Henry VII
(1457–1509)

Thomas
Duke of Exeter
(d.1426)

Joan = Ralph Neville
(d.1440)   Earl of
     Westmorland
     House of Neville

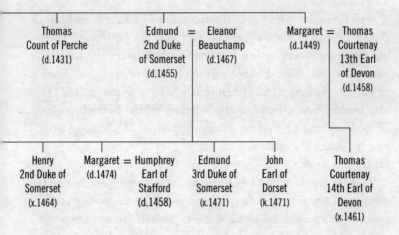

Thomas
Count of Perche
(d.1431)

Edmund = Eleanor
2nd Duke   Beauchamp
of Somerset (d.1467)
(d.1455)

Margaret = Thomas
(d.1449)   Courtenay
     13th Earl
     of Devon
     (d.1458)

Henry
2nd Duke of
Somerset
(x.1464)

Margaret = Humphrey
(d.1474)   Earl of
     Stafford
     (d.1458)

Edmund
3rd Duke of
Somerset
(x.1471)

John
Earl of
Dorset
(k.1471)

Thomas
Courtenay
14th Earl of
Devon
(x.1461)

of Eu, captured at Agincourt, whose ransom John purchased from the crown for £24,000 [£15.26 million]. The debt was crippling, as even after inheriting the Holland lands from his mother John's annual income was only £2,250 [£1.43 million].

In his absence Edmund, after his courtship of Queen Catherine was thwarted, was made Count of Mortain, near the border with Maine in western Normandy, and took service under Bedford. He saw some action in 1427 and a great deal in 1429, a year of multiple English defeats following Jeanne d'Arc's relief of Orléans, during which Bedford made him a constable of the army. Edmund formed part of the escort for Henry VI from Rouen to Paris for his coronation as king of France in November 1430, during which he first met Richard, Duke of York, at the time a member of the young king's household.

After returning to England Edmund married Eleanor Beauchamp, dowager Baroness Roos, without obtaining the required royal licence. The dates are uncertain, but it seems Edmund forced the issue by getting her pregnant. Eleanor was the middle of three daughters of the very wealthy Richard Beauchamp, Earl of Warwick, and his also wealthy first wife, Elizabeth Berkeley, heiress of the baronies of Berkeley and Lisle. After Elizabeth died in 1422 Beauchamp married another wealthy heiress, Isabel Despenser, who bore him Henry and Anne.

While he lived, Warwick blocked the royal licence for Edmund's marriage. Determined to deny his unwanted son-in-law any profit from it, he entailed his entire estate to his son Henry, depriving the daughters of his first marriage of what they (and their outraged husbands) regarded as their due inheritance from their mother. The ultimate beneficiary was Richard Neville, betrothed to Anne Beauchamp in 1434 when he was six and she was eight. He was to become Earl of Warwick by marriage and one of the wealthiest men in England after Anne's older brother Henry died in 1446, followed by his only child in 1448.

Though his matrimonial fortune-hunting failed, Edmund benefited greatly from his uncle Henry's wealth. It bought him his first independent command in March 1436, when the cardinal loaned the crown the money to equip a 2,000-man expedition to Normandy, conditional on his nephew being in command. Edmund's role, however, proved to be less autonomous than he had hoped, as the king required him to join the Duke of Gloucester at Calais.

Gloucester, the king's lieutenant in France following the death of his brother Bedford, thirsted to punish Duke Philippe of Burgundy, who at Arras the previous year had reneged on his treaty with England and entered into a military alliance with France. Under Gloucester's command Edmund led damaging raids (known as *chevauchées*) into Picardy, the province ceded to Burgundy by Charles VII at Arras, and performed so well that Gloucester left him in command while he returned to England to gather reinforcements.

Stung by Edmund's raids, Philippe raised a huge army, mainly Flemish militia, and besieged Calais and the frontier fortress at Guînes. Edmund conducted an aggressive defence, and thwarted an attempt to close Calais harbour with rock-filled blockships by sending men to dismantle them. When he learned that Gloucester was returning with 10,000 men, Philippe was compelled to lift both sieges and retreat south. Gloucester then embarked on a massive *chevauchée* into Flanders while ships out of Calais plundered along the coast, prompting a two-year revolt by the Flemish cities against Philippe's policies, which forced him to abandon any further military action against the English.

On his triumphant return to England, Edmund was made a Garter knight and constable of the royal castles of Aberystwyth and Kidwelly in Wales. Subsequently he was made warden of Windsor Castle, where the king charged him with guarding his late mother's lover Owen Tudor after he 'escaped' from Newgate prison.

For a few years Edmund achieved the remarkable feat of being highly esteemed by Gloucester as well as enjoying Cardinal Beaufort's continuing patronage. In 1438 he was appointed governor of the county of Maine, and four years later was awarded the land rights.

Along with his county of Mortain it made him the principal English lord in the area conquered from the Duke of Anjou.

This steep rise of Edmund's fortunes increased John Beaufort's resentment when he returned to England in late 1438. It was bad enough to have had his own career put on hold for seventeen years, but galling to find his youngest brother had flourished so outstandingly during his absence. John's return forced his uncle to switch political and financial influence away from the abler and more charismatic Edmund during the crucial years when the cardinal emerged the winner in his long feud with Gloucester.

In the spring of 1439 the cardinal funded an expedition led by John to join Edmund in Normandy. John was made captain of the fortresses of the Cotentin peninsula in the face of a Franco-Breton offensive that captured Harfleur and Montvilliers, and besieged Avranches. In April, after the death of Edmund's hostile father-in-law the Earl of Warwick, John became the acting overall military commander in France.

In November John returned to England, where his uncle tried to have him formally appointed the king's lieutenant in France in succession to Warwick. Gloucester thwarted him and John was only made senior commander on a temporary basis. In early 1440 he was sent to prove himself with an army of 2,100 men, again financed by his uncle. His subordinate commanders were his brother Edmund and Lord Talbot, each married to one of the late Earl of Warwick's daughters and fellow litigants against the terms of his will.

With Charles VII distracted by a rebellion, Edmund recaptured Harfleur and Montvilliers, stabilizing the situation in western and central Normandy. Meanwhile, on the eastern front, John led a *chevauchée* into Picardy. The aim was to provoke Franco-Burgundian conflict by drawing in the French, but he encountered no opposition. John could not know it, but this marked the beginning of a new strategy by Arthur de Richemont, Constable of France, designed to wear down the English without risking the new standing army he was building.

John's chance of being appointed lieutenant in France was a casualty of Gloucester's last attempt to discredit Cardinal Beaufort, before Gloucester was himself discredited by the prosecution of his wife in 1441. During the 1439–40 parliament Gloucester submitted an indictment of Cardinal Beaufort's entire career, arguing it was characterized by corruption and accusing him of putting the interests of the papacy ahead of his loyalty to the crown. Unsurprisingly, given that at this point the war in France was being maintained by the cardinal's wealth, the indictment did not prosper.

Henry VI was the first English king never to command an army in battle. He was a passionate hunter, by no means a risk-free activity, but took no part in martial tournaments. This may have been because those entrusted with his care as a minor did not dare expose him to the dangers, but the outcome was a man who regarded warfare with distaste. Henry's parliaments increasingly took a similar view, and became less and less inclined to vote for the necessary taxes. Henry could not expect his subjects to make sacrifices for a war to which he was not prepared to commit himself.

Furthermore, after the exhilaration of Henry V's conquest of Normandy had passed, there was scant enthusiasm among the professional fighting men for the grinding war that followed. Without much prospect of winning lands for themselves, commanders and men alike needed to be sure they would be paid, and their physical and military needs supplied, if they were to cross the Channel at all. Bedford, Gloucester and Warwick had deep pockets and could afford to advance money against sporadic royal reimbursement; John Beaufort could not.

One man who seems not to have been considered for the role of lieutenant in France was John Mowbray, Duke of Norfolk and hereditary Earl Marshal of England. He suffered from ill health brought on by debauchery and was afforded little respect by his peers throughout his life. That left only one man with the rank and wealth required to replace Warwick: Richard, Duke of York, who had already served as lieutenant in France in 1436–7. Humphrey,

Earl of Stafford, was appointed Captain of Calais and three years later made Duke of Buckingham.

Denied the prospect of glory and enrichment in Normandy, John and Edmund Beaufort returned to England at the end of 1440. John was made a Garter knight, and not long afterwards married Margaret Beauchamp (only distantly related to Edmund's wife), sole heir of the barony of Bletsoe and a widow with seven children. In May 1443, at the manor at Kingston Lacy, lent by the king and close to John's own lands in Dorset, Margaret bore him a daughter, also named Margaret, who was to become the most influential royal matriarch in English history.*

John preferred to reside at his own Corfe Castle, which broods over the peninsula known as the Isle of Purbeck, 90 miles directly north of Cherbourg in Normandy. From there he supervised the assembly at Portsmouth of the last army he was to lead. Faced with a French offensive against Guyenne, the king agreed to a major counter-attack out of Normandy in 1443. It was the largest expedition since Gloucester's in 1436 and was intended to draw the French away from Guyenne and bring them to battle. It was financed entirely by Cardinal Beaufort to the tune of £22,666 [£14.4 million] on condition it was led by his nephew John.

The Beaufort expedition was a departure from the previous strategy of forcing Charles VII to negotiate by making Normandy too hard a nut to crack. Two years previously York had provided his brilliant field commander Talbot with enough men to blunt a major French offensive into Normandy. Even so, they could not prevent the fall of Pontoise, a key fortress in the strategically vital Oise valley, and the case for persisting with this strategy was decreasingly persuasive. It required more money than Henry VI could obtain from Parliament, or wished to spend, and he wanted a quicker fix.

Cardinal Beaufort's offer to assume the entire cost of a counter-offensive in 1443 was therefore irresistible. Although it meant York's

* Margaret would be married to Edmund Tudor in 1455, when she was just 12 years old. Their only child, born in 1457, was the future Henry VII.

siege of Dieppe must be abandoned, he was assured the new expedition would operate in enemy territory, outside his area of authority, and accepted that John Beaufort's raid in force would relieve pressure on the rest of Normandy as well as Guyenne. The hope was that John could also defeat the French army in the field and force them to negotiate.

While Henry VI held Edmund Beaufort in high esteem, only their uncle's money and influence obtained royal favour for his older brother John. Somerset was made Baron of Kendal in Cumberland with an income of £400 [£254,500], but he was not promoted to duke until his delayed arrival at Cherbourg in late August 1443. This was to grant him parity of status with York, a quid pro quo demanded by Cardinal Beaufort.

PEERAGE PARTICIPATION IN SELECTED CAMPAIGNS 1415–53*

	Dukes/Earls			Barons	
Date	Commander	Summoned	Response	Summoned	Response
1415	Henry V	15	14	28	18
1430	Bedford	10	8	25	11
1436	Gloucester	10	8	27	17
1441	York	9	York + 1	26	3
1443	Somerset	14	Somerset	29	0
1452–3	Talbot	14	Talbot + 1	40	3

Henry V and his brothers had drawn a vigorous response from the peers summoned by Parliament for military service in France, but their successors could not. This reflected the deteriorating strategic situation, but in addition York and Somerset were not regarded as charismatic leaders. York did not actually recruit the

*Table from Adrian Bell et al. (eds.), *The Soldier in Later Medieval England.*

three barons listed for 1441 – Lords Talbot, Scales and Fauconberg – as they were already in Normandy. John Beaufort's 1443 expedition attracted no barons at all and was joined by only one banneret (a knight commanding his own company), Thomas Kyriell, and six other knights.

In sharp contrast to the speed with which Gloucester mobilized his massive 1436 expedition, those led by York and Somerset took a long time to assemble. Delay severely eroded the effectiveness of such ventures, as indentures (contracts) were for a limited time, and soldiers and horses cost much more to maintain in England and occupied France than they did in enemy territory, where they could live off the land.

Mounting a cross-Channel expedition was a major logistical challenge. Even a mounted archer needed at least two horses, esquires three and knights and above four or more. Soldiers' stipends covered their own costs, but if the horses could not graze – for example, while waiting to board ships – they consumed tons of feed at an additional cost to the chief contractor. Shipowners, also contracted for a limited time, needed to be paid whether or not they were used to transport the expedition during the stipulated period.

John's long-delayed expedition was a dismal failure. Forced to spend too much of his uncle's money before setting out, he needed to replenish his war chest as soon as possible. On his way south he crossed the border into neutral Brittany to attack the town of La Guerche, which he believed was owned by the Duke of Alençon, the local French commander. Alençon, however, had sold La Guerche to the Duke of Brittany in 1429. The 20,000 *saluts d'or* [£2.9 million] John demanded to spare the town from being sacked were paid by the enraged duke, who sent a strongly worded protest to Henry VI.

John marched on through Edmund's lands in Maine into Anjou, where he laid siege to Pouancé, one of Alençon's fiefs. A small French relief force was easily defeated, but Alençon himself refused to be drawn. Despite having carted boats from Cherbourg to bridge the Loire, John flinched from crossing the river to bring about the battle that was the strategic purpose of his expedition. Instead he marched east to Rouen, paying off his troops as he went, some of whom took service with the frontier garrisons.

After a frosty reception from York, John received a copy of the Duke of Brittany's protest from Henry VI, who ordered him to make full restitution. Compelled to disgorge whatever he had not spent, in January 1444 he returned to England in disgrace, sick, and once more in straitened circumstances. Barred from court, he spent his remaining months at Corfe and nearby Wimborne, where he died in May 1444, aged 42, probably by his own hand.

Edmund, created a marquess when his brother was made a duke, inherited the earldom and Corfe Castle, but the barony of Kendal and John's French fiefs reverted to the crown. John's entailed estate went to one-year-old baby Margaret, who remained with her mother. However the king broke a solemn undertaking given to John prior to his expedition, that her mother should also have the right to decide whom the child should marry. Instead, he made Margaret Beaufort the ward of his chief minister William de la Pole, at this point still only Earl of Suffolk, who promptly betrothed her to his two-year-old son John.

Edmund, to some extent, shared his brother's disgrace at this time, and may have traded off his niece's future in order to regain favour. On the other hand he must have secretly despised Suffolk for exploiting the situation to his own advantage, and the king for permitting him to do so. Some of Edmund's future behaviour may have been conditioned by this sordid episode.

HOUSE OF
VALOIS-ANJOU

I N THE FIRST ACT OF THE THIRD PART OF HIS *HENRY VI*
trilogy Shakespeare dubbed Marguerite d'Anjou the 'she-wolf of
France'. Her demonization by Tudor propagandists had its roots
in the efforts of Henry VII to have his namesake Lancastrian predecessor declared a saint, which required the transfer to Marguerite
of much of the blame for the catastrophes of her husband's reign.
Although the Bard did not mean it as a compliment, she-wolves are
in fact admirable animals that mate for life and are fiercely protec-
tive of their young.

Thus also Marguerite, who was a loyal and supportive consort to
Henry VI until it became apparent his weakness was endangering
their son's birth right, after which she felt compelled to provide
the necessary leadership. Her relentless determination, and the loyalty she commanded from some seriously hard men, leads one to
wonder whether her son Edward of Westminster might have made
a great king.

Marguerite was born in Lorraine, the duchy inherited by her
mother Isabelle in 1431. Her father was René of the House of
Valois-Anjou, second son of Louis II, Duke of Anjou, Count of
Maine and Count of Provence, and Princess Yolande de Aragón.
Louis devoted most of his energies to wider dynastic ambitions and
left the government of Anjou almost entirely to Yolande. After he
died, Yolande became regent for her young sons and fought the

English invasions of Maine and northern Anjou.

This she continued to do for the rest of her life, while her sons were mainly occupied elsewhere. She was also the surrogate mother of the disinherited Dauphin Charles, who married Yolande's daughter Marie six months before he claimed the kingdom in 1422. Later, Yolande was closely involved in the emergence of Jeanne d'Arc, with whom her son René rode to the 1429 relief of Orléans, the first major French victory over the English.

Yolande recruited and ran a network of courtesans who became the mistresses of high-ranking men in the courts of Brittany, Burgundy and Lorraine, and in the French royal household. In the process of detaching Brittany from its alliance with England, she won the loyalty of Arthur de Richemont, younger brother of Duke Yann VI of Brittany. Richemont became Constable of France in 1425, with Yolande's own subject Pierre de Brézé by his side.

In 1433, at Yolande's instigation, Richemont and Brézé expelled Charles VII's Grand Chamberlain Georges de la Trémoille, who had frittered away the military momentum won by Jeanne d'Arc in pointless negotiations. Richemont and Brézé were the architects of the 1435 Treaty of Arras with Burgundy, which marked the definitive turning-point of the war, and of the policies that earned Charles VII the sobriquets 'Well-Served' and 'Victorious'.

It would be hard to overstate how important Yolande was to the final stages of the Hundred Years War, or the significance for our story of the fact that during the last four to five years of Yolande's life (she died in 1442), her granddaughter Marguerite came to live with her during her transition to adolescence.

Marguerite's mother Isabelle was cast in the same mould as her mother-in-law and placed Agnès Sorel, who became the first officially recognized royal mistress, in Charles VII's household. It was thanks to Agnès's influence that Brézé rose so rapidly in the king's service from 1444 until her death in 1450. In 1435 Isabelle led an army in an unsuccessful effort to rescue her hapless husband from Burgundian captivity. In return for freeing René, the Burgundians

HOUSE OF VALOIS-ANJOU

Jean II = Bonne of Bohemia
King of France   (d.1349)
(d.1364)

Charles V   John   Philippe
King of France   Duke of Berry   Duke of Burgundy
(d.1380)   (d.1416)   (d.1404)

Louis I = Marie
Duke of Anjou   of Blois
(d.1384)   (d.1404)

Louis II = Yolande of
Duke of Anjou   Aragon
(d.1417)   (d.1442)

Louis III   Marie = **Charles VII**   René = Isabelle   Charles = Isabelle of
Duke of   (d.1463)   King of   Duke of   Duchess of   Count of   Saint-Pol
Anjou   France   Anjou   Lorraine   Maine   (d.1472)
(d.1434)   (1403–61)   (d.1480)   (d.1453)   (d.1472)

Louis XI   Charles IV
King of France   Duke of Anjou
(1423–83)   (d.1481)

Jean II = Marie du   Yolande = Frederick   Marguerite = **Henry VI**
Duke of   Bourbon   (d.1483)   Count of   (1430–82)   King of
Lorraine   (d.1488)   Vaudémont   England
(d.1470)   (d.1470)   *House of Lancaster*

Nicholas   René II
Duke of Lorraine   Duke of Lorraine
(d.1473)   (d.1508)

not only required a hefty ransom but also took his two sons hostage, one of whom would die in prison. Left impoverished, René and Isabelle sent young Marguerite to live with her grandmother Yolande.

Marguerite's father René became Duke of Anjou and Count of Provence on the death of his elder brother Louis in 1434. Four years earlier he had become (by marriage and adoption) Duke of Bar and Count of Piedmont. He also claimed the kingdom of Naples, but lost it to Alfonso V of Aragón in 1442. René was also titular King of Hungary and Jerusalem, and in 1466 made a futile claim to the throne of Aragón through the right of his mother.

He went through the motions of being a prince, but after his formidable mother and wife died he devoted himself to artistic pursuits. He looks remarkably like a toad in the only portraits we have of him, but they were painted when he was older. The striking portrait of Isabelle of Lorraine in the Uffizi Gallery leaves no doubt about the source of their daughter's looks.

Both genetically and through training by experts, therefore, Marguerite had the potential to be a dynamic queen consort, and grew up witnessing how strong women could make something of weak men. Lamentably for her and for England, while her husband Henry VI was even more ineffectual than her father he was also less pliable, and circumstances completely beyond her control doomed her attempt to emulate her grandmother.

Properly handled, a marriage alliance with the House of Valois-Anjou had much to offer the English crown. Charles VII had no eligible daughter, and his queen's niece was as good a French match as Henry VI could hope for. That said, England's best chance of imposing a negotiated settlement evaporated in 1440, when it failed to exploit the opportunity presented by a rebellion against Richemont's centralizing policies by the Duke of Bourbon and the deposed Grand Chamberlain Trémoille, who enticed the Duke of Brittany and Charles VII's teenaged heir apparent Louis to join them in a rebellion known as the 'Praguerie' (by analogy with a revolt that had recently occurred in Bohemia).

Henry's first choice had been to marry a daughter of Count Jean IV of Armagnac, one of the few remaining French magnates not of royal blood. This would have strengthened England's position in south-west France, off-setting the deep commitment to Charles VII of the Lord of Albret, whose lands lay within and adjacent to English Guyenne. Charles VII put an end to the count's dalliance with the English by invading Armagnac, imprisoning him and installing royal officials to administer La Marche, Rodez and Armagnac-Comminges (see Map 4).

So it was that when Suffolk was sent to treat for the hand of Marguerite in 1444, his negotiating position was weak and he insisted on the explicit backing of the Council and Parliament. At the time it was recognized that his contacts among the magnates of France made him uniquely qualified for the task; later they were viewed in a more sinister light. Suffolk's embassy met Charles VII and Richemont at Tours, the capital of Touraine, with René d'Anjou in attendance. At the end of May a two-year truce was agreed and a betrothal ceremony, with Suffolk as proxy for the king, was performed.

Suffolk also made a number of informal proposals authorized by Henry, including a temporary suspension of the English claim to the French throne in return for an extension of the truce, and the possibility that lands seized by the English in Maine and Anjou might be returned to René. These proposals were, rightly, interpreted by the French as evidence of Henry's lack of the will to prosecute the war, and Richemont used the truce to accelerate the establishment of the first standing army in French history.

Suffolk, by then a marquess, returned to collect the new queen the following November with a large retinue including 28-year-old Jacquetta, newly delivered of her second son, and her husband Richard Woodville. In 1443, Jacquetta's younger sister had married Marguerite's uncle Charles, the dispossessed Count of Maine, so she was able to greet the young queen as a kinswoman. As foreigners married into the English ruling family they had much in common and became good friends.

• ∽ •

A key member of Suffolk's retinue was his duchess, 40-year-old Alice de la Pole, granddaughter of the poet Geoffrey Chaucer. Marguerite would form a daughterly bond with Alice who, like Jacquetta, would become one of her ladies-in-waiting. The Chaucer connection reveals how Suffolk became part of the Beaufort affinity. Geoffrey Chaucer was married to the sister of John of Gaunt's mistress and later wife Katherine Swynford, mother of the Beaufort clan.* Alice's father Thomas, elected Speaker of the House of Commons five times between 1407 and his death in 1434, was a key intermediary between Henry IV and his son, and as a result was Henry V's most trusted official. After the king's death, Thomas worked closely with Bishop Beaufort to deny Gloucester the regency.

Alice was Thomas's sole heir, having previously inherited a large estate from her short-lived first husband, whom she married when she was 11 years old, and an even larger one from her second, Thomas Montagu, Earl of Salisbury, whom she married when still a teenager. He was killed in 1429 at the siege of Orléans, after which Suffolk, Salisbury's second-in-command, was defeated and captured by Jeanne d'Arc herself. He was released a year later after payment of a £20,000 [£12.7 million] ransom and promising to do all he could to obtain the release of the Count of Angoulême, a hostage since 1412, and his older brother the Duke of Orléans, captured at Agincourt in 1415.

Impoverished Suffolk became betrothed to now very wealthy Alice immediately after his release. Although she sensibly insisted on a 'what's mine is mine and what's yours is mine also' prenuptial

---

* If to Chaucer's robust appreciation of female sexuality we add the evidence of John of Gaunt's infatuation, it is reasonable to assume that the Swynford sisters were also passionate princesses.

settlement, theirs was a genuine love-match, strongly suggesting there may have been a previous relationship. Suffolk became lord of the Woodville estate at Grafton as Alice's husband, not in his own right, so it is reasonable to assume she and Jacquetta knew each other before they formed part of the young queen's retinue.

• ℘ •

The bridal party made a progress through occupied Normandy, during which Marguerite was greeted as queen of France. At Rouen, pleading illness but possibly ashamed of the poverty of her wardrobe, she did not take part in a procession and pageant organized by the Duke of York, the king's lieutenant in France. Although Jacquetta was of senior rank as dowager duchess of Bedford, she stood aside to let Alice represent the queen.

The most commonly reproduced likeness of Marguerite is from a magnificently illustrated book given to her at Rouen by John Talbot, by now Earl of Shrewsbury and Marshal of France. Although the depictions of Talbot himself and of his superior Richard of York (among the spectators) would have been taken from life by the Rouen miniaturists, the illustration shows Talbot presenting the book to Marguerite as crowned queen, holding hands with a depiction of Henry VI that bears no resemblance to any other portrait of him.

Sadly, the charming portrait of Marguerite bears no relation to her appearance, either. The loose hair represents virginity, and by convention all English queens were portrayed as fair-haired. She was described as dark-haired, and as 'handsome' rather than beautiful. The only reliable likeness of Marguerite is her profile on a medallion made for René d'Anjou by the sculptor Pietro da Milano in 1464, after she had fled England.

After her arrival at Southampton on 9 April, genuinely ill after a rough crossing, Marguerite was visited by the king in disguise, a convention of courtly love she was too distracted to recognize.

Henry ordered she should be bedecked and adorned as befitted a queen, and on 22 April they were married at Titchfield Abbey in Hampshire by his confessor, Bishop William Ayscough of Salisbury. Pageants and tableaux celebrating peace marked her entry into London on 28 May, and she was crowned in Westminster Abbey two days later.

Three days of feasts and tournaments followed. Not only was 15-year-old Marguerite herself rapturously received, but Suffolk was unanimously commended by the Lords, led by the Duke of Gloucester, and by the Commons. He was later to be made the scapegoat for the failure of English policy in France, but in mid-1445 he was applauded for accomplishing the king's commission, and for acting in accordance with the consensus of the political nation.

Tragically for Marguerite and fatally for Suffolk, her marriage was the keystone of a peace policy based on wishful thinking. It was not politically possible for Henry VI to surrender his dynasty's claim to the throne of France (not formally renounced by the British crown until 1801), or to pay homage to Charles VII for Normandy and Guyenne. With the strategic balance tipping more in his favour every year, however, Charles was not going to accept anything less.

If not often active allies of France, Burgundy and Brittany were no longer making common cause with England, and French royal authority was stronger than ever after the 1440 rebellion was crushed. Previously dependent on revenues from the ravaged royal domain and exceptional grants from the Estates General, in 1438 Charles helped himself to the substantial proportion of Church revenues previously paid to Rome.

The following year the Estates General voted to make permanent the *taille*, a previously exceptional tax on land, specifically to pay for a standing army.* Charles's appointment in 1436 of the talented

---

* As John Fortescue observed in his near-contemporary *On the Laws and Governance of England, or the Difference between an Absolute and a Limited Monarchy*, the *taille* and the standing army defined the French monarchy.

merchant Jacques Coeur as Master of the Royal Mint had brought rip-roaring inflation under control, and in 1438 he made him Steward of the Royal Expenditure. Improving fiscal order helped to sustain a boom in production and commerce sparked by the inflation, taxes from which further enhanced the royal exchequer.

The final factor dooming the English empire in France was demographics. Although reduced by pandemics from a peak of 17 million a century earlier, at 10 million France still had a population four times as large as England and Wales in the mid-fifteenth century. However, the estimated 'French' population includes Brittany, Burgundy, English Guyenne and the vast areas occupied by the Anglo-Burgundian alliance in northern and north-eastern France. Until the Burgundians changed sides in 1435 the demographic imbalance was not great, but Duke Philippe's desertion of his former allies tipped the scales decisively in France's favour.

The most fought-over areas, in particular Normandy, Maine, Alençon and the Île-de-France, suffered population declines of 70–75 per cent against an average of 40 per cent for the rest of the country. Unlike stable and prosperous Guyenne, the northern areas conquered after Agincourt became so devastated by marauding armies and endemic banditry that the cost of holding them outstripped the surpluses that could be extracted from them.

For all the certainty of England's impending defeat, the manner in which they were bundled out of Normandy within five years of the royal marriage, followed by the loss of neglected Guyenne, was a national humiliation. Suffolk and Edmund Beaufort were to be made the scapegoats, because to blame the king would have been high treason. In their innermost thoughts, however, all knew that the manner in which England lost its continental empire was primarily attributable to Henry VI's incompetence.

The failure of her marriage to bring peace and the consequent loss of Normandy and Guyenne therefore did not affect Marguerite's popularity, which soared against a backdrop of the collapse both of English rule in France and her husband's fragile morale. Her response was the first occasion on which she would step in to fill the void of authority left by her husband. Thereafter she played an increasingly activist role, as one would expect of a woman born of Duchess Isabelle of Lorraine and prepared for life by Princess Yolande de Aragón.

HOUSE OF
YORK

THE ARMS OF RICHARD, THIRD DUKE OF YORK, PROVED predictive of his life. The first and fourth quarters proclaimed him the great-grandson of Edward III, the second quarter was his grandmother's arms of Castille and León, and the third quartered the arms of the Mortimer earls of March and the Burgh earls of Ulster. The most potent element, however, was the central inescutcheon of the arms of England.

As the only son of two direct descendants of Edward III, the burden of ancestry lay heavily on him. His father Richard of Conisbrough, Earl of Cambridge, was the grandson of Edward III's fourth son Edmund, Duke of York. His mother Anne Mortimer, who died bearing him, was the great-granddaughter of Lionel, Duke of Clarence, Edward's second son. As Henry IV's father John of Gaunt was only the third son of Edward III, the Mortimer claim to the throne was stronger than the Lancastrian.

In 1415, when his namesake son was three years old, Cambridge was involved in a plot to put his brother-in-law Edmund Mortimer, 5th Earl of March, on the throne. Alas, he had failed to consult Edmund, who informed Henry V of the plot as soon as he learned of it and was a member of the court that condemned Cambridge to death. Even so, Henry V pointedly pardoned Edmund for his entirely unwitting role in the plot, to leave him in no doubt about the thinness of the ice under his feet.

The complicated backstory to the 1415 conspiracy began with the 1st Earl of March, Roger Mortimer, who was executed and attainted in 1330 after seizing power and murdering Edward II. After the title and Mortimer lands were restored to the 2nd earl in 1354, in 1368 the 3rd Earl of March married Philippa, only child of Lionel, Duke of Clarence, through whom he became Earl of Ulster. As the next in line to the throne after the Black Prince's son, the future Richard II, March was a leader of the nobles opposed to John of Gaunt's influence over Edward III during his final, senile years.

The 4th Earl of March was heir presumptive to Richard II until he was killed in an Irish ambush in 1398. Richard went to Ireland the following year to avenge his death, and on his return found he had lost his kingdom to Henry Bolingbroke, John of Gaunt's eldest son. In 1402, the 4th earl's brother was captured by Owain Glyn Dŵr and, after Henry IV refused to ransom him and looted his estate, joined the Glyn Dŵr-Percy rebellion, proclaiming his nephew Edmund, the 5th earl, to be the true king of England.

To thicken the plot further, Constance of York and Edward, Duke of York, the daughter and eldest son of Edmund of Langley, Edward III's fourth son, were involved in a plot to spring March from custody in Windsor Castle. Henry IV imprisoned York for four months; but he kept Edmund Mortimer in custody for the remaining years of his reign. There were good reasons for distrust of the Mortimers to be practically written into the DNA of the Lancastrian dynasty.

Edward of York was not involved in the later plot that led to the execution of Richard of Conisbrough, his younger brother, and shortly afterwards died heroically at Agincourt. Having saved his neck by denouncing Richard's plot, Edmund Mortimer was released from custody and restored to his inheritance by Henry V, under whose supervision he served in France. Although subsequently a member of the regency Council, he was never fully trusted by the Lancastrians and was sent to Ireland, where he died of the plague in 1425.

HOUSE OF YORK

k. = killed in battle   x. = executed

Edmund of Langley = Isabella of Castille
(1364–1402)   (d.1392)

Edward of Langley
2nd Duke of York
(k.1415)

Thomas Despenser = Constance = *Unmarried*
1st Earl of Gloucester   of York   Edmund Holland
(d.1400)   (d.1416)   4th Earl of Kent
                                    (k.1408)

1. Richard = Isabel = 2. Richard
Beauchamp (d.1439) Beauchamp
1st Earl   13th Earl
of Worcester   of Warwick
(k.1422)   (d.1439)

Eleanor = James Tuchet
Holland   5th Baron
(d.1459) Audley
          (k.1459)

Elizabeth = Edward
Baroness   Neville
Bergavenny *House of*
(d.1448)   *Neville*

Henry = Cecily
1st Duke Neville
of Warwick *House of*
(d.1446)   *Neville*

Anne = Richard
16th Countess Neville
of Warwick   *House of*
(d.1492)   *Neville*

Anne = Henry Holland
(1439–76) 3rd Duke Exeter
           (k.1477)

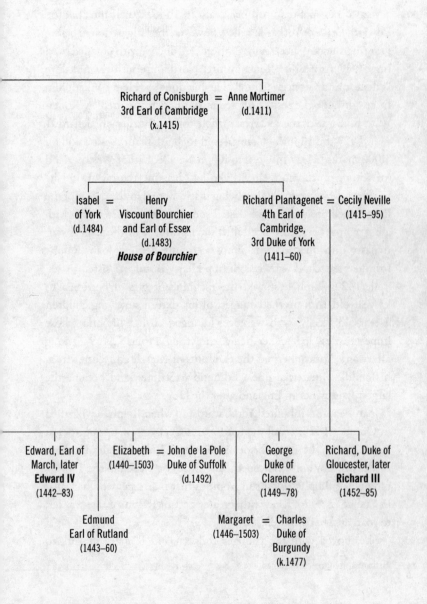

Henry V had not attainted Richard of Conisbrough, so his name-sake son inherited the earldom of Cambridge, although his young stepmother, Maud née Clifford, occupied Conisbrough Castle and several other manors until her death in 1446. When the childless Edward, Duke of York, was killed, however, the king hesitated before granting the boy succession to his uncle's duchy, with entailed hold-ings in Hertfordshire, Lincolnshire, Northamptonshire, Yorkshire, Wiltshire and Gloucestershire.* Having done so, Henry V kept him in custody for the rest of his reign, ominously guarded by Robert Waterton, one of the men responsible for the murder of Richard II.

In 1423 the minority Council sold Richard of York's wardship for 3,000 marks [£1.27 million] to Ralph Neville, Earl of Westmorland (of whom much more later), who had become the greater of the northern Marcher lords after being instrumental in the defeat of the Percy rebellions. That the Council should have entrusted him with a boy whose very existence called the legitimacy of the Lancastrian dynasty into question was almost certainly because Joan, Ralph's formidable second wife, was Bishop Henry Beaufort's sister.

In 1424 Ralph bestowed the magnificent gift of betrothal to 13-year-old York on the youngest of his sixteen surviving children, 9-year-old Cecily, who was over-indulged all her life and whose imperiousness led to her being known as 'Proud Cis'. Not long afterwards York inherited the earldoms of March and Ulster from his childless maternal uncle Edmund Mortimer, and became the largest landowner in England after the king.

Joan Beaufort inherited York's wardship when Ralph Neville died in October 1425. Until then, York and Cecily grew up together at Raby, one of the finest castles in England. The title, the Durham castles of Raby and Brancepeth, and little else passed to the 19-year-old heir of Ralph's eldest son from his first marriage, who had died in France in 1420. The vastly greater part of Ralph's estate was left to Joan and her children.

She moved with the younger children and Richard of York to

* Richard also inherited York's earldom of Rutland, a landless, courtesy title.

London. York had been presented at court earlier, but from this time he was able to observe at first hand the power struggle between Bishop Beaufort and Gloucester. When Bedford returned to part the warring princes in 1426, he took the time to knight York and other young lords who travelled back to France with him. In 1429 York sailed back to England to take up residence in the royal household and, in May, he and Cecily were married. Later in 1429 they were present at the coronation of 7-year-old Henry VI in Westminster Abbey, and then formed part of the cortege that accompanied him to Rouen and then to Paris, where he was crowned king of France in December 1431.

Twenty-year-old York finally came into his inheritance in May 1432. The 5th Earl of March had left the Mortimer estate heavily encumbered, but the deaths of the dowager Duchess of York in 1431 and of the dowager Countess of March in 1432 gave York the cash flow to settle with his debtors, among them Cardinal Beaufort, who behaved benevolently towards his nephew by marriage. With the Beauforts disqualified, York was next in line to the throne after the king's aging and childless uncles, and the cardinal was keen to win him.

York's estates in England and Wales plus annuities were worth about £4,600 [£2.92 million] per annum. He also had estates in Normandy, and although revenues from them and his Irish earldom of Ulster and the lordships of Connacht and Trim were meagre, his total annual income was well in excess of £5,000. The administrative centre for his holdings in Wales, the Middle March and the West Country was at Ludlow Castle in Shropshire, for Yorkshire at Sandal Castle, and for his eastern holdings at Fotheringhay Castle in Northamptonshire.

To put this in perspective, crown rents from its own lands in England and France, plus church subsidies, feudal and other dues (including payments in lieu of military service), and customs receipts from the export of wool, were about £70,000 [£44.52 million] per annum during 1438–53, the period of Henry VI's personal kingship prior to the loss of English France. The loss of Guyenne, in particular, was a severe blow and reduced annual crown revenues to about £44,000 up to 1461, when the first round of the Wars of the Roses came to a climax.*

York did not, therefore, approach the 'over-mighty subject' standard set by John of Gaunt. There was no reason for Henry VI's entourage to regard him as even a potential threat until, the king being still childless, he became the heir presumptive following the death of Gloucester in 1447. Initially York was treated with deference, and he was described as a 'great prince of our blood' in a royal commission of May 1436, by which he was first appointed the king's Lieutenant of Normandy following the death of Bedford.

The appointment pitched him into a potential disaster. As we saw in Chapter 2, Edmund Beaufort's separate expedition, funded by his uncle Cardinal Beaufort, which might have drawn French forces to the west, was diverted to the Calais theatre, where Gloucester was confronting the treaty-breaking Duke of Burgundy. Meanwhile the French had recaptured Paris and most of the Île-de-France, and had taken the Channel port of Dieppe and its hinterland along the eastern flank of Normandy.

The forces York brought with him permitted Talbot, whom he appointed Marshal of France, to blunt the French offensive. He himself led a campaign to restore English authority in the rebellious Pays de Caux, the large area between the northern Seine valley and the Channel. York's principal contribution, however, was political and administrative. He restored the shaken confidence of the Norman Estates General, and in the process of stripping out reinforcements for Talbot he imposed discipline on predatory English garrisons. He inherited Bedford's military and administrative staff, and continued his custom of hearing grievances in person, assuming the role of viceroy without having been authorized to do so.

Neither in 1436–7 nor during his second lieutenancy in 1441–5 did York command men in battle. His was the leadership of an

* From the table in Peter Karsten, *The Military-State-Society Symbiosis.*

able administrator and an even-handed magistrate, who chose good subordinates and made sure they stayed good. Although he did not command the tribal loyalty that exalts the warrior prince, he was widely respected. He had a clear idea of how things should be done, but a high sense of his own worth made him a poor politician. He also regarded greed and corruption with lofty disdain, which made him no friends among his less high-minded peers.

After Talbot went home following the 1436 campaign, York appointed Richard Neville, Earl of Salisbury and his wife Cecily's oldest brother, as his military lieutenant. York had already requested permission to return home, and although his successor Richard Beauchamp, Earl of Warwick, was nominated in May 1437, he did not relieve York until November. Salisbury came at the request of Warwick, with whom he had recently concluded a double matrimonial alliance, but it gave York and his brother-in-law – who was eleven years his senior – an opportunity to get to know each other.

York cited the expiry of the indentures of the men he had brought with him and the inability of the Norman exchequer to cover the cost of renewing them as the reason for wishing to relinquish his post. He was substantially out of pocket, as by the terms of his own indenture he was supposed to be reimbursed from the Norman exchequer, which was now bankrupt.

When Warwick and his wife died in April 1439, Salisbury returned to England to administer their estate and to look after his own children's interest in the succession, which was to keep him busy through the next decade. Asked to resume the lieutenancy, York demanded and was granted a promise of an annual subsidy of £20,000 [£12.72 million] from the English exchequer, plus the viceregal powers previously enjoyed by the Duke of Bedford.

Although York was unable to recruit the nobles summoned by Parliament, a trio of effective field commanders were already in place. William Neville, Baron Fauconberg, another brother-in-law, had come with York in 1436 and was now Lieutenant-General of central Normandy. Thomas, Baron Scales, had spent his entire adult life in Normandy and was marshal and Lieutenant-General of western Normandy. York was to make him godfather to Edward, his eldest son.

However the star, once again, was the newly returned Talbot, 53 years old in 1440. He had fought in Wales and Ireland before first being sent to Normandy in 1420 to separate him from the violent disputes with his peers in which he revelled. York now handed him the troops he had brought with him from England, and also thinned the Norman garrisons to provide him with additional forces. His role was to deal with the eastern sector, facing the main French thrust. Talbot's fast-moving 1441 campaign was a tactical masterpiece that demoralized Charles VII's new army and came close to capturing the king himself.

In early 1442, anticipating the French would renew their offensive, York sent Talbot to England to request urgent reinforcements. This was the only period when the king devoted his full attention to events in France, and he gave Talbot all he asked for. He also created him Earl of Shropshire (although he became known as the Earl of Shrewsbury), and recreated the barony of Lisle for his namesake son. Talbot's expedition did not, however, deliver the hoped-for returns. Royal enthusiasm for the strategy pursued by York and Talbot waned, leading to John Beaufort's ill-fated 1443 expedition.

• ∽ •

On 28 April 1442 Cecily gave birth to the future Edward IV. Given the dynastic significance later attached to the circumstances of his birth, they repay close consideration. The marriage had been barren for ten years when Anne was born in August 1439 in Fotheringhay, York's Northamptonshire castle. After the couple moved to Rouen, baby Henry was born in February 1441, but died unbaptised. Edward was baptized immediately after birth, without ceremony, in a side chapel of Rouen Cathedral. By contrast, after the next boy,

Edmund, was born in May 1443, his baptism was a lavish occasion for public celebration.

Nine months before Edward's birth, York had been dealing with the Pays de Caux rebellion. He could perhaps have made a brief but fruitful visit to Cecily at Rouen in late July 1441, but many years later Edward's youngest brothers (George, born in Dublin in 1449, and Richard, born at Fotheringhay in 1452) were in no doubt that Edward was the product of their mother's adultery. In 1483 the Italian chronicler Dominic Mancini was told that when Cecily learned of Edward's secret marriage to the commoner Elizabeth Woodville in 1464, she 'fell into a frenzy' and threatened to expose him as illegitimate.

One has only to contrast the depiction, from life, of York in the book Talbot presented to Marguerite at Rouen in 1445, with portraits of Edward IV to doubt they could have been father and son. Furthermore, when Edward IV's skeleton was measured in 1789 it was found he was 6ft 4in, much the tallest monarch in English history, and built in proportion. Following the recent discovery of the skeleton of York's namesake youngest, the future Richard III, we know he was slightly built and were it not for severe scoliosis, which reduced his standing height below 5ft, would have been about 5ft 8in. This corresponds closely with a contemporary description of his father as small, dark and 'spare'. Height is almost entirely hereditary, and although there are other cases where short men have had immensely taller sons, there are compelling reasons to doubt that this was one of them.

Cecily, bereft and vulnerable after the death of baby Henry and left alone while York was fire-fighting the 1441 crisis, may well have looked for comfort from someone else. Perhaps the individual was indeed a strapping archer called Blaybourne, named in 1469 by her nephew Richard Neville, Earl of Warwick, without contradiction from her son George, allied with him at the time against Edward. However, the most persuasive indication that Edward was a cuckoo is York's coldness towards him. When they fled England in October

1459 he took Edmund with him to Ireland while Edward, the heir he should have wanted by his side, went with the Nevilles to Calais.

So much of what followed fits the cuckoo hypothesis that to reject it requires the greater leap of faith. Had York denounced Cecily's adultery it would have made him a laughing stock and would have caused a rift with both the Nevilles and the Beauforts. Conversely, by not doing so, he put his haughty wife in his debt. Perhaps working on the principle that if he kept Cecily pregnant she could not cuckold him again, he made sure she bore him Edmund a year later, and Elizabeth the following year.

• ∾ •

Following the failure of John Beaufort's expedition the king veered back to York, paying the £20,000 due to him at the end of 1443 unusually promptly. The truce negotiated at Tours in May 1444 greatly reduced York's military expenses and permitted him to exercise a benevolent government that won him the lasting loyalty of the Anglo-Normans. Although he was not paid his dues for 1444, he was granted an appanage (a form of tenure traditionally awarded to younger sons of the French monarchy) of lands around Évreux in south central Normandy, worth £650 [£413,400] a year. In 1445 the king also gave his consent for York to pass his earldoms of March and Cambridge to Edward, and Rutland to Edmund, and even endowed Edmund with lands to go with what was an otherwise hollow title.

York was never a member of a supposed 'war party' led by the Duke of Gloucester – who was anyway, by this time, a spent force. To the contrary, he fully embraced the alternative strategy accomplished by Suffolk at Tours in May 1444 and, as we have seen, organized a lavish reception for Marguerite d'Anjou at Rouen early in 1445. He also sent troops to support a 1444 French invasion of Alsace in 1444, led by the dauphin. Nor did he voice any criticism of the king's decision to appease Charles VII with the cession of

Maine – which was, after all, Edmund Beaufort's fief.

The reason York returned to England in September 1445 was straightforward: he was owed a great deal of money, his indentures were about to expire and he would not renew them unless his own contract was honoured. It was not a case of abandoning a sinking ship: Normandy was at peace, he was enjoying his viceregal role and was willing to resume it. At the suggestion of the king, he had even opened negotiations for a marriage between his son Edward and Princess Madeleine, Charles VII's youngest daughter.

York's claim of £38,666 [£24.6 million] in arrears was a bargaining position. In the end he settled for £26,000 [£16.54 million] plus the borough of Waltham in Essex and the wardship of his 17-year-old son-in-law Henry Holland, who became Duke of Exeter when his father died in 1447. As a descendant of Edward III through both John of Gaunt and Thomas of Woodstock, Holland's claim to being the heir presumptive after Gloucester's death was as good as, and in Holland's opinion better than, York's. The king's consent to the marriage between Holland and York's 8-year-old daughter Anne in 1445 had been a mark of unqualified trust.

Unable to obtain the terms he wanted to return to Normandy, York had no reason to object to the appointment of Edmund Beaufort, and, in the light of subsequent events, must have judged he was well out of it. Nor was he necessarily piqued not to be granted a prominent role in government, as he would have been well aware of Suffolk's magpie-like attitude to power, and of the king's aversion to disagreement. As it was, he attended numerous Council meetings and was a witness to most of the charters issued in 1446–8.

In mid-1446 Bishop Adam Moleyns, Bishop of Chichester, Lord Privy Seal and a key member of the king's inner circle, attempted to attribute the deteriorating situation in Normandy to York's mismanagement. The duke petitioned the king to clear his name and in reply, Moleyns swore he never said such a thing, nor would he of a prince as eminent and highly respected as York. He had merely, he said, reported the opinion of unspecified others. This was, perhaps, a shabby bargaining ploy in the negotiation of the crown's outstanding debt to York – but if so, it was singularly ill-advised.

York was appointed Lord Lieutenant of Ireland in July 1447. It has been argued that this posting was intended to 'get him out of the way', but it manifestly did not. He was permitted to appoint a deputy and did so, not moving to Dublin until two years later. By that time the writing was on the wall for Normandy. Like many of his peers, York wisely sought to put as much distance as possible between himself and the doomed Suffolk administration.

Trying to pacify Ireland was like ploughing the sea, but in the fourteen months York was there he received the submissions of several Irish clan leaders, and showed 'good lordship' to his tenants in Ulster. He also ensured the election of one of Queen Marguerite's chaplains to the archbishopric of Dublin, and sided with James Butler, Earl of Ormonde, in his bitter dispute with Thomas Fitzgerald over the succession to the earldom of Kildare. This was a politically astute display of deference on York's part: Ormonde's namesake son was a member of Henry's inner circle, and was created Earl of Wiltshire the same month that York finally moved to Dublin.

Although hindsight permits us to see some straws in the wind, there is no evidence before 1450 that Richard of York was anything other than a loyal subject, who benefited greatly from the king's 'good lordship', or that the king's councillors believed him to be a threat even after he became the heir presumptive. Ironically, the break came about because, by governing Normandy and Ireland competently in the king's name, he won a reputation around which those who had suffered as a result of the king's fecklessness could rally.

FACTION AND FEUD

IT WAS NOT ONLY IN FRANCE THAT HENRY'S DITHERING unwillingness to deal with inconvenient reality created a combustible situation. Failure to impose order on his unruly nobles, and to restrain the rapacity of his household, undermined royal authority at home as well. During the 1440s, fear of legal retribution eroded to the point that nobles and knights increasingly resorted to arms in territorial disputes and competition for local influence.

The most serious breakdown was in the West Country, where a local rivalry was inflamed by Henry's intervention. In 1441, he awarded the prestigious stewardship of the royal duchy of Cornwall to Thomas Courtenay, 13th Earl of Devon, a descendant of Edward I and husband to Margaret Beaufort, Henry VI's aunt. This was the year Eleanor Cobham, the Duke of Gloucester's wife, was convicted of witchcraft and Devon's appointment was just one of several similar awards designed to affirm the Beaufort clan at a national level.

The rather large fly in the ointment was that the office had previously been awarded, for life, to William Bonville, a member of Suffolk's affinity. Bonville was the most prominent of a group of gentry and lesser nobility whose influence in the West Country had grown during Devon's long minority (1422–33), when his mother devoted her best efforts to frustrating her son. She continued to reside at Tiverton, the seat of the earls of Devon, and to control half the revenues from the estate until her death in 1441.

Bonville's second marriage, in 1427, was to Margaret Courtenay, widow of John, Baron Harington, and daughter of the 12th Earl of Devon – hence Thomas Courtenay's aunt. Bonville also married his namesake son from his first marriage to Margaret Courtenay's daughter from hers.* From Devon's point of view, it was bad enough that Bonville had gained so much from marriage with his own family. What made it all the more galling was that the dowager duchess's occupation of Tiverton obliged him to make his residence at Colcombe Castle, 2 miles from Bonville's main residence at Shute, which he had obtained by his marriage to Courtenay's aunt.

The Earl of Devon saw the appointment of Bonville in 1437 as royal steward in Cornwall for life as reflecting the government's belief that his rival was now the pre-eminent political figure in the West Country. Despite the erosion of his family's status, however, Devon's electoral and legal patronage remained more extensive than Bonville's. To prove the point he sent his retainers out to provoke Bonville's, secure in the knowledge he could frustrate any legal recourse by his rival.

Low intensity brawling began in 1439 and continued into 1441 despite a feeble royal attempt at arbitration. This was when the king appointed Devon to the stewardship of Cornwall, without revoking his prior grant to Bonville. Although the new appointment was promptly withdrawn, it was a classic illustration of the king's unerring instinct for getting the worst of both worlds. The consequences could have been more immediately dire had chance not intervened through the death of Devon's mother. Being able at last to take up residence at Tiverton Castle seems to have mollified him. In December 1441 Devon and Bonville were formally reconciled and required to post bonds for future good behaviour.

It is not clear whether Bonville renounced the stewardship of

* Their son became Baron Harington in 1458 following the death of his maternal grandfather. When all the male Bonvilles were killed his daughter Cecily became sole heir of both the Harington and Bonville estates.

Cornwall, but Courtenay was definitely re-awarded it in 1444. Bonville, meanwhile, had been appointed seneschal (steward) of Gascony and sailed to Bordeaux in March 1443, not returning to Devon permanently until 1447. Possibly he judged the Cornwall office not worth the aggravation and concentrated instead on strengthening his political connections. He was with Suffolk at the betrothal of Marguerite d'Anjou in May 1444, and married his eldest daughter to William Tailboys, a member of the king's household and Suffolk's most notorious henchman.

• ❧ •

As a living embodiment of the collapse of the rule of law under Henry VI, Tailboys almost merits a chapter in his own right. He was a wealthy man with estates in Lincolnshire and in Northumberland, where he owned the large moorland estate of Redesdale. Yet he chose to become the leader of a gang of thugs that rampaged through southern Lincolnshire during most of the 1440s. He overreached himself in March 1448 when he assaulted a servant of Robert, Baron Willoughby, who had the influence to get writs issued against Tailboys and his followers. Suffolk, however, prevailed on the sheriff of Lincolnshire not to enforce them.

Tailboys also developed a murderous hatred of Ralph, Baron Cromwell, another major Lincolnshire lord and a member of Richard of York's ducal council. In 1443 Tailboys' patron, Suffolk, had forced Cromwell to resign as Lord Treasurer after ten years' service, and Cromwell returned the favour by leading parliamentary attacks on Suffolk. Incensed by this, in November 1449 Tailboys physically assaulted Cromwell as he emerged from Parliament.

There followed the first impeachment by the House of Commons since 1386, in which Tailboys was 'named and famed for a common murderer, manslayer, rioter and continual breaker of [the king's] peace'. He was held in the Tower of London for twelve months while the case against him was prepared. He spent the next five years in prison while a series of judgements were made against him, notably damages awarded to Cromwell in the amount of £2,000 [£1.27 million].

• ☙ •

Bonville's long association with Suffolk paid off in July 1449, at the end of the first Parliament summoned that year, when he was created Baron Bonville of Chewton. In a defiant signal to Thomas Courtenay, Earl of Devon, Bonville chose a coat of arms modelled on the arms of the duchy of Cornwall. The same Parliament saw the royal favourite James Butler, son of the Earl of Ormonde, created Earl of Wiltshire. He and Bonville were to make common cause against Courtenay. These were, however, among the last significant acts of patronage by Suffolk.

The impeachment of Tailboys started the rockslide that swept Suffolk from power, but the build-up of instability had been many years in the making. He was never as powerful as he seemed, evidence of which was his inability to maintain order even in East Anglia, his area of greatest influence. By far the richest contemporary source for our period are the Paston letters, a collection of over a thousand letters and papers to, from and relating to the Paston family of Norfolk between 1422 and 1509. They contain a detailed account of an outrageous breach of the peace committed against the family, which we may take as representative of the lawlessness prevailing in the county.

It involved the manor of Gresham, 4 miles inland from the north Norfolk coast. In 1427 William Paston bought Gresham from Thomas Chaucer, father of Alice, Duchess of Suffolk. After William's death in 1444 his son John enjoyed unchallenged possession of the manor until 1448, when it was forcibly seized by 17-year-old Robert, namesake eldest son of Baron Hungerford and, by right of his wife, Baron Moleyns. Although heir apparent to the wealthy barony of Hungerford, with the expectation of inheriting an even larger estate from his mother, sole heir of William, Baron Botreaux, he chafed at the relatively minor extent of his Moleyns estate.

Moleyns' teenaged hormones and aristocratic arrogance made him a willing listener to the malicious advice of John Heydon of Baconsthorpe, a lawyer who, in association with the Keeper of the King's Wardrobe Thomas Tuddenham – both members in good standing of Suffolk's affinity – exercised a predatory ascendancy at the expense of the local gentry. Heydon, no doubt seeking to promote lucrative litigation, persuaded Moleyns that John Paston's title to the manor of Gresham could be challenged. Instead of suing, however, Moleyns simply took possession of the manor by force in February 1448.

It being pointless to bring a legal action in a jurisdiction run by Heydon and Tuddenham, John Paston obtained the intercession of William Wainflete, Henry Beaufort's successor as Bishop of Winchester and the king's right-hand man in the projects dearest to him, the building of colleges at Eton and Cambridge. Moleyns' solicitors made no serious attempt to defend the spurious title Heydon had created for their principal at a conference sponsored by Wainflete, and urged Paston to put his case to Moleyns directly. Paston tried to obtain an audience with him at several places, but was never received.

Accordingly, in early October 1449 he simply reoccupied his property, which the absentee Moleyns had failed to guard adequately. Paston did not make the same mistake and remained in possession with armed retainers. It took time for news of his coup to reach Moleyns in Wiltshire, and for him to plan his response, but in late January 1450 upwards of a thousand armed men hired by Moleyns launched a full-scale assault while John Paston was in London on business.

Margaret Paston held out with twelve servants, who put up stout resistance but were soon forced to surrender. Margaret was carried bodily from the mansion, which was then thoroughly ransacked and left in ruins. Paston estimated the damages at £200 [£127,200].

Before they left, Moleyns' rent-a-mob told Margaret that if they had found John or his solicitor, they would have killed them.

Paston sent a petition for redress to Parliament, and another to Wainflete, but 1450 was to be a year of unending crises for the regime and neither petition prospered. In subsequent years, Paston's insistence on obtaining redress was thwarted by Moleyns' seven-year captivity in France and the influence at court of the Duke of Norfolk, who made common aristocratic cause against Paston. In the end, all Paston could obtain was Moleyns' tacit abandonment of a claim he should never have made. His spiteful vandalism remained unpunished.

The swaggering behaviour of the knightly class has a flavour of the American Wild West about it. Then as later, men trained at arms and very little else, many with what today we coyly call anger management issues, were a very present danger. Still, we should beware of believing that anything like a complete breakdown of legal authority occurred. Trouble was concentrated in counties where there was no locally dominant lord, or where he was not normally resident. The biggest offender in this respect was Suffolk, permanently in attendance on the king, who perforce delegated the management of his local interests and affinities to crooks like Tuddenham and Heydon.

• ☙ •

The Harcourt–Stafford feud can be taken as representative of many local disputes that flourished in the absence of a dominant magnate or any realistic legal deterrent. Robert Harcourt of Stanton Harcourt in Oxfordshire enjoyed the 'good lordship' of Suffolk, while Humphrey Stafford of Grafton in Worcestershire was a distant kinsman of the Duke of Buckingham. In May 1448, the two knights, each with an entourage of armed retainers, encountered each other in Coventry. An exchange of insults between Harcourt and Stafford's eldest son Richard led to a brawl in which Richard and two of Harcourt's men were killed. Stafford himself was unhorsed and only narrowly escaped death.

The next day Harcourt, who had initiated the violence by striking Richard with his sword, was charged with murder by the city coroner and detained. Suffolk abused the Privy Seal to order the local sheriff not to proceed against Harcourt, who was released. After Suffolk was impeached, Stafford with 200 men made an overnight march on Stanton Harcourt. Harcourt took refuge in the tower of the parish church and withstood a six-hour siege during which the tower was peppered with arrows, killing one of his men. After a failed attempt to burn him out, Stafford withdrew.

In 1450, faced with the popular uprising known as Jack Cade's Rebellion, the king quickly pardoned all involved in the Harcourt–Stafford affray. Less than two months later Humphrey Stafford and his brother were killed after leading a column of the king's forces into an ambush set by Cade. Retribution for the killing of Richard Stafford was delayed until 1470, when Humphrey's illegitimate son murdered Robert Harcourt.

Cade's Rebellion itself drew its strength from the chronic abuse of power by agents of James Fiennes, Lord Saye and Sele since 1447, the king's bosom friend, Lord Treasurer and household chamberlain. Saye was represented in Kent by his son-in-law William Cromer, whose underlings duplicated the nefarious activities of Tuddenham and Heydon in Norfolk. Although there were no outrageous assaults comparable to Moleyns' attack on the manor at Gresham, rapacious lawlessness prevailed across Kent and East Sussex.

The king's regular progresses through East Anglia and the southeast were not replicated in the West Country, the Welsh Marches and the North, which were a law unto themselves. However, even when he did visit a region he was not accompanied by judges to hold assizes (properly 'commissions of oyer and terminer'), nor did he receive complaints or dispense justice himself. Henry's neglect of his duty as first magistrate was to prove particularly damaging in areas like Kent, where his household members were most dominant.

• ❧ •

We should also consider the Ampthill dispute, out of historical sequence but a classic illustration of the continuing undercurrent of aristocratic lawlessness. According to a petition later presented to Parliament, in June 1452 Henry Holland, Duke of Exeter, with 300 men seized a Bedfordshire estate, including the manor and castle of Ampthill, owned by Lord Cromwell. During his years as Lord Treasurer Cromwell had built up holdings that gave him an income only exceeded by the greater magnates. By contrast Exeter's landed patrimony produced an income well below the amount expected of a duke, and he did not even inherit the whole of it until the death of his stepmother in 1457. He was consumed with envy.

Exeter's claim was entirely spurious, concocted with the suborned help of three servants of the previous owner of Ampthill, now dead, and by one of his executors. Possessed to an even greater degree of the aristocratic arrogance that motivated Moleyns' seizure of Gresham, Exeter calculated he could spin out legal wrangling over Ampthill until the elderly and heirless Cromwell died, after which possession would be the proverbial nine-tenths of the law. Exeter was not clever enough to have conceived the scheme, and it was probably Tailboys who suggested manufacturing the claim as part of his feud with Cromwell.

The supposition hardens into certainty when we consider the second prong of Exeter's assault, which was to make a charge of treason against Cromwell, his allies the Bedfordshire and Marcher Lord Edmund Grey of Ruthyn, and John Fastolf, an East Anglian knight. The accusation was made by Robert Collinson, parson of Chelsfield in Kent, who swore that the leader of a post-Cade revolt in Kent, condemned for treason, had confessed, on the hurdle drawing him to be hanged and quartered, that Cromwell and the other two were traitors. Deathbed confessions carried a great deal of legal weight, as it was assumed nobody would wish to go into the afterlife with a lie on their lips.

Cromwell was ordered to appear in the Lord Chancellor's office and was suspended from the Council. However, in February 1453 Cromwell submitted a dossier that damned Collinson as a liar, a trickster and an epic whoremonger. Collinson's charges were dismissed, but Exeter's purpose had been achieved: a high-level panel of arbiters appointed by the king to decide the Ampthill dispute had been unable to proceed while a charge of treason was pending, and now events pushed it to the bottom of a pile of more urgent business.

Exeter countered Cromwell's suits with counter-suits and intimidated the sheriff of Bedfordshire, while juries could not be empanelled to hear the suits for fear of what Exeter might do to them. This moved the king to make one of his sporadic and typically ineffectual efforts to bring his nobles under control by briefly detaining Exeter at Windsor Castle, Cromwell at Wallingford Castle and Grey at Pevensey Castle.

Cromwell, who died in 1456, is a deeply unsympathetic figure, only somewhat redeemed by the fact that Exeter was even more loathsome. He did, however, leave us an excellent summary of the legal anarchy that increasingly characterized the reign of King Henry VI:

> Where any of so great estate puts any man out of his lands and tenements and wrongs him of his goods, the aggrieved party suing for his remedy in that behalf by special assize or otherwise there will be no judge, learned counsel nor jury [that will] take upon them to sit, come or appear, nor sheriff to make any restitution or mediate or do anything appertaining to his office in such case at any special or general assize or other place where remedy by course of law should be had.

DEFEAT AND HUMILIATION

ALTHOUGH APPOINTED TO THE LIEUTENANCY OF Normandy for three years in December 1446, Edmund Beaufort did not move there until early 1448. His own men took over from York's Anglo-Normans during 1447, but the province was essentially leaderless during a period of great uncertainty about the peace policy launched in 1444. Charles VII had agreed to extend the two-year truce agreed at Tours, but Henry failed to follow through with a journey to meet him in France in 1446. The main reason was financial – he had exhausted his credit to pay for Suffolk's two embassies and could not afford the magnificence the occasion demanded.

A greatly aggravating factor was Edmund's insistence that he be compensated for the loss of his holdings in Maine before he would consent to handing over the county, as privately agreed by Henry in a letter to his 'dear uncle of France' dated 22 December 1445. The letter stressed entreaties by his 'most dear and well-beloved companion the queen', who had been assured by her father and Charles himself that the cession of Maine would lead to a lasting peace.

Finally Edmund obtained a settlement of 10,000 *livres tournois* [nearly £1 million], to be paid annually by the already hard-pressed Norman exchequer. Only then did he move to Rouen, perhaps to ensure he received the agreed compensation. Although he was supposed to share it with the Anglo-Normans who would also be dispossessed, he did not. Consequently a deputation of English knights and squires obstructed the negotiations for the handover, to the point that in February–March 1448 they were besieged at Le Mans and even bombarded by a French army commanded by Pierre de Brézé. The knights handed over the town on 15 March after Charles VII agreed to compensate them himself, but of course they never saw a penny.

Henry was so greatly relieved that on 31 March he recreated the dukedom of Somerset for Edmund. This was further salt in the wounds of the dispossessed Anglo-Normans, particularly those of Richard of York's affinity, some of whom trickled back to England seeking his 'good lordship'. The trickle became a flood in 1449–50, and was the reason York became such a determined enemy of Somerset; which, since Somerset enjoyed the unconditional support of the king, brought York into ultimately mortal conflict with the house of Lancaster.

Somerset's performance of his duties as Lieutenant of Normandy was abject. When all the arguments about the inevitability of the outcome are weighed, the outstanding fact is that he made no serious preparation to resist French aggression. He appears to have shared Henry's wishful thinking, in the teeth of abundant evidence that Richemont's military organization was well advanced and could only have one purpose. Even if there might have been some doubt previously, there can have been none after the siege of Le Mans.

Possibly he thought the French would continue to nibble at the edges of Normandy through a process of armed negotiation. This would have granted him time to accumulate as much money as he could before returning to England, leaving his successor to deal with the consequences. The French did not oblige, and Somerset's ruin would have been complete were it not for the king's dogged loyalty to him, which may have been born in part of guilty knowledge that he should never have appointed Somerset to an office which required great personal wealth.

Another, stronger reason was that the collapse of the truce was

7. THE FALL OF NORMANDY 1449–50

© Hugh Bicheno

SEQUENCE OF EVENTS

1449

24 Mar.	Surienne takes Fougères
19 Jul.	Brézé invests Verneuil
30 Jul.	Declaration of war
24 Aug.	Fall of Verneuil
25 Aug.	Fall of Mortain
End Aug.	Fall of Évreux
	Fall of Harcourt
Early Sep.	Fall of Fécamp
	Start Avranches siege
	Fall of Coutances
Sep.	Alençon reconquers his duchy
	Fresnay holds out
Late Sep.	Fall of Argentan
	Start Château Galliard siege
16–22 Oct.	Siege of Rouen
23 Nov.	Fall of Château Galliard
	Fall of Fougères
8 Dec.	Start Harfleur siege

1450

1 Jan.	Fall of Harfleur
17–18 Jan.	Fall of Honfleur
15 Mar.	Kyriell lands Cherbourg
22 Mar.	Fall of Fresnay
15 Apr.	Battle of Formigny
12 May	Fall of Avranches
16 May	Fall of Bayeux
5–25 Jun.	Siege of Caen
6 Jul.	Start Falaise siege
	Start Cherbourg siege
21 Jul.	Fall of Falaise
23 Jul.	Start Domfront siege
2 Aug.	Fall of Domfront
12 Aug.	Fall of Cherbourg

precipitated by a personal decision made by Henry. During the night of 23/24 March 1449, the Aragonese captain known as François de Surienne, a Garter knight for his services to the English crown, took the Breton border fortress of Fougères in a daring escalade. The purpose was to force the Duke of Brittany to release Gilles of Brittany, Henry VI's childhood friend, imprisoned since June 1446. Henry knew Gilles had been arrested in the first instance by French soldiers acting on the orders of Charles VII. He regarded it as a breach of the truce, and the seizure of Fougères as therefore justified.

Charles, however, saw it as the opportunity he had been waiting for to conclude an explicitly anti-English alliance with Brittany, denounce the truce, and to declare war on 31 July. A year and a fortnight later, to the exhilarated satisfaction – and no small surprise – of the French commanders (among them Marguerite's father, René d'Anjou), the last of Henry V's and the Duke of Bedford's conquests were in French hands.

Hardly any of the smaller fortified towns put up a fight. In most, the inhabitants opened their gates and welcomed the French armies or, as at Verneuil, helped them scale the walls. Most of the English garrisons that prevented this were persuaded to capitulate on generous terms. One such was Regnéville, a port on the coast of the Cotentin peninsula near Coutances, where the king's stepfather Owen Tudor surrendered to the Bretons after six days. He was permitted to take ship to England with his men, their dependants and possessions.

Obdurate garrisons were bypassed, to fall like ripe fruit in due course. The outstanding example was Fresnay-sur-Sarthe, a small town on the border of Maine. Fresnay held out from September 1449, when the Duke of Alençon recovered his long-lost county in a whirlwind campaign, until March 1450, when the last hope of relief was extinguished. Somerset must have expected many more such hold-outs to buy him time, but Fresnay was held by Anglo-Normans dispossessed in Maine, who judged they had nothing more to lose. Somerset's own fief of Mortain welcomed the French invaders with open arms, as did Évreux, the chief town of Richard of York's appanage.

The English were vastly outnumbered. Not counting the Bretons, the four French armies numbered over 30,000 against 6,000–8,000 English in scattered garrisons. But the crowning humiliation was that they were defeated by equal numbers in the only pitched battle of the campaign. On 15 April 1450, about 4,500 men sent from England under Thomas Kyriell (the only knight banneret to respond to John Beaufort's summons in 1443), joined by 1,500 drawn from the Cotentin peninsula garrisons, were routed at Formigny by two French armies totalling about 5,000. The French commanders were Richemont himself and the Duke of Bourbon, leader of the 1440 revolt against Charles VII.

There is a common belief that Formigny was the first battle won by field artillery, but its role was only indirect. It was an encounter battle in which neither side had been well served by scouts. Taken by surprise and outnumbered, Bourbon did employ a couple of light cannon: but his aim was to keep the enemy out of longbow range. After the English archers rushed the guns he was in serious trouble and was on the verge of defeat when Richemont, marching towards the sound of the guns, appeared on Kyriell's flank. So, although the guns brought about the timely convergence of the French armies, it was tactical agility, supposedly the decisive advantage enjoyed by the English, which won the day.

The new French guns did, however, bring about the rapid capitulation of major fortresses that in former times had confidently withstood prolonged sieges. In 1414–15 the port of Harfleur held out against Henry V's primitive bombards for over a year. It fell in three weeks in 1450. Massive Château Gaillard, built on an immensely strong position overlooking the Seine, resisted Henry V for a year in 1419. In 1449 it was battered into submission in less than two months, and was never rebuilt.

Accordingly, when in 1452 York accused Somerset of treachery for capitulating at Rouen after a siege lasting barely a week, and seven months later at Caen after twenty days, he could not argue that further resistance would have affected the final outcome. By convention a fortress commander would hold out while there was hope his own side might send an army to lift the siege, and there was no dishonour in seeking terms when there was no such prospect. It was Somerset's haste and the terms he negotiated that York judged contemptible.

Somerset had thoroughly alienated the people of Rouen, probably because he needed to wring every penny out of his lieutenancy. Even though the Norman capital had much the largest garrison, commanded by none other than Somerset's fearsome brother-in-law John Talbot, Earl of Shrewsbury, in October 1449 they abandoned the city to a popular uprising and pulled back to the enormous castle. The main French armies were elsewhere and their heavy guns were at Château Gaillard, so even the minimum precondition of an effective siege had not been met when Somerset capitulated.

Along with the castle, he surrendered the fortified towns of the Pays de Caux and the port of Honfleur on the southern bank of the Seine estuary, which would have isolated Harfleur, on the north bank. In addition, he agreed to pay a ransom of 50,000 Norman *saluts d'or* [£7,314,000] for himself and his family to travel to Caen. As a guarantee he left Talbot and four other officers as hostages.

Intriguingly, Talbot bore Somerset no ill will; indeed he and his sons were to support him against York in the following years. A hypothesis to fit these facts is that by becoming a hostage for Somerset's debt Talbot avoided being held to ransom in his own right. What is generally judged to have been an exceptionally shameful act turns out, on closer examination, to have been probably an act of clever collusion between the two peers.

The captain of Honfleur refused to obey Somerset's order and held out until after Harfleur surrendered, capitulating on 18 January 1450. Talbot remained a hostage until July, when Andrew Trollope, one of his retainers and captain of Falaise, one of the last Norman towns still in English hands, made his release a condition of capitulation. Talbot swore never to bear arms against France again, and was to abide by the letter of his oath. He was unarmed when killed three years later during the last battle of the Hundred Years War.

The Earl of Oxford's son Robert Vere, commanding the Caen garrison, was able to prevent a revolt by the inhabitants. Besieged during June 1450 by an army led by Charles VII himself, he conducted an active defence of the city that may have included a bribe to Scots members of Charles's bodyguard to kill him. This, at least, was the charge levelled against them in 1453. One of the illustrations in the 1487 *Vigiles du roi Charles VII* shows an English sortie against the French bombards (the modern guns had not yet arrived), which finally put a stone shot through the window of the room where Somerset's duchess and children were sheltered.

Somerset immediately agreed terms of capitulation including an astronomical ransom of 300,000 écus *d'or* [£43,884,000], with 18 hostages as surety, to permit Somerset, his family and the garrison to evacuate by sea. The ransom was totally unrealistic – it would have wiped out both the Norman and English exchequers – and the hostages were later released for the derisory sums they raised themselves. Understandably uncertain of the loyalty of his troops or of the reception awaiting him in England, Somerset sailed separately to Calais.

With the Normandy debacle well under way, the Parliament summoned to vote emergency funds in November 1449 was in a vengeful mood. Driven by Lord Cromwell, the Tailboys impeachment segued into a full-scale parliamentary attack on Suffolk. The first notable rat to desert the sinking ship was Adam Moleyns, Bishop of Chichester, who in early December resigned the office of Lord Privy Seal, pleading ill health and a belated desire to attend to his neglected diocese, which he had visited only to be invested in 1446.

A month later, he was in Portsmouth delivering wages to the troops assembling for Kyriell's expedition when a group of Normandy veterans seized him and announced he must die for his role in handing over Maine. He tried to save himself by accusing Suffolk of embezzling the money intended for the defence of Normandy, but was slaughtered regardless. The murder of a bishop was a deeply shocking act in itself; but for the royal household the more worrying aspect was that the killers were men who had served under York, who may have been avenging Moleyns' attempt to blame him for the parlous state of Normandy's defences.

Suffolk issued a statement denying Moleyns' accusation at the opening of the new session of Parliament on 23 January 1450, but it backfired. The Commons cited his own words as proof 'there was an heavy noise of infamy upon him', which required he should be brought to trial. Suffolk's response was worded in a way to imply that the murdered bishop was indeed to blame for the surrender of Maine. This was demeaning: everybody knew the king was personally responsible, but it was treasonable to say so. The feeling was that Suffolk, having profited so greatly from being the king's chief minister, should now manfully accept his role as chief scapegoat.

On 7 February, the Speaker read out a very long indictment accusing Suffolk of a fantastical plot with the French king to depose Henry VI and to replace him with Suffolk's son John, whom he had betrothed to his ward Margaret Beaufort to give him a claim to the throne. This and other wild accusations about dealings with the French were simply embellishments to the core charges, which concerned the alienation of crown lands and rights to himself and his affinity. The result, said the indictment, was that there was not enough left to support the king's government, requiring the Commons to make good the deficit with taxation.

Suffolk was consigned to the Tower to await trial. When he was brought out on 9 March, he did the only thing he could and cast himself on the king's mercy. On 17 March the king summoned the lords to his inner chamber. In their presence, Suffolk knelt before him to assert his innocence, and once again threw himself on his mercy. Henry made no judgement on the charges against him, but banished him for five years from 1 May. The intention, clearly, was to recall him when the heat had died down.

Suffolk departed for his home in Ipswich, heavily guarded against a London mob intent on lynching him in revenge for what they believed was his murder of 'Good Duke Humphrey' in February 1447. When he got home he put his affairs in order and wrote a loving valedictory letter to his young son. The second paragraph, couched as advice, gives us an insight into how Suffolk himself had won the unreserved confidence of the king (my italics):

> Next [to God], above all earthly things, be a true liegeman in heart, in will, in thought, in deed, unto the King, our elder, most high, and dread Sovereign Lord, to whom both ye and I be so much bound; charging you, as father can and may, rather to die than to be the contrary, or to know anything that were against the welfare and prosperity of his most royal person, but that so far as your body and life may stretch, ye live and die to defend it *and to let His Highness have knowledge thereof,* in all the haste ye can.

Suffolk sailed from Ipswich on 30 April, bound for Calais. His two ships were intercepted by a flotilla led by the 'great ship' *Nicholas of the Tower,* flying the royal colours, which summoned him. He had himself rowed across without hesitation, perhaps believing the king had changed his mind, only to be seized, 'tried' for treason by the crew and his head hacked off with a cutlass. His torso was cast ashore at Dover.

Although Henry and Marguerite were devastated by the news, the circumstances of Suffolk's death were not investigated. It was clearly not an act of piracy – there must have been collusion with the master of Suffolk's ship for the interception to take place at all, and no pirate operated a 'great ship'. One is inescapably drawn to the conclusion that the murder was the work of young Henry Holland, Duke of Exeter. As Lord Admiral, Exeter's father had enjoyed a unique naval affinity, which made him, in practice, pirate-in-chief. The shamelessly corrupt Court of Admiralty was an extremely lucrative operation that provided his principal source of income, and continued to do so for his successors well into the seventeenth century.

When the older Exeter died, Suffolk added the Court of Admiralty to his own bag of offices. As we saw in Chapter 5, without the income from the court the younger Exeter was decidedly poor. Not only did this give him reason to hate Suffolk, but he would also still have had contacts within the seafaring community made while his father was alive. The remaining members of the royal household would not have dared suggest to the king that a prince of his blood would be capable of such a thing, and the office of Lord Admiral now reverted to the psychopathic young man.*

The household's suspicion that Exeter had assassinated Suffolk would have been subsumed into a growing panic about what they believed was a greater threat. Their fear, which soon infected the king himself, was that the murders of Moleyns and Suffolk were the product of a conspiracy with Richard of York at its heart. Suffolk's downfall had been initiated by Lord Cromwell, one of York's councillors, and Exeter was York's son-in-law. To their fearful minds it looked a lot like two plus two adding up to a deeply ominous four.

After the leader of the London riot against the release of Suffolk suffered the gruesome fate reserved for traitors, his quarters were sent to Coventry and Winchester, where there had been disturbances of the peace, and to Newbury and Stamford, where there had not. They were, however, boroughs owned by York. Further panicked by a lightning strike that severely damaged his favourite palace at Eltham, and by an outbreak of the plague, the king fled to Leicester. On his way there, another man earned a traitor's death by lashing the ground in front of Henry's horse, calling for York to do the same to the king's government.

* As Constable of the Tower he took such pleasure in torturing people that the rack became known as 'the Duke of Exeter's daughter'.

There is not the slightest evidence that York had anything to do with any of the shocks suffered by the court at this time. Barring the lightning strike, they were the result of a long period of misgovernment. This was not, however, an explanation the king and his household were prepared to contemplate. Much better to blame an external agency of infinite cunning and resource – the essential ingredient of every conspiracy theory throughout history.

HENRY AND
RICHARD

S UFFOLK'S ASSASSINATION ON 2 MAY 1450 WAS THE CAT-
alyst for a cascade of events that ripped apart the cocoon
around the king. William Cromer, sheriff of Kent and Sussex
and son-in-law of Lord Saye and Sele, took custody of Suffolk's body
and threatened retaliation against the people of Kent. Summoned
by commissioners of array on their own authority, and led by their
local constables, in June several thousand minor Kentish gentry,
yeomen and labourers assembled at Ashford and marched on
London, joined by a smaller contingent from east Sussex.

The host, at this point without a conspicuous leader, camped
at Blackheath, where the main roads from Kent converged south
of the Thames. When ordered to disperse by the king's heralds on
15 June, they said they were not rebels but petitioners, and would
remain until their grievances were heard. However, the spokesman
they elected was a bold ex-soldier, possibly of Irish origin, called
Jack Cade – who had chosen to call himself Mortimer 'for to have
the more favour of the people'.

The name was a red alert. By blood, the Mortimer claim to the
throne was better than the ruling dynasty's, and Richard of York
was the heir to the claim. Lest there should be any doubt why Cade
chose the name, the first item in the 'The Complaint of the Poor
Commons of Kent' denounced those said to be spreading rumours
that York wished to seize the throne. Their purpose, the petition

declared, was to make the king 'hate and destroy his real friends and to cherish the false traitors that call themselves his friends'.

This appears to be an accurate appreciation. The king's household were now a leaderless rabble, and rather than accept their responsibility for the widespread unrest it suited them to blame York, now out of the way in Ireland and unable to defend himself. The Kentish petition went on to denounce the abuses committed by the agents of the absentee lords of Kent, with particular venom directed at Lord Saye. It demanded that the king banish Suffolk's 'false progeny and affinity' and replace them with York, the Dukes of Buckingham and Norfolk, and 'all true earls and barons of this land'.

It is not for this but for the immortal dialogue with Dick, a confederate, put in their mouths by Shakespeare, that the spirit of Jack Cade lives on among the English-speaking peoples:

> Dick: The first thing we do, let's kill all the lawyers.
> Cade: Nay, that I mean to do.

While still at Leicester the king summoned Buckingham, who had been awarded Gloucester's palace at Penshurst, near Tonbridge in Kent, and Jacquetta's husband Richard Woodville, created Baron Rivers in 1448, with lands around Maidstone on the road from Ashford to London. They were commissioned to raise troops from their estates and meet the king in London, where he returned on 8 June. Joined by troops from royalist Cheshire under Lord Stanley, and the personal retinues of Henry Percy, Earl of Northumberland, the Neville Earls of Salisbury and Warwick, and the veteran Thomas, Baron Scales, the king rejected the petition and led his army across the river to confront the Blackheath encampment.

The massed petitioners melted away that night – and then Henry overplayed his hand. He sent punitive columns into Kent under Percy, Woodville, Scales and Buckingham's kinsmen, the brothers Humphrey (he of the recent attack on Stanton Harcourt) and William Stafford. The Staffords' column was ambushed by Cade and the two brothers killed in woods near Sevenoaks. Henry then compounded his error by ordering Buckingham's and Woodville's Kentish men to avenge the defeat. Instead they mutinied and declared solidarity with Cade.

From browbeating arrogance to abject panic was for Henry but a short step, and he fled to Westminster via Marguerite's (previously Gloucester's) palace at Greenwich. All would have contrasted his behaviour with the regal courage of young Richard II in 1381, when he rode out of London with only an escort to face down the so-called Peasants' Revolt. Henry also ordered Lord Saye and William Cromer detained in the Tower, and issued a proclamation echoing the petition's denunciation of unspecified traitors.

Once given into, fear is uncontrollable and this was the moment when Marguerite first stepped up to provide the courage her husband lacked. Despite the entreaties of the mayor and aldermen of London, Henry could not be persuaded to stay and she guided his further flight to the comforting security of her castles at Berkhamsted in south Hertfordshire and Kenilworth outside Coventry, the latter at the heart of her substantial Midlands dower. She, however, heroically remained at Greenwich, no more than a mile from Blackheath.

Henry tried to save Saye, but Exeter, the Constable of the Tower, refused to release him because the king had earlier ordered a formal trial for his friend. Cade returned to Blackheath on 23 June wearing the armour of one of the slain Staffords. Now that the fear of reprisals seemed to have been confirmed, his following – stripped of the respectable element – was far more radical. Another large gathering of petitioners emerged from Essex and on 2 July the two groups converged on the city. Cade occupied Southwark, next to London Bridge, whose ropes he cut so it could not be drawn against him, while the Essex men advanced north of the river to Mile End, opposite Aldgate.

Named by the rebels as one of the 'false traitors', Bishop William Ayscough of Salisbury, who had officiated at the king's wedding and was his revered confessor, fled London in mid-June for his castle at

Sherborne in Dorset, with a caravan bearing his personal wealth. He got only as far as the monastery at Edington, in Wiltshire. On 29 June a mob dragged him out of the church where he was celebrating Mass, stripped him of his finery and hacked him to death. They then looted his caravan of goods and cash worth about £4,000 [£2.5 million] and sacked the monastery, while others despoiled his palace at Salisbury.

Other senior churchmen found themselves under attack around this time. Only their armed retainers saved the Bishops of Bath and Wells, Coventry and Norwich, and the Abbots of Gloucester and Hyde, from sharing Ayscough's fate. Intriguingly, the king's close friends Reginald Boulers, Abbot of Gloucester and soon to be Bishop of Hereford, and John Sutton, Baron Dudley, fled for sanctuary to Richard of York's castle at Ludlow.

It is telling that – with the exception of Hyde (today in Greater Manchester) – all these attacks took place in areas where Lollardy remained strong. Lollardy was also strong in Sussex and Essex, but not so in Kent or Surrey, the counties that provided the majority of Cade's followers. Their anger was triggered less by the wealth and corruption of the church than by the thuggish behaviour of royal officials and their agents, and was exacerbated by the influx into these counties of destitute soldiers evacuated from Normandy.

The events we have been reviewing merely caused the cup of unrest to overflow – it had been filled by an economic contraction that began in the late 1430s and ran on until the 1480s. The north and Wales were hit by several harvest failures and the decimation of livestock, which sharply reduced income from rents. The south was adversely affected by a slow collapse of trade across northern Europe, mainly as a result of war. English cloth exports fell by over a third at the end of the 1440s, with the West Country particularly hard hit. The incomes of those who murdered Ayscough and looted Church property in Wiltshire had quite recently fallen precipitously, escalating chronic resentment of ecclesiastical tithes and excessive wealth to a peak of murderous hatred.

Cade's men crossed the river into London and Exeter ordered Lord Scales, the Keeper of the Tower, to hand over Saye and Cromer for a formal trial at the Guildhall. Cade now lost control of his men, who dragged the two men out of the Guildhall for summary execution. Saye was beheaded at Southwark and Cromer at Mile End, perhaps seeking to tie the Essex contingent to the Kentish men in common guilt. Instead the Essex group, which had not gone through the same process of radicalization, went home. Cade's men then began behaving like a conquering army and on 8–9 July, after a day of looting and indiscriminate violence, Scales led out the Tower garrison to win back control of London Bridge in a savage battle.

The next day – very bravely, given that it seemed to be open season on bishops – Cardinal Archbishop John Kemp of York (who had replaced John Stafford, Archbishop of Canterbury, as Lord Chancellor after the fall of Suffolk) and Bishop William Wainflete of Winchester crossed the bridge and persuaded Cade and his men to sign up for a royal pardon. Although Kemp proposed it and prepared the documents, he did so at the instigation of Marguerite.

The leader of the rebellion signed the pardon as Mortimer, but would be killed as Cade five days later. He fled when a 'Writ and Proclamation by the King for the Taking of Cade' was issued shortly after the rebellion, placing a price on his head, and was fatally wounded when resisting arrest on 12 July. His body was brought back to London and underwent a mock trial before being beheaded and quartered. The head was displayed on the bridge he had once crossed in triumph, and his body parts were sent to Blackheath and to Norwich, Salisbury and Gloucester, three cities whose senior clergy had been attacked.

This was the sole reprisal for the rebellion – the pardons were respected for everyone else who did not rebel again. Kemp emerged from the crisis with his prestige greatly enhanced, and with the deepest respect for Marguerite. It was one of her many great misfortunes that he was to die in the midst of the next great crisis to envelop the Lancastrian regime.

As reports of these events filtered across the Irish Sea, York became increasingly worried. The fate of his Mortimer ancestors and his father's death on the block for conspiring to put Edmund Mortimer on the throne were burned into his psyche. Although only 3 years old when his father was executed, York himself had spent the next eight years in the custody of the regicide Robert Waterton. He had every reason to be alarmed that his name was on so many seditious lips, and was enraged to learn that members of the king's household were seeking to deflect their culpability onto him.

York also felt that the collective honour of English chivalry had been defiled by the manner in which Somerset surrendered Normandy, the details of which lost nothing in the telling by destitute members of his old Anglo-Norman affinity who came to him in Ireland. They, supported by his chamberlain William Oldhall, fixed in York's mind the erroneous belief that the uprisings in England were caused by discontent over the loss of Normandy.

The only real link between Normandy and the disturbances was a widespread belief that the increases in taxation to maintain the province had been misappropriated by the king's rapacious household. Apart from the displaced Anglo-Normans, few in England felt the humiliation of defeat as strongly as York. For most, including his peers, the Normandy crisis had been like a festering boil, brought to a head by the failure of the king's misguided peace policy, and lanced by the deposition and murder of Suffolk.

The Commons still had scores to settle with the king's government, but these were over money. The parliaments of 1449–51 made the king's resumption of alienated crown lands and revenues a condition of voting further taxation. Henry fought a rearguard action to protect his household, until he lost his nerve across the board in the face of Cade's revolt. The murders of Suffolk and Saye did the crown a backhanded favour, as they had indulged the king's whims so that his household could continue to enjoy its privileges and extortion rackets. With them dead, it was easier for Henry to distance himself from his own previous behaviour.

One can only keep reality at bay for so long, and the dam broke in 1449–50, taking with it the painfully maintained illusion of the king's majesty. He was revealed as a rather pitiable figure, not hated but certainly not revered. The loss of crown income from the French provinces was the ultimate reality check, although this was offset to a certain extent by a drastic decrease in military expenditure. The appointment as Lord Treasurer of wealthy John, Baron Beauchamp of Powick, announced an intention to restore order to the royal finances.

York was one of the magnates most affected, in absolute terms, by the loss of Normandy and the Acts of Resumption, but it was a small proportion of his overall wealth. In relative terms the biggest loser was Somerset, who lost a great deal more than York in Normandy, and who needed those lands to maintain the income required of a duke. Although he lacked the means to develop an affinity, common interest gave him a ready-made following among the minor nobles – particularly those created during the 1440s – who also stood to lose much of their wealth if resumption was pursued too vigorously.

Once Marguerite recovered from the shock of bereavement following the murder of her father figure Suffolk, she must have looked with very cold eyes indeed on the household men whose failures had exposed her husband's frailties so cruelly. Henry remained away from London from July to the end of September 1450. At some point the queen joined him at Kenilworth, and brought him back to Westminster in the first week of October.

She then accompanied him to the palace of William Wainflete at Bishop's Waltham in Hampshire. She probably suggested the visit to lift Henry's spirits, as Wainflete was the inspiration and executor for the king's beloved Eton College project. The royal couple returned to London at the end of October and spent most of the next three months in Westminster, at last attending to business.

The timings are important, because hindsight permits us to see that the first substantial domino in the descent to civil war fell during this period. Somerset had returned to England in early August with no expectation of further royal favour, but his prospects were transformed when the king learned that York intended to make an unauthorized return from Ireland. Henry must have gone into panic mode again: nothing else can explain why he sent orders to his officers in north Wales and Cheshire to prevent York landing, and to arrest him if he did so.

Finding other ports closed to him, York landed at his lordship of Denbigh in north-east Wales on 7 September 1450 and proceeded south to Shrewsbury, in Shropshire. There, on the 12th, he met John Talbot, Earl of Shrewsbury, his namesake son Baron Lisle, and Lord Lionel Welles, a Lincolnshire baron who had married John Beaufort's widow. We do not know why they were there and what was said, but after the meeting York sent a letter to the king, explaining his reason for returning: 'I have been informed that diverse language has been said of me to your most excellent estate which should sound to my dishonour and reproach, and charge of my person.'

After asserting his unqualified loyalty, he humbly requested the king to permit him to confront his detractors and clear his name. The letter came too late. On 11 September Henry appointed Somerset as Constable of England, a post previously held by the totally loyal and militarily unsullied Duke of Buckingham. Possibly Buckingham had tried to reason the king out of his panic, and had resisted the move towards confrontation. The appointment also offended John Mowbray, Duke of Norfolk and hereditary Earl Marshal, who was outraged to be made subordinate to a man he despised.

York learned of this and more when he reached the capital of his Marcher lordships at Ludlow, and his second letter to the king was considerably less conciliatory. In it he demanded an explanation why orders had been given to arrest him and for a jury to be empanelled to indict him for treason. He also alleged that orders had been issued to imprison his stewards Walter Devereux and Edmund

Mulso, and to execute his chamberlain, William Oldhall.

All these allegations appear to be true, and confirm that the king and his entourage had convinced themselves that York was bent on seizing the throne. The murder of William Tresham, Speaker of the 1449–50 Parliament, while travelling to meet York wearing the king's livery chain, further fed their paranoia. In fact Tresham's killing was carried out by retainers of Lord Edmund Grey of Ruthyn (whom last we saw involved in the Ampthill dispute) over yet another Bedfordshire property dispute. Henry fled to Kenilworth again.

By the time York reached London in late September, the die was cast. He was received graciously when the king returned (pausing at St Albans to learn if it was safe to do so), but the presence of Somerset was a red rag. York issued a widely circulated 'bill', in effect a manifesto, which echoed the terms of the Kentish petition and requested full authority to salvage the regime from enemies internal and external.

Although York's bill was a blunt assertion of the king's incompetence to choose his own ministers, Henry did not reject it outright. As usual flinching from face-to-face confrontation, he had said nothing during their meeting, but replied in writing that the duke's request would be put to the Chancellor, and promised a greater role in government for a 'sad [solemn] and substantial council in which we have appointed you to be one'.

Marguerite had a good relationship with Duchess Cecily, dating back to their first meeting at Rouen in 1444, and must have suspected the arrest orders of August–September were a tactical error on Henry's part. However, now that he was overcompensating for his earlier weakness, she would have prudently kept her views to herself. After learning that York's primary purpose had been to clear his name, and that his demands had only hardened in response to the king's appointment of Somerset as Constable of England, she may have regretted not being more forthcoming with her husband.

Sadly, there was now no going back. York had thrown down the gauntlet and it remained to be seen what support he commanded from his peers and the Commons. It may be that Marguerite proposed the visit to Bishop's Waltham not only to get her brittle husband away from the febrile atmosphere at Westminster, but also to show confidence in Somerset by giving him a free hand to rally a household unmanned by mortal terror.

HOUSE OF
NEVILLE

AMONG THE STRONGEST SUPPORTERS OF HENRY VI'S prerogative to choose his own ministers were the father and son Earls of Salisbury and Warwick. They were to play a decisive role in the Wars of the Roses, and Warwick has gone down in history as 'the Kingmaker'. They were the junior branch of the great northern Neville clan, and owed their rise to national prominence to a combination of relentless dynastic ambition and astoundingly good fortune.

The Nevilles also owed much to Henry VI's favour, and the large retinues they brought to London in June 1450 played an important part in quelling disorder and securing the capital. Salisbury and Warwick remained in London for the rest of 1450, seeking to ensure that the lands they held by favour of the king were exempted by him from the Acts of Resumption passed by Parliament. This brought them into collision with York after he demanded wholesale resumption as a first step to restoring good governance.

Consequently they supported Somerset as a less-bad alternative to the 'sad and substantial council' promised by the king, in which York's influence might have predominated, as it already did in the Commons. York's chamberlain William Oldhall – whom the king had ordered hanged earlier in 1450 – had been elected Speaker in replacement of the murdered Tresham. Although nobody could have predicted it at the time, Oldhall's election marked the high tide of York's campaign to be formally recognized as the heir presumptive, and to make himself the king's chief minister. It would ebb quickly.

The Duke of Norfolk, who had struggled against the Suffolk affinity in East Anglia and the South East, and wanted the king's household purged of its remaining members, supported York. However, ranged against them were lords outraged by York's solidarity with the Kentish petition. These included the Duke of Buckingham, whose palace at Penshurst had been attacked, and Lord Scales, who had battled Cade on London Bridge. The defection of Scales, long one of York's councillors and godfather to Edward, his eldest son, was painful.

In addition, York's determination to ruin Somerset through acts of resumption earned him the opposition of all the other lords who stood to lose from them. Among the minor peers ranged against York, one who stood out both as a Kentish lord and as one who owed everything to royal favour was Richard Woodville, recently created Lord Rivers thanks mainly to the fact that his wife, Jacquetta, had been Queen Marguerite's lady-in-waiting since 1444.

On 1 December 1450 Yorkist supporters (presumably Anglo-Normans) attempted to kill Somerset at his lodgings at the Dominican monastery of Blackfriars, which the mob looted on finding him gone. The next day York rode in with a large force of retainers to restore order. He arrested one of the ringleaders and handed him over to the king, who passed him on to Salisbury for execution. York also lodged Somerset in the Tower, and then had him spirited away by river on a barge belonging to the Earl of Devon. Despite York's prompt action the damage was done and his standing as the champion of good order was tarnished.

It all went downhill for him very quickly in the new year. As a first step to undermine York's influence the king – no doubt at the urging of Somerset – nominated York to a commission charged with conducting assizes in order to quell continuing unrest in Kent. If he obeyed the king's summons he would lose popular support, so York did nothing. Then, at the end of January, another Kentish rebellion was sparked by a man who had been a member of York's household in Ireland, who revived the fears of royal retribution that had sparked Cade's rebellion, and once again portrayed York as the man to restore good governance.

The king at last acted decisively, riding into Kent with Somerset, Exeter, Shrewsbury, Lisle, Roos and Cromwell, the last now anxious to disassociate himself from York. According to William Gregory, Mayor of London in 1451, they conducted assizes at Canterbury that concentrated on punishing those of Cade's men who had rebelled again after taking the king's pardon, and for:

> Having more favour towards the Duke of York than to the king, and the condemned men were drawn hanged and quartered. Nine men were beheaded, at the same time, at Rochester, their heads sent to London at the king's command, and all set upon London Bridge; and at another time twelve heads were similarly brought to London at the king's command. Men in Kent call it the harvest of heads.

On return to London, the king dispensed with all talk of a 'sad and substantial council' and York found himself increasingly marginalized. In part this was because the French had embarked on the conquest of Guyenne and Gascony, and to continue to remonstrate with the king about the loss of Normandy would have seemed unpatriotic. Somerset was appointed Captain of Calais and Lord Rivers was commissioned to assemble reinforcements to send to Guyenne in Devon.

When Parliament was summoned in early May to vote money for Rivers' expedition, Thomas Young, one of York's MPs, tried to link the funds to a declaration that his master was the heir presumptive. This led to Young's arrest, the suspension of Parliament, and a series of measures making it abundantly clear that the king not only rejected York's pretension to become his first minister, but also

THE HOUSE OF NEVILLE

Descendants of Ralph Neville and Margaret Stafford

k. = killed in battle   x. = executed

Ralph Neville
1st Earl of Westmorland
4th Baron Neville of Raby
(1364–1425)
= 1. Margaret Stafford
(d.1396)

John
(d.1420)
= Elizabeth Holland
(d.1423)

Ralph
2nd Earl of
Westmorland
(d.1484)
= Elizabeth
Percy
(d.1436)

John
5th Baron
Neville of Raby
(k.1461)
= Anne
Holland
(d.1486)

Thomas
(d.1461)
= Elizabeth
Beaumont

John
(d.1450)
= Anne
Holland
(d.1486)

Ralph Neville
3rd Earl of
Westmorland
(d.1499)

Humphrey
(x.1469)

Charles
(x.1469)

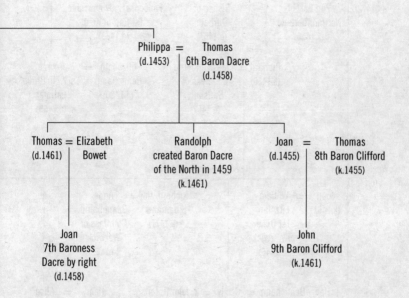

Philippa = Thomas
(d.1453) | 6th Baron Dacre
(d.1458)

Thomas = Elizabeth   Randolph   Joan = Thomas
(d.1461)   Bowet   created Baron Dacre   (d.1455)   8th Baron Clifford
                         of the North in 1459   (k.1455)
                              (k.1461)

        Joan   John
   7th Baroness   9th Baron Clifford
   Dacre by right   (k.1461)
     (d.1458)

THE HOUSE OF NEVILLE

Descendants of Ralph Neville and Joan Beaufort

k. = killed in battle   x. = executed

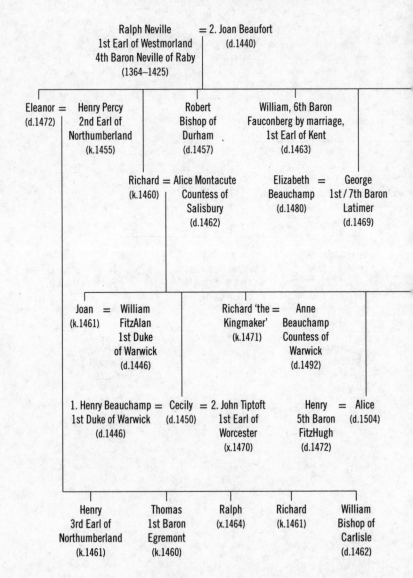

Ralph Neville = 2. Joan Beaufort
1st Earl of Westmorland   (d.1440)
4th Baron Neville of Raby
(1364–1425)

Eleanor = Henry Percy
(d.1472)   2nd Earl of
Northumberland
(k.1455)

Robert
Bishop of
Durham
(d.1457)

William, 6th Baron
Fauconberg by marriage,
1st Earl of Kent
(d.1463)

Richard = Alice Montacute
(k.1460)   Countess of
Salisbury
(d.1462)

Elizabeth = George
Beauchamp   1st / 7th Baron
(d.1480)   Latimer
(d.1469)

Joan = William
(k.1461)   FitzAlan
1st Duke
of Warwick
(d.1446)

Richard 'the = Anne
Kingmaker'   Beauchamp
(k.1471)   Countess of
Warwick
(d.1492)

1. Henry Beauchamp = Cecily = 2. John Tiptoft
1st Duke of Warwick   (d.1450)   1st Earl of
(d.1446)   Worcester
(x.1470)

Henry = Alice
5th Baron   (d.1504)
FitzHugh
(d.1472)

Henry
3rd Earl of
Northumberland
(k.1461)

Thomas
1st Baron
Egremont
(k.1460)

Ralph
(x.1464)

Richard
(k.1461)

William
Bishop of
Carlisle
(d.1462)

Edward = Elizabeth Beauchamp
(d.1476)   Baroness Bergavenny
                (d.1448)

Anne = 1. Humphrey Stafford
(d.1480)   1st Duke of Buckingham
                (k.1460)
            House of Stafford

Katherine = 1. John Mowbray
(d.1483)   1st Duke of Norfolk
                  (d.1432)

Richard = Cecily
Duke of York   (d.1495)
(k.1460)
House of York

John Mowbray
3rd Duke of Norfolk
(d.1461)

John
1st Baron Montagu,
1st Earl of
Northumberland
(k.1471)

Eleanor = Thomas
(d.1482)   2nd Baron
                Stanley
                (d.1504)

Thomas = Maud
(k.1460)   (d.1456)
                co-heir of
                Ralph, Baron
                Cromwell
                (d.1455)

George
Bishop of
Exeter
(d.1476)

William = Katherine
Bonville   (d.1504)
6th Baron
Harington
(k.1460)

John Vere, = Margaret
13th Earl   (d.1506)
of Oxford
(d.1513)

intended to exclude him from any role in his government whatsoever. The worm had turned with a vengeance.

• ❦ •

A high proportion of all the peers and peers' offspring killed in battle or executed during the Wars of the Roses were first- or second-generation descendants of Ralph Neville, 1st Earl of Westmorland. Furthermore, it is improbable that tensions would have escalated to full-blown civil war if Henry VI had retained the loyalty of the main branch of the Nevilles.

There was a Beaufort ingredient in this mix, as well. Within months of the death of his first wife in 1396, Ralph married 18-year-old Joan Beaufort, sister of the future cardinal and a recent widow with two daughters of her own. Joan captivated her 32-year-old second husband, bore him fourteen children, and had him wrapped around her little finger.

Three years after their marriage, Joan's half-brother Henry IV seized the throne. Although Ralph owed his title to Richard II, he supported Henry's usurpation and held the North for him against the rebellious Percy clan in 1403, 1405 and 1408. Finally, in 1415, while Henry V was away on the Agincourt campaign, Ralph defeated an invading Scots army much larger than his own at Yeavering in Northumberland.

Ralph's family by his first marriage did not stand a chance against Joan. John, Ralph's eldest son from his first marriage and heir to the earldom of Westmorland, agreed a settlement sometime before his death in 1420, whereby he would inherit only the ancestral Neville castles and manors of Raby and Brancepeth in Durham.

Richard, Joan's eldest son by Ralph, got almost everything else – which by 1425, when his father died, was a great deal. He became the largest secular lord in Yorkshire with his seat at Sheriff Hutton, and the largest in the county of Richmondshire with his seat at Middleham. He also inherited the wardenship of the West March with his seat at Penrith in Cumberland, and the stewardship of most of the northern duchy of Lancaster estates.

Ralph added to his second family's prosperity by means of matrimonial larceny. He married William, his third son by Joan, to the feeble-minded heiress of the barony of Fauconberg. After the death of his brother, Baron Latimer by marriage, he claimed the title and took effective possession of the lands of the barony, both assigned to George, his fourth son. He married his fifth son, Edward, to Elizabeth Beauchamp, Baroness Bergavenny by right. He also used his influence to accelerate the ecclesiastical career of his second son, Robert, who became Bishop of Salisbury at the age of 23 in 1427, two years after Ralph's death.

Ralph and Joan also arranged brilliant marriages for their daughters: Anne to the Duke of Buckingham, Katherine to the Duke of Norfolk and, as we have seen, Cecily to the Duke of York. Eleanor, the eldest of their children, was married to Hotspur's son Henry. Joan designed the marriage as a means to reconcile the Percys with Henry V, who in 1416 restored Henry Percy to his grandfather's attainted title, to the wardenship of the East March and to those of the Percy estates not previously awarded to others, principally to Ralph Neville himself.

Of all these unions, the prize was the marriage in 1420 of Richard, the eldest, to Alice, heiress of Thomas Montacute, 4th Earl of Salisbury, Alice Chaucer's second husband. Richard became a regional magnate when he inherited his father's lands and offices; but when Montacute was killed at the siege of Orléans in late 1428, he became one of the richest peers in England. The Salisbury inheritance included the huge manor of Bisham in eastern Berkshire and a broad spread of estates from Somerset through Wiltshire and Dorset to Hampshire.

We know very little about the man who became, by marriage, 5th Earl of Salisbury. The only surviving likeness is a figurine of him as one of the 'mourners' around the magnificent tomb of Richard Beauchamp, Earl of Warwick, in the Church of St Mary, Warwick.

It makes him look like a benevolent priest, which is hard to square with his harsh reputation. On the other hand, although he was 20 when he married Alice Montacute, seven years his junior, he had the decency to wait a few years before consummating the union. Between 1423 and 1444 she bore him many children, ten of whom survived infancy.

Other than that we really only know he was supremely blessed by good fortune and much favoured by the king's Council. This naturally bred envious resentment, not least among Ralph's first family. The new Earl of Westmorland tried to obtain a modification of the lop-sided settlement agreed by his father, but could not prevail in the face of Salisbury's power. Many years later the dispossessed Nevilles were to eat the dish of revenge very cold indeed.

Contrary to what most histories allege the feud that developed between Salisbury and the Percys took a long time to gestate. Despite the Nevilles having grown so greatly at his family's expense, until 1453 the Earl of Northumberland combined with Salisbury against Scots incursions, and the two frequently worked together on royal commissions and in other regional legal capacities. There was, however, no doubt which of the two was the dominant partner.

Northumberland itself remained a solidly Percy fief, but in every other northern county the 'good lordship' of Salisbury predominated, and most of the lesser local peers were drawn into his gravitational field. Two who looked instead to Percy for leadership were the intermarried families of Lord Clifford and Ralph Dacre of Naworth, in Cumberland. Among the reasons why they resisted Salisbury's hegemony must have been Dacre's marriage with one of the daughters of Ralph Neville's first marriage.*

The cascade of royal favour for the Earl of Salisbury continued after Henry VI assumed personal kingship, with the promise of the

---

* Ralph Dacre was not in the direct line of succession to the Dacre barony, which in 1458 went by marriage to Richard Fiennes of Herstmonceux Castle in Sussex. To avoid confusion Ralph was known as Dacre of the North after he was made a baron in his own right in 1459.

lands (but not the title) of the earldom of Richmond in heredity, and the lifetime grant of the West March wardenship for himself and his eldest son, as well as the remaining stewardships of the duchy of Lancaster in Yorkshire.

Suffolk, the king's chief minister, did not view Salisbury's growing power with equanimity. Towards the end of the 1440s he directed royal favour towards the long-neglected Percys in an effort to balance the Nevilles. In November 1447, Northumberland's second son, Thomas Percy, was granted the recreated title and the meagre lands of the barony of Egremont, to part of which Salisbury had laid claim. Suffolk also put the payments due to Northumberland as warden of the East March on a par with those due to Salisbury for the West March.

By this time Northumberland had become a more assiduous courtier. He really did not have the means to maintain a suitably grand presence in London, but had learned he must try to do so. He also spent a much higher proportion of his relatively modest income on maintaining his remaining influence in Cumberland and Yorkshire, as otherwise he could not hope to recover the assets lost by his family following the 1405 attainder.

It was, therefore, a crushing blow to Northumberland's hopes – as well as those of quite a few others – when in 1448 the Nevilles won the matrimonial lottery yet again. It began in 1435, when Salisbury and the Welsh Marcher magnate Richard Beauchamp, Earl of Warwick, agreed a double matrimonial alliance, with Salisbury's daughter Cecily (aged 10) betrothed to Warwick's heir Henry (9), and his eldest son Richard (6) to Warwick's daughter Anne (8).

When both Beauchamp and his wife died in 1439, Salisbury became the lead administrator of his estates on behalf of Henry and Anne, until Henry was granted his majority in 1444. Because his father had been the tutor chosen by Henry V for his infant son, Henry Beauchamp had been Henry VI's closest friend since childhood. In 1445, the king made him Duke of Warwick and also declared him King of the Isle of Wight, in order to put him on a more equal standing. It was a terrible blow to him when Henry died, aged only 21, the following year.

Not long before his death Henry and Cecily had a baby daughter, named Anne after her aunt, Henry's sister and the younger Richard Neville's wife. When Henry died the baby became Countess of Warwick by right, but three years later, in 1449, she also died. Salisbury was perfectly placed to ensure that Anne, his daughter-in-law and the sole full blood heir, secured as much as possible of an enormous inheritance.

At the age of 21 the younger Richard Neville became Earl of Warwick by marriage and inherited, through Anne, lands that rivalled his father's in acreage, although poorer. Apart from Barnard Castle in Durham and one or two other scattered holdings, the Beauchamp estate was concentrated in Wales and the South March, in Gloucestershire, and in Warwickshire itself.* The new Earl of Warwick's aunt Cecily did him one last favour by dying in 1450, with the reversion of her dower lands to the estate.

Another timely death – for Warwick – was that of his wife's half-sister in 1448, which in 1450 enabled him to gain control of the lands of the barony of Bergavenny on behalf of her minor son, supplanting her widower, his uncle Edward. Salisbury also ceded to him the guardianship of George, Baron Latimer, another uncle, who had been declared mentally incompetent in 1447, which gave him control of the lands of the youngest of the daughters from Richard Beauchamp's first marriage.

He was also outstandingly fortunate in the timing of the Beauchamp succession. The claims of the eldest daughters of Richard Beauchamp's first marriage were swept aside more easily because their husbands, the Duke of Somerset and Earl of Shrewsbury, who would have violently resisted Warwick's takeover, were so deeply involved in the Normandy debacle.

Another key factor in Warwick's rise and rise was the fall of

---

* For a fuller appreciation of this hotly contested succession, see Appendix F: The Beauchamp Inheritance.

Suffolk, who viewed the union of the Salisbury and Warwick earl-doms as highly undesirable and might have restrained Henry VI, who regarded the new earl as a close friend. Warwick had been in attendance at court alongside Henry Beauchamp, and some of the glow of his double brother-in-law's lifelong friendship with the king rubbed off on him. Overwhelmed by the crisis of 1449–50 and by his growing fear that York was plotting to overthrow him, the king gave Warwick's succession his unreserved blessing.

What sort of a man was the new Earl of Warwick, this sudden meteor in the English political firmament? Like Salisbury, his father, the only likeness we have of him is one of the figurines around the funerary monument of Richard Beauchamp, his father-in-law. Since he oversaw the construction of the tomb, we must assume he thought it portrayed him to best advantage. If so, he must have been strikingly ugly in real life – although we should not, perhaps, read too much into the strange face, which makes him look like a discontented cat.

As with all medieval biography, we must pick and choose among hagiographic and hostile commentaries. Two characteristics are common to both: even by the standard of his age, Warwick was extremely ruthless, and he was also highly charismatic. The Greek root of the word charisma means 'gift of grace', and it is not much of a leap of imagination to assume he saw the hand of fate in the improbable sequence of events that thrust greatness upon him at such an early age. His history bears the mark of a man convinced he was destiny's child, with no need to compromise with those who opposed him.

MARGUERITE

IN *The Treasure of the City of Ladies*, written in about 1405, the Venetian-French writer Christine de Pisan sought to buttress what she saw as an erosion of respect for the role of women as mediators and peacemakers between their husbands and the rest of the world. Their supportive role, she wrote, was to advocate chastity, charity, patience and humility, to which end rhetorical skill (her own forte) was an indispensable attribute. However, she also argued that a noble lady must play an active role during her husband's absences, not only employing her well-honed administrative skills but also, if necessary, as a military leader.

Marguerite of Anjou was a queen straight out of *The Treasure of the City of Ladies* until circumstances obliged her to take hold of the reins falling from her husband's hands. It was his failure that forced her to 'act like a man'. Although she was just 20 years old in 1450, Marguerite handled the moral collapse of her 28-year-old husband with remarkable maturity and aplomb. She had received a thorough education on how to rule through weak men from her mother and grandmother, and that training now paid off.

Henry VI had grown up crushed by knowledge that he could not possibly live up to the idealized example of his father, the alpha male of a warrior aristocracy in which natural selection had distilled an abundance of testosterone. Deficient in that respect, he had willingly surrendered his institutional power to Suffolk, twenty-five years older and a distinguished veteran of the Normandy conquest. Now, with Suffolk and Ayscough brutally murdered, his carefree cocoon ripped away and his entourage behaving like the proverbial headless chicken, he desperately needed someone to supply parental guidance. Who better than his wife, who had acted so bravely and decisively to defuse Cade's Rebellion?

The evidence points to Somerset being the queen's choice to replace Buckingham as Constable of England and as the new chief minister. Marguerite was probably not immune to his charm – few women were – but his principal attraction to her was that he owed everything to the crown. Without royal protection he would be hounded to death by York and the vengeful Anglo-Normans, and following his losses in Normandy and the Acts of Resumption, without royal favour he could not sustain the standard required of a duke.*

The collapse of the peace policy she symbolized made it all the more important for Marguerite to adopt a low profile, for which she needed a front man. Although she had been as much wrapped in Suffolk's cocoon as Henry, she would have been better informed about the true state of his realm through ladies-in-waiting such as Jacquetta and Alice Chaucer, and the other noblewomen who attended her court. They would have functioned as an intelligence service at a time when Henry's retinue was feeding him panic-inducing rumours.

We may also infer there was considerable scope for women to play a major, if informal, role in government if they could persuade their men to keep their testosterone under control. While we should not presume aristocratic women were any less ruthlessly ambitious than their male kin, their instincts would oppose a drift towards combat. The marital alliances in the list of 'Protagonists and Marriages' and the family trees do not, unfortunately, give us any indication of how effective they were, of who were the strong women and who

---

* Starting early in 1451, the queen began to pay him an annuity of £100 [£63,600] from her own exchequer.

the weak. What they do show, however, is that in less fraught times Marguerite might have made herself the hub of a powerful sorority working for compromise.

The immediate task was to see off the threat from York, and he was firmly put back in his box during 1451–2. We have seen how little the support of the Commons mattered once the Lords realized their interest was best served by opposing the cause of reform espoused by York. Somerset required no encouragement from Marguerite to go after the man who wanted to destroy him and, not surprisingly for a man far more accustomed to warfare than to government, he chose to run the political equivalent of a *chevauchée* against him.

York was far too eminent for someone like Somerset, admired by few and lacking the means to buy followers, to attack directly. Instead, he set out to erode York's prestige and popularity by showing he could not protect his own people. In June 1451, following the vehement rejection of his petition to recognize York as heir presumptive, Thomas Young and other Yorkist councillors were sent to the Tower. In July, Somerset turned his guns on William Oldhall, York's chamberlain and Speaker of the Commons. The arrest for sedition of the vicar and others of Standon, a Hertfordshire manor held by Oldhall from York, was the first shot. In November Oldhall took sanctuary in St Martins-le-Grand in London.

Even though there was credible evidence Oldhall had conspired against him, the king was outraged when, in January 1452, Somerset had him dragged out, and ordered him returned to sanctuary. It was an unheeded warning that Somerset's impatience could bring royal authority into further disrepute. The king was right to overrule him, not only because the violation of sanctuary was impious, but also because it was unnecessary. Oldhall no longer posed a threat. Even so he was impeached, and on 22 June found guilty of treason, outlawed and attainted. He remained in sanctuary under close supervision until 1455.

Adding to the sense of crisis, in September 1451 the dormant feud between the Earl of Devon and the recently created Baron Bonville erupted into open warfare. It is not entirely clear why it did so, but there must be a strong assumption the main culprit was Bonville, if only because he was now allied with the restless James Butler, Earl of Wiltshire. Devon was now supported by the hot-headed Lord Moleyns, whose arbitrary actions against the Paston family we reviewed in Chapter 5, and by Edward Brooke, Baron Cobham. After failing to capture Wiltshire at Bristol, they ran Bonville to earth at Taunton Castle in Somerset.

A short while previously the Berkeley–Lisle feud* had also burst into flames when John Talbot, Lord Lisle, seized Berkeley Castle and kidnapped Berkeley's wife. York intervened against Lisle, and then took 2,000 men south to separate the combatants at Taunton. Devon had been one of his few aristocratic supporters, while Bonville and Wiltshire were strongly associated with the court party. By taking Bonville into custody he saved Devon from being tainted by murder, and by submitting the dispute to royal arbitration he demonstrated that he could keep the king's peace where Somerset could not.

Fed false reports that York's people were responsible for outbreaks of unrest in East Anglia, the king reacted angrily to the actions taken in his name by York in the West Country. Marguerite's imperfect understanding of how England was governed may have led her to see a parallel with her cousin Charles VII's humbling of his overmighty nobles in France. For whatever reasons, the royal couple accepted uncritically Somerset's interpretation of York's actions as a usurpation of the king's prerogative, when most would have seen it as the justified exercise of regional lordship to restore law and order.

Although Lisle had plainly been in the wrong at Berkeley Castle, he was created a viscount. York was also insultingly cast as a party to the Courtenay–Bonville feud when the king summoned all involved to court. Moleyns, Cobham, Bonville and Wiltshire obeyed and were briefly detained, separately, in the queen's castles at

---

* See Appendix F: The Beauchamp Inheritance.

Berkhamsted and Wallingford. Devon and York ignored the summons, and it was probably because the king refused to pursue the matter any further that Somerset vented his frustration on Oldhall.

By January 1452 York was sufficiently alarmed by reports of the king's anger towards him to send a grovelling declaration of loyalty, and took the further step of publicly swearing to it in the presence of the Bishop of Hereford and the Earl of Shrewsbury. Then came Somerset's violation of sanctuary, after which York became convinced his enemy would stop at nothing to destroy him. Accordingly, he summoned his tenantry from all over England to join him in a march on London. A manifesto dated 3 February recited the now tired accusation against Somerset for the loss of Normandy, and continued:

> After my coming out of Ireland, as the king's true liegeman and servant (as I ever shall be to my life's end), I brought to his royal majesty's attention certain articles concerning the well-being and safeguard both of his most royal person and the tranquillity and conservation of all this his realm. These terms of advice... were laid aside, to have no effect, through the envy, malice and untruth of the Duke of Somerset [who]... labours continually about the king's highness for my undoing, and to corrupt my blood, and to disinherit me and my heirs and such persons as are about me.

Since Somerset 'ever prevails and rules about the king's person', York announced his intention to proceed 'in all haste against him', and called on his kinsmen and friends to join him. For all the protestations of loyalty to the king this was a call to armed rebellion, and seen as such even by peers such as Norfolk, who had hitherto supported York against Somerset. Such an extraordinary misjudgement must have been the product of obsession, nurtured by York's isolation at Ludlow with men who could see their own fate in Oldhall's.

After London shut its gates to him at the king's command, York took his force, which included artillery, south of the river and established a fortified camp at Dartford in Kent. He may have expected the Kentish men to rally to his standard, but if so he was disappointed. Only Devon and Cobham were with him. Ranged against them were the Dukes of Buckingham, Norfolk, Exeter and Somerset, the Earls of Salisbury, Warwick and Shrewsbury, the viscounts Bourchier and Lisle, the Bishops of Winchester and Ely, and a dozen barons including the veteran Scales and the new creations Bonville and Stourton.

The ensuing negotiations were designed to grant York and his confederates a face-saving formula to escape a charge of treason. They were permitted to submit their accusations against Somerset – which were dismissed by an arbitration panel packed with the king's men – a royal pardon for their followers was agreed, and then York had to kneel before the king in St Paul's cathedral on 10 March and swear a humiliating oath of allegiance (my italics):

> I, Richard Duke of York confess and acknowledge that I am *and ought to be* a humble subject and liegeman to you, my sovereign lord, King Henry VI, and *ought* therefore to bear you faith and truth as my sovereign lord... [and when summoned] *to come in humble and obeisant manner*. I shall never hereafter make any assembly of your people without your command or licence, or in my lawful defence. In the interpretation and declaration of my lawful defence, I shall report at all times to your highness...

York undertook to confine himself to his own estates and departed for Ludlow on the 24th. He was compelled to depart for Fotheringhay when the king came to Ludlow to conduct assizes after a judicial progress through Devon, accompanied by Bonville and Moleyns, to punish the Earl of Devon's followers. At Ludlow tenants who had followed York were indicted and found guilty of treason before being told of the pardon negotiated at Dartford. It was a demeaning trick to play on men who had no choice but to obey their lord's summons, and done to demonstrate York's powerlessness.

York had to move again when Henry, accompanied by a retinue of lords including York's erstwhile ally Norfolk, made a judicial progress through Hertfordshire, Cambridgeshire, Huntingdonshire, Northamptonshire and Lincolnshire. These areas had provided the bulk of York's army at Dartford and the assizes at his boroughs of Grantham, Newbury and Stamford were harsher than at Ludlow. At least one man suffered a traitor's death and his quarters were displayed in Yorkist towns.

Sadly for Marguerite, her husband's new-found self-confidence did not lead to a fresh start, but instead to a stubborn repetition of the mistakes of the past. He had learned nothing from the debacle in 1450 and the survivors of Suffolk's regime were permitted to resume the old pattern of abuses. Objectively, Somerset had fulfilled his function and should have been let go after Dartford. Unfortunately Henry was unwilling, perhaps indeed psychologically unable, to deal with the stress of being a hands-on king and, once again, fell into the damaging error of over-investing in his chief minister. By delegating too much of his power to Somerset, Henry risked confirming to the world the correctness of York's opinion of him.

The king awarded Somerset several benefits York had lost to resumption, including the lease of the Isle of Wight. York also lost offices he previously held, with the lieutenancy of Ireland going to his enemy Wiltshire, who had become Earl of Ormonde on the death of his father in August 1452. York's office of Justice of the Forests south of the Trent went to Somerset in July 1453, the grant gloatingly stating it was for good service 'on both sides of the sea' to rub in the king's opinion that he had done no wrong in Normandy.

At the same time the government did address some of the grievances that had shaken the country in 1450. An executive council was set up to manage the royal finances and to handle routine matters of administration, and the Commons became more amenable once the king was seen to be putting his house in order. They may also have been abashed that, after they refused to vote the money for Rivers' expedition, Guyenne and Gascony had fallen easily to the armies of Charles VII in mid-1451.

The people of the conquered province had been governed by distant English kings for 300 years and resented their new overlords, who did not even speak the same language.* They sent emissaries to London and, with Parliament now willing to vote the necessary funds, an expeditionary force of 3,000 men was rapidly assembled by inspiring 66-year-old John Talbot, Earl of Shrewsbury, and sailed for Guyenne in October 1452.

Timing his assault to coincide with a rebellion by the citizens of Bordeaux, Talbot quickly seized the city, after which other towns and castles along the Garonne and Dordogne valleys fell like dominoes. Further funding was voted for 3,000 reinforcements led by his son Viscount Lisle, accompanied by Lord Moleyns, to face the inevitable French counter-offensive in 1453.

Given her husband's over-investment in Somerset, it was probably Marguerite's initiative to dilute the new favourite's status by promoting two more princes of the blood. In late 1452 the king's bastard half-brothers, previously commoners, were vaulted to earldoms. The elder, 21-year-old Edmund Tudor, was created Earl of Richmond, and his one-year-younger brother Jasper was created Earl of Pembroke. An Act of Parliament lifted the stigma of illegitimacy from them the following year.

Pembroke was no great prize, but the honour of Richmond was a wealthy endowment where the benefit of the king's many manors had been granted for decades – with the promise of hereditary right – to Salisbury. Once again Henry was guilty of awarding the same patronage twice, with the added aggravation that Edmund Tudor was also declared the premier earl over the head of Warwick, to whom the king had awarded the status only a year earlier.

For a family as dependent on royal favour as the Nevilles, who must have been expecting reward for their robust support of the

---

* The Occitan languages of southern France have completely different roots from metropolitan French.

king against York, the promotion of the obscure – and Welsh – Tudors at their expense was a very unpleasant surprise. In conjunction with royal support for Somerset's machinations with regard to the Beauchamp inheritance, however, it took on a far more sinister complexion.

Once confirmed in office Somerset wasted no time in attacking the rulings made in the Beauchamp inheritance case while he and Shrewsbury had been extricating themselves from Normandy. In typical Henrician fashion, two royal grants made to Warwick in 1450 were reversed in favour of Somerset in 1451. The first was the wardship of the minor George Neville, heir to the barony of Bergavenny; both awards were disgraceful, as they usurped the natural right of the boy's father. The second was the office of Chamberlain of the Exchequer, awarded to Warwick before Christmas and given to Somerset a few months later.

Somerset and Shrewsbury also obtained a grotesque ruling on behalf of their wives that they were entitled to equal shares with their half-sister Anne, Warwick's wife, of the dower lands of her – not their – mother. If Somerset thought he could simply take possession of over half the dower lands as well as the whole of the Bergavenny estate, he was mistaken. Warwick, in possession of both, let him know the only way he could get any of it was by force. Ordered to submit and surrender Cardiff and Cowbridge castles to the king's friend Lord Dudley, Warwick refused him entry and increased their garrisons.

Taken together, the estates of Warwick and Salisbury put them on a par with the Dukes of York, Norfolk and Buckingham. Having made an embittered enemy of York it was breathtakingly foolish of Henry to alienate the Nevilles as well. One would be inclined to believe it was a case of the Somerset tail wagging the royal dog, were it not for the promotion from nowhere of the Tudor brothers, which was clearly not in Somerset's interest. Marguerite simply did not appreciate that it would be perceived by the Nevilles as further evidence of a concerted royal plot to undermine them.

MITRE AND CROWN

THE ELEMENTS OF STATESMANSHIP THAT LEAVENED THE febrile squabble between the houses of Lancaster and York were largely the work of Cardinal Archbishop John Kemp, who became Lord Chancellor in 1450 and was promoted from York to Canterbury in 1452. John Stafford, his predecessor in both offices, had been Chancellor since 1432, but had been excessively accommodating to the Suffolk regime, even granting Lord Saye and the infamous William Cromer stewardship of all the estates of the Canterbury archbishopric.

Kemp was unsullied by association with the fallen regime and was also a notably able administrator. The pope had made him a cardinal-priest as early as 1439, and he had previously been Lord Chancellor in 1426–32. He was the obvious candidate to deal with the crisis of 1450, as he also was to succeed Stafford at Canterbury two years later, when Rome made him a cardinal-bishop. His only price was the appointment in 1450 to the bishopric of London of his (genuine) nephew Thomas, which had been opposed by Suffolk.

As we have seen, it was Kemp in combination with Marguerite who defused Cade's Rebellion, and it was certainly he and not Somerset who introduced fiscal restraint and more rational admin-istration through the new executive council, and won back the support of the Commons. It was Kemp who devised the face-saving formula that averted bloodshed at Dartford, and he was also instrumental in obtaining the taxes from the Commons and the clerical subsidy which had made possible Talbot's initially successful expedition to Guyenne.

In sum, it was practically entirely thanks to Kemp that the regime won back a considerable degree of popular acceptance. When Parliament assembled at Reading in March 1453 it voted the king, for life, customs dues, increased wool subsidies and a poll tax on aliens (later revoked), along with the customary tax on the value of moveable goods (a fifteenth for rural and a tenth for urban areas). The last time the Commons had shown this much honour to their monarch was to Henry V after Agincourt. They even voted an additional three fifteenths and tenths to raise a force of 20,000 archers, an invitation for Henry to lead an army for the reconquest of the lost empire in France.

• ☙ •

The emergence of Kemp as the regime's saviour is perhaps the most unreported aspect of the crisis, and the reason is not hard to identify. Even today journalists report the easy stuff – the public doings of politicians – and hardly ever mention the senior permanent officials without whom the inadequacy of their political 'masters' would become apparent. Although historians may eventually be able to draw on the minutes of today's confidential discussions, there were no such records in earlier times.

The Church's moral and social power was in decline, but churchmen were valued as civil servants for a number of interrelated reasons. As the clergy were, in theory, celibate, there was less chance they would advance their families' interests at the expense of the state. The priesthood was also a career open to talent, and provided a pool of literate and numerate individuals from which the monarchy and the aristocracy preferentially drew their clerks and accountants. They were the 'technocrats' of the Middle Ages.

Senior churchmen also represented a powerful constituency and

8. ARCHDIOCESES AND DIOCESES OF ENGLAND & WALES

See also Appendices D and E

SCOTLAND

Durham

Carlisle

YORK

Bangor

St Asaph

Chester

Lincoln

Lichfield

Hereford

Coventry

Ely

Norwich

St David's

Worcester

Dorchester

London

Llandaff

Bath

Salisbury

Rochester

CANTERBURY

Wells

Winchester

Chichester

Exeter

© Hugh Bicheno

were no less self-serving than today's permanent officials. Since the 1430s the archdioceses of Canterbury and York, under constant pressure to finance secular government, had merged their convocations (assemblies). While most frequently summoned in response to royal requests for subsidies, ecclesiastical matters had also become subject to the approval of the convocation. The Archbishop of Canterbury, whose own see was relatively poor, was in a position vis-à-vis his bishops and lesser clergy somewhat akin to the king and his Lords and Commons.

Bishops played an active part in secular political life through membership of the House of Lords, and traditionally occupied two of the three most senior non-ceremonial offices of state. The first was the Lord Chancellor, Keeper of the Great Seal and Chief Royal Chaplain. He was not only the king's senior adviser in matters spiritual but also the senior legal officer, without whom the business of government could not be conducted. The second was the Lord Keeper of the Privy Seal, the king's personal signet, which travelled with him while the Great Seal remained in Chancery, the Lord Chancellor's London office. Almost all non-judicial documents requiring the Great Seal were first warranted by the Privy Seal.

Beyond these office-holders we know little of the role of the clergy in government. Some questions are easier to answer than others. The relatively tiny diocese of Ely was prized out of proportion to its size in part because, like Durham, the Isle of Ely was a county palatine – one ruled by a magnate with special authority elsewhere possessed only by the sovereign. Its principal attraction, however, was that although it was only the fifth most richly endowed see, it had much the lowest outgoings. The handsome surplus could be spent to buy influence.*

Bishops also enjoyed the rights by which a later age defined constitutional monarchy: to be consulted, to encourage, and to warn. Perhaps above all, the Church provided institutional memory and

* In 1454 Pope Nicholas V took advantage of the paralysis of English government to appoint William Grey, one of his own officials.

continuity. If to these attributes we add that about a third of the land in England was held by the Church, whose members were immune from civil or even criminal prosecution by the secular authorities, the wonder is not that a figure like Kemp should emerge in a crisis, but rather that it was not a more common occurrence.

Although most people compartmentalized religion apart from their worldly pursuits, everyone took it seriously. This had practical consequences. Throughout the Middle Ages, rebellion against the monarch was justified as an action taken against 'evil councillors' because the rebels had sworn allegiance to the king himself. When York finally articulated his claim to the throne he stressed the prior Lancastrian violation of divine order in a bid to absolve himself of the sacramental oaths he had sworn to Henry VI. Nobody was convinced.

• ∞ •

Kemp would have disapproved of the king's provocative assizes in the Yorkist heartlands and his support for Somerset's perversion of legal process in his attack on the Beauchamp settlement. They indicate that after Dartford Henry was no longer paying as much attention as previously to his Chancellor's political advice. Kemp did not tell the king what he wanted to hear, and could not prevail against a household of sycophants led by Somerset, a man even more rapacious and considerably less politically astute than Suffolk had been.

Then came a totally unforeseeable event, which threw everything into the melting pot and brought Kemp to the forefront again. On or about 7 August 1453, at his hunting lodge at Clarendon, east of Salisbury in Wiltshire, Henry VI went into a frenzy, followed by a deeply catatonic state from which he could not be aroused. The breakdown is commonly ascribed to his learning that Talbot and his son Lisle had been killed and their army destroyed at the Battle of Castillon on 13 July. Six weeks earlier, the news of the fall of Constantinople to Ottoman Sultan Mehmed II must also have been a terrible shock.

Henry may have been building up to a psychotic episode for some time. It would be in keeping with a diagnosis of schizophrenia that the harbinger of his catatonic withdrawal from reality was his acute sense of persecution in 1450, followed by his surrender of personal autonomy. Possibly Marguerite, alarmed by the purpose-less agitation that characterizes the disease, suggested Henry should unwind at Clarendon, far from London, as he had in 1450 when she whisked him off to Bishop's Waltham.

Henry's collapse brought Kemp back into play. Although gen-uinely concerned to protect the dynasty, he had his own agenda. The king was effectively the supreme governor of the Church in England long before Henry VIII expropriated the monasteries and, like all European princes, regarded it as a dependable cash cow. After being ruthlessly milked by Henry V, the bishops had become accus-tomed to far greater indulgence under Henry VI. Consequently the bishops were even more anxious than most lay lords that cold-eyed York should not become the king's chief minister, still less replace the king himself.

Over the coming months Kemp did all he could to buy time for Henry to recover. Although of supreme dynastic significance, the birth on 13 October 1453 of baby Edward, the long-awaited heir apparent, did not address the immediate problem of governance. Marguerite chose Kemp and Somerset as the baby's godfathers (his godmother was Anne, Duchess of Buckingham and older sister of Cecily, Duchess of York), but Kemp could not put himself forward as Protector, and Somerset lacked the prestige to do so.

Despite the fact that her uncle had just extinguished English hopes of recovering their empire in France, motherhood exalted Marguerite's status and popularity – already high following her her-oism in 1450 – to an extraordinary degree. Cecily, Duchess of York, captured the public mood in her letter of congratulations when she learned the queen was pregnant. It was, she wrote, 'the most precious, most joyful, and most comforting earthly treasure that might come into this land and to the people thereof'.

Politically, however, there was to be a serious downside to the queen's confinement (from which men were strictly excluded). For a month before the birth and for forty days after it Marguerite was out of the loop at a crucial time, when the severity of her husband's incapacity could no longer be concealed and Parliament was becoming alarmed about the power vacuum it created.

What Marguerite and Kemp needed, and did not get, was domestic tranquillity. The Lord Chancellor could not provide executive leadership. Somerset could only act with the authority of the king's warrant and could not forge one because the Privy Seal was under the control of Thomas Lisieux, Dean of St Paul's and a Kemp protégé. The accepted role for the queen, as for any noble lady, was to intercede with her husband to prevent or repair injustice, and to reward faithful service rather than to punish transgressions. Unfortunately, even before Henry's catatonia, transgressions were what had to be dealt with.

First, there was the continuing defiance of royal authority by Warwick's refusal to surrender Cardiff and Cowbridge. The issue was taken off the boil because, in the face of Kemp's disapproval and without the king's warrant, Somerset could not push his spurious claims any further. His ambition to undo the Beauchamp settlement had, anyway, been dealt a severe blow by the deaths of Shrewsbury and Lisle at Castillon. Had they returned in triumph from Guyenne they would undoubtedly have supported him against Warwick, in arms if necessary, with every possibility of success.

Secondly, and potentially more threatening to royal authority, the tinder of conflict in the North between the houses of Percy and Neville began to smoulder. It was a generational thing. Sixty-year-old Henry Percy, restored to the earldom of Northumberland in 1416 through the good offices of Joan née Beaufort, Countess of Westmorland, and married to her eldest daughter, had to accept that he must play second fiddle to 53-year-old Salisbury, his much wealthier and better connected brother-in-law.

His sons, however, yearned for the days when the Percys were 'Kings of the North', and chafed at Neville supremacy. The spark to the tinder was the marriage in August 1453 between Thomas Neville, Salisbury's youngest son, and Maud Stanhope, niece and joint heir of Lord Cromwell. Cromwell's many estates included Burwell in Lincolnshire and Wressle in south-east Yorkshire, both

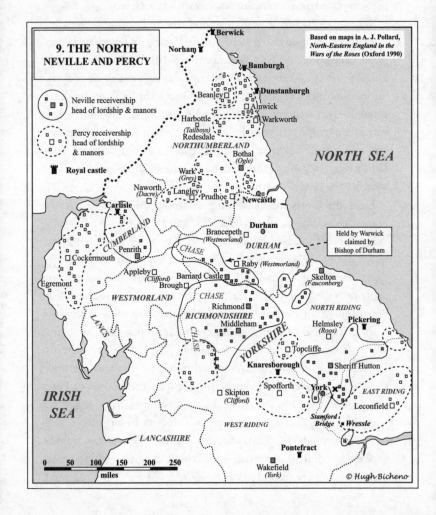

9. THE NORTH
NEVILLE AND PERCY

Based on maps in A. J. Pollard, *North-Eastern England in the Wars of the Roses* (Oxford 1990)

Neville receivership head of lordship & manors

Percy receivership head of lordship & manors

Royal castle

Held by Warwick claimed by Bishop of Durham

Berwick
Norham
Bamburgh
Beanley
Dunstanburgh
Alnwick
Harbottle
Warkworth
(Tailboys)
Redesdale
NORTHUMBERLAND
Bothal
(Ogle)
Wark
(Grey)
Naworth
(Dacre)
Langley
Prudhoe
Newcastle

NORTH SEA

Carlisle
CUMBERLAND
Penrith
Cockermouth
Appleby
(Clifford)
Brough
Egremont
WESTMORLAND
LANCS
Brancepeth
(Westmorland)
Durham
DURHAM
CHASE
Raby (Westmorland)
Barnard Castle
CHASE
Richmond
RICHMONDSHIRE
Middleham
CHASE
Skelton
(Fauconberg)
NORTH RIDING
Helmsley
(Roos)
Pickering
Topcliffe
Knaresborough
Sheriff Hutton
Spofforth
York
EAST RIDING
Skipton
(Clifford)
Leconfield
IRISH SEA
Stamford Bridge
Wressle
WEST RIDING
YORKSHIRE
LANCASHIRE
Pontefract
Wakefield
(York)

0   50   100   150   200   250
miles

© Hugh Bicheno

previously owned by Thomas Percy, Earl of Worcester, who had been beheaded and attainted in 1403 after the failure of his nephew Hotspur's rebellion.

Wressle, where Worcester had built a splendid castle-mansion, was among the properties the Percys most wanted to recover, and Northumberland's second son (also Thomas Percy) believed the Stanhope–Neville marriage would lead to the permanent loss of the castle and manor. Bearing in mind how Thomas Percy had been created Baron Egremont over the objections of Salisbury in the last flourish of Suffolk's ascendancy, and that the title brought with it very little land, it is possible some assurance about Wressle had been given to Thomas. He certainly reacted as though he had been robbed after the king gave consent to the Neville–Stanhope marriage.

Egremont issued his livery to a gang of hard cases recruited in York and, joined by his younger brother Richard, began to maraud Neville lands, ignoring orders from the king to desist and to take his men to Guyenne. Salisbury's second son, John Neville, retaliated by riding through the Percy manor of Topcliffe with a column of armed retainers.

Egremont's anger over Wressle is usually seen as the culmination of growing tension between the two families, but he had a genuine and specific grievance. Apart from Ampthill, which we reviewed in Chapter 5, Lord Cromwell was a party to a number of other disputes, and when he died in 1456, his executors returned lands worth £5,500 [£3.5 million] to illegally dispossessed owners. Probably he and the Nevilles were indeed planning some chicanery over Wressle, although it was a royal manor only granted to him for life. Common hostility towards Cromwell later brought together the younger Percys and the 23-year-old Duke of Exeter, making them enemies of York as well.

On 24 August Egremont and Richard Percy, joined by John Clifford, the eldest son of Thomas, Baron Clifford, waylaid the Neville–Stanhope wedding party, which included Salisbury himself, at Heworth, outside York. Although there was much shouting and jostling, no blood was spilt – but the affront to Salisbury brought the fathers openly into the dispute. They called out their retainers, and on 20 October the two armies came into dangerous proximity 4 miles north of Topcliffe. The younger men may have been champing at the bit, but Salisbury and Northumberland sought the mediation of Archbishop William Booth of York, and disbanded their forces for the winter.

Even though blood did not flow, the salient political fact was that both parties had ignored repeated injunctions and indictments issued under the Great Seal, just when Marguerite played the top dynastic trump card by giving birth to a healthy baby boy. Ironically, by taking the issue of York's possible succession off the table, it made him more acceptable as the champion of good governance he had always claimed to be. An orderly realm might be governed by a council – as it had been during Henry's minority. However, one where great lords were circling each other with fur bristling required a firmer hand than even a council guided by Kemp could provide.

RICHARD

I**N NOVEMBER 1454 YORK RODE INTO LONDON ACCOMP-**
nied by the king's Tudor half-brothers, the Earls of Richmond
and Pembroke. What makes this doubly significant is that
no other peers wished to be publicly identified with the duke.
Furthermore, although Somerset had tried to prevent it, York had
come because members of the royal household and bishops closely
associated with the regime had voted to include him in a summons
to a Great Council, which was to decide on governance during the
king's incapacity.

It is possible, indeed probable, that the queen had in mind the
creation of a royal 'centre', above faction, a project which remained
viable until the king emerged from catatonia around Christmas
1454. Discarding Somerset was the price she had to pay to bring
York on board, and there is no reason to believe she hesitated to pay
it. Somerset had become a political liability, and a distraction from
the serious business of deciding how to cope with the constitutional
conundrum of a living king who was unable to rule.

York had almost ruined himself pursuing the Anglo-Norman vendetta against Somerset, and would not have wanted to expend any
of his diminished political capital in reopening old wounds. It was
Norfolk, with his own axe to grind, who formally accused Somerset
of treason. Although York took advantage of Norfolk's accusation
to argue that Oldhall's conviction for treason should be set aside, he

did not pursue the matter after Kemp ruled the Council lacked the legal authority to do so. The Chancellor did, however, agree that York's councillors had been unlawfully purged from the Commons.

Somerset was sent to the Tower to await the preparation of the terms of impeachment, which Norfolk insisted should be by English law only for abuses of power as the king's chief minister. His alleged treasonous dealings with the King of France were to be judged by Norman law, which would have put his fate in the hands of nobles who had lost their French estates. We cannot know whether this was a genuine effort to see him punished for the loss of Normandy, or a ploy to drag out the proceedings indefinitely. Somerset's retainers took up residence around the Tower, and there he remained for the next fourteen months. York may have had few lords on his side, but Somerset had even fewer. He was neutralized.

By the end of November 1453 some forty-six lords had obeyed the summons to the Great Council. They all solemnly swore to abstain from and to suppress lawlessness, but evaded discussion of the constitutional crisis. On 5 December a mere fourteen peers put their names to a minimal agreement that the Council should act when required to maintain 'politic rule and governance'. The first such action, supported by York and voted the next day, was to make provision for the on-going functioning of the king's household.

York would not have subscribed to this if he believed the household was hostile to him. He and his wife certainly must have paid their respects to Marguerite and her baby after she emerged from confinement, so either face-to-face at that time or indirectly later he may have received the queen's assurance that she wanted to work with him. This would explain a number of things, not least why he did not pursue the impeachment of Somerset during 1454.

More intriguing is that York made no attempt to bring forward discussion of constitutional matters, the very reason why the Great Council had been summoned. The reason for his reticence was to avoid a clash with Kemp, who was determined to delay any such discussion for as long as possible. To make sure the Council did not try to grant itself royal prerogatives, Kemp kept Privy Seal, his man Lisieux, away from Westminster, thus maintaining a veto for the Great Seal.

The only move to fill the political void was an astonishing proposal circulated in mid-January that has Kemp's fingerprints all over it. Evidence of it is limited to a single report from one of Norfolk's informants in London, but it is plausible:

> The Queen hath made a bill of five articles, desiring those articles be granted; whereof the first is that she desireth the whole rule of this land; the second is that she may make the Chancellor, the Treasurer, the Privy Seal, and all other officers of this land, with sheriffs and all other officers that the King should make; the third is that she may give all the bishoprics of this land, and all the other benefices belonging to the King's gift; the fourth is that she may have sufficient livelihood assigned her for the King, and the Prince and herself. But as for the fifth article, I cannot yet know what it is.*

Marguerite and Kemp must have known that a Council reluctant to address substantive matters of governance would be hostile to the constitutional novelty they were proposing. They were setting out a strong negotiating position, designed to pre-empt any discussion of a regency unless it were hers. Some of the lords will have understood this, but it would have added to their resentment of a chancellor who was exceeding his traditional authority, and an emerging consensus in favour of York.

On 13 February, the day before Parliament convened, Kemp moved that the Council should decide 'to whom the king's power should be committed', with the Council retaining the right to prorogue and dissolve Parliament. The councillors overrode him and included the right 'to dissolve the said parliament and to do all

---

* The fifth item probably concerned her custody of the prince and matters to do with his upbringing.

things that shall be necessary thereto or to any of the premises' when they nominated York. Undeterred, Kemp altered the wording back to what he had originally proposed before affixing the Great Seal.

At about the same time York made a shrewd legal thrust to ensure the neutrality of the Commons. One of the charges brought against Oldhall to depose him as Speaker had been that he stole property worth about £2,000 [£1.27 million] from Somerset. York now obtained a judgement against Somerset's man Thorpe, who had replaced Oldhall, for stealing property to the same value from him, and had him consigned to the Fleet prison. When Parliament convened, the Commons sent a delegation to the Lords to protest, but accepted York's argument (which Kemp might perhaps have ruled invalid, but did not) that since Thorpe's arrest had taken place during the recess, it did not infringe on parliamentary privilege.

The new Speaker, one of the royal household MPs, made no advocacy for Thorpe or Somerset. York also obtained the acquittal of the Earl of Devon of the charge of high treason pending since Dartford. In a quid pro quo, he then led the lords in reciting an oath of allegiance as 'true and faithful Liegemen to the King our Sovereign Lord', and the next day subscribed to the Act by which 5-month-old Edward was created Prince of Wales.

Simultaneously with these developments, on 19 March 1454 the Commons refused a request from the Chancellor for a grant of £40,000 [£24.44 million]. They argued that they had been generous already and had not received in return the 'sad and substantial council' promised several times since the king first agreed to it in 1450. It is quite possible Kemp had made the request to provoke an excuse to dissolve a Parliament now unresponsive to his will, and to return power to a Council he could override; but whatever he intended to do became moot when he dropped dead on the 22nd.

The next day the Lords sent a deputation led by Buckingham to visit the king at Windsor, and, after they reported that he remained catatonic, the political log-jam constructed by Kemp was washed away. On the 27th, the Lords elected York Protector of the Realm

and Chief Councillor. He obtained an Act of Parliament to confirm the appointment, which cited the example of the arrangements
made after the death of Henry V in 1422. That is, he was to receive
all lawful and reasonable assistance in the service of the public good,
but the Council reserved the right to define the public good. His
only specifically defined duty was to defend the realm against foreign or domestic enemies.

The true novelty was the election on 28 March of Richard Neville,
Earl of Salisbury, as the first secular Lord Chancellor since 1412,
when Henry IV appointed his half-brother Thomas Beaufort as a
shot across the bow of a politically activist episcopate. The same
consideration applied in 1454: the election of Salisbury was retaliation by the secular lords for Kemp's frustration of the Great Council.
Salisbury was, however, a most inappropriate choice for the senior
legal officer of the kingdom. He had very recently defied royal
authority in his family's squabble with the Percys, and he was also a
party to other on-going disputes in the Midlands, and through his
son in south Wales.

We can only speculate how this appointment, which led to the
fateful alignment of the Nevilles with York, came about. It was certainly not due to York's influence, as he had barely managed to
achieve a highly circumscribed authority for himself. It was most
likely the result of wholesale bribery by Salisbury and Warwick, who
wanted to ensure that those seeking to challenge their supremacy
should have no legal recourse and would resort to arms, for which
they could be condemned for rebellion.

Even though they were brothers-in-law, Salisbury had not previously shown any indication of sympathy with York, and it is
not beyond the bounds of possibility that the queen could have
instructed her party to vote for him, to balance York. Likewise the
promotion from Ely to Canterbury of Bishop Thomas Bourchier,
the Duke of Buckingham's maternal half-brother, may have been
a move towards the creation of a 'centre' in which the country's
greatest magnates were in equilibrium.

If so, it constitutes evidence of a political project too sophisticated to have been the product of the rather dull minds of the household sycophants. It may have been a policy legacy from the wily Kemp, but its continuation must have been driven by Marguerite, advised by Laurence Booth, her own chancellor and holder of the sinecure archdeaconry of Richmond. Further evidence of a carefully planned project is that Booth's brother William, Archbishop of York, did not to seek his own promotion to Canterbury, the more normal progression.

York's most immediate challenge was the captaincy of Calais, held by Somerset since 1451. With the support of the garrison, which had not even received payment on account since July 1453, Somerset's deputy, Lord Rivers, and his subordinate captains Lords Welles and Stourton, refused to admit York as the new captain. We shall discuss this in greater detail in a later chapter. For now let it suffice to say that York delegated negotiations to his brother-in-law Henry, Viscount Bourchier, who was acquainted with the problems from his own service as governor-general of Picardy during York's lieutenancy of Normandy.

York treated the king's appointment of Wiltshire to replace him as lieutenant in Ireland as though it had never been made. Although the Council refused to rule between the two claimants, York asserted his right under the unrevoked terms of his own 1448 patent, appointed his own officials and collected the salary. Wiltshire was infuriated by the affront, which must have involved the complicity of John Tiptoft, the new Lord Treasurer. Previously a king's man and as such created Earl of Worcester in 1449, Tiptoft had become a member of the Neville affinity through his love-match in 1450 to Salisbury's daughter Cecily, the dowager Duchess of Warwick, tragically cut short by her early death.

In the North, Egremont obliged the Nevilles by embarking on a new round of depredations, in which the Duke of Exeter joined him. That the two men found themselves in such perfect harmony suggests Egremont's hold on sanity was also not too firm. Their cunning plan was for Exeter to assert his superior right by blood to challenge York's protectorship, and to claim the duchy of Lancaster. When Richard of York came north with a light escort in mid-May 1454, he had to retreat from York itself after learning of a plot to assassinate him. He gathered forces from his own estates and returned in mid-June to hold assizes, which condemned the two rebels and their supporters as traitors.

Consistent with his opinion of his own importance, Exeter had meanwhile obeyed a summons to appear before the Great Council. Finding the councillors did not share his opinion, he sought sanctuary in Westminster Abbey. When York returned to London on 8 July, he had his son-in-law snatched from the abbey and sent him north for imprisonment at Pontefract, a royal castle administered by Salisbury. To have put Exeter in the Tower with Somerset would have been folly, but the choice of Pontefract, where the deposed Richard II was starved to death, may have been intended as a reminder that royal blood did not confer immunity.

Reality caught up with Egremont and his brother Richard Percy when they ventured once too often into the concentration of Neville manors north-east of York. On 31 October, their small band of raiders was surrounded at Stamford Bridge by Neville retainers led by Thomas and John Neville, and after a brief struggle they were captured. Held first at Middleham in Richmondshire, they were sent to London to face trial for criminal trespass. Found guilty and unable to pay impossibly large fines, they were imprisoned as common debtors in Newgate.

The reason why no action was taken on their earlier conviction as traitors seems to have been a deal made among Salisbury, Northumberland, Clifford and York. Clifford was brought on board by appointing him to investigate and punish Egremont's accomplices, in the certain knowledge that he was one of them, while York promised to support Percy's petitions to recover estates held by the crown since the 1405 attainder. Meanwhile York obtained payment, equal to the amount he received as Protector, for each of the two Wardens of the Marches and promised to pay the arrears due to Percy. Salisbury also obtained recognition of his claim to Hawarden Castle in Flint, but overall York's even-handedness took the heat out of the Percy–Neville conflict.

York showed the same diplomatic skill in handling the void in command of naval matters created by Exeter's escapade. He did not seek to replace him as Lord Admiral, which would have required a vote by the Council. Instead, under his authority as Protector, on 3 April 1454 he appointed six keepers of the sea for three years, for which he obtained the necessary funds from the Commons. The eastern approaches, including Calais, were assigned to Warwick, the Channel to Lord Treasurer Worcester, and the Irish Sea to John Talbot's namesake son, now Earl of Shrewsbury, also Earl of Waterford and hereditary Lord High Steward of Ireland.

Bringing Talbot into government was cunning. Although he was a party to the Beauchamp inheritance imbroglio he was a rival to Somerset in the matter of the barony of Bergavenny. Also, although he was brother-in-law to Wiltshire/Ormonde, whom York had just brushed aside as Lieutenant of Ireland, Talbot's marriage to Ormonde's sister had been an attempt to heal the feud between their respective fathers. It was very much in York's interest to revive it by giving Talbot, who had inherited his father's fierce temperament, an Irish bone to chew on.

What York did not do was enrich himself, or show favour to his affinity. Unfortunately his allies Norfolk and Devon completely misread him, and took his appointment as a green light to settle scores with those who had encroached on their local supremacies under Suffolk and Somerset. These were very tricky issues and York appears to have handled them informally, presumably by appealing to Mowbray and Courtenay not to make his job more difficult.

He was probably not too exercised by Courtenay's renewed attack on Bonville, because the latter, as seneschal of lost Gascony, was waging a naval war against French shipping, which included seizing French cargoes carried by neutral ships. His actions were denounced as piracy by the Duke of Burgundy, who retaliated by putting an embargo on the Calais wool trade through his surrounding counties of Artois and Flanders.

Burgundy's embargo actually gave York some much-needed leverage in the Calais impasse, as it dawned on Rivers and Welles that their continued rejection of the Protector's authority could get them included in the accusation levelled against Somerset, their patron, of a treasonous intent to sell Calais to Burgundy. The loss of Calais would have been devastating to York's protectorship, but even if Somerset considered it a price worth paying, Rivers and Welles knew it would cost them their heads.

One problem York did not have to deal with was hostility from the royal household. In recognition of the reduction of the king's needs to doctors and carers, the money voted for his household was drastically reduced – but the reduction was matched by a corresponding increase in the votes for the households of the queen and the Prince of Wales. Marguerite, of course, controlled both, and was also the beneficiary of substantial transfers of assets, cleared of encumbrances by resumption, from the duchy of Lancaster to her son's endowment. She could not be regent for the king, but nobody questioned her right to be regent for their son. While Henry remained catatonic it made her a major player in her own right.

Perhaps most notably, York did not make any effort to proceed to the impeachment of Somerset, although he successfully resisted efforts to release him on bail. It is reasonable to assume he could have obtained the necessary articles from a Commons in which Somerset's erstwhile supporters were anxious not to draw attention to themselves, so why did he not? One reason would have been to avoid being seen as vindictive, but another may have been because the queen asked him to let sleeping dogs lie.

One of the most valuable primary sources for this period is contained in the commonplace book written in Latin by the priest John Benet. The duke, he wrote, 'governed the entire kingdom of England well and honourably for a whole year [actually nine months], and miraculously pacified all rebels and malefactors, in accordance with his oath and without great severity'. Allowing for Benet's Yorkist bias, this is still a fair summary. York had achieved as much as he could have realistically hoped, not least the mutually respectful modus vivendi he worked out with the queen.

HENRY

HENRY VI EMERGED FROM CATATONIA AT CHRISTMAS 1454 and within weeks destroyed the neutral royal centre painstakingly constructed by Marguerite and York. He had no memory of anything that had happened in the interim and so, disastrously, resumed personal kingship as though he had never relinquished it. Worse, he overcompensated for once more having abandoned his duties as a king and a man, and tried to act as he imagined his father would have done. On finding the queen had coped very well without him, he foolishly spurned what she had achieved and tried to turn back the clock.

We may feel some residual sympathy for the wretched man because of his mental condition, but there can be none at all for the fecklessness of his conduct in the following months. He acted as though he were still riding high after humbling York, the bogeyman created by his panicked entourage in 1450, and was deceived by the rejoicing at his recovery into believing it reflected widespread dissatisfaction at the way the country had been governed in his absence. Perhaps so, but there was no less widespread awareness that York had been honest and even-handed, qualities the king's personal kingship had always conspicuously lacked.

Rescued from political eclipse by his recovery, Henry's inner circle nurtured his delusion and urged him to make his priority the release of Somerset, their leader. He was duly freed on 26 January

1455 by the king's warrant. In truth, he had been detained for too long without formal charges, and when the Great Council reassembled on 5 February it declared his continued detention violated the clause against arbitrary imprisonment in the Magna Carta. The bishops had been vocally uneasy about this for some time, and the Council might well have insisted he be formally impeached or released even if York had still been Protector.

As soon as Somerset was back at Henry's side his priority was to ensure his survival should the king lapse back into catatonia. A second York protectorate would finish him, so he had to destroy his rival as soon as possible. As a first step, on 4 March Somerset persuaded Henry to dismiss all criminal accusations against him, recasting the remainder as civil suits to be decided by an arbitration panel. The panel included the now rabidly anti-Yorkist Wiltshire/Ormonde, but its findings would be irrelevant because the king stated he believed the matters left pending were vexatious suits, without merit.

On the same day York, who had resigned the protectorship as soon as the king's recovery was confirmed, was dismissed as Captain of Calais and Somerset restored to the office. Three days later, on being ordered to release Exeter from Pontefract, Salisbury refused to do so and resigned as Lord Chancellor. Without seeking licence to do so, York and Salisbury withdrew to their estates in Yorkshire. Warwick, who resigned from the Council on 5 February, had already gone north, probably to Middleham. When he joined his father later, it was with a contingent led by Robert Ogle, whose family held several castles in Northumberland and had a history of bitter rivalry with the Percys.

On 13 March, Henry ordered his new Chancellor, Archbishop Bourchier, to release Exeter from Pontefract, ludicrously stating that he had only been imprisoned because of 'sinister information made upon him by certain persons not well disposed'. Two days later he dismissed Tiptoft as Lord Treasurer and appointed Wiltshire/Ormonde in his place. Egremont and his brother had defied the king before his catatonia, and so remained in Newgate, but this was scant consolation to the Nevilles. The king could not have made his ill will towards York and anyone associated with him any clearer.

• ❧ •

If Henry had appreciated the need for conciliation he would have given Somerset a blanket pardon and a golden handshake, and made Humphrey Stafford, Duke of Buckingham, his chief minister. It is worth examining why he did not. Fifty-three years old in 1455, Stafford was descended from Edward III's youngest son, was married to Anne, one of Salisbury's sisters, and was half-brother to the Bourchiers. With estates in twenty-two counties producing an annual income of about £5,000 [£3.18 million], roughly the same as York's, he had a large affinity and could have played a much more prominent role in affairs of state than he did.

Stafford had served with Henry V and was knighted by him in 1421. Despite marrying one of Cardinal Beaufort's nieces, as a member of Henry's minority Council from 1425 he was not a partisan in the cardinal's rivalry with the Duke of Gloucester. Made a Garter knight in 1429, in 1431 he returned to France with the king and was involved in several military operations as governor of Paris, Constable of France and Lieutenant-General of Normandy. He was also made Count of Perche, worth 800 marks [£340,000] a year.

It must have been galling to Stafford when York, nine years his junior and with negligible military experience, was appointed Lieutenant of Normandy in 1436. However, the appointment was made not only because York was a prince of the blood, but because he also had possession of his estates and could afford it, whereas Stafford's mother controlled all except £1,250 [£795,000] of his landed income until her death in 1438. After Stafford came into the whole of his inheritance he was made Captain of Calais in 1441, and in 1444 he was made Duke of Buckingham.

As we saw in Chapter 4, York had been stung in 1436–7, and he

HOUSES OF
STAFFORD AND BOURCHIER

k. = killed in battle   x. = executed

1. Thomas = Anne of = 2. Edmund
3rd Earl of Stafford   Gloucester   5th Earl of Stafford
(d.1392)   (d.1403)

Humphrey = Anne Neville
1st Duke of
Buckingham
(k.1460)

Humphrey = Margaret   Catherine = John Talbot
Earl of   (daughter   (d.1476)   3rd Earl of
Stafford   of Edmund   Shrewsbury
(d.1458)   Beaufort)   (d.1473)

Henry = Margaret   William = Joan
(k.1471)   (daughter   2nd Viscount   (d.1484)
           of John   Beaumont
           Beaufort)   (d.1507)

Anne of = 3. William Bourchier
Gloucester   1st Count of Eu
             (d.1420)

Henry, 1st Viscount = Isabel
Bourchier, 1st Earl   of York
of Essex   (d.1484)
(d.1483)

William   Henry = Elizabeth   Humphrey   Edward
2nd Viscount   (k.1459)   Baroness   (k.1471)   (k.1460)
Bourchier   Scales
(d.1480)   (d.1473)

Children of Anne of Gloucester (1383–1438)

Eldest daughter of Thomas of Woodstock, Edward III's youngest son. Her mother was Eleanor, Bohun co-heiress. Mary, Eleanor's younger sister and co-heiress, was snatched from a nunnery, where Thomas had placed her, by his brother John of Gaunt to marry his eldest son, Henry of Bolingbroke, later Henry IV. Anne was thus Henry V's aunt.

Anne (d.1432) = John Holland, 2nd Duke of Exeter (d.1447)

Henry Holland, 3rd Duke of Exeter (k.1475) = Anne of York (d.1476)

Anne Holland (d.1486) = 1. John Neville (d.1450) 2. His uncle John, 1st Baron Neville of Raby (k.1461) 3. James, 9th Earl of Douglas (d.1488)

Anne (d.1472) = 1. Aubrey, heir to John Vere, 12th Earl of Oxford (both x.1462) 2. Thomas, 5th Baron Cobham (d.1471)

Eleanor (d.1474) = John Mowbray, 3rd Duke of Norfolk (d.1461)

William (d.1470) = Thomasine Hankeford, Baroness Fitzwarine (d.1453)

John, 1st Baron Berners (d.1474) = Margery Berners

Thomas, Archbishop of Canterbury (d.1486)

John Mowbray, 4th Duke of Norfolk (d.1476)

Humphrey (k.1471) = Joan (d.1490), co-heir of Ralph, Baron Cromwell (d.1455) negotiated financial conditions permitting him to relinquish the lieutenancy when the money stopped coming. Although Stafford, too, had previously experienced difficulty in getting the money he was due from the exchequer, he did not take the same precaution. He loyally completed his ten-year Calais appointment, even though for the last few years he had to pay the garrison out of his own pocket. Having in the meantime lost the income from Perche, he was owed over £20,000 [£12.72 million] in 1451, and had managed to collect less than half of it by 1455.

Not, one would have thought, an experience likely to make Stafford's heart grow fonder of the feckless king. Yet he remained devoted to him, and his loyalty was rewarded. We have seen how, having connived as Constable of England in the disgraceful downfall of Gloucester, he received the duke's magnificent palace of Penshurst in Kent. He was also made Constable of Dover and Warden of the Cinque Ports, which, together with his captaincy of Calais, should have made him the dominant lord in Kent. Cade's revolt had revealed this was not the case, and may explain why he did not enjoy the king's confidence.

Stafford was loaded with offices but continued to have difficulty collecting the salaries supposed to accompany them. His eldest son married one of Somerset's daughters, but the dowry was never paid, and it did little to increase his influence at court. His wife was made godmother to Prince Edward, but he seems to have held aloof from Marguerite's attempt to construct a non-partisan centre. In sum, if we look for a reason why Henry did not even consider Buckingham as a compromise chief minister, it is that the duke was taken for granted but not taken seriously. The clever ones in his family were his Bourchier half-brothers.

• ↜ •

Following the absolution of Exeter in March 1455, events moved rapidly to a bloody climax and other magnates took sides. John

Mowbray, Duke of Norfolk, inherited 150 properties across twenty-five counties, but outside East Anglia none formed a sufficient concentration for him to develop a significant local affinity. He also suffered from chronic bad health, the given reason why he did not attend the Council after Henry's recovery. Forty years old in 1455, he was the son of Katherine, Salisbury's eldest sister, and was married to Eleanor, full sister to Viscount Bourchier and the new Archbishop of Canterbury.

Norfolk inclined to York because the king's party included 46-year-old Viscount Beaumont, who held large estates of his own in Lincolnshire, Leicestershire, Norfolk and Suffolk, and had married Norfolk's widowed mother. It galled the duke that, as a result of the marriage, Beaumont enjoyed the fruits of more than a third of Norfolk's patrimony. Beaumont had been one of York's councillors before 1450 and was not closely associated with Somerset, but he was a lifelong friend of the king, and head of his much-reduced household during 1454.

The motives of 38-year-old William FitzAlan, Earl of Arundel, and 47-year-old John Vere, Earl of Oxford, are more obscure. Arundel was married to Salisbury's eldest daughter, which inclined him to support his father-in-law, but he was a cautious player who went with whatever tide was flowing during the whole period of the Wars of the Roses. Oxford had been an ally of Norfolk against Suffolk and disliked Somerset, and in the early stages of the conflict followed the example of the prudent Arundel. Later, for reasons of his own, he made some fatally bad choices.

Among the barons, in addition to Lord Cromwell, whose landed income was as great as an earl's, two of the most powerful were Thomas, Baron Clifford, and Thomas, Baron Roos. Clifford's lordships were adjacent to Neville strongholds in Cumberland, Westmorland and Yorkshire, and he had backed Egremont's attacks on Neville manors in the north-west. Roos, with the oldest continuous title of nobility in England, held Helmsley in Yorkshire, Belvoir in Lincolnshire and other estates in Leicestershire. Eleanor née Beauchamp, his widowed mother, had married Somerset, and consequently Roos was involved in the Beauchamp inheritance imbroglio. Roos had supported the rebellion by Egremont and Exeter, and became one of the most tenacious enemies of the York–Neville alliance.

The event that did most to crack the body politic irreparably was Salisbury's and Warwick's gamble that the king's incapacity would be permanent. When this proved not to be the case a wiser king would have offered them a way back. Instead, by unconditionally embracing Somerset and all he stood for, Henry doomed him. Somerset continued to believe York was his principal enemy, but it was the Nevilles, whose power and fortune depended on royal favour, who most needed him dead.

In mid-April the king summoned a Council to which York, Norfolk, Salisbury and Warwick were not invited. The small gathering voted to convoke an exceptional Council at the queen's borough of Leicester on Whitsun (25 May), with the stated purpose of providing for the king's safety. Messengers were sent far and wide to pack the Leicester Council with regime loyalists, something York and the Nevilles would have known about before they received their own summons.

They could not construe it as anything other than an attempt by Somerset to repeat the charade engineered by Suffolk to bring down the Duke of Gloucester. Assuming, with some justification, that the deliberations of the exceptional Council were likely to place them in mortal danger, York and Warwick gathered their retinues and prepared to march south – to prevent Henry from reaching Leicester.

The king, however, seems to have believed they would tamely submit. We can take this either as evidence of simple-mindedness, or else as a manifestation of the assertive, over-confident state of mind with which he had emerged from catatonia. Right up to the moment war arrows began to hammer into his entourage, Henry was convinced York and the Nevilles would not dare use violence against their 'king anointed'. Somerset seems to have concurred, and as a result grossly overplayed his hand. The stage was now set for the first military encounter of the Wars of the Roses.

We are better informed about the run-up to the first Battle of St Albans than for any other battle of the Wars of the Roses.* The evidence is partial and often contradictory, but the details are insignificant beside the astounding fact that the king's entourage was unprepared for combat, even after the king raised his banner. To unfurl the royal standard was to declare that those against whom it was displayed were rebels and traitors. It was an action demanding immediate and unconditional submission – or war.

How could such a dislocation of cause and probable effect have come about? Even if Henry, who knew nothing of war, did not fully appreciate its significance, the experienced warrior nobles around him would have fully understood what raising the standard meant. The only possible reason why most of them were not in full harness when the attack came was their shared belief that an outright assault on the king's person was unthinkable.

It was only the last of a series of miscalculations by Henry and his retinue. The first, the decision to relocate the exceptional – and handpicked – Council to the Lancastrian Midlands, arose because of concerns about Somerset's unpopularity in London and a concomitant uncertainty that he could control the outcome of a normal election. The second was their assumption that the retainers summoned by York and the Nevilles were intended merely for a show of strength at Leicester. Only on the eve of departure from London, when the king received a letter from York at Royston in Hertfordshire, did they awake to the possibility the royal party might be intercepted before reaching Leicester.

The Roman roads radiating out of London were still the main highways of the realm at this time, as was the pre-Roman Icknield Way, which linked Ermine and Watling Streets laterally. The high road from London to Leicester necessarily passed through St Albans,

---

* Thanks to Charles Armstrong's brilliant 'Politics and the Battle of St Albans, 1455' in the *Bulletin of the Institute of Historical Research*.

where the king wished to spend the night and to pray at the shrine of the martyr, towards whom he had a particular reverence. He may also have wished to pray for the soul of the Duke of Gloucester, victimized in his name, whose tomb was next to the shrine.

Somerset had earlier summoned loyalists to come to Leicester with armed retinues, but now he sent messengers urgently requiring them in the king's name 'to be with us wheresoever we be in all haste possible'. The departure from London could not be delayed if the royal party was to arrive at Leicester by Whitsun, but the choice of the Watford over the more travelled Barnet road was probably made to get further away from the Great North Road, down which York and the Nevilles were presumed to be marching. A second letter from York and the Nevilles, sent from the Neville manor of Ware on 21 May, seemed to confirm it.

It was a deception – by the time the letter arrived at Watford in the early morning of 22 May, York and the Nevilles were marching

10. APPROACH TO ST ALBANS
May 1455
Approximate distances shown in miles

© Hugh Bicheno

west through Hatfield towards St Albans. Somerset must have presumed as much, for he now argued strongly that the king should remain at Watford until reinforcements arrived. A large contingent led by the Earl of Shrewsbury was two days' march away, while the Earl of Oxford, Lord Cromwell and Lord Stanley had also indicated they would join the king shortly. On the other side, the Duke of Norfolk was also closing in on St Albans in support of York. None of them arrived in time, and Shrewsbury was probably the only one who really tried.

The king's retinue included the Dukes of Somerset and Buckingham, and their heirs with the courtesy earldoms of Dorset (Henry Beaufort) and Stafford (Humphrey Stafford). The substantive earls were Pembroke, Northumberland, Wiltshire and Devon. There were also six barons: the king's old friends Lords Dudley and Sudeley, plus Roos, Clifford, Salisbury's brother William, Lord Fauconberg, and Buckingham's half-brother John Bourchier, newly created Lord Berners. The party included only one bishop, William Percy of Carlisle, who was Northumberland's brother. The best estimate for the sum of their retinues, of which the king's would have been the largest, is 2,000 men.

Closing on St Albans from the east were York, his 13-year-old heir Edward, Earl of March, Salisbury and Warwick. They had been joined by Buckingham's eldest half-brother Henry, Viscount Bourchier, and his son Humphrey, plus the Northamptonshire lord John, Baron Clinton, and Edward Brooke, Baron Cobham. They had at least 3,000 men, of whom York perhaps raised half in his progression from Yorkshire, past his manors in Lincolnshire and Hertfordshire. Most of the rest were Neville retainers with experience of the border wars.

With Salisbury's brother Fauconberg and the younger Bourchier in the king's party, it is reasonable to assume that York, the Nevilles and the older Bourchier were well informed about its numbers and composition. Since Somerset did not even know they had come south until York's Royston letter arrived, it is also reasonable to suppose the king's men were as much in the dark about their opponents' numbers as they were about their intentions.

After receipt of the Ware letter, the king took Buckingham's advice not to show fear by proceeding as planned to St Albans. At this point he replaced Somerset with Buckingham as Constable of England. There is much room to speculate about why Henry did this. At the simplest level, if there were to be negotiations, Somerset could not be a party to them, as he was completely unacceptable to York and the Nevilles. At another level, it may have been intended as a signal that the king was not wedded to Somerset. As we know he was, it follows Buckingham's appointment was a stratagem, to buy time until reinforcements arrived.

If this was the purpose of the Buckingham appointment, however, Somerset should have kept keep his head down. Instead, he sent insulting messages to York and Salisbury through an emissary he knew would be obnoxious to them. To understand the provocation, it is necessary to understand the function of heralds in medieval warfare. Their task was to communicate terms before a battle and to issue challenges if terms were not agreed. The herald had four junior officials under him known as poursuivants. They all wore surcoats, called tabards, which displayed the coat of arms of their master.

It was common for the principals in any imminent trial of arms to parley using their political allies' heralds – at St Albans, York used the Duke of Norfolk's – because their own heralds could not pose as neutral intermediaries. Quite the opposite intention can be firmly deduced from Somerset sending one of Exeter's poursuivants. This was a red rag to his opponents' bull, and the use of a junior official may have been insulting as well. The message he brought was blunt: submit or face attainder.

There are three possible interpretations of Somerset's actions. The first is that Somerset had agreed to the venerable negotiating tactic of playing bad cop to Buckingham's good cop. Given what we know about the chilly relations between them, this seems unlikely.

The second is that Somerset, knowing the only issue was his political future, wanted to prevent meaningful negotiations. This would imply he was afraid the king might fold under the pressure and act as he had with Suffolk in 1450, sending him away with a promise of reinstatement when tempers had cooled down. Suffolk's fate would have loomed large in Somerset's mind, and he may have been trying to pre-empt a repeat performance.

Related to the second, the third and most probable alternative is that Somerset was running a bluff, based on an underestimation of his enemies' resolve. He had been a gambler all his life, so why play it safe now, when he was riding a winning streak? Accordingly, the last message York and the Nevilles claimed to have received from the king may have been an invention they produced to justify their actions.* But it could also have been a further bluff by Somerset, taking the king's name in vain, or a last display of the false hair on the chest Henry had been flaunting since he emerged from catatonia:

> I, King Henry, charge and command that no manner of person, of what degree or state or condition that ever he be, abide not but void the field and not be so hardy to make any resistance against me in mine own realm for I shall know what traitor dare be so bold to raise a people in mine own land, wherethrough I am in great dis-ease and heaviness. And by the faith that I owe to St Edward and to the Crown of England I shall destroy them every mother's son and they be hanged and drawn, and quartered that may be taken afterward of them to have example to all such traitors to beware to make any such rising of people within my land, and so traitorly to defy their King and governor. And for a conclusion rather than they shall have this day any Lord here with me at this time I shall this day for their sake and in this quarrel myself live or die.

---

* The source is the strongly Yorkist *Stowe Relation*. Perversely, textual details like 'every mother's son' are so contrary to what one would expect from Henry that a forgery would have omitted them.

COUP D' ÉTAT

MEMBERS OF THE KNIGHTLY CLASS WERE REARED FOR war from childhood – it was what had won them their lands and titles, and the justification for their place in society. At St Albans on 22 May 1455 there were men on both sides who also had considerable experience of command in war, in France and along the Scottish border. We should, therefore, expect to find evidence of intelligent calculation in the way the battle was fought.

On the king's side, Buckingham was not only the senior duke but also the most experienced senior commander on either side. He chose to advance to St Albans partly because he believed the king should not be seen to flinch in the face of a challenge to his authority, but also because he knew the town was highly defensible. It was surrounded by a trench and embankment known as the Townman or Tonman ditch, and where roads crossed it there were structures into which heavy beams could be inserted to bar access to the town. He also knew from his experience in France that fighting in a built-up area gave the advantage to the defenders.

York and the Nevilles – for convenience the 'Yorkists' – either arrived after the royal party, or else chose not to enter St Albans to avoid the strong possibility that the two sides' troops might clash spontaneously. They turned left off the Hatfield road and formed up in an area known as Keyfield, halfway to the Barnet road and about 250 yards from the ditch. York was nearest the Hatfield road,

Salisbury nearest the Barnet road, with Warwick in between.

They had achieved strategic surprise by advising their affinities along the way to be ready to join them but not to alert the authorities by gathering beforehand, and operational surprise by intercepting the king before he reached Leicester. They knew the king could not possibly accede to their minimum demand, which was to abdicate his authority and hand Somerset over to them. Therefore, they arrived at St Albans intending to fight, and the only remaining questions were how to disguise their intent, and how to avoid a knock-down, drag-out battle with heavy casualties. That required tactical surprise.

If not before, then soon after arriving they would have known the ditch and the barred roads ruled out the use of cavalry. They would have seen the banners of Northumberland and Clifford at the barriers, and knew they were held by tough northerners who would make them pay dearly should they launch a frontal assault. A breakthrough at Sopwell Street, or a right hook through Cock Lane, would have involved a further advance along streets where they could be sure the royalists would have posted archers in the houses on either side – because that was what they would have done. The weaker of the two barriers was on Butts Lane, flanked by market gardens, but it was consequently more heavily manned.

Keyfield was in full view of the defenders at the barriers and along the embankment, and from the bell tower overlooking the marketplace, where the king and his retinue were located. We have no way of knowing where the retinues of the other lords might have been, but some may have been posted along the embankment between the two barriers. It was a clear day and the royalists must have been confident it would be impossible for the Yorkists to achieve tactical surprise. Both sides knew the obvious tactic would be a strong feint at one of the barriers to draw in the reserves, followed by the main thrust at the other.

And that, following an hour or two of heralds pointlessly trotting back and forth, was exactly what the defenders saw coming

**11. BATTLE OF ST ALBANS
22 May 1455**

Sandridge

St Peter's Church

Catherine Lane

Cock Lane

Wall Close

Hatfield
Ware

Townman Ditch

St Peter's Street

Townman Ditch

The Castle

Dunstable

Dagnal Street

Butts Lane

Percy

King

Bell
Tower

Market

The Chequers

Warwick

York

Eleanor Cross

Holywell Street

The Cross Keys

Keyfield

Abbey Church

Sopwell Street

Clifford

Salisbury

Abbey Precinct

Holywell Hill

Barnet
London

Abbey Mill

Fishpond

River Ver

Watford

N

0   100   200   300   400   500
Yards

© Hugh Bicheno

at them. First, a column led by Salisbury, banners displayed and drums beating, attacked the Sopwell Street barrier. A while later, a larger column led by the banners of York and Warwick marched to attack the Butts Lane barrier. So far so predictable – a third of the force to make the feint, two-thirds to make the main attack. The lords and knights with the king in the marketplace still did not hurry to get into harness, so confident were they that Clifford and Northumberland would easily repel the attacks.

Although his banners were at the front of the column with York, Warwick was at the back with Ogle's 600 archers. After the head of the column had been become fully engaged, and the nearby enemy troops along the embankment drawn towards the barrier, he and Ogle peeled off. Without banners or fanfare, they crossed the now lightly defended ditch 100 yards below the barrier, into the market gardens on the other side. If the townscape was indeed as portrayed in Map 11, the manoeuvre was in plain sight of the men at the Butts Lane barrier. They, naturally, would have seen it as an attempt to outflank their position.

The first reaction of whoever was in command in Butts Lane – probably Somerset, who seems to have joined Northumberland once the Yorkist attack began – would have been to reposition archers to cover the flank of the men-at-arms at the barrier. Some of Ogle's men would have loosed a volley or two to maintain the illusion, but Warwick's main force was charging for a gap between two of the many inns along Holywell Street that catered to the pilgrim trade.

With the observers in the tower frantically clanging the curfew bell overhead, Warwick's men burst into the centre of the town, making as much noise as possible to increase shock. In the words of *The Stow Relation*: 'They ferociously broke in by the garden sides between the sign of the Key and the sign of the Chequer in Holywell Street, and immediately they were within the town, suddenly they blew up trumpets and set a cry with a shout and a great voice "A Warwick! A Warwick!"'

The essence of tactical surprise is the dislocation of expectations. An enemy is never so vulnerable as when he believes victory is in his grasp. The men at the Butts Lane barrier believed they had stopped the main Yorkist attack, and thought they had beaten off a flank attack. Nothing, however, can keep troops in line when they hear the noise of battle to their rear. After Warwick's men erupted into Holywell Street, Northumberland's men broke and fled across the market gardens towards the road leading north, back to their homes. A group of men-at-arms, including Somerset and his son, fell back towards the town centre, but were cut off by Warwick's men and took refuge in the Castle Inn.

If there was one thing above all the Yorkists did not want to do, it was to kill the king. It would have put them irretrievably in the wrong and they could expect the moral power of the Church to turn on them. The Scriptures were unequivocal (I Samuel 26): '…who can stretch forth his hand against the Lord's anointed, and be guiltless?… The Lord forbid that I should stretch forth mine hand against the Lord's anointed.'

Yet, possibly because the king's standard-bearer fled and his banner dropped to the floor, Ogle's archers shot indiscriminately into the mass of royalists in the marketplace. Four of the king's bodyguard were killed in his presence, and an arrow grazed Henry's neck before he was hustled to cover in a tanner's cottage. Buckingham and his son, badly wounded, were taken by their men to the abbey church.

Northumberland was probably killed somewhere along Butts Lane, and Clifford in Sopwell Street. The only one whose fate we can be sure of was Somerset. Called upon to surrender, he sortied from the Castle Inn and is said to have killed four men before he was brought down and clubbed to death. His son Henry, badly wounded at his side, survived. Abbot Whethamstede, an appalled eyewitness, wrote, 'here you saw one fall with his brains dashed out, there another with a broken arm, a third with a cut throat, and a fourth with a pierced chest, and the whole street was filled with dead corpses'.

Lord Dudley, who must have been near his friend the king, was hit in the face by an arrow. The other lords – Pembroke, Devon, Sudeley, Roos, Fauconberg and Berners – presumably took cover until it was safe to emerge. Wiltshire fled first to the abbey church and then, disguised as a monk, got clean away. Another notable royalist casualty was John Wenlock, who had served as the queen's chamberlain until 1453. He recovered remarkably rapidly from a disabling wound to become Speaker of the Commons in the Parliament elected seven weeks later. Deeply wounded in his dignity was Bishop Percy of Carlisle, who was stripped of his possessions and driven out of the town on foot and in his underclothes.

We know the names of sixty of those killed, practically all royalists and many of them members, some quite humble, of the king's household. Apart from them, the casualty list is top-heavy with knights and esquires who fell with Northumberland, Clifford and Somerset – proof, if any were needed, that it was a decapitation strike as well as a *coup d'état*. Men in harness were not easily killed, and there can be little doubt the York and Neville retainers were settling old scores. Another contemporary account states 'all who were on the side of Somerset were killed, wounded or at least despoiled'.

Before Somerset was killed, York had found the king and escorted him to safety in the abbey church. After the fighting ended and his troops turned to stripping the dead and looting, he made his way back to the church and demanded that Buckingham and Wiltshire should come out, or else they would be taken out by force. Buckingham duly emerged but Wiltshire had by now wisely fled. York, Salisbury and Warwick then entered the church and knelt before their king to beg his forgiveness for putting his life at risk. They had, they said, only wished to free him from the clutches of the traitor Somerset.

Showing surprising realism and presence of mind, Henry did not waste time with protests and received their homage, asking only that the fighting should cease. One can discern behind this the entreaties of the abbot that the rampaging Yorkists should be brought under control before they turned their attention to the abbey and its many treasures. Order was restored, and the wounded and dead brought into the abbey precinct for treatment and burial. Somerset, Northumberland and Clifford were buried in the Lady Chapel, and the proper reverence for their memories was to be the cornerstone of the king's last, sadly unsuccessful attempt to stop the slide into all-out war three years later.

York and the Nevilles escorted Henry back to London, where a ceremonial parade was staged with York and Salisbury riding on either side of the king, while Warwick rode in front bearing the royal sword, point uppermost. Henry was lodged at the Bishop of London's palace, and agreed that writs be issued for a Parliament on 9 July. The Whitsun celebrations went ahead as usual, and on Whitsunday (27 May), at the crown-wearing ceremony at St Paul's cathedral, the king insisted it should be Richard of York, not the Archbishop of Canterbury, who placed the crown on his head. It was a subtle move. Archbishop and Chancellor Bourchier might construe it as a snub engineered by York, but it also underlined that York had usurped the authority granted to Henry by God.

Henry's biographers have devoted few pages to the remainder of his reign, and it is true he scarcely features as a leading protagonist in the following years. Yet here we have him, only days after the brutal shock of St Albans, perpetrating a highly symbolic act of passive aggression. Although his brief spasm of active leadership had led to disaster, it is unwise to believe he ceased trying to influence events. Unfortunately for him and for his kingdom, the time for subtle hints and signals was over: the rules of the game had changed irrevocably.

MARGUERITE'S COUNTER-COUP

MARGUERITE SAW WITH CRYSTAL CLARITY THAT York's action at St Albans must lead, sooner or later, to the usurpation of the crown. A puppet monarch, no matter how benign the puppet master, offended intolerably against the medieval concept of kingship by divine right. Henry and Somerset had blown away her attempt to create a neutral royal centre, and the polarization resulting from Henry's connivance in Somerset's efforts to destroy York now left her with no option but to build up a Lancastrian faction.

Of the dukes, she could count on the unconditional support of the rabid Exeter and the slain Edmund Beaufort's vengeful son Henry, now Duke of Somerset, but both were affinity-light. Buckingham should have been ripe for recruitment after St Albans, but she did not, at this time, try to win him. Possibly she blamed him for persuading Henry to go there in the first place, and his Bourchier half-brothers may also have compromised him in her eyes.

Of the earls, the king's half-brothers Richmond and Pembroke had not had time to develop useful affinities. Only Wiltshire, Shrewsbury and the new Earl of Northumberland could summon numbers to support the Lancastrian regime. The Nevilles of Raby and Brancepeth were led by the ineffectual Westmorland, and Oxford was still a maybe. Marguerite could also count on the unconditional support of Viscount Beaumont and several barons, notably Rivers, Roos, Welles, the veteran warrior Scales and, in particular, John, the new Lord Clifford, who shared Somerset's and Northumberland's passionate desire for revenge.

Marguerite's greater strength lay with the bishops, several of whom owed their promotions to her influence. Firmly on her side were Archbishop William Booth of York, previously her chancellor, and her confessor Walter Lyhert at Norwich. Beckington at Bath and Wells, Percy at Carlisle, Boulers at Lichfield and Coventry, Chedworth at Lincoln and Dorchester, Kemp at London, the king's confessor Stanberry at Hereford, and Wainflete at Winchester were all king's, and by extension queen's men. They controlled vast wealth, and Bishops Booth and Percy were also authorized to maintain armed forces.

The Yorkists could count on only one bishop, Salisbury's brother Robert Neville at Durham, although Salisbury obtained the election of his youngest son, 23-year-old George, to Exeter in November 1455. The Duke of Norfolk, the Earl of Worcester, Viscount Bourchier and Barons Clinton and Cobham supported them, but the rest of the secular peerage was at best lukewarm. The blatant insult to the king's majesty at St Albans was impossible to overlook, and weak national government suited most lords very nicely. Their principal concern – devoutly shared by the bishops – was to avoid the tax increases that any attempt to recover England's empire in France must require.

The Yorkists' first order of business on returning to London was to establish a justification for their actions. Parliament grudgingly accepted a patently false story about the Yorkists' just petitions being kept from the king, with Somerset, his deposed nominee as Commons Speaker Thomas Thorpe and another low-ranking household member made the scapegoats. A popular gloss was applied by the posthumous rehabilitation of the Duke of Gloucester – and the promise to settle his debts, left unpaid after his assets were seized by the crown and distributed by Suffolk.

The second priority was to allocate the offices made vacant by the death of Somerset, with the plums going to Warwick. He was appointed Lieutenant of Calais and was given three castles on the border of Monmouth and Abergavenny, consolidating his south Wales holdings. Viscount Bourchier replaced the fugitive Wiltshire as Lord Treasurer, and his youngest son Edward got Kidwelly Castle in Carmarthen. Lords Fauconberg and Berners, who had been with Henry at St Albans, were made joint Constables of Windsor Castle, where it was expected the king would reside. He chose not to, once again demonstrating that in small matters he could still do as he wished.

Salisbury seized the opportunity to obtain a judgement in his favour over the Oxfordshire estate of the abeyant barony of Camoys, in the wardship of the crown since 1426. Also, the prosecution of the Percys for their attacks on Salisbury's interests in 1453–4 went ahead and they were fined 9,000 marks [£3.8 million], which they could not pay. He also made sure that the payments due to him as Warden of the West March continued to be paid promptly, while the new Earl of Northumberland found it more difficult than ever to collect for the East March.

By contrast with his Neville and Bourchier allies, York once again pointedly refrained from rewarding himself or his affinity. He replaced Somerset as Constable of England and of the largest royal castles in Wales, but these were necessary adjuncts for a protectorship. The reason for his forbearance is not hard to identify. The new crop of MPs were certain to insist on a radical resumption of crown revenue sources before they would vote new taxes, and York did not want to find himself obliged to seek exemptions for himself or his affinity. With the Lords sceptical of his motives and intentions, he needed the Commons on his side.

This was admirably nuanced politics on York's part; but it was incomprehensible to his peers and to his loyal followers. What was power for, if not to enrich yourself and your friends? To the despair of those who wish human nature were other than it is, people may respect but never love an austere ruler. It is the reason why politicians who make promises they know cannot be kept routinely defeat those who attempt to tell the truth about the allocation of limited resources. York's lofty integrity was his Achilles heel – and Marguerite knew it.

She was determined he should not be made Protector again, since to do so would acknowledge the king was incompetent even when not catatonic. Unfortunately for her, a tacit consensus was forming that Henry was 'unworldly'. How else could he be absolved of personal responsibility for humiliating defeats abroad and borderline anarchy at home? Sovereignty could not, at this time, be detached from the person of the sovereign himself, and an unfit monarch posed a constitutional conundrum not finally resolved until Parliament judged Charles I guilty of treason and detached him from his head two centuries later.

With the king not free to act, and York unable to act with the king's authority, there was a power vacuum during the six months between St Albans and the appointment of York as Protector on 17 November 1455. Disorder surged, notably in the West Country, but it requires a deep faith in conspiracy theories to believe, as the queen and her party did, that any of it was engineered by York to bring about his appointment. That was indeed the outcome, but correlation was not causation in 1455 any more than it had been in 1450.

Although he had been with the king at St Albans, York's longtime supporter Devon judged the moment opportune to re-open the Courtenay–Bonville feud, to the point of open warfare. However, although this was the immediate cause of York's appointment, Devon was a chronic loose cannon and had reasons of his own. Backing York in 1452 had cost him dearly, and over the following years Bonville had replaced him as the leading magnate in the West Country. Devon's attempt to regain royal favour explains why he was on the losing side at St Albans. Now he had less than ever. The final straw came when Devon's cousin, Philip Courtenay of Powderham Castle, married his son to Bonville's daughter.

In late October 1455, retainers led by Devon's son murdered Nicholas Radford, Bonville's senior councillor, and in early November Devon himself, at the head of 1,000 men, threw Bonville's men out of the royal castle at Exeter. The castle had been traditionally held by the earls as hereditary sheriffs of Devon, but the king had appointed Bonville to punish Devon for backing York in 1452. Devon now marched south to besiege Powderham, while Bonville gathered forces at Shute, his stronghold. Devon marched back through Exeter to confront him, and on 15 December smashed Bonville's army at Clyst Heath. He then vengefully sacked Shute, lost to Bonville by his marriage to Devon's aunt.

York himself owned land in Devon but, mindful of how he had been humiliated after resolving the last outbreak of Courtenay–Bonville violence, he would do nothing unless specifically empowered to do so by Parliament and the king. The first protectorship did not provide a precedent, as it lapsed automatically when the king recovered his faculties. The king suffered some kind of relapse in late 1455, but York resisted appointment on the same terms as before. On 10 November, a Great Council of Lords appointed him the king's lieutenant, but the Commons refused to conduct any other business until a Protector was formally appointed to resolve the situation in Devon. The only candidate was York.

He was duly appointed on 17 November, having obtained the terms he wanted. These were that a Council should be nominated 'to whose advice, council and assent I will obey and apply myself', and that his appointment should last until Prince Edward came of age, or earlier if revoked by the king 'with the assent of the lords spiritual and temporal in Parliament'. Of the eight lords elected to form the protectorate Council, the Archbishop of York and the Bishop of Norwich were out-and-out queen's men, and the Bishops of Rochester and Ely were neutral. The others were the royalists Buckingham and Lord Stourton, balanced by Warwick and Viscount Bourchier. If York believed this would reassure the queen he did not mean to act against her interests, his hope was misplaced.

One of York's first actions as Protector was to quell the private war raging in the West Country. A letter signed by the king was sent ordering all involved to 'obey [York] and keep his command-ments as you would and ought to obey us as if we were there in our own person'. Bonville immediately appealed in person to the king, who told him to submit to York. Devon continued his siege of Powderham but was eventually arrested and brought to London, where he spent some time with York before being brought before the protectorate Council. Devon and Bonville were imprisoned, not by the king or York, but by the Council, a constitutional nov-elty that in better times might have prospered.

In a reversal of the situation during Henry's period of catatonia, the queen now rejected compromise. York had backed the Commons' demand for a radical resumption and, once the immediate issue for which he had been elected was resolved, she used the issue to rally the lords against him. The first – and much quoted – reference to Marguerite's newly prominent political role was made with refer-ence to her actions at this time. One of the *Paston Letters*, dated 8 February 1456, describes her as 'a great and hard-working woman who spares no pains to pursue her interests with the purpose of increasing her power'.*

The Lords brought the king to Parliament to repudiate resump-tion and to receive York's resignation as Lord Protector on 25 February 1456. York immediately left London, and we can readily imagine his thoughts. Resumption was unquestionably necessary to restore solvency to the royal finances, and there had never been any suggestion it might impinge on the endowments of either the queen or the Prince of Wales. The queen's actions, therefore, must have been dictated by personal animosity, without regard for the national interest.

York then got into man-think. Whence came Marguerite's fury? It must be because Somerset had been her lover, and she was irrational

---

* The actual words are 'a grete and strong labourid woman spareth noo peyne to sue hire things to an intent and a conclusion to hir power'.

with grief. It would not have occurred to him that a nubile young woman might have made a cold political calculation to forgo a short-term gain for a longer-term objective. The next, short hop of reasoning was perhaps coloured by York's own matrimonial experience: his people begin to circulate rumours casting doubt on the paternity of the Prince of Wales.

Taking away York's formal title did not diminish the need for his services, because St Albans had cured Henry of any illusion that he could be a strong leader. In a decision we may be sure infuriated his wife, the king retained York as his chief councillor and sent him north to deal with a new threat from Scotland. The Battle of St Albans had persuaded King James II the time was ripe to renew the 'auld alliance' with France, and he wrote to Charles VII proposing concerted action to seize, respectively, Berwick and Calais. To muddy the waters, James also announced that York was the rightful king of England, before declaring war and sending raiding parties across the border. Marguerite would have believed York engineered the whole episode – but Henry did not.

In the absence of support by Charles VII, James scuttled back across the border after York moved to his stronghold at Sandal Castle in Yorkshire and issued two stern warnings, the first in Henry's name and the second in his own. Meanwhile the queen took the prince with her to Tutbury in Staffordshire, the westernmost of the triangle of castles at the heart of her Midlands dower, leaving Henry behind. It was an intimate power play and in late August, Henry left London to join her at Kenilworth Castle, outside Coventry, impregnable within its man-made lake, but which Marguerite ostentatiously equipped with additional artillery. A further twenty-six long guns (serpentines) would be brought from the Tower in 1457.

Since York, Salisbury and Warwick were all busy about the king's business at the time, it is worth pondering the motives behind Marguerite's retreat to the Midlands. It is hard to escape the conclusion that she was dramatizing a non-existent threat – although she may have convinced herself it was real – to pressure Henry into taking a harder line with York. Her message could not have been clearer: only *she* could take care of her husband, and he should trust no one else.

The inevitable result of the semi-permanent removal of the court to the queen's Midlands was to indicate distrust of London, which, however deserved, in the end turned out to be a gross strategic error. That, perhaps, is more apparent in hindsight than it was at the time. Marguerite would have had in mind her uncle Charles VII's ability, as dauphin, to rally support at Bourges after his father lost Paris. Unfortunately it was a false analogy. London was more central to the life of England than Paris was to France. It was by far the largest city, not only the political but also the commercial capital, and the hub of all the Roman roads that still provided the country's principal highways.

Marguerite completed her counter-coup at a Great Council summoned to Coventry on 16 October 1456. In the presence of York and Salisbury, the Bourchier Lords Chancellor and Treasurer were sacked and replaced by Bishop William Wainflete and John Talbot, Earl of Shrewsbury. The late Archbishop Kemp's man Lisieux was dying, and he had previously been replaced as Lord Privy Seal by Laurence Booth, the queen's chancellor and younger brother of the Archbishop of York.

Having control of the Privy Seal permitted Marguerite to appoint the officers of her son's estate. John Morton, a previously obscure doctor of civil law, became the prince's chancellor, while the ultra-loyalist Viscount Beaumont became his chief steward, as he already was the queen's. Other offices were filled by members of Marguerite's household.

On 28 January 1457, a formal minority council was set up for Prince Edward, which a month later was given control of his patrimony: the principality of Wales, the duchy of Cornwall, the county palatinate of Chester and select parts of the duchy of Lancaster. Chester and the northern duchy estates were complementary to the queen's Midlands dower, a factor that will help to explain some of her subsequent initiatives.

The ecclesiastical members of the council were the queen's former chancellor Archbishop Booth of York, the new Lord Chancellor Bishop Wainflete, the king's confessor Bishop Stanberry of Hereford, Bishop Boulers of Coventry and Lichfield, and her chancellor Laurence Booth, the new Lord Privy Seal, who was made Bishop of Durham when Salisbury's brother Robert died later in 1457. Three of the six lay members were the king's new Lord Treasurer Shrewsbury, Beaumont again, and Lord Dudley who, like Boulers, had been a member of the king's inner circle since he first assumed personal kingship.

The other three were the Lancashire magnate Lord Thomas Stanley, Humphrey, Earl of Stafford, and, as Treasurer, James Butler, Earl of Wiltshire, whom the Yorkists would have killed at St Albans if they had managed to lay their hands on him. Stanley's lordships and royal stewardships were also complementary to the prince's Cheshire estates. The appointment of Stafford, Buckingham's heir, was clearly intended as a gesture to smooth the duke's feathers, ruffled by the dismissal of his Bourchier half-brothers, without bringing in the reluctant duke himself. Wiltshire's appointment was equally clearly a defiantly rude gesture towards the Duke of York and, at this early stage, surprisingly provocative.

Thus, less than two years after St Albans, Marguerite had totally outmanoeuvred York to set up a parallel government responsive to her will. Nobody questioned her right to act as regent for her son, which she turned into a de facto regency for the kingdom. She controlled the greater part of the unencumbered royal revenues, and all of Henry's senior officials were now hers as well. The bureaucracy in London, as well as the unruly London mob, had been disempowered, and she was free to develop a compact affinity in areas where loyalty to the crown, and to her person, ran deep.

What she lacked, and to her sorrow always would lack, was someone to fill the office much better described in the *Game of*

Thrones saga by George R. R. Martin's invented 'Hand of the King' than by 'lieutenant' or 'constable'. Of the dukes, Buckingham was insufficiently partisan, Exeter too wild and the 20-year-old Somerset too young to be her champion. The Earls of Shrewsbury, Northumberland and Wiltshire were old enough at 39, 35 and 34 respectively, but they would have pursued their personal vendettas against York and the Nevilles without sufficient regard for the queen's overall strategy.

For all the mystique of divine right, the Yorkists had demonstrated at St Albans that power ultimately depended on brute force, intelligently applied. For all her political skill, Marguerite was disqualified by her sex from overtly leading the royalist faction because, until very recently, combat has always been an exclusively masculine activity. She needed a loyal man of rank with brains as well as brawn – and she never found him.

LORD OF
CALAIS

S T ALBANS WAS THE MOMENT WHEN THE YOUNGER Richard Neville, known to history as Warwick 'the Kingmaker', first took centre stage. He was to remain there for the next sixteen years. His rise is bound up with Calais, the English outpost across the Channel surrounded by the Duke of Burgundy's domains. While the military significance of the enclave is apparent, unless we fully appreciate its economic, strategic and diplomatic importance we cannot understand why Warwick once said he would give up all his lands in England if he could keep Calais.

The Calais garrison was the English crown's only standing army, and the outpost itself was virtually impregnable. It was protected to the east by the undrained marshes of the Aa River. The marshes to the south and west were drained, but where the drainage canals emptied into the sea, the Newenham bridge, guarded by Nieulay fort, provided the only road into the town.* Under the bridge were sluice gates that could be used to flood the approaches. The canals were a barrier to an attack through the counties of Ponthieu and Boulogne to the west, while a fort at Hammes and a castle at Guînes guarded the wooded hills to the south.

The sea entrance was guarded by a large fort at Rysbank, while

---

* When Calais was finally lost on 1 January 1558 it fell to a night attack that began with the capture of the sluice gates – by that time strongly fortified – while the garrison was drunkenly celebrating the New Year.

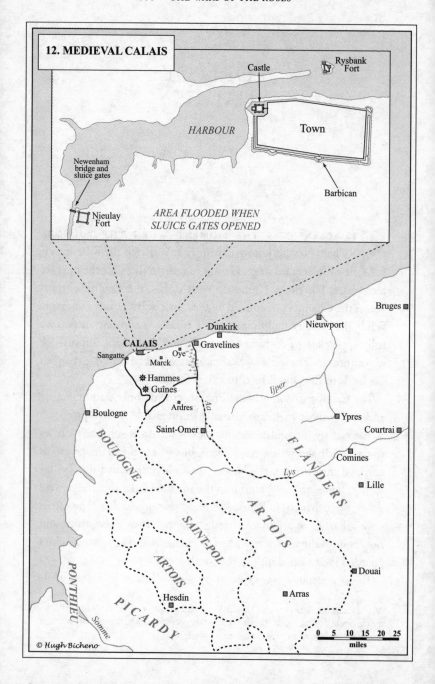

12. MEDIEVAL CALAIS

Castle

Rysbank Fort

HARBOUR

Town

Newenham bridge and sluice gates

Nieulay Fort

Barbican

AREA FLOODED WHEN SLUICE GATES OPENED

Bruges

Dunkirk

Nieuwport

CALAIS

Gravelines

Sangatte

Oye

Marck

✷ Hammes

✷ Guînes

Ijper

Ardres

Boulogne

Saint-Omer

Ypres

Courtrai

Comines

Lille

BOULOGNE

FLANDERS

SAINT-POL

ARTOIS

ARTOIS

Aa

Lys

Douai

PICARDY

Hesdin

Arras

PONTHIEU

Somme

0 5 10 15 20 25
miles

© Hugh Bicheno

the harbour was dominated by powerful Calais Castle. The walled town itself was surrounded on the landward side by a double wet ditch, with outworks between the two channels. The port could not be starved into submission, as distant naval blockade was not possible with the sailing ships of the era, and shifting sandbanks made a close blockade too perilous to contemplate.

Rowing galleys and other shallow draft vessels that could have operated close to shore required a nearby base of operations, but Gravelines and Dunkirk were not available for as long as the prosperity of neighbouring Flanders depended on the English wool trade. This was Calais' strategic defence in depth, as seen after the failed siege of 1436, when a revolt of his Flemish cities forced Duke Philippe to abandon his military alliance with France.

The siege of 1436 had illustrated a further aspect of Calais' military/diplomatic significance, as a potential base for offensive operations. The reason the garrison was so expensive was that it contained a high proportion of men-at-arms and mounted archers, who could launch raids against Burgundian or even French territory at short notice. If reinforced from England they could spearhead devastating *chevauchées*, something Duke Philippe and King Charles VII were not likely to forget.

This aspect of Calais' strategic importance only came to the fore after Duke Philippe ended the Anglo-Burgundian alliance in 1435. Somerset seems to have been the first to realize the outpost could become an independent power base, perhaps when he sailed there after surrendering Caen in 1450. When he returned to England he left behind his bodyguard, later joined by others of his Norman affinity including Andrew Trollope, the Captain of Falaise who had made the release of John Talbot a condition of surrendering the town.

In September 1451, when Somerset became constable at the end of Buckingham's ten-year tenure, he replaced the entire garrison with his own men. In December, he sent Richard Woodville, Lord Rivers, with sixty men-at-arms, to act as his deputy. Subordinate captains at Guînes (Thomas Findern), Calais Castle (Lord Welles),

Hammes (John Marney) and Rysbank (Osbert Mountfort) indented for themselves and for, respectively, 100, 50, 41 and 18 men. Trollope commanded the barbican at the sole gate into the town.

By the end of 1452 Somerset had increased the numbers he could indent for by 160 men-at-arms and 511 mounted archers. This alone was an additional daily cost of £25 per day, £9,125 [£5.8 million] per annum, an increase of about 75 per cent above the peacetime establishment. In addition, the crown already owed Buckingham £20,000 [£12.72 million] for the last years of his captaincy, making Calais much the largest single charge to the exchequer at a time of desperately straightened royal finances.

Somerset almost certainly chose Rivers as his deputy because his wife Jacquetta was the sister of Louis of Luxembourg, Count of Saint-Pol 25 miles south of Calais. Louis inherited Saint-Pol and Brienne in 1433, and continued his family's policy of supporting the English after Duke Philippe renounced his alliance with England in 1435 in return for Picardy, which left Saint-Pol buried deep within Burgundian territory. Louis was also the heir to his uncle, Count of Ligny and Guise, but when he died in 1441 Charles VII seized the counties and only let Louis have Ligny after he swore fealty and ceased helping the English. He was also required to join in the reconquest of Normandy.

Rivers' dealings with Saint-Pol were probably the reason Richard of York believed Somerset intended treason with regard to Calais. Marguerite, also, may have had doubts about his motives. Her father owed fealty to the rulers of France, Burgundy and the Empire for his scattered domains, and she would have had a greater understanding of how the game was played at the borders of rival kingdoms than any other member of the English court.

So, what was Somerset's game? First, Calais was a cash cow, although getting the milk was problematic. In 1457, two years after Somerset's death at St Albans, the crown recognized a debt to his estate of £23,000 [£14.6 million], separate from the arrears separately paid to the garrison. This was a staggering amount for a mere four years' service, and vastly greater than his landed income. The king's aim had been to put him on a financial par with the great magnates, but Somerset exploited his benevolence further by indenting for more soldiers than were actually serving in Calais.

Somerset must have known the cost to the crown was unsustainable, and it is hard to dismiss the suspicion that he had a fall-back position in case he lost the king's favour and was obliged to flee England. It could well have been to enrich himself and those who chose to remain with him by handing over the enclave to the highest bidder, perhaps with Louis of Luxembourg acting as broker, and to remain as Count of Calais.

Whatever plans he had were aborted by his imprisonment during York's first protectorate. Denied emergency taxation by the Commons, the exchequer could no longer pay Somerset's men in Calais. This provoked a mutiny, which, had he been free to attend to it in person, might have served as a step towards whatever outcome he had in mind. Instead, it became a means of undermining his rival's authority, a tricky hand for Somerset's deputies to play when York was the legally appointed authority for the defence of the realm.

The key to resolving the impasse was the Company of the Staple, set up in Calais in 1399 to handle the export of all English wool to northern Europe. Like any monopoly, it depressed producer income and inflated the price paid by consumers, in this case the great textile manufacturing towns of the Low Countries, which paid in gold and silver. After several other expedients had failed, the Staple was set up to provide the crown with a single point of tax revenue from the wool trade, and practically its only source of bullion, without which the English could not have waged the last half of the Hundred Years War.

So great was the difference between the purchase and sale prices that Cardinal Beaufort's great wealth had come largely from the sale of wool to southern Europe, less than a fifth of all wool exports, through his port of Southampton. The Calais Staple could do nothing about that; what infuriated the Staplers were the exemptions from their northern European monopoly, granted by the crown to pay debts to favoured individuals. York, for example, was granted one such exemption to recover some of what he was owed for his Normandy lieutenancy.

Consequently, when in May 1454 the garrison seized the entire stock of wool warehoused in Calais as a guarantee of its unpaid wages, the Staplers were not in a mood to compromise. As we have seen, York had pressing calls on his time in England, and he delegated negotiations to Viscount Bourchier. Bourchier set about driving a wedge between the troops, whose grievances were financial, and their politically motivated commanders. This tactic appears to have been on the brink of success when the king recovered from his catatonia and restored Somerset to all his offices.

One of the reasons Somerset did not pay enough attention to the gathering Yorkist storm may have been because his eyes were fixed on affirming his hold on Calais as a bolt-hole should Henry relapse. Not long after the king dismissed the charges against him, he sent Lord Roos and his two most trusted household officers to arrange for his return. The arrears continued to mount and the Staple was no more interested in backing him than it had been to commit to York. For this reason, on 14 May 1455 Somerset appointed shire commissioners throughout the land to raise a loan to pay the garrison.

This would have encountered considerable resistance, but the issue became moot after Somerset was killed at St Albans eight days later. Anxious not to repeat his previous error of trying to do too much himself, one of York's first acts was to get the king to appoint Warwick as Captain of Calais. With Somerset gone, political resistance from the Calais commanders was limited to a non-negotiable demand for immunity for previous actions, including the theft of the wool. York no longer had cause to find evidence of Somerset's frauds, beside which any his subordinates might have committed were minor. So it came down to money.

With all claims to be honoured at face value, the amount in

question was enormous. The arrears due to the captains and soldiers, net of £17,366 deducted for the stolen wool, were calculated on 20 April 1456 to be £48,080 [£30.6 million]. A cash settlement was provided by the Staple, which accepted £23,000 in crown IOUs ('tallies') held by the treasurer of Calais in part payment. Exemptions from the Staple's monopoly were to cease and, once Buckingham's debt was cleared, the Staple's advance was to be paid down by the customs receipts of Sandwich, Calais' main corresponding port in England. The Staple was also promised the customs receipts from Southampton, although it never collected a penny.

A pardon was issued by the Council on 1 May, and shortly afterwards Warwick entered Calais with his own retinue of 300 men, paid for by a further crown-guaranteed loan from the Staple. He adopted a light-handed approach, and apart from terminating the employment of Rivers, Welles and Mountfort, there was no purge of the remaining Somerset loyalists. Warwick was confident he could win them over – and they were content for him to believe he had. He was to find his confidence misplaced in 1459–60, when Trollope and his men deserted him at a crucial moment, and Findern and Marney handed over Guînes and Hammes to Somerset's heir, Henry Beaufort.

Previous Captains of Calais had been absentees, governing through deputies, and at first it seemed Warwick might follow the same path. After his ceremonial taking of possession he returned to England to consolidate his gains in Wales and to attend Council meetings. As control slipped progressively from York's hands, however, Warwick saw Calais was a good place to sit things out. It would take him away from the danger of assassination by the heirs of the men killed at St Albans, and permit him to continue his pose as the king's loyal servant by distancing himself from active factionalism.

Warwick was a supremely lucky man in an age that believed Lady Luck (the pagan *Fortuna*) ruled over all. How much of his luck was the product of careful planning is hard to say, but in the peculiar circumstances prevailing after Marguerite's counter-coup he strengthened his hand by creating tension with Burgundy. The mechanism was raids from Calais across the border into Artois, falsely reported as a response to Burgundian aggression. After a preliminary meeting between representatives of the two sides at Ardres in late 1456 and early 1457, in April the king commissioned Warwick to negotiate in his name with Duke Philippe.

By this time Warwick had made the momentous decision to move his household to Calais, which made him the idol of the townspeople. He was a big spender, which of course pleased the local merchants, but by establishing a glittering court in what had always been a rather drab garrison town, he and Countess Anne also greatly enhanced the social life of the local aristocracy, the very wealthy members of the Company of the Staple and their wives. This marked him as among the first English nobles to appreciate the political advantages of princely magnificence, a feature of the contemporary Italian Renaissance but late in coming to northern Europe.

In July 1457 Duke Philippe's personal envoy came to meet Warwick between Oye and Marck, inside the pale of Calais. This was Philippe's eldest illegitimate son Anthony, known as 'the Grand Bastard of Burgundy' to differentiate him from his younger brother Corneille, who was merely 'the Bastard of Burgundy'. Anthony was brought up with Philippe's legitimate heir Charles, Count of Charolais, and the two were close. More remarkably they were both loyal sons, a rare occurrence among the Valois. Warwick hosted a splendid banquet, and obtained compensation for the border incidents he had provoked.

In August Lady Luck dealt him the ace of trumps in the shape of a large-scale amphibious raid on Calais' supply port Sandwich led by Pierre de Brézé, Grand Seneschal of Normandy since the reconquest. Although Brézé had lost influence at court since the death of Agnès Sorel, the king's mistress and his patron, he was still the Charles VII's go-to man in military matters. The raid underlined Exeter's complete failure to maintain a fleet to justify his title of Lord Admiral, and Warwick successfully argued for the extension of his power to include Calais' maritime communications.

He was strongly supported by the inhabitants of Sandwich and many other ports, whose trade was suffering from a great increase in French piracy since the fall of Normandy. Although Brézé claimed his raid was retaliation for English piracy, to Henry VI it confirmed he had a naval war on his hands. Exeter kept his title, but in early October 1457 the king and Council made Warwick Keeper of the Seas, de facto Lord Admiral, 'for the resistance of [the king's] enemies and repressing their malice' and 'the comfort and relief of his subjects, friends and allies', with an initial advance of £3,000 [£1.9 million].

Subsequent patents richly gilded the lily. He was authorized to do the king's enemies 'all hurt and annoyance' by sea and, remarkably, by land as well, to issue (for which read sell) safe conducts on his own authority, and to keep a third of any spoils for himself, with another third for his crews, and a wishful thinking third for the crown. He was required to recruit 3,000–5,000 men and to lease or build ships at will, for which he was not only assigned the customs receipts of every port except Sandwich and Southampton (already committed to the Staple), but also to appoint his own customs agents to collect them.

There were an almost infinite number of ways to make money from this astonishingly broad remit. For example, Warwick was already a ship-owner as a result of his lordship (through his wife) of the Channel Islands, and we may be certain the first ships he leased for the crown, no doubt on extremely generous terms, would have been his own. He was not required to render accounts, and we can be sure he would also have received kick-backs from every individual involved in the building, equipping and maintenance of the ships. Not least, the right to issue safe conducts and to collect customs – or not – gave him the option to develop a nationwide coastal and naval affinity.

The powers vested in Warwick, at a time when Marguerite's star was in the ascendant, were enormous. He was made virtually sovereign of Calais, where he controlled the principal source of bullion for England and even had his own mint. He was empowered to negotiate with other sovereigns in the name of the king, with only remote oversight. He had the only standing army in English territory, as well as a navy he could use to make war, commit piracy, or to trade on his own account. All of this in principle paid for by the crown.

Why, after her assumption of leadership of the Lancastrian faction, did Marguerite not seek to clip the wings of the man responsible for the lethal attack on the king's retinue at St Albans and the butchery of Somerset, Northumberland and Clifford? I believe the answer is that he was really the only candidate for a 'Hand of the King', with no claim by blood to the throne, who was capable of facing down York on behalf of the Lancastrian dynasty. Warwick had been a most assiduous courtier before the king's illness – why not try to win him back?

Unlike Suffolk and Somerset, Warwick was not a man who could be won by an accumulation of offices, wardships and other small privileges. He had shown no desire for a role in the administration or the other mundane occupations of indirect power. He fancied himself as a prince, so why not encourage him to seek glory, riches and renown – outside England? Just because we know it backfired does not mean Marguerite was wrong to gamble on building Warwick up in the hope of splitting the Nevilles from York. She was looking for a way to win without incurring the risks of a war in which her gender would preclude her from playing a leading role, and really had no other option.

Her hopes were in vain, as Warwick remained in close communication not only with his father, but also with York. Edmund Mulso, previously York's Midlands steward, came to Calais with Warwick in 1456 and was his marshal until he died in 1458. He was replaced by Walter Blount, another Yorkist councillor whose family home was sacked in 1454 by anti-Yorkists, and who went on to become the treasurer of Calais in 1460.

Even if there had been exploitable differences among Warwick, his father and York, the crown's finances were in such a parlous state that payments for Calais could not be sustained, and soon ceased. The king's government also broke its agreement with the Staple and continued to issue exemptions, persuading the Staplers their future lay with the Yorkists. Warwick was to use his fleet not only to generate income for the garrison by piracy, but also to seize ships carrying non-Staple wool, and to fence the stolen property through Calais.

Warwick won an even wider following by acting as the champion of English merchants against foreign competition. A particularly shrewd blow was the seizure of three exempt Genoese ships with cargoes worth £4,000 [£2.5 million] at Tilbury, down-river from London, cheered by local merchants deeply resentful that their own government was favouring foreign inroads into their trade. At another level he appealed to bruised patriotism by demanding foreign ships should dip their flags to England's, and attacking them if they did not.

Warwick was a phenomenon quite outside the normal run of English history. He was indeed a prince, and a quick-witted warlord who would have been quite at home in Renaissance Italy. Most of the English sources for his life are hagiographic, but reports by Burgundian, French and Milanese agents to their masters support the view that he was not only popular, but also a man of exceptional intelligence, personal charm and steely determination. That he was also a serial killer was, if anything, considered a mark in his favour.

He remained devoted to his wife even though they never had the son for whom he yearned, and she is one of the unexplored aspects of his story. She was, after all, the source of his wealth and a considerable peeress in her own right. He did not appoint a formal deputy to govern Calais during his absences in the crucial early years of his captaincy, which strongly suggests Countess Anne must have played an active political role, as well as being the hub around which his court revolved. They were a formidable partnership.

Warwick's withdrawal to Calais left Wales, the source of his original contention with what was now the Lancastrian party, very much up in the air. It was to play a crucial role, but it is a mistake to see it as simply one more stage on which the evolving rivalry between the English magnates was played out. There was more to it than that.

HERE BE DRAGONS

WALES MIGHT WELL HAVE BEEN MARKED 'HERE BE dragons' on the Anglo-Norman mental map. Barring rims of settlement along the north and south coasts, it was a mountainous, wooded territory, thinly inhabited by miserably poor and deeply resentful peasants. It preserved its own legal system, with feudalism still the dominant form of land tenure, and of course its own language, thanks to which a separate Welsh identity survives to this day. It is only through translations of the oral history contained in bardic poems that English speakers can even glimpse what was going on in the hearts and minds of the conquered people.

The border marked on Map 13 was not legally defined until the mid-1500s, by the same series of acts that made Wales part of England, granting it representation in Parliament for the first time, but abolishing its legal system and banning the Welsh language from any official role or status. 'The March' occupied most of what we now call Wales. During the prolonged Norman conquest from 1067 to 1283 it was dotted with a profusion of motte and bailey timber castles. These were gradually replaced by a smaller but still large number of masonry castles and walled towns, with the heaviest concentration in the south.

Monmouth and Glamorgan corresponded approximately to the old kingdoms of Gwent and Morgannwg. The royal counties of

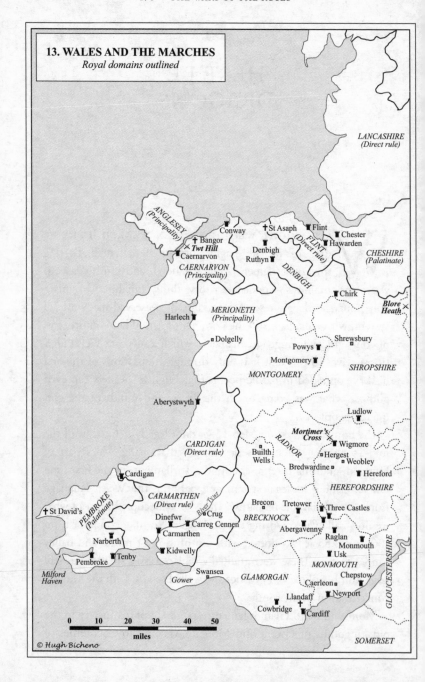

13. WALES AND THE MARCHES
Royal domains outlined

LANCASHIRE
(Direct rule)

ANGLESEY
(Principality)

✝ Bangor
✗ *Twt Hill*
♜ Caernarvon

♜ Conway

✝ St Asaph

♜ Flint
FLINT
(Direct rule)

♜ Chester
♜ Hawarden

CHESHIRE
(Palatinate)

♜ Denbigh
♜ Ruthyn

DENBIGH

CAERNARVON
(Principality)

♜ Chirk

Blore
Heath ✗

MERIONETH
(Principality)

♜ Harlech

◻ Dolgelly

♜ Powys

♜ Shrewsbury

♜ Montgomery

MONTGOMERY

SHROPSHIRE

♜ Aberystwyth

♜ Ludlow

Mortimer's
Cross ✗ ♜ Wigmore

CARDIGAN
(Direct rule)

RADNOR

◻ Builth
Wells

◻ Hergest
◻ Weobley

◻ Bredwardine
♜ Hereford

♜ Cardigan

PEMBROKE
(Palatinate)

HEREFORDSHIRE

✝ St David's

CARMARTHEN
(Direct rule)

♜ Brecon

♜ Tretower

♜ Three Castles

River Tywi

♜ Dinefwr
♜ Crug
BRECKNOCK

♜ Narberth

♜ Carreg Cennen

♜ Carmarthen

♜ Abergavenny

♜ Raglan

♜ Pembroke
♜ Tenby

♜ Kidwelly

♜ Monmouth

♜ Usk

Milford
Haven

Gower

♜ Swansea

GLAMORGAN

MONMOUTH

♜ Caerleon

GLOUCESTERSHIRE

♜ Chepstow

♜ Llandaff
♜ Newport

♜ Cowbridge
✝ Cardiff

| 0 | 10 | 20 | 30 | 40 | 50 |

miles

© *Hugh Bicheno*

SOMERSET

Cardigan, Pembroke and Carmarthen had once been the kingdom of Deheubarth, while the borders of the Principality (Anglesey, Caernarvon and Merioneth), along with Denbigh and royal Flint, were those of Gwynedd, the last independent Welsh kingdom. Cheshire, Shropshire, Herefordshire and Gloucestershire were English, but Welsh gentry predominated along the borders. Many adopted English surnames only during our period, under the pressure of penal laws enacted by Henry IV.

The most famous Anglicization was by Owen, son of Maredudd ap Tudur, hence properly Owain ap Mareddud (Meredith), Catherine of Valois' consort. His was not a Marcher family – the Tudors were from north-west Wales. When given Englishman's rights for service in Normandy, Owen chose to use his grandfather's name as his English surname. This was probably in tribute to the role of the three ap Tudur brothers in the last great Welsh revolt, led by their first cousin, Owain Glyn Dŵr, after whom he was named.

The peculiar circumstances of the Wars of the Roses gave Wales a role in English history it had never played before – or has since – thanks to which a Welsh dragon was one of the shield supporters of the royal coat of arms from 1485 to 1604. The Tudor dynasty descended from Edmund, the first-born son of Catherine of Valois and Owen Tudor, but he did not even live to see the future Henry VII born. It was his brother Jasper who piloted the boy to the throne, through vicissitudes that would have broken the spirit of a lesser man.

As Pembroke was so poor and much of it was owned by the Bishop of St David's, the English nobles appointed to senior posts within Wales never performed in person the duties for which they were paid, delegating them to local officials instead. The most outstanding of these was Gruffudd ap Nicholas of Crug, in the Tywy valley, who made himself so useful to successive absentee lords and bishops that by the late 1440s he and his sons Thomas and Owain dominated Carmarthen, Pembroke and much of Cardigan.

Although some of Gruffudd's lands were granted in theory to

Jasper Tudor in 1452, he did not set foot in the county until 1456. Gruffudd resided at Carmarthen Castle and acted in all respects as the lord of south-west Wales until Somerset was killed at St Albans, after which Gruffudd and his sons were replaced by new Yorkist stewards, constables and justiciars throughout the area. York himself became constable of Aberystwyth, Carmarthen and Carreg Cennen. Kidwelly and Dinefwr, held by Gruffudd since the 1430s, went to Edward Bourchier and to the Yorkist retainer William Herbert of Raglan in Monmouth.

Herbert was the son of William ap Thomas, who fought at Agincourt and was made a knight banneret, but never anglicized his name. The older William had been Chief Steward of Usk and Caerleon, York's largest Welsh estates, and High Sheriff of Glamorgan. When he died in 1445 his namesake son, who adopted the surname Herbert and was also knighted for service in Normandy, inherited his offices along with the manor of Raglan, which his father had begun to fortify. Herbert, who made a fortune from the Gascony wine trade, was to make it the last of the great Welsh castles, as a proud display of wealth and power.

Although Gruffudd and his sons were summoned on pain of treason to appear before the Council in London, he had seen it all before and ignored York's authority and appointments, confident that, as always, his isolated corner of the kingdom would be very low on the squabbling English lords' lists of priorities. Thus it came as a nasty surprise when Edmund Tudor, Earl of Richmond, was sent in late 1455 to restore royal authority in south-west Wales.

Jasper was the more obvious choice, but unlike Richmond he had formed part of the king's retinue at St Albans and York did not trust him. In the confrontation with Somerset, who despised them as upstart bastards (what a difference a generation makes!), the Tudors had been, if anything, Yorkist in their sympathies. In early 1453, to Somerset's fury, the king gave them the lucrative joint wardship of the estates of Margaret, sole heir of John Beaufort, Edmund's older brother and predecessor as duke of Somerset. The wardship had previously been awarded to Suffolk, and after his death was exercised by Marguerite, so this concurs with the hypothesis that she built up the Tudors to counterbalance Somerset.

The death of Somerset at St Albans removed any impediment to Richmond marrying his 12-year-old ward, and to the Tudors becoming wholeheartedly associated with the queen's faction. Either York did not fully appreciate this, or else he thought to win Richmond to his own side by entrusting him with gaining control of the castles defiantly held by Gruffudd. Richmond did not do so, however, moving first to the bishop's palace at Lamphey, near his brother's castle at Pembroke. There, so great was his anxiety to guarantee his life interest in his wife's estate that he got her pregnant despite her age and slight build.

Edmund must have been anxious indeed: convention dictated that men of refinement waited until their child brides were in their late teens before consummating their marriages. Such forbearance was practical as well as ethical. Although twelve was the legal age of consent, simply because a girl had reached puberty did not mean her body was fully developed. An early pregnancy risked the girl's life or, as proved to be the case with Margaret Beaufort, could wreck her ability to bear more children.

When Richmond finally took possession of Carmarthen Castle in August 1456, it was by agreement with Gruffudd ap Nicholas. By then York had lost patience with him and sent 2,000 men under William Herbert to do the job properly. With him went Walter Devereux of Weobley, Herbert's father-in-law and constable of York's castle at Wigmore, and the Vaughan brothers of Bredwardine, Hergest and Tretower, who had been brought up with the Herbert brothers after their widowed mother married William ap Thomas. Carmarthen and the other castles were not prepared for defence and quickly surrendered. Richmond was briefly imprisoned, but he was at liberty when he died of the plague in Carmarthen on 1 November.

Jasper Tudor moved to Pembroke Castle in late 1456 and there, on 28 January 1457, his brother's posthumous son was born. It was a difficult birth yet within two months, escorted by Jasper, Margaret travelled to meet the Duke of Buckingham at his manor of Greenfield in Newport in Monmouth. She negotiated her betrothal to his younger son, Henry Stafford, and they were married on 3 January 1458. Confusingly, Buckingham's heir Humphrey had earlier married Margaret's namesake first cousin, the daughter of Eleanor Beauchamp who had been the cause of her 'shot-gun marriage' to Edmund Beaufort.

In the face of the Yorkist onslaught Gruffudd made submission to the queen, and after her counter-coup of October 1456 the king issued a pardon to him and his sons. Jasper Tudor took back the lands pertaining to his earldom, but when he replaced York as the constable of Aberystwyth, Carmarthen and Carreg Cennen in April 1457, things continued as before with Gruffudd's family operating as his agents. The last record of Gruffudd is in late February 1460, when he made a will bequeathing the castle and lordship of Narberth to his son Owain. Along with Jasper Tudor, Gruffudd's family were to be the most tenacious of Lancastrians throughout the Wars of the Roses.

All politics is local and, as was the case throughout the kingdom, it was clan rivalries rather than any overarching commitment to York or Lancaster that tended to define what side noble and gentry families took. The most inveterate opponents of Gruffudd were the Dwnns of Kidwelly, Carmarthen, and they perforce became beleaguered but fanatical Yorkists. The Kynastons and Eytons of Shropshire were rivals of the Talbots of Shrewsbury, and so became York's main supporters in the North March. The Skydmores of Herefordshire had chronic disputes with York and Herbert, and the Pulestons of Denbigh with York's unpleasant ally Lord Grey of Ruthyn, and so became firm Lancastrians.

An exception to the general rule was the Principality of Wales. More than was the case with the royal counties of Wales, there was genuine popular commitment to the Prince of Wales as the successor to Llewellyn the Great in Anglesey, Caernarvon and Merioneth. Unfortunately for his cause they had been wretchedly governed during his father's reign: 'Lawlessness was everywhere rampant, and Merioneth subsisted on cattle stealing, private feuds, burning of houses and murders. Market day at Dolgelly and Conway was a festival of looting and plunder.'*

Thanks to Jasper Tudor, south-west Wales proved a greater asset. He quickly appreciated the strategic importance of the Pembroke peninsula and the great harbour of Milford Haven. Even before it became apparent that war was inevitable, he entered into an agreement with the citizens of Tenby, on the southern side of the peninsula, to build up the fortifications of the port. He also governed fairly. Winning the loyalty of the people of Pembroke proved to be the wisest long-term investment made by any of the participants in the wars.

The Middle and South Marches were the heartland of York's power and, as we have seen, after the failure of his demonstration at Dartford, Henry and Somerset had held assizes in Ludlow to humiliate his tenants. They never turned out in force for York again. From 1457, Marguerite resumed the attack, singling out York's supporters in the South March. In April, at Hereford, William Herbert and Walter Devereux were arraigned before the king, with Marguerite at his side, not for their actions on behalf of York in south-west Wales, but for an arbitrary act committed on their own initiative a year earlier.

Following the murder of Walter Vaughan, Herbert and Devereux had intimidated the coroner's court at Bredwardine and seized Hereford, imprisoning the mayor and pressuring the king's justices to convict the men they said were responsible, whom they promptly hanged. The members of the commission that tried Herbert and Devereux at Hereford were the leading lights of the royalist faction: Buckingham, Shrewsbury, Wiltshire, Beaumont and James Tuchet,

* Quote from Howell Evans' indispensable *Wales and the Wars of the Roses*.

Baron Audley, joined by William FitzAlan, Earl of Arundel, trimming his sails to the prevailing wind in the manner that was to serve him well in the future.

Herbert and Devereux were found guilty of treason, but their subsequent treatment was markedly different. Devereux, who had already been condemned and pardoned for his part in York's armed protest in 1452, was imprisoned and his goods declared forfeit. Herbert, the principal instigator, was granted his life and restored to his property in return for swearing allegiance to the king. The purpose was plainly to divide the two men and to weaken Herbert's allegiance to York.

Herbert was the steward of York's castle at Usk and manor of Caerleon, which together with Herbert's own large estate of Raglan occupied the strategic centre among Buckingham's large holdings in Brecknock and southern Monmouth, and the lands held by Somerset, Wiltshire and the junior Talbots in Gloucestershire. If the Vaughans followed Herbert's lead, a wedge would also have been driven between York's strongholds in the Middle March and Warwick's lordships of Abergavenny and Glamorgan. Herbert was also Warwick's High Sheriff for Glamorgan, and if he could have been won to active support of the king, it would have been a spectacular coup.

• ↀ •

There is little doubt that Marguerite's policy of chipping away at York's support without confronting him directly, and carefully refraining from taking any similar action against Salisbury and Warwick, offered the best chance of achieving her objective. Time was not on her side, however. Keeping the court away from the Westminster bureaucracy was unsustainable, as although Shrewsbury and Wiltshire were able to collect taxes directly from the Midlands, the mobile court lacked the staff to conduct national administration. The struggle against York might be won, but only at the cost of accelerating the fragmentation of a kingdom that could only function as a unitary state.

With the court living hand-to-mouth, Marguerite could not use royal patronage to win followers or to buy conformity to her designs. She became a coalition manager, hostage to the interests of its component parts. While those of her son's Council broadly corresponded to her own, any hope of breaking up the alliance between York and the Nevilles was dashed by the actions of the heirs of the nobles killed at St Albans and their allies, who at this stage must be seen as constituting a third party, and a damagingly loose cannon on Marguerite's deck. She would need them if push came to shove, but they made sure it came to shove.

The heirs were Henry Beaufort, 3rd Duke of Somerset, 21 years old in 1457, Henry Percy, 3rd Earl of Northumberland (36), and John, 9th Baron Clifford (22). Driving them on were the trio who had caused so much trouble in the earlier 1450s: Henry Holland, 3rd Duke of Exeter (27), Henry Percy's brother Thomas, 1st Baron Egremont (35) and Thomas, 9th Baron Roos (30). The Percys and Cliffords had intermarried several times, and Roos was the son of the first marriage of Eleanor Beauchamp. Hence he was the maternal half-brother of Henry Beaufort, and shared his hatred of Warwick for the disinheritance of their mother.*

Politics was not only local, but also highly personal. Although Clifford's and Roos's main grievances were with the Nevilles, they had their own reasons to hate York. Both had been born in York's own birthplace, Conisbrough Castle, when it was part of the dower of his stepmother Maud, Countess of Cambridge. She was the daughter of the 6th Baron Clifford and Elizabeth, daughter of the 5th Baron Roos, and along with her extended family lived there sumptuously while running up debts using the castle as collateral. When she died in 1446, York reclaimed his heavily encumbered property with icy contempt for Maud's heirs.

* For the Beaufort-Roos connection see Appendix F: The Beauchamp Inheritance.

The product of all these and other resentments and provocations too numerous to list was a critical mass of unappeasable hatred that demanded bloodshed. Exeter and Egremont had tried to assassinate York during his first protectorate, and they were probably the authors of a sinister threat in September 1456, after Egremont escaped from Newgate. Five dogs' heads were impaled on the railings of the London home of Richard Beauchamp, Bishop of Salisbury, where York was staying. The verses in the dogs' jaws said that although York, the son of a traitor, deserved to die, others had paid the price for his treason:

> What planet compelled me, or what sign
> To serve that man that all men hate?
> I would his head were here for mine
> For he hath caused all the debate.

This was a killer jibe, because it was true. So far, York had paid no material price for seeking to impose himself on the king – but the persecution of his followers after Dartford had seriously eroded their collective loyalty. At the same time, nobody seeking a legal judgement in his favour or public office would now seek York's 'good lordship', and consequently he had to spend more of his own money to maintain influence. The quest for power was a further large drain on his resources, and he was compelled to mortgage more and more of his estates to sustain the regal style his ambition demanded. Added to which, after St Albans he had pressing reasons to retain a considerable number of bodyguards on a permanent basis.

In October 1456, at the Coventry Council where Marguerite staged her counter-coup, Somerset had to be restrained from assaulting York in person, and on 1 December, still at Coventry, his retainers attacked York's party, and were themselves attacked by citizens outraged by their behaviour. Before then, an attempt was made on 5 November to ambush Warwick, returning to London from

Calais, by retainers of Somerset, Exeter and Shrewsbury. It was this episode that persuaded Warwick to appoint deputies to administer his interests in England, and to move to Calais.

There were several other such attacks over the next two years, forcing York and Salisbury to travel with large armed retinues and to reside only in their own castles or fortified manors. If the purpose had been assassination, there were many better ways of accomplishing it than through the very public clash of retainers. There were few if any casualties and one does wonder whether the supposed ambushes were not just threatening displays, akin to the behaviour of male animals in the wild.

To pursue the analogy, the aim of intimidation is to achieve dominance without fighting. If, however, neither party backs down, then the issue has to be settled by force. There may have been an element of bravado in the young lions' challenges to the Alpha males, but at some point the urge to find out who was the stronger would become irresistible. To avoid this, Henry VI made a last effort to dissuade his nobles from tearing his kingdom apart.

MARGUERITE AND HENRY

HENRY VI'S SITUATION IN 1457 MIRRORED YORK'S, ON a larger scale. Decades of fiscal irresponsibility had shrivelled his possibilities of exercising patronage, although he remained the fount of the judicial powers that might be exercised to buttress the 'good lordship' of his loyalists. However, if York's inability to protect his own followers had diminished his authority, it paled beside the towering fact that the murder of the king's most eminent supporters at St Albans remained unpunished. Few had respect for Henry as a man, or any faith he would keep his word, or honour the tallies littering the country.

Henry's struggle to employ his inadequate resources and negligible personal authority to palliate the confrontational determination of his queen is, I believe, the reason why, in the words of York's biographer, 'the tone of English political life in 1457 is… peculiarly elusive'.* Henry believed, beyond reason, that it was still possible to negotiate a peaceful settlement of the blood feuds born at St Albans. Consequently York was not entirely excluded from favour, with financial compensation promised for the loss of the Welsh castles, and the award of one or two profitable privileges that cost the crown nothing.

In March, York's appointment as Lieutenant of Ireland was

---

* From P. A. Johnson, *Duke Richard of York 1411–1460*.

renewed, six months before it was strictly necessary, along with a payment on account of £446 [£283,656]. This must have been in the form of a tally, as by this time the court was subsisting almost entirely on credit. There may have been an element of wishful thinking involved, with Henry entertaining the hope that York could be persuaded to exercise his kingly pretensions in Ireland, as Warwick's restless ambition was now focused on Calais. Ireland, however, offered no comparable attractions.

The truth, squarely faced by Marguerite but intolerable to her husband, was that nothing he did could fill the void of authority created by his compound personal deficiencies. For a man so profoundly convinced that God's will was paramount, he must have believed his troubles were akin to the biblical trials of Job by Satan. Deprived of everything he previously enjoyed, Job utters one of the most famous biblical aphorisms: 'The Lord gave, and the Lord hath taken away; blessed be the name of the Lord'. Thus also Henry, desperately hoping that if he, too, steadfastly maintained his faith in the face of adversity, he would be rewarded.

During 1457–8, therefore, the king resisted pressure from Marguerite to take a harder line with York. Henry spent most of 1457 in the queen's Midlands domain, yet he was clearly not under her control, even though this was widely perceived to be the case. No doubt there were tense scenes in the royal apartments at Kenilworth, but Marguerite knew better than anyone that once her husband was set on a course of action, the peculiar workings of his mind were impervious to argument. She would also have been haunted by the ever-present fear that, if pushed too hard, he might withdraw once more into catatonia.

The emergence of the royalist faction during this period was characterized by the fundamental contradiction between a quietist king and an activist queen. It was precisely analogous to driving with the brakes and accelerator applied simultaneously. The only question was whether the brakes would burn out before the motor exploded – but neither outcome could avoid a wreck.

To take the brakes first, the product of Henry's prayers and consultation with his confessor, the Carmelite monk John Stanberry, Bishop of Hereford, was the 'Loveday' of 24 March 1458. The good faith of Stanberry, whose diocese covered much of the ancestral Mortimer lands that were York's Marcher stronghold, was at this time still respected on both sides of the factional divide, and probably no one else could have brought the rival nobles together. York and the Nevilles would not have trusted Henry's unsupported word that they were not simply being lured into an ambush.

Henry summoned a Great Council of the entire peerage to meet in Westminster on 27 January, to discuss a wide range of governance issues, leading up to a settlement of the vendettas born at St Albans. York and Salisbury arrived separately to stay at their London palaces, but as they rode out together to the opening session of the Council, surrounded by over 1,000 guards, they encountered a hostile demonstration by a larger number of retainers wearing the livery of Somerset, Exeter, Clifford and Egremont. The two groups were kept apart by a special force of 5,000 armed men that the king had prudently commissioned the Lord Mayor to recruit and equip.

Other nobles, including Warwick (who arrived from Calais with 600 men), were late in coming and Henry withdrew to Chertsey, 25 miles south-west of Westminster, for a week. After Warwick arrived, the king returned to Westminster to declare the main purpose of the Council was 'to set apart such variances as been betwixt divers lords of this our realm'. Discussion of the core issue, St Albans, was again postponed until the arrival of Northumberland. On 26 February the king withdrew even further, to the queen's castle at Berkhamsted. There, he granted an audience to the aggrieved lords, and another to Northumberland when he arrived.

The details of the deal eventually agreed are revealing. York was to pay Somerset 5,000 marks [£2.12 million], Salisbury was to forgo the fines of 9,000 marks awarded to him against the Percys for their breaches of the peace and Warwick was to pay Clifford 1,000 marks. The only reciprocal undertaking was that Egremont's conviction and his escape from Newgate were set aside in return for posting a 4,000 mark bond to keep the peace. The payment York agreed was far from onerous – it was made with royal tallies owed for his lieutenancy, and he was granted a licence to export wool on his own account to a customs value of 10,000 marks, of which about half would be profit.

No doubt similar arrangements were made with regard to the Nevilles' indemnities. Simply put, they were bribed to accept a semblance of culpability for the St Albans killings. Contrition was to be shown with an annuity of £45 [£28,620] to pay for a permanent chantry for the souls of those killed at St Albans, in the abbey church where they were buried. A single payment of £45 was made before these arrangements were overtaken by events.

The terms were published on 24 March, the day the proceedings were crowned by a procession from Westminster to St Paul's in which Warwick walked hand in hand with Exeter (presumably in representation of the Percys and Clifford), Salisbury with Somerset, and York with the queen. In an age that attached great importance to symbolism, the king had arranged a pageant unequivocally reserving the role of arbiter to himself alone, casting the queen, who should have walked by his side, in the role of one of the plaintiffs.

During the remaining months of 1458 Henry resumed his peregrinations. Immediately after the 'Loveday' he spent three weeks at St Albans abbey, to which he returned for a month in September–October, and again for ten days in March 1459. There can be little doubt he went there to pray that the spirits of his uncle of Gloucester, dishonoured by his authority, and of the men who died for his mistakes in May 1455, should rest in peace and cease troubling his realm. Shakespeare was no historian, but his three-part *Henry the Sixth* portrays the tragic fate of a man born to a role no amount of prayer could make him competent to play:

> O God! methinks it were a happy life,
> To be no better than a homely swain.

The 'Loveday' did not, indeed could not, answer what Humpty Dumpty rightly posited as the only question of importance: 'which is to be master – that's all'. One gets tired reading the ceaseless invocations of God to witness their loyalty to the king from men who were evidently disloyal, and constrained from seizing power only because they were deeply distrusted by almost all their peers. Most histories have portrayed the following eighteen months as a period in which the queen forced the issue, yet the issue – and the force – were entirely of the Yorkists' making. With regard to Marguerite, the French saying 'this animal is very wicked: if you attack it, it defends itself' springs to mind.

There was a limited amount Marguerite could do when shackled to a supine king, but she had proved adept at shaping the political environment to strengthen her husband's hands, should they cease to be clasped in prayer. Amid a sea of uncertain loyalties, the seldom savoury but usually sound maxim 'my enemy's enemy is my friend' compelled her to work with men hated by York, among them the egregious Wiltshire and the infamous Thomas Tuddenham and William Tailboys. They used the same techniques to raise money for the cash-strapped court they had employed during Suffolk's ascendancy.

The giving of royal consent to noble marriages and the granting of wardships were areas in which the queen's influence was undisputed, and she made full use of it. In September 1456, she arranged the marriage between the namesake heir of Thomas Courtenay, Earl of Devon, and Marie of Anjou, illegitimate but dearly loved daughter of her brother Charles, Count of Maine. Devon, whose alliance with York had brought him little but grief, was ripe for plucking because the Nevilles favoured Bonville, his mortal enemy. He died on his way to the 'Loveday' Council, and his son became one of the queen's unconditional supporters.

Although Margaret Beaufort, Edmund Tudor's teenaged widow, negotiated her own marriage to Buckingham's younger son Henry, it required royal approval and the price was the queen's wardship of the infant Henry Tudor, Earl of Richmond. Margaret was a considerable heiress in her own right, but the Richmond estates were a strategic royal asset and needed stronger wardship than Henry Stafford could provide. Marguerite entrusted it jointly to Henry's uncle Jasper, Earl of Pembroke, and to John Talbot, Earl of Shrewsbury, Lord Treasurer and the senior lay member of the Prince of Wales's council.

The desire to drive a wedge between York and the Nevilles, which had led to Warwick becoming the virtual lord of Calais and Lord High Admiral in all but name, seems to have lain behind Marguerite's consent to the marriage in April 1457 of her 15-year-old ward Isabel Ingoldisthorpe to John Neville, Salisbury's second son. Isabel had eight manors in East Anglia from her recently deceased father, and was also co-heir of her childless uncle by marriage John Tiptoft, Earl of Worcester, previously and briefly married to Cecily Neville, dowager Countess of Warwick. The expected benefit to John Neville from this marriage can be measured by his agreement to pay the queen £1,000 [£636,000] in ten instalments.

One of the more intriguing matrimonial alliances made at this time was arranged between York and Alice de la Pole née Chaucer, widow of the murdered Duke of Suffolk. She remained, as she had been before she married Suffolk, an acquisitive landowner in her own right, with estates in twenty-two counties. Although the dukedom had been revoked, her only son John was still an earl, and Alice remained a member of the Order of the Garter, a lady-in-waiting to Marguerite, and castellan of her castle at Wallingford. Fifteen year-old John de la Pole was the most eligible bachelor in the kingdom, and his marriage in early 1458 to York's 13-year-old daughter Elizabeth was a highly significant political event.*

The most noteworthy matrimonial initiative of this time came in late 1458, with a proposal for multiple marriages with the French

---

* John de la Pole had previously been married to 7-year-old Margaret Beaufort in 1450. Henry VI declared the marriage annulled in 1453 when he bestowed her wardship on Edmund Tudor, who married her himself.

and Burgundian royal houses for the Prince of Wales, York's eldest son Edward, and Somerset. It did not proceed beyond a preliminary embassy by John Wenlock, lately Speaker of the House of Commons. Although he had extensive diplomatic experience, he was not of sufficient stature to lead such a high-level mission and King Charles VII sent his own herald to London to assess the seriousness of the proposal.

His findings were startling: after meeting with Warwick in Calais, Wenlock had totally subverted the peace-making purpose of the mission by stirring up trouble between Burgundy and France, and by falsely reporting to his own government that a French attack was imminent. Application of the 'who benefits?' test suggests Warwick saw that the embassy, if successful, would undermine his own status as the indispensable man in the confrontation with France. Wenlock's emergence as a committed Yorkist in 1459 strongly suggests Warwick bribed him to make sure the embassy failed.

The Wenlock mission marked the abandonment of the queen's gamble that Warwick might be tempted to break with York, to pursue power and glory on his own account. Marguerite was now faced with a monster of her own creation, and the possibility cannot be dismissed that she authorized an attempt on Warwick's life in November 1458. The attack took place at Westminster after Warwick responded to a personal summons from the king under the Privy Seal. Along with his father and York, Warwick had ignored a previous, more general summons to a Council in which, among other matters, his predation of neutral shipping in the Channel and the failure of Wenlock's mission were to be discussed.

The details of the episode were, of course, disputed. According to the court, Warwick got caught up in a fracas between his retainers and the Westminster kitchen staff. He agreed that the incident took place in the kitchen, but said it was a carefully prepared ambush in which the would-be assassin, posing as a cook, lunged at him with a roasting spit. There are two good reasons to believe Warwick's version was correct. The first is that several of his retainers were killed

Funerary effigy of Catherine de Valois.

Henry VI, *left*, and a young Henry VIII, *right*, share certain facial features with, respectively, their mother and great-grandmother.

A contemporary Flemish sketch of the young Humphrey, Duke of Gloucester.

A portrait by Jan van Eyck, *c.* 1431, believed by some to portray an Italian cardinal named Niccolò Albergati and by others to depict Cardinal Henry Beaufort.

Marguerite d'Anjou's mother, Isabelle, Duchess of Lorraine by right and of Anjou by marriage.

Marguerite d'Anjou's father, René, Duke of Anjou and Bar, Count of Provence and unsuccessful claimant to the kingdoms of Sicily, of Jerusalem and of Aragon.

Detail of a miniature from the Shrewsbury Book, with John Talbot, 1st Earl of
Shrewsbury, presenting the book to Marguerite d'Anjou. Richard, Duke of York,
is the figure wearing a coronet on the far left, behind Henry VI.

A medallion of Marguerite d'Anjou by Pietro da Milano, 1464.

Charles VII 'the Victorious', king of France from 1422 to 1461.
During his long reign Charles would expel the English from all of the
territories they occupied in France, with the exception of Calais.

Duke Philippe 'the Good' wearing the Order of the Golden Fleece. Ruler of Burgundy from 1419 until 1467, Philippe's desertion of his English allies in 1435 tipped the balance of the Hundred Years War decisively in favour of France.

Isabella of Portugal, Duchess of Burgundy and granddaughter of John of Gaunt, wearing a headdress typical of the court clothing of the day.

Funerary monument of Richard Beauchamp, Earl of Warwick, in the Collegiate Church of St Mary, Warwick. His daughter Anne's marriage to Richard Neville would bring the future 'Kingmaker' huge wealth, a prestigious earldom – and immense political influence.

Mourners around Richard Beauchamp's tomb: Richard Neville, Earl of Salisbury, and his namesake son, Richard Neville, Earl of Warwick.

Images illustrating the fall of Normandy as depicted in the fifteenth-century manuscript *Vigiles du Roi Charles VII*.

Top The mercenary François de Surienne takes the Breton border fortress of Fougères for the English.

Centre Modern French artillery batters the English fortress of Château Gaillard.

Below Crude stone-firing bombards at the siege of Caen.

and he only got away thanks to the intervention of other lords. The second and conclusive reason is the presence at the scene of the royalist thug Thomas Tuddenham, who was later rewarded by promotion to treasurer of the household.

Warwick escaped by boat down the Thames, and never returned in peace. The Lancastrian version of what followed is that he, Salisbury and York had *previously* agreed a plan whereby Warwick would make a sudden advance from Calais to capture Kenilworth, to support a charge of conspiracy to kill the royal family and to seize the throne. The conspiracy had to have been hatched *before* the attempt on Warwick's life, because if not the fuse for war was lit in the Westminster kitchens.

Further dominoes fell steadily in 1459. As the household had done in 1450, so now the queen orchestrated a campaign of disinformation designed to convince Henry that York and his allies intended his downfall. There is no evidence of any such conspiracies, the least believable of which implicated Alice, Countess of Salisbury. Possibly aware of how he had been manipulated nine years earlier, Henry refused to be panicked into precipitate action.

The queen, meanwhile, put the young lions on standby and prepared to recruit her own army in the name of her son in Cheshire, by issuing the knights and squires of the shire the swan livery badge of Henry V's Bohun mother. He had adopted it when he was Prince of Wales, and it was talismanic to English chivalry.

Finally, even appeaser-in-chief Buckingham was convinced. He accused York, the Nevilles, the Bourchiers, the Bishops of Ely and Exeter and several others of conspiracy at a Great Council summoned to Coventry in June 1459. Two Acts, unfortunately lost, were passed, but the king refused to sanction the recommended punishments. In a staged melodrama, Buckingham and the loyalist lords knelt before him and begged:

> Seeing the great jeopardy for your most noble person, and also
> [seeing] the Lords so often charged, and disturbing so often the

great part of your Realm, that it should not please you to show grace hereafter to the said Duke of York, nor none other, if they attempt to do the contrary to your Royal estate, or disturbing your Realm and the Lords thereof, but to be punished as they deserve, and have deserved, for the good of You, Sovereign Lord, and for the good of all your Lords and people.

Henry indicated his assent, and with it all the offences supposedly wiped clean by the 'Loveday' were back on the table. Salisbury and York began to gather forces respectively at Middleham and Ludlow, and Warwick prepared an expedition. The Yorkists issued repeated professions of loyalty, and assurances that they were acting in self-defence. For Henry, this must have been all-too reminiscent of the events leading up to St Albans, and the king could only conclude that another *coup d'état* was in preparation.

Were the Yorkists, as they declared, simply acting in order to pre-empt further false accusations leading to their condemnation and attainder? The assumption that such measures were likely to be taken was an entirely reasonable one. By this stage the only thing that could restore the political standing and financial credit of the Lancastrian dynasty was a massive acquisition of lands and wealth. The lands of the duchy of York and the earldoms of Salisbury and Warwick would have fitted the bill nicely.

Faced with a similar situation, Richard II doomed himself by dispossessing Henry VI's grandfather Henry Bolingbroke, but the precedent was ignored. One of the constants of history is how effortlessly people persuade themselves that, however disastrous a particular course of action was when first attempted, they will achieve a favourable outcome by doing exactly the same thing again.

The Nevilles agreed to join York at Ludlow for two reasons. The first was that York was a royal duke, and still a figure around whom those discontented with the king's government could be expected to rally. The second, however, was that his standing in the Welsh Marches had been successfully undermined by the 1452 and 1457 assizes, and his Marcher affinity was understandably reluctant to sign up for what might prove another Dartford. The arrival of strong contingents from the North and from Calais would provide concrete evidence that, this time, York was not isolated.

This time, however, what we may now regard as the Lancastrian faction was alert and prepared, and Henry gave evidence of an unwonted purposefulness. Whatever methods of persuasion Marguerite used to urge her husband to take decisive action – on past form some encouragement in the bedchamber would have been involved – he now dressed for war, and for a month led his army in the field, not merely as a show of force but with the clear determination to bring his enemies to battle.

THE ENGLISH
WAY OF WAR

O UR STORY NOW MOVES FROM A MAINLY POLITICAL TO a preponderantly military sphere, and a brief digression now will save much explanation later. It is relatively easy for the modern reader to relate to the dynamics of ambition, pride and the bonds of kinship and affinity we have been reviewing. Medieval warfare is another matter.

English military superiority and democratic institutions both owed much to the longbow. Used en masse, its rapid shooting rate (as many as eight aimed arrows per minute) made it an awesomely effective battlefield weapon, while knowledge that common men could puncture their hauberks (mail coats) may have done much to convince the Norman-French ruling class they should not push the English-speaking majority too far. It was the latent power of the independent yeoman class, the distinguishing glory of English social history.

Many other societies had similar weapons, but nowhere else were they as powerful as in the hands of the English. The technique of using the whole body, not just the arms, to draw the bow was first developed in Wales, where Edward I had found it necessary to clear the forests 100 yards on either side of roads to prevent deadly sniping by the Welsh. From there, the technique spread throughout England.

Boys in fourteenth- and fifteenth-century England grew up training with bows of increasing power to accustom their bodies to their demands, and forensic anthropologists have no difficulty identifying medieval archers from their skeletal remains. Constant practice also made them deadly accurate, and their tremendous upper body strength served them well in hand-to-hand combat, when they commonly used the lead-headed mauls also used to drive in the stakes with which they protected their shooting positions.

Properly deployed, massed longbowmen removed cavalry as well as skirmishing by light troops from the battlefield equation. Plate armour evolved to protect those who could afford it, and fully armoured knights could march into an arrow storm with a reasonable expectation of coming to hand strokes, although they had to lean into it, heads down to hide their eye-slits. However, even if the rain of arrows did not find the proverbial chink in their armour, their punishing impacts sapped the strength of the men enduring it.

Longbowmen also greatly diminished enemy command and control. A commander who lifted his visor to look around or to shout orders risked an arrow in the face, as happened to both Harry 'Hotspur' Percy and to the future Henry V at Shrewsbury in 1403. The most effective use of the longbow was direct fire with heavy arrows at 50 yards or less, comparable to the crossbow but with an overwhelmingly faster shooting rate.*

Armour ('harness') was worn over and attached to padded garments ('arming jacks') with fabric or leather laces at the appropriate places. The wealthy wore bespoke harness made in England, which would have been brightly polished hardened steel, with an outer garment (tabard) bearing the heraldic device of the wearer (hence 'coat of arms'). 'Off the peg' hardened steel armour generally came from Italy, while those of more limited means might wear cheaper armour, painted to combat corrosion.

Steel armour of any kind was valuable and common soldiers often wore partial harness looted from enemy casualties. These

---

* For a full assessment see Mike Loades' splendid *The Longbow*.

trophies aside, foot soldiers and archers wore thickly padded fabric jacks with detachable sleeves, some with strips of armour incorporated, or a canvas garment reinforced with rivets called a brigandine. Either could be worn over a hauberk, although multiple layers of fabric alone are surprisingly effective.

Although some preferred the two-handed sword, the man-at-arm's premier weapon for close-quarter battle was the poleaxe, a reinforced wooden shaft 4–5 feet in length, with a steel head comprising a spike, an axe and a war hammer. Either weapon could be used to lunge, or like a quarterstaff to defend and attack the upper body, but with the poleaxe you could hook an opponent's feet from under him. He could then be dispatched with a jab between plates by the spike on the butt of the shaft, or with a swing of the war hammer.

Billmen used longer-shafted weapons topped with a wide range of variations on the basic agricultural billhook. Most combined a spike, a blade and some kind of hook to drag men off their feet. The principal role of the billmen was area denial, to prevent opponents getting around the men-at-arms from different directions. To finish off the fallen, all would have had daggers in their belts, with pommels to permit a two-handed punch through mail.

Hand-to-hand fighting was exhausting, and battle lines would ebb and flow as combatants backed off from each other to take a breather. As far as we know, there was no formal procedure for men in the rear ranks to relieve those at the front when they grew tired, but it certainly took place continuously during a battle, causing a rippling effect. Fighting in full harness was also hot and thirsty work, and several cases are known of knights killed with arrows through the throat when they removed their bevors (armour worn to cover the lower face and neck under a half-helmet called a sallet) to take a drink.

Although the era of decisive heavy cavalry charges was over, a significant proportion of an army was still mounted. The knights and men-at-arms all rode, as did mounted archers and hobilars (mounted spearmen who rode and fought with the archers). Light cavalry performed essential functions. Lancers (prickers) scouted ahead of an army, as did foragers and harbingers, whose job was to source supplies and to identify places for the army battalions (the contemporary term was 'battles') to bivouac.

These men would be concentrated in the leading battalion (Vanward/Vanguard) on the march, but would revert to their parent battalions, the Main (often, confusingly, called 'the Battle') and the Rearward/Rearguard, when the time came to fight. As in every war, the vast majority of casualties were inflicted on a broken army as it ran away, when the winning side's men-at-arms, hobi-lars and mounted archers would regain their horses to harry the fleeing men. Pursuit would end at the enemy baggage train, because looting trumped everything.

In England, the bulk of the rank-and-file came from levies raised under commissions of array, a royal order sent to county sheriffs, usually through a local magnate, to summon all adult males for a period of military service. They had an obligation of thirty days' annual service, paid for by their communities, and were expected to muster with the weapons appropriate to their station. This was a fairly well oiled system, as the levies were often summoned for inspection and basic training.

The obligation was for service at home only. Overseas service was voluntary and involved contracts known as indentures. This was ruinously expensive, and lack of money was the main reason the English were so easily bundled out of France. However, even though the wage bill for a campaign at home was reduced, a commander still had to pay surgeons, armourers, bowyers, fletchers, farriers, wheelwrights, blacksmiths, saddlers, masons and carpenters.

Added to which would be the cost of several hundred wagons to carry tens of thousands of arrows, supplementary feed for horses, several days' hard rations for the troops, anvils, tools and tents. If required, siege guns, their specialist crews and ammunition were an additional expense and increased the number of wagons required;

but their greater cost was that they slowed the army's progress, adding further to the per diems.

Two means of reducing the cost of warfare were denied to commanders during the Wars of the Roses. One was the *chevauchée*, which was expected to be profitable as well as self-supporting through plunder once it entered enemy territory. During the Wars of the Roses neither side could afford to plunder the people whose best interests both claimed to represent. The other was ransoms paid by captives, but civil wars are notoriously savage, and chivalrous conventions died at St Albans.

While not entirely dictated by financial considerations, the English way of war diverged from the continental norm by its willingness to stake all on a climactic battle. The exemplar for all the commanders during the Wars of the Roses was fierce old John Talbot. His death and the destruction of his army, attacking artillery-equipped fieldworks at Castillon, cast doubt on the continuing validity of the paradigm and was taken to heart by, in particular, the Duke of Buckingham. But overall the emphasis remained on seeking a decision as quickly as possible.

MARGUERITE'S ARMY

STARTING FROM MIDDLEHAM, SALISBURY HAD TO PASS through the royalist heartland to join York at Ludlow in the Middle March. He had to move fast, and would have marched around the Clifford stronghold of Skipton (Craven) to regain what I have called the Western Spur of the Great North Road (Map 4) before it reached Halifax. If he then chose to continue east of the section of the Pennines we now call the Peak District, he would necessarily have had to turn west at Derby or Nottingham and march through the Lancastrian Midlands.

However inappropriate as a location from which to rule the country, the Midlands were ideal in military-strategic terms. In the light of the highly fragmented and dispersed distribution of the main estates of the king, the queen, the Prince of Wales and the principal magnates, generalizations about areas of influence need to be made with caution (see Map 2). Still, the queen's fortress triangle of Tutbury, Kenilworth and Leicester gave her the interior lines beloved of strategists, and in 1459 they worked as the textbooks say they should.

Believing that Salisbury did intend to march through the Midlands, on 20 September the king marched from Coventry through Market Harborough to Nottingham. He had earlier made a circuit from Coventry to Nuneaton, Burton upon Trent, Lichfield and Coleshill to rally supporters. This was the main royalist army,

14. THE APPROACHES TO BLORE HEATH
Approximate distances in miles

and he would have been accompanied by the peers most identified with his cause, with the exception of Somerset and Devon in the West Country, and Shrewsbury in the Welsh Marches.

Salisbury had knights from Lancashire, Cheshire and Shropshire in his entourage, but none from Nottinghamshire or Derbyshire. Accordingly there is no reason to believe he ever contemplated marching east of the Pennines. Instead, he marched west from Halifax and then turned south to skirt the western side of the Peak District, with royalist Lancashire on his right flank. Given that Thomas, Baron Stanley, the local commander of the king's forces, was married to Salisbury's daughter Eleanor, and that his younger brother William rode with Salisbury along with the Cheshire knights Robert Bold and Henry Radford, probably as guides, it is fair to assume a laissez-passer had been arranged in advance.

Stanley's treachery is another illustration of the adverse *fortuna* that dogged Marguerite. His namesake father, handpicked by the queen for her son's Council, had died in February, aged only 54. There are no grounds for doubting the elder Stanley's loyalty to the crown. If he had lived, the outcome of the Blore Heath campaign would have been very different.

Armies commonly bivouacked outside towns for the night, and Hyde, Macclesfield and Newcastle under Lyme are plausible candidates for stopping-points for Salisbury's army. At Newcastle under Lyme, at latest, his scouts would have informed him that he was in the middle of a closing ring of royalist armies. Following him at a prudent distance were Stanley's Lancashire men, while the king was marching west from Nottingham, the queen and her Midlands retainers were approaching from the south, and barring his way were Lords Audley and Dudley with the 'Queen's Gallants' of Cheshire.

Fifty-nine-year-old John Sutton, 1st Baron Dudley, has cropped up at regular intervals in preceding chapters. Originally one of the courtiers who became part of the king's inner circle as a member of Suffolk's affinity, he remained close to the king after his mentor's fall and was wounded by his side at St Albans. A member of the prince's council, he had limited military experience dating back to the 1420s. Sixty-one-year-old James Tuchet, 5th Baron Audley, had considerably more experience, but had last commanded troops in 1431. The queen trusted him, but he also owed his appointment to the retainers he could draw from his estates in Cheshire, Shropshire, Staffordshire and Derbyshire.

The list of ninety-nine known or probable royalist casualties compiled by Blore Heath guru Mark Hinsley is revealing. One would have assumed the Cheshire army came mainly from the queen's and the Prince of Wales's lands, with some drawn from Audley's and Dudley's estates, in particular Dudley's manor of Malpas,

15. CLOSE APPROACH TO BLORE HEATH

© Hugh Bicheno

through which the army marched on its way from Chester to Market Drayton. Yet thirty-six of the named casualties came from the manor of Gawsworth outside Macclesfield, held by the Fitton family since 1316, among them Thomas Fitton and eight of his kin. He must have marched to join Audley before it was known that Salisbury had crossed the Pennines.

Estimates of the numbers on either side vary too widely to be useful, but something like 8,000 versus Salisbury's 5,000 seems likely. As to quality, although Robert Ogle and his tough Northumbrians remained in the north, experienced Marcher soldiers once again formed the core of Salisbury's force. They were trumped on the Lancastrian side by thousands of Cheshire archers, famed for their deadliness during the Hundred Years War, formed up along a hedgerow running down from Blore village – much of which still exists.

A battle has at least four identities. The closest to reality is the mosaic of participants' perceptions, soon subsumed into the second, which is a body of accepted facts to which memories retrospectively conform. The third is the canonical version, coloured by the propaganda use to which it is put at the time and later. The fourth seeks to rediscover the first, but is shaped by the intellectual climate of the time in which it is written. There are few accounts from either of the first two categories of the battles of the Wars of the Roses, and the third category source for Blore Heath is the *The Attainder of Richard Duke of York and others*, from the rolls of the Parliament that met in Coventry two months after the battle.

16. BLORE HEATH
23 September 1459
Contours in feet

Based on 1333 tithe map
Distances from Audley's Cross

Mucklestone
3 miles

Newcastle under Lyme
12 miles

Audley's Cross
Farm

Modern A53

Rounhay
Wood

Salisbury
Reserve

Eccleshall
9 miles

Market Drayton
2.5 miles

Archers and footsoldiers

Netherblore

Dudley

Hemp Mill

Wagons
& guns

Reserve

Audley

Wemberton Brook

Archers and footsoldiers along hedgerow

Reserve

Audley

N

Blore

500 yards

© Hugh Bicheno

The Burgundian Jehan de Wavrin wrote the closest fourth category account in about 1470. It is wildly inaccurate in many respects, yet so curiously exact in its description of the battlefield that it is reasonable to assume he had spoken with participants. This does not mean what they told him was accurate with regard to the tactical calculations of the rival commanders. The most influential history has been Edward Hall's *The Union of the Noble and Ilustre Famelies of Lancastre and York*, first published in 1548, republished in 1809 as *Hall's Chronicle*. He drew on oral family history: his grandfather, one of York's councillors, would have heard accounts of the battle from Salisbury's men when they arrived at Ludlow.

Men in combat understandably focus on their immediate surroundings. Even for modern battles, with dozens of 'I was there' memoirs to draw on, the only dependable witness remains the terrain. Although the battlefield of Blore Heath is almost pristine, the standard account of the battle is two-dimensional, and points the finger of blame at Audley for tactical incompetence. He is supposed to have abandoned an impregnable position to make a mounted charge across the brook to utterly predictable destruction, supposedly tricked into doing so by a feigned retreat by Salisbury's right wing. He did not.

The valley of the Wemberton Brook was described as 'not very broad, but somewhat deep'. As it is today, so in 1459 the brook itself would have been lined with bushes and trees. Even after 556 years of erosion, the modern contours answer a number of questions. The road Salisbury wished to follow would have taken him across a steep-sided ford that would have slowed deployment to a crawl, up a long slope overlooked by the royalist right wing commanded by Audley himself, his banners visible on the Blore village plateau.

This was also the logical place for his guns. The ridge and the hedgerow not only concealed Audley's numbers, but at the western end also permitted troops to move behind the lines without being seen by Salisbury, who would have been with his reserves on the high ground at the edge of Rounhay Wood, between the Newcastle under Lyme and Eccleshall roads.

Salisbury's situation could hardly have been more unfavourable. He knew the queen and her retainers were at Eccleshall, 9 miles to the south-east, with the king and the main royalist army not far behind. He also knew the complicity of his Stanley son-in-law would not extend to permitting him to fall back through Newcastle under Lyme, and that he would come off the fence against him if a Lancastrian victory seemed assured.

He was trapped, yet any assault across the brook would certainly be annihilated. Worse, Audley's left wing extended beyond the Hemp Mill pond to another crossing where the contour lines open up and the brook bed becomes less of an obstacle. This is the point where modern roads cross the brook, and is certainly the *passage* described by Wavrin, where an outflanking move by mounted men was practicable.

Even if he could not see them, Salisbury would have assumed, correctly, that the Lancastrians would have a strong force concentrated on their left wing. Thus the most likely sequence is that he paused at the top of the hill while he brought up the wagons and guns, and then sent them together with the Van towards the lower crossing. At the same time the Main and Rear advanced down the hill to form a line within bowshot of the brook and the track along its northern bank. The wagons and guns went to form an artillery fort beyond the mill pond, to cover the crossing and to anchor his right flank. His left flank was reasonably secure behind the steeper slopes to the east of the upper ford, and he would have had an outpost at Netherblore, covering the approach from Eccleshall.

Why did the Lancastrians not interfere with this deployment? Probably because their plan was to stop Salisbury while reinforcements closed in on him. In the usual preliminary parleys they would have called on Salisbury to capitulate on terms. With these rejected and Stanley dawdling at Newcastle under Lyme, Audley and Dudley would have been in a quandary. The queen had given them explicit instructions to bring her Salisbury, dead or alive. If he slipped away during the night they were sure to be branded as cowards for not seeking battle with the odds so greatly in their favour.

The defensive strength of their position worked against offensive action. Bearing in mind the terrain and the fact that all contemporary armies were organized in three 'battles', an interpretation that does not assume Audley was a blunderer would run as follows. The Van on the right wing would advance downhill towards the upper ford to fix Salisbury's left. Audley would then charge with the Main at a diagonal to cross the brook east of the mill pond, the first wave being mounted men-at-arms who would have ridden rapidly down to the brook, hoping to gain tactical surprise. Nobody had ridden into an arrow storm since the early years of the Hundred Years War, and nobody (bar the Heavy Brigade at Balaclava) ever launched a cavalry charge uphill. Therefore, they dismounted and the advance to contact was made on foot, angling towards Salisbury's right flank.

Meanwhile the Rear would have redeployed behind the ridge to join the reserves commanded by Dudley on the royalist left wing. Once Audley's attack had engaged the attention of Salisbury's right wing, Dudley was to advance across the brook and take the fort by frontal assault. The principal drawback to the plan was that it slighted the Lancastrian advantage in archery, but it is hard to see how they could have used their numerical advantage to better effect. It was a good plan and should have worked – but nothing in battle is certain.

Audley's attack was repulsed and he was killed in hand-to-hand combat by a man thirty-five years his junior, 26-year-old Roger Kynaston of Hordley in Shropshire, who thereafter quartered the Tuchet arms with his own. As noted previously, the Kynastons and Eytons were York's confederates in Shropshire, and Roger was the constable of his castle at Denbigh. He and Roger Eyton had probably joined Salisbury only recently, to guide him along the back roads around Shrewsbury, the Talbot clan's stronghold in the Welsh Marches.

The ancient cross marking where Audley fell is well within 50 yards of where I believe Salisbury deployed his archers, so the charge was first slowed by an arrow storm and then driven back by Kynaston and other knights and men-at-arms. This would have created a shambles in the brook bed, as the Main struggled to advance through a hail of arrows from the archers who advanced with the men-at-arms, and from the unengaged centre of Salisbury's line, which would have swung forward like a door to hit them in the flank.

The overthrow of Audley's attack happened so swiftly that Dudley's advance, which was supposed to be a coordinated, knockout punch, went in too late. He could not be seen to hold back while the Main was slaughtered, but with the attention of the men and guns in the wagon fort no longer engaged by Audley, Dudley's chances of success were greatly diminished. Also, the success of his attack required Salisbury to have committed his reserves already. If he did, they were not required to defeat the first attack, and so were free to ride around the fort to hit the second in the flank.

Dudley's men would already have been unsettled by artillery fire, a novelty to most of them, which began to hit them well outside archery range. They would also have seen their comrades of the Main thrown back. Finally, the Lancastrians again suffered the misfortune of losing their commander early. Once Dudley fell, badly wounded, the Cheshire knights and esquires fled, leaving their foot soldiers to be harried mercilessly back towards Market Drayton. The field next to today's bridge over the Tern, against which they were trapped, was once known as 'Deadman's Den'.

The first battle in a war generally sets the tone for what follows: you do not get a second chance to make a first impression. By any abstract calculation of numbers, strategic planning and operational advantage, the Lancastrians should have annihilated Salisbury's army at Blore Heath on 23 September 1459, and snuffed out the Yorkist revolt. Instead, the flower of the queen's army was shattered, and with it her hopes of being able to control events.

Casualty figures for medieval battles are notoriously unreliable, even when the victorious army took the time to bury the dead. In this case Salisbury had no time to devote to such niceties, and even abandoned his own wounded and his guns. Perhaps 1,000 of Salisbury's men, a fifth of his army, would have fallen, consistent with a battle fought at point-blank range by many skilled archers on both sides, followed by a brutal hand-to-hand struggle. The Lancastrians would have lost more than twice as many, the imbalance coming, as always, from the massacre of fleeing men.

There is a believable anecdote that Salisbury left a 'stay behind' party, possibly including the Augustinian friar mentioned in *Gregory's Chronicle*, to fire the captured royalist guns on the far side of Blore Hill at intervals during the night, in order to discourage an advance by the Lancastrians from Eccleshall. Pausing only long enough to loot the royalist baggage train in Market Drayton, he marched the remnant of his army, severely depleted by casualties and desertion, across the Tern bridge to camp at a place still called Salisbury's Hill.

Among the wounded Salisbury left behind were his sons John and Thomas, and the Lancashire knight Thomas Harrington. They were captured 25 miles north of Market Drayton, presumably on their way to the Harrington manor of Brierley in western Yorkshire. Their captor was the 17-year-old namesake son of John Done of the nearby manor of Utkinton in Cheshire, who had been killed along with his eldest son Richard at Blore Heath.

The three men were held at Chester Castle but released not long afterwards, allegedly in the face of a threat of force by local sympathizers, but almost certainly by order of Stanley. When they were captured they were carrying a note from him to Salisbury, congratulating the earl on his victory and offering further assistance. It would have been difficult to sweep the matter under the carpet if the captives had been brought before magistrates and interrogated.

Although it was an astonishing feat of arms, Blore Heath was a pyrrhic victory. Salisbury had to abandon his equipment and brought relatively few men to Ludlow; but in addition the Yorkist line that they were only in rebellion against the 'evil councillors' around the king lost all credibility once they had destroyed the queen's personal army. The offence was judged so heinous that the terms subsequently offered to the Yorkists specifically excluded Salisbury and his subordinate commanders at Blore Heath from all possibility of grace.

As things turned out, however, the greater effect of the battle was that the talismanic swan livery was discredited and the county palatinate of Cheshire never again responded in such numbers when summoned in the name of the prince. Had Audley won, Marguerite would have ensured he became one of the king's principal military councillors, offsetting and perhaps supplanting the temporizing Buckingham. That weapon had now been dashed from her hand, and her ability to influence military decisions greatly diminished.

LANCASTER
RESURGENT

THE LANCASTRIAN NARRATIVE, SET OUT IN THE PRE-
amble to the Acts of Attainder that followed, was that the
Yorkists had plotted to march on Kenilworth to capture or
kill the king. In fact York remained at Ludlow and, as we have seen,
Salisbury's route was designed to skirt the Midlands. Warwick's
line of march from London to Ludlow did, however, pass through
Marguerite's fortress triangle. His force of 300 Calais veterans (half
the number he brought to the 'Loveday'), swelled by Kentish men
who joined them on the march from Dover, had a near miss with
a Lancastrian force led by Somerset at Coleshill, 13 miles north of
Kenilworth.

On the face of it this would seem to support the Lancastrian
accusation – but in fact the fastest route from London to Ludlow
followed Watling Street (Map 3), which arches through northern
Warwickshire, well to the north of Kenilworth. However, to continue on Watling Street much beyond High Cross would have
lengthened his journey considerably, as well as bringing him dangerously close to Lancastrian Shrewsbury. Assuming he cut the corner,
his line of march would indeed have passed through Coleshill. That
said, Warwick knew it was a highly provocative route, and took it to
distract the Lancastrian armies from closing in on his father.

Somerset may have been leading troops from the South West
to join the queen, making the near encounter accidental. Another

17. LUDFORD CAMPAIGN
SOUTH AND CENTRAL WELSH MARCHES

■ **Responsive Yorkist castle or borough**

□ **Unresponsive (Herberts & Vaughans)**

SHROPSHIRE

Clun

Teme

■ **Ludlow**

Leintwardine
Orleton □
Wigmore ■ Croft ■

Lugg

Presteigne ■ Kingland ■
Pembridge ■ Leominster ○

New Radnor ■
Kington ■
Hergest □

Arrow

Stone Street

Weobley ■

Lugg

■ Bredwardine

Wye

□ Hay

Hereford ○

HEREFORDSHIRE

Ledbury ○

*Warwick did not
summon troops
from Glamorgan
and Abergavenny*

□
Three
Castles □
Tretower
Crickhowell □ **Abergavenny**
□

MONMOUTH

Monmouth ○

□ Raglan

Usk

□ Usk

Wye

Caerleon □

Newport ○

Chepstow ○

Severn Estuary

Watling Street

Salisbury

Warwick

Bridgnorth ○

Royal army

Kidderminster ○

Yorkists

Teme

Worcester ○

Royal army

Yorkists

Unnamed Roman road

Malvern ○

Tewkesbury ○

Severn

Gloucester ○

Severn

N

0   50   100
miles

© *Hugh Bicheno*

possibility is that he had already joined Marguerite and, when they learned of Warwick's movements, Somerset led a column south to keep him under observation. A perceived threat from the south might also explain why the army at Eccleshall did not advance to join the attack on Salisbury at Blore Heath. Such a stratagem would have required a military sophistication Warwick did not possess, and its author would probably have been the veteran Andrew Trollope, commander of the Calais contingent.

On arrival at Ludlow, Warwick found that with the exception of the younger Thomas Vaughan of Bredwardine, already accused of treason in the alleged conspiracy involving Countess Alice, the Herberts and Vaughans had not answered York's summons. Despite the queen's efforts to divide and rule, this was not an act of disloyalty to York. They had valid reasons to stay at home in the face of the threat from Jasper Tudor in Pembroke, and from Buckingham's retainers in Brecon and Newport. The same consideration kept Warwick from summoning his own retainers from Glamorgan and Abergavenny.

Viscount Bourchier was absent, but his brother John, Baron Berners, and his son Edward were there. They were joined by the ever-faithful John, Baron Clinton, and the younger Walter Devereux, *de jure* Baron Ferrers of Chartley; also by Edmund, Baron Grey of Ruthyn, and Henry, *de jure* Baron Grey of Powys, who was married to the late Lord Audley's daughter.* Grey had joint possession of Powys Castle with his cousin John Tiptoft, Earl of Worcester, who went on pilgrimage to the Holy Land early in 1458 and did not return until late 1461. Also present were two previous Speakers of the Commons: John Wenlock, who may have come with Warwick, and York's much-persecuted chamberlain William Oldhall.

With the king were the Dukes of Buckingham, Somerset and Exeter, the Earls of Shrewsbury, Wiltshire, Northumberland, Devon,

---

* *De jure* means that they had not yet been summoned to Parliament by the titles they had inherited, in Devereux's case by marriage. Tiptoft had received the summons that might otherwise have gone to Grey.

Oxford and Arundel, Viscount Beaumont and the northern Barons Clifford, Dacre of the North, Egremont, Greystoke and FitzHugh (another Salisbury son-in-law), plus Grey of Ruthyn's brother Grey of Rougemont, Rivers, Roos, Scales, Sudeley and John Tuchet, the new Lord Audley. Greystoke and FitzHugh were supposedly defectors from the Neville affinity, but with the exception of Arundel the rest were committed Lancastrians and the Yorkists should have expected them to turn out against them.

Clearly they did not, or else grossly underestimated the numbers their enemies would bring to the field. Vastly outnumbered, the Yorkists had brought about the conditions for their own defeat and attainder, the very situation they had mobilized to pre-empt. Any chance of another *coup d'état* was gone, and if they fought, they could expect no mercy from the heirs of the men they had killed at St Albans. It is not clear why they did not immediately disband their followers and go into exile, which they must have known was their only realistic option from the moment they came together at Ludlow.

Instead, they embarked on a peculiar peregrination, marching along the River Teme to Worcester, where they met Richard Beauchamp, Bishop of Salisbury, who brought the king's offer of a conditional pardon for all except Salisbury if they disbanded and made submission within six days. The bishop was accompanied by Garter King of Arms, acting as the royal herald, to emphasize that the alternative was war.

York and the Nevilles swore a solemn oath of loyalty to the king in the cathedral, but they rejected his terms. They replied that the reopening of past, pardoned offences at the Coventry Council in June had shown the worth of the king's grace. In addition, the unpunished and excused assassination attempt on Warwick in the Westminster kitchen had demonstrated the will of the king's councillors to destroy and dispossess them. It was all quite plausible, and it was couched in language that presaged its future use as a manifesto.

When the king advanced towards Worcester the Yorkists retreated down the Severn valley to Tewkesbury, presumably hoping the royal coalition would fall apart through lack of leadership and money. Henry was now in warrior mode, however, and his march from Worcester towards Malvern, threatening their line of retreat to Ludlow, left them in no doubt that he was seeking battle. The Yorkists made a forced march to Ledbury, after which they probably followed the line of a Roman road that once ran from Cirencester to Ludlow.

Passing behind the retreating Yorkists, the king marched to Leominster, where he would have lodged at the Benedictine abbey that owned the borough. It was prime campaigning season, with barns and grain stores full from the recent harvest, and religious establishments probably provided the supplies to maintain an exceptionally large army in the field. Once in the Yorkist heartland, however, they would have been released to forage at will, not quite a destructive *chevauchée*, but painful for York's tenants nonetheless.

When the Yorkists reached the bridge over the River Teme at Ludford, about 600 yards from Ludlow Castle, they could retreat no further. The river was in flood and they dug a wet ditch and rampart around the bridgehead, with artillery mounted in wagons around the perimeter. The Yorkists' collapse is traditionally ascribed to the defection of Trollope and the Calais contingent, supposedly induced by Somerset's appeal to their old loyalty to his father, but by this time desertion was the only rational choice. What followed was described with contempt in the preamble to the Act of Attainder:

> [During the night of 12 October] Almighty God smote the hearts of the Duke and Earls from the most presumptuous pride to the most shameful fall of cowardice that could be thought, so that about midnight they stole away out of the field under colour that they would have refreshed them a while in the town of Ludlow [and], leaving their Standards and Banners in their battle directly opposite [the king's] field, fled out of the town unarmed with few persons into Wales.

York also abandoned Duchess Cecily, his younger sons George and Richard, and his youngest daughter Margaret, found standing forlornly at the market cross when the king entered Ludlow. On the face of it a pragmatic decision to spare them the dangers of accompanying (and slowing) York's flight, it was not an action any wife or child was ever likely to forgive. They were placed in the custody of Cecily's older sibling Anne, Duchess of Buckingham, the wife of a man who now detested York, and who could not resist gloating over their father's over-indulged favourite.

According to *Gregory's Chronicle* the royal army sacked Ludlow – if true, probably a breakdown of discipline provoked by lack of pay. Still, it was the traditional reward for soldiers when they captured an enemy town, and the crowning achievement of the queen's long campaign to demonstrate that York's 'good lordship' was worse than valueless:

> The misrule of the king's gallants at Ludlow, when they had drunken enough of wine that was in taverns and other places, they full ungodly smote out the heads of the pipes and hogsheads of wine, that men went wetshod in wine, and then they robbed the town and bare away bedding, cloth and other stuff, and defouled [sic] many women.

There was further evidence of logistical failure and indiscipline when the royal army continued to loot on its way back to Worcester, even though York and the Nevilles had no estates along the Teme valley. This was probably the work of levies discharged at Ludlow, but the result was that the political outcome of the 'rout of Ludford' was more ambiguous than the phrase implies. In the competition for hearts and minds it was a serious error for the king's forces to be seen to have treated any part of his kingdom like conquered enemy territory. It showed him to be either spiteful, or else too weak to control his men.

The pros and cons of what followed are set out in arguably the most illuminating single document to survive from this period. It was discovered bound with other unrelated papers and listed, presumably from a lost title page, as *Somnium Vigilantis* (the reference is to the Latin aphorism *spes est vigilantis somnium* – 'hope is the dream of the vigilant'). Written in Latin, English and French and clearly intended for the eyes of the highest in the land, it is a lawyerly brief, awkwardly crammed into the literary form of a dream about a debate in the presence of the king between advocates of pardon and attainder for the Yorkist lords. At the end a French-speaking arbitrator (a proxy for Marguerite?) calls for exemplary punishment.

The case for the defence is that mercy is a cardinal virtue in a king, and the Yorkists should also be pardoned because the consequences of attainder would be more harmful. They took up arms for the good of the kingdom, and meant no harm to the king. Those who had died were regrettable collateral damage. At a time when foreign enemies threatened, their power should be harnessed to defend the kingdom. Finally, and going to the heart of Henry's dilemma, they commanded support in the country and 'if they be not received into mercy while they are inclined to accept it, it is to be doubted that at another time they will ask for any'.

The rebuttal is comprehensive: mercy shown to notorious and recidivist offenders would undermine the rule of law; the prospect of reconciliation with such wicked men was a chimera; they posed a greater threat than foreign enemies; any support they enjoyed was won by lies; and they were motivated by insatiable ambition, not by any concern for the general welfare. So far so reasonable, but the concluding indictment restated the patently false accusation that had undone whatever chance the 'Loveday' ever had of bringing about a peaceful settlement:

> Furthermore, was it no harm to kill that merciful and most gracious king that now is? And although the blessed grace of God saved him at that time and suffers him as yet to be alive, they nevertheless did their utmost to undo him, and proceeded as far

as they might within the limits of concealing their pernicious intent.

The 'arbitrator' fully supports the case for the prosecution and also sets out the political argument in favour of attainder. It would strike weapons from the hands of the king's enemies and – properly administered – strengthen his own. By handsomely rewarding his supporters from the proceeds of attainder, their interests and lives would become bound to the survival of his regime. To strengthen the bonds further, all who spoke out against the king's supporters should be put to death as though they had impugned the king himself.

The author of *Somnium Vigilantis* was probably Lawrence Booth, Bishop of Durham and Lord Privy Seal, the queen's chancellor and a member of the Prince of Wales's council. To the modern eye, the realpolitik of the 'arbitrator' is simply common sense. Perceptions were radically different in the Middle Ages, however, and more so in the case of Henry VI. He was still haunted by the injustice committed in his name against his uncle Gloucester, and perhaps more aware of how he had been manipulated in 1450 than historians have been willing to consider.

The handpicked Parliament that met in Coventry in November 1459 was primed to attaint the Yorkists and their supporters root and branch – but the king was not. Acts of Attainder were passed against ten peers present at Ludlow plus Salisbury's countess, but Grey of Ruthyn had got his submission in early, swore he had been deceived and dodged the bullet. The king reserved to himself the application of the judgements against Grey of Powys and Ferrers of Chartley (Walter Devereux, whose much-persecuted namesake father had died in April), who had also submitted. Both were pardoned, but while Powys was promptly restored to his lands, Ferrers had to pay a fine and was not pardoned until March 1460.

Also attainted were twelve knights who fought for Salisbury at Blore Heath including William Stanley, although the king rejected the attainder of Lord Stanley. There was, however, an order under

Privy Seal releasing the knights captured after Blore Heath to Stanley's care – which was pointedly ironic as they were long gone, and the court knew it. The administrators of the dukedom and the two earldoms were largely spared, with the exception of those who were at Blore Heath, plus York's treasurer John Clay and Warwick's chamberlain Thomas Colt. Rounding off the list were Wenlock, Oldhall and others who had accompanied York and the Nevilles into exile, a total of thirty individuals.

Thanks to the prior accusation against Countess Alice, and because the only blood had been shed at Blore Heath, the attainders hit the earldom of Salisbury particularly hard, to the benefit of their local rivals. Northumberland was owed £17,000 [£10.8 million] in back pay as Warden of the East March and Constable of Berwick Castle, and the revenues from many of Salisbury's northern manors were assigned to him – but not the titles. Clifford was made Warden of the West March, Beaumont was made steward of Knaresborough Castle and the duchy of Lancaster lands in the West Riding, and Shrewsbury of the castles at Pontefract and Pickering (see Map 9).

Another beneficiary of the crown's recovery of lands previously entrusted to Salisbury was his son-in-law Henry, Lord FitzHugh, who was made steward of Middleham and Richmond. He was among the most lukewarm of the king's supporters, and the appointments only make sense if the aim was to win over others of Salisbury's affinity. To complete the picture, John, made Baron Neville in July 1460 and acting head of the Nevilles of Raby and Brancepeth by the incapacity of his brother, the Earl of Westmorland, was made steward of Sheriff Hutton. Most of the offices vacated by Salisbury's attainder, however, went to royal officials.

Bishop Booth moved to take possession of Warwick's Durham manors, long claimed by his diocese, even before Warwick was attainted, but otherwise the distribution of spoils went ahead at a glacial pace. In Wales, Warwick's retainers refused to give up his castles in Glamorgan and Abergavenny. Elsewhere due legal process was generally respected, which prevented any rapid transfer of property. Even Somerset's and Shrewsbury's mothers were permitted only to reopen their suits with regard to the Beauchamp inheritance, an admission that previous judgements had been flawed but not a reversal in their favour. A number of those attainted had taken the precaution of settling their lands on Lancastrian trustees, and those properties were specifically excluded in the Acts of Attainder.

Practically all of York's manors were heavily mortgaged and the titles would have brought no immediate benefit, so there was little point in redistributing them. Wiltshire was awarded some unencumbered lands in the South West and drew revenues from them, but Beaumont and Exeter, made stewards of Stamford and Fotheringhay respectively, encountered stubborn popular resistance. York's officials found ways to frustrate the new owners, even when it was the king himself. For example, Henry appointed Egremont constable of forfeited Conisbrough Castle, but a year later it was still held against him by York's lifelong retainer Edmund FitzWilliam. In Wales, Denbigh Castle held out against Jasper Tudor until mid-1460.

From the Yorkist point of view the 'Parliament of Devils', responding to the will of the spiteful queen, committed a monstrous injustice against the king's loyal subjects. Marguerite's view would have been that the attainders were a good start to the restoration of order to the kingdom, but the process failed because the policy advocated by 'the arbitrator' in *Somnium Vigilantis* was not fully implemented. To do so, however, would have sparked countless local rebellions, and Henry knew he lacked the military means and the leadership qualities required to impose it.

The same consideration explains why Stanley got a pass for his treachery during the Blore Heath campaign. He was so greatly the dominant lord in southern Lancashire that only military force could evict him. He was also lord of the Isle of Man, and with York himself now in Ireland the prospect of the island becoming a Yorkist base was unthinkable. All Henry could do was to prevent Parliament from including Stanley in the Acts of Attainder, and (vainly) hope he would be grateful.

The favour shown to the two Lords Grey fits the pattern of Marguerite's strategy of trying to weaken York's hold on central and north Wales. It worked with Powys, who was made steward of Montgomery, later raised troops for the crown in Shropshire, and remained loyal for as long as it was practicable. Ruthyn was a much higher risk gamble. It was worth trying to detach him from his alliance with York in Denbigh, but it was deeply unwise to trust him. He was at daggers drawn with the Duke of Exeter over Ampthill, and he was also responsible for the murder of Speaker Tresham in 1450. Possibly the court's judgement was influenced by his Lancastrian ancestry: he was a great-grandson of John of Gaunt.

A third view of the aftermath of Ludford Bridge is that the settlement, as pursued, was the only viable option. The attainted estates were kept intact as an incentive for the exiled lords to submit, and resume their titles and their essential local functions without presuming to dictate to the king how he should govern. There was little chance they would, but in the meantime, the revenues from the forfeited lands could begin to pay off the crown's debts. The alternative would have been to award the estates to today's loyal lords, who would in all probability prove to be tomorrow's over-mighty subjects.

Although almost every lord spiritual and temporal apart from those in exile swore an oath of loyalty to Henry and his son during the Coventry Parliament, Marguerite's triumph was more apparent than real. Every legal right was on her side, but in the end the case for the defence, rejected in *Somnium Vigilantis*, proved prophetic. The rebel lords were not received into mercy, and subsequently did not seek it. The author of the document should have remembered the Latin aphorism *inter arma enim silent leges*: laws are silent in matters of arms.

WARWICK'S APOTHEOSIS

THE YORKISTS SPLIT UP WHEN THEY FLED LUDLOW. Warwick, his father, York's eldest son Edward, Wenlock, Colt and Pickering made their way to south Wales, sailed across the Bristol Channel to Devon, and travelled overland to the Channel coast. They were assisted by John Dynham of Nutwell, a manor on the bank of the River Exe, for which he later joined them in attainder. He provided them with a balinger, a single-masted vessel similar to a Viking longship, and sailed them to Jersey in the Channel Islands, where they were warmly received by Warwick's governor, John Nanfan. Presumably they then boarded one of Warwick's own, more substantial ships.

They sailed into Calais harbour on 2 November, only days before the arrival of about 1,000 men including Anthony Trollope and others who deserted at Ludlow. This expedition was led by 23-year-old Henry Beaufort, Duke of Somerset, appointed governor of Calais by the Coventry Parliament, with Lords Roos and Audley and Humphrey Stafford of Hooke. While he was away in England Warwick had left his uncle, Lord Fauconberg, and Countess Anne in charge, but with no news of him in the twenty days since the Ludford debacle, they would have had difficulty persuading the garrison to hold out if he had not arrived opportunely.

As it was, Thomas Findern and John Marney, Beaufort loyalists from Somerset's father's time as governor of Calais in the early 1450s, opened the gates of the castle at Guînes and the fort at Hammes to him (see Map 12). Findern and Marney were no more motivated by loyalty to the son of their old commander or to the House of Lancaster than Trollope and Clifton had been at Ludford. They simply placed the wrong bet on the eventual outcome, having failed to appreciate that the Company of the Staple would go the other way after the king pronounced an embargo on all trade with Calais.

Bearing in mind that by this time customs officers in every port except Southampton were Warwick's nominees, the embargo may have been the most counter-productive of all the exercises of the royal prerogative during Henry's reign. Trade with Calais was not affected and, far from cowing the Staplers, it resolved any remaining doubts they may have entertained. Somerset arrived with a war chest of 200 marks [£85,000], all Wiltshire had been able to scrape together in addition to the first payment of Somerset's indentures for troops. In contrast the Staplers made Warwick a personal loan of £3,850 [£2.45 million] and became his financial partners in the military exploits that followed.

Almost as tellingly, the Duke of Burgundy also backed Warwick. He renewed the truce negotiated at Marck in 1457, and ignored a delegation sent by King Henry. At the same time his heir Charles, Count of Charolais, became fascinated by Somerset's bold playing of a very weak hand. One gets the impression that, for the Burgundian court, reports from their agents about the doings of the English at Calais became something like a soap opera, or at least a large-scale chivalric tournament with wonderfully entertaining characters.

Warwick's quid pro quo for the truce had been to desist from attacking Burgundian shipping, while continuing his naval war against France, and the English court could offer nothing of comparable value. In addition he now provided political cover for Burgundian raids into north-eastern France by claiming them as his own, burnishing his credentials as the champion of England against the hated French, at no expense to himself.

The asking price of a warlord in contemporary Italy reflected his cunning (*furbizia*) more than his military prowess. Thus also Warwick. The key to understanding his international stature is that he embodied the paradigm shift which took place during the Renaissance, from lip service to Christian values to the unashamed exaltation of Classical manliness – bravery, strength, pride and ruthlessness (Niccolò Machiavelli's amoral *virtù*). Pope Pius II lamented the change in his autobiographical *Commentaries* (my italics): 'While men live they take pleasure in the glory of the present, which they hope will continue after death. It is this which sustains the most brilliant intellects, *and even more than the hope of a celestial life*, which once begun shall never end, cheers and refreshes the heart of man.'

Adding to Warwick's already extravagant *fortuna*, Charles VII of France was by now very ill with what sounds like diabetes, and beset by other problems. Chief among them was that the Dauphin Louis had sought asylum with the Duke of Burgundy in 1456, and furiously rejected all his father's attempts at reconciliation. Louis of Luxembourg, Count of Saint-Pol, Jacquetta's brother and Marguerite's brother-in-law, was also involved in a military-diplomatic rats' nest too off-topic to unravel here. Suffice it to say that the chronic problems England had with Scotland were fully replicated in France's north-eastern March.

Charles also had to deal with Jean V, Count of Armagnac, one of the more outrageous French nobles. Jean embarked on a relationship with his sister Isabelle, who bore him three children, and they were excommunicated after Jean forged a Papal Bull to permit them to marry. When he also rejected the candidate for Bishop of Auch agreed between the king and the pope, and installed his own bastard half-brother, Charles VII had no option but to invade Armagnac once more.

Somerset's campaign must have been covertly subsidized by Charles VII because Warwick, decisively assisted by his Kentish supporters, prevented any significant support reaching him from England. Some of Warwick's most important warships had been impounded at Sandwich, where a second expedition of 1,000 men was being assembled by Richard Woodville, Baron Rivers, and Gervase Clifton, the previous Calais treasurer and another Ludford defector to the royalists. Rivers had replaced Buckingham as Warden of the Cinque Ports, and was accompanied by Jacquetta and 19-year-old Anthony, their eldest son.

Warwick gambled by sending his remaining ships and his most trustworthy troops under Dynham and Wenlock to make a combined assault on Sandwich. Wenlock landed nearby during the night of 14/15 January and in the morning, when Dynham sailed into harbour firing his guns, achieved tactical surprise by attacking from the landward side. Clifton got away, but Rivers, Jacquetta and Anthony were captured. Warwick's men sailed back to Calais with them, and with the ships, money, equipment and no few of the troops so painfully assembled. The exploit marked the apotheosis of Warwick among the Kentish men, and they were to remain his most devoted followers in the years to come.

Among the men captured at Sandwich were men who had deserted Warwick at Ludford, and they were brought to Calais for execution in a barbaric night-time ritual that included parading Rivers and his son through the streets by torchlight. They were spared, but brought before Warwick, Salisbury and March, sitting on a dais in the central square, who berated and humiliated them as parvenus while boasting of their own royal blood and ancient lineages.

Warwick now had his fleet back and put it to good use. Piracy resumed, the good times rolled once more in Calais, and defections to Somerset ceased. The traffic in fact reversed. In one of Somerset's frequent attacks on the Calais perimeter, Lord Audley and Humphrey Stafford of Hooke were captured. Honourably treated by Edward, they became two of his most devoted followers. Warwick felt so secure that in late February he set out to meet York in Ireland, leaving his father and March behind and seizing prizes indiscriminately as he went, to arrive magnificently on 16 March. As York's biographer acutely comments:

It must have been evident, as Warwick's twenty-six ships sailed into Waterford harbour, that the earl was not only a very able commander, but that whole companies of men and ships were defecting from the Lancastrian regime to serve him. Such defections had been singularly absent from York's career hitherto. The duke may have had the blood of kings in his veins, but it was Warwick who knew his way to his potential subjects' hearts.

Warwick's mother, Countess Alice, was among those who welcomed him. It is not recorded how she made her way from Middleham to Ireland, but reasonable to assume, since she had to pass through Lancashire, that Lord Stanley had much to do with it. Unlike 'proud Cis' in the less than tender care of her sister, Alice bore her husband no ill will, so it is also reasonable to assume she and Salisbury had prepared an escape plan before he set out for the ill-fated rendezvous at Ludlow. Of course it helped that Alice had no minor children, although 17-year-old Margaret, her unmarried youngest, probably accompanied her.

York, Warwick and the fleet soon transferred to Dublin, where the Irish Parliament was in session from 7 March to 5 May. The concrete evidence in the harbour of the strength of the Yorkist cause must have influenced the proceedings, which were entirely favourable to York's cause. As Earl of Ulster he was already strong, and even before Warwick's arrival the Parliament had ratified his appointment as lieutenant, and declared that in the absence of the king himself, York was due all the rights and privileges of royalty.

This was heady stuff both for York and the Anglo-Irish under the leadership of York's deputy, Thomas Fitzgerald, Earl of Kildare, who emerged with a far greater degree of self-government than they had previously enjoyed. It may have been at the suggestion of Warwick, applying the lessons learned from his control of the money supply in Calais, that York also created an autonomous Irish currency to halt the outflow of silver to England. The effect of this and other measures designed to boost Irish trade, however, did little to address

York's immediate need of money and men with which to return to England.

The Irish economy was mainly subsistence-agrarian, and Parliament struggled even to collect the annual subsidy of £360 [£230,000] voted in 1458. Given that Ireland was in a perpetual state of war, and the local lords needed their armed retinues to defend their own lands, the best they could do was grant York a mounted archer for every twenty freeholders – while he was in Ireland. York raised some money from the English merchants of Dublin by the sale of a royal charter to form a guild, and some Anglo-Irish families did contribute men-at-arms to his eventual return to England – but the initiative plainly lay with Warwick.

Before Warwick departed in early May the two men agreed a manifesto listing twelve grievances. The first concerned the abuse of the church, the significance of which is explained below. The second and fourth concerned the crown's abuse of purveyance, the right of the sovereign to fix the price of provisions and transport below market price in time of war. Indeed, much of the manifesto dwelt on the increasingly arbitrary expedients to which the court had been driven by its rejection of resumption, including repeated accusations that the dreaded French *taille* (land tax) was being introduced by the back door.

Taken together the charges had the propaganda virtues of being reasonably close to the truth, and also harking back to the arguments used by Henry IV to justify overthrowing Richard II. They also fastened culpability around the neck of Marguerite, doubly guilty of being both French and a 'designing woman'. She and Beaumont, Shrewsbury and Wiltshire were alleged to have enriched themselves at public expense, and to be seeking to abolish ancient English liberties.*

After Warwick sailed back to Calais, driving a fleet hastily assembled by the Duke of Exeter back to port, the papacy provided the

---

* Anyone who thinks there is anything modern about artfully spinning naked self-interest as a boon to humankind would be well advised to study this document.

cherry on the top of his brimming sundae of *fortuna*. As in everything to do with the medieval Church, the backstory is wonderfully intricate; but as it affects our narrative the key component is that Pius II had become obsessed with launching a crusade against the Ottoman Empire. In 1459 he appointed Francesco Coppini, made Bishop of Terni in 1458 at the instigation of Duke Francesco Sforza of Milan, as his legate to England, charged with obtaining King Henry's support for the crusade.

Pius was deeply misogynist, probably from self-disgust over his sexual incontinence as a young man. In the course of political missions to Scotland, England and Strasbourg in the 1430s, he had sired two bastard children. During 1459–61 the pope's opinion of events in England, as recorded in his *Commentaries*, seems to have been based on Coppini's reports. These, in turn, reflected Coppini's ambition to win an English bishopric and/or a cardinalate, in which he was encouraged by Warwick after they met in Calais in May 1460.

Pius would not have promoted Coppini to legate *a latere* (plenipotentiary) in England and its dominions without the consent of Archbishop Bourchier, who had his own axe to grind with the Lancastrian regime. In February 1460 the pope granted Coppini the right to 'compel the disobedient by ecclesiastical censure and deprivation and to appoint preachers' to proselytize the crusade, and to offer indulgences for all their sins to those who made even modest financial contributions.

Yet, a month later, Coppini wrote to Sforza from Bruges, alleging he had left England on the advice of Warwick – who was at the time embarked on his expedition to Ireland. So, Coppini lied to his patron but not to his employer, as the pope continued to show confidence in his ability to raise funds in England for the crusade, something he would not have done if Coppini's departure had been unauthorized.

What was it Coppini could not tell Sforza, but had no need to explain to Pius II? The most likely answer is that he was acting on the advice of Archbishop Bourchier, who had convinced the pope that Marguerite was the greatest obstacle to England contributing to the crusade.

Forensic analysis of correspondence between Canterbury and Rome may reveal secret writing (commonly used by Renaissance princes when plotting nefarious deeds) in which the archbishop committed secular treason, and which influenced the pope to support the Yorkist cause. Using the vainglorious Coppini as their cat's-paw gave pope and archbishop deniability, while the ambitious legate, frantic for advancement, had every reason to conceal the source of his instructions. It was no less significant that wealthy Bishop William Grey of Ely, a papal appointee and previously neutral, came out for the Yorkists at this time.

Archbishop Bourchier's full siblings were committed Yorkists, and he was also acutely aware that the sympathy of his dangerously volatile Kentish flock was overwhelmingly favourable to Warwick. Thus it came about that when Warwick invaded England in June 1460, Bourchier had summoned a convocation in London to vote the ecclesiastical tenth requested by the pope for his crusade. Presumably it went to Warwick instead, as Pius never saw a penny of it.

Whether or not the hypothetical backstory can be established, when Coppini and Warwick met in May the legate became an active partisan of the Yorkist cause, without rebuke from the pope at the time, or subsequently in the *Commentaries*. On 24 June Fauconberg and Dynham launched another pre-emptive raid on Sandwich, where Osbert Mountfort, previously in command of Rysbank and dismissed by Warwick in 1456, was gathering reinforcements for Somerset. This time there was no surprise and Dynham was seriously wounded in the fighting, but Fauconberg prevailed. Mountfort was sent back to Calais and beheaded.

Two days later Warwick, Salisbury and March arrived at Sandwich and set out on a triumphal progression to London. Kentish men flocked to their banners, and two lords sent to oppose them defected. They were the perennial Yorkist Cobham, who had gained some measure of Lancastrian trust by not joining the Ludlow rebellion, and Bergavenny, the uncle whom Warwick had dispossessed. An explanation why Buckingham had been replaced by Rivers as Warden of the Cinque Ports emerges from the modifications made to the Yorkist manifesto as they marched towards London: the Kentish men demanded Buckingham be added to the short list of evil councillors to be done away with, for being 'fat of grease' from profiteering.

If it were not that Warwick had given himself so little time to prepare it since returning from Ireland, one would be tempted to believe the unbridled popular joy at his return reported by Wavrin had been carefully orchestrated. The Yorkist lords swept into London, where a popular uprising forced Lord Scales and several other Lancastrian lords to retreat to the Tower. The Yorkists were welcomed by the mayor and aldermen, the Bishop of Ely and Warwick's brother, the Bishop of Exeter. They then went to St Paul's, where the Canterbury Convocation was in session, and renewed their oath of allegiance to the king, swearing they had come to rescue him from his wicked entourage.

As though the loss of Kent and London was not enough, Coppini now made public the text of a long letter from him to the king, copies of which had been sent to the pope and to Marguerite. It portrayed the Yorkist lords and their motives in the best possible light, and called on Henry to accept Coppini's mediation, or else bear full responsibility for the consequences: 'You can prevent this if you will, and if you do not you will be guilty in the sight of God in that awful day of judgement in which I shall also stand and require of your hand the English blood, if it be spilt.' In his covering letter to Pius II, Coppini waxed eloquent about his own skills as a conciliator:

> Since fate and necessity had caused me to be as it were an angel
> of peace and a mediator, [the people] looked upon me also with
> incredible applause, with reverence and tears, welcomed me,

honoured me, praising the Lord and giving thanks with clasped hands to Your Holiness because you had sent back and restored to them your legate, whose departure with his work undone they had lately mourned.

Self-seeking charlatan he may have been, but Coppini's authority as papal legate *a latere* was unquestionable. The effect of his letter on the deeply pious Henry – if he were permitted to read and respond to it – would almost certainly have been capitulation. It follows that either it was kept from him, or else he was no longer a free agent. Either way, it helps to explain what happened in one of the most enigmatic battles of the Wars of the Roses.

BETRAYAL

FOLLOWING THEIR TUMULTUOUS WELCOME IN KENT and unopposed admission to London, Warwick, Salisbury, Fauconberg and Edward of March were joined by John Mowbray, Duke of Norfolk and Henry, Viscount Bourchier. The bigger turn-out, however, was by the lords spiritual conveniently convoked by Henry's brother Thomas, Archbishop of Canterbury. Along with Coppini, they were to play a uniquely public role in the following campaign.

Within a few days, on 4 July, Fauconberg set out for the Midlands along Watling Street with a Van of mounted archers and hobilars. Word had come that the king's army was trundling south from the queen's triangle of Kenilworth, Tutbury and Leicester with about 80 guns previously taken from the Tower and used to equip her castles. Fauconberg's task was to cause the royal army to halt well short of London, to give time for Warwick to recruit more troops and to gather guns. We know Warwick set out from London with perhaps thirty guns, and with the Tower armoury still in enemy hands he probably got them from his fleet.

Humphrey Stafford, Duke of Buckingham, commanded the royal army, which, by the time it halted just south of Northampton, included John Talbot, Earl of Shrewsbury, John, Viscount Beaumont, Thomas Percy, Baron Egremont, and Edmund, Baron Grey of Ruthyn. It was probably not Fauconberg who caused them to halt where they did. Northampton was 67 miles from London and roughly equidistant from Kenilworth and Leicester. It was close to some of Buckingham's larger manors, notably Oakham, and to Beaumont's estates in Lincolnshire and Leicestershire. Fatefully, however, it was also very close to the Bedfordshire lands of the recently pardoned Grey of Ruthyn, which explains his presence in an army otherwise composed of unswervingly loyal Lancastrians.

We have no idea how many men each side brought to the field. Since Buckingham adopted a static defensive position he must have been outnumbered, and an educated guess is that he had 10,000 or less against the rebels' 15,000 or more. Much of the Shrewsbury affinity would have been on guard to prevent York landing in north Wales while Jasper Tudor guarded the south, and Egremont had no significant following. He was there in representation of the Percys while the northern lords rallied to his brother Northumberland at York. Possibly the idea was to hold off the rebels until the northerners could join the royal army.

Warwick, Fauconberg, March and Viscount Bourchier left Salisbury and the other Yorkist lords to besiege the Lancastrian lords in the Tower and to secure London. The rebel army was not only more numerous but also had a high proportion of volunteers, including many veterans of the fall of Normandy. They caught up with Fauconberg at Dunstable and then marched together on Northampton, accompanied by Archbishop Bourchier, Papal Legate Coppini and several bishops. The rebel army camped for the night of 9/10 July at a 'mountain', possibly Hunsbury Hill, 2 miles south-east of Northampton.

In terms of eyewitness or at least close contemporary testimony, on a scale of one to ten among the battles of the Wars of the Roses, Northampton is the ten.* Since the combat was almost perfunctory, the principal interest lies in locating exactly where it took place. I beg the reader's indulgence while I illustrate the difficulty medieval

* Mortimer's Cross, as we shall see, is the zero.

Northampton

COW MEADOW

Derngate

Sandyford Road

Nunn Mills

River Nene

Menthynfeld?

Cotton End

FLOOD PLAIN

COW PASTURE

Bedford Way

Fishponds

Dispersed course

Church?

Meadow Leys

Delapre Abbey and enclosure

London Road

COW LEYS

Windmill Hill

Fauconberg

Warwick

Battle Dyke

March

Battle Dyke Furlong

Eleanor Cross

Fulbrook

Grey of Ruthyn

HILL

DELAPRE WOOD

Hardingstone

N

18. BATTLEFIELD OF NORTHAMPTON

Based on 1740 & 1756 maps

0   250   500   750

yards

© Hugh Bicheno

historians encounter even when dealing with apparently well-documented events.

According to *An English Chronicle of the reigns of Richard II, Henry IV, Henry V and Henry VI*, written by a Yorkist Londoner: 'The king at Northampton lay at Friars, and had ordained there a strong and mighty field, in the meadows beside the Nunnery, armed and arrayed with guns, having the river at his back.' Warwick's Burgundian hagiographer Jehan de Wavrin locates it 'in a park outside the town beside a little stream'. Dating from 1471, *An English Chronicle* states it took place 'beside Northampton in the Newfield between Hardingstone and Sandyford'.

Written between 1462 and 1471, *Benet's Chronicle* says Henry had 20,000 men in a fortified camp between Hardingstone and Delapre Abbey, but Benet's figures are always exaggerated. Finally, and possibly reflecting comments by Archbishop Bourchier, who viewed the battle from the top of the hill crowned by the Eleanor Cross (erected by Edward I in 1292 and still there, albeit headless, today), the Canterbury monk John Stone wrote: 'And for the field's name on the one part on the north-east side is called Cowemedewe. And that other part is called Menthynfeld. And for the other part is called Sandyngford bridge next to the towne. On the east side there is a water mill called Sandford mill.'

This is not helpful. As Map 18 shows, Cow Meadow was north of the River Nene outside the town walls, bounded by the Sandyford Road, which entered Northampton through the south-western Derngate. Possibly Stone confused it with Cow Pasture, the name given to the flood plain south of the river in a 1740 map. This map also identifies a 'Moorfield', which might have been 'Menthynfeld' 280 years earlier. The only water mills were on an island in the river, with bridges to both banks. The fundamental problem with Stone's description is that he seems to locate the battlefield between the abbey and the river, which would not have been observable from the Eleanor Cross.

A 1756 map identifies a 'Battle Dyke' on the west side and the adjacent 'Battle Furlong' on the east side of the Fulbrook, a stream born of a spring on Hardingstone Hill, on top of which the Eleanor Cross is located. Over time the brook may have altered its course to follow the line of excavation behind the rampart once built along its eastern bank – in fact it may have begun to do so during the battle, as one account says the rain was so heavy 'the guns lay deep in the water', which would be consistent with the stream overflowing.*

The hypothesis portrayed in Map 18 accepts that Benet's description of the location is correct and that Wavrin was right about the topographical details. Thus the Fulbrook was the 'little stream', and the abbey farmlands, which might be described as a 'park', stretched to the woods running from the Eleanor Cross towards the township of Hardingstone. Another source states that Bishop Wainflete resigned as Lord Chancellor and returned the Great Seal to the king three days before the battle in 'Hardingstone Field', next to Delapre Abbey.

The artillery fortification along the Fulbrook commanded the London Road, with the woods covering the left flank and the abbey enclosure the right. Another stream, feeding two fish ponds, presented a further obstacle to a frontal assault, while any attempt to outflank the position along the Hardingstone Road would have been vulnerable to ambush from Delapre Wood. It was a strong position, akin to the one at Castillon on which Talbot's last charge broke in 1453.

The fullest account of the battle is in *An English Chronicle*, which also illuminates the role played by Archbishop Bourchier:

> The earls… sent certain bishops to the king beseeching him that
> to avoid the effusion of Christian blood he should admit and
> suffer the earls to come to his presence to declare themselves
> as they were. The Duke of Buckingham that stood beside the

---

* My reconstruction draws heavily on Northampton Council's online *Site of the Battle of Northampton 1460: Conservation Management Plan*, and on 'War in Writing' in *Medieval Warfare* (June 2015) by battle of Northampton guru Mike Ingram.

> king said to them, 'You come not as bishops to treat for peace
> but as men of arms', because they brought with them a notable
> company of men of arms. They answered and said, 'We come
> thus for the security of our persons, for those that be about the
> king are not our friends'. 'Forsooth', said the duke, 'the Earl of
> Warwick shall not come to the king's presence, and if he comes
> he shall die'.

The *Registra* of Abbot Whethamstede of St Albans identifies Richard
Beauchamp, Bishop of Salisbury, as the leader of this episcopal delegation. The other bishops were probably Grey of Ely and Neville
of Exeter. However, *An English Chronicle* adds that the archbishop
then sent Bishop Stanberry of Hereford, the king's confessor, who
instead of appealing for the king to accept mediation, 'exhorted
and encouraged the king's party to fight'. Stanberry did not return
from a second visit 'but privily departed away'. As a result, 'after the
battle he was committed to the castle of Warwick, where he was
long in prison'.

In his *Commentaries* Pope Pius II states that Coppini was with
Warwick's army and 'raised the standard of the Church of Rome,
and on the ground that they were to do battle against the enemies
of the Faith, he granted plenary remission of sins to those who
were to fight on the side of the Earl of Warwick'. He also 'pronounced anathema on their enemies, exhibiting before the camp
an Apostolic letter which was believed to contain this formulation,
though in reality its contents were quite different'.

Six months later, when the tide of war seemed to have turned
against the Yorkists, Coppini sent an indirect message to Marguerite
frantically denying he had excommunicated the king's army. But
why would Pius II have lied in his private journal? He did dismiss
Coppini from his bishopric in 1462, but for other reasons. Unless
we are to believe the pope was attempting to deceive himself, there
can be no doubt Coppini acted in an outrageously partisan manner,
and that Pius II approved.

Apoplectic fury that the Church had come out for the Yorkists would, of course, explain why Buckingham refused the bishops access to the king, and Stanberry would have warned the duke and Beaumont of their likely fate if Henry accepted Coppini's mediation. Buckingham's baffled rage was further inflamed by seeing his Bourchier half-brothers openly among the enemies in arms against him, many of them Kentish men who would kill him on sight.

The Yorkists formed the usual three battles parallel to the earthworks along the London Road, and Wavrin says the attack was led by the 'advance guard, commanded by Lord Fauconberg'. Warwick's battle arrived at the Fulbrook a little later, and March's later still. If accurately described, this was an oblique attack of the kind later made famous by Frederick the Great. It works by drawing the enemy's attention and reserves to the first flank attacked and then to the centre, leaving the remaining flank vulnerable to the knockout blow. In this case, the last flank attacked, on the Lancastrian left, was held by Grey of Ruthyn.

Grey was probably a Yorkist Trojan Horse from the start, and must also have insisted that his submission should be made to March as his father's representative; such a vital role would not otherwise have been entrusted to an 18-year-old who was leading men into battle for the first time. While the rain had silenced the royal artillery, it also made the earth rampart impossibly slippery, and Grey's men had to help March's troops climb over it.* The royalist position collapsed immediately and the levies fled towards the bridges over the Nene, where the crush pushed hundreds to drown in the river.

As their army collapsed the Lancastrian lords made a last stand around the king's tent and were slaughtered. Apart from them, however, there were remarkably few combat casualties – one source estimates as few as fifty-eight. This would be consistent with a battle in which the rain not only silenced the guns but also wet the archers' bowstrings, so they could only loose a shaft or two with the

---

* His reward for this well-designed act of cold-blooded treachery was the definitive award of Ampthill and, eventually, the earldom of Kent.

spare strings they kept in their hats. If the earthworks were too slick to climb, then Fauconberg's and Warwick's battles may not have come to hand strokes at all, but rather milled around in the mud on the other side, making a lot of noise. As at St Albans, the battle was decided by a distraction followed by an abrupt dislocation of expectations.

The defeat was an unqualified disaster for the Lancastrian cause. The king was now in their enemies' possession and they had also lost three of their greatest magnates. Buckingham was succeeded by his 5-year-old grandson and Shrewsbury by his 12-year-old son, leaving two of the largest Lancastrian affinities leaderless. Only Beaumont's affinity still had a leader in his 22-year-old son, who was with his father at Northampton. He was wounded but survived to join the other lords bent on avenging the deaths of their sires.

Of the named 'evil councillors' only Wiltshire had escaped the net. Following the failure of the Duke of Exeter to intercept Warwick on his return voyage from Ireland to Calais, Wiltshire had been entrusted with raising a fleet to guard the Irish Sea and to rouse the Butler affinity against York's authority in Ireland, meeting with success in neither endeavour. Not long after Northampton he sailed to Brittany on instructions from Marguerite to ask the new Duke Frañsez II to back the Lancastrian cause. The death of Arzhur III, his immediate predecessor, was a heavy blow to Marguerite as he was none other than the Count de Richemont, erstwhile Constable of France and a loyal supporter of the House of Anjou.

Two weeks after Northampton the Lancastrian lords holding the Tower of London capitulated. Although their leader, Lord Scales, was granted a safe conduct, it was not respected by the watermen supposed to row him to safety. They murdered him and dumped his body in the grounds of a riverbank priory. He was 63 years old, a distinguished Normandy veteran who had led an army for York in the later stages of the Hundred Years War, and godfather to Edward of March.

Warwick and March attended his funeral and deeply regretted

the murder; but they also executed – for treason – six of the Duke of Exeter's retainers who had fought their way into the Tower. They had acted in the service of their legitimate sovereign, which clearly could not be treason, but the Yorkist lords needed to throw the mob a bone. They could only hope to channel popular fury – they could no more control it than a surfer controls a wave.

The other lords who had held the Tower with Scales were more fortunate. Henry Bromflete, Baron Vescy, had not previously participated, and after this wisely retired from the conflict. Richard West, Baron de la Warr, temporarily defected to the Yorkist cause. John, Baron Lovell, held multiple titles of nobility and had landholdings in the Midlands an earl might envy. He continued to fight for Lancaster. Robert, Baron Hungerford, had only recently returned from French captivity after payment of a ruinous ransom. He was released to go on a pilgrimage.

Northampton also destroyed any hope Somerset retained of capturing Calais. Warwick returned and on 8 August met Somerset to agree terms of capitulation for Guînes and Hammes. As the alternative was that Somerset might sell them to France, the terms were generous. Somerset, Roos, Trollope and their men were paid to march unhindered to France with their equipment, and Rivers and his son were released to join them.* They were welcomed by Charles VII, who gave them more money and lent them ships and an escort to take them back to England. Somerset had sworn not to bear arms against Warwick in the future, but saw no reason to keep his word to an oath-breaker.

Following the battle Marguerite and her son fled from Kenilworth with what remained of the royal plate and jewellery, and a small escort. According to William Gregory she was robbed near Malpas in Cheshire by a member of her entourage whom she had raised from nothing to the status of gentleman, and completed the journey to Harlech Castle riding pillion behind a young squire. The people

---

* Jacquetta would have been sent back to England soon after capture.

of north Wales received their prince and his mother warmly, but she could not remain once the Yorkist lords learned where she was:

> And from there she moved in secret to Lord Jasper, Lord and Earl of Pembroke, for she dared abide in no place openly. The cause was that counterfeit tokens were sent to her as though they had come from [her husband]... but she gave them no credence; for at the king's departing from Coventry toward the field of Northampton, he kissed her and blessed the prince, and commanded that she should not come to him until he sent her a special token that no man knew but the king and she. For the [Yorkist] lords greatly wished to bring her to London, as they knew full well that all the workings that were done were her doing, for she was much more clever than the king...

Some spirit remained in the defeated and captive king, it seems. Despite his many failings, one cannot withhold sympathy for him, miserably aware his life hung by a thread and humiliatingly paraded through London in a cynical mockery of a triumphal procession. Most devastating of all would have been to discover that not only his bishops but even the pope had turned against him. The following passage in the *Commentaries*, although its words are attributed to Warwick by Pius II, reflects the pontiff's own opinion and crusading hopes:

> Our king is a dolt and a fool who is ruled instead of ruling. The royal power is in the hands of his wife and those who defile the King's chamber... Many feel as I do, among them the Duke of York, who would now be on the throne if there were any regard for justice... If God gives us victory, we shall drive our foes from the King's side and ourselves govern the Kingdom. The King will retain only the bare name of sovereign... before long, when the Kingdom is again at peace, we will equip a fleet in defence of religion.

If Pius believed the already bankrupt English crown would be able to contribute to his crusade after a further round of civil war, he had parted company with reality. It is a sobering thought that the papacy's decisive intervention in the internal affairs of the kingdom was based on a delusion as profound as any of poor Henry's wishful thinking.

MARGUERITE
AND SON

A FTER NORTHAMPTON MARGUERITE'S SITUATION WAS desperate. Her husband was now a prisoner and, although this freed her to take personal command of the defence of her son's right, it permitted her enemies to issue orders in the king's name. Financially, the loss of London and the South East, and the defection of the Canterbury Convocation, were body blows. Strategically, the battle had nullified the power base she had built up since 1455: her Midlands domain around the fortress-triangle of Kenilworth, Tutbury and Leicester was lost, as were her castles at Wallingford and Berkhamsted.

Any chance of limiting Stanley's influence in Cheshire had gone with the death of Shrewsbury and the ensuing defection of the previously dog-loyal Dudley. Her attempt to undermine York's influence in the Marches was also undone, but in Wales itself loyalists held a crescent from recently taken Denbigh Castle around the coast to Carmarthen. Grey of Powys held Montgomery for her, and Buckingham's affinity was still strong in Brecknock, but the only really safe area was Jasper Tudor's isolated Pembroke.

Possession of the Welsh coast would have been more useful if there had been any hope of supplanting York in Ireland, but that was a pipe dream. Wiltshire had neglected his earldom of Ormonde, and leadership of the Anglo-Irish was now exercised by the firmly Yorkist Earl of Kildare. Money might persuade the Gaelic lords to provide troops, but they were mainly concerned with fighting among themselves. The ports on the Pembroke peninsula were, nonetheless, among the few geostrategic assets remaining to the Lancastrian cause.

With the return of Somerset to Corfe the situation in the West Country was more promising. Henry Beaufort was a vigorous and now militarily experienced 24-year-old, and loyal to the House of Lancaster in a way his father had never been. Marguerite also had the unqualified support of 28-year-old Thomas Courtenay, who was married to her niece and had succeeded his namesake father as Earl of Devon two years previously. A Yorkist triumph would see his efforts to drive Bonville out of Devon reversed. Lastly, she could count on Alexander Hody, a major landowner around Yorkist Bridgwater in north-central Somerset and, for what he was worth, the Duke of Exeter, who had lands in Somerset and Dorset.

Wales and the West Country aside, the principal hope of the Lancastrian cause now lay in the North. With Stanberry imprisoned, apart from her confessor Walter Lyhert at Norwich and Thomas Bird at St Asaph, she could no longer count on the support of any of the bishops in the archdiocese of Canterbury. In contrast, with the Booth brothers at York and Durham, and William Percy at Carlisle, the archdiocese of York was solidly hers. While far poorer than Canterbury, in the absence of any other major source of revenue it can be assumed the church in the North subsidized the Lancastrian cause in 1460–1.

Added to which Yorkist influence in the North had been curtailed to the benefit of the Percys and their allies. However, the degree to which Neville influence had been supplanted in the region should not be overestimated. Before he set out from Middleham Castle in 1459, Salisbury appears to have secretly agreed that Ralph, Baron Greystoke, would act as his Trojan Horse within the Lancastrian ranks should the rebellion not prosper. It is probable that Salisbury had also made a similar arrangement with his son-in-law Lord FitzHugh, but it seems FitzHugh's head may have been turned when he benefited so greatly from Salisbury's attainder.*

With the king now the hostage of their enemies, Northumberland and the other northern lords needed no urging from Marguerite to cast off the restraint he had imposed on them, and they raided Yorkist manors across the North. The raids were not destructive and were more akin to peremptory tax collections. Although the Parliament summoned by Warwick had repealed the 1459 attainders, the letter of the law was now irrelevant in the North.

What Marguerite could and did do, using dispatch boats out of Tenby, was to coordinate the mobilization of her own West Country followers and officials. She begged Somerset, Devon and Hody to gather their followers and march north to meet her at the port of Hull, on the River Humber in the East Riding of Yorkshire. To 'all those servants that loved her or wished to keep and enjoy her office', she wrote, 'all excuses ceasing and other occupations left, you shape yourselves to be with us [at Hull] in all haste possible, for certain causes that move us, which shall be declared to you at your coming'. This they did, marching up the Fosse Way past Bath, through Cirencester and past Coventry to join the northern lords.

The Lancastrians quickly agreed they would all wear the Prince of Wales's livery, and one of the very few surviving Lancastrian proclamations from this time took the form of a letter from Prince Edward to the inhabitants of London. It was written after York dropped the pretence of being a loyal subject and tried to claim the throne for himself (see following chapter). In it the prince denounced 'that horrible and falsely forsworn traitor calling himself duke of York, mortal enemy unto my lord, to my lady and to us, [who] has blinded my lord's subjects and, to [the end of] obtaining his subtly contrived treason, by untrue means often times provoked them to commotions, stirrings and unlawful assembly against his royal estate'.

Aware that Warwick's propaganda machine was already cranking

---

* Greystoke did well out of it, but several years passed before Warwick forgave FitzHugh.

up atavistic fear of 'the Northmen' among the southern English, Marguerite herself wrote a rebuttal addressed to the council of the City of London, in which she announced her intention to rescue her husband:

> We will have you know for certain that at such time as we and our son shall be disposed to see my lord, as our duty is and so binds us to do, that none of you shall be robbed, despoiled or wronged by any person that at that time we or our son shall be accompanied with, or any other sent in our or his name, praying to you in most hearty and desirous wise that you will diligently extend all earthly means to the security of my lord's royal person in the meantime.

The designation of Hull as the rendezvous point suggests Marguerite had already received a favourable response to a request for a meeting with Mary of Guelders, queen mother and regent for 8-year-old King James III of Scotland. If the aim was only to join the northern lords, she could have sailed to Cumberland, bypassing Stanley in Lancashire, even though that would have put her on the wrong side of the Pennines in mid-winter. The choice of Hull indicates Marguerite already knew she would sail to south-eastern Scotland, then cross to the North Sea and take another ship down the coast.

It was politically impossible for Marguerite to accept open support from her uncle Charles VII of France. With Yorkist propaganda branding her a French whore, her Valois parentage was something she needed to downplay in the competition for hearts and minds. As for the allegations of infidelity, such evidence as we have supports the view that it was not believed. She continued to enjoy considerable popular sympathy as the wife of the man all regarded as the legitimate king, and the mother of a no less legitimate Prince of Wales. Sympathy would evaporate, however, if she made any overt alliance with England's foreign enemies.

Wiltshire/Ormonde had her authority to treat with the Duke of Brittany and to recruit foreign mercenaries, but that was at suitably arm's length and, anyway, she had nothing to offer Brittany in exchange for more substantial support. She did, however, have something to offer Scotland, but could entrust no one else with the task. Having first obtained a private letter from her uncle Charles VII supporting her mission, and leaving Jasper Tudor to await the arrival of Wiltshire and whatever forces he had gathered, she sailed with her son from Tenby to Kirkcudbright, then travelled to Lincluden Abbey, near Dumfries.

• ❧ •

The Scottish backstory is in many respects a mirror image of events in England. It will be recalled that the first (of six successive) King James fell in love with and married Joan Beaufort when he was a hostage in England. James was murdered in February 1437 by assassins sent by the Earl of Athol, his uncle and nearest adult relative. Joan was wounded but escaped with her 6-year-old son to the protection of Alexander Livingston, warden of Stirling Castle. The *coup d'état* failed and Athol and his co-conspirators were executed.

The chronic threat came from the over-mighty Black Douglas dynasty. The 5th Earl of Douglas acted as regent until he died in 1439, but a year later his 16-year-old heir and his next eldest son were invited to the infamous 'Black Dinner' by James II and murdered by his Lord Chancellor, whom the king promptly ennobled.* Twelve years later James II himself murdered the 8th earl at Stirling Castle. James Douglas, the 9th earl, was attainted for rebellion and for conspiring with the English in 1455. After his brothers were killed in battle by the Red Douglas Earl of Angus, James Douglas took refuge in England. Angus was awarded the Douglas title and core domain, but James II prudently retained the wider Black Douglas estates.

* The inspiration for the 'Red Wedding' in George R. R. Martin's *A Storm of Swords*.

Also in 1455, as we have seen, James II proposed a joint war against England to Charles VII of France to take advantage of the Yorkist rebellion, and tried to stir the pot by falsely alleging that York had been in treasonous correspondence with him. Charles refused the invitation but James followed up the defeat of the Black Douglases by leading a raid into England. He withdrew when York was made Protector and marched north, only to launch a six-day *chevauchée* into Northumberland the following year, after York's protectorship was ended. James agreed to a one-year truce in July 1457 mainly because he needed to assert royal authority in the Highlands and to initiate far-ranging institutional reforms.

Although the 2nd Duke of Somerset, his maternal uncle, had been killed at St Albans, sentiment played no part in James II's calculations. War with England was one of the few policies capable of uniting his unruly nobles, and in conjunction with his reforms rallied the common people behind him. He was also a pioneer in the use of siege artillery, the bane of the castle-based feudal order, and had used it to complete the destruction of the Black Douglases and their allies.

In July 1460, following the Battle of Northampton, James set out to remove the irritant of Roxburgh, an English stronghold on the north bank of the upper River Tweed, which was regarded by the Scots as their natural frontier. The Anglo-Scottish border shown on the maps in this book is today's; in the fifteenth century it was more like a wide ribbon of no man's land running on either side of a line from Berwick to Carlisle, populated by infamous border 'reivers' and studded with fortified houses and Pele towers.

Roxburgh town fell quickly, but James had to bring up his guns to reduce the castle. In early August, while supervising the bombardment, he was killed by a fragment when one of the guns exploded. He was only 29 years old, and the timing of his death could not have been more fortunate for the Lancastrians.

• ∾ •

Marguerite sailed to Scotland in December 1460 to win peace on the border so her supporters could concentrate against the Yorkists. Like Marguerite with Henry, Mary of Guelders had been 15 years old when she was betrothed to James II in 1449. Unlike Marguerite, however, she came with a magnificent dowry of 60,000 crowns [£9.54 million] provided by her cousin Duke Philippe of Burgundy, in whose household she had grown up. The Scots regarded her as such a splendid asset that the palace of Holyrood House was built to receive her, and her dowry underpinned her husband's consolidation of royal power.

Mary was well regarded by all strata of Scots society, especially after producing the required heir in 1452. When she learned of her husband's death she took her son, now King James III, to Roxburgh, arriving five days later to direct the successful conclusion of the siege and the demolition of the hated castle. Having thus established her credentials as a leader, she had no difficulty in assuming the role of regent to the infant king and quickly appointed her own men as keepers of the most strategically located royal fortresses.

The only significant opposition she had to deal with for the remaining three years of her life came from her principal minister, Bishop James Kennedy of St Andrews. Superficially their differences concerned the correct manner to exploit the situation south of the border, with Mary to some extent swayed by the Yorkist sympathy of her surrogate father the Duke of Burgundy, and Kennedy fiercely advocating the 'auld alliance' with France. The real problem was that Kennedy was another episcopal misogynist who tried to smear Mary with the usual allegations of promiscuity, for no better reason than his own psychology and the Church's hostility towards women it judged insufficiently submissive.

Understandably, given that their countries were at war, the December meeting at Lincluden Abbey was conducted in the strictest secrecy, between the two queens alone. They had much in common. Marguerite was still only 30 years old, Mary four years her junior, and their sons were respectively 10 and 8 years old. The

Auchinleck Chronicle, the sole source for what was discussed, states they tentatively agreed a marriage alliance between the Prince of Wales and one of Mary's daughters. We can deduce from subsequent events that they also discussed the cession of the fortress at Berwick if Mary helped the Lancastrians to defeat the Yorkists, but all we can be sure of is that Mary agreed to an immediate truce.

While they were still at Lincluden, electrifying news arrived from south of the border – news that made it imperative for Marguerite and her son to join the army raised in his name as soon as possible. An agreement, presumably relating to the marriage, was signed by the two queens on 5 January, after which Mary arranged for Marguerite and Edward to be rushed across Scotland to the port of Leith. Here they boarded a royal ship provided by Mary and accompanied by an escort, and sailed south – for Yorkshire.

RICHARD'S
HUMILIATION

WARWICK ACTED AS THE KING'S CHIEF MINISTER following Northampton and, using Henry as a rubber stamp, summoned Parliament to revoke the Acts of Attainder passed nine months previously. Salisbury was obsessively concerned with recovering and adding to his vast estate, and content to leave the politics to his son. Nor is there any evidence that Edward of March acted as his absent father's deputy; to the contrary, both before and after York's belated return from Ireland, Edward plainly acted as Warwick's apprentice.

Warwick petitioned the pope to appoint Coppini cardinal, and for permission to award him an English bishopric, but neither was forthcoming. Archbishop Bourchier remained benevolent and Viscount Bourchier replaced Wiltshire/Ormonde as Lord Treasurer. The office of Lord Chancellor, resigned by Bishop Wainflete three days before Northampton, went to Bishop George Neville of Exeter, and Bishop Robert Stillington of Bath and Wells replaced Bishop Laurence Booth of Durham as Lord Privy Seal.

Any pretence that the king could command even his own household was swept away, a situation also facilitated by so many of the household having joined the queen. The only survivor was the neutral figure of Lord Beauchamp of Powick, who remained as steward because his expertise was irreplaceable. Warwick's brother John became the king's chamberlain and other Warwick appointees filled the lesser household offices. Warwick also made himself and his father joint chief stewards of the king's duchy of Lancaster estates.

Warwick recovered the governorship of the Channel Islands and had himself appointed Warden of the Cinque Ports. He got Parliament to renew his commission as Keeper of the Seas, now supported by the customs revenues of Sandwich and Southampton as well as all other ports. The Staplers were delighted to surrender their nominal right to the receipts from the two great wool ports in return for the resumption of uninterrupted trade. The City of London Corporation and the individual livery companies were likewise grateful, and lent Warwick large sums in the months ahead. He also collected £7,000 [£4.45 million] in a forced levy from all crown servants who wished to retain their offices.

Warwick was a whirlwind on a tightrope, with every move designed to maintain the momentum won at Northampton, and he expended no political, still less financial capital to address the chronic problems that had brought successive kings' governments into disrepute. The Commons were not required to vote any new taxation, which would have opened the door for a reiteration of demands for radical resumption to put royal finances on a sustainable basis.

One unpostponable reckoning was the issue of legitimacy. Marguerite may have been the first to see that a puppet king could not long survive, but now the Yorkist lords ran into the contradiction at the heart of their rebellion. If, as they had repeatedly sworn by the most sacred oaths, they were the loyal liegemen of the anointed sovereign, then by what authority did they presume to dictate to him how he should rule? A present-day historian of the period offers a perfect summary of the issue:

> The real problem of Henry's reign was that an authority which should have been whole and located in one man, was actually fragmented and dispersed: royal blood, personal lordship, executive power and the capacity to represent the public were

scattered among a host of magnates, clerks and gentlemen of the household. The tragedy is that the efforts to restore this authority involved the great in conflicts among themselves, conflicts which were actually between the constituent parts of the monarchy. From these conflicts, unmodified by the saving power of genuine royal grace, there was no escape.*

Every argument the Yorkist lords had used to justify their defiance now backfired. As they had at all times acquitted the king of personal responsibility for the chronic ills besetting the nation, they found themselves promoted to the role of the 'evil councillors' who must, perforce, be to blame for everything. Added to which, the avidity with which the Nevilles awarded themselves lucrative offices made it clear they were just Suffolks writ large, and that their claim to uphold the greater good had always been a cynical pretence.

York did not return to England from Ireland until 9 September 1460 when, his lordship of Denbigh still held against him, he stepped ashore at the Wirral, Stanley's manor on the peninsula between the Mersey and Dee rivers. Like Grey of Ruthyn, Stanley had not yet received any significant reward for his treachery, and he made a further effort to curry favour from York by organizing a civic reception for him at Chester, the administrative capital of the Prince of Wales's county palatinate of Cheshire. Blore Heath cast a long shadow.

From the time of his arrival York assumed the full arms of England and omitted Henry VI's regnal year in the dating of his correspondence. He had come to claim the throne, and Warwick's later protestations that it had come as a complete surprise were false. The two men had probably agreed he must do so when they met in Dublin, and York delayed his arrival for a triumphal progress to London to be organized. In mid-September Warwick travelled to meet him in Shrewsbury, where they spent four days together

* From John Watts' brilliant essay in Kekewich et al., *The Politics of Fifteenth-Century England*.

before he returned to London. He did not, however, prepare the ground along the route later followed by York.

If York hoped to replicate Warwick's triumphal procession through Kent he was soon disappointed. He had gone to the well too many times. The loyalty he once commanded had been eroded by his failure to protect his supporters over the preceding decade, and only his retainers turned out to greet him at Ludlow. Although Cecily and, presumably, his younger children joined him at Hereford, Edward of March pointedly did not come to replace his younger brother Rutland at their father's side.

Whether or not York perceived it, there was a fundamental weakness at the heart of his relationship with the Nevilles. What would Warwick have gained if York became king? He stood only to lose if his rubber-stamp king was replaced by a man he could not control. York's ambition was to establish strong, orderly government, whereas Warwick and his father had done very well indeed out of weakness at the centre. It did not require a crystal ball to see that the alliance the Nevilles had made with York would survive only as long as they faced a common enemy.

Conversely York knew that the only alternative to claiming the throne was to become, once more, the Protector of a king he did not control and a government differing only in personnel from those against which he had rebelled. It is irrelevant whether he was coldly calculating or deluded by arrogance of ancestry and the urgings of his Irish and Marcher entourage, or to what degree he was encouraged – or not – by Warwick. What followed is best seen as a power play within the Yorkist alliance.

When York entered London, his sword held before him point upward in royal style, he was not greeted by the popular enthusiasm Warwick could have organized had he wished to do so. Even though things were clearly not proceeding to plan, York still went ahead as though his acclamation as king was a foregone conclusion, which strongly suggests Warwick misled him about the reception he could expect from the handful of lords assembled in Westminster Hall.

On 10 October York entered the Hall, walked to the throne and laid his hand on it. There was a deafening silence until Archbishop Bourchier spoke, to ask him if he sought an audience with the king. York blustered 'I know of no person in this realm whom it does not behove to come to me and see my person rather than that I should go and visit him', but his humiliation was as complete as it was, to him, unexpected. He had been hung out to dry.

After the debacle a furious altercation took place in private between York and the Nevilles. Edward of March was present and did not support his father, but it was probably Salisbury who prevailed on the duke to accept the logic of 'hang together or all hang separately', and that they must make way for younger blood. Salisbury was 60 years old, but York was not yet 50 and it was a bitter pill to swallow, made worse by the galling knowledge that March's young blood was not his. We can readily imagine his rage.

A charade of parliamentary consultation ensued before Warwick proposed a compromise the bishops could accept. Very few secular lords had responded to the summons, and the Act of Accord agreed on 31 October was probably a deal worked out with Archbishop Bourchier. Even though York's attempt to supplant Henry was ruled out for several reasons, not least the many oaths of allegiance he had sworn, it was judged expedient to accept the validity of his claim to a superior hereditary right, as the matrilineal descendant of Edward III's second son. Henry was eleven years younger than York, so the most likely heir would be March, who carried none of his father's baggage of sacred undertakings.

Modelled on the 1420 Treaty of Troyes, the Act required the king to recognize York and his issue as his heirs. Pope Pius II recorded that it was the egregious Coppini who prevailed on Henry to accept it, arguing it was his Christian duty to do so in order to avoid further bloodshed. Fear for his own life may have influenced Henry less than is commonly supposed. Without even his confessor to advise him, he may have reasoned that no agreement reached under duress was binding, and that he should buy time for his beloved son to grow up and for York and the Nevilles to turn on each other, as they inevitably must.

Sugaring the pill for York, the Act also appointed him Protector for life, with an annual salary of 10,000 marks [£4.24 million], of which 3,500 was for March and 1,500 for Rutland, to be drawn from disinherited Prince Edward's lands in Wales, Cornwall and Chester. In point of legal fact the accord was never formally enacted – it was not even submitted to the Commons, which underlined that it was no more than a face-saving expedient. Underlining it further was that Warwick, not York, carried the king's sword before him in the procession to St Paul's to celebrate the Accord, while March carried his train.

York's claim and the Act of Accord caused widespread outrage. York and the Nevilles seriously underestimated the extent of the opposition they had aroused, and the only explanation for the carelessness that characterized the next act in the drama is if they were seriously misinformed about the situation developing in the North. All they had to work with were reports – which would have lost nothing in the telling – of raids, mainly against Salisbury's estates, which seemed to follow the pattern of defiance last seen in 1454.

As Protector York had to move quickly to suppress the disorder and Salisbury, as the person most directly affected, accompanied him. The crucial factor in the conduct of the ensuing campaign in the north was probably York's state of mind. He behaved in a lackadaisical and rash manner; if depression is anger turned inward, he was probably deeply depressed. Also, his relations with Salisbury, brother and father of the woman and the man who had first intimately and now publicly humiliated him, may have been barely civil.

The composition of their army suggests that York was not pleased to be leading an expedition whose main purpose was to re-establish Salisbury's authority in Yorkshire. Apart from the duke, his son Rutland and Edward Bourchier, the youngest son of York's brother-in-law Viscount Bourchier, the notables who marched north with him were members of Salisbury's affinity, including his son-in-law William Bonville, Baron Harington.

When they set out from London on 9 December they may have had a siege train, intending to recover Pontefract Castle, but at some point they abandoned the guns and decided to march instead to Sandal Castle, in York's south Yorkshire manor of Wakefield. Why they went there rather than to his larger castle at Conisbrough, less than a day's march to the south-east, is a mystery. Along the Great North Road they passed through or close to several of York's boroughs in Hertfordshire and Lincolnshire, but he made no great effort to summon his affinity. Nor did he ensure that Sandal was adequately provisioned, so when they arrived on 24 December 1460 there was little in the way of Christmas cheer.

Sandal was a compact fortification that could only accommodate a few hundred men within its walls. The adjacent village of Sandal Magna was also small, so the bulk of the Yorkist forces must have camped in the open, probably clustered around the entrance to the castle, overlooking the plain leading to the River Calder, with Wakefield on the other side across a narrow bridge. There was a 40-acre, wooded and fenced deer park close to the castle, but the earliest land use maps show no evidence of woods anywhere on the plain.

York and Salisbury were unaware that there was a large Lancastrian force at Pontefract, where the West Country lords had met up with Northumberland, Clifford, Roos and Lord John Neville, acting for his demented brother the Earl of Westmorland. There also cannot have been outposts stationed in every direction to give early warning of an enemy approach. The omission of such an elementary pre-caution strongly suggests the weather was appalling. Bad visibility would also have discouraged the lookouts atop the castle keep.

So, we have perhaps 5,000–6,000 men, cold, wet and ill fed, hud-dled around a castle where their leaders had brought them for no discernible purpose. Meanwhile, 9 miles away at Pontefract, at least twice and perhaps three times as many Lancastrians were gathered under leaders who knew exactly what they wanted to do. Somerset,

19. BATTLE OF WAKEFIELD
Contours at 8-feet intervals

Wakefield

Clifford

✗ Kirkgate

Medieval road (or both)
Modern road

Modern railway

Old bridge

River Calder

Pontefract 9 miles

Foragers attacked?

John Neville

Modern A638

✗ Rutland killed
✝ York monument
☐ Site of Portobello House

Agbrigg

Yorkist rout

Milnthorpe

Mangates

York's sortie

Sandal Magna

Sandal Castle

Modern A61

Wood?

Lancastrian main force

N

Barnsley

0   250   500   750   1000
yards

Walton

© Hugh Bicheno

Northumberland and Clifford could scarcely believe their luck to find two of the three men responsible for the deaths of their fathers on their doorstep, and were determined they should not get away.

The hatred between the Nevilles of Raby and of Middleham ran deep, and Lord John Neville had also deeply offended York by obtaining a commission of array from him to raise troops and then joining the enemy camp. It may well have been he who proposed using himself as bait in a trap. By this time his men had teamed up with Clifford's elite force of mounted archers and hobilars, known as the 'Flower of Craven' from the district around Skipton. It was probably they who scouted Wakefield and Sandal, and reported that the enemy was sending foraging parties north of the river.

Clifford and Neville proposed to make a rapid advance north and south of the river to trap the enemy foragers and, if that failed, Neville would make a provocative display in front of the castle to lure the Yorkists out. The main Lancastrian force, having set out during the night, would march well to the south to approach from the direction of Walton, halting out of sight below the (possibly wooded) southern end of the ridge on which Sandal Castle stood. Once the Yorkists sortied they would charge around both sides of the ridge to cut off their retreat.

On 30 December, whether because one of their foraging parties was cut up in full view of the castle, or in response to jeers and taunts from Neville's men – or both – York led a mounted charge out of the castle and chased the coat-trailing enemy force. When the trap was sprung York and his men tried to fight their way back to safety, but were slaughtered. Some made a last stand on the riverbank, where centuries later excavations for Portobello House (see Map 19) found a great deal of battle debris. Seventeen-year-old Rutland managed to flee across Wakefield Bridge, but not far beyond it he was killed after surrendering by Clifford.

Shakespeare made the event one of the most dramatic scenes in Part III of *Henry the Sixth*. Despite the pleas of Rutland's tutor to spare 'this innocent child', the fictional Clifford overflows with a hate that was probably not far from the historical truth:

> Had thy brethren here, their lives and thine
> Were not revenge sufficient for me;
> No, if I digg'd up thy forefathers' graves
> And hung their rotten coffins up in chains,
> It could not slake mine ire, nor ease my heart.
> The sight of any of the house of York
> Is as a fury to torment my soul;
> And till I root out their accursed line
> And leave not one alive, I live in hell.

York might have made a good king, or even a good 'Hand of the King' if Henry VI had emerged from catatonia with sufficient wit to continue the work of conciliation begun by Marguerite. As it was, the traditional mnemonic for the sequence of colours in a rainbow provides a sadly accurate epitaph: Richard of York gave battle in vain.

Salisbury, his son Thomas, his Harington son-in-law and some of their retainers survived the battle and surrendered on terms. It is possible they never left the castle, which would indicate a last, fatal disagreement with York. They were taken to Pontefract, but their captors did not protect them from a mob that dragged them out and beheaded them. Salisbury's death was dishonourable, but then so was his life: there was no shortage of people who passionately wanted him dead.

The heads of the fallen lords were taken to York and mounted on spikes on the Micklegate Bar. Richard of York's head was adorned with a paper crown and mocking placards were hung below the grisly trophies. We should not make too much of this. It was traditional for traitors' heads to be displayed on Tower Bridge, but since it was in the possession of Warwick, Micklegate would have to do for the time being.

When Marguerite and young Edward arrived at York, it must have been exhilarating to have hundreds of fierce warriors wearing the Prince of Wales's livery kneel before them, with their enemies' heads grimacing down on them. Free at last from the constraint of trying to work through her dithering husband, Marguerite could work with men as determined as she was herself. The northern lords were delighted by the truce she had obtained at Lincluden, which permitted them to summon their whole strength.

All the Lancastrian lords wrote a joint letter to Charles VII endorsing the agreement. They would not have done so had it contained any suggestion that Berwick, the gateway to the North, might be ceded to the Scots. There is also no evidence there were any Scots in their army. It was never likely that English Marchers would put aside a hatred nurtured by centuries of raid and counter-raid to conduct a joint *chevauchée* deep into England with their ancestral enemies. Yet both of these allegations were made in Yorkist pronouncements.

The primary sources for the climax of the first phase of the Wars of the Roses must be treated with caution. All of them were written under Edward IV, when to record anything other than the 'party line' might have had severe consequences for the author. If we add that the most generally trusted source for the period 1459–61 is the *Registra* of John Whethamstede, Abbot of St Albans, a subtle apologia for the Duke of York written to curry favour with his son, it is not at all remarkable that the black legend of Marguerite put down deep roots.

The Lancastrians' strategic objective was to recover the king, and the operational design was a fluid concept, regularly reviewed by assemblies of the most experienced officers. Prince Edward was the nominal commander-in-chief, which finessed any issue of precedence that might have caused friction between the Dukes of Exeter and Somerset. And if the prince was present at the councils of war, then so was Marguerite. Her mother, who herself once led an army in an attempt to liberate her own ineffectual husband, would have been proud of her.

EDWARD OF MARCH

WHILE YORK, RUTLAND AND SALISBURY MADE FOR the North, 18-year-old Edward, Earl of March set out, separately, to affirm the new regime's authority in the South West and to counter the threat posed by Lancastrian Wales under the leadership of Jasper Tudor. With him went the Marcher retainers who had accompanied York to London, at whose urging he had tried to claim the throne even though the popular acclaim promised by Warwick had failed to materialize. Thus during Edward's first independent command he was surrounded by men who would have been outspokenly scornful of Warwick's duplicity.

Edward was seen as 'one of their own' by the Marcher retainers in a way his father had never been. We know nothing of his childhood and very little about his adolescence – apart from the very salient fact that he spent his teens at Ludlow and the other Yorkist Marcher manors. From a joint letter sent by Edward and his brother Edmund to their father complaining about being bullied by the somewhat older Croft brothers, it is clear they were brought up with the sons of York's retainers rather than, as customary, in a noble house. The reason is evident: by the time they were old enough to leave their mother's household their father was locked in a power struggle with the court, and there was no senior peer to whom he could entrust them.

The result was more practical training in military matters than

Edward would have received in a court-oriented household, where the emphasis would have been on tournament skills. As the acting lord of Ludlow Edward would have received guidance from York's steward, the elder Walter Devereux, and would certainly have spent time at York's other manors in the March. He could not have prayed for a better place to exercise his first independent command, or for more militarily experienced and dependable advisers and nominal subordinates.

The principal Yorkist Marchers were Herbert of Raglan, steward of York's manors of Caerleon and Usk (also Warwick's Sheriff of Glamorgan), the younger Walter Devereux (*de jure* Lord Ferrers) of Weobley, who had succeeded his father at Ludlow, and Roger Vaughan of Tretower and Crickhowell in the Usk valley. Other Vaughans were Thomas of Bredwardine in the Wye valley and his uncle Thomas of Hergest and Kington in the Arrow valley. The older Thomas and Philip Vaughan were also stewards of the Buckingham manors of Huntington (between Hergest and Kington) and Hay, respectively. With them was Reginald, Lord Grey of Wilton in south Herefordshire.

Making his first appearance in our narrative is William Hastings, who had been at Ludford Bridge and was among those who stayed and obtained a royal pardon. Like his father, he was a Yorkist retainer with lands in Leicestershire and Warwickshire, who became involved in the Marches as ranger of York's vast Wyre forest and chase in Shropshire. As such he would have played host to young Edward on several occasions. Hastings was twelve years older, but the cascade of honours bestowed on him as soon as Edward became king argues that they had formed a very close friendship before the events of 1461.

As they had during the Ludlow campaign, Warwick's Abergavenny and Glamorgan retainers stayed at home to guard his estates. The only notables with Edward who were not his father's retainers were Lord Audley and Humphrey Stafford of Hooke, who had defected to him in Calais, and John Wenlock, whose loyalty Warwick had

20. MORTIMER'S CROSS CAMPAIGN
January–February 1460

N

0   50   100   150
miles

825 Mountain pass
═ height in feet

▪ Yorkist castle
or borough

Shrewsbury

MONTGOMERY

◉ Montgomery

◉ Bridgnorth

SHROPSHIRE

Kidderminster ◉

Wyre
Forest

Clun

Teme

▪ **Ludlow**

Leintwardine ▪
Knighton ◉   Wigmore ▪

Lugg

Teme

Presteigne ▪   ✕ *Mortimer's Cross*

1250 New Radnor ▪   Leominster ▪

Arrow   *WORCESTER*

RADNOR   Kington ◉
Hergest ◉   Weobley ◉   *-SHIRE*

Eardisley ◉   **Worcester** ◉

▪ Builth Wells

▪ Bredwardine   *Unnamed Roman road*

950

◉ Hay   *Wye*

← Llandovery   Glasbury   Holme Lacy ◉   **Hereford**

◉ Talgarth   *HEREFORDSHIRE*

825   *735*   Kentchurch ◉   **Tewkesbury** ▪

Trecastle ◉ *Usk* ◉ **Brecon**   Wilton ◉

BRECKNOCK   Three
Castles ▪   **Gloucester** ▪

Tretower ◉
Crickhowell ◉   ◉ **Abergavenny**   *Stone Street*

BRECON
BEACONS   ◉ **Monmouth**

MONMOUTH

GLAMORGAN   ▪ Raglan

Usk   *GLOUCESTERSHIRE*

▪ Usk

Caerleon ◉   **Chepstow** ◉

Newport ◉   *Severn Estuary*

Wye

© *Hugh Bicheno*

bought in 1459. Wenlock may have acted as Warwick's eyes and ears, but it is remarkable he did not also send a member of his own Marcher affinity to represent his considerable interest in the area.

Edward moved first to Gloucester, to control the Severn valley and to discourage the West Country from sending any more support to the queen's army, although most would already have joined the march north by Somerset, Devon and Exeter. The town was in the midst of many Buckingham, Wiltshire and Talbot manors, but with their lords either recently killed or absent, they would have been easily overawed. Gloucester was also a good base from which to counter an advance through south Wales by Jasper Tudor, on whose doings the Yorkists were kept informed by the Dwnns of Kidwelly.

Thanks to Jasper's good lordship and close alliance with Thomas and Owain, the heirs of Gruffudd ap Nicholas and stewards of the absentee Bishop of St David's, he had a firm hold on south-west Wales. Before departing for Scotland Marguerite had also made him her son's deputy for the Principality, but required him to wait for the arrival of Wiltshire/Ormonde, who was supposed to be recruiting an army with funds provided by the Duke of Brittany. If instead she had authorized him to march north at the same time as Somerset, Exeter and Devon, Jasper would have been able to fall on York's Marcher domain while he and his principal retainers were away in London.

Now, his situation was unenviable. The Skydmores of Holme Lacy and Kentchurch in Herefordshire should have been able to keep him informed about Edward's strength and movements, but do not appear to have done so. Perhaps, menaced by their Yorkist neighbours, they had already fled to join Jasper in Pembroke. It was mid-winter, so although there were more men available for war, provisioning was meagre everywhere in Wales, and any march through the barren interior was out of the question. Jasper's options, once Wiltshire arrived, were either to march up the coast through the miserably poor Principality into Cheshire, or along the south coast into the rich heart of the Yorkist Marches.

Time was not on his side, but Wiltshire was delayed. When he finally arrived, late in January 1461, he brought with him a force of Irish mercenaries and, perhaps, some Breton men-at-arms as well. These were troops who had to be employed as soon as possible, before supplies ran out and they began to plunder indiscriminately. The Roman road from Carmarthen through south Wales offered the fastest route, but Glamorgan and southern Monmouth were solidly Yorkist, and the Lancastrians would have had to fight their way through, dissipating their strength before they encountered Edward's main force.

Accordingly they had to march north of the Brecon Beacons through Llandovery, after which they could either continue north through Builth Wells, or east through Brecon. There really was no choice. The Builth route would take them through two high mountain passes that might be choked with snow, along a route studded with Yorkist manors. At Brecon they could obtain supplies and possibly also recruits from Buckingham's bereft retainers, after which the first Yorkist manor they would encounter was Weobley. Both routes met at the bridge over the River Lugg at Mortimer's Cross where, unless they could achieve operational surprise, they were certain to encounter Edward's army.

The element of surprise was denied to them. Jasper ranked the Dwnns among his most damaging enemies, acknowledging the crucial role played by the information they provided on his movements. By this time both sides had learned of York's defeat and death at Wakefield, and Jasper may have believed that Herbert and the other Yorkist Marchers had gone north with him to destruction. He may also have discounted Edward's ability to rally and lead what he hoped was the remnant of the Yorkist affinity, as otherwise he would not have attacked a larger army, deployed in an immensely strong position.

In fact, nothing could have united the Marchers more than an incursion by 'deep' Welshmen, and Edward's appeal to turn out against the men of Pembroke coming to ravage the Yorkist estates ensured that every able-bodied flocked to his banner. At dawn on the bitter cold battle day a phenomenon occurred that Edward made his own. Three suns appeared to be rising together, the effect of light refraction through atmospheric ice crystals known as a parhelion, or 'sundogs'. Although he does not even mention the ensuing battle, Shakespeare described the apparition superbly in Part III of *Henry the Sixth*:

> Three glorious suns, each one a perfect sun;
> Not separated with the racking clouds,
> But sever'd in a pale clear-shining sky.
> See, see! they join, embrace, and seem to kiss,
> As if they vow'd some league inviolable:
> Now are they but one lamp, one light, one sun.
> In this the heaven figures some event.*

Noting uneasiness among his men, Edward rode among them to pronounce it a favourable omen, claiming that the phenomenon was symbolic of his rise to glory, flanked by his two younger brothers. Another account has him saying it was a divine blessing and symbolized the Trinity, but the first version must get the nod, as Edward thereafter adopted a sunburst as his personal badge. It was his command moment, and he seized it with both hands.

It is fortunate the terrain at Mortimer's Cross is so eloquent, because our only source of tactical information is two stanzas from Michael Drayton's epic poem *The Miseries of Queen Margaret*, published in 1627, which is scraping the bottom of the military-historical barrel. For dramatic effect Drayton described Jasper as 'young Tudor', although he was 30 years old. Wiltshire was ten years older and Jasper's father Owen, commanding the third Lancastrian battle, was at least 60.

---

* Shakespeare puts these words in the mouth of the future Richard III. The real Richard was 8 years old at the time, and in Burgundy.

**21. BATTLE OF MORTIMER'S CROSS
2 February 1461**

Contours at 5-feet intervals

© Hugh Bicheno

The Earl of Ormond, an associate then
With this young Tudor, for the king that stood,
Came in the vanguard with his Irish men,
With darts and skains; those of the British [Welsh] blood
With shafts and gleaves them seconding again,
And as they fall, still make their places good:
That it amaz'd the Marchers, to behold
Men so ill-armed upon their bows so bold.

Now the Welch and the Irish so their weapons wield,
As tho' themselves the conq'rors meant to call;

Then are the Marchers masters of the field,
With their brown bills the Welchmen so they maul;
Now th' one, now th'other, likely were to yield;
These like to fly, then those were like to fall:
Until at length (as Fortune pleas'd to guide)
The conquest turned upon the Yorkists' side.

The 'darts' were throwing spears and the 'skains' (actually *scians*) were long dirks, the characteristic secondary armament of the Irish gallowglasses (*gallóglaigh*). They were mercenary heavy infantry who wore mail coats over padded jackets and fought with two-handed axes or the huge swords known as claymores. Although they also used bows, they were not longbows. Each of them had a boy to carry whatever weapons they were not using at a given moment and their battle tactic was to fire their arrows first, then close in to hurl their spears before charging to close quarters, where they were terrifyingly effective. The *scians* were for use in the crush, when there was no room to swing the heavier weapons.

If Drayton's description is accurate, Ormonde's gallowglasses were the Lancastrian shock troops, backed by Pembroke's Welsh billmen, none of them wearing adequate harness. They would have been hopelessly outranged and decimated by the Marcher bowmen, and any who managed to come through the arrow storm would have been rapidly dispatched. It is possible Herbert positioned a group of mounted men in a re-entrant on the wooded hill crowned by Mortimer's Rock, to charge into the rear of the Lancastrian left wing once it approached the Yorkist line. If so, it was the icing on the cake of an already lopsided battle.

If even the Welsh bards barely refer to it, we may be sure the battle saw no feats of derring-do. No notable Yorkist was killed, as there certainly would have been if the gallowglasses had managed to get to hand strokes. Battlefield archaeology may eventually reveal more, but it seems likely the Lancastrian left wing crumbled first, possibly precipitated by the flight of Wiltshire/Ormonde. If the monument at the entrance to Kingsland along the modern A4110 does indeed mark a place of special interest, it may be where the right-hand battle commanded by Owen Tudor made a last stand, covering the retreat of his son's battle along the Leominster road.

In the pursuit following the battle no mercy was shown to the defeated Lancastrians, in revenge for the slaughter at Wakefield and Pontefract. Owen Tudor and other captured Lancastrian knights were summarily beheaded in Hereford marketplace. The lists of men killed in the battle or executed are undependable, but the definitely dead included Marguerite's steward of Harlech, two of John Skydmore's sons and his brother William of Kentchurch, and Thomas ap Gruffudd ap Nicholas.

Edward's forces did not, however, pursue Jasper Tudor and his Pembrokemen, who retreated in good order. Most of them made it home and were to turn out for their lord again and again in the years to come. Instead, the victorious army returned to Gloucester, and stayed there while events in England unfolded. It is not clear whether Wenlock was at Mortimer's Cross, and it could be he is first recorded with Edward now, at Gloucester, because Warwick sent him. The message he brought was that Marguerite and the main Lancastrian army was marching south, and that Edward should join him as soon as possible. Warwick may have worded his request as an order to a man who was now a duke and outranked him.

Edward had left London with commissions of array for Somerset and Gloucestershire as well as Hereford and Shropshire, but with a war chest of only 650 marks [£275,600]. This was enough to keep his modest army of volunteers supplied for about a month, but a larger force for a longer period required more. The attraction of Gloucester was that all five of the major monastic orders had large abbeys there, making it a pot of gold for anyone who held the city. No threats were necessary, because the oppressively taxed people of Gloucester were violently Lollard and the abbots, who never ventured out without a strong bodyguard, were highly motivated to ingratiate themselves with the civil power.

It was not, therefore, lack of men or money that kept Edward from marching to join his mentor. He bided his time, and in the end Warwick was forced to come to him. It must have come as a nasty shock to discover that the young man was coldly willing to put the entire Yorkist enterprise at risk in order to assert his own leadership so soon after the death of his father.

Edward's rise in the English political firmament was as sudden as a shooting star. There had been no previous indication that he was anything other than a loyal lieutenant to Warwick, even siding with him against his own father. But therein, I believe, lies the key. York quite clearly favoured his second son Edmund over Edward. Even if Salisbury and Warwick did not know that Edward was the product of their, respectively, sister and aunt's adultery, he was of their blood and they gave him the adult male approval denied him by his coldly distant father.

More than his victory at Mortimer's Cross, therefore, the death at Wakefield of his father and his favoured younger sibling would have had a galvanically liberating effect on Edward. There is little indication he mourned their loss. He perfunctorily reunited their heads with their bodies at Pontefract, but did not rebury them in the family vault at Fotheringhay until 1476, and even then the leading role was played by Richard, his youngest brother, who also commissioned the construction of their tomb monuments. In an era when the aristocracy practised thinly disguised ancestor worship, Edward could not have made it plainer that he felt no debt of filial gratitude to the man who was not, in fact, his blood father.

If this interpretation is correct, Edward would have been transformed to learn of York's death, to win his first independent battle, and to see his surrogate father Warwick come to him with his tail between his legs, all in a period of little more than a month. In a wider sense, despite his youth Edward now assumed the stature of the king English society needed to enforce the law, without which there could be, in Thomas Hobbes's famous phrase, 'no arts; no letters; no society; and which is worst of all, continual fear and danger of violent death; and the life of man, solitary, poor, nasty, brutish, and short'.

Although modern research indicates that the Wars of the Roses impacted less than one would expect on the general population, Hobbes' aphorism sounds like a pretty good description of what England had become by 1461. What we are looking at, therefore, is the coincidence of Edward's emancipation from a father who did not love him with the final breakdown of the limited amount of order the Lancastrian regime had been able to provide.

Henry, the anointed father of the nation, had utterly failed to enforce the law and so permit his people to prosper. Looming chaos made it imperative to anoint another, and suddenly to hand there was a victorious, noble, physically imposing and sexually potent candidate. In the absence of Sigmund Freud to explain how it was all a function of their libidos, many – not least Edward himself – saw it as proof that the forefinger of God had reached down to designate him.

THE BUBBLE
REPUTATION

THE PARADOX OF RICHARD 'THE KINGMAKER' NEVILLE'S epic life is that his brilliance as a politician was not matched by similar skill as a general. At St Albans in 1455 he was a subordinate, and Northampton, his one great victory, had been won by intrigue before the armies ever came into contact. Subsequently, he seems to have been guided by the maxim (devoutly practised by contemporary Italian *condottieri*, who were above all businessmen) that battle should be the last resort.

This was the principle the French finally adopted to win the Hundred Years War; but it was completely at variance with the English way of war. The English were renowned for their ferocity and were not temperamentally suited to positional warfare, which may explain why castles played such a peripheral role in the conflict. It is hard to think of any other reason why siege artillery, so crucial in the fall of English Normandy, had to be deployed against only two English castles between 1455 and 1485.

The strategic value of castles was that a few men could tie down a large force for months, dissipating the besieger's resources and exposing his troops to attrition through camp diseases. An example of what might have been achieved was set by Lord Lovell's castle at Thorpe Waterville in Northamptonshire, the only significant Lancastrian hold-out south of the River Trent in early 1461. Edward had to send John Wenlock with three bombards and commissions of array for five counties to deal with it, but he cannot have used the guns because the castle was undamaged when it was surrendered two months later. Just a few more like that and Edward would not have been able to march north with sufficient strength.

Isolated Harlech, supplied by sea, held out for Lancaster from 1461 to 1468, and the only other castles held for any considerable time were also coastal. Inland, we simply do not know why Pontefract, ferociously Lancastrian at the time of Wakefield, was not held against the Yorkists only three months later. It was folly not to use castles to slow down opposing armies as they marched the length of the country, yet neither side appears to have believed it worth attempting. The only obvious explanation is that, apart from Calais, none had a permanent, professional garrison, which in turn reflected the English fixation on the quick campaign and climactic battle as the be-all and end-all of warfare.

A climactic battle was what Marguerite's army of allegedly ravening 'Northmen' marched south to seek in January 1461, supposedly wreaking havoc as it went. Contrary to Yorkist propaganda, there were no Scots or French contingents in Marguerite's army: her supporters came from all over England. There is also no evidence whatever to support the over-the-top tales of Lancastrian atrocities recorded in the rolls of Edward IV's first Parliament.*

Considering the treasonous support given to the Yorkists by the Canterbury Convocation, systematic looting of the wealthy abbeys and churches along the line of march might have been an understandable act of vengeance – but it would not have been queenly. Marguerite's behaviour was governed by the need not to burn any bridges of allegiance over which today's Yorkist supporters might cross back to her husband once she recovered him, or, if he were killed, to her son. Likewise, it made no sense to sack the previously Yorkist boroughs and manors through which her army passed because, following the 1459 attainders, they were legally crown estates.

---

* Bonita Cron took a well-researched war-hammer to that interpretation in the December 1999 issue of *The Ricardian*.

This is not to say that her army did not take what it needed in the way of food and other supplies against an uncertain promise of reimbursement, or that looting did not take place; but it was no *chevauchée*. Several edicts issued by Warwick at this time clearly point to the Lancastrians receiving significant voluntary support in Leicestershire, Lincolnshire and Cambridgeshire. A general order was issued to all sheriffs to raise the shires to repress 'the malice of riotous people', which may have been a precaution against a general breakdown of law and order, but could have been aimed at suppressing Lancastrian supporters.

Warwick was acutely aware how thin popular support for the Yorkist cause was outside Kent and London. Having the church on his side was financially beneficial, but in strongly Lollard areas like Sussex, East Anglia and the South West it was probably harmful. Edward's primary mission had been to shore up support for the regime in the South West as well as the Marches, assisted by the fact that the more determined Lancastrians had already marched north; but his assignment was only one of Warwick's initiatives.

Warwick's most notable coup was to bring about Yorkist near-hegemony in traditionally fractured East Anglia. The cornerstone was to entice John Mowbray, Duke of Norfolk, out of political hibernation, and to reconcile him with 19-year-old John de la Pole, Earl of Suffolk, who had married York's daughter Elizabeth in early 1458, but who only now became an active Yorkist. Added to the other Yorkist lords' affinities in the region, this alliance persuaded the Lancastrian Earl of Oxford to keep his head down.

For Sussex, Warwick persuaded William FitzAlan, Earl of Arundel, to come off the fence, joined by Richard Fiennes, Baron Dacre of the South. Warwick also convoked the Order of the Garter and had himself elected, along with three others: John Wenlock and Thomas Kyriell for services rendered, and William, Lord Bonville, mortal enemy of the Courtenay Earls of Devon, whose heir, Lord Harington, had died with York at Wakefield.

The picture that emerges is not one of the Yorkist south united against the Lancastrian north, but of frantic coalition building by Warwick – which is what one would expect after a *coup d'état*. The peers who took sides after the coup were evenly divided, but all the Lancastrians fought at the climactic Battle of Towton except for Oxford, Pembroke cut off in Wales and Wiltshire who was in transit. In contrast many Yorkist peers did not, even though all had burned their bridges with Lancaster. Warwick probably judged it more important for them to stay in their shires to control the populace, a further indication that he was far from confident of having won southern hearts and minds.

During the Lancastrians' march south they were accurately informed about enemy numbers and movements, and the Yorkists were not. There is no way this could have happened if the Yorkists had enjoyed the southern support against the northern bogeymen that their propaganda sought to generate. For example, although Grantham and Stamford had been York's boroughs, the affinities of Lords Beaumont, Roos, Welles and Willoughby made Lincolnshire, through which Marguerite's army marched south from York, a strongly Lancastrian county. Furthermore, if the people had indeed fled before the Lancastrian advance, refugees would have kept Warwick fully informed about their movements.

This quite evidently did not happen. Consequently, instead of marching north from London to meet Marguerite's army head-on, Warwick reacted uncertainly and tentatively. He sent the Van under his younger brother John to St Albans with most of the guns. The Main, with Warwick himself, his 55-year-old uncle Lord Fauconberg and the king, marched through Waltham Cross to Ware. Thereabouts they rendezvoused with the Duke of Norfolk, whose East Anglian contingent constituted the third battle of an army 10,000–15,000 strong.*

At Ware, Warwick learned that Marguerite's army had left the

---

* The Earl of Arundel, Earl of Suffolk and Viscount Bourchier took part in this campaign, probably joining forces with Norfolk. The recently turned Baron de la Warr also participated, after which he went home and stayed there.

**22. APPROACH TO
ST ALBANS
February 1461**
Approximate distances shown in miles

© Hugh Bicheno

Great North Road at Royston, turning west along the Icknield
Way. Convinced she would turn south again between Baldock and
Luton, he set out his battles accordingly. John Neville left most of
his archers in St Albans and marched about a mile north-east to a
massive Iron Age earthwork known as Beech Bottom Dyke, with
a commanding view of the surrounding area. There, he set up an
artillery fort seemingly modelled on the one that gave victory to the
French at Castillon. Warwick's battle was at Sandridge, a mile further to the north-east, and Norfolk's another mile along the same
road, covering roads from Hitchin and Welwyn/Baldock.

It was not necessarily a bad idea to cover a wide front while
keeping the three battles within supporting distance of each other
– if adequate advance notice of an impending enemy attack could
be obtained. Although a mile is no great distance, it takes time to
create a column of march at one end and to deploy at the other. It
appears Warwick was failed by his scouts, as they clearly did not

maintain a close watch on the enemy. As a back-up he would have had outposts covering all the roads running south from the Icknield Way. No doubt he had them on the Baldock, Hitchin and Luton roads, and believed Watling Street was well covered by several hundred local levies at Dunstable.

Fortuna notoriously favours the bold. Moving fast, the Lancastrian Van – probably Lords Clifford and Neville again, accompanied by Andrew Trollope, the most experienced officer in the Lancastrian army – surrounded and annihilated the Dunstable levies. Their unfortunate commander, a local butcher, survived but later hanged himself for shame. Watling Street was a well-defined thoroughfare

23. BATTLE OF ST ALBANS
17 February 1461
FIRST PHASE

© Hugh Bicheno

and the Lancastrians then did something unheard of in medieval warfare: they marched by night to St Albans, arriving at dawn.

Crossing the River Ver at St Michael's Mill, they first attempted to rush the town by charging along Fishpool Street, but were stopped by an arrow storm as they tried to debouch into the marketplace. Dead and dying men and horses soon blocked the street and they fell back. However, another force raced along Folly and Catherine Lanes to cut off the defenders' retreat. Attacked from two sides, the Yorkist archers were doomed. Some got away to warn a shocked John Neville, but Clifford's 'Flower of Craven' would not have been far behind.

The second battle of St Albans enjoys the distinction of having left us not one but two accounts written by men who were there. The first witness was, as before, the Abbot of St Albans, whose ornate Latin is sometimes enlightening. The second was the anonymous and regrettably laconic continuator of *Gregory's Chronicle*, who may have served in Warwick's army. His explanation for the operational surprise achieved by the Lancastrians is a priceless variant on the infantryman's eternal grumble about the cavalry: 'As for spearmen [lancers], they are good for riding before the footmen and to eat and drink up their victuals, and many more such pretty things they do, [but] hold me excused though I say the best, for in the footmen is all the trust.'

Neville did not have time to reposition his artillery and could only turn his battle through almost 90 degrees to take up a new position on a broad stretch of flat ground known as Bernard's Heath. He had with him a great novelty in English warfare: after Wakefield, Warwick had appealed for help to the Duke of Burgundy, who sent him a contingent of hand-gunners. *Gregory's Chronicle* gives a detailed description of these professional soldiers:

> For the Burgundians had such instruments that would shoot both pellets of lead and arrows of an ell [45 inches] of length with 6 feathers, 3 in the middle and 3 at the other end, with a

great mighty head of iron at the other end [he then asserts that these 'instruments' exploded in the gunners' hands if loaded in haste]. Also they had nets of great cords of 4 fathoms of length and 4 foot broad... and at every second knot there was a nail standing upright such that no man could pass over it without the likelihood of hurt. Also they had pavises, like doors with a folding strut that they could set down where they wished, and loop-holes with shutting windows to shoot out of [and bristling with] three penny nails. When their shot was spent and done, they cast down the pavises in front of them [so that] no man could come at them over the pavises for the nails that stood upright, without mischief to himself.

The weapons described are hook guns [Dutch *hakebusse*, hence 'arquebus'], man-portable cannon with a brutal recoil, which had to be fired hooked over a solid support, in this case the traditional crossbowman's propped *pavise* or heavy wooden shield. Gregory adds that the Burgundians also set out ground nets to tangle horses' hooves, and scattered caltrops – four spikes welded together, such that one always stood upright.

Neville expected his Burgundians to halt the Lancastrian attack, but they failed to do so. Gregory snorts that all this new-fangled defensive array had to be abandoned, and the matter was decided by 'mauls of lead, bows, swords, glaives [pole arms topped with single-edged blades] and axes'. Reading between the lines, his message is clear – Neville tried to fight the battle according to the best practice developed on the European mainland, and was overcome by good old English speed and ferocity.

The battle on Bernard's Heath was over so quickly that Warwick, whilst marching to support his brother, encountered only the fleeing remnants of Neville's command. At which point many of the levies in his own battle recalled an urgent appointment else-where, and he was left to fight a desperate rearguard action back through Sandridge. He was not able to make a stand until later on

24. BATTLE OF ST ALBANS
17 February 1461
SECOND PHASE

Based on Burley, Elliott & Watson
The Battles of St Albans (Barnsley 2007)

Hitchin

Norfolk

Nomansland Common

Luton

Welwyn

Sandridge
Village

Warwick

Ware →

Beech Bottom Dyke
Neville

Bernards Heath

- - Lancastrian attack - -

FIRST PHASE

Hatfield →

N

1 mile

© Hugh Bicheno

when he reached Norfolk's intact battle on Nomansland Common.

By this time, the epic Lancastrian attack had run out of momentum. They had been marching and fighting hard for twenty-four hours or more, and were exhausted. A strong counter-thrust would now have inflicted a severe reverse on them, but the Yorkists' will was broken. Warwick later tried to blame the defeat on treachery by a Kentish captain called Lovelace, but it was glaringly evident to all that he had been comprehensively out-generalled and out-fought. Shakespeare called it 'the bubble reputation', and Warwick's had burst.

Either at Bernard's Heath or during the retreat, Thomas Kyriell was killed and John Neville, Lord Berners (John Bourchier) and Lord Bonville were captured. The greatest prize, however, was the king. The most plausible explanation for how Henry was recovered safely is that his guards abandoned him in the chaos of the Yorkist retreat through Sandridge. Clifford's outriders found him sitting alone under a tree, singing to keep his spirits up, and brought him back to their lord's tent, where he was reunited with Marguerite and his son. According to Gregory:

> The night after the battle the king blessed his son the Prince, and Doctor Morton brought forth a book that was full of prayers, and there the book was opened and blessed that young child and made him knight... And the Prince made many knights. The first that he made was Andrew Trollope, for he was hurt and might not go for a caltrop in his foot; and he said 'My lord, I have not deserved it for I slew but fifteen men, for I stood still in one place and they came unto me, but they abode still with me.' And then came Whittingham, Tresham and many more others, and were made knights that same time.

The precedence granted to Robert Whittingham is suggestive: he was from Salden in Buckinghamshire, only a few miles north-east of Dunstable, and may have been instrumental in sealing off the town so that none should get away to give warning. Thomas Tresham of Rushden in Northamptonshire was the son of the Speaker murdered by Grey of Ruthyn's men in 1450, and had himself been the Speaker of the 1459 'Parliament of Devils' at Coventry.

There was also justice of another kind to be dispensed. The Earl of Devon demanded Bonville's head, and Marguerite could not afford to deny him. Henry might have done so, but after agreeing to the Act of Accord his personal authority was nil. Marguerite made sure it was, instead, 7-year-old Prince Edward who pronounced sentence. Neville and Berners were spared because Warwick retained hostages, including Edmund, the second of the Beaufort brothers, captured trying to holding the Isle of Wight for his brother.

Yorkist propaganda made much of the execution of Bonville, claiming Kyriell was beheaded as well. It was alleged that he and Bonville had remained behind to guard the king, and Henry's promise that they would be held harmless was overridden by Marguerite. One can forgive Shakespeare for typecasting Marguerite for reasons of dramatic licence, but there is no reason to believe she would have undermined her husband's authority. The anecdote is of a piece with Yorkist accounts of Marguerite's supposedly undisciplined, looting and pillaging army, which somehow became a tightly organized and fast-moving fighting force for long enough to win at St Albans and Bernard's Heath, before reverting to rabbledom once more.

Warwick's army was scattered and his reputation for invincibility destroyed. The East Anglian lords' levies having returned to their homes, he cannot have had more than 4,000 men under command when he marched west to meet Edward near Chipping Norton in Oxfordshire, 35 miles from Gloucester but 70 miles from the scene of his defeat. Edward by now commanded a Marcher army perhaps twice as large, and had money to pay his troops independently. Furthermore the men around him had seen Warwick humiliate York, and were coldly determined that history should not repeat itself with his son.

TWO KINGS

MARGUERITE'S PURPOSE HAD BEEN TO RECOVER THE king, and with him the legal authority of the state. This had been achieved at relatively little cost. Only one Lancastrian of rank was killed at second St Albans: John Grey, heir to the barony of Ferrers of Groby and husband to Elizabeth Woodville, eldest daughter of Lord Rivers and Jacquetta. However, since setting out from Pontefract the Lancastrian army had marched 180 miles in mid-winter. The levies were at the end of their enlistment period and many of them had gone home before the battle, which Gregory affirmed was won by no more than 5,000 'household men and feed men'.

Supplies were scarce, money to pay the troops even more so, and there is no evidence to indicate the Lancastrians could have continued the march south to London even if they had wished to. Although Marguerite had written the capital off as a political dead loss since 1457, there is a near-unanimous consensus among historians that she committed a strategic blunder in not marching her army into London, there to await the arrival of the combined forces of Edward and Warwick. In effect, she stands accused of failing to put her head into a noose.

She was certainly guilty of not committing that stupidity. Her army never moved from St Albans, where it blocked the fastest route – Roman Akeman Street – by which Edward could reach London from the west. He notably did not accept the challenge, which is only remarkable if we accept the view that a Lancastrian occupation of London would have been devastating to his cause. Clearly he did not think so, and his veteran Marcher councillors probably persuaded him to mark time in Oxfordshire, hoping Marguerite would march into London so they could cut off her retreat.

Understandably, the mayor and aldermen of London did not share Edward's relaxed view of the situation. Warwick's propaganda had generated a healthy fear of the northern army, and the mayor sent a delegation to St Albans led by the two most senior ladies in the land after Marguerite: the dowager Duchesses of Bedford (Jacquetta, Lady Rivers) and Buckingham. Their Lancastrian loyalty was unquestionable, and their warning about the temper of the people of London would have confirmed there was no hope of conducting the king on a procession through the city.

It is not clear whether the first Lancastrian emissaries were sent after the duchesses arrived at St Albans, or crossed paths with them. Either way, the Lancastrians brought only a request for supplies, which the mayor made haste to provide. A convoy of wagons set out from Cripplegate (today's Barbican), but was set upon by a mob and looted. It would be unwise to read any political intent into the violent behaviour of the London underclass at a time of political instability. The mob is a wild beast, and any excuse to commit mayhem will do.

What happened next, however, was definitely partisan. A party of Lancastrians carrying a warrant from the king declaring Edward a traitor was assaulted, resulting in a street battle with many casualties, after which the mayor announced a curfew 'in order that the king and his forces might enter and behave peacefully'. This provoked a riot, at which point the authorities unleashed the city guard and the rioters were violently dispersed. Meanwhile, a second Lancastrian delegation skirmished with an advance party of Yorkists outside the city gates, now closed against them both.

The king's warrant, dated 'at Westminster', never achieved the form and the signet of law and so did not have to be officially recognized as valid by the London authorities. It was, instead, published as a proclamation on 26 February, the same day a demand for admittance arrived from Edward and Warwick, now close to London after taking the cross-country route from Chipping Norton through Oxford and High Wycombe. The mayor replied that the Yorkist lords might enter the city, but not their troops.

On the same day the Lancastrian army departed St Albans, heading for York. Although they did not expect the Yorkists to be able to trump their possession of the king, in purely military terms it was essential to fall back on their area of greatest popular support. It was also a strategic retreat. Hoping to recreate the circumstances that gave them victory at Wakefield, their aim was to oblige the Yorkists to pursue them through a countryside emerging from winter, which could offer little in the way of supplies. It would have worked better if they could have conducted a scorched-earth campaign, but that was politically unthinkable.

With the loss of the king's person the Yorkist regime could make no claim to the obedience of royal officials and the general populace. With remarkable aplomb, Edward now styled himself 'by the grace of God of England, France and Ireland the true and just heir'. He based his claim not on the unratified Act of Accord, but on his superior right of descent from Lionel of Clarence over the usurping House of Lancaster. The claim, seen as patently contrived when made by York after all his sacred oaths of fealty, had far greater credibility coming from his heir, who had made no such solemn undertakings.

Edward and his captains took up residence at Baynard's Castle, the York family's grand Thames-side palace, but the Nevilles handled the stage-managing of his accession. On 1 March the Chancellor, Bishop George Neville, addressed a large crowd, composed mainly if not exclusively of Yorkist troops, outside London at St George's Fields (today's Bayswater), and set out Edward's claim. Popular acclamation was an important prerequisite for claiming the throne, and the partisan crowd duly cheered when required.

Next day the articles of Edward's title were published and announced throughout London, and on the following day a hastily convened 'Great Council' consisting of Archbishop Bourchier, Bishops Beauchamp of Salisbury and Neville of Exeter, Norfolk, Warwick and the most prominent of Edward's Marchers met at Baynard's Castle and formally begged Edward to assume the throne. Henry IV had based his claim on conquest, and Henry VII was to do the same. Edward claimed the throne by hereditary right.

On 4 March Edward rode the short distance to St Paul's Cathedral to hear a *Te Deum*, then rode in a magnificent procession to the Palace of Westminster. In the Great Hall he swore to uphold the laws and customs of England, after which, duly robed, he took his seat on the king's bench and personally proclaimed his title to the throne. After the sparse assembly acclaimed him, he formally 'took possession of the realm of England'. He then walked to Westminster Abbey, where he sat on the throne and received St Edward's sceptre, and again declared his title.

The ceremonies served the purpose of absolving the assembled lords from their previous oaths of allegiance. This was particularly important to the bishops, who had previously found them an insuperable obstacle to York's claim. A proper coronation would have to wait until Edward had made good his claim against Henry VI, now recast as a usurper after nearly forty years during which his right to reign had never been impugned.

However contrived the formula to justify his usurpation, the young and virile Edward was a dream come true for those yearning for the glory days of Henry V, and from this time forward Warwick could only hope to be the first among equals, all illuminated by the rising sun of York. The abrupt reversal of roles could be finessed while they had a common cause, but in the end Warwick was sure to find it intolerable to be subordinate to his younger cousin and one-time apprentice.

For the time being, however, they had to win the war they had begun together. With the loss of Bonville at St Albans, preceded by his heir, killed at Wakefield, they no longer had a local counterweight to Lancastrian sympathizers in the West Country. Also, despite Mortimer's Cross, much of Wales remained loyal to the Prince of Wales and Jasper Tudor. There were also the Beaumont and Oxford affinities in East Anglia to be considered. All might erupt behind them when they marched north, and several important Yorkist lords remained behind to prevent this.

On 6 March proclamations in Edward's name were sent to the sheriffs of all the counties south of the River Trent, ordering them to prevent any support to pass over the river 'towards our adversary'. Any follower of Henry VI who submitted within ten days was to have 'grace and pardon of his life and goods', except for those with an annual income of more than 100 marks [£42,000] – which was to say all peers and greater gentry – and twenty-two named individuals. Finally, a bounty of £100 [£63,600] was offered for each of the heads of eight individuals.

The named men were not particularly prominent, but all had given personal offence to one or other of the Yorkist leaders. But then, the whole conflict was highly personal in nature. It is as well to recall how much it was a Neville family matter. Warwick was brother-in-law to Arundel, Worcester, FitzHugh, Stanley and Bonville, while the Dukes of Norfolk, Buckingham and York were or had been his uncles by marriage. Ranged against him, the entire Percy clan, the Nevilles of Brancepeth, Clifford, Dacre of the North and Beaumont were all cousins of one degree or other.

Nor should we forget the Beaufort connection. Somerset and his two brothers were the only descendants in the male line, but one great-aunt had been the matriarch of the Nevilles of Middleham and guardian of Richard of York, and another the mother of the Earl of Devon. Through the marriages of their father and uncle, and the subsequent marriages of their widows, they were related to Roos, Welles and to the Talbots and Lisles, all of them Warwick's mortal enemies from the Beauchamp inheritance feud.

PARTISAN PEERS IN 1461

k. = killed; x. = executed; * = peers not present at Towton

Lancaster			York		
Title	Age	Main estates	Title	Age	Main estates
Dukes					
Exeter	31	Southwest	York	19	Many counties
Somerset	25	Southwest	Norfolk	46	Most counties
Earls					
Devon (x.)	29	West Country	Warwick & Salisbury	32	North; Glamorgan; Southwest; Bucks
Northumberland (k.)	40	North; Sussex			
Shrewsbury	13	Shropshire; Derby	Suffolk	19	East Anglia; Oxford
* Oxford [1]	53	East Anglia; Oxford	* Arundel	44	Sussex; Dorset
* Pembroke	30	Wales			
* Wiltshire (x.)	41	Southwest; Cambridge			
Viscounts					
Beaumont	23	Lincoln; Norfolk	* Bourchier [2]	56	East Anglia
Barons (excluding de jure)					
Clifford (k.)	26	Yorks; Westmorland	Clinton	30	Northants
Dacre North (k.)	49	Cumberland	Dacre South	46	Sussex; Dorset
FitzHugh	32	Yorkshire	Dudley	60	Cheshire
Grey of Codnor	26	Midlands	Fauconberg	56	Yorkshire
Lovell	28	Midlands	Grey of Ruthyn	45	Denbigh; Bedford
Neville (k.) [3]	41	Durham	Scrope of Bolton	24	Yorkshire
Rivers (Woodville)	56	Kent; Northants	Scrope of Masham	33	Yorkshire
Roos	34	Midlands; Yorkshire	* Audley	41	Shropshire; Midlands
Rougemont Grey (x.)	43	West Country	* Bergavenny	49	Monmouth
Scales (Woodville)	21	Norfolk	* Bonville (x.)	68	West Country
Welles (k.)	55	Lincolnshire	* Cobham	50	Somerset
Willoughby [4]	33	Lincolnshire	* Grey of Wilton	40	Herefordshire
			* Saye and Sele	33	Kent
			* Stanley [5]	26	Cheshire; Lancashire

1. Contained; only his third son, George Vere, fought for Lancaster at Towton.
2. Brother John, Baron Berners, was a POW. Sons William and Humphrey fought for York.
3. Led the affinity of the Earl of Westmorland, his demented brother.
4. Richard Welles, also heir to his namesake barony.
5. Brother William fought for York.

There was no such complexity in the York family. Edward had only one aunt, married to Viscount Bourchier. Other than that, he was brother-in-law to Suffolk, now an ally, and to Exeter, who could not have been a more furious enemy. His desire to create a substantial extended family to rival Warwick's was to define his subsequent reign.

Although the Lancastrian army that retreated from St Albans to York was relatively small, Edward and Warwick knew it would swell rapidly once back in the North. They could not ignore the challenge, but once they, too, crossed the Trent, they knew the northerners would see them as an invading army and react accordingly. There was, therefore, a premium on acting as fast as possible.

Warwick departed immediately after the coronation to raise troops in the Midlands. Less than a week later, on 11 March, the Van, mainly consisting of the mounted men who had ridden to London in late February, set off up the Great North Road under Fauconberg. Meanwhile, Norfolk summoned his own and allied East Anglian lords' followers to rejoin him in London or on his way north.

Edward also remained in London, to raise a further loan of £4,000 [£2.54 million] from the City, plus contributions from individual merchant houses. Money worked its usual magic and volunteers flocked to London from all over the Home Counties. They were equipped from the royal armouries, and an enormous wagon train assembled to supply the army on its way north.

The contemporary poem 'The Rose of Rouen' is virtually the only source for who actually fought on the Yorkist side at the Battle of Towton, identified by their heraldic banners. Edward's retainers fought under Lionel of Clarence's Black Bull, Edmund of Langley's Falcon and Fetterlock, and the White Lion of the Mortimer Earls of March. The Duke of Burgundy sent a contingent led by a representative of the French Dauphin Louis, under the dolphin banner of the Dauphiné. In addition to the banners of the nobles listed in the 'Partisan Peers' box, the poem describes the banners of Bristol, Canterbury, Coventry, Gloucester, Leicester, Northampton,

Nottingham, Richmond, Salisbury, Windsor and Worcester.

We have no way of knowing how the different contingents were distributed among the battles, but Edward led the Reserve, Fauconberg the Van, Warwick the Main and Norfolk the Rear. Fauconberg, with the majority of the mounted archers and hobilars, did not need to recruit. He raced ahead to clear the way along the Great North Road, springing Lancastrian ambushes as he went. Warwick went to draw on his own and other Yorkist lords' extensive holdings in the Midlands. Edward and Norfolk set out along the Great North Road on 13 March, guarding the main wagon train and recruiting from their own and other Yorkist lords' manors along the way.

The core of the Reserve would have been the army recruited by Edward before and after Mortimer's Cross, with the addition of an unknown number of Burgundians. Those who marched with Warwick to the Midlands would have been the Calais veterans, the Londoners and Kentish men who had stuck with him despite St Albans. Norfolk was in bad health – he died eight months later – but his own and associated affinities turned out in sufficient strength under his cousin, the Essex squire John Howard, to form a fourth battle.

Sadly there are no records on the composition of the Lancastrian army or how it was organized. A reasonable assumption is that Somerset, ably advised by Trollope, was in overall command and would have led the tactical reserve under the banners of King Henry. Exeter must have been with him, as his ego would not have tolerated being under the Earls of Northumberland and Devon, who perforce commanded the other two battles.

Devon fell ill and could not lead his battle to Towton, so the army fought broadly divided into two groups, with Northumberland and the northerners forming on the right, and Somerset, Exeter and the southerners on the left. As before, the mounted archers and hobilars under Clifford and Neville had a roving commission to keep the Yorkists under observation, and to attack any enemy scouting or foraging groups that ventured too far away from their army.

Warwick's battle joined Edward's and Norfolk's before Doncaster and they arrived together at Pontefract on 27 March. There were too many alternative crossings to make the Don a defensible line, but the next place where the Great North Road crossed a river, the Aire at Ferrybridge, a little over 2 miles from Pontefract Castle, was another matter altogether. The Romans never bridged it because the river meanders through a broad flood plain, and there was a serviceable alternative crossing where it ran wide and shallow at Castleford. The Normans replaced the ferry with a bridge in 1198, but it was not until the end of the fourteenth century that it was rebuilt with seven piers, a chapel, and a causeway over marshy ground to Brotherton, on a peninsula of firm ground north of the river, with flood plain on either side.

It was an ideal chokepoint, yet Fauconberg found it undefended. The wooden upper works of the bridge had been demolished, but as long as the piers are still standing any bridge can be easily repaired. With no evidence that the Lancastrians intended to contest the crossing, Fauconberg must have assumed they intended to make their stand at the Wharfe, a bigger river and the last before York, 12 miles further north. He had no engineers or building materials, so rode on to establish whether the crossing at Castleford was passable. Finding it was, he sent squadrons of fore-riders across to reconnoitre north of the river.

The Van, therefore, was astride the Aire at Castleford before the other battles arrived at Pontefract. Edward occupied the castle, while Warwick camped at Ferrybridge and sent workmen and materials to repair the bridge. The workmen set up their camp at the southern end of the bridge, guarded by a small force commanded by a Norfolk lord, John Radcliffe, *de jure* Baron FitzWalter, accompanied by Richard Jenny, one of Warwick's illegitimate brothers. By the evening of Saturday 28 March the engineers had repaired the bridge and returned to camp for the night. They were not destined to enjoy their rest.

KNIGHT'S GAMBIT

BEFORE THE DAWN OF PALM SUNDAY, CLIFFORD'S AND Lord John Neville's men crept along the causeway from Brotherton and silently disposed of any sleepy sentries there may have been at the southern end of the repaired bridge over the Aire. Once the rest of the raiders had crossed, they attacked the engineers' camp. According to *Hall's Chronicle*: 'The Lord Fitzwalter hearing the noise, suddenly arose out of his bed and unarmoured, with a poleaxe in his hand, thinking that it had been an affray among his men, came down to appease the same, but before he could say a word, or knew what the matter was, he was slain, and with him the bastard of Salisbury, brother to the Earl of Warwick.'

The survivors fled towards Warwick's camp at Ferrybridge, pursued by Clifford's men. Panic is particularly contagious in low-light conditions, and with arrows raining down on them from an unseen enemy, several thousand men milled around, some probably fighting each other. Gregory says that Warwick, who cannot have had time to don harness, was wounded in the leg by an arrow, but whether he was or not, he did not stay to steady his men. Hall again:

> He like a man desperate, mounted on his hackney and came blowing to King Edward saying, 'Sir I pray God have mercy on their souls, which in the beginning of your enterprise hath lost their lives, and because I see no success of the world, I remit the

vengeance and punishment to God our creator and redeemer'
and with that he alighted down and slew his horse with his
sword, saying 'Let him fly that will, for surely I will tarry with
him that will tarry with me' and he kissed the cross hilt of his
sword.

Although obviously embellished – Hall was much given to putting
words in his subjects' mouths for dramatic emphasis – if any part of
this account is true it reflects appallingly badly on Warwick, com-
pounding his panic and desertion of his men with an histrionic act
that would have made any fighting man's lip curl.

Having created chaos and inflicted a gratifying number of casualties, the raiders retreated once Warwick's battle recovered from its
initial disorder and began to fight back. They would have been too
closely pursued to tarry on the bridge long enough to damage it
again, but would have taken up positions on the other bank to cover
the bridge, slowly falling back towards Brotherton and shooting at
the Yorkists as they advanced along the causeway.

Although most histories assume Clifford retreated on learning
that Fauconberg's men were approaching from Castleford, there is
no reason to doubt the passage along the causeway to Brotherton
was forced by Edward's men-at-arms, led by hand-gunners and
crossbowmen protected by their pavises. Clifford's men would then
have mounted up and ridden off along the Great North Road, well
satisfied with as neat a delaying action as anyone could wish to have
carried out.

Several hundred crack archers would have done terrible execution among crowds of sleepy and unharnessed men spilling from
their tents, and casualties must have been heavy. This would
explain why Yorkist-inspired accounts gloss over the battle at
Ferrybridge. Clifford would have sent messengers back to Somerset
and Northumberland in York with an account that would have lost
nothing in the telling, and they set their army in motion.

Two things spoiled the party for them. First, Edward was no

Warwick. Knowing the enemy would expect him to pause to lick his wounds, he ordered an immediate general advance. He sent Warwick's shaken battle to Castleford, to advance along the Roman Ridge Road screened by Fauconberg's Van, while he led his battle from Pontefract across the bridge and north along the Great North Road, leaving Norfolk to follow with the wagons.

Secondly, Lady Luck did not smile on the Lancastrians. It seems Clifford had not sent scouts to check the crossing at Castleford, perhaps assuming it was not viable because the river was in spate. Therefore, unaware that Fauconberg had sent squadrons of fore-riders across the Aire the day before, he conducted a leisurely retreat

25. APPROACH TO TOWTON
March 1461

York

Tadcaster

Grimston

Afternoon 29 March

Towton

Cock Beck

Midday 29 March

Lead

Aberford

Saxton

Church Fenton

Scarthingwell

Barkston Ash

Leeds

Micklefield

Sherburn in Elmet

River Wharfe

River Ouse

Castleford

Brotherton

Ferrybridge

Early morning 29 March

River Aire

River Calder

Pontefract

Wakefield

Sandal

0   5   10

miles

© Hugh Bicheno

along the Great North Road, dropping off pairs of riders to watch for pursuit.

As the miles passed without any of them riding back to him, the pace would have dropped to a comfortable walk, and his tired men would have relaxed in their saddles. It is probable Clifford had received confirmation that the main Lancastrian army was on its way and would rendezvous with him at the hill overlooking the village of Saxton. Turning west at the crossroads of the Great North Road and the lane leading to Saxton, he led his command into an ambush in the little valley called Dinting Dale.

Leadman, the best of the Victorian historians of the battle,

26. ROAD DISTANCES & MARCHING TIMES
At 3 mph

N

York

9 miles
3 hrs

Tadcaster

River Wharfe

River Ouse

3 miles
1 hr

Towton

Cock Beck   Saxton

10 miles
3:20 hrs

9 miles
3 hrs

River Aire

River Aire

3.7 miles
1:15 hrs

Castleford   Ferrybridge

River Calder

3.5 miles
1:10 hrs

2 miles
40 mins

Pontefract
Castle

© Hugh Bicheno

says 'they met with some that they had not looked for, and were attrapped', in a context which suggests the trap was set by men sent racing up the Roman Ridge Road by Fauconberg after the battle at Ferrybridge. Alternatively they may have been fore-riders who had narrowly missed encountering Clifford's men on their way south, and had plenty of time to prepare an annihilating ambush for them when they returned. Clifford, Neville and most of their men were killed.

Not only was this a severe loss of inspiring leaders and elite troops, it also caused Somerset and Northumberland to slow their advance after the survivors reached them. As a result, Fauconberg's Van was the first substantial body of troops to arrive at Saxton. His scouts would have fanned out towards Tadcaster and kept him informed about the progress of the Lancastrian army, while preventing theirs from providing the same service.

The most recent research argues persuasively that Ferrybridge, Dintingdale and Towton all took place on the same day, it being understood that a medieval 'day' was calculated very differently from the way it is today.* The proper anniversary of the battle is 6 April, which was 29 March in the Julian calendar then in use, and the day when the moveable feast of Palm Sunday was celebrated.

As to timings, the medieval day began 6 a.m. with the liturgical Prime (first hour), a fixed time of prayer of the traditional Divine Office. Lauds marked actual daybreak, and so varied in time from place to place and season to season. Prime was timekeeping, as were the daytime offices of Terce, Sext, None and Vespers at three-hourly intervals, and Matins punctuated the night hours. Variable Compline marked actual nightfall.

The chart shows the timings of dawn and nightfall in Yorkshire on 6 April 2014. I have no idea what, if any, variation there may have been in the rotational axis of the Earth in the intervening 553

---

* See Tim Sutherland's brilliant online article 'Killing time: challenging the common perceptions of three medieval conflicts – Ferrybridge, Dintingdale and Towton', *Journal of Conflict Archaeology*.

24 hour	By the clock	Liturgical	Julian calendar
0600	6 a.m.	Prime	*Start 29 March 1461*
0625	*Variable*	*Lauds*	*Dawn*
0900	9 a.m.	Terce	
1200	Midday	Sext	
1500	3 p.m.	None	
1800	6 p.m.	Vespers	
1950	*Variable*	*Compline*	*Nightfall*
2100	9 p.m.	Matins	
2400	Midnight	Matins	
0300	3 a.m.	Matins	
0600	6 a.m.	Prime	*Start 30 March 1461*

years, but it will not have made more than a few minutes of difference. The point is there would have been nearly fourteen hours of sufficient light for fighting, and that the medieval Palm Sunday ran on to what we would consider 0600 the following Monday.

In a letter to Papal Legate Coppini, his physician wrote: 'the battle was begun on Palm Sunday, at the hour of prime, at Pontefract'. The Lord Chancellor, Bishop George Neville, wrote the earliest account, also to Coppini, in which he stated: 'on Palm Sunday, near a town called Feurbirga… there was a great conflict, which began with the rising of the sun, and lasted until the tenth hour of the night'. 'The Rose of Rouen' also contains a highly significant timing. The stanza goes as follows (my italics):

> The northern party made them strong with spear and shield,
> On Palm Sunday, *after the none*, they met us in the field
> Within an hour they were right fayne to flee, and eke to yield.

The highlighted phrase has generally been misunderstood as 'afternoon', whereas it means very specifically 'after 3 p.m.' If the battle that took place between Saxton and Towton began between 3 and 4 p.m., then 9–10 hours had already elapsed since the battle of

Palm Sunday began. That was more than double the time the two armies required to march to the battlefield from, respectively, York and Pontefract, without guns or wagons to slow them down. It is not only entirely possible but highly likely that fighting began at Ferrybridge at 0600–0630, and continued until 0600 the next day by modern reckoning.*

Coppini had fled to Flanders after Wakefield, but those who wrote to him knew he would share the information they sent with the pope and the Duke of Burgundy. Accordingly Bishop Neville's letter was what we now call 'informal communication', which also explains why he ridiculously alleged that 28,000 had died in the battle. He wanted to reassure Pius II and Duke Philippe that they had backed the right horse, and sought to evoke Pharsalus, Julius Caesar's crushing victory over Pompey in 48 BC, which brought their civil war to an end.

• ∾ •

A death toll 28,000 would have been not only vastly more than for any other battle of the Wars of the Roses, but also 40 per cent more than the British Army suffered on the first day on the Somme, 455 years later. Furthermore, if 28,000 were killed, at least as many suffered survivable wounds, for a minimum total of 56,000 combat casualties. Just to account for these, each side would have had to field an army more than twice as large as any other in the Wars of the Roses.

A combined total of 56,000 men would also have been nearly twice as many as Charles VII of France assembled for the reconquest of Normandy, after years of preparation, drawing on a larger population, possessed of superior organization and enjoying greater resources. Since a minimum casualty rate of 100 per cent is an

---

* *John Benet's Chronicle* does state that it was a battle in three phases, all on Palm Sunday, but his account contains too many serious errors about the numbers and commanders involved to be accepted as corroboration.

evident absurdity, the actual number of combatants would have had to be greater even than the hallucinatory 100,000 claimed in Edward Hall's *Chronicle*, allegedly based on the original muster rolls.

The largest army assembled during the Wars of the Roses was probably Henry's during the Ludford Bridge campaign, in which he was supported by three dukes, six earls, a viscount and at least eleven barons, all of whom had been issued commissions of array. Even though there appears to have been a bigger turn-out of the gentry for the Towton campaign, there is no way they could have compensated for the notably lower number of peers. The city of Coventry only sent forty men initially and sixty more later, and the average knight or squire would have brought far fewer.

If each army at Towton, including non-combatant personnel, numbered between fifteen and twenty thousand, it would have been pushing the upper limit of what the country could provide and sustain. As to the number killed, the estimate of 9,000 in William Worcester's 'Annales Rerum Anglicarum' is at least possible – if it includes all those killed in the three separate battles that day.

With regard to the battle itself, everything written about it before 2000 (and some since) must be revised in the light of the findings of the Towton Battlefield Archaeological Survey (TBAS). For the purposes of establishing how the battle was fought, the principal value of the TBAS has been the belated recognition it brought to the outstanding private enterprise of Simon Richardson, who since 1985 has scrupulously plotted many hundreds of metal detector hits over the entire area where fighting may have taken place.

In the following chapter I propose a battle development to match the areas where Richardson found dense concentrations of hits. Some will be metallic debris from later dates, but not many: there were no hits at all in areas where we know no fighting took place. That he found so few near the Cock Beck in Towton Dale and Bloody Meadow is probably attributable to the unsystematic work of metal detector hobbyists, who will have concentrated their efforts in these areas on the basis of the canonical account of the battle. Other artefacts in this area will have washed into the Cock Beck, which I have shown in Map 25 (next chapter) swollen by spring run-off, with pools in the two places where modern contours suggest it could have been backed up on Palm Sunday 1461.

Richardson also found no hits in the area where the lane now called the Old London Road once crossed the Cock Beck, supposedly the site of the 'bridge of bodies' massacre. This is another legacy of Victorian historiography, which had the Great North Road doglegging at Towton to cross the stream west of the town, before turning sharp right to Tadcaster and York. The lane does not appear in the earliest road maps, which all show the Great North Road following the line of the modern A162, bridging the Cock Beck not far from where it runs into the River Wharfe, close to Tadcaster.*

For several reasons we can dismiss the tale told in Hall's *Chronicle*, in which Fauconberg provoked the Lancastrians out of their defensive posture by sending his archers forward, with the wind and snow at their backs, to fire a long-range volley:

> The northern men feeling the shoot, but by reason of the snow not knowing the distance between them and their enemy, like hardy men shot their sheaves of arrows as fast as they might, but all their shot was lost and their labour was in vain. When their shot was almost spent, the Lord Fauconberg marched forward with his archers, which not only shot their own full sheaves, but also gathered the arrows of their enemies and let a great part of them fly against their own masters.

Archers would not have wasted their arrows in blind, parabolic flight: they would have saved them for use in the accurate killing range of 50 yards or less, and few arrows driven deep into the ground would have been immediately reusable. As to the snow, spring was well under way, hence the streams and rivers in spate.

* See John Davey's online article 'The Battle of Towton 1461 – A Re-Assessment'.

Temperatures were declining from the Medieval Warm Period, but the Little Ice Age, from which we are still emerging, only really got going in the sixteenth and seventeenth centuries. If any snow did fall, it was a light, unseasonal flurry. Since Hall's account depends on the Lancastrian archers being blinded by the snow, he may have invented it as the necessary *deus ex machina*.

Furthermore, if the Lancastrians had arrived first with the intention of taking up a strong defensive position, they would have formed up on the hill overlooking the village of Saxton. The position is so strong, facing south, that two late Victorian historians argued it *must* have been held by the Lancastrians. Archaeology, however, has confirmed the Lancastrian start line was indeed on the next hill to the north, on the other side of Towton Dale, between the two roads that converge on the village of Towton.

Indisputable truth is not something to look for in any military-historical reconstruction. What follows is a hypothesis that accepts some of the more general parts of contemporary reports, but which is shaped above all by the testimony of the only reliable witnesses: geography, topography and archaeology.

YORK TRIUMPHANT

AUCONBERG WOULD HAVE QUICKLY APPRECIATED THAT the Great North Road and the offshoot of the Roman Ridge Road along which he had advanced were both dominated by the hill north of Saxton. He would have occupied its eastern end, with Warwick's battle pounding up the road behind him to form up on his left. Believing the Lancastrians intended to make a stand at the Wharfe, Edward would have had no reason to hurry his advance along the Great North Road until he was made aware of the developing situation, and so his battle arrived last.

Long before then, messengers would have galloped frantically back down the Great North Road to tell Norfolk at Brotherton to abandon the wagons and close up as fast as his East Anglians could foot it. If not previously, Norfolk's battle now came under the operational command of John Howard, the duke's cousin. Without the hand-over of command to the more vigorous Howard, the East Anglians would not have arrived in time.

The view across Towton Dale was alarming. As Northumberland's men peeled off to form opposite Warwick, followed by the southerners under Somerset and Trollope, with Rivers coming up with the reserve, the Yorkist commanders would have seen that they were badly outnumbered. As more and more Lancastrians poured down the Great North Road, they extended their left wing well beyond Fauconberg's battle.

This was the moment when Fauconberg would have sent his archers forward to disrupt the orderly deployment of the Lancastrian left. Fortuitously, Warwick's battle, the least steady of the Yorkist formations, was separated from Northumberland's men by the deepest section of Towton Dale. The hill also fell off quite steeply to the right of Fauconberg's position, but the ground between the centres of the two armies was almost flat. Edward would have positioned his reserve there, behind Warwick's right flank and Fauconberg's left. According to Wavrin:

> [Edward] jumped from his horse and told them, sword in hand, that on this day he would live or die with them in order to give them courage. Then he came in front of his banners [that is, in full view of the whole army] and waited for the enemy which was marching forward with great noise.

Somerset attacked as soon as his army had formed for battle, the outflanked and outnumbered Yorkist right wing falling back before him. Richardson's metal detecting hits indicate that the fighting on the eastern end and the centre of the hill was ferocious, much less so on the Yorkist left. This may help to extract some value from what is otherwise one of Wavrin's wilder embellishments:

> When Lord Rivers, his son and six or seven thousand Welshmen [?] led by Andrew Trollope, following the Duke of Somerset himself with seven thousand men, charged [Edward's] cavalry who fled and were chased for about eleven miles. It seemed that Lord Rivers' troops had won a great battle, because they thought that the Earl of Northumberland had charged on the other side, unfortunately he had not done so and this became his tragic day for he died that day. During this debacle many of [Edward's] soldiers died and when he learned the truth of what had happened to his cavalry he was very sad as well as very annoyed.

27. TOWTON ARTEFACTS

Results of decades-long metal detecting by Simon Richardson

Area of dense concentration

x   Individual hit

Tadcaster

Old London Road

Towton

Towton Hall
Chapel Hill

Mass grave

Renshaw Wood

Wayside Cross

Mass graves

N

Castle Hill Wood

Great North Road

Modern A162

Cock Beck

Modern

Modern B1217

Scarthingwell

Dinting Dale

Ferrybridge

Castleford

Saxton
Dacre tomb

© Hugh Bicheno

28. BATTLE OF TOWTON
29 March 1461
Contours at 5-feet intervals

0   250   500   750
yards

Probably not
contemporary

Towton

(A) Initial Yorkist deployment

(B) Archer advance/arrow storm

(C) Yorkist last stand

(D) Late arrival of Norfolk

(1) Initial Lancastrian deployment

(2)(3) Lancastrian advance

Renshaw Wood

45   35   25   15

Towton Dale

Bloody
Meadow

Northumberland   (1)   Rivers
Somerset

Castle Hill
Wood

North Acres

Warwick   (2)   (A)   (B)
Edward   Fauconberg

(C)   (3)

45

Cock Beck

35

Norfolk

25

(D)

Saxton   25   Clifford

35   trapped

© Hugh Bicheno

Indeed he would have been, if his cavalry had ended up back at Pontefract! Let us assume Wavrin collected threads of the truth, but without a map to hand failed to understand them and so was unable to weave them into a coherent narrative. If for 'Welshmen' we read 'West Countrymen' and if for 'Edward's cavalry' we understand Fauconberg's battle, which had most of the Yorkist light horse, the opening sentence makes sense. Roughly three-fifths of the Lancastrian army under Somerset and Rivers crunched into Fauconberg's men, who were driven back hundreds of yards to the line of the modern B1217.

On the other flank, the northerners made less progress against Warwick's men, in part because of Towton Dale but also because of the early loss of Northumberland, who was mortally wounded, and Dacre, who was killed by a crossbow bolt in the throat when he lifted his bevor to take a drink. The earlier loss of Clifford was now felt strongly, as the senior remaining northern peer was the semi-Trojan Horse FitzHugh, who could not compensate for the disheartening loss of Percy and Dacre, even if he tried. FitzHugh quite possibly did not – he would have had no stomach for a fight with Warwick, his brother-in-law.

In this scenario, the Yorkist army was kept from defeat by Edward's battle, which held the centre and drew the greater Lancastrian effort, permitting the other two battles to fall back in an orderly manner. There is not much doubt that Edward himself, towering over his men and dealing out death under his family's ancestral banners, was the glue that kept his army together. This all happened very quickly. Not many Yorkists of note fell, however, which must mean their billmen held together, leaving few of the men-at-arms exposed.

Men with nowhere to run will fight to the bitter end, whereas those who see open country behind them are more tempted to flee. The rapid retreat of Fauconberg's battle meant that the Yorkist army soon found itself backed up into a large bend in the Cock Beck and fighting for their lives. It was at this moment that Lady Luck dealt them the ace of trumps with the belated arrival of Norfolk's battle along the Great North Road, behind the Lancastrian left.

There is no possibility this was planned. Edward did not expect to fight another battle this day, otherwise he would not have divided his army in the advance from the Aire. It was a battle in which expectations were dislocated three times. Edward's rapid advance dislocated the Lancastrians' assumption that the battle at Ferrybridge would delay him, and permitted the Yorkists to occupy the hill where the Lancastrians had intended to form up. Edward's assumption the Lancastrians would wait for him behind the Wharfe put him at a grave disadvantage when they advanced to meet him instead. The final, devastating dislocation was Norfolk's arrival behind the Lancastrians when they thought victory was in their grasp.

One minute the exultant Lancastrians were pressing forward to deliver the *coup de grâce*, and the next they had to extricate themselves from a trap. Some would have panicked, but others closed up on their banners and made a fighting retreat across the fields where so many of their comrades already lay dead and wounded. These twice fought-over areas are where Richardson found the densest concentration of hits. The formed units making their way to the Great North Road would have been left alone by the now feral Yorkist foot soldiers, who would have pursued disorganized prey fleeing from the battlefield.

As the door swung back, it would have been the northerners on the far right of the Lancastrian line who were the last to realize that their army was collapsing. Some, trapped against the Cock Beck, gave Bloody Meadow its name. Others on this wing, cut off from the Great North Road, would have been the ones who left the pathetic trail of debris extending north past Renshaw Wood.

Excavation of a mass grave under Towton Hall by the TBAS has added grim detail to what took place during the pursuit phase. It is a product of the hunting instinct provoked by a fleeing enemy and the explosive release of the pent-up rage required for hand-to-hand combat. The skeletons show evidence of frenzied hacking and stabbing, and the injuries to the skulls suggest the butchered men had thrown away their helmets as well as their arms to speed their flight. Not enough to outpace their over-adrenalized pursuers, however, as many of the injuries were inflicted by poleaxes, the preferred weapon of men-at-arms fighting on foot.

Once the horses were brought up a more systematic pursuit ensued. There was no baggage train to distract their pursuers, so the men retreating along the Great North Road were harried through the night. No major fighting could take place in the darkness, but with riders snapping at their heels the pace of the retreat would have been unsustainable for many exhausted men, and their screams out of the murk would have caused the others to hurry even more. Cohesion would have been impossible to maintain, leading to mass panic and the final disaster following the collapse of the bridge over the Cock Beck near Tadcaster.

Most of the lords, including the dying Northumberland, got away. Apart from Dacre, only Welles was killed on the field, while Rougemont Grey and (possibly) Beaumont were captured. Otherwise this was a battle in which, for once, the knights did not ride away, leaving the foot soldiers to be massacred. Trollope and some others were killed during the fighting, but a large number of gentry from all over England fell during the pursuit. Many of them were later attainted and their families ruined.

Henry, Marguerite and Prince Edward fled to Scotland accompanied by Somerset, Exeter, Roos (who had remained with the royal family in York) and Ralph Percy, Northumberland's remaining brother. Devon was captured in York, too ill to travel. He had to pay for Bonville and was executed on 3 April in Edward's presence. So was Rougemont Grey, brother of the turncoat Grey of Ruthyn, for what particular offence is not recorded. Young Viscount Beaumont was spared, perhaps because Edward was ashamed at the manner in which his father had been killed at Northampton.

Elsewhere, the flying Earl of Wiltshire's luck finally ran out. Following defeat at Mortimer's Cross he had made his way back to Pembroke, then took ship to join the northern army. He was not with it at Towton, however, and was trying to board a ship again when he was captured at Cockermouth. Edward saw him beheaded at Newcastle on 1 May.

Captured along with Wiltshire were Marguerite's clerks, Doctors John Morton and Ralph Mackerell. Morton was one of the men specifically excluded from pardon in the proclamation of 6 March, so it was his great good fortune to be brought before Edward a month after Towton, when his thirst for vengeance had been assuaged by the execution of Wiltshire. He ordered Morton and Mackerell imprisoned in the Tower while a commission investigated their treasons, from which they escaped to rejoin Marguerite in France a year later.

While Edward was replacing the Yorkist heads on the Micklegate Bar with Lancastrians, Lords Montagu and Berners, captured at second St Albans, were found alive and well. Possibly because their lives had been saved by the city authorities, they interceded with Edward not to exact collective punishment, and a pattern was set for the generous treatment of all boroughs and individuals who submitted to his grace.

On past and future form we may be sure that Warwick was not so magnanimous. The Trojan Horse Lord Greystoke, who had stayed clear of the final battle, now dropped his Lancastrian mask and advised Warwick which of the Neville tenants had been disloyal. If Lord FitzHugh did betray the Lancastrian cause at Towton, he gained nothing from it except immunity for having too willingly taken possession of Neville lands during the 1459–60 attainder.

Edward rode on to Durham, where he made Bishop Lawrence Booth, previously Lord Privy Seal and Marguerite's chancellor, his confessor. He even promised 'good lordship' to the Prior of Durham, who had lent the queen 400 marks [£170,000] and now had the chutzpah to ask the new king to reimburse him. Thirteen years later he was still trying to collect. Edward rode no further north than Newcastle, where he remained only to see Wiltshire executed, then rode back to Durham.

He then embarked on a progress through Lancashire, Cheshire and Staffordshire. Continuing south-east, at Stony Stratford he received the submission of Lord Rivers, who came from his nearby manor of Grafton. Rivers and his son Anthony, Lord Scales, had been imprisoned in the Tower after Towton but were released in July, probably through the intercession of Jacquetta. Edward sent a letter to Bishop Neville, the Lord Chancellor, stating he had 'of our grace especial pardoned and remitted and forgiven unto Richard Woodville, knight, Lord Rivers, all manner of offences and trespasses of him done against us'.

Among those trespasses was breaking his parole, given to Warwick when he was released from captivity in Calais. Edward may have taken a liking to Rivers during his Calais captivity, as he certainly behaved with remarkable generosity towards a man who had come close to killing him at Towton – although this was not a demerit in knightly terms. Three years later he married Rivers' and Jacquetta's stunningly beautiful eldest daughter Elizabeth, and ushered in a whole new round of woe.

From Stony Stratford Edward rode to Sheen, where he was immediately beset by the host of problems that Henry had never addressed, and which the last two years of war had greatly exacerbated. Parliament was summoned for 6 July and Edward's formal coronation was scheduled to take place six days later. What seemed to be a perfect storm of combined threats from France and Scotland, detailed in the next chapter, caused him to postpone the summons until 4 November, and to bring forward the coronation to 28 June.

Edward made his state entry into London on 26 June and was escorted to the Tower by the mayor, aldermen and 400 leading citizens. That evening and the next morning he created thirty-two new knights. They included Norfolk's cousin John Howard, Norfolk's 17-year-old heir John Mowbray and the late Duke of Buckingham's son John, Lord Stafford. Others honoured were the Treasurer of Calais Walter Blount and Lord Stanley's brother William. Edward also knighted his younger brothers, 11-year-old George and

8-year-old Richard, newly returned from the Burgundian court, where their mother had sent them after Wakefield.

The following day, Sunday 28 June, was fully taken up by a magnificent ceremony in which Archbishops Bourchier of Canterbury and Booth of York anointed and crowned him, and by a sumptuous banquet. No expense was spared, but as the crown's secular revenue stream had dried up completely, it was all with money borrowed against the security of a further tenth voted by the Canterbury Convocation. We may be sure the new king also received gifts in cash and kind from those anxious to win or keep his favour.

On Monday, Edward created his brother George Duke of Clarence, and four months later he made Richard Duke of Gloucester. A month later Norfolk died, his heir still a minor. With the dukedom of York now merged with the crown, the heir to the dukedom of Buckingham also a minor, and Exeter and Somerset attainted, no adult dukes remained. Despite this, Edward did not make Warwick a duke, either now or later, on the face of it an outstandingly ungrateful act of omission. Perhaps he felt that Warwick's behaviour at second St Albans and Ferrybridge had cancelled out his previous achievements – or maybe he just wanted to show Warwick who was the boss. Whatever his reasons, it was a slap in the face.

On Tuesday 30 June he made Viscount Bourchier Earl of Essex, and Lord Fauconberg Earl of Kent. By summons to Parliament Edward created six new barons in their own names: William, Baron Hastings, William, Baron Herbert, Thomas, Baron Lumley, Robert, Baron Ogle, Humphrey, Baron Stafford of Southwick (previously known as 'of Hooke') and John, Baron Wenlock, and confirmed Walter Devereux as Baron Ferrers of Chartley by marriage.

All the new creations had distinguished themselves in the recent battles, most of them at Mortimer's Cross. Edward's intention was plain – he wished to refresh the nobility with men of proven courage and loyalty. Apart from Ogle, Lumley and Wenlock, they were unequivocally his men, not Warwick's. Some were to become Edward's closest councillors and even companions in debauchery.

Acts of Attainder in late 1461 deprived Northumberland, Devon, Wiltshire, Pembroke, Clifford, Dacre of the North, Neville, Rougemont Grey and Welles, the majority killed on Palm Sunday or executed shortly afterwards. Of the living peers attainted, Somerset, Exeter and Roos were still in rebellion, but Beaumont was not, and was probably attainted because Hastings wanted his lands. Thirty-nine of the seventy-one attainted knights, squires, gentlemen, yeomen, clerks and two tradesmen had also been killed. Most attainders of the nobility were later reversed, but Edward had less compunction in permanently depriving commoners.

Edward did not become personally involved in the suppression of continuing Lancastrian resistance. This showed a precocious understanding that kings should lend their presence only to great enterprises, and that a war of sieges and skirmishes offered no prospect of gain commensurate with the risk of death or disgrace. It was a surprisingly mature appreciation for a man who had only just, on 28 April, celebrated his twentieth birthday.

• ☙ •

Objectively Henry VI's reign ended on Palm Sunday 1461, but he lived on for a further ten miserable years. It would have been infinitely better for the Lancastrian cause if he had been killed at the second battle of St Albans, leaving his son as king. After Marguerite recovered him she had to step back from the leading role she and her son had been playing. The dithering at St Albans during February 1461 seems more typical of Henry than his consort, as does the fact that no progress was made to conclude a Scottish alliance on the foundations laid at Lincluden Abbey.

Now, too late, Marguerite finally stopped trying to make her husband behave like a king, and resumed acting as though she were queen in her own right. Behind the scenes she had not ceased to do so: after St Albans she sent Morice Doulcereau to France to conduct clandestine negotiations with her uncle Charles VII through Pierre de Brézé, Grand Seneschal of Normandy and Charles's foremost military commander. Brézé owed his eminence to Agnès Sorel, placed in the king's bed by Isabelle of Lorraine. He was to prove a devoted friend to Isabelle's daughter, whom he had known since childhood.

Doulcereau was a Brézé retainer and had been with Henry VI at Northampton. Given that Brézé had played such a prominent role in the fall of Normandy, and had led the attack on Sandwich in 1457, the appearance of his personal emissary among the Lancastrian courtiers suggests he was there at Marguerite's invitation. What passed between them before 1461 we do not know, but in February 1461 Doulcereau brought secret offers to Brézé which, had they become known in England, would have destroyed Marguerite's credibility.

In a letter to his king dated 24 February, Brézé warned Charles not to send letters to Marguerite 'by any hands except Doulcereau's, because, if his letters were captured and the queen's intentions discovered, her friends would unite with her enemies, and kill her'. There is no reason to doubt that the secret offers Doulcereau brought were an outright gift of the Channel Islands to Brézé if he could conquer them, and to sell Calais to Charles in return for his financial support against the Yorkists.

By a Dominican friar sent directly to Charles VII, she requested 80,000 crowns [£12.72 million], and that he should mobilize a fleet to wrest control of the Channel from Warwick. Another Dominican went to Rome to denounce Coppini. Charles agreed to Brézé recruiting an army and a fleet to seize the Channel Islands, but told Marguerite he was not in a position to send the money she needed, and that the matter of Calais must await a successful suppression of the Yorkist insurgency.

Brézé sent his son-in-law to conquer the islands, Warwick's through the right of his wife, Anne Beauchamp. John Nanfan, the warden who had welcomed Warwick and his party after their flight from Ludlow, was taken by surprise and surrendered Mont Orgueil Castle, a fortress on the eastern coast of Jersey. Although a simultaneous attack on Guernsey failed, Brézé proclaimed himself Lord of the Isles of Jersey, Guernsey, Alderney and Sark. In fact his rule did not even extend to the whole of Jersey; the Lord of St Ouen in the north-west of the island never bent the knee to him.

Marguerite's luck continued to be unfailingly bad. Whatever Charles VII might have done to help her after Towton became moot when he succumbed to the illness that had been crippling him for years. He became delirious, an abscess in his mouth prevented him from eating, and he died on 22 July. His son, who refused to be reconciled with him even on his deathbed, became Louis XI, and among his first acts was to strip Pierre de Brézé of his offices.

Before that blow landed, Marguerite had been tending another iron in the fire. As soon as the royal party fled to Scotland after Towton, she renewed her friendship with Mary of Guelders. Henry was sent out to Linlithgow Palace, 18 miles west of Edinburgh, while Marguerite and her son were made welcome by Mary 50 miles away at Falkland Palace in Fife, with Bishop Kennedy also excluded from the proceedings. There, the two queens made a deal they may have discussed at Lincluden Abbey, but which could not have been concluded while Marguerite's Marcher lords lived.

Trusting to the truce previously agreed, Northumberland had drawn his retainers from the border and left Berwick with a skeleton garrison. Now that he was dead and his 12-year-old heir was in Yorkist custody, Ralph Percy, as the senior member of the family, consented to the hand-over of Berwick on 25 April. Nothing could better illustrate the depth of northern bitterness after Towton than that a Percy should have remained loyal to the Lancastrian dynasty despite the surrender of Northumberland's border fortress.

In addition, Marguerite's remaining supporters not only agreed Scotland should have Carlisle, gateway to the western March as Berwick was to the eastern, but also to march with Scots troops to capture it. Along with Brézé's assault on Jersey, this constituted the 'perfect storm' referred to in the last chapter, which caused Edward IV to postpone the summoning of Parliament and to bring forward the date of his coronation.

Although the Scots border levies cannot have been happy to find themselves under the command of such as Dacre's brother Humphrey and other English knights, they cheerfully laid waste the countryside around Carlisle. With remarkable stupidity (if, that is, they ever intended to mount a siege) they then burned the town, simplifying the castle garrison's task while depriving themselves of shelter. The raiding force retreated back over the border at the approach of Montagu with a locally raised army.

There, in a nutshell, was the conundrum posed by Marguerite's Scottish alliance. The Marcher commons may have hated the Yorkists, but they hated the Scots even more. Regional identities were very strong, but an emerging national identity trumped them in any confrontation with foreigners. Although there were strong local dialects, almost all who lived within the kingdom of England spoke the same language, unlike France with its four major and several minor language groups.

Yorkist propaganda insisted that Marguerite was not English, and that support for her was not only treason to the new king but also treason to England. Having spent her entire adult life in England without once returning to France, Marguerite was a thoroughly naturalized Englishwoman, and in many ways an exemplar of the profound English belief expressed in the clichéd phrase 'I know my rights'. The Yorkist portrayal of Marguerite gained little traction until she was compelled to ally with England's foreign foes. Even then, awareness of the great wrong done to her may have inclined many to forgiveness.

Yet she remained the guiding light to the small band of Lancastrians who continued to fight for her in a right-angle triangle of land north of Hadrian's Wall and south of the border. At the western tip of the triangle, in Cumberland, Humphrey Dacre forted up in the family castle at Naworth. East of Naworth, the lord of the large but sparsely populated Harbottle and Redesdale estates in north-central Northumberland was none other than William Tailboys, whose ceaseless troublemaking in the 1440s and 1450s had done so much to undermine Henry VI's authority. The main body of the triangle, however, consisted of Percy lands.

The main focus of the war shifted to the royal castles of Bamburgh and Dunstanburgh, each on a headland jutting into the North Sea, and the great Percy castle at Alnwick. Alnwick was on the Great North Road, but the other two were in such remote locations that the only strategic threat they posed was as staging posts for seaborne invasion. They had harbours, plentiful water from wells dug deep into the rock on which they stand, and the walls of Dunstanburgh enclose one of the largest spaces of any castle ever built in England.

Bamburgh had been the capital of the Anglo-Saxon kingdom of Bernicia and of the preceding British kingdom, and is only a few miles from the Holy Island, Lindisfarne, from which the north of England was evangelized at the invitation of Oswald, king and saint. Today we live detached from our history, and 'folk tale' is a term of derision. Not so in the fifteenth century, and Bamburgh's talismanic quality may account in some measure for the tenacity with which it held out against the Yorkist tide.*

Alnwick, Bamburgh and Dunstanburgh all initially capitulated to Warwick in the summer of 1461 on the easiest of terms. Ralph Percy was left in command of all three, in the hope of reconciling the Percy affinity. He did not, however, regard an oath of loyalty extracted under duress as binding, and when a Lancastrian force under Tailboys marched south in October, he opened the gates. The castles now fulfilled their purpose by obliging the new regime to expend treasure and political credit, while buying time for Marguerite to raise an army.

Her problem, underlined by the ignominious performance of the Scots at Carlisle, was that her hosts could not, even if they wished to do so, field an army capable of defeating the English, or even march far beyond the border. The Lancastrians could mount

---

* Bamburgh's significance as the very heart of historic Northumbrian identity is made clear in Max Adams' brilliant *The King in the North*.

troublesome raids, one of which got as far as the Clifford manor of Skipton in the West Riding of Yorkshire before turning back; but without the credibility needed to rouse popular support, they were just pinpricks. With Duke Philippe of Burgundy fully committed to the Yorkists, there was only one place where she could hope to obtain the resources to recover the kingdom.

She sent her first formal embassy to France before news of Charles VII's death arrived. She probably knew he was dying, as she also sent Somerset to the Burgundian court to make contact with Duke Philippe's heir Charles, Count of Charolais, with whom he had formed a warm friendship during his attempt to seize Calais. To Paris she sent Lord Hungerford, recently returned from his pilgrimage and a rare example of a rat boarding a sinking ship, and Robert Whittingham. They had safe conducts from Charles VII, but Somerset did not.

When they disembarked at Le Tréport in the County of Eu, at the border of French and Burgundian territory, they were arrested and their papers seized by men sent by Louis XI, who was on his way to Reims for his coronation. Somerset was taken inland to the castle at Arques, outside Saint-Omer in Artois, whence he could as easily be handed over to Warwick's men at Calais as to Duke Philippe. Hungerford and Whittingham were moved to Dieppe, from where they sent desperate letters to Marguerite warning her not to come to France herself, still less with the king and the prince, as Louis had disbanded the fleet his late father had assembled to wrest control of the Channel from Warwick.

Marguerite was now trapped in the web of intrigue Louis XI began to spin across Europe from the moment his father died, which was to earn him the well-deserved nickname 'the Universal Spider'. Although there is hot competition for the title of the most devious prince of the Renaissance, Louis probably edges out the likes of the della Rovere Pope Sixtus IV and the Borgia Pope Alexander VI, who would otherwise have little secular competition. Warwick was a babe in arms by comparison with any of them.

Marguerite's last opportunity to act as a free agent came in 1462, when Louis' machinations very nearly provoked the hostile Anglo-Burgundian alliance he most feared. She travelled to France and her cousin agreed to prepare a fleet and an army for an invasion of England, to be led by Brézé, now conditionally back in favour. The moment passed, and she and Brézé set out with only 800 men, in an expedition Brézé had to finance himself. Their arrival at Bamburgh in October finally persuaded Edward he must lead an army himself to suppress the northern rebellion and to intimidate Scotland.

As for Marguerite, no one could have done more than she did, at any time since she first stepped into the void created by her husband's abdication of responsibility in 1450. No one could have animated him more and sustained his cause longer, but he was too great a burden to carry. It is hard to identify any moment in her life when she was blessed with unalloyed good fortune, but like all the great women of history she scorned self-pity and never saw herself as a victim. Her indomitability should be a source of inspiration to men and women alike.

PART II

LEGITIMACY

ENRY VI'S CAUSE SHOULD HAVE BEEN IRRECOVERABLE after the crushing defeat of his followers at the Battle of Towton on Palm Sunday 1461. Even before that bloodbath, the Lancastrians had lost the support of the Church and the mercantile class, in particular the vital Calais-based Merchants of the Staple: all had swung solidly behind Edward IV, the Yorkist usurper. Yet a hard core of Lancastrians fought on and lost everything, though they could have retained their lives, titles and property by making peace with the new order.

What motivated them? It was certainly not devotion to dispiriting Henry VI, or even to charismatic Marguerite d'Anjou, his admirable queen. The modern mind finds it difficult to comprehend their motives because the concepts of shame and honour play a reduced role in our society. Most of us are Sir John Falstaff's children:

> Well, 'tis no matter; honour pricks me on. Yea, but how if honour
> prick me off when I come on? How then? Can honour set-to a
> leg? No. Or an arm? No. Or take away the grief of a wound? No.
> Honour hath no skill in surgery, then? No. What is honour? A
> word. What is in that word 'honour'? What is that 'honour'?
> Air. A trim reckoning! Who hath it? He that died o' Wednesday.
> Doth he feel it? No. Doth he hear it? No. 'Tis insensible then?

> Yea, to the dead. But will it not live with the living? No. Why?
> Detraction will not suffer it. Therefore I'll none of it. Honour is
> a mere scutcheon.

It may seem absurd to suggest that honour played a life-defining role among men who schemed incessantly against each other, stole by force when they could not subvert the law to their advantage, and regularly broke the most sacred oaths. Yet it did, and provides the key to understanding why the new Yorkist dynasty was insecure and ultimately unsuccessful.

There was no shame in surrendering to a worthy opponent. For example Robert, Lord Hungerford, was captured by the French in 1453 and fully accepted his obligation to pay a ruinous ransom to obtain his release. The same rules did not apply during the Wars of the Roses for several reasons, chief among them personal hatreds. Thus when leading Yorkist Richard Neville, Earl of Salisbury, surrendered on terms at Wakefield, he was butchered in cold blood even though he had surely promised his captors an enormous ransom.

Denied the prospect of ransom, common soldiers had little incentive to take prisoners. The expensive armour and distinctive tabards that once advertised that their wearers were worth taking alive were now just desirable spoils of war to be stripped from their corpses. In some instances commanders may have promised their troops a financial reward for the capture of named opponents, but usually because they wished to inflict a more ignominious fate.

That some still surrendered was probably the result of combat exhaustion – also the reason why the hand-to-hand fighting phase of battles was relatively short. Towton marked the nadir, with no mercy shown even to the humble conscripts who made up the vast majority of armies. We dwell on the blood feuds of lords because their doings are known – but desire for revenge also seared the souls of the sons of slaughtered men whose names were not recorded.

As in the aftermath of any civil war, the victors were faced with the imperative need to reverse the pitiless polarization that had been necessary to prevail. This proved particularly difficult for Edward IV and his principal supporter, the Earl of Salisbury's namesake heir Richard Neville, Earl of Warwick, because the Lancastrians regarded them as unworthy opponents. It was the reason why some Lancastrians refused to accept the verdict of Towton, and why the war dragged on intermittently for another generation.

Was the Yorkist cause dishonourable? Well – yes. The Lancastrian Henry IV seized the throne in 1399 because his cousin Richard II, the legitimate king, expropriated Henry's inheritance from his father, John of Gaunt. That was an invitation to a trial of strength, which the king lost. Richard of York had no such justification to rebel against Henry VI, whose only offence (other than chronic weakness) was a cautious refusal to hand over the administration of his kingdom to a haughty cousin with as good or better right by blood to the throne.

The issue of blood right became crucial after York was killed at Wakefield on 30 December 1460, because there were good reasons to believe that Edward, his heir, was not his son. He did not resemble Richard in any way: parents of slight build and average height do not engender burly sons 7–8 inches taller than they. Richard conspicuously slighted Edward in favour of his second son, Edmund, who was also killed at Wakefield, while contrary to the medieval norm Edward made no great effort to honour the memory of his supposed father until several years after the question of his true parentage nearly cost him the throne.

Not for nothing is the word 'legitimacy' employed to describe a government's legal and moral right to rule. The suspicion that Edward's mother, Cecily née Neville, was an adulteress and he a bastard was more damaging to his authority than the evident fact that he had usurped an anointed king. In 1469–70 it was whispered to discredit him by Warwick (her nephew) and Edward's brother George, Duke of Clarence. Thirteen years later, until he concocted an alternative to spare his mother's blushes, it was also the legal premise that Richard, her youngest son, thought to advance when he seized the throne from Edward's namesake heir.

Added to which, Edward was barely 19 years old when he became king in 1461 and, regardless of his precocious brilliance as a battlefield commander, he undoubtedly owed the throne to the machinations of his 38-year-old cousin Warwick. It was Warwick who made Calais a Yorkist stronghold, won over the Company of the Staple and persuaded Pope Pius II's legate Francesco Coppini to back the Yorkist cause with the full might of the Church, and Warwick who commanded the loyalty of the ever-rebellious men of Kent.

Like his father, Warwick owed his eminence to favour shown him by Henry VI, built up further by Queen Marguerite's desperate effort to turn him into the Lancastrian regime's strongman in the later 1450s. This made him a greater traitor than Edward in Lancastrian eyes, compounded to loathing when he engineered the battlefield treachery that precipitated the rout and slaughter of Lancastrian nobles at Northampton in 1460.*

In addition to the intense hatred the Nevilles of Middleham had earned by their insatiable avarice, Warwick's devouring ambition also made him an uncertain prop for the new regime. He was like an Italian Renaissance warlord miscast in late medieval England. Despite being showered with offices and with lands taken from the defeated Lancastrians, he calls to mind King Louie's song in Disney's version of *The Jungle Book*:

> I've reached the top and had to stop
> And that's what's bothering me

In 1463 Bishop Kennedy, regent for King James III of Scotland, wrote that Warwick was 'governor of the realm of England'. A year later the Governor of Abbeville in Picardy wrote to King Louis XI of France, 'in England they have but two rulers – M. de Warwick and

---

*Also for a similar selective massacre after the First Battle of St Albans in 1455.

another whose name I have forgotten'. Warwick has been known as the 'Kingmaker' ever since Shakespeare put these words in the mouth of Marguerite in *Henry VI, Part 3*:

> Peace! Impudent and shameless Warwick, peace;
> Proud setter up and puller down of kings;

The encounter with Marguerite crowned a series of acts of the blackest treachery, whose aim was to achieve for Warwick the status Bishop Kennedy incorrectly attributed to him, and which Warwick thought he deserved. This appears to have been his sole motivation – he said he felt dishonoured by Edward, who not only did not make him a duke but also rubbed salt in the wound by refusing permission for his brother Clarence, at the time next in line to the throne, to marry one of Warwick's daughters.

Clarence is a very modern figure. He was driven by an over-powering sense of entitlement, a now common condition that was limited to princes of the blood in the late Middle Ages. Favourable circumstances he did nothing to shape spared him the reality checks that normally correct adolescent whininess and self-absorption, until at last he pushed his luck too far.

Warwick did not seek power because he believed, as Richard of York did, that he would be a more just and competent ruler, but because his pride would settle for nothing less. It also blinded him to his own shortcomings. While he fully possessed the *furbizia* (unscrupulous cunning) indispensable to contemporary Italian princes, it was Edward's great good fortune that in the military sphere Warwick's cleverness took the form of over-elaboration.

Behind Warwick was Edward's contemporary Louis XI, the greatest of the Valois kings, who was to *furbizia* what the Grand Canyon is to valleys. He was a man who lived only for power, and cared nothing for luxury or any other of its secondary rewards. His father expelled the English from Normandy and Aquitaine, but it was Louis – despite a near-fatal stumble in 1465 over his own hubris – who achieved the more difficult task of forging a nation from the semi-autonomous feudal fragments he inherited.

Edward's reign coincided with Louis XI's almost exactly. Although nineteen years older, Louis became king five months later than Edward and died five months after him. Even their male heirs were born five months apart. All the major political upheavals of Edward's reign were influenced, when not initiated, by Louis. The Hundred Years War between England and France did not officially end until the Treaty of Picquigny in 1475, when Edward and his closest associates were bought off with pensions.

Given the enormous disparity in wealth and population between the two kingdoms, Edward could only aspire to be more than an inconvenience to Louis by combining with Burgundy and Brittany. Conversely, Louis did not have to invest very much to stir the pot across the Channel because the English supplied the ingredients and the heat themselves, while the Scots generally required only modest financial inducement to cause trouble.

These, then, were the main structural elements of discord with which Edward had to wrestle throughout his reign. It was an era of personal kingship and although he was a more 'hands-on' monarch than his hapless predecessor, maintaining order in England and Wales was like trying to herd cats. He had neither the income nor the inclination to create a national bureaucracy, and for regional government had to depend on established local magnates, or endow others to make them first among equals, and hope they would repay him with loyalty.

Unlike the norm under Henry VI, the interests of Edward's inner circle seldom diverged significantly from his own. Outstanding among them were William Herbert, effectively his viceroy in Wales, and William Hastings, his closest friend and chamberlain, who controlled access to the king throughout his reign. Hastings' even-handedness was widely commented and his only enemies appear to have been Edward's queen and her family.

Thanks to unique rights of property ownership and inheritance, women played a more important role in the history of England than they did elsewhere. The recent work of female authors has shed much-needed light on the role of women during the Wars of the Roses. Unfortunately most of it is necessarily speculative, as no narratives by women survive and they seldom feature in chronicles written by men. When they do 'intrude' into the male narrative, it is as active players in moments of crisis; but, obviously, if they had the power to affect events at such moments, their influence in normal times must have been considerable.

If one could choose a single item that would do most to illuminate this poorly documented period, it would be a diary or memoir written by Jacquetta de Luxembourg. Married at 17 to the Duke of Bedford, Henry VI's elder uncle and next in line to the throne, she was widowed at 19 and two years later married handsome Richard Woodville without obtaining the legally required royal licence. Anthony, their first child, was born rather less than nine months later, and thirteen more children testified to her robustness and their abiding passion.

Jacquetta became a confidante of Queen Marguerite and secured the advancement of her husband in the Lancastrian hierarchy. She also accompanied her husband – by now Baron Rivers – to Calais in a vain effort first to deny and later to wrest it away from Warwick. Her standing as the second most senior lady at court under Henry VI (after Marguerite) and, until he started his own family, Edward IV (after his mother) undoubtedly facilitated the reconciliation between her husband and the new king soon after Towton.

There can be no doubt that Jacquetta had a great deal to do with the dynastic bombshell of Edward's secret marriage to her daughter Elizabeth, a widow with two young sons. Edward's companions noted his state of blissful exhaustion in the days following the marriage, and anyone who doubts that Elizabeth's sexual virtuosity closed the deal simply does not know much about young men.

It is prissy as well as unhistorical to underplay traditional female strengths. Also, given the appalling rate of death in childbirth and infant mortality, a proven record of bearing healthy sons was certainly an asset we should not undervalue. Nor should we doubt the influence of mothers on their children. There is little doubt Cecily poisoned her younger sons' minds against Edward, but the outstanding example was Lady Margaret Beaufort, who was to be the most intimate and influential adviser to her only child Henry VII throughout his reign.

Marriages among people of property were regarded as the cement of family alliances, and love matches were extremely rare. Arranged marriages, such as Warwick's with Anne Beauchamp, which made him the heir to most of the large Beauchamp, Montague and Despenser estates, were active partnerships. Wives retained their property rights, and for wealthy widows there was a brisk sellers' market in which, barring royal interference, they could dictate the terms of new partnerships.

It has been a more demanding task to organize this colourful cast of characters into a coherent theme for the quarter century following Edward's accession than it was for an equal period preceding it. There was a grim inevitability in the steady slide from the start of Henry VI's feeble and erratic personal kingship to the chaos and war that ended it. By contrast, Edward had done much to restore stability before Warwick rebelled in 1469–71, and had done so again by the time he died in 1483.

Yet his story ends with arguably the most tragic and certainly one of the most disputed events in English history. The recent discovery of Richard III's bones has only underlined the durable fascination of a period that culminated in one king being buried with full honours in the magnificent chapel he built at Windsor, and his successor brother's naked body cast into an unmarked grave and historical obloquy twenty-eight months later.

There was nothing inevitable about the outcome, but it is difficult to dismiss the suspicion that the fate of the Yorkist dynasty was written from the moment Edward was conceived. In the end it is wonderfully ironic that the issue of legitimacy should have fatally undermined the House of York, because the only Plantagenet blood in the veins of the Tudors came from Cecily Neville and Margaret Beaufort, both descendants of the family John of Gaunt bred with his mistress Katherine Swynford while he was married to Constance of Castille.

EDWARD

W HEN WE REVIEW THE ACTIONS OF YOUNG EDWARD IV during his early reign we should consider the possibility that the appalling experience of Towton may have influenced him profoundly. He was at the forefront of a prolonged hand-to-hand battle, much of it spent grimly retreating in the face of superior numbers, his height, distinctive tabard and banners making him a magnet for war arrows, while hacking down determined warriors who burst through his bodyguard, seeking to claim the glory of killing the usurper king.

Historians are often faulted by combat veterans because 'they were not there' – that while hindsight may permit them to see the big picture better than those who were involved, they lack the personal experience to get the details right. This is undeniable; but the antiseptic nature even of most accounts written by combatants suggests the main obstacle is the almost universal reticence of the veterans themselves.

Such reticence, born of a once general belief that feelings are a private matter, is the overt manifestation of the mind's ability to 'seal off' traumatic events, which, for some, can have a disabling psychological or even physiological cost. Ancient Mesopotamian texts reveal that the symptoms of post-traumatic stress disorder (PTSD) following combat had been identified over 3,000 years ago. Herodotus wrote of an unwounded Greek hoplite who went blind after a comrade was killed next to him at the Battle of Marathon in 490 BC.

No amount of training or mock combat in tournaments could have prepared Edward for the reality of thousands of men snarling and screaming around him, or for the experience of trampling over dead and dying men, or being spattered with blood and brains, or the overpowering stench of bowels voided in terror and agony. Add the stunning effect of repeated heavy blows to helmet and harness and sheer physical exhaustion, and it would be strange indeed if it did not affect his thinking and behaviour for many years to come.

Some men thrive on combat, but – probably because of Towton – Edward was not one of them. He fought well, when it was necessary, but he lacked the thirst for war that distinguished Edward III, the paternal and maternal great-great-grandfather after whom he was named. No doubt royal sycophants evoked the memory of his very distant ancestor Edward I, known as 'Longshanks', to explain the young king's exceptional physical stature, but he notably lacked the implacable ferocity of the dread 'Hammer of the Scots'.

The canonical view is that Edward pursued a policy of reconciliation to the point of endangering his regime – but would a harder line have stamped out the Lancastrian embers sooner? There is abundant evidence that well-established regional lords commanded deep loyalty, often reinforced by ties of kinship, and that beheading the lords did not decapitate their following. Indeed, some families were so deeply entrenched as to be seemingly untouchable. The outstanding example was the Stanleys of Lancashire and Cheshire, who retained their titles, lands and even royal offices despite serial betrayals of successive kings.

• ❦ •

This loyalty is commonly attributed to the network of patronage or 'good lordship', which some call 'bastard feudalism'. If that had been all there were to it, decapitation and legal dispossession (attainder)

HOUSE OF YORK

Descendants of Richard of York and Cecily Neville

k. = killed in battle   x. = executed

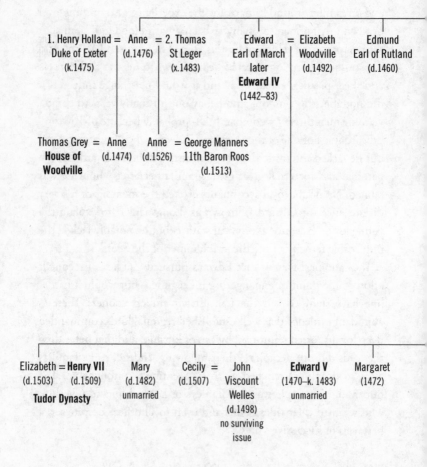

1. Henry Holland = Anne = 2. Thomas   Edward = Elizabeth   Edmund
   Duke of Exeter   (d.1476) St Leger   Earl of March   Woodville   Earl of Rutland
   (k.1475)   (x.1483)   later   (d.1492)   (d.1460)
                                         Edward IV
                                         (1442–83)

Thomas Grey = Anne   Anne = George Manners
House of   (d.1474) (d.1526) 11th Baron Roos
Woodville   (d.1513)

Elizabeth = **Henry VII**   Mary   Cecily = John   **Edward V**   Margaret
(d.1503)   (d.1509)   (d.1482) (d.1507) Viscount   (1470–k. 1483)   (1472)
Tudor Dynasty   unmarried   Welles   unmarried
                                                  (d.1498)
                                                  no surviving
                                                  issue

[1] Margaret's eldest son Henry, Baron Montagu, was executed 1539 and his young son was imprisoned until his death *c.*1542. Her second son Cardinal Reginald Pole was Archbishop of Canterbury under Queen Mary. Margaret was beatified in 1889.

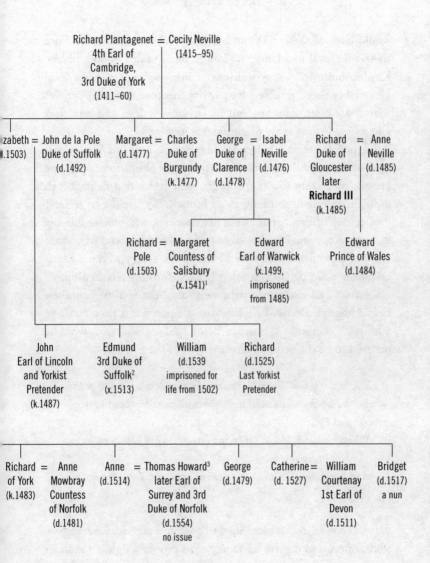

Richard Plantagenet = Cecily Neville
4th Earl of   (1415–95)
Cambridge,
3rd Duke of York
(1411–60)

zabeth = John de la Pole   Margaret = Charles   George = Isabel   Richard = Anne
.1503)   Duke of Suffolk   (d.1477)   Duke of   Duke of   Neville   Duke of   Neville
          (d.1492)   Burgundy   Clarence (d.1476)   Gloucester (d.1485)
                                              (k.1477)   (d.1478)   later
                                                                                       Richard III
                                                                                       (k.1485)

                                  Richard = Margaret   Edward   Edward
                                  Pole   Countess of   Earl of Warwick   Prince of Wales
                                  (d.1503)   Salisbury   (x.1499,   (d.1484)
                                             (x.1541)[1]   imprisoned
                                                                from 1485)

          John   Edmund   William   Richard
          Earl of Lincoln   3rd Duke of   (d.1539   (d.1525)
          and Yorkist   Suffolk[2]   imprisoned for   Last Yorkist
          Pretender   (x.1513)   life from 1502)   Pretender
          (k.1487)

Richard = Anne   Anne = Thomas Howard[3]   George   Catherine = William   Bridget
of York   Mowbray   (d.1514)   later Earl of   (d.1479)   (d. 1527)   Courtenay   (d.1517)
(k.1483) Countess   Surrey and 3rd   1st Earl of a nun
          of Norfolk   Duke of Norfolk   Devon
          (d.1481)   (d.1554)   (d.1511)
                                   no issue

[2] Edmund was demoted to earl in 1493 and deprived of the earldom in 1504.
[3] Howard was uncle to Anne Boleyn and Catherine Howard, Henry VIII's second
and fifth wives, both executed.

would have worked, since no practical benefit could derive from remaining loyal to a family no longer able to offer 'good lordship'. Kinship built up over generations of intermarriage with the local gentry was also a double-edged sword, because extended families were more often than not rent by envious rivalries and vendettas. Clearly something more profound was involved.

The phenomenon is better described by the term 'affinity', which, born of the faithful performance of reciprocal obligations, over time became more akin to a deeply ingrained custom that defined each individual's way of thinking about himself. We use the term 'land-lord' to describe mere possession of a property, without considering its etymology. Smallholders were no less lords to those who share-cropped their fields than were nobles to the gentry who prospered under their tutelage. It was a deeply habit-forming relationship.

Custom and customary right were once the soul of Common Law. Although Rudyard Kipling cast the poem at a time not long after the Conquest, 'A Norman Baron's Advice' describes what he believed to be the defining characteristic of the English:

> The Saxon is not like us Normans. His manners are not so polite.
> But he never means anything serious till he talks about justice
>   and right.
> When he stands like an ox in the furrow – with his sullen set
>   eyes on your own,
> And grumbles, 'This isn't fair dealing', my son, leave the Saxon
>   alone.

It was considered 'fair dealings' to execute a man for his transgressions, but not to deprive his family of its property rights. Attainder, also known as 'corruption of blood', was a legal way around this. It declared an individual a non-person, and so without rights of any kind for his heirs to inherit. However, punishing the innocent sat so ill with the medieval concept of kingship that attainder was rarely sustained to the point of permanent deprivation.

There was also an element of practical politics involved. Members of attainted families with no hope of a reversal had every reason to seek the overthrow of the regime responsible for their deprivation as soon as possible, before whoever had been granted their lands could establish himself as the customary lord and win over their affinity. The longer a family had been in possession the deeper the roots, and so Edward's attainders tended to 'stick' in the case of newer creations, and to be reversed for those with older titles.

• ⟡ •

Contemporaries and historians have generally been critical of the supposedly over-indulgent policy of reconciliation Edward pursued with those lately his mortal enemies. It would not have seemed so to Thomas Courtenay, Earl of Devon, and James Butler, Earl of Wiltshire in England and of Ormond in Ireland, both executed and attainted after Towton. Also attainted were Henry Percy, Earl of Northumberland, John Talbot, Earl of Shrewsbury, and Lords Clifford, Welles and Dacre of the North, all of whom had fallen in battle.

Of those who lived, the titles and lands of the deposed king, his queen and their son were of course forfeit. Dukes Henry Beaufort of Somerset and Henry Holland of Exeter, and Lords Roos and Hungerford, who fled to Scotland with the royal party, were also attainted. So was Jasper Tudor, Earl of Pembroke, who remained at large in Wales after defeat at Mortimer's Cross. Though William, Viscount Beaumont, was not still in rebellion, his attainder was sustained because Lord Hastings, Edward's closest friend, coveted his lands.

Edward offered an amnesty to those who had the prestige and affinity to cause him serious trouble. All they had to do was submit, swear allegiance to him, and prove the sincerity of their conversion through service to his cause. A different policy governed the lower-level attainders after Towton, which were part of a general score settling demanded by Edward's followers and tended not to be reversed because they contributed to stability by resolving minor vendettas. The 'hearts and minds' strategy was mainly applied to magnates.

Somerset was to prove the most notable failure, but Ralph Percy, brother of the slain Earl of Northumberland, repeatedly abused the king's mercy. Percy's recidivism showed indifference to the fate of his young nephew Henry, heir to the earldom, who was held in the Fleet prison as a hostage. This could be because, with older brothers Henry and Thomas killed in battle and his only other brother George a priest, Ralph and his sons would become the heirs to the earldom if young Henry were executed.

The back story is that the royal castles of Bamburgh and Dunstanburgh, along with the Percy stronghold of Alnwick, all in Northumberland, initially resisted the Yorkist tide after Towton. Alnwick and Dunstanburgh capitulated to Warwick in the autumn of 1461. Ralph Percy, royal constable at Dunstanburgh, was pardoned and reappointed, only to declare for Lancaster again in November after a Lancastrian-Scots force led by the proscribed and attainted William Tailboys recaptured Alnwick.

Tailboys was a knighted thug who had contributed greatly to the climate of lawlessness that undermined Henry VI's regime – in 1449 he was the first man impeached by the Commons in nearly seventy years, for assaulting a peer inside the parliamentary precinct. His principal properties were in Lincolnshire, but he also held a large moorland estate in Northumberland between Harbottle on the upper Coquet River and Redesdale, home to some of the most notorious border bandits. For the Yorkists, he was a dead man walking.

Percy continued to hold out after Alnwick and Bamburgh capitulated again in July 1462. Dunstanburgh is built on a headland jutting into the North Sea and encloses the largest space of any medieval English castle, but port facilities were better further north at Bamburgh. There, on 25 October, Henry VI, Queen Marguerite and an entourage including the attainted Earl of Somerset, Earl of Pembroke, Lord Roos and Lord Hungerford, landed with an 800-man French force led by Pierre de Brézé.

Brézé was once the most powerful man at the court of Charles VII, who made him Grand Seneschal of Normandy in recognition of his leading role in the 1449–50 reconquest of the province. He had also led a damaging amphibious raid on Sandwich in 1457, and to the English he was the French bogeyman personified. Nonetheless, he had been devoted to Marguerite's mother Isabelle, and his loyalty carried over to her embattled daughter.

In late March 1462 Marguerite had travelled, alone, via Brittany, to meet Louis XI, and obtained a limited amount of support in exchange for the promise to cede Calais once she regained the throne. Louis released Brézé, whom he had dismissed and imprisoned after he became king, and provided ships and a modest war chest. Brézé was permitted to mount a partially successful invasion of the Channel Islands, the right to which Marguerite also ceded, and to raise troops for the expedition to Northumberland.

They sailed first to Leith, Edinburgh's port, to pick up Henry VI and the other exiles, before landing at Bamburgh. Even though Marguerite had already surrendered the border fortress of Berwick to the Percys' ancestral Scots enemy, the Percy affinity still turned out for her in force. The massacre at Towton had created a blood feud that outweighed historical animosities, and it was the strength and depth of the Percy affinity that led Edward to show such seemingly reckless magnanimity to Ralph Percy.

Edward had to remain near the levers of power in London, learning on the job and trying to create an aura of permanence and stability. He also understood that a war of sieges and skirmishes offered no prospect of gain commensurate with the risk of death or disgrace. Consequently he did not become involved in the pacification of the North and delegated the task to Warwick, whose own regional hegemony was most directly challenged.

In early December 1462 Warwick began sieges of the three

☐ Percy Manors and
■ Heads of Lordship

**29. SIEGES & BATTLES
IN THE NORTH-EAST
1462–4**

0   5   10
miles

Tweed

⚑ **Berwick**

⚑ **Norham**

Lennel

*Holy
Isle*

CHEVIOT

Milfield

Belford

⚑ **Bamburgh**

Wooler

Till

**Hedgeley
Moor** ✕

■ Beanley

Dunstanburgh ⚑

HILLS

Breamish

Alnwick ⚑

Aln

Warkworth ⚑

Harbottle
(Tailboys)

Rothbury

Amble

*Redesdale
(Tailboys)*

Coquet

Otterburn

Font

Ashington

Morpeth

Wansbeck

Bellingham

North Tyne

Bothal
(Ogle)

Blyth

Wark
(Grey)

Belsay

Cramlington

Hadrian's Wall

Heaton
(Grey)

Tynemouth

Langley

Corbridge

Bywell

Hexham ✕

Prudhoe

Tyne

Newcastle

Gateshead

© Hugh Bicheno

castles. Based at the Percys' Warkworth Palace he directed the siege of nearby Alnwick by his ailing 57-year-old uncle William, now Earl of Kent, and his thirty-five-year younger deputy, the reconciled Lancastrian Anthony Woodville, Lord Scales. John Tiptoft, Earl of Worcester, and local magnate Ralph Grey besieged Dunstanburgh. Grey's family had a long history of affiliation with the House of York, but he had failed to hold Alnwick for Edward in 1461.

The main effort was at Bamburgh under Warwick's brother John, Lord Montagu, and Lord Ogle. Percy had moved there to join the Lancastrian high command, and as the northernmost of the castles it would be the first to be relieved should the Scots march south from Berwick. No such timely support developed thanks to Warwick's diplomacy and squabbles among the Scots, and with supplies running short Bamburgh capitulated on 26 December.

To shore up Scots support, Henry VI and Marguerite, along with Brézé and 400 of his men, had embarked on 13 November intending to make their presence felt at the Scots court. With their customary bad luck their little fleet was assaulted by a storm soon after it left Bamburgh. The French men-at-arms were wrecked on Holy Isle and were put to the sword by some of Ogle's men, led by his bastard brother. Their leader Jean Malet, lord of Graville in Normandy, was a prisoner in London for many years.

The ship carrying the royal couple and Brézé foundered, taking with it part of their war chest of gold crowns provided by Louis XI. They made it to Berwick in a small boat, but were now unable to influence events in Edinburgh. Meanwhile Edward, who had at last felt compelled to march north at the head of a large army, was incapacitated by measles at Durham. Fortunately by that time his show of force had produced the desired effect, and the alarmed Scots court requested and was granted a truce.

Brézé and the Earl of Angus defied the truce, cobbled together an army at Berwick and marched south, but word of their relief effort did not reach the defenders of Bamburgh and Dunstanburgh in time to prevent their capitulation. Warwick was only too well aware that Brézé was coming, and consequently the terms of capitulation were outrageously generous. To the bitter chagrin of Ralph Grey who, like Ogle, had struggled against Percy hegemony in Northumberland for many years, Ralph Percy was not only restored as royal Constable of Dunstanburgh, but appointed Constable of Bamburgh as well.

The rest of the Lancastrian high command were given the option of safe conduct to Scotland, or a full pardon if they swore allegiance to Edward. Pembroke and Roos, given no guarantee their lands would be restored, chose the first option. Somerset, Percy and several Lancastrian knights travelled to Durham, paid homage to Edward and were 'taken into the king's grace'. Somerset and his followers immediately joined the siege of Alnwick, where the defenders rejected all blandishments.

Warwick's army contained several other lords who had fought for Lancaster. They included his unattainted (but on probation) brother-in-law Lord FitzHugh, who had commanded the Lancastrian division opposite him at Towton – with little conviction – after Northumberland was mortally wounded. Three others, Lords Lovell, Grey of Codnor and Willoughby – the last also heir to the still-attainted barony of Welles – had benefitted from the reversal of their post-Towton attainders conditional on service against their old comrades.

Consequently it is not even slightly remarkable that Warwick broke off the siege and took up a defensive position when Brézé and Angus arrived at Alnwick on 6 January 1463. Apart from the doubtful loyalty of some of his subordinates, his army had suffered considerable attrition from exposure and desertion. The relief force must have been in little better shape after a rapid march south across inhospitable terrain in the dead of winter, but even so Brézé wanted to seek battle. Angus, who was mortally ill, settled for collecting the Alnwick garrison and marching back to Berwick.

Despite the setback at Alnwick, Edward had reason to believe that the policy of reconciliation was working for him. His offer of an open hand as an alternative to the mailed fist is the way lasting peace is normally made. It was also a notably mature policy for such a young man to pursue. Perhaps more to the point, with regard to the pacification of the North he acted in full agreement with the Earl of Warwick, who would not have hesitated to behead his defeated opponents had he believed it the wiser course of action.

WARWICK

WARWICK BENEFITTED HUGELY FROM THE RELATIVE failure of reconciliation. It permitted him to win a geographic concentration and regional hegemony akin to those enjoyed by cadet branches of the Valois dynasty in France, a fragmentation that weakened them so significantly in the confrontation with the English Plantagenets. One of the greater ironies of this saga is that by crushing their resistance in 1461–4, Warwick won the independent power that later made him the Lancastrians' last hope for reversing the verdict of Towton.

He was a schemer, not a warrior. His victory at Northampton was won by the treachery of Lord Grey of Ruthyn, and a similar odour emanates from FitzHugh's performance at Towton. Along with Lord Greystoke, FitzHugh had been encouraged to become Trojan Horses within the Lancastrian ranks by seeming to rally to Henry VI in 1459. Warwick's talents were not best suited to the grinding war against adamant enemies in the North, although intelligence from Greystoke did help him to identify covert Lancastrians among the Yorkshire gentry and burgesses, who were forced to take oaths of allegiance.

Warwick was able to depend at first on his veteran warrior uncle William, newly created Earl of Kent, and, following his death in January 1463, on his brother John, whom Edward had created Lord

Montagu as one of his first acts on seizing the throne.* With his uncle and brother largely taking care of military business, Warwick was free to play the statesman, a role he had relished as the virtually independent Captain of Calais and Keeper of the Seas during the last years of the Lancastrian regime.

The northern rebellion of late 1461 was supposed to be followed by a rising in East Anglia led by John Vere, Earl of Oxford, commanding his own and the Beaumont affinities, taking advantage of the fact that the Norfolk affinity was leaderless following the death of the sickly duke in late 1461. The plan may have been to attack Edward from the rear after he had been drawn north, or perhaps to join his army and assassinate him. They were also expecting Somerset to land in East Anglia with troops recruited in France or provided by his admirer Charles, Count of Charolais and heir to the dukedom of Burgundy.

Edward learned of the plan and Oxford, his eldest son, Thomas Tuddenham and a dozen accomplices, all of whom had previously avoided attainder, were arrested and imprisoned. Tuddenham had been a key player in a thuggish gang that terrorized East Anglia during the Lancastrian regime. To deal with them Edward appointed John Tiptoft, Earl of Worcester – already Lord Treasurer and Constable of the Tower – as Constable of England, with the power to try cases of high treason without reference to Parliament.

Tiptoft stood out among the generally philistine English peers. William Caxton, who brought the first printing press to England in 1475, wrote of him 'I knew none like [him] among the lords of the temporality in science and moral virtue'. After a pilgrimage to Jerusalem in 1458 Tiptoft spent two years studying at the University of Padua and brought the texts of the 'new learning' back to England. Something else he brought back from Italy was total ruthlessness in defence of the state, and he had Oxford, his heir and their fellow conspirators executed in a cruelly protracted sequence.

*John had been captured at the Second Battle of St Albans; his ennoblement was a signal that there would be reprisal against captured Lancastrian nobles if he were executed.

THE HOUSE OF NEVILLE

Descendants of Richard Neville and Alice Montacute

k. = killed in battle   x. = executed

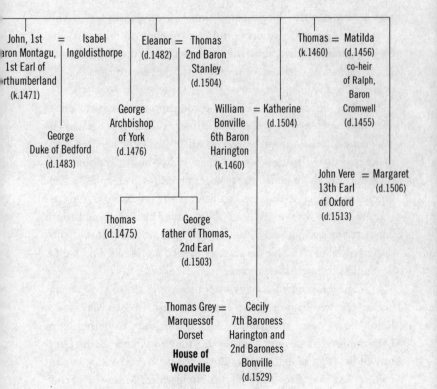

John, 1st = Isabel
Baron Montagu, Ingoldisthorpe
1st Earl of
Northumberland
(k.1471)

Eleanor = Thomas
(d.1482) 2nd Baron
Stanley
(d.1504)

Thomas = Matilda
(k.1460) (d.1456)
co-heir
of Ralph,
Baron
Cromwell
(d.1455)

George
Duke of Bedford
(d.1483)

George
Archbishop
of York
(d.1476)

William = Katherine
Bonville (d.1504)
6th Baron
Harington
(k.1460)

John Vere = Margaret
13th Earl (d.1506)
of Oxford
(d.1513)

Thomas
(d.1475)

George
father of Thomas,
2nd Earl
(d.1503)

Thomas Grey = Cecily
Marquess of 7th Baroness
Dorset Harington and
2nd Baroness
House of Bonville
Woodville (d.1529)

Bereft of support elsewhere, the 1461–2 rebellion in the North swiftly collapsed, leaving only Percy holding out at Dunstanburgh. When, as we have seen, it flared up again later in 1462, both Warwick and Edward were drawn north – but with the Lancastrian leadership now concentrated in Bamburgh they no longer feared a hostile landing to their rear. Following the capitulations of Dunstanburgh, Bamburgh and Alnwick, Warwick delegated the Wardenship of the East March to his brother Montagu while he and the king returned to London.

They had to deal with a mountain of decrees and legislation required to revoke or revalidate all the acts of the Lancastrian regime, now legally declared illegitimate from its inception in 1399. The crown was also vastly in debt, and even interest on the sums lent by the Calais Staplers, crucial to the success of the Yorkist insurgency, had to be declared 'in respite' until the royal finances could be sorted out.

This was no easy task. Even the resumption of crown lands alienated by Henry VI was not straightforward, as it generated an avalanche of petitions for exception, which had to be handled with delicacy. Edward made no fewer than eighty-four exceptions, no doubt grimly aware that each favour created several enemies and an ingrate. At the same time he had to deal with pleas from Yorkists seeking redress for wrongs done them under Henry VI, and from Lancastrians seeking relief from abuses committed by Yorkist supporters after Towton. He desperately needed a prolonged period of domestic and international peace.

Of course his enemies knew this, and combined to strike again before the new regime could establish itself. In late May 1463 Ralph Percy raised the banner of Lancaster over Bamburgh and Dunstanburgh once more. At the same time embittered Ralph Grey turned his coat, seized Alnwick castle and welcomed a Lancastrian column led from Scotland by Lord Hungerford. Meanwhile Scots queen mother Mary of Guelders and young James III, accompanied by Marguerite and Henry VI, marched with a Scots army to besiege the Bishop of Durham's border fortress of Norham, which was held by Lord Ogle.

With Ogle bottled up, the combination of the Percy, Grey, Tailboys and related affinities now dominated Northumberland. Montagu managed to prevent them seizing Newcastle, while ships under his command intercepted a French fleet before it could land supplies at Bamburgh; but he could only hold the southern border along the Tyne. At the same time there were Lancastrian risings in other parts of England. It was a well-coordinated offensive and, unlike the previous effort, took Edward and Warwick by surprise.

Montagu's situation was made even more precarious by the fact that the archdiocese of York had been solidly Lancastrian. Carlisle was not a problem, as Bishop William Percy died in August 1462 and his replacement died a year later. Archbishop William Booth had been Marguerite's chancellor, but the greater danger came from his half-brother Laurence, Prince-Bishop of Durham. Laurence had succeeded William as the queen's chancellor and had been Lord Privy Seal from 1456 to 1460. He had military obligations throughout the Marches, and retained a significant armed force.

Edward neutralized the prince-bishop by assigning his temporalities to Warwick, who immediately travelled north to raise his own Yorkshire and Richmondshire affinities. The Scots army at Norham fled before his approach and he chased it into Scotland. Meanwhile his brother George, Bishop of Exeter and Lord Chancellor, led a high-level delegation to negotiate a truce with France. Warwick was made plenipotentiary to deal with Scotland, and George was given almost unlimited negotiating discretion, including the prospect of a marriage between Edward and a suitable French princess.

Unusually, Parliament voted Edward the specific sum of £37,000 [£23.5 million], rather more than the usual fifteenth and tenth.* Stung by the fact that he had not made war on Scotland with the

---

*The basic form of direct taxation in late medieval England, on the assessed value of movables: one-tenth in towns and one-fifteenth in the shires. Land taxes were furiously rejected until the late seventeenth century.

taxes raised for the purpose in 1462, the new grant came with the proviso that the money was to be used solely for the defence of the realm. For the second time in three years the Church Convocations voted him a tenth of ecclesiastical revenues, over and above the loans individual bishops had made since he seized power. The City of London, whose leading citizens had also been generous to the new king, voted him additional funds to feed his army, and other cities did likewise. It was a massive, if conditional vote of confidence.

So it was that Edward marched north at the head of the best equipped and provisioned army he had ever led. The suspicion must be that he had tricked his loyal subjects into giving him money for a war he had no intention of fighting. He and Warwick knew the Lancastrian threat was ephemeral without French and Scots support, thus the solution would be diplomatic. Instead, to their chagrin, they had to spend much of the money to stamp out brush fires all over England.

The political ace Edward thought to play was Henry Beaufort, Earl of Somerset, whom he made every effort to win as a supporter and friend. He restored his lands, granted him a cash settlement to help pay his debts, and gave him a handsome annuity. Somerset played along so convincingly that he was made a Companion of the Bedchamber and appointed head of a new King's Guard, some 200 men recruited from his own retainers. It was an extravagantly trusting gesture, intended as a propaganda coup to dishearten the Lancastrians.

Edward's subjects were not impressed. Outraged to see their king surrounded by men they believed might kill him, the citizens of Leicester rioted and Somerset barely escaped with his life. Ruefully accepting that his gambit had backfired, Edward pacified the rioters with a tun [252 gallons] of wine and thanked them for their concern. He sent Somerset to the nearest of the duke's properties at Chirk Castle in Denbigh, and ordered the King's Guard to march on ahead to Newcastle. Edward himself proceeded to pay his respects to his mother at the family seat at Fotheringhay, then went to the royal castle at Pontefract, and finally to York.

The citizens of Leicester may well have saved Edward's life, as Somerset always planned treachery. He did not stay long at Chirk, stealing away by night with the intention of joining his men at Newcastle. He was identified when he stopped for the night in Durham and an angry mob formed. He had to flee the inn in his night-clothes, leaving his armour behind. His retainers were primed to seize Newcastle when he arrived, but by now Montagu was fully alerted and those of Somerset's men who did not flee in time were executed.

Somerset himself managed to reach Bamburgh, where the royal family had fled after the debacle at Norham. Henry VI remained, but in August Marguerite and their son sailed to Flanders. They were destitute and rescued by Charles, Count of Charolais, who helped them and their small band of followers to reach her father's duchy of Bar. Somerset was re-attainted in December and his estates awarded to Richard, Duke of Gloucester, Edward's 10-year-old brother.

Thus the sum total of Edward's contribution to the pacification of the North was a failed propaganda coup that could have cost him his politically irreplaceable life, and which cast strong doubts on his judgement. Thereafter he became little more than a spectator to a show run by the Neville brothers. First they cut off the Lancastrians from their French and Scots life support, and then they methodically crushed them.

Edward summoned Parliament to assemble at York in early February 1464, intending it to coincide with a peace treaty with the Scots. Things did not go to plan. While Somerset was posing as the king's friend his agents had been busy organizing revolts all over the country, which flared up as soon as he dropped the pretence. Though the coup at Newcastle failed, while at Chirk Somerset had set in motion local uprisings serious enough for Edward to send the young Duke of Norfolk to suppress them, with the power to execute and pardon at will. That he did not empower Lord Stanley, the nominally Yorkist local magnate, is significant.

Our only source for this rebellion is a letter in February 1464 from the younger John Paston, who rode with the king's friend John Howard, the real commander in Norfolk's name. Paston wrote that they had 'great labour here in Wales', where 'the commons in Lancashire and Cheshire were up to the number of ten thousand or more… but now they be down again'. There was obviously more to it than that. Many of the rebels would have come from Marguerite's dower lands in the region, where Lancastrian affinity ran deep, but the presumption must be that Stanley played an important part both in the rebellion and its suppression.

There was also dangerous unrest in the Midlands. In January Edward moved from York to Coventry, where Warwick and other Yorkist lords, plus his two chief justices, joined him. Their presence had the desired effect of overawing the city and the surrounding area. He then ordered his chief justices to Gloucester, where a revolt had broken out, and joined them in early February to conduct assizes (properly 'commissions of oyer and terminer'). Then came word of the intimidation of a commission appointed to deal with unrest in Cambridgeshire, presumably by members of the Oxford and Beaumont affinities, and Edward had to ride with Tiptoft and other lords to lend his personal authority to the proceedings.

Parliament, already postponed once, assembled at York on 20 February but had to be prorogued until 5 May with the humiliating explanation that unrest in the kingdom made it impossible for the king to be present. In fact he rode from Cambridge to London to meet a delegation from King Enrique IV of Castille, which brought him an offer of marriage to the king's sister and heir presumptive. This was none other than the lady known to posterity as Isabella of Castille, but one of history's more intriguing 'might have beens' became moot when Edward politely declined the offer.

With Edward buzzing around like the proverbial bluebottle fly (actually, as we shall see, more like a bee around a nectar-laden flower), it was left to the Nevilles to rip the heart out of the Lancastrian insurgency. At some point, in the absence of Lord Ogle, the Bishop of Durham's men at Norham mutinied, and it became imperative to conclude a truce with the Scots before they snapped up the border fortress. In April Montagu assembled a force of about 5,000 men and marched north to escort a Scots delegation from the border to York.

The march took him through the heart of the Percy lordship of Beanley, and on 25 April, at a place called Hedgeley Moor, he found his way barred by a Lancastrian army of about equal numbers commanded by Somerset. The bulk of the army was made up of northerners, but Roos and Hungerford led a battalion of supporters from elsewhere in England, including some of Somerset's affinity.

The difference in morale and determination between men fighting on their own ground and the rest became apparent once battle was joined, when the left wing under Roos and Hungerford broke and fled as Montagu's men advanced after an initial exchange of arrows. Abandoned by the other lords, Ralph Percy made a last stand and was killed. His dying words were 'I have saved the bird in my bosom', and historians have puzzled over them ever since.

Having failed to prevent the Anglo–Scots peace negotiations, Somerset's last throw, this time accompanied by Henry VI himself, was to march south in the hope of rallying the men of the Percy lordships of Langley and Prudhoe on the Tyne. On the night of 14/15 May the small Lancastrian force camped outside Hexham, and the next morning was dispersed with ease by a considerably larger force from Newcastle under Montagu, accompanied by Lords Greystoke and Willoughby.

All the Lancastrian high command were captured. Somerset and four others were immediately beheaded at Hexham; Hungerford, Roos and three others at Newcastle on the 17th. Seven more (presumably Neville turncoats) were executed at Middleham on the 18th, and fourteen more at York on the 26th, after being tried and convicted by Tiptoft. The last to be captured was Tailboys, found hiding in a Redesdale coal mine with the remains of Louis XI's gold. He was beheaded at Newcastle.

Henry VI, who had remained at Bywell Castle on the north bank of the Tyne, got away and, accompanied initially by Richard Tunstall and Henry Bellingham, two dog-loyal knights, wandered from one Lancastrian household to another in West Yorkshire, Westmorland and Lancashire for the next fourteen months. He was betrayed in July 1466 by Richard Tempest of Waddington Hall, near Clitheroe in eastern Lancashire. After a humiliating ride through London, riding a nag with his feet tied to the stirrups, he was imprisoned in the Tower.

At York on 27 May 1464 a delighted Edward created a new earldom of Northumberland for Montagu, endowed with the Percy estates not previously awarded to Warwick and Clarence. After Edward signed a fifteen-year truce with the Scots on 1 June, the new earl set out to reduce the Northumbrian castles. The Norham garrison's mutiny ended when they were paid, and the garrisons at Alnwick and Dunstanburgh capitulated in return for pardons on 23 and 24 June.

There remained Bamburgh, where the turncoat Ralph Grey knew he had no hope of pardon. With him was Warwick's cousin Humphrey Neville, whose father Thomas, brother and guardian of the demented Earl of Westmorland, had died with Clifford at Dintingdale, a few hours before the Battle of Towton. Humphrey had twice broken his parole to Edward and led damaging raids as far south as Yorkshire, so he also had no expectation of mercy.

Because of their strategic location Edward had been loth to see the Northumbrian castles damaged. This time the gloves came off and Montagu blasted Bamburgh's walls with huge bombards shipped years earlier to Newcastle from London and Calais, but only now brought along the coast by barges and put to work. After they brought down the roof of the central keep on Grey's head, Humphrey called for parley.

Perhaps believing Grey was dying, he gave up the castle in exchange for a pardon for himself. In fact Grey survived and was taken to Doncaster, where he was put on trial before the fearsome

Tiptoft. In recognition of his family's services to the House of York he was not degraded from the Order of the Garter or attainted before he was beheaded on 10 July. All the men around whom further resistance to the Yorkist regime might have coalesced were now either dead or reconciled.

In order not to burden the narrative I have set out the honours, offices and lands accumulated by Warwick in Appendix H. From the Warwick and Salisbury inheritance alone he held lands that had once endowed four historic earldoms, with estates in Welsh Glamorgan and Brecknock, and in every English county except Cheshire, Derbyshire, Lancashire, Lincolnshire and Shropshire. He had more land and enjoyed a higher income from it than any nobleman since John of Gaunt, the prototype of the 'over-mighty subject'.

To this he added revenues from the many offices he accumulated as the indispensable man in winning and securing the throne. He had more disposable income than the king, whose estates were heavily encumbered and whose overheads were vastly greater. While this may have rankled, it remains incomprehensible that Edward refused him a dukedom. It was possibly the least expensive gesture he could have made to ensure Warwick's loyalty.

Perhaps he intended to do so eventually, maybe even as a reward for pacifying the North; however, well before Hexham Warwick had made it clear that he considered himself the king's chief minister and the power behind the throne. Nowhere was this more evident than in his dealings with France, a role that appealed irresistibly to his grandiosity.

LOUIS

I F A RULER'S SUCCESS OR FAILURE DEPENDS AS MUCH ON THE ineptitude of his opponents as on his own skill, then Louis XI of France, wonderfully nicknamed 'the Universal Spider', was one of the luckiest monarchs in history. His principal antagonists were the last independent Duke of Burgundy Charles, nicknamed '*le Téméraire*' (which translates as 'the Rash' as well as 'the Bold'), Duke Frañsez II of Brittany, described by a contemporary Breton chronicler as 'weak in body and even weaker in mind', and the insecure usurper Edward IV.

On the minus side, the curse of genealogy lay heavily on the Valois dynasty. The legalistic justification for the devastating Hundred Years War was the English kings' claim to the throne of France, based on a superior right of succession through the marriages of the first two Edwards to the eldest daughters of the House of Capet. The powerful Dukes of Bourbon and Counts of Bourbon-Vendôme also had a separate but junior line of descent from the Capetian King Louis IX.* The greater problem was that the extended Valois clan, 'the princes of the blood', made the English Plantagenets seem like happy families.

The Dukes of Valois-Alençon were a cadet line descended from Count Charles of Valois, whose eldest son became the first Valois

---

* Thus becoming a new royal dynasty in 1598, after both the Valois and Valois-Orléans lines became extinct.

king. The Dukes of Valois-Anjou and of Valois-Burgundy were descendants of the second Valois king, and the Dukes of Valois-Orléans and of Valois-Orléans-Angoulême from the third. Their bitter rivalries had permitted relatively small English armies to conquer northern France. Even after Jeanne d'Arc shamed some of them into turning the tide, many years of ego massaging were required before they could be united to expel the invaders.

They were soon back to squabbling amongst themselves; but now, instead of hindering Charles VII (Louis's father), their divisions helped him to reduce their importance by building on the foundations of absolutism. The king's new measures included the 1438 Pragmatic Sanction, by which he 'nationalized' the Papacy's right to appoint French clergy and the revenues deriving from it, and a standing army paid for by a land tax (*taille*) on non-nobles. The *taille* was awarded to the monarchy in perpetuity by the Estates General in 1439, thereby rendering themselves irrelevant: Louis XI summoned them only once in twenty-two years.

Charles VII's reduced need to accommodate his nobles did not pass unnoticed, and the steps he took to rationalize the administration of justice and tax collection were seen for what they were – the thin end of a wedge of encroachment on traditional aristocratic prerogatives. His reforms provoked the short-lived 1440 Praguerie rebellion nominally led by Louis, his 17-year-old heir apparent, involving the Dukes of Bourbon, Alençon and Brittany, and the Count of Vendôme. There was a formal reconciliation, but Charles never forgave his son.

In 1441–3 Louis distinguished himself in operations against the English and the Count of Armagnac, and in 1444 Charles sent him to fight the fearsome Swiss at the head of an army of *écorcheurs*, savage and fiercely meritocratic French irregulars. Louis emerged with credit from the campaign, but received no reward. At court, relations between him and Agnès Sorel, Charles's influential mistress, became so bad that in 1446 he was sent to govern the Dauphiné, the traditional principality of the heirs to the throne, and a nest

30. KINGDOM OF FRANCE 1461

Calais
B
St
Flanders
Artois
E
Picardy
Rethel
S E E M A P 3 1

Normandy
Île de
France
□ Paris
Champagne
Bar
Alençon
Perche
Maine
D
Nemours
Brittany
Anjou
V
Orléans
Touraine
Blois
S
Berry
Burgundy
Nevers
SMALL
COUNTIES
B   Boulogne
C   Comminges
D   Dunois
E   Eu
M   Mirande
S   Sancerre
St   Saint-Pol
V   Vendôme
Poitou
La Marche
Bourbon
Saintonge
Angoulême
Limoges
Forez
Duchy of
Savoy
Périgord
Auvergne
Turenne
Dauphiné
(semi-autonomous)
Guyenne
Albret
Rodez
Gascony
Armagnac
Papal
State
Béarn
M
Provence
Kingdom
of
Castile
Kingdom of Navarre
Bigorre
C
Languedoc
Foix
Narbonne
Kingdom of Aragon
Rousillon &
Cerdagne
© Hugh Bicheno

International frontiers
.... Territories of Burgundy-Nevers and Brittany
Royal demesne in bold italics. Comminges and Mirande were semi-autonomous.
The Duke of Valois-Orléan's lands included Valois, Blois and Dunois
The Dukes of Angoulême were a cadet branch of the House of Valois-Orléans
The Duke of Valois-Anjou's lands included Provence and Bar
The Count of Maine was the son of Valois-Anjou
The Duke of Valois-Alençon's lands included Perche
The Duke of Bourbon's lands included Auvergne, Forez and Vendôme
The Counts of Sancerre were a cadet branch of the House of Bourbon
The Count of Armagnac's lands included Rodez and La Marche
The Counts of Nemours were a cadet branch of the House of Armagnac
The Count of Foix's lands included Béarn, Bigorre and Narbonne
The Lord of Albret's lands included Limoges, Turenne and Périgord

31. BURGUNDIAN LANDS 1461

Frontier with Holy Roman Empire
Burgundian lands
Internal borders
✝ Toul Prince-Bishoprics
Italics Other principalities

Friesland
Zuiderzee
Holland
✝ *Utrecht*
Guelders
Zutphen
Cleves
Guelders
Zeeland
Bruges
Antwerp
Neuss
Calais
Ghent
Duchy of Brabant
Cologne
Flanders
St Omer
Ypres
✝ *Tournai*
Brussels
Duchy of Limbourg
Boulogne
Artois
Ligny
✝ *Liège*
HOLY
St Pol
Hainault
Namur
Frankfurt
Arras
✝ Cambrai
Mainz
Hesdin
Guise
Duchy of Luxembourg
Picardy
Amiens
Liège
Trier
Eu (Nevers)
Brienne
Rethel (Nevers)
ROMAN
Reims
Lorr.
Palatinate
Île de France
Champagne
Bar
✝ *Verdun*
✝ *Metz*
Lorr.
Paris
Montlhéry
Duchy of Bar
Lorr.
EMPIRE
Nancy
Strasbourg
Troyes
Bar and Lorraine governed by House of Valois-Anjou
✝ *Toul*
Metz
Lower Alsace
Iles (Nevers)
Bar
Duchy of Lorraine
Auxerre
✝ *Luxeuil*
Upper Alsace
Breisgau
County of Nevers
Duchy of Burgundy
Dijon
Free County of Burgundy
Basle
Zurich
Berry
Grandson
Berne
Charolais
Morat
Mâcon
Swiss Confederacy
Bourbon
Geneva
0 25 50 75 100
miles
Duchy of Savoy
© Hugh Bicheno

of interlocking feudal and ecclesiastical jurisdictions calculated to break the spirit of any ruler.

Once again Louis rose to the challenge. He humbled the local lords, favoured the gentry and the bourgeoisie, and introduced reforms such as the first regular postal service in Europe. He also ignored frequent attempts to recall him and in 1451, in defiance of his father's orders, he made a dynastic marriage with the House of Savoy. Charles intended to enforce Louis's obedience by invading the Dauphiné the following year, but had to turn aside to deal with the English reconquest of Guyenne. When the delayed invasion went ahead in 1456, Louis fled to the court of his uncle Duke Philippe of Burgundy.

Despite Charles's threats, Philippe set Louis up with his own establishment at the castle of Genappe in his sub-duchy of Brabant, a prudent arm's length south of the provincial capital at Brussels. By Valois standards Philippe's heir Charles, Count of Charolais, was a loyal son: but he questioned Philippe's benevolence towards Louis. He argued that it would be better to surrender the dangerously capable Louis to his father. If he lived he would promote sedition, and if killed his twenty-three-year younger brother would become Dauphin. Philippe thought otherwise, and fondly believed he was creating a bond of gratitude.

Louis's policy over the next five years was straightforward: he opposed anything his father did, thus he backed the Yorkists against the Lancastrians in England's civil war. Philippe took the same view, but Charolais was fascinated by the struggle between Warwick and Somerset over Calais. He became enamoured of handsome Henry Beaufort, and when he had to abandon the struggle for Calais gave him 1,400 livres [£135,000] to get himself and his men back to England and continue the fight.

I use the word 'enamoured' advisedly. Charolais's intense admiration for Somerset led him to support Lancastrian resistance after Towton, seemingly in defiance of his father's pro-Yorkist policy.* He felt Somerset's execution deeply, and once he became duke he sheltered Somerset's brothers and was reluctant to ally with the Yorkist regime. While he was also influenced by his adored mother Isabella of Portugal, a granddaughter of John of Gaunt, father of the Lancastrian dynasty, his motives appear to have been more personal.

The link may be that he was repelled by his father's monumental promiscuity – at least twenty-four mistresses and eighteen recognized bastards. Although Charolais managed to overcome his revulsion and engender a daughter in 1457, in general he shunned female and sought out exclusively male company. In 1470 his illegitimate half-brother Baudouin fled to France and accused him of 'unnatural vices'; but while he was almost certainly homosexual, it is more likely he sublimated his urges in violent sports and warfare.

During his time at Genappe Louis was at all times respectful of his uncle Philippe and also won over his sceptical son through their mutual passion for the chase. He even managed to remain friendly with Jacquetta's brother Louis de Luxembourg, Count of Saint-Pol, who had been his comrade-in-arms in 1441, even though they backed different sides in the English civil war. During his time in exile Louis obtained an intimate knowledge of the strengths and weaknesses of men who would later oppose him, without permitting any of them to catch more than occasional glimpses of the workings of his own mind.

On the other side of France, Duke Frañsez of Brittany seems to have calculated (if, indeed, any coherent mental process was involved) that his interests were best served by stirring the English pot. After the Lancastrian defeat at Northampton he welcomed Marguerite's emissary the Earl of Wiltshire, gave him the money to recruit Breton and Irish mercenaries, and the ships to transport them to join Jasper Tudor, Earl of Pembroke, in Wales. Few survived the rout that followed their defeat by Edward at Mortimer's Cross. Frañsez continued to support Jasper, as well as the last Lancastrian

---

*There may be less to this than meets the eye. Charolais lacked the means to conduct an independent foreign policy and Philippe could have stopped him if he wished. He was probably using his son to hedge his bet.

holdout of Harlech Castle in Wales, for many years.

When Marguerite's army marched on London after defeating and killing Richard of York and Warwick's father at Wakefield, Philippe gave generous sanctuary to Richard's two youngest boys. He also sent a contingent of hand-gunners, who shared Warwick's defeat at the Second Battle of St Albans. Arguably more significant was the choice of one of Louis's retinue, Lord de la Barde, to represent Burgundy to the Yorkists, and that he led a contingent of Burgundians to fight for Edward at Towton under the Dauphin's banner.

Philippe's greater contribution was to keep Charles VII in check. Charles was in poor health – he died four months after Towton – and desperate to be reconciled with his heir. Louis refused to go to him even when he was dying, and after he died shocked Philippe by making only a perfunctory gesture of mourning during the elaborate ceremonies the duke organized. Louis went along with the charade, making it clear he did so only to please his uncle, but eventually could bear it no longer and slipped away to get on with the business of ruling.

He immediately adopted many of the policies he had opposed while his father lived, among them support of the Lancastrians. Having been at the heart of the informal alliance between Burgundy and the Yorkists, Louis fully appreciated the threat it could pose to France. Also, France's allies the Scots had obtained Berwick by helping Marguerite after Northampton – could he not obtain title to Calais now that she was truly desperate? Yet, having obtained her undertaking to cede the enclave if she recovered the throne, he did the bare minimum to keep the Lancastrian resistance alive.

This was because he did not wish the issue of who governed England to become a major bone of contention between France and Burgundy. He was coldly pragmatic and the sole purpose of his limited support for the Lancastrians was to keep England divided and weak for as long as possible, in order to diminish the value of an English alliance in Burgundian eyes. In this he was successful, leaving both Philippe and himself free to deal with more important bilateral matters and their own internal problems.

· ∽ ·

The Burgundian lands were separated by the duchies of Bar and Lorraine and by the Prince-Bishopric of Liège. Bar was ruled by Duke René d'Anjou, Marguerite's father, and Lorraine – in succession to his mother – by René's eldest son Jean. About half of Bar and all of Lorraine lay within the boundaries of the historic Holy Roman Empire, such that René and Jean owed nominal homage to the Emperor for them.

Considerably more significant was the homage René owed to the King of France for part of Bar, and all of Anjou and Provence. He was also titular King of Naples, having been expelled by the King of Aragon in 1441, a can of worms best left unopened here. More germane to our story is the war fought between René and Philippe over Lorraine in 1431, in which René was captured. He was eventually released in 1436 after agreeing a ransom that ruined him, even though he was never able to pay the whole amount.

Power abhors a vacuum, but the Angevins and their descendants clung on to Bar and Lorraine until 1766 because they were recognized as the legitimate rulers by both the Empire and France. The price of powerlessness was that their territory was regarded as a thoroughfare, and Nancy as an occasional alternative location for the courts of the French kings.

The existential threat to the Dukes of Burgundy was not so much that every duchy, sub-duchy and county recognized his overlordship according to its own laws and customs, a feudal overhang common to all the proto-nations of Europe. Their particular problem came from the example set by the autonomous Rhine valley cities outside their borders. Burgundy depended heavily on revenues from the commercial and industrial cities in Flanders, where a desire for comparable autonomy was never far below the surface.

• ❧ •

Louis XI added two substantial territories to his kingdom in 1462–3, both by purchase. The first opportunity came about in early 1462 when the province of Catalonia overthrew the authority of King Juan II of Aragon, who had exhausted his credit in a war over Navarre. In May Juan signed treaties with Louis XI for the loan of 4,200 knights plus their retainers and led by the Count of Foix for an agreed price of 200,000 gold crowns [£25.4 million]. As surety Louis was to hold Roussillon and Cerdagne, Catalan counties north of the Pyrenees.

The Catalans, hard pressed by King Juan's French army, invited King Enrique IV of Castille to become their ruler. He denounced the cession of Rousillon and Cerdagne and threatened to conquer the kingdom of Aragon in its entirety. In an adroit move, Louis persuaded Enrique to accept his arbitration, then prevailed on Juan to cede disputed territory in Navarre to keep Castille out of the war. The war dragged on for another decade though permutations including the Catalans' election of René d'Anjou, who ruined himself again by trying to make good his claim; but by 1474 Rousillon and Cerdagne were permanently incorporated into France.

Louis's other purchase seemed at first to be more straightforward. In 1435 his father had ceded the rich towns of the Somme valley in Picardy to Duke Philippe as part of the price he paid to break up the Anglo–Burgundian alliance.* The terms were that the towns would revert to the French crown in return for 400,000 gold crowns [£51 million].

Louis completed the supposedly prohibitive payment and, with the help of high-placed agents at Philippe's court, recovered the towns by the end of 1463. The complications here were that the taxes vigorously collected across France to raise the money were

---

*From west to east, the cities were Abbeville, Saint-Riquier, Amiens, Corbie, Péronne and Saint-Quentin. Also, south of the valley, Roye and Montdidier, and north of the valley Doullens, Arleux and Mortagne.

deeply unpopular, and that Philippe's son Charolais violently opposed the deal and swore to reverse it.

Not only Burgundian feathers were ruffled. As before in the Dauphiné, Louis had been a whirlwind since becoming king, constantly touring and making no effort to cultivate his nobles. Indeed, he seemed at times to go out of his way to offend them, and spoke rather too freely about their personal shortcomings. He also enforced royal prerogatives at their expense, notably by revoking the patronage previously enjoyed by secular and ecclesiastical lords under the terms of the 1438 Pragmatic Sanction.

Louis certainly knew he was playing with fire. He had, after all, helped to derail his father's more modest attempts to assert royal authority in the 1440 Praguerie rebellion. Since then Charles VII had committed the *taille* to setting up the salaried *compagnies d'ordonnance*, drawn from the lesser nobility and gentry. This was the standing army with which Charles threw the English out of France in 1449–51 and Louis, confident of his own military skill, believed it would deter his nobles from resorting to arms.

It did not deter the Duke of Brittany, who inspired little enthusiasm among his subjects but could depend on their unqualified support in resisting any attempt by the French king to infringe on Breton autonomy. So, when Frañsez defied him in 1463 and Louis found he needed the support of the French nobility, he did not get it. The step too far was to make an enemy of Charolais at the same time, when Philippe was showing signs of senility and could no longer be depended on to keep his intemperate son under control.

The paradoxical result was that England moved to the front and centre of Louis's diplomacy. He had created a critical mass of enemies and the last thing he needed was for an English army with its dreaded longbowmen to descend on Normandy. Thus the embassy sent by Edward IV, led by Chancellor George Neville, was manna from heaven. Louis agreed a one-year truce with Neville in October 1463, deluged the embassy with expensive gifts, and showed himself warmly disposed to the idea of a matrimonial alliance.

Not least, he expressed extravagant admiration for Warwick and requested he should lead a subsequent delegation to a peace conference to end the state of war that still existed between the two kingdoms. In what he thought was a masterstroke, Louis asked Duke Philippe to host the conference. Philippe, who, unlike his son, was rather pleased with the immense addition to his treasury from the redemption of the Somme towns, was flattered and moved almost permanently to his palace at Hesdin, the designated venue.

Warwick could not come because the Lancastrians and Scots continued to cause trouble well into 1464, and everybody – except Marguerite and Bishop Kennedy in Scotland, who begged in vain for further support – believed Louis was responsible. This was no longer the case: the Lancastrian gambit had outlived its usefulness. His aim was to prevent an Anglo–Burgundian alliance, and what better way than by winning over the man said to be the power behind the English throne?

In March 1464 Louis sent Lord de la Barde, who had fought for Edward at Towton, with an offer of marriage to Bona of Savoy, Louis's 14-year-old sister-in-law. Edward coolly replied that he would give it serious consideration. Warwick, on the other hand, leapt for the fly and promised to go to Hesdin to agree the final terms of the treaty. As spring gave way to summer, letters arrived from Warwick excusing himself because negotiations with the Scots required his presence in York, and Louis became increasingly nervous.

Meanwhile Philippe was becoming restless, and Louis rode to Hesdin to soothe his uncle's increasingly clouded mind. Finally an embassy arrived, but it was led by Warwick's retainer Lord Wenlock and had only come to negotiate a one-year extension of the truce due to expire in October. Warwick would certainly come, Wenlock said, before then. By now Louis was genuinely desperate. His diplomacy was unravelling, reports from his spies indicated serious trouble brewing among his nobles, and now he had involved Duke Philippe in a fiasco. Louis left Hesdin on 9 July, never to see his uncle again.

'I never saw a lord so ardently desire anything as this King desires this peace with the English', reported Louis's confidante Alberico Maletta, the Milanese ambassador. 'I believe that if the earl of Warwick came he would obtain anything from the King to obtain this peace'. 'Anything' almost certainly included a French title and lands to go with it.

Then rumour swelled to certainty – Edward had secretly married Elizabeth Woodville, a beautiful English widow, and had announced it at a meeting of his Great Council after first permitting the oblivious Warwick to extol the virtues of Bona of Savoy. It was a brutal rejection of the French alliance, and Duke Philippe exploded with rage when he learned of it. Then Charolais announced he had arrested a spy sent by Louis – a nephew of the Croy brothers, Louis's agents at the Burgundian court and the blackest of Charolais's *bêtes noires*. The Universal Spider's web had been torn apart.

ELIZABETH

LIKE MOST WOMEN OF HER TIME ELIZABETH WOODVILLE has no voice in the historical record. Inevitably, most of what we 'know' of her as a person is based on gossip, because that is all there is to work with. There are records of a few acts of charity, patronage and household management, but none that illuminate her closest relationships. Her presumed influence must be inferred from the better recorded actions of those around her, in particular Edward IV, because had she not become his queen we would know even less about her.

One incontrovertible fact is that, like her mother Jacquetta, Elizabeth was astonishingly fertile. Between 1466 and 1480 she bore Edward ten children, eight surviving infancy. Since Edward was an inveterate womanizer, clearly something more than sex continued to draw him back to Elizabeth's bed. Perhaps, like Shakespeare's Cleopatra:

> Age cannot wither her, nor custom stale
> Her infinite variety. Other women cloy
> The appetites they feed, but she makes hungry
> Where most she satisfies…

Edward would not have been easily impressed. He would have started early with servants and worked his way up the social scale as he grew older. He was young, tall, handsome and rich, and would have had little difficulty seducing lonely widows and women married to men who thought to profit from the liaison. The floodgates would have opened after he became king. Royal courts could be hothouses, and adultery was easily incubated behind the stylized flirting of courtly love, accompanied by staggering amounts of wine and spirits.

Married women were the safest option, as any by-blows could not definitely be attributed to him, and Edward is reputed to have bedded the wives of many London merchants. His taste ran to mature, sexually experienced women, but no doubt a fair number of maidens were happy to be deflowered by him. He had at least two recognized bastards.* English kings never adopted the well-ordered continental custom of 'official' mistresses (*maîtresses en titre*), but the families of their lovers still had much to gain, and their cast-offs could expect to make good marriages to men likewise seeking royal favour.

So – Edward lived any young man's dream of concupiscence, and if foreign observers were still commenting on his sexual appetite when he was approaching 40, he must have been truly voracious in his late teens and early twenties. It may have contributed to his reluctance to subject himself to the hardships of campaigning, and might help to explain his sluggishness in all except the most challenging situations. These were not qualities that inspired respect. However indulgent society might otherwise be of youthful exuberance, as king he had an obligation to ensure the succession and to set an example.

Accordingly, Edward was under pressure to marry and settle down. Warwick's earnest efforts to saddle him with Bona of Savoy were irksome, and Edward's decision to marry someone 'unsuitable'

*Elizabeth Lucy née Wayte, a widow, gave him a daughter, also Elizabeth, in the early 1460s, and may have died giving birth to a son, Arthur, *c.*1476. Elizabeth married Thomas Lumley and their son Richard (born *c.*1478) became the 4th Baron Lumley. In 1511 Arthur married Elizabeth Grey, Baroness Lisle by right, and was made a viscount in 1523.

THE HOUSE OF WOODVILLE

k. = killed in battle   x. = executed

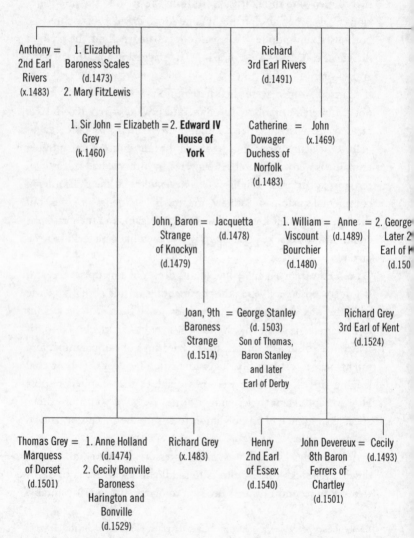

Anthony = 1. Elizabeth
2nd Earl   Baroness Scales
Rivers   (d.1473)
(x.1483)   2. Mary FitzLewis

Richard
3rd Earl Rivers
(d.1491)

1. Sir John = Elizabeth = 2. **Edward IV**
Grey   **House of**
(k.1460)   **York**

Catherine = John
Dowager   (x.1469)
Duchess of
Norfolk
(d.1483)

John, Baron = Jacquetta
Strange   (d.1478)
of Knockyn
(d.1479)

1. William = Anne = 2. George
Viscount   (d.1489)   Later 2
Bourchier   Earl of H
(d.1480)   (d.150

Joan, 9th = George Stanley
Baroness   (d. 1503)
Strange   Son of Thomas,
(d.1514)   Baron Stanley
            and later
            Earl of Derby

Richard Grey
3rd Earl of Kent
(d.1524)

Thomas Grey = 1. Anne Holland
Marquess   (d.1474)
of Dorset   2. Cecily Bonville
(d.1501)   Baroness
               Harington and
               Bonville
               (d.1529)

Richard Grey
(x.1483)

Henry
2nd Earl
of Essex
(d.1540)

John Devereux = Cecily
8th Baron   (d.1493)
Ferrers of
Chartley
(d.1501)

Richard Woodville = Jacquetta of Luxembourg
Earl Rivers   Duchess of Bedford
(1405–69)   (1415–72)

Lionel
Bishop of
Salisbury
(d.1484)

Eleanor = Anthony
(d.1512) Grey
         (d.1480)

Edward
Known as
Lord Scales
(k.1488)

Mary = William
(d.1481) Herbert
          1st Baron
          Dunster[1]
          (d.1491)

Margaret = Thomas FitzAlan
(d.1491)   Lord Maltravers
           (d.1524)

Henry Stafford = Catherine
2nd Duke of   (d.1497)
Buckingham
(x.1483)

Elizabeth = Charles Somerset
3rd Baroness   Later Earl of
Herbert   Worcester,
(d.1507)   legitimized son of
               Henry Beaufort,
               Duke of Somerset

Edward
3rd Duke of
Buckingham
(x.1521)

Elizabeth
Countess of
Sussex
(d.1532)

Henry
3rd Earl of
Wiltshire
(d.1523)

Anne
Countess of
Huntingdon
(d.1544)

William
18th Earl
of Arundel
(d.1544)

Margaret = John de la Pole
(d.1493)   1st Earl of
           Lincoln
           (k.1487)

Joan = George
       5th Baron
       Berganvenny
       (d.1535)

[1]Eldest son of Lord William Herbert, 1st Earl of Pembroke. William Jr. surrendered the earldom of Pembroke in 1479 when made Earl of Huntingdon.

was undoubtedly a defiant gesture both to him and to convention. Although it was a snub to Warwick, it was also a humiliating slap in the face to his aunt, Edward's insufferably proud mother. Duchess Cecily liked to think of herself as 'queen by right' and had no doubt been looking forward to dominating a young foreign-born queen. Her chagrin at being replaced by a mature and self-assured Englishwoman was boundless.

It went deeper than that: Jacquetta and Richard Woodville filled an emotional void in Edward's life before he ever set eyes on Elizabeth, and his close relationship with them preceded his marriage to their daughter by several years. When his reign began he was, just, 20 years old, Richard was 56 and Jacquetta 46. Edward's nominal father – had he lived – would have been 50 and Cecily was also 46. To some degree, the older Woodvilles became surrogates for the loving parents he never had.

Edward first got to know them when he was with Warwick in Calais. In January 1460 Lord Rivers, Jacquetta and their eldest son Lord Scales were captured in a raid on Sandwich. Jacquetta seems to have insisted on being taken with them to Calais, where Warwick and Edward submitted Rivers and Scales to a public humiliation, sneering at Rivers for marrying above himself. Jacquetta's presence may have saved their lives, as she was not only dowager Duchess of Bedford, thus outranking both Edward and Warwick, but also the sister of Louis, ruler of the neighbouring county of Saint-Pol. She would have demanded honourable treatment of her husband and son before returning to England.

While he did not bond with Rivers at this time, Edward did win over two other Lancastrians captured during his sojourn in Calais. John Tuchet, Baron Audley, and Humphrey Stafford of Hooke (later Southwyck) formed part of the expedition sent under Henry Beaufort to take Calais back for Lancaster. Captured in a skirmish, they were treated so well by Edward that they changed sides and became his devoted followers.

Edward's next encounter with the Woodvilles was at Towton,

where Rivers and Scales led the division that outflanked the Yorkist right wing and nearly won the battle before the tide was turned by the late arrival of the Duke of Norfolk's men. It was therefore remarkable that only ten weeks later Edward should have visited Rivers's manor of Grafton in Northamptonshire on his way back to London. Before departing he wrote to Chancellor George Neville saying he pardoned Rivers 'all manner of offences and trespasses of him done against us'. A month later he also pardoned Scales, conditional on service against the Lancastrians in the North.

Even Somerset was required to prove his loyalty – why not Rivers? The answer is almost certainly Jacquetta. Her feisty performance at Calais no doubt made a positive impression, but it would have been her subsequent actions that turned Edward into an admirer. She was one of the two noblewomen, both ladies-in-waiting to the queen, who were sent by the mayor and aldermen of London to beg Marguerite not to assault the city after her victory at the Second Battle of St Albans on 17 February 1461.*

In fact Marguerite's army was in no condition to fight its way into the city. It would also have been madness to do so with Edward's army approaching from the west following his victory at Mortimer's Cross. Contemporaries did not see it that way. They believed Marguerite was at the head of a horde of ravening English and Scots borderers, intent on rape and pillage. Consequently, when Jacquetta returned to reassure them the alleged horde would not try to enter the city, she became a secular saint to Londoners.

Arriving a few days later, Edward would have believed she had made it possible for him to occupy the capital peacefully, with all the political, financial and military benefits that flowed from this. Although her husband and eldest son tried earnestly to kill him at Towton, he owed Jacquetta a considerable debt of gratitude and went to Grafton to pay his respects – to her. No doubt she told her doting husband, in no uncertain terms, how he should behave.

---

*At which Jacquetta's son-in-law John Grey, Elizabeth Woodville's first husband, had been the only prominent Lancastrian killed.

Rivers was soon regularly employed on royal commissions and in 1463 became the first ex-Lancastrian to become a member of the Privy Council. Even so, Elizabeth did not judge her parents close enough to the king to plead her cause in a well-documented event immediately preceding her marriage to Edward, which may be crucially illuminating. It involved a negotiation with William Hastings, Edward's closest friend.

Hastings was an inveterate lecher and Edward had learned much from him when he was a lusty teenager enjoying the older man's hospitality as ranger of the Duke of York's chase at Wyre in Shropshire. Given Hasting's reputation, when we find Elizabeth appealing to him in 1464 to use his influence on her behalf in a lawsuit involving the fourth son of Viscount Bourchier, the king's uncle, it is a safe assumption that he demanded something more than the goodwill of a highly desirable widow in return.

The suit came about because Elizabeth's mother-in-law, Baroness Ferrers of Groby in her own right, tried to cheat her of a settlement made on her by the baroness's first husband, who had died in 1457. The baroness was urged on by her second husband John Bourchier, nineteen years her junior, both of them emboldened by the death of Elizabeth's husband at the Second Battle of St Albans and the sudden prominence of John's father, now Earl of Essex. At stake were not only three manors allocated by the terms of a trust, but also the Ferrers lands, which should eventually go to Thomas, Elizabeth's eldest son and heir to the barony.

By the terms of a contract signed on 13 April 1464 Hastings acquired the right – for which he paid 500 marks [£106,000] – to marry a daughter of his family to Thomas, or if he died to his younger brother Richard. If both died Elizabeth was to repay 250 marks. Hastings was also to have an equal share of the income from any Ferrers lands secured (implicitly by his influence) for Thomas before his 12th birthday.

It was an almost priceless warning shot across the bow of John Bourchier from the heaviest gun at Edward's court. As to the settlement, half of something is, after all, a great deal better than all of nothing, and 500 marks was not chicken feed. If part of the price Hastings demanded to ensure her son's inheritance was for Elizabeth to bed him, it would explain her hostility towards him in the years to come. It would, of course, have been very greatly in the interest of neither to tell Edward about it.

Given that the contract became moot after Elizabeth married Edward, he cannot yet have been a prospect. He was probably first smitten seventeen days later during a visit to Grafton, when Elizabeth is alleged to have petitioned him for justice in her dispute with Lady Ferrers. As early as 1468 an Italian author stated the marriage took place the next day, but it is just too neat to have it take place on May Day, the spring festival of fertility. The marriage took place after Edward returned from signing the Scots truce, at one of two subsequent visits to Grafton in June and July.

Jacquetta probably pimped her daughter, as any aristocratic mother would have done. Edward was always on the quest for nubile widows, but he would have hesitated before seducing the daughter of a couple he respected. No doubt the usual game of love was played out, with Edward becoming increasingly ardent. Jacquetta was the only family member to witness the informal marriage that preceded the consummation, after which Elizabeth set the hook so well that Edward's travelling companions remarked on his blissful exhaustion.

In the context of his policy of reconciliation it was politically shrewd for Edward to marry the daughter of Lord Rivers, the most prominent of the genuinely reconciled Lancastrians. But there was also an overwhelming dynastic argument with reference to the looming power struggle with over-mighty Warwick. With his older sisters already married, in mid-1464 Edward could dispose of only three siblings as matrimonial assets: 18-year-old Margaret, 14-year-old George and 11-year-old Richard.

By marrying Elizabeth he acquired two stepsons and nine brothers-and sisters-in-law, all except one, Elizabeth's sister Jacquetta, unmarried. The significance of this becomes apparent when we contrast the wave of marriage alliances that ensued with those of the Nevilles when they were seeking to affirm their power a generation earlier. Edward married his new in-laws to every eligible bachelor in the peerage to strengthen his family ties, and the grooms in turn expected to benefit from becoming members of the extended royal family. It was a transaction well understood by all concerned.

Petit bourgeois preoccupation with class has never bothered the nobility when money and power are involved, and despite sniffy comments by some contemporary chroniclers and most historians, Elizabeth's lineage was acceptable to the old aristocracy. Led by the Earl of Arundel, whose title dated back to 1138 and who had married one of the Nevilles a generation earlier, they were only too willing to enter into matrimonial alliances with the Woodvilles.

Some have suggested that Warwick was outraged by the marriage between 19-year-old John Woodville and wealthy, 65-year-old Katherine née Neville, dowager Duchess of Norfolk, Duchess Cecily's sister and Warwick's aunt. Yet Warwick did not object to his sister Katherine marrying newly created Lord Hastings or another aunt, the dowager duchess of Buckingham, marrying Lord Mountjoy, an even more recent creation.

The canonical accounts have it that Edward, like a guilty schoolboy, was forced to admit his marriage at the meeting of the Great Council in mid-September when pressed by Warwick to make a decision about Bona of Savoy. This is unlikely. The assembled peers would have regarded any proposal from Louis XI with extreme suspicion, and Warwick's sales pitch would have been addressed to them. The more likely reason why Edward delayed the announcement of his secret marriage is because there had not previously been an occasion when he could inform his magnates collectively.*

If it was always Edward's intention to announce his marriage to Elizabeth, then it was malicious to have permitted Warwick to

---

*The reason given for summoning them to Reading Abbey was to agree a recoinage, not to discuss royal matrimony.

NEVILLE MARRIAGES

Joan married (1438) William FitzAlan, Earl of Arundel.

Cecily married (1434) Henry Beauchamp, heir to the earldom of Warwick.

Richard married (1434) Anne Beauchamp, eventual heir of Henry, Earl of Warwick.

Alice married (1448) Henry FitzHugh, heir to the eponymous barony.

John married (1457) Isabel Ingoldisthorpe, wealthy heiress.

Eleanor married (1457) Thomas Stanley, heir to the eponymous barony.

Katherine married (1458) William Bonville, Baron Harington, heir to the Bonville barony.

William married (1422) Joan, *suo jure* Baroness Fauconberg (congenital idiot).

Edward married (1424) Elizabeth Beauchamp, *suo jure* Baroness Bergavenny.

Thomas married (1454) Matilda, co-heiress of Ralph, Baron Cromwell.

Margaret married (1458) John Vere, Earl of Oxford.

WOODVILLE MARRIAGES

Elizabeth married (1455) John Grey of Groby, heir to the barony, and (1464) Edward IV

Thomas Grey married (1466) Anne, heiress to the dukedom of Exeter

Anthony married (1459) Elizabeth, Baroness Scales

Jacquetta married (1450) John, Baron Strange of Knockyn

John married (1466) Katherine Neville, dowager Duchess of Norfolk

Anne married (1467) William Bourchier, heir to the earldom of Essex

Mary married (1467) William Herbert, heir to the earldom of Pembroke

Margaret married (1465) Thomas FitzAlan, heir to the earldom of Arundel

Eleanor married (1465) Anthony Grey, heir to the earldom of Kent

Catherine married (1465) Henry Stafford, Duke of Buckingham argue the merits of the French alliance in the presence of his peers. Thus it was not so much the supposed unworthiness of Elizabeth, nor even differences of opinion on foreign policy that lit the fuse for Warwick's future treason: it was the gratuitously insulting manner in which Edward let the assembled nobility of England know that he no longer heeded Warwick's advice.

Only one or two already knew. Rivers, a royal councillor since 1463, certainly; also Hastings, and one would have liked to have been a fly on the wall when Edward told him. The king would not have informed the other members of his household, as such a juicy piece of gossip would have spread like wildfire. Accordingly, the sound of mental gears changing would have been almost audible in the Council chamber after Edward's announcement until someone, probably Hastings, broke silence to be the first to congratulate the king.

Escorted by Warwick and Edward's brother Clarence, on the 29th Elizabeth was introduced to the Great Council and saluted by all present as Queen of England. The royal couple stayed at Reading after the Council disbanded, then moved to the royal palaces of Windsor in November and Eltham in December. Edward ordered her paid £466 [nearly £30,000] to cover her Christmas expenses, and later endowed her with lands producing about £4,500 [£2.86 million] per annum. Christmas gifts included the palaces of Greenwich and Sheen.

Elizabeth was crowned at Westminster Abbey on 26 May 1465, the date delayed to accommodate a high-ranking delegation from Burgundy, among them her brother Jacques de Luxembourg, lord of Richebourg. Edward rode into London on the 23rd and knighted thirty-nine men in her honour, including Elizabeth's brothers Richard and John. The City put on a splendid display at London Bridge. There was music and singing and a tableau of men dressed as St Paul, St Elizabeth and Mary Cleophas, the Virgin Mary's half-sister, flanked by angels with wings of peacock feathers.

Elizabeth spent the night at the Tower and the next day rode in an open litter through the streets of London to Westminster Hall, escorted by the new knights. During her procession to the abbey the following day the dowager Duchess of Buckingham, whose husband had been killed at Northampton by Warwick's men, carried her train. At the ceremony of bridal washing back at Westminster Hall after the coronation, John Vere, who had been permitted to succeed as Earl of Oxford and hereditary chamberlain after Tiptoft executed his father and older brother in 1462, poured the water.

Warwick and Tiptoft were away on conveniently timed official business. While obviously the ex-Lancastrian guests would have been glad not to rub shoulders with men who had killed their kin, one suspects Warwick was also sent away lest he spoil the joyous occasion by glowering. Also pointedly absent, of her own volition, was Cecily Neville, dowager Duchess of York and the king's mother.

The family of Henry Bourchier, Earl of Essex, the king's uncle by marriage, dominated the new queen's household. Her chamberlain was John, Lord Berners, the earl's brother, the most senior of her ladies-in-waiting was her sister Anne, wife of the earl's heir William, Viscount Bourchier, and one of her carvers was Humphrey, Baron Cromwell, the earl's third surviving son. Another lady-in-waiting was her brother Anthony's wife Elizabeth, Baroness Scales – but even she had a Bourchier connection, as she was the widow of Henry, the earl's second son. The only male Woodville was her brother John, her Master of Horse.

After the ceremony Edward created his new father-in-law Earl Rivers, and recreated the earldom of Kent for Edmund Grey of Ruthyn, whose timely treachery had given him victory at Northampton. He also ennobled Walter Blount, who became Lord Mountjoy, and gave him £666 [£42,400], perhaps to soften the blow of losing the lucrative office of Lord Treasurer to Rivers two months earlier. Like Grey of Ruthyn before him, Blount had done well out of his time in office, and in 1467 he married the dowager Duchess of Buckingham.

So many wheels within wheels. One of the biggest barriers to modern understanding of the late Middle Ages is how far from straightforward everything was: even the art of the period is layered with allusions and arcane symbols. So also the statements and actions of princes: they were always seeking to achieve more than one thing at a time, and form was often as important as substance. Whatever the original spark of Edward and Elizabeth's relationship, the marriage itself was a complex act of dynastic calculation and theatre.

In sum, Elizabeth was a beautiful and sexually skilled woman who could be expected to produce a healthy heir. Choosing her over Bona of Savoy delivered a deserved snub to Louis XI and strengthened Edward's ties with Burgundy, while announcing his emancipation from his mother and Warwick. She brought with her sons and siblings to expand the matrimonial links of a royal dynasty with shallow roots. Finally, she symbolized Edward's desire to heal the wounds of fratricidal strife.

It was a heavy load for a pair of slender shoulders to carry.

───────────── V ─────────────

HENCHMEN

THE PROPAGANDA SPIN PUT ON THE EVENTS OF THE
next few years by Warwick and his partisans at home and
abroad has weighed heavily on historiography. Supposedly
entranced by Elizabeth and her mother, Edward is alleged to have
showered preferment on his grasping and parvenu in-laws, to the
exclusion of the great lords (for which read Warwick) whose ancient
lineage made them the custodians of historic customs, and thus of
the nation's best interests.

It should not be necessary to refute such evidently self-serving
piffle. There is little evidence any of the Woodvilles were promoted
above their level of competence, and even less that they exercised
undue influence on the king. It was hardly likely Edward should
have declared his independence by marrying Elizabeth, only to
become overly dependent on her family. He favoured them when it
served his purposes to do so – but that is all he did.

The key men of his regime were three who rode with him after
Mortimer's Cross, whom he ennobled after Towton. They were
William Herbert, 38 years old in 1461, the first full-blooded
Welshman to be made an English peer; 30-year-old William
Hastings; and 22-year-old Humphrey Stafford of Southwyck. Also
part of the group though less prominent was 30-year-old Walter
Devereux, Baron Ferrers of Chartley by marriage. An outlier, not
ennobled until 1470, was 36-year-old John Howard, whose timely

arrival at the head of his cousin the Duke of Norfolk's men decided the outcome at Towton.

• ❧ •

Although Hastings was Edward's closest friend and fellow voluptuary, Herbert was the man on whom he depended most – after the Nevilles – to affirm his regime in the face of adamant Lancastrian resistance. The struggle for the North gets more attention because of the presence of the usurped royal family, but the challenge was more intractable in Wales. Only the south-eastern part of Wales was ever truly reconciled to Yorkist rule.

It is generally believed that the 'deep' Welsh never truly accepted English rule until the Tudors seized the throne, but it was more complicated than that. Underlying the York-versus-Lancaster rivalry was a blood feud among Welshmen whose forefathers had fought for or against Owain Glyn Dŵr, the last Welsh Prince of Wales. Superimposed on both were local clan rivalries, with the parties choosing sides in the greater conflict for tactical reasons.

Things were simplified after Towton. Herbert, who provided the best of Edward's army at Mortimer's Cross, was immediately appointed Chief Justice for South Wales and steward of royal Carmarthen and Cardigan. He, his brother and his Vaughan half-brothers also took possession for the king of the local lands of the variously killed Earl of Wiltshire (Laugharne and Walwyn's Castle in Wales), Earl of Shrewsbury (Goodrich and Archenfield in Herefordshire) and James Luttrell in northern Somerset. They also took possession of the lands of still living Jasper Tudor, Earl of Pembroke, and John Skydmore of Herefordshire.

Walter Devereux was a not a member of Herbert's affinity, but they acted in concert. Herbert was married to his sister, but Devereux was a Herefordshire and Leicestershire landowner in his own right and, through his wife, acquired the title and lands of the barony of Ferrers of Chartley in Staffordshire and Lincolnshire. Consequently he was content to play second fiddle in Wales to his brother-in-law, although Edward built up Ferrers's holdings in Herefordshire by making him steward of Goodrich and Archenfield, and adding his manor of Richard's Castle to Devereux's own manor of Weobley.

In 1461 Herbert and Ferrers received nominally joint custody of the Stafford lands in south Wales during the Duke of Buckingham's minority, but Herbert was appointed Chief Steward of the main manors of Brecon, Hay, Huntington and Newport.* In 1463 Edward created the Marcher lordship of Crickhowell and Tretower in Brecknock for Herbert (delegated to the Vaughans) and in 1465 another lordship, the last ever created, of Raglan, Carleon and Usk in Monmouth. Both were areas long held for the House of York by the Herberts and Vaughans, now made feudal fiefs.

A glance at Map 32 will reveal that Edward's intention was to build a *cordon sanitaire* around Warwick's Marcher lordship of Glamorgan and the lands of the barony of Bergavenny appropriated by Warwick from his compliant uncle Edward Neville. Fully occupied as he was in the North and with playing the statesman, Warwick could not object when Herbert was entrusted with pacifying Wales and was showered – as he himself had been in the North – with the appropriate royal offices.

Warwick's break with the Lancastrian regime had come about when his wife Anne Beauchamp's inheritance in south-east Wales and the Marches was assailed by the claims of her half-sisters and their husbands, the now dead and attainted Duke of Somerset and Earls of Shrewsbury and Wiltshire. His local affinity was shallow because of this and neglect during the war, and the promotion of Herbert further devalued his 'good lordship'. If to this we add that Herbert had been for many years his steward and Sheriff of Glamorgan, and it is clear why Warwick came to hate him.

The Herbertification of Wales was not confined to the south-east. After their ennoblement, on 30 September 1461 he and Ferrers

*Newport became a venomous bone of contention with Warwick – presumably to do with port rights.

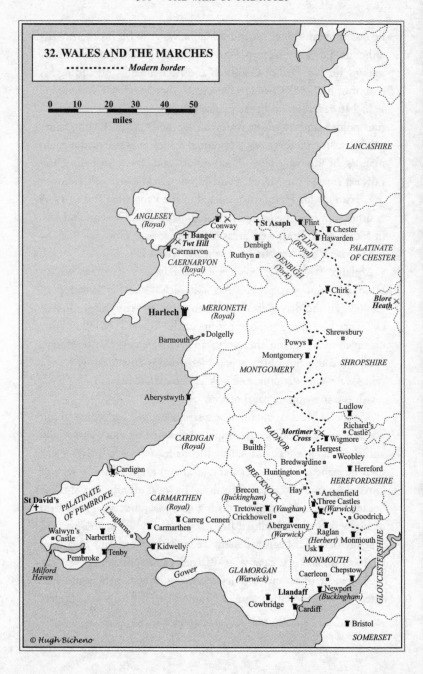

32. WALES AND THE MARCHES

-------------- *Modern border*

0 10 20 30 40 50
miles

LANCASHIRE

ANGLESEY
(Royal)

✝ Bangor
✕ *Twt Hill*
Caernarvon
CAERNARVON
(Royal)

Conway

✝ St Asaph

Flint
Chester
Hawarden
PALATINATE
OF CHESTER

Denbigh
Ruthyn

FLINT
(Royal)

DENBIGH
(York)

Chirk

*Blore
Heath* ✕

Harlech
MERIONETH
(Royal)

Barmouth   Dolgelly

Powys
Montgomery

Shrewsbury

MONTGOMERY

SHROPSHIRE

Aberystwyth

CARDIGAN
(Royal)

Ludlow

Richard's
Castle
*Mortimer's
Cross* ✕ Wigmore
Hergest
Weobley

RADNOR

Builth

Bredwardine
Huntington

Hereford

BRECKNOCK

HEREFORDSHIRE

Cardigan

St David's
✝

PALATINATE
OF PEMBROKE

Walwyn's
Castle
Narberth
Pembroke
Tenby

*Milford
Haven*

Laugharne

CARMARTHEN
(Royal)

Carreg Cennen
Carmarthen

Kidwelly

Gower

Brecon
(Buckingham)
Tretower *(Vaughan)*
Crickhowell

Hay

Archenfield
Three Castles
(Warwick)

Goodrich

Abergavenny
(Warwick)

Raglan
(Herbert) Monmouth

Usk

GLAMORGAN
(Warwick)

Caerleon

MONMOUTH

Chepstow

GLOUCESTERSHIRE

Llandaff
✝
Cowbridge
Cardiff

Newport
(Buckingham)

Bristol

SOMERSET

© Hugh Bicheno

secured the surrender of Tenby and Pembroke Castle from John Skydmore, Jasper Tudor's most trusted lieutenant, who was promised a pardon. Although Skydmore's attainder was revoked, by a separate bill he was pardoned only his life and goods – Ferrers kept his forfeited Herefordshire lands.

A bonus from the capture of Pembroke Castle was that 4-year-old Henry Tudor, Earl of Richmond, came into Herbert's custody. He placed him in the care of his wife at the great show castle he was completing at Raglan, and paid the king £1,000 [£636,000] for the boy's wardship and marriage. This was further grit in Warwick's eye, as the young earl's estates would have nicely complemented his own.

Herbert then rode north to recruit another army, with which on 16 October he defeated a force led by Jasper Tudor and the Duke of Exeter (who joined him after fleeing Towton) at Twt Hill near Caernarvon Castle. Jasper and Exeter fled to Ireland, whence Jasper continued the fight with support from Duke Fransez. Exeter eventually reached Burgundy, where he remained until 1471, initially in a state of beggary but later in receipt of a pension from Charolais.

Three Welsh castles still held out for Lancaster. In the north, Edward declared the temporalities of the rebel bishops of Bangor and St Asaph forfeit, and without support from the surrounding area or hope of relief Denbigh Castle surrendered in January 1462.* In the south, Carreg Cennen capitulated in May. This left only Harlech in Merioneth, the most formidable of Edward I's castles and of enormous symbolic importance to the Welsh. It had capitulated to Glyn Dŵr in 1404 to become his headquarters for the remainder of the dying kick of Welsh independence.

Although now separated from the sea by a half a mile of sedimentary deposition, at the time Harlech had a functioning water-gate at the base of the cliff on which it stands, through which it was kept supplied by Jasper, first from Ireland and later from Brittany. Even if Edward had been prepared to ship his bombards to Merioneth, it

---

*The bishop and parishioners of St Asaph were so recalcitrant that in 1463 he was deprived of his see, which remained vacant until 1471.

is hard to see where they could have been sited. The county was also desperately poor and notoriously unruly, such that maintaining a siege was an expensive and risky proposition. Harlech's commander David ap Eynon, latterly joined by Richard Tunstall and Henry Bellingham, easily held out until late 1468.

In February 1462 Edward awarded Herbert the lands of Jasper Tudor's attainted earldom of Pembroke and custody of the Welsh estates of the Mowbray dukedom of Norfolk, including Chepstow and Gower. In 1468 he acquired them permanently, the first when he was made Earl Palatine of Pembroke, and the Mowbray manors in exchange for properties he held in East Anglia, a sensible act of territorial consolidation for both lords. Already a wealthy merchant in 1461, control of the south Wales ports made Herbert wealthier still.

By that time he had also replaced Tiptoft as chief justice and chamberlain for north Wales and had been given custody of the lands of Lord Grey of Powys, who had backed the wrong horse in 1463. Herbert was now either the dominant lord or the senior crown official of every county in Wales except Warwick's lordship of Glamorgan. In addition, in September 1466 Edward revived the extinct barony of Dunster for Herbert's 15-year-old namesake son prior to his marriage to Mary, the queen's youngest sister, and endowed him with lands confiscated from the late Earl of Wiltshire and James Luttrell in Somerset.

• ∽ •

The most cold-blooded injustice committed by Edward during the early years of his reign was the permanent dispossession of William, 2nd Viscount Beaumont. His father, the first viscount ever created in the English peerage, was a childhood friend of Henry VI, thanks to whom he built up large estates in Lincolnshire, Leicestershire, Norfolk and Suffolk. He also married the Duke of Norfolk's mother, Warwick's aunt Katherine, and enjoyed her dower of more than a third of Norfolk's patrimony. He was one of the lords killed at Northampton.

The sole reason for confiscating William's lands was to build up the Midlands lordships of William Hastings, who remains an enigmatic figure. The standard attack on the sacred person of a medieval monarch was through his favourites, the canonical 'evil councillors'. Hastings was certainly qualified for the role, yet with the notable exception of the queen and her family he was well regarded by everyone. This appears to be because he refused any title higher than baron and, content with Edward's generosity, did not abuse his influence to take more.

He had much to be content about. In addition to the Beaumont lands, some of which were entailed during her lifetime to the now widowed dowager Duchess of Norfolk, Edward awarded him the Midlands estates of the late and attainted Earl of Wiltshire and Baron Roos. Although Hasting's barony was a new creation, Edward also awarded him the lands recovered by the crown from the previous barony of Hastings, extinct in 1389.

Complemented by the stewardship of the local duchy of Lancaster and duchy of York lordships, Hastings became a prominent lord in Leicestershire, Rutland, Northamptonshire and Huntingdonshire, and even had a strong presence in Warwickshire. Additional estates in Norfolk, Suffolk, Cambridgeshire and Hertfordshire gave him an income appropriate for an earldom, which he was almost certainly offered but prudently declined.

Unlike Herbert, Hastings was not assigned a role that required him to tread on Warwick's toes, and they were potential allies against the Woodvilles. Perhaps because of this, in 1468 Warwick appointed Hastings steward of his own holdings in Leicestershire, Rutland and Northamptonshire. This should be highlighted, as it has a bearing on later events.

• ❧ •

One of the more persistent myths about the Woodville ascendancy is the supposedly scandalous nature of the marriage in 1465 between the elder of two dowager duchesses of Norfolk, 65-year-old Katherine née Neville, and the queen's 19-year-old brother John. This is based on a misunderstanding of women's property rights. What actually took place was that Katherine – who had another notorious liaison between her marriages to Norfolk and Beaumont – bought herself a young husband, and with him influence at court to offset Hastings' designs on the Beaumont estates she retained.

She was also a player in Edward's scheme to ensure the loyalty of East Anglia, which had not enjoyed the stability of a dominant lord for many years. When the 3rd duke, dissolute John Mowbray, died in 1461, his 17-year-old namesake heir became Edward's ward. Granted possession of his estates in 1463, he proved as ineffectual as his father. As a prince of the blood and hereditary earl marshal of England he should have provided a 'regime lock' on the region. In practice the dowers of previous duchesses consumed two-thirds of the revenues from his estates and he never played a role commensurate with his rank.

Also in 1463, Edward restored the dukedom of Suffolk to 19-year-old John de la Pole, whose father had been Henry VI's chief minister until murdered in 1450. In 1458 Richard of York had bound the teenager to his cause by marrying him to Elizabeth, his second daughter. Young Suffolk had at least one thing in common with his neighbour Norfolk: over half of his inheritance was held by his formidable mother Alice, granddaughter of Geoffrey Chaucer of *Canterbury Tales* fame. John himself proved to be a nonentity.

It was because the Mowbray and de la Pole affinities were temporarily leaderless that the third most important East Anglian lord, John Vere, Earl of Oxford, had dealt himself a hand in the Lancastrian conspiracy of 1461–2. His was one of the poorer earldoms and apparently genuine illness kept him side-lined during the battles of 1460–1, although his third son George fought for Lancaster at Towton. Urged on by Aubrey, his eldest, Vere rashly boarded the sinking Lancastrian ship in 1462, and both paid with their heads.

Vere's 20-year-old namesake second son thus became the 13th earl and, as we saw on the occasion of Edward's marriage, the king made every effort to win him over. But with regard to East Anglia, one of the richest and most strategically vital regions of his kingdom, there was no single lord Edward could back secure in the knowledge that he could keep the peace. It is for this reason the marriage between young John Woodville and the older of the two dowager Duchesses of Norfolk deserves reconsideration – Edward needed her on his team.

His chief agent in the region was John Howard, whom he had knighted on the battlefield of Towton. Howard's mother was the eldest daughter of the 1st Duke of Norfolk, and his paternal aunt was married to John Vere, Earl of Oxford. His sister was married to Warwick's dispossessed uncle Edward Neville, Baron Bergavenny. During 1461 Edward took Howard into his household and appointed him Constable of Norwich and Colchester castles, as well as High Sheriff of Norfolk and Suffolk. He may have hoped Howard could coordinate the fragmented Norfolk affinity and/or keep an eye on the Oxford affinity.

Howard built up a moderate estate around his inherited manor of Stoke-by-Nayland on the border of Suffolk and Essex, including seven manors granted him by Edward and six bought from his penurious Vere uncle after 1463. Like Howard and Hastings, he was a wealthy trader who did not depend on land rents – he was cash rich and relatively land poor. This may explain why he was not ennobled until 1470, although another reason may have been not to risk arousing resentment among the established but ineffectual regional lords.

• ᥫᨆ •

In addition to the North and Wales, Edward had to contend with persistent Lancastrian unrest in the West Country. The dominant lords had been the Earl of Wiltshire in Somerset and the county from which he drew his title, the Courtenay Earls of Devon, and Baron William Bonville, who feuded throughout the 1440s and 1450s. Courtenay declared for Lancaster and Bonville for York in 1459, but the war proved a catastrophe for both. Bonville's son and grandson, who had recently become Lord Harington, were killed at Wakefield, and Bonville himself was beheaded after the Second Battle of St Albans. When Courtenay and Wiltshire were executed a few weeks later and attainted, the West Country was leaderless.

The man who became Edward's principal agent in the region was only three years older than the king. Humphrey Stafford inherited a modest estate around Hooke in Wiltshire from his father, killed during Cade's Rebellion in 1450. By the time he fought at Mortimer's Cross and Towton, however, he was the heir apparent of his namesake cousin, the largest landowner in Dorset with sizeable estates in Somerset as well. His cousin died on 7 July 1461 and twenty days later Humphrey was summoned to Parliament as Baron Stafford of Southwyck.

The West Country was not a blank slate. The large Bonville-Harington affinity needed to be treated with respect, and rewards had to be found for local Yorkist barons like the Earl of Essex's brother William Bourchier, Lord FitzWarin, and Lords Cobham and de la Zouche. It was also necessary to build up the holdings of John Dynham, a south Devon landowner who had helped Edward and Warwick to escape to Calais after Ludlow and taken part in the capture of Sandwich, to justify his recent ennoblement.

Warwick resolved the issue of the Bonville succession with the king's approval. Cecily Bonville was only eight months old when the deaths of her father, grandfather and great-grandfather made her Baroness of Bonville and Harington by right and the richest heiress in England after Warwick's own daughters. The child's mother was another Katherine Neville, Warwick's younger sister, and in early 1462 he arranged Katherine's remarriage – to none other than William Hastings. Warwick retained a veto over the child's marriage, which he exercised to prevent her betrothal to William Herbert's heir.

There remained the larger problem of what to do with the Courtenay affinity, one of the oldest and deepest rooted in all England, which had suffered grievously at Towton. This was the task Edward set Stafford of Southwyck, starting with his appointment to the traditional Courtenay stewardship of the royal duchy of Cornwall, also as keeper of the royal forests in Dorset, Wiltshire and Somerset, and Constable of Bristol and Taunton.

If the plan was to give time for Stafford to grow his affinity, it went out of the window when the Earl of Oxford's co-conspirators revealed that the Courtenays were involved in the 1462 conspiracy. In February Edward awarded Stafford their principal estates in Devon, and although Stafford moved into the Courtenay family seat at Tiverton Castle the transfer of ownership never 'took'. Legal challenges forced Edward to regrant the awards in 1464, 1467 and again in 1468.

Further evidence of Stafford's failure to get a grip on the West Country can be seen in additional awards throughout the 1460s. These included his appointment in 1465 as keeper of the dowager Duchess of York's castle and manor of Bridgwater and Petherton Forest in Somerset, the award of further Courtenay lands in 1467, and in 1468 the stewardship of the estates of the minor John, Baron de la Zouche, in Dorset, Somerset and Wiltshire.

Like the Woodvilles, Edward's henchmen owed everything to him and were supposed to be his 'regime locks' on the most problematic regions of his kingdom – other than the North, where the Nevilles all but reigned in his place. There was, however, another individual to whom he entrusted a more general responsibility, the man immortally damned by Shakespeare as 'false, fleeting, perjur'd Clarence'.

CLARENCE

G EORGE, DUKE OF CLARENCE, WAS THE THIRD SON OF Richard, Duke of York and Cecily née Neville to survive infancy. He was born in Dublin in October 1449, when his father had wisely absented himself from a court about to suffer the consequences of the collapse of the English empire in France. York was the king's lieutenant in Ireland, a senior office usually awarded to princes of the blood but normally handled by a deputy.

Like his younger brother Richard, born two years later, George's early life was dominated by their father's struggle to take over the government of England. They were captured along with their mother when York abandoned them at Ludlow, and later sent to the Duke of Burgundy for safekeeping after their father and their older brother Edmund were killed at Wakefield and the Lancastrians marched on London.

George would have grown up with a deep-seated sense of insecurity, but apart from those two episodes we know next to nothing about him before his oldest brother became king. Suddenly he was elevated to the rank and status of heir presumptive to the throne, a role for which, as a third son, he had no preparation whatever. Far from celebrating his good fortune he appears to have been a more than usually sullen adolescent, petulantly resentful of his older brother and lacking any sense of loyalty or gratitude.

It is not difficult to deduce what tipped George into outright malignancy. At some point, probably not long after being replaced at court by Elizabeth Woodville, the enraged Duchess Cecily must have told him that Edward was not his father's son, and that he should properly sit in his place. The confirmation of what he probably already suspected would have had a dislocating effect even on a normal person: for Clarence it tied together all the inchoate strands of his emerging personality.

Two things made this catastrophic for the Yorkist regime. The first is that Elizabeth did not produce the expected male heir until November 1470. The second, closely related to the first, is that Edward needed Clarence to fill a void in his scheme of governance. Maps 9 and 10 seek to illustrate why this was the case. I am aware that they do not do justice to the complexity of English landholdings – they aspire only to show who was or had the potential to be a dominant lord in every shire.

There were only five noble houses with nationwide estates: the duchies of Lancaster, York, Norfolk and Buckingham, and the Warwick/Salisbury earldoms. No other came close – the independently governed ecclesiastical estates were a special case. Edward was duke both of York and Lancaster, and the young Duke of Buckingham was his ward. These holdings, combined with the crown estates, should have given him an overwhelming supremacy. In practice he had to delegate to subordinates of varying honesty, competence and loyalty, and the personal link essential to the maintenance of an affinity was tenuous.

The crown, Lancaster and York estates were all separately administered and as late as 1466 Edward had to call in returns from all his manors, honours, messuages, feudal rights and other forms of tenure just to establish where and what they were. Nor could he count on anything like the professional bureaucracy that might have knit the varied strands together. In fact the only unifying element was the law, and consequently the administration of justice was the touchstone of a monarch's reputation.

Royal progresses and assizes could only accomplish so much. For

33. PRINCIPAL ESTATES OF THE CROWN AND LEADING MAGNATES c.1455

A	Arundel (FitzAlan)
B	Buckingham (Stafford)
Bt	Beaumont
C	Clifford
Cr	Cromwell
D	Devon (Courtenay)
Da	Dacre
E	Essex (Bourchier)
G	Grey of Ruthyn
H	Hungerford
K	King (inc. Lancaster)
M	Norfolk (Mowbray)
N	Neville (Salisbury/Warwick)
n	Neville (Westmorland)
P	Percy (Northumberland)
Q	Queen's dower
Qp	Queen/Prince of Wales
R	Roos
S	Somerset (Beaufort)
St	Stanley
T	Talbot (Shrewsbury/Lisle)
V	Vere (Oxford)
W	Wiltshire (Ormonde)
Y	York (duchy)

The aim of this map is to illustrate the patchwork quilt nature of landholdings. Only named manors are shown in approximately the correct location. A third of all landholdings were ecclesiastical, but only the most important are marked with a cross.

© Hugh Bicheno

34. REDISTRIBUTION OF ESTATES *c.*1468

A Arundel
B Buckingham
C Clarence
Cr Cromwell (Bourchier)
E Essex (Bourchier)
G Gloucester
H Herbert

Ha Hastings
Ho Howard
K Kent (Grey of Ruthyn)
L Lancaster
M Montagu (Neville)
N Norfolk
n Neville (Westmorland)
O Ogle
P Suffolk (de la Pole)
Q Queen's dower
R Crown estates
S Stafford of Southwyck
St Stanley
T Talbot/Lisle
V Vere (Oxford)
W Warwick (Neville)
Y York (duchy)

© Hugh Bicheno

the day-to-day running of his kingdom Edward needed dependable local lieutenants. It was easier to deal with the blank slates of
authority created by death, forfeiture and attainder in the North,
Wales and the West Country than in the rest of the country, where
Edward needed to fill the random gaps created across the patchwork quilt. Local Yorkists filled many posts, but his pressing need
was to unite under one authority the scattered, nationwide distribution of the remainder. The sum of the parts was adequate to endow
dukedoms, and the only candidates were his young brothers.

After his coronation Edward revived the duchy of Clarence for
12-year-old George. The first duke had been Lionel of Antwerp,
Edward III's second son, descent from whom in the matrilineal
line was the basis of the Yorkist claim to priority over the House
of Lancaster, which descended from John of Gaunt, the third
son. A few months later Clarence was the first candidate inducted
by Edward to the Order of the Garter. There were a number of
vacant stalls thanks to attrition in the battles of 1459–61, but even
Hastings, Herbert, Tiptoft (Worcester) and John Neville (Montagu)
were not inducted until the following year.

Edward also made Clarence Steward of England and Lieutenant
of Ireland, and endowed him with a larger estate than any previous king had given a brother. As he was too young to exercise the
offices or receive the income directly, all were handled by officials
appointed by Edward. But for outward show, Clarence was provided magnificently. One could hardly design a programme more
likely to bring out the worst in any teenager.

It proves nothing about how he felt towards her that Clarence
played a leading role in the ceremonies of Elizabeth's introduction
to the nobles assembled at Reading and at her coronation. He was
still a ward of the king, and when not performing ceremonial duties
lived with his brother Richard and sister Margaret at Elizabeth's
palace at Greenwich. The test came after his minority was terminated early in July 1466, when he was still only 16, because Edward
needed him to balance Warwick in the Midlands.

Not for one moment after that date did Clarence show any indication of gratitude. He appears to have believed that everything he had was his by right, and by right he should have much more without doing anything to earn it. This element of unbounded entitlement so completely defined his life that it is fair to conclude he believed he was the legitimate king – and the only reason he can have been so fatally convinced of this is if his mother had told him so.

The most lucrative of the manors and boroughs assigned to Clarence were concentrated around Tutbury Castle in south Staffordshire, which was deeply associated with the House of Lancaster. The compact estate had previously been one of the jewels in the crown of Queen Marguerite's dower and produced about 30 per cent of the income from Clarence's own endowment. He moved there as soon as he was declared of age, a long way from his brother in London – but very close to Warwick's Midlands estates.

Clarence chose to regard Tutbury as an appanage, a form of tenure originating in France, where it was customary to assign a fief to the younger sons of a monarch. The system did not have a good record of discouraging rebellion and was the principal reason why so many French dukedoms became virtually autonomous. In England the results were no less inauspicious – suffice it to say that Edward III gave his sons Edmund of Langley and John of Gaunt the duchies of York and Lancaster as appanages.

There were several problems inherent in Clarence's belief, the first being that no part of his endowment was specifically given as an appanage. By regarding it as such, Clarence made apparent his belief that it came to him by right of his father, not his brother the king. Related to this, while Tutbury and the rest of the lands awarded to Clarence were an unprecedentedly generous endowment for a royal brother, they were inadequate if perceived as an appanage for the heir to the throne.

On 30 August 1464 Edward appeared to accept the logic of the last argument when he announced that he would grant Clarence the palatinate of Chester, traditionally part of the patrimony of the

Prince of Wales. This was no casual gift: a county palatine was an hereditary principality enjoying judicial autonomy from the rest of a kingdom. In England, apart from the duchies of Lancaster and Cornwall, only the bishoprics of Durham and the Isle of Ely and the abbacy of Hexham enjoyed similar status. Pembroke was the only formal palatinate in Wales, but the Marcher lordships were in most respects indistinguishable.

The timing of the grant also gives food for thought, coming as it did after Edward had married Elizabeth but before he made this public. When he did, the grant was left without effect and the Chester palatinate reverted to the endowment properly reserved for the future heir apparent. Perhaps there was an early pregnancy that did not prosper, another possible explanation for the timing of an announcement that marked a watershed in Edward's reign.

Less speculative is that the marriage deprived Clarence of the appanage he came to think he deserved, more than sufficient reason for him to resent Elizabeth. If Duchess Cecily, in her fury at losing her precedence at court to a woman she could not dominate, did indeed tell him at this time that Edward was the product of her adultery, it would explain a great deal of what ensued. It certainly explains the following:

> In 1468 he [Clarence] approved an ordinance that would have made his household the largest and most expensive known for any medieval nobleman. There were to be 399 staff, 188 in the riding household, and the annual cost was £4500 [£2.86 million]. This was considerably grander even than Edward IV's lavish endowment... The 1467 Act of Resumption reserved for Clarence a further 5500 marks [£1.16 million] a year and 1000 marks in reversions, three times the minimum qualification for a duke, but clearly insufficient to support Clarence's plans which, if implemented, must have left him short of money.*

*Extract from Michael Hicks, 'George, duke of Clarence (1449–1478)', *Oxford Dictionary of National Biography*, Oxford University Press, 2004.

• ☙ •

Clarence may have seen parallels between his own situation and that of Charles, Duke of Berry, who was 18 years old in 1465 when he did his best to depose and replace his twenty-three-year older brother Louis XI. When we left Louis he was contemplating the ruins of his diplomacy following Edward's marriage. Despite his own teenage rebellion against his father in the 1440, he did not anticipate that his brother and heir presumptive, notwithstanding his whining about Berry being an inadequate appanage, would reprise his disloyalty.

Most of Louis's domestic enemies were nobles he had offended, such as Duke Jean of Bourbon, Lord Charles of Albret, Count Antoine of Dammartin and Count Jean of Dunois, who were simply demanding respect. Incestuous Count Jean of Armagnac was eventually condemned and crushed by the Church. Finally Duke Jacques of Nemours and Jacquetta's brother Louis, Count of Saint-Pol, two relentless schemers, were long overdue an appointment with the headsman by the time Louis finally sent them to the block.

Louis did not think any of them posed a serious threat, but his greater error was to have believed that his deterrent, the *ordonnances*, were king's men, when their loyalty lay with the commanders who had led them to victory against the English. As he did with others who had served his father well, Louis dismissed the old commanders and they were understandably bitter. Fortunately for him Pierre de Brézé, one of the greatest of them and a man he had demoted as seneschal of Normandy and briefly imprisoned on coming to power, overcame his personal dislike of Louis and remained loyal to the crown.

To round things off, he was at daggers drawn with his bishops, outraged by their loss of patronage and revenues following his unilateral suspension of the Pragmatic Sanction. He cannot have underestimated how widespread resistance to his style of government had become, but he did not believe his opponents were capable of coordinated action, and expected to disarm or defeat them in detail. The most likely explanation for how he came to such a nearly fatal miscalculation of the danger he faced is that his enemies either 'turned' his informants or systematically fed them misleading information.

Even then, had he not simultaneously made it apparent to the Dukes of Burgundy and Brittany that he intended to assert his feudal rights over them, it was a storm he could probably have weathered without resort to arms. Working for him, in contrast to Edward IV, was that nobody doubted the sacred right of the senior branch of the House of Valois to occupy the throne – but that was precisely why the complicity of Louis's heir presumptive was vital to the rebel plan. Young Charles gave them a king they could control if Louis were taken off the board, and the only honourable way for him to be killed was by the judgement of God in battle.

Although Louis had won the fervent support of the new urban elites they were not militarily significant and the rebellion was as much directed at them as against the king. Indeed, the League of the Public Weal was socially reactionary – it was an attempt by the land-based aristocracy to assert their traditional political dominance over mere wealth creators. Nor was this conservatism limited to the socio-political sphere. The one major battle of the rebellion at Montlhéry, 17 miles south-south-west of Paris, was an affair of massed mounted charges, with archers and footsoldiers ridden down by heavily armoured lancers as though Crécy, Poitiers and Agincourt had never taken place.

What reasons did Berry have to lend himself to a rebellion that would ideally end with the death of his brother? Leaving aside the almost genetic predisposition to unrestrained sibling rivalry among the Valois, the most obvious explanation is the simplest. Between 1456 and the death of the father who had named him after himself, he was in effect Charles VII's only son, and grew up hearing the king vituperate against the defiantly absent Louis. Plus his doting mother, who died in 1463, was René d'Anjou's sister (thus Queen

Marguerite's aunt), and the Angevin interest was strong at court. When he became king, Louis dismissed anyone even suspected of loyalty to the House of Anjou.

René was one of the conspirators in 1465, but Louis was on his doorstep when the rebellion began and, as he thought, neutralized him by making René's brother Charles, Count of Maine, his deputy in the west. Maine was given command of the local *ordonnances* and assigned the task of containing Duke Frañsez of Brittany while Louis himself rode east to deal with the greater threat from his cousins of Burgundy and Bourbon/Auvergne. Instead Maine simply fell back in the face of Frañsez's slow advance, and deserted Louis at Montlhéry.

The signal for the rebellion to begin came when Berry slipped away from his royal minders to join Frañsez at Nantes. Simultaneously Louis learned that Count Jean of Dunois had shipped his valuables to Nantes and joined the Bretons. This was particularly bad news, as Jean was the renowned 'Bastard of Orléans' who had ridden with Jeanne d'Arc and played a key role in the expulsion of the English. Not even Brézé matched his stature among French fighting men, but fortunately for Louis he was crippled by gout and unable to fulfil the strategic objective of trapping Louis between the Breton and Burgundian armies.

Aided by Jean, Count of Nevers, who had deserted the Burgundian camp when his stepbrother Charolais became ascendant, and by his fanatically loyal followers from the Dauphiné, Louis forced Bourbon, Nemours and Armagnac to negotiate – but then had to make them generous concessions to free himself to march north to relieve Paris, besieged by Charolais. Thanks to Maine's treachery, the resulting battle of Montlhéry was a draw. What might otherwise have been the decisive stroke was delivered by Brézé, who was killed, against Saint-Pol's massed cavalry on the Burgundian right wing.

It was Charolais's first battle and he led a locally successful charge of his own against the right wing of Louis's army. In fact he was very nearly cut off and killed, suffering a wound in the throat, but thought he had won a great victory. Philippe de Commynes, who was in the thick of things with him, later commented:

> All this day my lord of Charolais remained very joyfully on the field, thinking the glory his. This has since cost him dearly because never afterwards did he heed the counsel of anyone except himself. Up to that time he had little use for war and liked nothing to do with it, but subsequently his attitude changed because he continued fighting until his death. By it his life was ended and his house destroyed.

The rebellion came to an end when Louis bought off Charolais with the return of the Somme towns. Berry was granted the duchy of Normandy as an appanage and Frañsez was given a formal undertaking to respect Breton autonomy. Bourbon was made governor of eastern France, other lords were granted pensions, and men Louis had dismissed were brought back into his service at the expense of those who had remained loyal. Thus Saint-Pol was made Constable of France, expensively married to Louis's sister-in-law, and granted the county of Eu, which Louis's ally Jean of Nevers had inherited from his mother.

It was a brutal check to Louis's ambition, but a Pyrrhic victory for the rebels. If they had killed him and put his brother on the throne they might have been able to turn back the clock. As it was, they left the Universal Spider free to devote his considerable *furbizia* to recovering lost ground. The first to fold was Berry, always the weakest link, who was overwhelmed by his new responsibilities and all but invited his brother to take Normandy back in early 1466.

To follow this thread further would diverge too far from our story. Where it impinges is that Louis was nearly fatally weakened in 1465–6 and knew his fate would have been sealed had the English come in on his brother's side. Accordingly, he persisted in his policy of preventing an effective Anglo–Burgundian alliance at all costs, while by insidious diplomacy he created alternative red rags for the Charolais bull to charge.

EDWARD

A T THE HEART OF THE 'EVIL WOODVILLES' MYTH LIES the same historical misogyny that has demonized energetic Marguerite d'Anjou, one of the greatest heroines of English history. The implicit innuendo underlying the myth is that Elizabeth was a succubus who could get Edward to do whatever she wanted, which is ridiculous. Until she bore him a male heir she could not even obtain an independently administered endowment half as great as that granted, on her marriage day, to Marguerite – who, like Elizabeth, brought no dowry with her.

Unlike previous kings and their favourites, Edward did not grant the Woodvilles lands that elevated them far above their 'station'. But had he done so, in what way would it have distinguished them from the origins of any other noble house? The oh-so-grand Neville family fortunes were built on royal favour, and Warwick himself owed his eminence to a ruthlessly opportunistic exploitation of his wife's fortuitously grand inheritance.

Scrape away the mould of snobbery, and what remains are the practical ways in which the Woodvilles served Edward's dynastic, diplomatic and political purposes. It was he, not they, who arranged their marriages, and he who used Jacquetta's family connections to pursue an alliance with Burgundy against France. With one exception the Woodvilles played no part in the king's policy of building up other lords to contain Warwick's power and frustrate his unconcealed desire to be the power behind the throne.

That exception was Anthony Woodville, Lord Scales, whom the king helped to exchange some of his estates in Essex for the lordship of the Isle of Wight and constableship of Carisbrooke Castle in November 1466, and Porchester Castle a year later.* Commanding as they did the approaches to Southampton and Portsmouth, and Portsmouth harbour itself, the castles were an indication that Edward intended Scales to command the main squadron of the royal fleet.

In terms of royal offices the only notable beneficiary was Earl Rivers, the Lord Treasurer. In August 1467 Edward purchased the life term of Constable of England from Tiptoft and awarded it to Rivers, with reversion to Scales. Rivers's income from all offices was in the region of £1,330 [£846,000], which, added to the rents from Jacquetta's dower as Duchess of Bedford, was sufficient to sustain the dignity of his earldom. However and by contrast, William Herbert's income from lands alone was about £3,300 [£2.1 million].

Scales's younger brothers Edward and Richard did not receive any offices, and Lionel's career in the priesthood was not unduly accelerated until the last years of Edward's reign. Thomas Grey, the elder of Elizabeth's sons from her first marriage, was married to Anne Holland, previously betrothed to Warwick's nephew, who was the only child of Edward's sister the Duchess of Exeter. Richard, the younger royal stepson, received nothing.

Although the marriages affected Warwick by denying him the opportunity to marry his daughters to the heirs in question, the Woodvilles were not otherwise rewarded to the point of challenging the local dominance of any other lord. Whence, then, the oft-quoted words of Dominic Mancini (writing in 1483) that they were 'certainly detested by the nobles, because they, who were ignoble and newly made men, were advanced beyond those who far exceeded them in breeding and wisdom'?

*The Isle of Wight and Carisbrooke had been previously awarded to Geoffrey Gates, Warwick's marshal at Calais. Gates was to cause a great deal of grief for Edward in 1469–71.

Mancini was simply repeating, almost word for word, Warwick's manifesto of 1469; but that, in turn, also echoed Yorkist propaganda of ten years earlier. On both occasions the real target was the monarch. The Woodvilles were attacked as proxies for Edward himself, and the particular venom with which their alleged lack of breeding was denounced in 1469 owed more to Clarence and Duchess Cecily than it did to Warwick.

It should never be forgotten that Cecily was a Neville and a descendant of John of Gaunt through her Beaufort mother, and that even as a child she was known as 'proud Cis'. The few documented facts argue that she was implacably hostile to the Woodvilles. One is her boycott of Elizabeth's coronation, another her complicity in Clarence's rebellion. A third was her boycott of the reburial of her husband in 1476 because Elizabeth would be present, a less than subtle assertion of her belief that she was 'queen by right' and Elizabeth a usurper.

From her evidently malevolent behaviour towards Edward it is not much of a stretch to conclude that Cecily probably resented him from birth as the undeniable evidence of a far from 'classy' indiscretion that permanently diminished her in the esteem of her august husband. We tend to judge political figures by the success or failure of their policies, but like everybody else their principal lifelong endeavour is to come to terms with the legacy of their parentage and upbringing.

From that perspective, Edward's lifelong philandering may be seen as an obsessive fixation on an unattainable partner by someone emotionally crippled from childhood. Pursuing the thread, another manifestation of the same psychological deprivation would have been a subconscious attempt to build himself an alternative family – which incurred the potentially murderous hostility of his biological mother and half-brothers.

Another under-commented aspect of Edward's character was the romanticism displayed in his attempt to revive the Arthurian ethos of the Order of the Garter. Chivalry developed from the Church's effort to temper the brutality of societies defined by military might. The essential virtues were faith, hope and charity, from which came the cardinal virtues of justice, prudence, temperance and fortitude. Ironically, the English monarch who came closest to living according to these ideals was the hapless Henry VI.

Henry's usurper had every reason to tip the balance back towards the martial virtues. During the first half of Edward's reign membership of the Order of the Garter was preferentially a reward for courage and skill at arms. After Clarence, the next man inducted was the obscure William Chamberlaine, in his time a famous jouster, belatedly honoured in the last year of his life. John Astley, inducted the following year, had been the English champion at a tournament in Paris in 1438 and another at Smithfield in 1442.

Notable warriors such as the exiled Gaillard, lord of Duras in the Narbonnais, John, Lord Scrope of Bolton – to whom Edward gave Richard of York's garter – Robert Harcourt and James, the last of the fabled Scots Black Douglases. followed in 1463. They were joined by men who had achieved eminence by force of arms, including the great *condottiere* Francesco Sforza, Duke of Milan, and the Aragonese King Ferrante of Naples. By the time Anthony Woodville was inducted in 1466 he too had become the tourney champion of England.

Thanks to Sir Thomas Malory, whose *Le Morte d'Arthur* gave the myth its modern form in 1469–70, King Arthur and the Knights of the Round Table will forever inhabit the late medieval era. The myth of course was much older: 150 years before Malory, in *L'Inferno* V, Dante linked the doomed thirteenth-century passion of lovers Francesca da Polenta and her brother-in-law Paolo Malatesta to their reading about Lancelot and Guinevere.

Dare one suggest that Arthur's conception by trickery was particularly appealing to Edward, the cuckoo in the Yorkist nest? Tending to support the hypothesis, in 1474 he made Federico da Montefeltro, Duke of Urbino, a Garter knight. Federico was not only a usurper but also a cuckoo in the Montefeltro nest, and modelled his court on the Arthurian legend – to the point that his daughter-in-law Elisabetta Gonzaga was a leading figure of the Renaissance Camelot in Baldassare Castiglione's highly influential 1528 treatise *Il Cortegiano*.

The ladies of Edward's court entered fully into the Arthurian fantasy. The famously handsome Scales features in an anecdote that grants us a unique glimpse of the light-hearted atmosphere Elizabeth brought to the court. In April 1465, a month before her coronation, Scales was speaking with his sister when the ladies of the court mobbed him, tied a garter of gold and pearls with an enamelled 'flower of souvenance' around his thigh and gave him a roll of parchment tied with a thread of gold containing a task he must perform.

The required deed was revealed to be a challenge to a nobleman of 'four lineages and without reproach' for a two-day encounter, the first on horseback and the second on foot, to take place in London in October. The nobleman chosen was Anthony, known as the Grand Bastard of Burgundy, hardly an impeccable pedigree, who had already written to Scales saying he would like to break lances with him. In other words, this was a diplomatic initiative thinly disguised as a celebration of chivalry.

The challenge was sent to the Burgundian court and accepted in the presence of Duke Philippe, Count Charles and Jacquetta's brother Jacques de Luxembourg. Anthony could not meet the deadline because he had to serve in his father's war with Liège, and further delays robbed the tournament of much of its diplomatic significance. Intended to initiate the diplomatic process leading to an alliance between the two countries, when the joust at last took place in June 1468 it merely coincided with the climax of a long courtship.

Even though on several occasions Edward used taxes specifically voted for war in order to repair the royal finances, there can be no doubt that he was intent on creating and maintaining a credible threat of war with France. One motive was revenge for Louis having kept the Lancastrian resistance going for the first years of their respective reigns; but another was that no other enterprise would do more to heal the wounds of civil war and unite the English nobility and people under Edward's leadership.

Nobody could forget that Henry V's conquests would have been impossible without the Burgundian alliance, and that they were ultimately doomed after Philippe ended the alliance in 1435. Edward was also grateful for Philippe's support in 1459–61, and single-mindedly pursued a renewed alliance against France. Philippe's Valois sympathies and Charolais's infatuation with Somerset were an impediment, but the main obstacles were commercial.

• ⁊ •

Especially for a period when the political actors were so entertaining, it is easy to forget how ephemeral they were. The dynastic conflicts in England engaged a decreasing number of the barons and, apart from those directly involved, the rest of the nation just wished it would all go away. The real, deep-seated changes took place in the economic and social spheres.

The driver of economic and social change in England was the wool trade. It constituted the principal wealth of the country and created a new upper middle class of merchants and financiers. The commercial relationship between the Calais-based Company of the Staple and the great, mainly Flemish textile manufacturing cities had been the cash cow that permitted the English to sustain the Hundred Years War, and in 1436 it was the rock on which Duke Philippe's attempt to conquer Calais broke. Its historic importance was so great that to this day the Lord Chancellor sits on the Woolsack in the House of Lords.

Like all monopolists the Staplers abused their privilege, paying suppliers as little as they could get away with, while charging buyers as much as possible. Consequently a cottage textile industry grew up in England to compete for raw wool with the Staplers, while greatly undercutting imported Flemish textiles on price. The Flemings could live with losing England as an outlet for their finished products, but were adamantly opposed to permitting competition from high-quality English textile exports in the western European market.

The Staplers were the principal suppliers of raw wool to the Flemish cities and their interests were inseparable. The crown also owed them enormous sums, and by the Act of Retainer of 1466 their monopoly was extended to the collection of all customs duties on their own wool, both to repay themselves and to cover the likewise burdensome arrears and future wages of the Calais garrison. Consequently the strategically vital but declining traditional wool trade absolutely required the preservation of the status quo, but freer bilateral trade would benefit a growing new class of merchants seeking to export English manufactures.

• ∾ •

Thanks to education and facilitation by Herbert, Howard and Hastings, Edward was the first English monarch to draw significant revenues from personal participation in trade. Exactly how much is hard to establish, but it was sufficient for him to assure Parliament in June 1467 that he intended to 'live of his own'. Of course 'his own' included revenues regularly 'volunteered' by the nominally tax-exempt Church, which owned a third of the land in England; but it indicated his desire to achieve financial independence.

The conflict of interest was manifest. Edward, trading on his own account, was also solely responsible for concluding commercial agreements with the nation's trading partners. It is impossible to say to what degree his diplomacy was conditioned by considerations of personal gain, but there is no reason to suspect he had any more ethical reservations in commerce than in his pursuit of women. Despite his Arthurian pretensions he was sleazy, and this was the main reason he commanded little respect from his peers at home and abroad.

The clearest example we have of his dubious trading is that Italian merchants continued to enjoy unilateral trading privileges in England. We know Edward made extensive use of Italian ships to carry his own trade goods, mainly wool, to the hugely profitable Italian market, without demanding reciprocity from the Italians for English merchants in general. The special deal the Italian merchants offered him was, in effect, a massive bribe to act against the interests of his own subjects.

This said, no hint of rent-seeking contaminated Edward's desire for a Burgundian alliance. It was a purely strategic choice and actually cost him a great deal. The decision was also plainly his to make, and Warwick's opposition to his sovereign's clearly expressed will in this matter went well beyond merely flirting with *lèse majesté*. Before turning to his motives for doing so and the pros and cons of the alternative he proposed, it is essential to bear in mind that it was an outright challenge to the king's prerogative.

WARWICK

THE CASE FOR WARWICK'S DEFENCE IS THAT HE WAS denied the honour due to him and acted to prevent a clearly signposted attack on the sources of his power. That hypothesis can only be sustained if taken in isolation from Warwick's no less clearly signposted desire to dominate. Unarguably Edward could have taken back Warwick's offices and the lands he held by royal favour – but to assume he intended to provoke an inevitable rebellion by doing so is to brush aside the entire theory and practice of deterrence.

Edward desperately needed domestic peace, and depended on Warwick to ensure it in the most troublesome area of his kingdom. Once the North was pacified, the question was whether being the king's virtual viceroy for the region would satisfy Warwick's grandiosity. Edward's policy of containment indicates he was certain it would not. Close collaboration with Warwick had given him an unequalled opportunity to study the man, and it is most unlikely he misread him.

To unconstrained egos any limit placed on their freedom of action is intolerable, and aggressive individuals will indeed perceive deterrence as an imminent attack – because that is what they would do if the roles were reversed. Rational people are always at a disadvantage when dealing with such people, because compromise is impossible. Concessions are taken as no more than their due and as a sign of weakness, therefore requiring no quid pro quo. It is a psychopathic condition known as malignant narcissism – and the only cure for it is death.

Not coincidentally, Warwick was a pioneer of mass propaganda. The 'big lie' was first deployed against Henry VI, but that was just a rehearsal for the full force of the technique he was to unleash on Edward. One can forgive the contemporary commons for believing him because, in the words of Adolf Hitler, the master practitioner, 'it would never come into their heads to fabricate colossal untruths, and they would not believe that others could have the impudence to distort the truth so infamously'. Historians should not be so credulous.

Nobody understood better than Warwick how fragile Edward's authority was, or had more to lose if his erstwhile apprentice managed to unite the country behind him in a successful military campaign against France. Louis XI perceived this early, and shaped his diplomacy accordingly. Their common interest was cemented when Edward insultingly rejected Warwick's guidance. A less grandiose individual might have accepted it as a warning not to presume too much – but to Warwick it was an unforgivable affront.

Bitter at the loss of the titles and lands Louis had promised him for delivering a marriage alliance with France, and enraged to have lost face, Warwick immediately wrote to Louis and said he hoped soon to have news that would please him. An oral message would, as usual, have accompanied the letter, and afterwards Louis told the Milanese ambassador he believed Warwick intended to seize the throne, and that he would help him.

So yes, the marriage and the matter of the Burgundian versus the French alliance were indeed the issues that led to war between Warwick and Edward – but because they were a trial of wills. Warwick could only be the power behind a throne occupied by a weak king, and looking back at the compromise he brokered in 1459, which left captive Henry VI on the throne and denied it to Richard of York, we can see he was always guided by that calculation.

The benefits to Louis were immense. During the Public Weal revolt Warwick thwarted Edward's efforts to profit from it by secretly assuring Louis there was no danger of an English invasion of Normandy. The Universal Spider was wary at first, finding it hard to believe that Warwick and his brother the Lord Chancellor should be so naive as to leap into his web by committing treason. In the event he never had to use the leverage they gave him: he had only to encourage them to do what they were set on doing anyway.

When George was made Archbishop of York in 1465, Warwick turned the week-long celebration of his installation into a display of magnificence intended to outshine the festivities following Elizabeth's coronation four months earlier. There were over 6,000 guests, including six bishops, five abbots and their retinues. Apart from Richard, Duke of Gloucester, whom Edward had placed under Warwick's tutelage, and the king's easily influenced brother-in-law John de la Pole, Duke of Suffolk, the rest were members of the Neville affinity.

The earls were Warwick himself, his brother John of Northumberland, his future brother-in-law John Vere of Oxford and the newly restored John Talbot of Shrewsbury. Barons FitzHugh, Stanley, Lumley and Hastings – who was made comptroller of the event – were Warwick's brothers-in-law, while Scrope of Bolton, Greystoke and Ogle were retainers. Young Lovell, who was wealthier than many earls (he was also Baron Holland, Deincort, Bedal and Grey of Rotherfield), was also living at Middleham, and Willoughby was a kinsman through his wife, to whom he owed the title that remained to him after the attainder of his father, Lord Welles.

Most of them had benefitted from Warwick's good lordship. Northumberland, Lumley and Ogle owed their titles to him, and he had saved FitzHugh, Greystoke and Lovell's father from attainder after Towton. His role in the restoration of Shrewsbury to his attainted title, Oxford's immunity following his father's treason and Willoughby's later recognition as Baron Welles is less clear, as they were in keeping with Edward's policy of reconciliation. What matters is that they believed Warwick had persuaded Edward to show them grace.

Hastings's prominent presence is intriguing. Edward could not very well have forbidden him to attend the installation of his brother-in-law, but would have been displeased by his acceptance of a leading role in such a defiant celebration of Neville power. The most likely explanation is Hastings's guilty certainty that he could never be reconciled with the Woodvilles. The key to Hastings's behaviour in 1465, as it would be again in 1469 and 1483, was the conflict between his personal loyalty to Edward and his justified fear of Edward's queen.

George's elevation to the archbishopric of York was the last of the grand concessions Edward made to the Nevilles. This was partly because he had no more major offices or substantial forfeited estates to award, but also in the hope that they would be satisfied with their virtual hegemony in the North. Even so, he would have expected that his brother Clarence, whose estates included the ex-Percy lordship of Spofforth in Yorkshire and royal Richmond Castle, would act as his loyal representative. He could not have been more mistaken.

Elizabeth bore Edward three daughters, Elizabeth in February 1466, Mary in August 1467 and Cecily in March 1469, before producing Prince Edward, the required male heir, in November 1470.* Each pregnancy might have ended Clarence's status of heir presumptive, and with it his aspiration to the appanage he thought he deserved. In the absence of any prospect of further endowments from his brother, he was highly receptive to the alternative offered by Warwick, who had his sights set on Edward's brothers as husbands for his daughters Isabel and Anne.

The heir to Warwick's Salisbury patrimony in Yorkshire, the South-West and the Home Counties was his brother John, now Earl of Northumberland, who did not produce a male heir until

*Louis XI's first surviving son, the future Charles VIII, was born in June 1470.

1465. Through their mother Warwick's daughters were heirs to the rest, including the entirety of the Beauchamp/Despenser estates in the west Midlands, the Welsh Marches and Barnard Castle in County Durham. These were complementary to the lands Edward had given Clarence, and best of all would become his by right of marriage and not by royal favour.

Warwick was not a personally attractive man. He completely failed to win over Richard of Gloucester and Francis, Lord Lovell, two young men who grew up in his household at Middleham. Outside his family and the northern retainers he inherited from his father, his principal following was in Kent, which was economically symbiotic with his Calais stronghold and whose men had been well rewarded after turning out for him in 1460. In general his free-spending magnificence was much admired by the common people, but not by his peers.

His immensely high opinion of himself was not something he could conceal beyond superficial acquaintance and, in an age that believed the face was the mirror of the soul, he was strikingly ugly. The only likeness we have of him is an ill-visaged figurine on the funerary monument of Richard Beauchamp, his father-in-law. Since Warwick oversaw the construction of the tomb, presumably he thought it portrayed him to best advantage. At a purely personal level it is not surprising he believed Louis XI, almost as ugly as himself, a kindred spirit, and that he envied Edward and felt a reciprocal loathing for handsome Charles of Burgundy.

Apart from making the French king a gift of priceless intelligence, whatever else Warwick may have intended to do was put on hold while Louis was fully taken up with the Public Weal revolt and its aftermath. Louis retreated to the Loire valley for a year and put his reform programme on hold while he built up the standing army from seventeen to twenty companies of heavy cavalry and established an artillery factory and park so that he should never again be outgunned, as he had been at Montlhéry.

Louis had also been shocked by the presence of several hundred mercenary English longbowmen at Montlhéry. Although Count Charles wasted the advantage they might have given him, the prospect of a larger contingent taking part in a future war under competent leadership was something that must have given Louis sleepless nights. If he could not prevent an Anglo–Burgundian alliance, Edward must be kept distracted by other challenges, to make it impossible for him to embark on the expedition against France for which Parliament was only too willing to vote the necessary funds.

It took Edward an unconscionably long time to subtract the Nevilles from the diplomatic initiatives they invariably sabotaged. Chief among them was the opportunity that opened up when Charolais's second wife died in late September 1465. Louis promptly offered him the hand of his 4-year-old daughter Anne along with an enormous dowry, but the count did not wish to reaffirm the Valois link. Even though the exiled Lancastrians had served in his army and Somerset and Exeter were still pensioners at his court, in early 1466 Charolais put out diplomatic feelers for a marriage with Edward's sister Margaret.

The Nevilles argued that the suggestion had not been made in good faith, and Warwick got himself appointed to lead a delegation, which included Lords Hastings and Wenlock, to discuss Charolais's initiative but also to treat with Louis, supposedly to strengthen Edward's bargaining position. Warwick clashed with Charolais when they met at Boulogne on 15 April, but all was sweetness and light when he met Louis's representatives at Calais three days later.

Louis, suspicious that Warwick was playing some unfathomably deep game, took the precaution of sending a copy of his ambassadors' instructions to Charolais. His doubts were resolved when Warwick agreed a truce to last until March 1468, in which both sides undertook not to support each other's enemies, with a final peace settlement to be negotiated in October. With Warwick's complicity, and in return for merely disowning the spent Lancastrian resistance, Louis had sabotaged Edward's hopes for a Burgundian marriage.

In the light of future events it is highly significant that Hastings, supposedly Edward's eyes and ears, went along with this attempt to subvert his king's intentions. Like Warwick, he associated Edward's pro-Burgundian policy with Jacquetta, and this is merely the first clear evidence we have of what we may presume was his constant effort to diminish Woodville influence, for fear that it might grow strong enough to drive him from Edward's side.

In further discussions Warwick and Louis's ambassadors drew up a draft treaty by which Louis would pay 40,000 gold crowns [£5 million] a year during the truce and for as long as it might be extended. He also undertook to arrange a suitable husband for Margaret, to provide her dowry and to pay for a magnificent marriage ceremony. The candidates discussed included Galeazzo Maria Sforza, the new Duke of Milan, and Prince Philibert of Piedmont, heir to the duchy of Savoy and Louis's nephew by marriage.

The Nevilles were now in the awkward position of arguing that the notoriously slippery Louis was more trustworthy than Charolais. It did not help their cause that the deal Warwick brought back was transparently aimed at derailing Anglo–Burgundian understanding, and that he had plainly exceeded his instructions. Also, while he was away Edward had rebuked Chancellor George Neville for obstructing safe conducts for the Grand Bastard of Burgundy to come to England for his contest with Anthony Woodville. As it happened, the event was again postponed because the Burgundian was required to serve in the siege of Dinant.

If Count Charles had made a formal offer for Margaret's hand in 1466, the showdown between Edward and the Nevilles would have been brought forward by a year. He did not because Louis sent him a copy of the draft treaty. Having himself just spurned a far greater bribe, Charles's lip must have curled. Far from strengthening Edward's hand in his dealings with Burgundy, the Nevilles had deliberately undermined him by giving the impression he was only toying with Charles in order to increase the money he could obtain from Louis.

Edward let the Nevilles think he remained amenable to a French alliance because his own position was not strong. The reconciliation with the Lancastrians had not been popular among the Yorkist nobles, and the advancement of newly created peers, particularly the Welshman Herbert, had generated further resentment. Regional magnates such as his uncle the Earl of Essex, the Earl of Arundel and Lord Stanley did not feel they had sufficient influence.

By over-rewarding Warwick and subsequently finding himself obliged to build up his henchmen in order to contain him, Edward had dangerously narrowed the scope of his patronage. Every attainder he reversed also reduced the spoils available for distribution, and after endowing his brothers there was little left over for his other supporters. They did not become hostile, but rather were neutral between Edward and Warwick, although many would have let Warwick know they shared his disappointment with the king.

The result was that Edward had to move carefully, and while pursuing the tournament and the Burgundian marriage he did not reject the French alternative. Just prior to the long-heralded arrival of the Grand Bastard of Burgundy, he again commissioned Warwick to treat with Louis. In early June 1467 Warwick sailed up the River Seine with a 200-man retinue to meet the king himself in Rouen. Louis went to greet him at La Bouille, about 15 miles (24km) downstream from Rouen, and then let him go on by river while he followed by road. He had organized a royal reception for his guest and did not want the effect diluted by his own presence.

For eight days Warwick and his followers were showered with expensive gifts. During their daily meetings Louis suggested his guest could better control England with a Lancastrian restoration, but Warwick was adamant that he was still the power behind the throne. They drew up a draft treaty by which in return for a military alliance against Burgundy Louis would pay a yearly pension of 4,000 marks [£845,000]. The spoils of the conquered Netherlands would be shared, and Louis floated the idea that Warwick should become Prince of Holland and Zeeland. The king also repeated his offer to provide a fitting groom for Margaret entirely at his own expense, and free access to French markets for English goods.

The love fest broke up when news arrived that Duke Philippe was dying. Both judged that Warwick should hurry back to London and on 16 June he departed, accompanied by a high-level French delegation. On their way back they learned that on the 8th, the very day the Rouen conference had begun, Edward had ridden with Clarence, Herbert and other henchmen to Archbishop Neville's palace and required him to surrender the Great Seal. The following day Edward had signed a thirty-year truce with Duke Frañsez of Brittany, promising him military support if Louis attacked him.

Warwick could not have been more humiliated.

KINGSHIP

THE DEATH OF DUKE PHILIPPE BROUGHT AN ABRUPT end to the tournament designed to strengthen Anglo–Burgundian ties, as the Grand Bastard had to return for his father's funeral. Charles's accession also ushered in a new, more urgent phase of French diplomacy, as it revived the hopes of the nobles dissatisfied by the outcome of the League of the Public Weal. So keen was Louis on keeping England out of the mix that the French delegation Warwick brought back with him even offered to submit Edward's territorial claims to papal arbitration.

Birds in a bush proffered by Louis were of no interest to Edward. Whether or not he genuinely aspired to recovering Normandy and/or Guyenne, in the short term it made eminently good dynastic sense to seek an alliance with Burgundy. With the exception of Marguerite's shabby court in Bar and Jasper Tudor in Brittany, the main Lancastrian exiles were now pensioners of Duke Charles. Burgundy was also England's most important trading partner and its territories surrounded Calais.

On 14 July, after being treated as unwanted guests, the French ambassadors went home. Warwick escorted them to the coast, assuring them he would reassert control of the realm, and then rode to his estates in the North. Unfortunately, no record survives of where he went and whom he met; but it is a safe bet they included his brother John and Lord Ogle in Northumberland, Lords FitzHugh, Scrope of Bolton and Greystoke in Yorkshire and Richmondshire, and Lord Stanley in Lancashire.

Warwick did not make direct contact with teenaged John Talbot, Earl of Shrewsbury, whose father he had killed at Northampton. Shrewsbury's involvement came through Clarence, who was the same age and held adjacent lands. Clarence had been seduced by the prospect of marriage with 16-year-old Isabel, Warwick's elder daughter, some time in 1466. The mission sent that year to follow up Charles's suggestion of a marriage alliance proposed an additional match between Clarence and Charles's only child, Marie of Burgundy. It was an unrealistic proposal, its purpose to justify Edward's rejection of Clarence's betrothal to Isabel.

Edward put himself in the wrong by continuing to block it – having married an English wife it was hypocritical to oppose Clarence marrying another. Isabel was the best prospect Clarence could hope for, and sympathy for him was not limited to his mother and sister. The Bourchiers saw no harm in it, and other senior Yorkists would have agreed. When they were eventually married it was with Archbishop Bourchier's blessing and with a papal dispensation (they were second cousins) obtained by Bourchier's representative in Rome.

If we broaden our focus beyond the growing tension between Edward and Warwick, we can see that Edward had been reasonably successful in repairing his deeply fractured kingdom. Political stability seemed to have been restored, the royal finances were improving and flagrant abuses of authority by the nobility were restrained. Public order and the impartial administration of justice remained very distant ideals, but if any proof were required that he had succeeded in returning the genie of anarchy to the bottle, it came after Warwick pulled the cork.

The main source of unrest was that the economy was still in the recession that began around 1440, exacerbated by the initial contraction of the money supply and exchange rate confusion following the debasement of the coinage in September 1464. It was actually a devaluation of about 25 per cent, agreed with rare unanimity by the heavily indebted members of the Great Council. As the country's greatest debtor, Edward had the most to gain from it, and he also charged a fee for the new coinage; but it did make English exports more competitive.

The same desire to act in concert with his nobles inhibited him from a more vigorous style of kingship. He could have made royal progresses to every corner of his realm in the manner of Louis XI, but he did not. This is commonly attributed to indolence, but a less facile explanation is that he needed to avoid any perception of seeking to undermine the authority of local magnates. Given that Louis was nearly overthrown for doing so, it is hard to fault Edward's judgement.

Edward's greatest weakness as a politician was that he lacked his opponents' insatiable will to dominate. With relatively little effort he had achieved all the wine, women and song a man could wish for, his life punctuated by leisure activities and peregrinations from one palace to another, with teams of people devoted to making his existence as pleasurable as possible. He was a self-confident, spoiled child of fortune, revelled in it and had no burning desire for more.

It follows that he resented the Neville fly in his brimming pot of ointment mainly because it would not stop buzzing. He did not anticipate how far Warwick was prepared to go, and one cannot fault his reasoning. Objectively, the earl had nothing to gain commensurate with what he stood to lose. The king's legitimacy might be questionable, but without him Warwick had none at all, and the only people who wanted to depose Edward hated Warwick even more.

Clarence supplied the missing ingredient, but again it is hard to see how Edward could have anticipated this. Clarence owed everything to his brother, he had no following among the nobles and any affinity he might have developed in his scattered domains since 1466 was wafer thin. There is every reason to suspect his mother's influence was crucial – and that was Edward's blind spot.

This said, we cannot acquit him and his courtiers of a failure to focus on the essentials. They only began to pay county sheriffs for political information in 1468, and they should have maintained the commissions of array. These were summons of all men between the ages of 16 and 60 for the defence of the realm, through royal orders sent to the sheriffs through local lords. Edward's predecessors regularly summoned the levies for inspection and basic training, a useful reminder of royal authority, but he let the custom decay. Consequently the permanent militias, responsive to the will of local authorities, assumed greater military significance.

Arguably a greater failure was to regard the Church as little more than a cash cow. If properly handled it would have been an invaluable source of intelligence as well as being the most important institutional foundation of the monarchy. Two of the three most senior non-ceremonial officers of state were traditionally clerics: the Lord Chancellor, who was the senior legal officer and also the king's senior adviser in matters spiritual – hence normally the Archbishop of Canterbury; and the Lord Keeper of the Privy Seal, the king's personal signet.

Thomas Bourchier, Archbishop of Canterbury, had been Lord Chancellor during Richard of York's Protectorship in 1455–6, but Edward did not reappoint him even after he dismissed George Neville. In part this may have been because the archbishop seems to have been an indecisive individual; but mainly it was because Edward wished to be his own chancellor, to which end he appointed the yes-man Robert Stillington, Bishop of Bath and Wells. Although he did petition the pope to make Thomas a cardinal, this was because George Neville was lobbying the pope to appoint him instead. When Thomas's nomination came through in September 1467, Edward maliciously forwarded the letter to his recently sacked ex-chancellor.

The Bourchiers were of royal blood and were a pillar of the Yorkist cause, but Edward appears to have taken them for granted. Although he did arrange the marriage of Viscount Bourchier, Earl Henry's heir, to Elizabeth's sister Anne, and packed the queen's household with Bourchiers, Edward did not bring the older Bourchiers back into government when he humiliated the Nevilles. The reason is uncomplicated – he wished to be surrounded by men unlikely to volunteer unwelcome advice. Consequently he did not pay enough attention to the nuts and bolts of the scaffolding on which he stood until it collapsed under him.

Warwick had not sought royal permission to withdraw to the North and Edward overplayed his hand by peremptorily summoning him to answer an accusation of treason made by a Lancastrian courier captured by Herbert. Warwick refused, and Edward had to back down. In January 1468 Warwick rejected another summons to a Council meeting in Coventry, saying he would not come while Rivers, Scales and Herbert were at the king's side, but Archbishop Neville persuaded him to attend. He was civil to Herbert and Stafford of Southwyck, but refused to have anything to do with the Woodvilles.

Edward resorted to appeasement. After Warwick rejected the first summons, he formally confirmed the earl's wardship and marriage of wealthy Francis, Lord Lovell. After Warwick ended his sulk and attended the Council meeting, Edward appointed him Constable and Steward of the nearby duchy of Lancaster castle and honour of Kenilworth, previously the jewel of Queen Marguerite's dower. Later in the year he also granted him a share of the profits from all the royal gold, silver and lead mines north of the river Trent.

Thus the carrot: it did not work because Warwick could not be won or even mollified by an accumulation of offices, wardships and modest territorial concessions. He had no desire for a subordinate role in the administration or the other mundane occupations of indirect power. Following further defiance, Edward reverted to the stick. After Warwick opposed an expedition to help Brittany against a French invasion in July 1468, the king appointed Scales to lead it – and made him Keeper of the Seas.

The office of Keeper of the Seas had been Warwick's since the late 1450s when Marguerite, in a vain attempt to win him over, had made him lord of Calais in all but name. In the peculiar circumstances then prevailing it had given him extraordinary power.

The trade conducted through the town was the crown's principal source of bullion, and it even had its own mint. The garrison was England's only standing army and Warwick was given full charge of the fleet. Warwick once said he would give up all his lands in England if he could keep Calais, and he could not now ignore a threat to the constellation of power built around it.

Insult was added to injury. Although the expedition arrived too late to help Duke Frañsez, it turned aside to help the locals retake Jersey from the heirs of Pierre de Brézé, who had seized it in 1461. The Channel Islands formed part of Warwick's wife's Beauchamp inheritance, so it was a further slap in the face when the king resumed them and made Scales Warden of Jersey.

Nothing Edward had to offer could compensate for this thrust at the heart of Warwick's power, but the king does not appear to have understood the gravity of what he had done. As late as February 1469 he granted Warwick three more Percy manors in Cumberland and two in Warwickshire. This sent entirely the wrong signal, as Warwick rightly concluded that Edward did not intend to attack his power further. He was mistaken, however, in believing that if he could get rid of the king's inner circle he would recover his dominance over him.

Fear will do in the absence of respect, but Edward inspired neither. This was a disappointment to his subjects, who had hoped for firm leadership once woeful Henry VI was deposed. Another factor in the growing disaffection among Edward's subjects was the reappearance of a virulent new strain of the plague in 1463–5 and again in 1467, which would have been seen as an indication of divine disapproval. But thence to rebellion and a return to the anarchy of 1459–61 was a very big step indeed, one nobody except Warwick and his affinity was prepared to take. Accordingly, he had to prepare the ground, and did so in a remarkably modern manner.

Latin-based languages use the same word for 'discord' and 'tares', the Biblical term for harmful weeds that grow in wheat fields. Warwick set his agents to sowing tares in the ever fertile ground of endemic discontent – much as left-wing 'grass roots organizers' do today. Sometimes this took the form of direct action. It is not difficult to identify the hidden hand of the Nevilles in a conspiracy among the London craft guilds to maim Flemish artisans resident in Southwark, discovered in September 1467. More blatantly, one of Clarence's retainers led a mob assault on one of Earl Rivers's manors in Kent in January 1468.

Meanwhile Warwick and his brother used their now assiduous attendance at Council meetings to steer government policy in unpopular directions. The most clear-cut example came when they prevailed on Edward to levy a huge fine backed by the seizure of Hanseatic League merchants and their goods, over what was actually an unrelated matter. This led to a guerrilla war at sea with the Hansards, who commanded a considerably larger fleet.

In this, the dog that did not bark in the night was the passivity of Warwick's Sandwich-Calais squadron, previously only too willing to maraud against Hanseatic shipping. The resulting losses were extremely damaging to the London merchants, to whom Edward was heavily indebted and on whom he depended to finance temporary shortfalls in his general revenues.

That Edward ignored so many indications of their ill will bears testimony to the personal plausibility of the Nevilles. He should have noticed that the 'great riots and oppressions done to our subjects' were increasing in counties where Warwick and Clarence were supposed to keep the peace. He did not join the dots even after he judged it necessary to travel with a large bodyguard to Coventry at the end of 1467. Again, he should have dealt with the situation in person; instead – and in keeping with his governing philosophy – he commissioned Warwick and Clarence to conduct assizes to deal with unrest in six Midlands counties.

To continue listing examples would merely labour the point that Edward sleepwalked into a world of trouble. Not all or even most of the ignored warning signals were engineered by the Nevilles. It was sufficient for them to sow their tares and let nature take its course, never openly espousing treason, such that their troublemaking blended into the normal background noise of grumbling dissatisfaction. Edward was also distracted by a revival of Lancastrian subversion, which could not have served Warwick's purpose better had he devised it himself.

In May 1468, two months before Margaret of York's long-delayed marriage to Charles, Chancellor Stillington informed Parliament that the king had concluded encircling alliances with Burgundy, Brittany, Castille and Aragon, and was now ready to lead an invasion of France. Despite previous disappointments, Parliament once again granted him an exceptional tax of three-sixteenths and tenths for the purpose. As before, there is no indication that Edward seriously contemplated jumping into the financial bottomless pit of a continental war.

Taxes voted by the Commons between 1461 and 1470 averaged about £10,000 [£6.36 million] per annum, with a further £7,000 per annum from the Church. Against this, regular annual charges against the royal purse – in peacetime – totalled about £50,000. To put this into perspective, the down payment on Margaret's dowry and the cost of her trousseau and related expenses was about £15,000. The peacetime military establishment demanded about the same amount annually until the Staplers assumed responsibility for the Calais garrison in 1466.

Edward was also still struggling to pay off the massive overhang of debts run up by Henry VI, and those incurred to overthrow him. Even quite modest military campaigns added significantly to the burden – in 1468 the relatively small expedition to Brittany under Scales cost about £18,000. Before condemning Edward's apparent embezzlement of funds voted for war, we should perhaps consider that the gulf between what people demand of their government and what they are prepared to pay was at least as great in the fifteenth century as it is today.

We have noted his neglect of the commissions of array, but one of the reasons for it highlights a military constraint on Edward's freedom of action. Service abroad had always been through paid indenture, and without the prospect of earning good money there was little incentive to put in the years of practice necessary to become a skilled longbowman. Many of those who did became mercenaries – Charles of Burgundy was a major employer – and as a result the military value of the unpaid levies declined. Even if it were possible to survey every subsequent battlefield of the Wars of the Roses as thoroughly and fruitfully as Towton has been, the number and concentration of arrowheads would be decreasingly informative.*

Although the levies still provided the billmen who made up the bulk of the armies, and the longbow still deterred mounted charges, the bow's slow eclipse increased the relative importance of the more expensive, fully harnessed (armoured) and more independent men-at-arms. In terms of the internal balance of military power, the dying out of the generation of southerners with experience of war in France shifted the preponderance of combat-tested men-at-arms to the North, where the years of war against the Scots and the Lancastrian die-hards had provided the Neville affinity with continuing on-the-job training.

Edward's promotion of Herbert to become the dominant lord of the Welsh Marches, the other area with a strong martial tradition, argues he was alert to the danger this posed. He could not himself maintain his father's affinity once the crown subsumed the duchy of York, and delegating to Herbert, Stafford of Southwyck and Hastings was his best option. The insuperable problem was that being a step removed from affinity maintenance meant he could no longer summon a large body of men-at-arms personally loyal to himself. This was to prove the decisive factor in the early stages of the storm that nearly washed away the Yorkist regime.

---

*Before investing in a metal detector, consider that differences in land use and soil chemistry make some sites considerably less promising than others. In many places the survival of battle artefacts would be miraculous.

TREASON

EDWARD BEGAN TO SUPPLY FUNDS TO THE COUNTY sheriffs to pay informers because there was no doubt that Louis would retaliate for the Anglo–Burgundian alliance. The harvest was not long in coming, contaminated by confirmation bias, a problem no intelligence service has ever resolved. If you demand details of a specific threat you will get it; and the more insistent you are, the more your informers will tailor their reporting to your demand. Also, by narrowing the focus of inquiry you shut out intelligence that might have led you to ask better questions.

To employ a phrase coined in a later age, Renaissance princes surrounded their intentions with a bodyguard of lies. The Universal Spider was a master of the craft, and his preferred outlet for disinformation appears to have been the Milanese ambassador. While dealing with more urgent threats nearer home, Louis confided in him that he was equipping Marguerite and the exiled Lancastrians with money, ships and troops. This was false, but after it leaked back to England it served the dual purpose of alarming Edward and encouraging unreconciled Lancastrians to give him something to be alarmed about.

The only hostile action that can be unequivocally attributed to Louis is the help he gave Jasper Tudor after he was compelled to leave Brittany following the Anglo–Breton treaty. The loss of support from Frañsez doomed Harlech Castle, the last Lancastrian toe-hold, and when Jasper sought alternative patronage from France, Louis made another of his small investments in the hope of creating disproportionate trouble for his enemies. In June–July 1468 Jasper sailed with fifty men in three small ships to the relief of Harlech, but finding it too closely invested he landed at Barmouth instead (Map 8).

The Principality was still so strongly Lancastrian and lawless that no rents had been paid to the monarchy since 1461, and with the peasantry flocking to his banner Jasper marched inland to strike at the Yorkist borough of Denbigh, which he sacked and burned. He retreated along the coast when a royal army under Lord Herbert's brother Richard approached, but was caught and crushed near Conway. Jasper escaped into Snowdonia, and thence back to France, but the royal army, 'pursued its course up the Conway valley, ravaging it with fire and sword. The entire Snowdon district experienced such unparalleled desolation that it had barely recovered more than a century later. Echoes of the slaughter survive in song and story'.*

The commissions of array for the Marches issued by Edward to the Herbert brothers in early July marked the abandonment of his hope that Lancastrian resistance in Wales would wither on the vine. While one would hesitate to attribute humanitarian concerns to any monarch of the period, Edward's patience with the unreconciled Welsh appears to have been based on an intelligent appreciation that, as several of his predecessors had discovered, scorched earth simply provided more fertile ground for future rebellions.

The Herberts' view was that the scorching had not been done thoroughly enough. Lord Herbert gathered an army in Pembroke and marched north through Cardigan, the passage of a large army alone sufficiently punitive for such a poor county. When he reached Harlech the defenders repulsed a first assault, but with no prospect of relief following Jasper's defeat they surrendered on 14 August.

---

*From Howell Evans's indispensable online *Wales and the Wars of the Roses*.

The garrison of about fifty men was sent to London to await the king's judgement. Only two, presumably turncoats, were executed.

Edward not only spared but also honoured David ap Eynon, the Captain of Harlech, and showed similar grace to Richard Tunstall and Henry Bellingham, who had fought against him in all the Northumbrian sieges and battles, and had also escorted Henry VI during part of his peregrinations. A general pardon followed on 1 December. Although Tunstall and Bellingham declared for Lancaster in 1470 and were subsequently attainted, they were pardoned again and Tunstall served Edward faithfully for the rest of his reign.

William Herbert was rewarded with the earldom of Pembroke and Edward confirmed his wardship and marriage of 11-year-old Henry Tudor, Earl of Richmond and Jasper's nephew. Herbert had married his namesake son to the queen's sister Mary, and also had the wardship and marriage of 19-year-old Henry Percy, heir to the attainted earldom of Northumberland, currently held by John Neville. It was clearly his intention to marry Percy and Tudor to his daughters, hoping thereby to supplant Neville supremacy in the North.

Louis must have been delighted with the return on his miniscule investment, but it is not possible to detect his or Warwick's hand in the other domestic troubles that distracted Edward. The first pebble of the landslide was the arrest of a Lancastrian courier named Cornelius, who was captured with incriminating documents. Handed over to the tender mercies of Tiptoft, under torture Cornelius implicated Thomas Malory, a number of prominent Londoners and John Hawkins, who in turn implicated London Alderman Thomas Cooke.

For Edward the timing could not have been worse. Hawkins was a servant of Lord Wenlock and claimed to have been acting with his approval. Wenlock was about to accompany Margaret on her journey to marry Duke Charles, and Cooke was one of the merchants who had stood surety for the payment of her dowry. After bidding farewell to Margaret, Edward returned to London for the trial of some of those accused by Cornelius and Hawkins. Clarence, Warwick, Northumberland and Rivers headed the commission, but the man really in charge was Chief Justice John Markham, renowned for his integrity.

Possibly convinced of Cooke's guilt but certainly anxious to lay hands on his wealth, Edward sent Lord Treasurer Rivers and house-hold treasurer John Fogge to loot Cooke's London and country homes. After the jury acquitted all the prominent Londoners Edward was particularly incensed by the verdict in the case of Cooke, who at the direction of Markham and despite royal pres-sure was acquitted of treason but found guilty of 'misprision' – a failure to report treason to the authorities. The king subsequently fined him £8,000 [£5 million] and Elizabeth added a demand for 800 marks under the ancient right of 'Queen's Gold'.

Before his execution Hawkins confessed he had defamed Cooke, but by then Edward was in too deep. Despite the fact that the goods taken and money extorted from Cooke were promptly paid to one of Edward's creditors, and that he dismissed Markham a few months later, this sordid tale has been spun as the work of the evil Woodvilles. One can understand why contemporaries would be extremely careful to avoid pointing the finger directly at the king; but not historians for seizing on it as, in fact, the sole example any of them has been able to produce to prove what nasty, grasping par-venus the Woodvilles were.

As though unhinged by the flagrant injustice he had committed against Cooke, Edward embarked on a witch-hunt based on hearsay evidence from paid informers. The victims were Henry Courtenay and Thomas Hungerford, heirs respectively to the attainted earldom of Devon and the barony of Hungerford, both arrested in late September and imprisoned at Salisbury to await trial. In January 1469 a special commission consisting of the king's brother Richard of Gloucester, the Earl of Arundel and Lords Audley, Scales, Stafford of Southwyck and Stourton presided over a trial in which the accused in desperation opted for a verdict by a local jury.

With no one to play the role of Markham and in the presence of the king, the provincial jurors found the two men guilty of plotting the king's overthrow and murder. Although Courtenay had availed himself of a general pardon dated subsequent to his alleged offence, they were hanged, drawn and quartered. It is hard to escape the conclusion that they had the misfortune to be brought to trial when Edward, frustrated in London, wanted to make an example of someone, and did not much care who it was.

The effect was wholly negative. The scholarly John Warkworth, whose *Chronicle* is generally unbiased and can be taken as a record of what well-informed Englishmen then believed, wrote that the two men were the victims of the malice of Stafford of Southwyck, who had been made Earl of Devon in May. Perhaps so, but the award of their lands fits the pattern of Edward's attempt to build up Stafford as his regime lock on the West Country. The blame and dishonour for an outrageous perversion of justice lay entirely with the king.

John Vere, Earl of Oxford, was detained and consigned to the Tower shortly after the arrest of Courtenay and Hungerford. There was no doubt of his guilt, as he promptly turned king's evidence and betrayed Thomas Tresham, a former speaker of the Commons. Oxford also identified three other men as Lancastrian couriers, one a servant of the exiled Duke of Exeter and the other two servants of the Duke of Norfolk. The three were convicted and executed in haste, but Oxford was Warwick's brother-in-law and so was released in January 1469. In April Edward pardoned him but kept Tresham in prison.*

After a regime falls it is tempting to explain the event by reference to a catalogue of grievances. Unfortunately reason plays a limited role in politics; what matters is the spirit of the moment, which is elusive. Having lived through such a moment a couple of times, I

---

*Also Thomas Malory, who wrote *Le Morte d'Arthur* during his two-year imprisonment in the Tower.

can only describe it as a form of psychic electricity that galvanizes and disorders each component part of a society in its own way, such that people think and act in a manner they later have difficulty reconciling with their self-image as rational beings.

To pursue the analogy, there was undoubtedly an ominous build-up of electricity in 1468–9, and Edward's behaviour may have been as much a symptom as a cause. As king he could do no wrong, and the contradiction that arose when he committed a flagrant injustice could only be resolved if he were not in fact, the legitimate king; which, if believed, explained everything. The deadliest of the tares sowed by Warwick's agents was that Edward was not Richard of York's son, which had the great advantage of being highly believable.

None of this was regime-threatening so long as the regional magnates were on board, but by 1469 Edward's support among them was fragile. Of the dukes, Norfolk was ineffectual and also offended by the execution of his servants. Suffolk, even though Edward had recreated the earldom of Lincoln for his 5-year-old son in 1467, continued to avoid becoming closely identified with the regime. The king had neglected to cultivate the extensive affinity of his ward Buckingham, and only in 1470 – far too late – sought to revive it by recreating the earldom of Wiltshire for John Stafford, the youngest son of the duke killed at Northampton.

The senior Yorkist earls felt excluded and Arundel, who was Warwick's brother-in-law, may have been disgusted by his enforced participation in the judicial murder of Courtenay and Hungerford. The rest, apart from Tiptoft, Rivers and Edward's recently promoted henchmen Pembroke and Devon, were at best neutral, while Oxford and Shrewsbury had family wrongs to right. Most of the barons kept their heads down while those who owed their titles to Edward and Warwick lined up behind their patrons in roughly equal numbers.

The key figure in the equation was John Neville, Earl of Northumberland, with whom Edward believed he had a special understanding. Why this should have been the case cannot be established with certainty, but John probably distanced himself from his ambitious brothers in private conversation with the king. This was eminently believable because, sitting atop the unreconciled Percy affinity, a long way from London and next to Scotland, he stood to lose everything if there were a breakdown of the Yorkist order. Edward had also made him a Garter knight, and perhaps put too much faith in the ancient tradition of blood brotherhood.

When reports filtered back to London of a rebellion in Northumberland in April–May 1469, led by a man calling himself Robin of Redesdale (notorious bandit country) or Robin Mend-All, Edward had no reason to doubt John Neville's report that it was just another minor revolt, dispersed without bloodshed. The truth of the matter is revealed in a letter to Louis XI from his chamberlain, the Scots William, Lord Monypenny, who was in England to liaise with Warwick:

> In the county of Surfiorkshire [South Yorkshire] more than three hundred archers were in arms, and had made themselves a captain named Bobin, and sent to the Earl of Warwick to know if it was time to be busy, and to say that all their neighbours were ready. But my lord answered bidding them go home for it was not yet time to be stirring.

Redesdale had been awarded to the Neville retainer Lord Ogle following the attainder of Tailboys in 1461. Thus the alias 'Robin of Redesdale' strongly suggests that the most experienced military commander in the Neville camp was primed to act on Warwick's signal, a plan put at risk by the impatience of some of those on standby to join him in Yorkshire. It is most unlikely these preparations could have been made without John Neville's complicity.

Happily for the Neville conspiracy, in late May a genuine rebellion erupted in Holderness, in the East Riding. It started as a protest against an ancient corn tax levied by the monks of St Leonard's hospital in York, supposedly for the benefit of the indigent but notoriously spent on luxuries. It grew into a revolt against the corruption that flourished in the archdiocese of York under George Neville, and thence to a demand for the reinstatement of the Percy family. The main landlord in Holderness was the Duke of Buckingham, and nearby Hull was one of the Duke of Norfolk's boroughs – but they abutted on one of the largest forfeited Percy estates around the head of lordship at Leconfield, which had been awarded to John Neville.

The leader of the revolt, who adopted the name 'Robin of Holderness', was Robert Hildyard, lord of Arnald and heir to his namesake father, lord of Winestead, which was located next to the ex-Percy manor of Partington. The Hildyards had fought for Lancaster but avoided attainder and were the largest resident landlords in the 'beak' of the East Riding. Massively joined by the Percy affinity, Robert marched through Leconfield towards York. Edward Hall's and Polydore Vergil's accounts are virtually identical:

> [Hall] When the fame of this great commotion and assembly came to the ears of the citizens of York they were first greatly astonished: but leaving fear aside they were in great doubt and

uncertain whether it were best for them to issue out of their walls and to give battle to the rebels, or to keep their city and repulse the violence of their enemy by manful defending of their walls and port [gate].

[Vergil] But [John Neville], lieutenant of that county for the king, delivered the city of that fear, who, taking a very fit way for avoiding further danger encountered with the commons as they came at the very gates of the town, where, after a long fight he took their captain Robert Hulderne and forthwith struck off his head, which when he had done he caused all his army to retire from the battle, very late in the night, and withdrew them into the town.

Robert Hildyard was still very much alive and seeking the king's pardon at York in late March 1470, so the report of his execution was Neville's attempt to put a brave face on what was, at best, a drawn battle. The truth was that he fell back into York and the rebels returned unmolested to their homes. Neville, an experienced commander at the head of family retainers, must have been deeply shocked to be fought to a standstill by men from lands that were nominally his, and this was to have repercussions two years later.

The episode – as reported to him – confirmed Edward in two related errors of appreciation. The first was that the threat to his regime in the North was simply a revival of the adamant Percy affinity, which had been the mainstay of Lancastrian resistance in 1461–4. The second was that he could depend on John Neville to suppress it.

COUP D'ÉTAT

HISTORY IS NOT A COURT OF LAW. THE BEST ONE CAN do is apply the Sherlockian dictum that when you have eliminated the impossible, whatever remains must contain the truth. Thence to proving something beyond reasonable doubt is usually beyond the historian's grasp. In the preceding chapters we have reviewed a deep background broadly agreed by historians, give or take a nuance. This one deals with the series of explosive events born of that background.

As had been the case with the Public Weal conspiracy in France, the inescapable logic of the Warwick–Clarence rebellion in mid-1469 was that Edward must die in battle. Warwick and Richard of York had failed to rule through docile and compliant Henry VI in 1460–1. Merely capturing a king as vigorous as Edward could not bring about the changes the conspirators desired, while assassinating him risked unleashing a free-for-all they were unlikely to win. Only if armed with evidence of God's judgement could they seize and retain power

While Warwick was nearly as clever as he believed himself to be, he had the psychopath's signature inability to think through the likely consequences of the crimes he planned so carefully. Removing Edward and his henchmen from the board would certainly create a void of authority, but it was a delusion to believe the Yorkist magnates would be so anxious to avoid chaos that they would tamely accept it being filled by Warwick's puppet king. It was also a certainty the unreconciled Lancastrians would seek to exploit the divisions in their opponents' ranks, so the civil war Warwick needed to avoid at all costs would have been inevitable.

Accordingly, the story of the coup is that the best laid plans of mice and men 'gang aft agley'. At the operational level it was a story of the mistaken preconceptions the two leading protagonists drew from the battles of 1461. Edward believed Warwick was a blustering coward who would not dare draw sword against him, and Warwick believed Edward was stupidly brave and would charge to destruction rather than surrender.

The precise timing of the rebellion was opportunistic. Edward was due to accompany Warwick to the blessing of his rebuilt flagship *Trinity* and to review the fleet at Sandwich, and then to visit Calais, but cancelled the expedition on learning of the Robin of Holderness rebellion. The trigger was Edward's precautionary issuance of countrywide commissions of array. Warwick took the opportunity to mobilize his followers in the North and the Midlands under royal warrant, and decided to strike before the king could gather sufficient forces of his own.

One of the unexamined factors in what followed is the generally accepted view that Edward did not know his brother intended to defy him and marry Isabel Neville – which is absurd. Given the certainty the king would learn of it from his own agents in Rome, Cardinal Bourchier could not have obtained the papal dispensation for the match – which was granted long before, on 14 March 1469 – without Edward's tacit approval. It follows that the king was also informed when Bourchier authorized Archbishop Neville to perform the marriage ceremony in Calais.

The significance of this lies in the fact that the furtive toing and froing by the conspirators before the event was probably regarded with wry amusement by Edward, who set off from Windsor on a pilgrimage to the shrines at Bury St Edmunds and Walsingham on 13 June. There is even a hint of sly humour in his choice of itinerary.

The first stop for the royal party was at Archbishop Neville's palace of More in Hertfordshire, where they had to be expensively entertained and which required the archbishop to hurry back from blessing the *Trinity*.

Edward would also have known that his mother went to Sandwich with Clarence in mid-June to give the young couple her blessing – the movements of the duchess and duke and their retinues could hardly have been kept secret. From his point of view it was an act of tolerable defiance by his own family, which spared him the necessity of officially revoking his prohibition of the wedding. His own secret marriage had, after all, set a precedent. No doubt he intended to accept the fait accompli gracefully, perhaps taking the opportunity to embrace Warwick as a brother-in-law when he received the newly-weds at court.

He clearly had no inkling that the preparations for Clarence's marriage were functioning as effective cover for the well-kept secret of the rebellion that Warwick initiated before sailing to Calais. Reports of a major northern uprising led by Robin of Redesdale reached Edward at Bury St Edmunds on 18 June, along with the disquieting news that the rebels had issued a manifesto comparing the current state of England to that prevailing under Edward II, Richard II and Henry VI when they were deposed. As usual it denounced 'evil councillors', naming the Woodvilles, the Herberts, Stafford of Southwyck and Edward's friend Lord Audley.

This was a bombshell – Edward still did not doubt John Neville's good faith, but clearly he had failed to keep the peace in the North. Working on the false assumption that the rebels had somehow slipped past Neville to march south, and that they were a spontaneous, probably Lancastrian rabble, Edward decided to deal with them from his own resources. He ordered the royal artillery to set out along the Great North Road and the royal wardrobe to send Yorkist banners and 1,000 liveries to his castle-palace of Fotheringhay in Northamptonshire, while he continued his leisurely progress through East Anglia.

Edward had very recently prevailed on his mother to exchange Fotheringhay, once the administrative centre for the duchy of York in eastern England, for the castle-palace of Berkhamsted in Hertfordshire, with nearby Kings Langley palace added to sweeten the deal. The Hertfordshire palaces had been royal residences, set in large parks and much nearer London, but Fotheringhay was particularly dear to Cecily, four of whose children had been born there and where she had spent much of the 1450s with her younger children. She would have been furious that even in this she was being supplanted, as she saw it, by Elizabeth.

The uprising was very far from being a rabble. The nucleus was made up of tough borderers led south by the highly competent Lord Ogle. They were joined by Warwick's Richmondshire and Yorkshire retainers, quietly summoned by Lord Scrope of Bolton and by John Conyers, Warwick's steward at Middleham. A proportion of the Neville affinity under John Neville, probably based at Pontefract, and in Westmorland and Cumberland under Lord FitzHugh and Richard Salkeld, Warwick's Warden of Carlisle, remained to guard against a genuine uprising by the Percy affinity. John Conyers also stayed behind for the same reason, although his brother and namesake eldest son marched with Ogle.

Despite this, starting with Warkworth, Hall and Vergil, historians have agreed Robin of Redesdale was the elder John Conyers, or failing that his brother William. Apart from the highly suggestive *nom de guerre*, the principal reason for believing he was more certainly Lord Ogle is the skill and boldness with which the campaign was conducted. Neither John nor William Conyers had experience of independent command, and the only other candidate with the necessary qualities was Scrope of Bolton, who dropped out of the conspiracy once he realized its lethal intent towards his king and Garter brother.

Warwick's initial plan was to draw Edward north so that he and Clarence should not encounter any opposition when they landed in south-eastern England and made a triumphal entrance into

London, just as he and Edward had done in 1460. If all went as anticipated he would then march up the western spur of the Great North Road (Map 4) to trap Edward between his anvil and Ogle's hammer. Meanwhile his retainers in the east Midlands would create a blocking force to prevent Edward escaping to the Yorkist heartland in the Welsh Marches.

Edward was remarkably ill-informed throughout the campaign. He had neglected to cultivate alternative eyes and ears in the North, such that Clarence's treachery meant the only news he received about events north of the Trent was what the conspirators wanted him to believe. For their purposes he needed to know about the Robin of Redesdale revolt, but not that it was sufficiently serious to warrant his prompt return to London, there to await reinforcement by the Yorkist magnates.

However, his fateful decision to deal with the rebellion from his own resources also suggests that someone close to him was giving him very bad advice indeed, and the only viable suspect is William Hastings. Not only was he Warwick's brother-in-law, he was also (since late 1468) steward for the earl's estates in Northamptonshire, Leicestershire and Rutland, where he was a major landowner in his own right.* Edward had also entrusted Hastings with stewardship of the Yorkist affinity in the east Midlands, including Stamford, Grantham and, most recently, Fotheringhay. Their peregrination had taken them through or close to Hastings's own estates in Norfolk and Lincolnshire.

Even though Edward was belatedly joined by the Dukes of Norfolk and Suffolk, they would have come only with their retinues and most of the troops who marched with him to Newark were Hastings's men. This would explain why Edward sent the Woodvilles away on 9 July, when he belatedly obtained accurate information about the size of Robin of Redesdale's army and learned that it was

*The core of his lordship were the castles at Ashby-de-la-Zouche, Bagworth and Kirby, occupying a broad band of territory running north-west from Leicester and equidistant from Nottingham and Coventry.

36. EDGCOTE CAMPAIGN 1469

Redesdale

Newcastle

Carlisle
Salkeld

Fitz-Hugh

Richmond
Scrope

Middleham
Conyers

Skipton

York
Neville

Halifax

Hull

Rotherham

Chesterfield

Lincoln

Newark

Nottingham

Grantham

Crowland

Castle Rising

Walsingham

The Wash

Bishop's
Lynn

Norwich

Caister X

Shrewsbury

Tutbury

Leicester

Stamford

Fotheringhay

Ludlow

Coventry

Warwick

Daventry **X**

Northampton

Olney

Bury St Edmunds

Hereford

Edgcote X

Banbury

Warwick

Edward

Raglan
Herbert

Gloucester

Cirencester

St Albans

Stafford

Bristol

More Palace

Barnet

Windsor

London

Canterbury

Sandwich

Bridgwater

Dover

Hythe

Warwick Clarence

Rye

Lydd

0   25   50   75
miles

© *Hugh Bicheno*

CHRONOLOGY OF THE 1469 EDGCOTE CAMPAIGN

End May	Edward learns of 'Robin of Holderness' rebellion, cancels plan to go with Warwick to Sandwich for the blessing of Warwick's rebuilt flagship *Trinity*, to review the fleet and travel to Calais.
Early June	Edward issues commissions of array to dukes, earls, barons and judges across the country.
9 June	Warwick is joined in Sandwich by Archbishop Neville.
12 June	The archbishop blesses the *Trinity*.
13 June	Edward, Gloucester, Hastings, Rivers, Scales *et al* depart Windsor on pilgrimage.
14 June	Edward visits Archbishop Neville at More Palace in Hertfordshire; Clarence at Canterbury.
15 June	Clarence and Duchess Cecily to Sandwich.
15–17 June	Edward at the shrine of St Edmund in Bury St Edmunds.
18 June	Edward first learns of Robin of Redesdale manifesto and uprising.
19 June	Edward at Norwich; Duchess Cecily to Canterbury.
20 June	Edward orders royal artillery sent from London up the Great North Road and royal wardrobe to supply 1,000 House of York liveries, banners, etc.
21 June	Edward at the shrine of Our Lady of Walsingham; Duchess Cecily in London.
22–24 June	Warwick at Canterbury, sends 'get busy' order to Yorkshire, travels to Sandwich.
24–28 June	Edward at Castle Rising, Bishop's Lynn and Crowland Abbey.
29 June	Edward at Fotheringhay, joined by Elizabeth; Warwick in London, announces he will join Edward after the forthcoming marriage of Clarence and his daughter Isabel.
1 July	Edward's party joined by Dukes of Norfolk and Suffolk.
4–6 July	Conspirators joined at Sandwich by Earl of Oxford, sail to Calais.

5–8 July	Edward marches up Great North Road through Stamford and Grantham to Newark.
9 July	Edward marches to Nottingham, sends Rivers, Scales and John Woodville away; summons Pembroke and Devon to join him in all haste, summons archers from Coventry.
11 July	Archbishop Neville marries Clarence and Isabel in Calais.
13 July	Conspirators to Sandwich, issue manifesto enlarging on Robin of Redesdale's.
16–19 July	Conspirators recruit at Canterbury.
20 July	Warwick's army enters London; Clarence and Isabel with Duchess Cecily.
26–27 July	Warwick and army march to Northampton.
26 July	BATTLE OF EDGCOTE
27 July	Warwick beheads Pembroke and brother Richard at Northampton.
28–29 July	Edward disperses his troops, departs Nottingham with Gloucester and Hastings, surrenders to Archbishop Neville at Olney.
10–12 August	Rivers and John Woodville captured near Monmouth, beheaded by Warwick at Coventry.
13 August	Thomas Herbert beheaded at Bristol.
17 August	Humphrey Stafford (the 'three-month earl') lynched in Bridgwater.

marching down the western spur of the Great North Road. Facing a far more serious challenge than he expected, the bad blood between the Woodvilles and Hastings made it impolitic to keep them by his side. No doubt Hastings also urged him to send them away, supposedly to make it easier to negotiate with the rebels.

The most likely explanation is that Hastings was privy to Warwick's plans, but only with regard to their common desire to depose the Woodvilles. Expecting the usual show of force followed by negotiation, he would have been as shocked as Edward by the size of the northern army and the purposeful speed with which it marched south. There is ample reason to suspect Hastings had crafted a situation where Edward would be powerless to protect his in-laws, but did not anticipate that the purpose of the revolt was to supplant the king as well.

Warwick must have assured Hastings that he would continue to enjoy his status at court in a Warwick-dominated administration. Now, when it became clear the threat from the North was far deadlier than he had anticipated, Hastings realized that Warwick intended the king's destruction. As he and Edward marched from Newark to Nottingham to stand across the rebel line of advance with what they now knew was an inadequate army, frantic summons were sent galloping to Herbert in south Wales and Stafford of Southwyck in the West Country.

Meanwhile the main thrust of Warwick's strategy went ahead. The first step was to cement his alliance with Clarence, who duly signed a prenuptial agreement to make Warwick his chief councillor and restore Archbishop Neville to the chancellorship when he became king. Clarence and Isabel were married on 11 July and on the 13th Warwick, Clarence and Archbishop Neville issued a manifesto echoing Robin of Redesdale's word for word, and expanding on it. Published under the seals of the two richest laymen and the richest prelate in the kingdom, the insolent audacity of the text was breathtaking:

> First, when the said Kings estranged the great lords of their blood from their private Council and not advised by them, and taking about them others not of their blood and inclining only to their counsel, rule and advice, the which persons take no consideration to the weal [welfare] of the said princes, nor to the commonweal of this land, but only to their singular lucre and enriching of themselves and their blood, as well in their great possessions as in goods; by which the said princes were so

impoverished that they had not sufficient of livelihood nor of goods, whereby they might keep and maintain their honourable estate and ordinary charges within this realm.

The proclamation went on to allege that Edward's alienation of crown lands – of which Warwick and Clarence had been major beneficiaries – had prevented him from living within his means, as he had promised, and so led to burdensome taxation, the misappropriation of money voted for war with France, and of church contributions intended for a crusade.

The 'evil councillors' were enumerated, to reassure Hastings and others that they were not threatened. They were Earl Rivers, his wife Jacquetta and their sons, the Earls of Pembroke and Devon, Lord Audley and John Fogge. Audley's inclusion probably stemmed from a desire to distribute his lands among Warwick's Midlands affinity. Fogge was Edward's household treasurer and had participated in the despoiling of Thomas Cooke, but he was also an unpopular landlord in Kent, the next stop for the conspirators.

The manifesto announced they would be at Canterbury on 16 July and summoned all 'true subjects' to be there in arms. As Warden of the Cinque Ports Warwick had prepared the ground in Lydd, Rye, Hythe and Dover, which sent contingents to meet him at Sandwich when he arrived with part of the Calais garrison on 13 July. The conspirators were already at the head of a large, well-armed force when they arrived at Canterbury, where the mayor paraded the militia to greet and join them. Their numbers swelled rapidly as the commons of Kent, led by their captains, flocked to join what promised to be a profitable party.

One of the stronger indications of Warwick's hope to kill Edward in battle is that he was careful to keep his new son-in-law uncontaminated. Clarence remained with his mother in London, and his retainers in Yorkshire did not join Ogle's army. It was still Warwick's intention to trap Edward in the Midlands, but the king's move to Nottingham and the speed with which Herbert and Stafford responded to his summons required a change of plan. Ogle left the western spur at Rotherham, marched south to Chesterfield and then rapidly across country to Coventry, bypassing Edward at Nottingham.

The next stage was crucial. When Ogle left Coventry he marched towards Northampton to rendezvous with Warwick, who was marching up the St Albans–Bedford branch of the western spur. Warwick's advance was slowed by the guns required to give battle to Edward, who was well equipped with them, so he sent his fore-riders on ahead to Northampton under Geoffrey Gates, his marshal at Calais. Among them were Thomas Parr, youngest son of William Parr, lord of Kendal in Westmorland (who was riding with Ogle), and John Clapham, one of Warwick's Midlands esquires of the body.

Ogle's march took him across the path Herbert and Stafford would have to follow if they were to join Edward at Nottingham, and their respective outriders soon came into contact. The stage was set for one of the most fiercely fought battles of the Wars of the Roses after Towton, which it uncannily resembled in terms of battlefield evolution. It may well have been even bloodier as a proportion of the men engaged, and its impact on English history may have been greater.

SHOWDOWN

N EITHER EDWARD NOR WARWICK WANTED THEIR subordinates to fight. Edward desperately needed reinforcements, and Warwick's revised plan was for a united army to stand on ground of his choosing between the king and London, forcing him to attack. The plan was the same as it had been when he was defeated at the Second Battle of St Albans in 1461 – it was typical of the man that he did not doubt its essential soundness. Instead, their subordinates sought each other out for reasons of their own – and what those reasons were defined the battle that ensued.

Ogle's decision to seek a battle was probably the result of learning Herbert and Stafford had divided their forces, with Herbert at Banbury and Stafford several miles away on the Fosse Way. This was the Roman road running from Exeter through Cirencester, where they had initially joined forces, which would take them most directly to Edward (Map 3). Ogle, immensely experienced in the fast-moving northern Marcher tradition, would have jumped at the opportunity to attack before they could join up again.

So, the key question is why the two royal contingents became separated. The generally accepted version, based on Edward Hall's account, is that Herbert and Stafford, responding to the urgent summons to join him as soon as possible by the king, inexplicably turned aside to seek battle with Ogle. They then fell out with one another when battle was imminent, allegedly over lodging at Banbury and/or a wench. As a result, Herbert fought the battle without archers, who were under Stafford's command.

To take the last point first, it is absurd to believe that Herbert, who won Mortimer's Cross for Edward with an arrow storm, would have marched without a full contingent of Welsh longbowmen, or that he might have transferred them to Stafford. It is far more likely that, surrounded by the flower of Welsh chivalry, Herbert saw it as a unique opportunity to save the regime singlehandedly and to smash the northern Neville affinity, paving the way for the restoration of Henry Percy, his ward and soon-to-be son-in-law.

Another – improbable but not inconceivable – explanation is that Stafford was a traitor, in keeping with Warwick's modus operandi of cultivating Trojan Horses within enemy ranks. This was the view of the mob in Yorkist Bridgwater that lynched Stafford when he returned there after the debacle, according to Hall on Edward's orders. The unanswerable objection to this theory is that Herbert rushed into battle knowing full well that Stafford was out of supporting range.

No – Herbert side-lined Stafford so that he should not share the glory, and both sides sought battle for the oldest of all reasons: from time to time men are overcome by an impulse to do reckless things simply because they are men. Herbert and Ogle were alpha males in their respective warrior cultures, in command of men trained for combat from childhood and accustomed to victory in battle. The intoxicating prospect of putting their skills to the test against a worthy opponent was irresistible.

The decisive pre-battle event was a major skirmish on the 24th, which came about after Herbert's fore-riders reported sighting enemy stragglers somewhere between Daventry and Northampton. He sent a large mounted force to attack them, which found that the alleged stragglers were the rearguard of a considerable army. Now aware of each other's presence, Ogle returned to Daventry and Herbert left the Fosse Way and marched towards Banbury, a distance of 12–15 miles. This is when he parted company with Stafford, after a violent disagreement over disregarding Edward's orders.

The 25th would have seen the two armies closing on each other behind screens of mounted scouts, and in one encounter Henry Neville, eldest son of demented Lord Latimer, was captured and beheaded. This announced there would be no prisoners taken in the impending battle. Ogle marched south from Daventry and diverged from the main Banbury road to camp for the night on Byfield Plain, next to a ford over the River Cherwell (today's Trafford Bridge), which at this point is only 20 feet wide and 2 feet deep.

That night Herbert rested his army at Banbury and the next morning marched through Upper Wardington to Edgcote Hill, knowing Ogle had crossed the Cherwell and formed up on a hill about a mile away between two rivulets and overlooking the plain of Danes Moor, an area of fields divided by another rivulet and belonging, according to *Hearne's Fragment*, to Richard Clarell, 'a gentleman of Edgcote', one of many villages depopulated by the Black Death.

By this time both commanders knew whom they were facing and in what strength, so if they sought battle it was because they were of roughly equal numbers – perhaps 6–7,000 each. If the planned high speed railway project (HS2) goes ahead it will create an unrepeatable occasion for archaeologists to obtain funding to excavate the Edgcote battlefield before it is destroyed. Should that come to pass we will have some definitive answers. Until then the following is an interpretation based on the terrain and the personalities involved.*

Supposedly Ogle induced Herbert to leave his strong position by harassing him with archery, to which he could not make reply because of Stafford's absence. This is a variant on Hall's account of the opening phase at Towton and is no less nonsensical. The killing range for heavy war arrows was not much greater than 50 yards, and archers did not waste their arrows in the long-range parabolic shooting beloved of film-makers. Herbert paused only long enough to dress his lines and then attacked. If anyone was short of archers it was Ogle, as the Welshmen came to hand strokes without any serious check to their momentum.

Ogle's men would have made a short charge down the hill to meet them and so, if my reconstruction is correct, the first brutal encounter would have taken place more or less exactly on the line planned for the HS2 railway. The northmen gave way and were driven back over the hill where they had first formed up, suffering terrible losses. Ogle himself was mortally wounded and with him fell the only son of Lord Greystoke and both John Conyers's namesake son and his brother William. The fall of so many senior officers was a sign their army was disintegrating, a view that supports an anecdote in Hall's account:

---

*N.B. The depth of the rectangles in this and other battle maps is dictated by labelling and bears no relation to the likely deployment, which would have been perhaps 5–6 ranks deep and far less ordered in attack.

The Earl of Pembroke behaved himself like a hardy knight and expert captain, but his brother Sir Richard Herbert so valiantly acquitted himself that with his poleaxe in hand (as his enemies did afterwards report) he was by fine force passed through the battle of his adversaries and without any mortal wound returned. If every one of his followers and companions in arms had done but half the acts which he that day by his noble prowess achieved, the Northmen had obtained neither valour nor victory.

But then it was Towton all over again – an army on the point of annihilation was saved by the last minute arrival of reinforcements who appeared to the enemy rear, and the sudden dislocation of expectations turned the exultant Welshmen into a fleeing mob:

> When the Welshmen were at the very point to have obtained the victory (the Northmen being in manner discomforted) John Clapham Esquire, servant of the Earl of Warwick, mounted up the side of the east hill accompanied only with 500 men gathered of all the rascals of the town of Northampton and other villages about, having borne before them the standard of the earl with the white bear, crying 'a Warwick, a Warwick'. The Welshmen thinking that the Earl of Warwick had come on them with all his puissance, so that as men amazed fled: the Northmen then pursued and slew without mercy for the cruelty they had shown Lord Latimer's son. So that of the Welshmen there was slain about 5,000 besides them that were fled and taken.

Some of Herbert's men crossed the Cherwell and were hunted down as they fled. The road running between Chipping Warden and Job's Hill is still known as the Welsh Road, and there are indications there may be mass graves in the nearby churchyard. Welsh sources confirm that Herbert's affinity, the cream of the south Wales aristocracy, was slaughtered, but not before doing terrible damage to the northern Neville affinity.

• ∾ •

Ironically, in defeat Herbert still achieved one of his objectives. The reduction in Neville military power permitted and to some extent demanded the restoration of Henry Percy as Earl of Northumberland, and he kept his word and did eventually marry one of Herbert's daughters. Neither William nor Richard Herbert lived to see it. The earl and his brother were captured and brought before Warwick at Northampton. Despite William's pleas that his brother be spared, both were beheaded without even the pretence of a trial.

Warwick also sent Clapham and others including Edward Grey, Queen Elizabeth's brother-in-law from her first marriage, to seize Earl Rivers at his manor of Grafton, 10 miles south of Northampton. On 12 August both he and his son John, the dowager Duchess of Norfolk's young husband, were summarily executed at Gosford Green outside Coventry. Even nobles who had resented the rise of the Herberts and the Woodvilles, and would have celebrated their fall from power, were appalled by these cold-blooded murders.

Warwick may have forced Edward to witness the death of his father-in-law, for by this time the king was his captive at Coventry. On learning of the disaster at Edgcote Edward had set off from Nottingham towards London, ordering his army to disperse. Suffolk and Norfolk returned to their counties. The king travelled only in the company of his brother Richard and Hastings, and at the village of Olney, 10 miles south-east of Northampton, he surrendered to Archbishop Neville, who arrived in full harness.

The surrender was probably negotiated by Hastings, by now horribly aware his friend might be killed should he fall into the hands of Warwick's servants. By accepting Edward's surrender George Neville became the guarantor of his life, which suggests he also feared his brother would commit the ultimate act of *lèse majesté*, which Cardinal Archbishop Bourchier would condemn in the strongest terms, and which risked turning every man's hand against them.

Sadly there is no record of what passed between Warwick and Edward at Coventry, whence the king was transferred to Warwick Castle. While there, a repellent individual called Thomas Wake, a Northampton man whose son had been killed at Edgcote and who was among those who seized Rivers, produced alleged proof that Jacquetta had employed witchcraft to bring about the marriage of her daughter and the king, and the destruction of Warwick. The 'proof' of the latter was a leaden figure like a man-at-arms, broken in the middle and wired together.

Jacquetta appealed to the mayor and aldermen of London, who demanded to examine the case against her. In due course Wake and a parish clerk who had testified to the existence of two other images, of the king and Elizabeth, were questioned and the clerk recanted his testimony. They were not punished for their perjury, but in January 1470 Jacquetta obtained a formal and published vindication by the Great Council, which both Warwick and Clarence signed.

Before travelling to London Warwick transferred Edward to the custody of John Conyers at Middleham, where he could be kept isolated. Warwick may have hoped for a popular apotheosis when he rode into London, similar to the last occasion he had rebelled against a king in 1460, but if so he was disappointed. He also found that the king's senior officials accepted his orders so long as they bore the king's signet, and gave him no excuse to dismiss them.

Accordingly, he could promote only one of his followers to high office. This was John Langstrother, acting Prior of St John's Hospital, a lucrative post Edward had wished to award to the younger Richard Woodville. Warwick made Langstrother Lord Treasurer to replace Rivers, while taking Herbert's Welsh offices for himself and, tellingly, making Hastings chamberlain of north Wales. To punish Archbishop Neville for having guaranteed Edward's life he chose not to appoint him Lord Chancellor, as previously agreed.

One can deduce that the Bourchiers and other leading magnates told Warwick that he had gone far enough, and that they would come out against him if he harmed the king. He must, perforce, govern with the king's consent. Baffled to find that victory had won him so little, on 8 August Warwick obtained Edward's signet on a summons for a Parliament to meet at York on 22 September. The stated agenda was to 'arrange the government of the realm', but the realm rapidly demonstrated that there was no time for such formalities.

First, there were riots in London that threatened to overwhelm authorities uncertain whether the disturbances were prompted by Warwick. They were only subdued when a large embassy of Burgundian knights, in town to arrange the reciprocal appointments of Duke Charles and Edward to their respective orders of chivalry (the Golden Fleece and the Garter), made it clear they would act if the authorities did not. Charles also sent a letter to the mayor and aldermen promising help and protection if they were faithful to Edward and to the Burgundian alliance, and dire retribution if they were not.

The London riots were only one of many breakdowns of law and order. Thanks to the *Paston Letters* we are best acquainted with the Duke of Norfolk's assault on Caister Castle. Having failed to win it by legal means, on 21 August Norfolk besieged the castle with a large force and artillery, and repeatedly rejected demands from the Council in London to submit to arbitration by Archbishop Neville. He also treated personal pleas from Clarence with contempt. 'He would not spare to do as he is purposed for no duke in England', he replied.

The defenders capitulated on 27 September and Norfolk held the castle until his death in 1476, when at last the Pastons secured possession of a property whose title they had obtained in the first place by prevailing on a dying old man to will it to them, or possibly forging the will. It is a fascinating story of stubbornly maintained legalistic skulduggery by commoners in the face of apoplectic outrage by two generations of one of the most eminent noble families in the land, something unimaginable in any other European kingdom.

As it affects our main narrative the siege of Caister simply serves to highlight that while Warwick had won a measure of control over the apparatus of government, he had failed to achieve authority. Warwick found himself at a loss, probably for the first time in his life, and then things got humiliatingly worse. He had to admit failure and cancel the Parliament because the next major challenge underlined the degree to which the coup had also eroded his own power, in his ancestral heartlands.

It will be recalled that Humphrey Neville, a nephew of the demented Earl of Westmorland, managed to negotiate a pardon when he surrendered Bamburgh Castle in 1464. Although his branch of the Neville clan was senior, they had lost much of their birth right when the 1st Earl of Westmorland willed it to the children of his second marriage to Joan Beaufort, who included Warwick's father and Cecily, the king's mother. As a result the Nevilles of Brancepeth and Raby hated their cousins of Middleham with an abiding passion.

Consequently, when Humphrey and his brother Charles raised the standard of Lancaster in Northumberland in August 1469 it was above all a threat to Warwick's northern hegemony. Despite this, the earl found he could not raise sufficient troops from his own resources to suppress the rebellion. This was a startling development and strongly suggests that, following the bloodbath at Edgcote, Warwick's most dependable retainers were no longer willing to go to war at his command. Even his brother John, Earl of Northumberland, held back.

Defied on every side, Warwick had to yield to pressure from his peers to release Edward, who regained freedom of action in calculated stages. On 10 September he was allowed to make a public appearance in York, where his call for men to join Warwick against the rebellion met with an immediate response. Warwick marched north and quickly dispersed the uprising, capturing Humphrey and Charles. In his absence Edward moved to Pontefract and summoned brother Richard, his uncle the Earl of Essex and the Earls of Arundel, Suffolk and, most tellingly, of Northumberland, plus Lords Hastings and Mountjoy.

When Warwick returned to York with his captives, who were beheaded in Edward's presence on 27 September, he found the king acclaimed by the populace and flanked by some of the highest in the land. There can be no doubt Edward was coldly determined to be avenged, but a combination of prudence and the unanimous urging of his loyal lords to avoid a civil war led him to do no more than announce he was returning to London, and that Warwick should remain in York to complete the pacification of the North.

Warwick tried to salvage something from the wreck by sending Archbishop Neville to join the king's party as it entered London, but when he and the Earl of Oxford approached, according to John Paston 'the king sent them a messenger that they should come [when] he sent for them'.

BITER BIT

THE BALANCE OF POWER HAD TIPPED BACK TO EDWARD, but not enough to permit him to punish the crimes committed against him. He promptly set about shifting it further in his favour, but he had to move carefully. Expecting more immediate retribution, Clarence joined Warwick in the North and they ostentatiously rode around the region with a small army of their respective retainers. Any military move against them would have precipitated the civil war that even the most loyal Yorkist magnates were anxious to avoid.

Since Warwick had done so little to change government personnel it was uncontentious to reverse the few appointments he had made. Langstrother was dismissed as Lord Treasurer but confirmed as Prior of St John's. William Grey, the immensely wealthy Bishop of Ely, was appointed in his place. With the Herbert affinity almost annihilated, Edward appointed 17-year-old Richard, Duke of Gloucester, with the guidance of Lord Ferrers, as the temporary custodian of the Welsh offices that Warwick had awarded himself and Hastings.

This was the only sign Edward ever gave that he disapproved of Hastings's conduct. Hindsight permits us to be tolerably sure his role during the early stages of the Edgcote campaign was disloyal, but the irresponsible behaviour of Herbert and suspected treachery of Stafford had been much worse. With his scheme for regional control of the West Country and Wales in ruins, Edward could not afford to alienate his remaining henchmen.

He did signal a major policy reversal with regard to the North by releasing Henry Percy, whom Warwick and Clarence had placed in the Tower, and accepting his oath of fealty on 27 October. The presence of Cardinal Bourchier, two bishops, two dukes and five barons underlined the importance of the ceremony. The Earls of Arundel and Kent, Lord Treasurer Bishop Grey, and Lord Ferrers in representation of the late Lord Herbert, whose ward Henry had been, posted surety of £8,000.

The writing was on the wall for Percy's restoration to the earldom of Northumberland in place of John Neville, whose loyalty Edward still seems not to have doubted. John had to go because he had failed to win over the Percy affinity, and who knew how long the Scots court, egged on by Louis XI, would resist the traditional temptation to take advantage of English weakness? Restoring Percy had become a geopolitical imperative, and all that could be done was to soften the blow for John Neville.

Edward strained the limits of appeasement to keep John from making common cause with his brothers. On 6 November he announced his intention to recreate the dukedom of Bedford, previously reserved for members of the royal family, for John's 4-year-old son George, effective on 5 January 1470. He also announced the betrothal of young George to his eldest daughter, 3-year-old Elizabeth. Edward ruled that the Yorkist claim to the throne through the female line would continue, and this was duly certified by the Great Council. If no male heir was born and the two children outlived Edward, a Neville would become king. George would also inherit the pick of Warwick's northern lands, which were entailed in the male line.*

Percy was restored to his family estates as the months advanced, at the expense of the Nevilles and Clarence. Edward compensated

*The large lordships of Penrith (Cumberland), Sheriff Hutton (Yorkshire) and Middleham (Richmondshire).

only John, awarding him many of the lands, offices and wardships previously enjoyed by Stafford of Southwyck. As well as making him an honorary member of the royal family, he was clearly being invited to become the regime lock on the West Country. Eventually, when Percy was restored as Earl of Northumberland, Edward created the new marquessate of Montagu for John, which gave him a higher rank than Warwick. It is hard to see what more the king could have done.

This has not stopped historians citing the alleged poverty of John's new endowment as the reason for his later disaffection, without considering how little income he had derived from the surly Percy estates. Edward failed to keep his loyalty because he never had it. John was guilty, at best, of 'misprision' in the Robin of Redesdale conspiracy, and of conflating it with the Robin of Holderness revolt. His misrepresentations persuaded Edward not to follow up on the nationwide commissions of array he had issued, and to embark on a pilgrimage with only a ceremonial retinue. There is more than sufficient reason to believe John Neville, not the unfortunate Stafford of Southwyck, had been Warwick's Trojan Horse all along.

Edward summoned Warwick and Clarence to attend the Great Council that convened on 18 November. They eventually came, no doubt persuaded to do so by Edward issuing commissions of array on 29 October to everyone except those who had lately rebelled against him. It was an imposing display of the king's latent power, attended by the Dukes of Gloucester, Norfolk and Suffolk, the Earls of Arundel, Kent, Essex and Northumberland, and Barons Dacre, Dynham, Ferrers of Chartley, Hastings and Mountjoy. Cardinal Bourchier and five bishops also attended. Polydore Vergil's account rings true:

> Both the authority and the entreaty of the nobility so moved the mind of the king and earl, that, upon mutual promise of assurance made, the earl himself and the Duke of Clarence came to London, guarded with a slender crew of soldiers in respect of so

great danger, and had at Westminster long talk with the king concerning composition [settlement].

The Council persuaded Edward to issue a general pardon for all offences committed before Christmas, an insolent demand by Warwick and Clarence that allowed a further month of impunity for crimes yet to be committed. Against this they were compelled to assent to a series of measures transparently aimed at them. The stinging vindication of Jacquetta was one, and they could hardly oppose either the promotion of young George, the sole legitimate male heir any of the Nevilles had produced, or the appointment of Richard of Gloucester to Herbert's Welsh offices and as Constable of England in replacement of murdered Earl Rivers.

Although Anthony, Lord Scales, did not attend the Council, he reappeared at court using his father's title, and there were other indications Edward regarded the 'composition' as no more than a truce, among them measures to repair the Herbert affinity. Herbert's widow, resident at her brother Lord Ferrers's manor at Weobley in Herefordshire, was granted the wardship of her 14-year-old son, now Earl of Pembroke and also married to Mary Woodville. The idea was that in due course he would fill his father's shoes, but he proved a disappointment and never assumed the offices held for him by Gloucester.

Further writing on the wall was the partial rehabilitation of Humphrey Dacre, heir to the attainted Dacre barony whose lordship around Norham Castle in Cumberland was exercised by Warwick. Although Dacre was not yet restored, the intention was plain and in conjunction with the return of the large lordship of Cockermouth to Henry Percy it would undermine the hegemony in the West March enjoyed by Warwick since 1461. Also, when Warwick's demented uncle Lord Latimer died on 30 December, Cardinal Bourchier was awarded the wardship of Latimer's baby grandson and heir, and Warwick lost the custodianship of the large estate around Corby in Northamptonshire he had exercised since 1447.

Clarence's situation was even more precarious. He held all his lands at the king's pleasure, what he had regarded as his appanage was shrinking, and his status as heir presumptive was officially revoked in favour of Princess Elizabeth. It is not remarkable, therefore, that he initiated the next roll of the dice – the only surprise is that Warwick went along with a scheme not under his complete control. This may be evidence of a fracture in his carapace of self-regard, brought about by the abject failure of his *coup d'état*.

The Council was dissolved in early February and Edward immediately initiated a sequence of events that was to end with Warwick and Clarence fleeing the country. The contemporary *Chronicle of the Rebellion in Lincolnshire* has so much corroboration from other sources that it was not until 1988 that any modern historian took a close look at the timing. This argues persuasively that Edward set a trap for his enemies and fabricated evidence, and that the *Chronicle* is a masterly work of propaganda. The chronology opposite Map 38 is based on the *Chronicle*, with the points of factual manipulation in italics.*

This being the case, the idea of Edward as merely a gonad-led playboy crumbles. There were no 'evil councillors' – Edward alone was the architect and protagonist of his cause. He showed intelligent resolution in working his way free of Warwick's control, and in the months that followed acted moderately at the urgent behest of the Council; but from the start he hoped to provoke his enemies into breaking the peace and, once freed of the Council's restraint, did so.

• ∽ •

---

*See P. Holland, 'The Lincolnshire rebellion of March 1470', *English Historical Review* (October 1988). In 1903 Charles Oman had come to the same conclusion, but on the basis of intrinsically fallacious 'after which therefore because of which' reasoning.

The fuse for the next round of violence was lit by Lord Welles, a supposedly reconciled Lancastrian and Lincolnshire magnate who had served (as Lord Willoughby, his secondary title) under Warwick in 1462–4, and owed him a debt of gratitude for the reversal of the Welles attainder. While Welles was of his affinity, Warwick had no local landed presence, whereas the king had given Clarence the extensive Lincolnshire lands of the attainted and executed Lord Roos and the infamous Tailboys.

Edward summoned Lord Welles and his brother-in-law Thomas Dymock to London to answer for the destruction of the main Lincolnshire manor house of Thomas Burgh, the king's Master of Horse. Burgh had risen to local prominence thanks to Edward's patronage, and the Welles affinity would not have dared attack him had they not believed the king too weakened by Edgcote and his captivity to retaliate. If, as seems likely, the assault took place in November or December 1469, it was covered by Edward's general pardon.

It is believable that Welles's defiance of Edward's authority should have prompted Clarence to invite him to join some future uprising; however, the chronology too neatly assigns this to early February, before Edward issued an order for his local retainers to meet him at Grantham on 12 March. The *Chronicle* had to make this assertion, because otherwise it was Edward's order that tipped the first domino. When he subsequently summoned Welles and Dymock they may have believed they were sheltered by the general pardon, and only fled to sanctuary at Westminster Abbey when they learned that the king did not share their view.

Clarence apparently did stir the pot by warning Welles's eldest son Robert that the king intended to lead a punitive expedition into Lincolnshire – but this was also the only interpretation that could be placed on Edward's military preparations. The pardon for the assault on Burgh's manor he issued on 3 March was belied by his order on the same day to start the royal artillery rolling up the Great North Road. There followed an episode that awoke Edward

38. LOSECOTE CAMPAIGN 1470

0   25   50   75
miles

Newcastle

Carlisle

Richmond
Scrope   *Neville*

Middleham
Conyers

York

Pontefract

Stanley

Manchester   Rotherham   Doncaster
                            Gainsborough
            Sheffield
Chesterfield   Retford   Ranby
                            Willoughby
                    Newark   Lincoln

Warwick & Clarence

Richard

Nottingham

Derby   Grantham
Burton
Shrewsbury   *Talbot*   Leicester   **Losecote**
                        Tutbury   Stamford
Ludlow   Fotheringhay   Norwich
            Coventry
        Warwick   Huntingdon

Hereford

Edward

Gloucester
Nibley Green
                        Ware
                More Palace
Bristol   **London**
    Wells   Canterbury

            Salisbury

Courtenay
Exeter   Southampton

                            To Calais

Dartmouth

© Hugh Bicheno

CHRONOLOGY OF THE 1470
LOSECOTE CAMPAIGN

2 February	Clarence invites Richard, Lord Welles, to join a 'great uprising'. *Some time before this* a mob incited by Welles, his son Robert and his brothers-in-law Thomas Dymock and Thomas de la Lande sack the manor house of Thomas Burgh at Gainsborough, Lincolnshire.
9 February	Edward orders Yorkist retainers to meet him at Grantham on 12 March.
22 February	Edward summons Lord Welles and Dymock, who seek sanctuary in Westminster Abbey.
3 March	Clarence warns Robert Welles the king is coming in force to punish Lincolnshire. Edward issues a general pardon for the sack of Burgh's manor, but also mobilizes the royal artillery.
4 March	Robert Welles summons the Lincolnshire commons to assemble at Ranby on 6 March. Clarence at Duchess Cecily's London palace – *they delay Edward's departure for two days.*
6 March	Edward, Clarence, the Earl of Arundel, Henry Percy, Hastings and other lords travel to Ware.
7 March	Edward to Waltham Abbey. *Clarence returns to London with commissions of array for himself and Warwick,* meets Welles, Dymock and John Langstrother, Prior of St John's Hospital.
8 March	Edward to Royston, learns of the rebellion and sends for Welles and Dymock. Receives first letter from Warwick and Clarence, who are together at Warwick.
9 March	Edward to Huntingdon, interrogates Welles and Dymock who confess *but do not implicate Clarence and Warwick.* Welles ordered on pain of death to instruct his son to stand down.
10 March	Warwick and Clarence send second letter. *Robert Welles marching to meet them at Leicester.*
11 March	Edward at Fotheringhay. Warwick and Clarence to Coventry, joined by William Parr. On receipt of his father's letter, Robert Welles turns south down the Great North Road towards Stamford.

12 March	Edward arrives at Stamford at midday, writes to Warwick and Clarence thanking them for their promised support, learns the rebels are arrayed for battle 5 miles to the north. BATTLE OF LOSECOTE FIELD – Lord Welles and Dymock beheaded.
13 March	Warwick and Clarence still at Coventry. *Captured letters confirm their treachery. Edward summons them to his presence, appoints Worcester Constable of England.*
14 March	Edward at Grantham. *Robert Welles's confession.* Warwick and Clarence write that they will join him at Retford. Scrope of Bolton and John Conyers disband troops assembled in Richmond.
16–17 March	Edward at Newark. Warwick and Clarence at Burton-on-Trent, Derby and Chesterfield.
17–19 March	Edward at Doncaster, executes Robert Welles and de la Lande. Warwick and Clarence march to Sheffield, hoping to rendezvous with Conyers.
20 March	Edward to Rotherham. Warwick and Clarence to Manchester, Lord Stanley stays away. Viscount Lisle killed in private battle with Lord Berkeley at Nibley Green.
21 March	Edward to Pontefract, Richard of Gloucester approaching Manchester from the west. Warwick and Clarence march south and collect Warwick's family. William Parr defects.
22–28 March	Edward at York. Scrope, Conyers, Parr and Robert Hildyard make submission and are pardoned. Henry Percy restored as Earl of Northumberland. Warwick and Clarence at Bristol with 5,000 men, they disband them and abandon their artillery.
29 March	Edward at Nottingham, marches south through Coventry and Warwick.
3–10 April	Warwick and Clarence at Exeter, then set sail from Dartmouth.
11–14 April	Edward at Wells and Exeter. Warwick's raid on Southampton defeated.

to the possibility of using the disturbance to smoke out his brother and Warwick.

The *Chronicle* would have it that Clarence invited Edward to meet him at Baynard's Castle, their mother's London palace, in order to delay his departure, giving time for Robert Welles to summon the Lincolnshire commons. Yet why would Edward have set out on the heels of his artillery? The guns needed several days' head start, and his aim was to be in Lincolnshire by 12 March, which indeed he was. Clarence's amiability and professed willingness to join him in the expedition was transparently a ruse – how best to take advantage of it?

Clarence set out with the royal party, but after the first stop at Ware he returned to London with commissions of array issued for himself and Warwick. Since Edward had returned from captivity they had been pointedly excluded from all judicial and military commissions, and he did not need their support to overawe Lincolnshire – indeed, he only learned of the uprising the following day; so what was this all about? Bearing in mind the manner in which Warwick had exploited commissions of array to prepare the 1469 *coup d'état*, much the most likely explanation is that Edward was enticing his enemies to try again.

The great unknown of the ensuing campaign is why Warwick let himself be carried away by Clarence's opportunism. Robert Welles certainly appealed to them for help, and he and many of his followers sported Clarence's livery. How many of Clarence's Lincolnshire affinity joined the rebellion is unknown – only two were later accused of participation, but this probably reflected Edward's desire to underplay his brother's role to Warwick's detriment. A mere eight days separate Welles's call for the commons to rally at Ranby and the Battle of Losecote, so the livery coats constitute prima facie evidence of Clarence's prior complicity.

Even the *Chronicle* does not claim that Lord Welles and Dymock, when summoned by Edward to Huntingdon, implicated Warwick and Clarence in their confession to having plotted treason. The uprising seems to have been a rash initiative by Robert Welles, seeking to precipitate the more general rebellion that Clarence's messages had led him to believe was in preparation. If there were any such preparation it was in its early stages and, even with commissions of array for the Midlands counties, Warwick and Clarence were finding it difficult to recruit an army. They were still at Coventry when the battle took place.

The *Chronicle* says Robert Welles was leading his men to a rendezvous with Warwick and Clarence at Leicester when he received the letter from Lord Welles begging him to desist, at which point he marched south to rescue his father. When the armies came face to face just north of Stamford, with a ruthlessness he had not previously displayed Edward had Lord Welles and Dymock beheaded in full view of both sides. Robert, to whom his father had earlier passed the subsidiary Willoughby title, thus also became – very briefly – Lord Welles.*

The battle barely deserves the name, as Welles's men broke under artillery fire and fled, those wearing Clarence's livery shedding it as they ran – hence 'Losecote'. Edward had his brother dead to rights, but needed to implicate Warwick. This he did with the impossibly convenient battlefield capture of a box of incriminating letters, never published, and an alleged confession by Robert Welles: '[without] the said Duke and Earl's provoking we at this time would nere durst have made any commotion or stirring; but upon their comfort we did that we did'.

It was time to slam shut the jaws of the trap Edward had set when he issued the commissions of array to Clarence. He did this *before* Robert Welles was captured, but allegedly after the box of incriminating letters was discovered. In the morning of the day after the battle he sent letters sealed with his signet to the sheriffs of twenty-six counties ordering them to proclaim the victory and to announce that:

*Both titles passed to Richard, Lord Hastings's younger brother, through his marriage to Welles's sister Joan.

> None of his subjects presume… to rise, nor make any assembly
> or gathering by reason of [commissions of array previously
> issued nor by the] commandment [of] any person or persons
> of whatever estate he be, unless it be by the King's commission
> newly issued after this 13th day of March.

It would not have taken long for Warwick and Clarence to have
sight of this letter and to appreciate the snare Edward had set for
them. Their efforts to recruit were being disowned and portrayed
in a sinister light, yet the day before the battle Edward had written
thanking them for their support and urging them to make haste to
meet him. Had they done so, he would have defeated and slaughtered them along with their retainers.

Even if historians for years to come have bought the king's version, Warwick and Clarence knew he had trapped them. Worse, he
had shown a previously unsuspected capacity for fair-faced deceit
and malevolent *furbizia*. Six months later they complained that
they had been the victims of 'false means and dissimulations', and
indeed they had. Edward had paid them back with their own coin,
and now they had to salvage what they could from the wreck.

NOISES OFF

READERS MAY BE WONDERING WHY LOUIS XI AND DUKE Charles abstained from involvement during the turmoil in England in 1469–70. The explanation is that they were fully occupied with matters that concerned them more, a reminder of how relatively unimportant England had become since losing its empire in France. Charles's attention was almost fully absorbed by his efforts to assert and expand his areas of authority, and Louis was still working to recover the authority he had lost by the Public Weal rebellion.*

As soon as Duke Philippe died on 15 June 1457, Louis began receiving reports of a revival of the alliance among Brittany, Burgundy, Alençon, Armagnac, Nemours and Savoy to replace him with his brother Charles. He was forced to negotiate short and humiliating truces with Burgundy and Brittany, later extended to 15 July 1468. In April he convoked the only assembly of the Estates General during his reign and listened to their grievances with every appearance of sympathy, and a ready wit that won over many.

He took only a little time out of his busy schedule to stir the English pot with Jasper Tudor's tiny expedition to Wales, mainly because Warwick was doing such a good job unprompted. He also vigorously libelled Edward's sister Margaret, but could not stop

---

*Readers will find it useful to bookmark Maps 6 and 7 for ease of reference while reading this chapter.

Duke Charles marrying her on 3 July, 'against his heart and nature' as Philippe Commynes put it. In the midst of the extravagant celebrations of the event Charles agreed to extend the truce for himself and his allies from 15 July to 1 August.

Duke Fransez, who was sheltering Louis's brother, omitted to ratify the agreement and on 15 July Louis sent three armies into Brittany. Edward's expedition, led by Scales, failed to provide timely support, and on 10 September Fransez was forced to sign the Treaty of Ancenis, by which he renounced all his alliances. Duke Charles was so enraged that Brittany Herald, the bearer of the bad news, feared for his life. Louis had created a situation where it was imperative to persuade the duke that, contrary to the evidence, he had not been duped.

There was no hope of renewing the truce whose spirit Louis had violated, and mercenaries flocked from all over Europe to join Charles's army in Picardy. Louis could see nothing he might gain that outweighed the likelihood of a revival of the Public Weal alliance should he suffer a military check, and was determined to avoid war. Confident he could charm the duke if they met face to face, he committed a potentially fatal error.

When Duke Philippe died the citizens of Liège, smarting from the loss of municipal privileges following a 1465 revolt against the installation of Louis de Bourbon as prince-bishop, and undeterred by the brutal suppression of the Dinant revolt the following year, rebelled again. They were crushed in battle and surrendered in November 1467, after which Charles made them degrade the city walls and declared Liège a Burgundian protectorate under his deputy Guy de Humbercourt.

Louis had encouraged the revolts with false promises of military support, but the Liègeois were slow learners. Incited by French agents, they rebelled again on 9 October 1468, capturing Humbercourt and the prince-bishop, whose palace was occupied by the rebel leader. On the same day Louis left behind the army that had lately overawed Brittany and rode to Charles's headquarters at

Péronne, 50 miles east of Amiens, with only a small retinue. If he had prior knowledge that the Liège revolt was imminent, it was a breathtakingly rash bluff.

We know a great deal about the sequel thanks to Philippe Commynes, who was closely involved in the proceedings. There is no reason to doubt that, as he boasted in his memoirs, he played a key role in the encounter between the king and the duke at Péronne. After he defected to Louis four years later the king's deed of gift to him specified that 'our councillor and chamberlain, without fear of the danger that could come to him, informed us of all he could for our welfare and so employed himself that by his means and aid we escaped'.

The meeting between Louis and Charles was arranged by Jacquetta's brother Louis, Count of Saint-Pol. While one would normally assume that anything involving Saint-Pol was steeped in treachery, Louis himself insisted on meeting Charles protected only by a safe conduct. His confidence was severely shaken on the day he arrived when four of his most bitter enemies, including his Savoyard brother-in-law Philippe of Bresse, rode past the splendid palace allotted to him. The mutual hatred of Louis and Bresse, born of reciprocal acts of treachery, was boundless, and the king immediately requested a move to the dilapidated castle of Péronne.

While assuring Louis that Bresse was merely on his way elsewhere, after negotiations on 9 October proved unsatisfactory Charles brought Bresse to their meeting the next day and insisted on presenting him to the king. This was considerably more than a nod as good as a wink, introducing an element of menace even before news of the Liège revolt arrived. Initial reports falsely asserted that Humbercourt and the prince-bishop had been murdered along with their retinues, and identified two royal emissaries among the rebels.

Although he soon learned that Humbercourt had been released and that the prince-bishop was being well treated, Charles was (allegedly) consumed with rage and ringed Péronne Castle with his English archers. Louis quickly professed himself shocked by the revolt and offered to accompany Charles to chastise the rebel city. If Commynes is to be believed Charles would have none of it and was only with difficulty dissuaded from violating his safe conduct by his half-brother Anthony and other knights of the Golden Fleece.

Louis was both appalled and relieved to learn of this – from Commynes. Now then: whose interest was Commynes serving? In all probability Charles never had any intention of harming Louis, but wanted him to believe he might. After all, Commynes's message was that Louis should agree to everything Charles demanded, on pain of death. There is ample reason to suspect that he was serving the interest of his master in falsely persuading Louis that his life was in danger.

On 14 October Louis presented Charles with a peace treaty by which the king promised to abide by the 1435 Treaty of Arras and the 1465 Treaty of Conflans. Charles would not be required to renounce his alliance with England, but each undertook to aid and defend the other against aggression by third parties. Full territorial restitution was to be made to Philippe of Bresse and reparations paid for the harm done to him. Louis surrendered his claim to Bruges, Ghent and Ypres in Flanders, and accepted that if he broke any of the treaties, all feudal obligations Charles owed for his French possessions would be permanently cancelled.

Louis also accepted an addendum Charles had perhaps put forward more as a negotiating tactic than a serious proposal. This was that Berry was to be granted the appanage of Champagne, the strategically vital province bordering on the principalities lying between the northern and southern concentrations of the Burgundian empire. To reassure Charles further, Louis ordered his army to disperse and repeated his offer to join him in the suppression of the Liège rebellion.

They signed the treaty under the reliquary cross worn by the Emperor Charlemagne, held aloft by Cardinal Jean Balue, Louis's chief negotiator and, although unknown to him at this time, a traitor. Charles, for the first time, grudgingly knelt before Louis in homage for his French dukedom, stating he did so on condition that the king kept his promises. They then put their hands on Charlemagne's cross and solemnly swore to uphold the terms of the treaty.

Louis could not wriggle out of his commitment to ride with Charles against Liège, and they set out the next day. Humbercourt and the prince-bishop soon joined them, the latter released by the rebels to negotiate a capitulation, having given his word to return. Charles forbade him to honour his commitment. He also tested Louis, saying he was free to go if he wished, but the king continued to ride alongside him, separated from his own councillors and bodyguard.

On 28 October, when they were lodged in the Liège suburbs, 600 rebels wearing Burgundian livery made a night raid that came close to killing or capturing both. The raiders were all killed and defenceless Liège fell to an unnecessarily massive assault on the 30th. Most of the citizens had fled, and those who had not, thinking to indicate their loyalty, suffered the same treatment as those who made a last desperate stand in the cathedral. Hundreds were put to the sword, hundreds more tied together and hurled into the river Meuse, and the city was torched.

By associating Louis with this barbarity Charles ensured he would not find it easy to stir trouble in the Burgundian back yard in the future. He was still reluctant to let him go, but the king pointed out that the peace treaty would not be valid until registered by the Paris Parlement, which required his presence. Before departing, Louis casually asked Charles what he should do if Berry was not satisfied with his new appanage. 'If he does not want it and you can satisfy him some other way, I leave it to you two', Charles replied, confirming that it had never been high on his list of priorities, probably because he knew how undependable Berry was.

When Louis returned to French territory he was startled to find his subjects celebrating the news of the treaty with unreserved joy. They were weary of wars and, like the prime ministers of France and

Britain after selling out Czechoslovakia at Munich in 1938, Louis found himself cheered for what he knew to have been a humiliating act of appeasement. This, as much as the terms of the treaty, explains why he was so quiescent during 1469, and refrained from meddling in the affairs of England.

He was also fully taken up with the protracted wooing of his brother. There was no question in France of the throne descending through the female line – that had been ruled out forever when the English Angevin claim was rejected and the Valois dynasty installed in 1328, kicking off the Hundred Years War. In eighteen years of marriage Queen Charlotte had born him only two surviving daughters; three sons had been stillborn or died in infancy. It seemed likely that Berry would succeed Louis, and reconciliation was a dynastic imperative.

It took Louis a year to overcome his brother's fear that he had committed an unforgivable act by his dalliance with Charles. Early in 1469 Louis offered him the far richer – but safely separate from Burgundy – province of Guyenne in exchange for Champagne. In the midst of the negotiations a treasonous letter written by Cardinal Balue came into Louis's possession, in which the cardinal urged Duke Charles to resist the proposed exchange by force of arms. Although the pope refused to revoke their clerical immunity, Balue and his confederate the Bishop of Verdun were imprisoned for the next eleven years.

In April Berry accepted the exchange, but still refused to meet. Louis's next gambit was to create the chivalric Order of Saint-Michel and to appoint the new Duke of Guyenne as its first member. The order was exclusive, such that members could not also accept the Burgundian Golden Fleece or the English Garter. On 7 September the brothers finally met on a bridge of boats across a river, with a fence in the middle. Overcome with emotion, the younger man got around the fence and threw himself at the king's feet. For a week they were inseparable and Louis had little cause for serious concern for the remaining three years of his brother's life.

Meanwhile, with his back now covered, Duke Charles presided over a conference at Ghent to arbitrate a long and violent dispute, which Charles had stoked, between Duke Arnold of Egmond and his son Adolf over the duchy of Guelders and county of Zutphen. In January Adolf kidnapped his father and a civil war ensued that drew in the Duke of Cleves and the Archbishop of Cologne. By appointing himself arbitrator Charles took a large step towards the occupation that followed in 1473. Friesland, flanked by the lands of Charles's bastard half-brother David, Prince-Bishop of Utrecht, was next on the list.

In the south, Charles acquired Upper Alsace by mortgage from Archduke Sigismund of Austria. The province was a rat's nest of sub-mortgages that created only liabilities for its nominal ruler, but Charles was not deterred. Like his father, he dreamed of re-creating Lotharingia, the central kingdom of the three into which the vast Carolingian empire was divided in 840. It ran from the Low Countries along a broad band of territory west of the Rhine, through western Switzerland and Savoy to Provence.

The difference between father and son was that Philippe's aspiration was long term and dynastic, while Charles, having overcome his repugnance long enough to engender a daughter in 1457, made no further effort to produce a male heir and thought only in terms of personal glory. Fatefully, this was to include subduing the formidable Swiss, now stronger than ever.

Sociological studies of the posturing hypermasculinity known as *machismo* concur in the paradoxical role of mothers in perpetuating it as a form of revenge on philandering fathers. They teach their sons that all women – apart from the sainted mother – are bitches on heat and all men treacherous dogs. Throw in the high testosterone levels commonly found in homosexual men, add almost unlimited wealth and power, and you get Charles 'the Bold'.

The dominant figure in Charles's life was his mother, Isabella of Portugal, who was obsessed by the fact that her grandmother had been John of Gaunt's eldest child. Charles was a mother's boy to such an extent that he used to speak of 'we Portuguese', and after the death his first wife in 1454 Isabella pressed him to strengthen his claim to the English throne by marrying one of Richard of York's daughters. In 1457 she became completely estranged from Philippe after he insisted Charles marry Isabelle of Bourbon instead.

When Charles became a widower again in 1465 he was free to indulge his mother's obsession. What Edward believed was a matrimonial alliance against France was seen in a completely different light by Charles and his mother, who handled the marriage negotiations. It was she who imposed conditions of such unilateral advantage to Burgundy that it undermined Edward's standing with his own people, and this may have been her intention. In her eyes the (junior) Lancastrians and Yorkists had lesser claims to the throne, and in a perfect world they would destroy each other to make way for her son.

Was this an unrealistic ambition? Perhaps – but no more than many other calculations in an age politically defined by genealogy. The clinching argument in favour of this interpretation is that on 11 November 1471, five weeks before his mother died, Charles ordered a notarized document drawn up in which he set out his right to the English throne as the sole remaining legitimate Lancastrian claimant, and promised to pursue it. One need look no further for an explanation of his ambivalent behaviour towards Edward.

Thus there were no 'noises off' when England fell into turmoil because the two most powerful princes of Christendom, who might have sought to turn the situation to their advantage, had backed away from confrontation and each had pressing reasons to do nothing to provoke the other. The eternal problem with peripheral disputes, however, is that the parties in conflict will draw you in, no matter how unwilling you are to get involved.

OUT OF THE ASHES

PERHAPS UNEASY ABOUT CLARENCE'S ATTEMPT TO
bounce him into exploiting the Lincolnshire rebellion,
Warwick only tried to mobilize his wider affinity after Losecote,
when Edward sprung the trap he had set for them. Warwick and
Clarence protested their innocence and said they would meet
him at Retford on the Great North Road, but instead set out for
Rotherham via Burton upon Trent, Derby and Chesterfield, gathering retainers as they went.

With Richard of Gloucester and the Yorkist Marchers on his
doorstep, John Talbot, Earl of Shrewsbury, declined to join
them. Their hopes were now pinned on John Conyers and Lord
Scrope of Bolton bringing reinforcements down the Western Spur
from Richmondshire. When Edward advanced from Newark to
Rotherham, Warwick and Clarence stopped at Sheffield. Learning
that Conyers and Scrope were not coming, in a last throw of the
dice they marched to Manchester in the vain hope that Lord Stanley
would come off the fence.

When they turned south their followers began to desert them,
notably William Parr of Kendal, a key figure in Warwick's north-
western affinity who had fought for him at Edgcote and who had
carried messages to and from the king after Losecote. Although
Warwick and Clarence still had 5,000 troops when they arrived at
Bristol, these were men from the region who only stayed with them

because they were returning home. Few accompanied them on the last stage of their flight, and the fact that they abandoned their artillery at Bristol suggests a general disbandment.

Meanwhile John Neville put on a show of loyalty by raising troops in the king's name from his own inherited estates in north Yorkshire and joined Edward at Doncaster. Soon afterwards Robert Hildyard joined Parr, Scrope and Conyers in seeking the king's pardon, and Edward learned that John had deceived him about the 'Robin of Holderness' revolt. This may have been why he chose this moment to announce the restoration of Henry Percy, who had accompanied him throughout the campaign, as Earl of Northumberland. Despite this Edward continued to trust John, and we must assume he believed the elevation of young George Neville to the dukedom of Bedford and his betrothal to the eldest royal daughter would keep his father loyal.

In March, in a matter unrelated to what was going on elsewhere, Thomas Talbot, Viscount Lisle, decided it was an opportune moment to bring to a head a longstanding family feud with William, Lord Berkeley, and he formally challenged him to battle. Berkeley unsportingly arrived at Nibley Green with a larger army and one of his archers killed Lisle with an arrow to the throat. Thus the male line of the Gloucestershire Talbots was extinguished in folly just when Thomas's Shrewsbury cousin was opting for discretion over valour.*

About a week later Warwick and Clarence rode past Nibley Green on their way to Exeter, where another local fracas awaited them. Clarence had a strong presence in Devon and may have encouraged this uprising in the same way he had in Lincolnshire. Although the senior Courtenay line was Lancastrian, following the judicial murder of Henry Courtenay its leader was his brother John, an exile at Marguerite's threadbare court. The rival Courtenays of Powderham Castle, 7 miles south-east of Exeter, were intermarried with the Lancastrian Hungerfords and Luttrells, whose lands had

*The Lisle–Berkeley feud is more fully explained in Appendix F. It was not resolved until 1609.

been seized without regard to the rights of, among others, James Luttrell's widow Elizabeth Courtenay.

Elizabeth later stood as godmother to Clarence's only child, and the Powderham Courtenays were probably members of Clarence's affinity in the hope of recovering family lands awarded first to Stafford of Southwyck and subsequently to the new Marquess Montagu. On 16 March Edward ordered Lords Dynham and FitzWarin, his chief representatives in the West Country following the lynching of Stafford, to arrest them and Hugh Courtenay of Bocconoc in Cornwall for a rebellion that must have started some time earlier, in the expectation that Edward would be overthrown and replaced by Clarence.

Things did not go well for Dynham and FitzWarin, and by 22 March they were besieged in Exeter Castle. Also in the castle was Isabel, Clarence's very pregnant wife, whom he had sent there from Tutbury before the Losecote campaign, which argues he prepared an escape route in advance. The siege was lifted when he and Warwick arrived, and Isabel was permitted to join them as they travelled to Clarence's borough of Dartmouth, where a fleet was assembled. The rebel Courtenays went with them.

While to this point Warwick had been scrambling to make something of the dire situation in which his new son-in-law had landed him, from the moment they sailed he was in total command and Clarence became increasingly irrelevant. The ships and crews were Warwick's and they sailed to Southampton intending to cut out *Trinity*, his flagship, now under the command of Anthony Woodville, Earl Rivers. Forewarned, Woodville's men not only killed or captured the raiding party, but took two of Warwick's ships as well.

The remainder sailed to Calais, where Warwick hoped to repeat the strategy he had followed in 1459 of using it as a springboard for invasion. Lord Wenlock, his deputy, and most of the garrison were his men; against which the commander of the garrison was Galliard, lord of Duras, who was fiercely loyal to Edward, while the garrison's Stapler paymasters were strong supporters of the Burgundian alliance. Consequently Warwick found the chain across the entrance to the port raised against him, and warning shots fired. Poor little Isabel endured the stillbirth of her baby on a ship tossing at anchor in the Calais roads.

Back in England Edward reached Exeter four days after Warwick had sailed. On learning of the Southampton raid he marched there and unleashed Tiptoft on what was by now a large collection of prisoners. John Clapham, whose arrival at Edgcote had doomed Herbert, was fortunate only to be beheaded. Geoffrey Gate, Warwick's Marshal of Calais, captor of Earl Rivers and leader of the Southampton raid, was inexplicably pardoned. Humbler rebels suffered the novel barbarity of being dismembered and having their torsos impaled upside down with their severed heads on their buttocks.

Edward's party now included two dukes, four earls, ten barons and about 10,000 men. With the Earls of Essex and Kent securing London and the Home Counties, Northumberland and Montagu having left to settle the North, Rivers organizing the fleet and three more nobles sent to arrest Archbishop Neville at his Hertfordshire palace, aristocratic solidarity was overwhelming. It was also opportunistic and ephemeral, as Henry VI had discovered after they all joined his triumphal Ludford Bridge campaign in 1459.

To return to the herding cats analogy, noble houses that do not put their own interests first, last and everywhere in between seldom last long. Loyalty, like respect for the law and paying taxes, is for the little people. While a monarch could not govern without the greater magnates, they needed him only to the extent that he could maintain the status quo at no expense to them. This is why Losecote proved to be such a hollow victory – it had been won very largely by Edward's cunning and by employing his own resources. Most of the glittering array of nobles that jumped on the bandwagon could be depended on only to jump off again at the first sign of trouble.

Warwick knew he had severely weakened Edward's regime and that he must strike again before the damage could be repaired.

He could probably count on his Trojan Horse brother, while Shrewsbury and Stanley would no doubt jump on his own band-wagon if he could get it rolling again. But Edgcote had diminished his northern affinity both in number and in their willingness to turn out for him again, especially after the restoration of Henry Percy, and the Losecote campaign had ended with a number of his Midlands retainers executed and the rest feeling abandoned.

With Calais closed to him Warwick's remaining bargaining chip was his fleet, soon joined by a squadron led by his illegitimate first cousin Thomas Neville, better known as the Bastard of Fauconberg, who had escaped from the Sandwich fleet, newly put under the command of John Howard. Warwick knew how fiercely Louis XI must resent his humiliation at Péronne, and used the fleet to put the shaky Franco–Burgundian détente under intolerable pressure.

Not long after Thomas joined him Warwick's warships raided along the coast of Flanders, Zeeland and Holland, capturing sixty to one hundred small vessels. Collecting the transports off Calais, they then sailed along the coast of Normandy but were intercepted by John Howard. Most of the recently pirated Burgundian prizes were lost, probably sacrificed to cover the retreat of the remainder. On 1 May they arrived at Honfleur, on the Seine estuary, where Warwick demanded sanctuary, and sent Louis a letter saying they must meet to discuss the restoration of the House of Lancaster, as the king had first suggested in 1467.

Back in England, Edward declared Warwick's lands forfeit but redistributed little of it apart from returning Barnard Castle to the Bishop of Durham, keeping for the crown most of the income from the remainder. He also made Henry Percy, whose restoration as Earl of Northumberland was still subject to confirmation by Parliament, Warden of the East March, leaving Richard Salkeld of Carlisle, Warwick's deputy, in charge of the West March. Showing that indifference to cause and effect characteristic of those who have conspired and failed, the Neville affinity in general and Montagu in particular felt aggrieved.

Elsewhere, apart from appointing Arundel Warden of the Cinque Ports, Edward did not bring the great magnates into his government and tried to rebuild his network of personally loyal key men. He brought Tiptoft back as Lord Treasurer and also appointed him Lieutenant of Ireland to replace Clarence – but, like the Woodvilles, Tiptoft had no significant affinity. Of Edward's remaining henchmen Hastings and Ferrers were only medium-size lords while John Howard, recently created a baron but not yet confirmed by summons to Parliament, was not even that. The king's brother Richard of Gloucester and John Stafford, created Earl of Wiltshire only in January, had not had time to develop their own affinities.

The gaping holes in the scheme were Wales and the West Country. Edward had bet so heavily on Herbert and Stafford of Southwyck that he was left scrambling for alternatives. Gloucester and Ferrers appear to have done a good job of containment with regard to Wales, but the shattered Herbert affinity would require many years to recover, if it ever did. In the West Country, even if Montagu had loyally accepted his new role the Courtenay affinity was no more likely to accept his lordship than it had Stafford's. Yet, for obvious reasons, Edward's main concern was whether his gamble on Percy had neutralized the threat from the North.

All of this is more apparent in hindsight than it was at the time. Whatever Warwick's failings as a tactician he was a masterly strategist. Bearing in mind that he had no following in the West Country and that his south Wales affinity had been deprived of his good lordship for most of the preceding decade, he still formulated a plan to strike not where he was strongest, but where Edward was weakest. He probably got a crash course in West Country politics from the Courtenays who joined him in exile, while for Wales he was soon to be joined by the indefatigable Jasper Tudor and other Welshmen driven into exile by Herbert.

The question was whether Louis XI could be persuaded first to bring about an alliance with the exiled Lancastrians, and secondly to provide Warwick with a large enough army to get the band-wagon rolling in England. Warwick succeeded because Louis's heart remained that of the innovative rebel he had been as a young man. His formative hero had been the *condottiere* Francesco Sforza, who won the duchy of Milan in 1450 and thoroughly reformed an administration that had become predatory under the extinct Visconti dynasty.

Louis saw Warwick as another Sforza and his English opponents akin to the reactionary nobles he himself had outmanoeuvred in the Dauphiné. He was wrong on both counts, but he was not the first nor would he be the last French ruler to underestimate the degree to which England diverged from the continental norm. Louis persuaded himself there was a groundswell in favour of regime change in England, and that Warwick could make it happen.

Accordingly, on receipt of Warwick's letter Louis summoned Marguerite d'Anjou to join him at court, currently at Amboise in the Loire valley, while seeking to show favour to Warwick without provoking Charles of Burgundy, who was outraged by Warwick's piracy and demanded Louis treat him as their common enemy, as required by the Treaty of Péronne.

Initially Louis requested that Warwick take his ships to Barfleur on the Cotentin peninsula or to the Channel Islands, where he could be resupplied and reinforced away from the eyes of Saint-Pol, acting Governor of Normandy, who hated Warwick for his shabby treatment of his sister Jacquetta and was keeping Charles fully informed about Louis's machinations. Warwick refused, holding out for an interview.

In the face of Charles's fulminations and threats Louis came to the conclusion that, given the opportunity of at least destabilizing England for many years, the time was ripe for war with Burgundy. We are seriously hampered in our understanding of what followed because our best sources are reports citing Louis himself by the Milanese ambassador, which may have been disinformation and which in key places contradict a subtle piece of Warwickian propaganda called *The Manner and Guiding of the Earl of Warwick at Angers in July and August 1470.*

As with the *Chronicle of the Rebellion in Lincolnshire*, one must read between the lines of *The Manner and Guiding*. Selling Warwick's alliance with the House of Lancaster to the English people was a difficult task, to put it mildly, and the military alliance with France was not even mentioned. The restoration of Henry VI would bring with it the reversal of an enormous number of property transfers, which would hit Warwick's and Clarence's affinities particularly hard. They had to be reassured that Warwick would be the real power in the land and would take care of their interests. For this and other reasons *The Manner and Guiding* had to portray Warwick, not Louis, as the principal protagonist in the negotiations.

In battlefield analysis the sole unimpeachable witness is the terrain. So also in political analysis the only dependable contours are who had the power, and what they sought to gain. Louis XI had all the power in the negotiations between Warwick and Marguerite, and while he was flatteringly polite to the pieces on his chessboard they moved because he willed it. What followed was a French invasion of England with Warwick as its figurehead, and with Lancaster providing its political justification and supplementing his popular appeal. There was not the smallest chance they would co-exist peacefully once they seized power.

The alleged details of how these irreconcilable enemies were brought to sink their differences long enough to seize power are unimportant. Louis may have hoped Warwick would prevail in the ensuing power struggle to become a firm French ally against Burgundy, but he was too shrewd to count on it. What he wished to avoid was the immediate threat of an English invasion of Normandy in support of Burgundy, led by the dangerously competent Edward. If the English king could be permanently removed from the board, so much the better; but simply tying him down and exhausting his resources would be gain enough.

The agreement between Warwick and Marguerite was confirmed

on 25 July at Angers, the capital of Anjou. There was no formal treaty, but the immediate betrothal of 14-year-old Anne, Warwick's younger daughter, and 17-year-old Edward of Westminster, Marguerite's son, was supposed to guarantee an agreed course of action. Warwick was to go ahead with Jasper Tudor, the Courtenays and his brother-in-law the Earl of Oxford, who had lately joined them. He would defeat Edward, restore captive Henry VI to the throne and govern as his lieutenant until Marguerite and Edward joined him. What was to happen then remained to be seen.

Warwick believed his status would not change, but it is as near an absolute certainty as any historical 'what if' can be that fiery Marguerite intended to kill him once his usefulness was over. Ten years of metaphorically – if not literally – sticking pins in his effigy could not be abolished by a marriage forced on her by her manipulative cousin Louis. She had fought like a wolverine to defend her son's right, and the forlorn expedition to Northumberland Louis had embarked her on in 1462 must have been acid-etched in her memory. Neither she nor the Lancastrian exiles whose kin Warwick had slaughtered would tamely submit to putting their prince under his tutelage.

BLOODLESS VICTORY

PRIMED BY LOUIS DE LUXEMBOURG, DUKE CHARLES bombarded Edward with warnings that an invasion was imminent, but could offer no useful intelligence about where Warwick planned to land and in what strength. Edward had to assume it would be at places where disaffection ran deep and so had the south-east coast covered by Arundel and Howard, while Ferrers and the Yorkist Marchers could be expected to defeat any landing in Wales. That left the North, and at the end of July word came of another Middleham-based insurrection led by Lord FitzHugh.

Henry Percy reported he could not persuade the family affinity to turn out in defence of the Yorkist regime and with fatal naivety the king issued a commission of array to Montagu, who just happened to be in the North, but heard no more from him. We may fairly question whether the alleged insurrection was ever more than a ruse to permit Montagu to summon the levies with royal authority. The northern Neville affinity in fact played no significant part in the events that followed.

Edward decided he must go north himself. Before departing he ordered guns brought from Bristol and extra munitions, bows and arrows to reinforce the Tower, where he installed pregnant Queen Elizabeth and their daughters. By 5 August he was in Leicester and he reached York on the 14th. From there he marched directly towards Middleham but at Ripon, 24 miles north-west of York, word came that the alleged insurrection had collapsed and FitzHugh had fled to Scotland. Edward returned to York and on 10 September issued a general pardon.

Inexplicably he stayed there, even after writing a warning to Arundel and Howard that a landing in Kent was imminent. That was not where it arrived. To explain how Warwick achieved strategic surprise a background weather report is in order. The prevailing winds in the English Channel are westerlies at 15 knots, but strong easterlies can blow for days if a high-pressure system settles over England. The tail end of Atlantic hurricanes sweep in from June to November, with the historic peak of activity around 10 September. Contemporary ships were square-rigged hulks and carracks, slow and unhandy at the best of times and with poor performance into the wind. Under normal conditions a fleet sailing from Normandy would sail with the prevailing wind to south-eastern England.

Most accounts state that a Burgundian fleet 'blockaded' the Normandy ports, but that would have been impossible without the ship and signalling technology of a much later age. They would have been cruising well out into the Bay of the Seine, and when the prevailing wind was blowing could swoop on ships tacking laboriously

39. THE CHANNEL 1470

out of Harfleur or Honfleur. When Warwick secretly moved his base of operations to Valognes, his followers left their own ships as decoys in Honfleur and transferred overland to Barfleur and Saint-Vaast-La-Hougue on the Cotentin peninsula. There, sixty French ships and about 5,000 soldiers, mercenaries hired by Louis, awaited them. The Burgundians were left guarding the wrong ports.

Strong easterlies were blowing in late August/early September, making exit from the Cotentin ports difficult, and the departure of the invasion fleet may also have been delayed because the French admiral had orders to avoid combat. But another explanation is that Warwick's strategic deception plan required a wind shift. If the fleet's departure were observed, with westerlies blowing his enemies would expect him to sail to the south-east and deploy accordingly to intercept him. Counting on that, he intended go in the opposite direction.

It was a fortunate bonus when the tail end of a hurricane dispersed both the Burgundian fleet and the high-pressure system over England, restoring the prevailing wind. On 9 September the invasion fleet sailed into the Channel then spent four days tacking *into* the wind to make landings at Dartmouth and Plymouth, near the centres of rebel Courtenay power. Unlike Duke Charles, who unjustly sacked his admiral, Warwick understood ships and the sea.*

Edward learned of the landing in mid-September and set out for London. At Doncaster he stopped to give Montagu time to catch up, but when the new marquess was 5 miles away loyalist deserters brought warning of his hostile intent. Edward was comprehensively wrong-footed, and not just by Warwick's Trojan Horse. He had not expected Louis to tear up the Treaty of Péronne by attacking him with a major expedition. Nor had he anticipated that the long bereft affinities of the attainted West Country earls would flock to Warwick's banner.

He could have turned and fought Montagu, but chose not to risk

*On Louis's orders the French admiral promptly sailed away.

the attrition of his closest followers. He could also have issued commissions of array to the southern lords, but his summons to local people at Nottingham had such a poor response that he chose not to put anyone else in a similar situation. He disbanded his army and fled to Bishop's Lynn accompanied by Gloucester, Worcester, Rivers, Hastings, Lord Saye and their retinues. On the way, in an echo of Kings John's mishap in 1216, the royal party was nearly wiped out by the notoriously fast-rising tide in the Wash.

Tiptoft chose to remain behind but on 2 October the rest set sail for the Netherlands. The little fleet scattered after encountering hostile Hanseatic ships the next day. The Hansards pursued Edward's group while Gloucester and Rivers sailed south to Walcheren island. Edward's ships ran themselves aground next to Texel island. With the Hansards waiting for the tide to turn, the islanders helped Edward and his party ashore (see Map 40).

Five days later Lodewijk van Brugge, fellow knight of the Golden Fleece and lord of Gruuthuse, welcomed them to his mansion at Alkmaar. Gruuthuse had been in London on several occasions and regarded the king as a friend. He gave the refugees clothes and money, and on 10 October sent letters from Edward to Duke Charles and to Edward's sister Duchess Margaret. On 11 October he rode with them to his palace in The Hague, where they were reunited with Gloucester and Rivers. We shall return to them in the following chapter.

Back in England the Yorkist regime was effortlessly supplanted, even though the only nobles to sail with Warwick had been Clarence, Oxford and Jasper Tudor, the attainted Earl of Pembroke. Jasper peeled off to rally his own people in Pembroke and the principality, but Clarence and Oxford stayed with Warwick. They were met at Bristol but accompanied no further by Shrewsbury and Stanley. The rest of the nobility stood down: the only, – failed – attempt to organize resistance was at Salisbury by Thomas St Leger, lover of Edward's older sister Anne, Duchess of Exeter.

Although Warwick was determined to prevent the outrages that commonly accompany a mercenary army and hanged offenders, his own people stained his cause. The commons of Kent erupted when they learned of his landing and marched on London, where they looted the premises of Dutch merchants and indulged in drunken debauchery. The authorities placed guns to cover the bridge and the gates, and volunteers swelled the ranks of the militia; but then recently pardoned Geoffrey Gates released imprisoned Lancastrians and hundreds of criminals from the city's jails, and blood ran in the streets.

Elizabeth and her daughters moved to sanctuary at Westminster Abbey before the Tower surrendered to Gates on 3 October.* On the 5th Archbishop Neville arrived to install a new garrison and found King Henry living in monkish squalor. Two days later, after making a triumphal entrance into London, Warwick led Henry in procession to the Bishop of London's palace. On the 13th he held the king's train in another procession to St Paul's, where he was crowned to mark the 'Readeption' of his reign before moving to the palace of Westminster.

The arcane term 'Readeption', meaning 'recovery', was proposed by Dr John Fortescue, Marguerite's closest advisor, who along with Dr John Morton had accompanied Warwick since Angers. Along with Dr Ralph Mackerell they became the king's councillors. All three had been repeatedly pardoned by Edward, Mackerell as recently as November 1469, but they were convinced of the legitimacy of the House of Lancaster to the depths of their learned souls.

Henry was still capable of independent action and imposed a tone of forgiveness on the new regime. An early edict was that sanctuary should not be violated, protecting not only Elizabeth but also Edward's chief office holders, the Bishops of Ely, Bath and Rochester, who had taken refuge in St Martin's Le Grand, near St Paul's. It was probably also at Henry's insistence that the Duke of Norfolk, the Bourchiers (the Archbishop of Canterbury, the Earl of

---

*Among others, Gates released Thomas Malory, who died the following March, aged about 55. *Le Morte d'Arthur* was published by Caxton in 1485.

Essex and Lord Cromwell), the Earl of Wiltshire, Lord Mountjoy and even Richard Woodville were released from arrest, pardoned, and their rights regranted.

Richard Tunstall, the king's faithful companion after Hexham and who had helped to hold Harlech for him for so long, was rewarded with the influential and profitable offices of Royal Chamberlain and Master of the Mints in England and Calais. Another sly flicker of independence may have been the special favour shown to the Earl of Oxford, who had contributed little to the campaign but was the only non-renegade in the triumvirate that liberated the king. Oxford carried the sword of state before him at the coronation and was made steward of the royal household.

It was Warwick, however, who also made Oxford Constable of England, so that he should have the pleasure of presiding over the trial and execution of John Tiptoft, Earl of Worcester, who had done the same to Oxford's father and older brother.* Although it was a popular act of public vengeance, there may have been another reason to make an example of Tiptoft. His death released the estates he had held from his late wife and Warwick's sister Cecily, dowager Duchess of Warwick, while by matrilineal succession Montagu's young son George, Duke of Bedford, was heir to half of Tiptoft's own family estate.

On 15 October Warwick summoned Parliament, with none excluded save the lords who had accompanied Edward into exile and the Stafford Earl of Wiltshire. Intriguingly, it was by this summons that John Howard was officially recognized as Baron Howard. This was supposed to reassure loyal servants of the deposed regime that, despite the execution of Tiptoft, they need not fear for their lives. It did not reassure those in sanctuary, who remained there.

The new regime was faced with the impossible task of restoring forfeited Lancastrian estates without creating a pool of discontent among those dispossessed. Fortescue, Morton and Mackerell

---

*Unusual to the last, Tiptoft instructed the executioner to behead him with three strokes to honour the Trinity.

performed prodigies of legal adjustment, and Fortescue had set out a plan of action for government to be conducted through a permanent Council that must approve all the king's decrees. The details need not concern us because the regime never had time to evolve.

There were two reasons for this. The first was that Edward would certainly be back, and nobody could put any faith in a settlement until one or other of the parties was dead and buried. The other was that Marguerite stubbornly refused to cross the Channel with her son and his new wife. At first the excuse was that papal dispensation for the marriage was delayed, which is deeply unconvincing. The degree of consanguinity between Anne and Edward was very tenuous indeed, and dispensation may not even have been necessary. Furthermore, although Louis could have obtained it in a heartbeat, it was not forthcoming until December 1470.

Did Marguerite insist on it to delay their departure, or was it yet another strand to the Universal Spider's web? Probably both: even after the marriage was formalized Marguerite and Prince Edward did not cross the Channel for another four months, and it stretches credulity to believe Louis could not have forced them to travel sooner. He can have been in no doubt about Marguerite's cold loathing for Warwick, and her unwillingness to lend him legitimacy coincided with his desire to give Warwick as much time as possible to secure his hold on power. Failing that Louis's aim, as always, was to keep England in turmoil.

In late October Jasper Tudor, the restored Earl of Pembroke, arrived in London with his 14-year-old nephew Henry, Earl of Richmond, whom he had taken from William Herbert's widow. Clarence held extensive property pertaining to the Richmond earldom and Jasper's request that his nephew should have it back could not be granted. Although Clarence's possession was only confirmed for his lifetime, when Jasper returned to Wales with his nephew in mid-November he was justifiably resentful. So was Henry Stafford, uncle to his namesake the young Duke of Buckingham and second husband of Margaret Beaufort, Henry Tudor's mother.

Clarence did lose all his duchy of Lancaster estates, notably Tutbury, which reverted to Marguerite. He was awarded the duchy of York, but it was encumbered by his mother's dower and Warwick was in no hurry to surrender the revenue of any part of what had been Edward's royal domain. As for compensation elsewhere, none was available because previously attainted estates were returned to Lancastrians – thus the exiles William, Viscount Beaumont, and Edmund, Baron Roos, recovered lands Edward had awarded to his henchman Hastings.

Although the threat to his Richmond estates was averted, Clarence would lose more if John Butler, Earl of Ormond in Ireland, were restored to the English title and lands of his father's earldom of Wiltshire.* Whichever way he looked, the man who had sniffed at his brother's generous endowment could see only a future in which, at best, he would be hard pressed to sustain the income required of a duke. More ominously, his permanent removal from the scene would obviously resolve quite a large number of problems for his father-in-law.

A Spanish aphorism about government and opposition translates as 'it is another matter with guitar in hand'. Like many another charismatic narcissist swept to power on a carefully orchestrated wave of popular euphoria, Warwick had not thought through what tune he would play once he was standing in the spotlight, with the audience eagerly awaiting the magical performance he had led them to expect. He had promised peace and an end to burdensome taxation and constraints on trade. He could deliver none of these, and his secret military undertaking with Louis obliged him to strum increasingly unpopular chords.

There is no record of Warwick sending back the French mercenaries who marched with him to London, and he almost certainly kept them to act as his regime guard. They must also have been intended to form the bulk of the 8,000-man army he had agreed

*It did not happen because Ormond wished nothing to do with a regime dominated by Warwick.

to lead against Burgundy, as there was no other way he could have made good on the promise. Warwick could only make war if France paid for it, and this we know Louis did not do – directly. But what if the mercenaries were his subsidy? If so, they would continue to prop up Warwick only as long as he kept faith with their paymaster.

One could continue indefinitely reviewing the number and vigour of the worms that erupted from the can Warwick opened by seizing power as he did. One that deserves mention was the murder of Warwick's friend and retainer Robert Harcourt, a Garter knight who had been among those attending the wedding of Clarence and Isabel. In 1448, in a brawl with the Staffords of Grafton, he had killed Richard Stafford. In November 1470 Stafford's bastard half-brother took his revenge by ambushing Harcourt in London, and Warwick could do nothing because the head of the Staffords of Grafton was also his retainer and a local MP.

Chaos reigned. Henry VI was as unconvincing as ever and the monarchy's authority was at an all-time low, while Marguerite and her son, the real strength of the House of Lancaster, were waiting in the wings for Warwick to stumble. This he was guaranteed to do, because he had been put in power by Louis XI to deliver an active military alliance against Burgundy, which ran counter to the deeply ingrained prejudices of the English people.

Power in England was a three-legged stool resting on the aristocracy, the Church and the merchant class. The monarchy was supposed to be the seat that held it all together, but had ceased to do so because of what was basically gang warfare among the Houses of Lancaster, York and Neville. Nations can endure most things but not prolonged uncertainty, and there was a general desire for the turmoil to end, one way or another.

THE ARRIVAL

HAVING INVESTED SO HEAVILY IN THE ALLIANCE WITH Burgundy, and after being overthrown by their common enemy, Edward had the reasonable expectation of rapid and immediate support from Duke Charles. It was not forthcoming. Not only the duke but also his wife Margaret, Edward's sister, proved reluctant to meet him, and for several months Gruuthuse alone stood between him and abject penury. Edward's anguish was made worse when he learned that Elizabeth had given birth to the long-awaited male heir in Westminster Abbey on 2 November.

Not far from the forefront of Charles's megalomaniac mind would have been the thought that it was 'one down and one to go' until he could add England to his heterogeneous empire. Duchess Margaret's motives were more rational – like their malignant mother, she yearned to see her whole-blood brother Clarence replace the cuckoo Edward on the throne. If that was no longer possible, her main concern was to save Clarence from the consequences of his treachery.

A third strand was the Lancastrian exiles, Charles's pensioners. The most prominent were the younger brothers of Charles's lost love Henry Beaufort. Edmund, Duke of Somerset, and John, Marquess of Dorset, served with Charles against Louis XI and had his ear. A third pensioner was Edward's erratic brother-in-law Henry Holland, the dispossessed and cuckolded Duke of Exeter, who appears to have been kept at arm's length.

The Beauforts had remained in contact with Marguerite's humble court in Bar and with Jasper Tudor in Brittany and France during the long years of exile. How closely and to what purpose we can only guess, but the traffic of messengers among the exiles and with Lancastrian sympathisers in England multiplied after the two great usurpers came to blows.

In early October 1471, at about the time the Yorkists were reunited at The Hague, Charles sent Commynes on a mission to Calais. The message he bore was that Charles regarded the Anglo–Burgundian treaty as between the kingdom of England and the

40. EDWARD'S ITINERARY 1470–1

duchy of Burgundy, and that he would accept whomever the English wanted as their king. This was also the view of the Company of the Staple, appalled at the prospect of a war with Burgundy.

Commynes found the garrison, which had already raided neighbouring Burgundian territory, wearing Warwick's livery. Duras, appointed governor by Edward, must by now have gone to join him at The Hague because Commynes dealt with Lord Wenlock. Wenlock gave evasive replies and Commynes reported that he had requested several hundred additional Warwick retainers to reinforce the garrison, and was openly preparing for war.

Charles ordered a crash programme of coastal fortifications – a new gatehouse built at Veere on Walcheren island was called 'de Warwijkse poort', making it clear what threat they were built to counter. Even so, Charles permitted reality to intrude on his dynastic delusion only after Louis XI declared war on 3 December. The king denounced the Treaty of Péronne, declared all Charles's French lands forfeit to the crown and mobilized the *ordonnances* against Picardy.

Louis should not have moved until his pieces were in place. It appears to have been a bad-tempered response to Charles's increasingly strident protests about the king's evident breach of the Treaty of Péronne by sponsoring Warwick, and it gave Charles time to assemble an army of mercenaries in Picardy. Louis's initiative was also diplomatically rash, as it put him in the wrong and also placed intolerable pressure on Warwick to deliver on his promise of armed support before he was in a position to do so.

In mid-December Charles requested his allies of the Hanseatic League to cease trading with France and England, to clear the way for his own fleet to attack any ship sailing to and from England. The aim was to prevent Warwick reinforcing Calais in order to attack the duke's army in Picardy from behind, but it also gave Marguerite another excuse to ignore Warwick's pleas to join him.

On 26 December Edward's party moved to Gruuthuse's castle at Oostcamp, near Bruges, and on 31 December he was summoned to meet Charles's mother Isabella, possibly accompanied by his sister Margaret, at Aire-sur-la-Lys in Artois, 35 miles south-east of Calais. Isabella informed Edward that her son, who was 25 miles south-west of Aire at Hesdin, directing his army in Picardy, had granted him a monthly pension of 500 *écus* [£53,000]. Charles himself came to Aire between 2 and 4 January, but what they discussed is unrecorded.

On 6 January St Quentin, one of the main Somme valley towns in dispute, declared for France. On 7 January Edward was at Saint-Pol with Louis de Luxembourg, his uncle by marriage and Constable of France. They were joined by Charles until the 9th, and although their talks are also unrecorded it probably involved an intricate negotiation whereby Luxembourg would not find himself obliged to come off the fence. Edward came away with the impression that Louis XI was disappointed with Warwick, and was not wedded to the new English regime.

Edward also wrote to Duke Frañsez asking for support. Whether related to this request or not, in January the Breton fleet under Frañsez's illegitimate brother intercepted a convoy carrying a French commercial delegation, returning from an attempt to win the support of the English merchants for the Anglo–French treaty. Louis XI was later obliged to pay 30,000 *livres* [over £7 million] to compensate Jean de Beaune, the cloth merchant who financed the expedition, for the loss of the cargo and the death of his son at the hands of the Bretons.

While Edward was at Saint-Pol, Duchess Margaret summoned her younger brother Richard to Lille, and twelve days later loaned him 6,000 gold florins [£11.4 million], advanced by five Dutch cities on her surety, with Charles's tacit approval, to be repaid in 1472 and 1474. Charles arranged it this way to disclaim responsibility to his Lancastrian pensioners, who had begged him to do nothing that might assist Edward to return to England.

Margaret's munificence was timely. On 19 January, after the two brothers returned to Bruges, Rivers had difficulty hiring ships at

Damme, a port downriver from Bruges, for lack of funds. Charles's pension took the form of credit and could not be spent without official approval. Not so Margaret's loan, but Edward and Richard kept secret the amount of cash at their disposal, both at her request and for fear of theft or piracy.

The exiles were joined by a stream of knights and esquires from England and two ships' captains who served at their own expense throughout the ensuing campaign. Edward also received at least £500 [£320,000] sent secretly by several of the Calais Staplers after Warwick signed a ten-year truce and mercantile alliance with France on 16 February. Warwick, Archbishop Neville, Clarence, Langstrother and the Earl of Kent signed for England.

In mid-February Charles did two things that showed his hand. He sent his Lancastrian pensioners to England, and he cut off Edward's pension, a signal that he wanted him, too, gone. Charles did not believe Edward would succeed, but at the very least he would distract Warwick from joining Louis, while the optimum result from his point of view would be if Edward, his brothers, Warwick, Henry VI and his son were all killed in a three-way civil war.

On 19 February Edward walked through cheering crowds from Bruges to Damme, thence by boat to Flushing on Walcheren island, where his invasion fleet was assembling. By 2 March Edward, Gloucester, Rivers, Hastings and Duras with about 2,000 troops, mainly English men-at-arms but including 500 hired Flemish hand-gunners, were embarked on thirty-six transports with an escort of Hanseatic warships. Edward had promised the Hansards great rewards once he recovered the throne, but the warships were hired by Charles. Their orders were to escort Edward to England and to remain at his disposal for fifteen days after he landed.

The flagship was the *Anthony*, property of the lord of Veere, Gruuthuse's father-in-law. Later Veere was to receive English trading privileges, and the captain an annuity of £20 [£12,720], but the most revealing reward was a munificent grant to the *Anthony*'s 'lodesman' (navigator), whose skills included identifying sediment brought up by soundings with a tallow-coated lead weight, essential for inshore navigation. He was Robert Michelson and his home port was Hull, fairly conclusive evidence that Edward always intended to land in the Humber estuary.

Our principal source for the following campaign, *The History of the Arrival of Edward IV in England and the Final Recovery of His Kingdoms from Henry VI*, was written immediately after the campaign by one of Edward's servants. As with Edward's propaganda about the Lincolnshire rebellion and Warwick's *The Manner and Guiding*, the *Arrival* adheres so closely to independently verifiable facts that the omissions acquire heightened significance.

The key omitted fact is that Edward had been in in correspondence with Henry Percy, Earl of Northumberland, since arriving at The Hague, and his invasion strategy was based on the earl's assurance that the Percy affinity hated Warwick more than they hated him. Edward planned to take a leaf out of Warwick's book and land where he was least expected.

After nine days of prevailing westerlies, the wind turned and Edward's fleet set out from Flushing on 11 March and made a fast passage to arrive at Cromer, on the north-east Norfolk coast, the next day. Here, the *Arrival* says, the landing party found there was no local support because the Dukes of Norfolk and Suffolk, the Bourchiers, the Earl of Wiltshire, Lord Mountjoy and Henry Stafford had been placed in the Tower and others forced to post surety. However, Edward would have known this before he sailed.

Also allegedly, Cardinal Bourchier had smuggled out a letter warning Edward that Oxford, based at Castle Hedingham in Suffolk, and Beaumont, from his east Midlands estates, controlled East Anglia. Again, Edward would have known this. The landing at Cromer was really a feint designed to draw Oxford and Beaumont to Norfolk, which it did. Edward lied about it because, like all good generals, he did not want to reveal the tricks of his trade.

On the run from Cromer to the Humber the fleet ran into a violent storm that sank one of the horse transports and scattered

41. BARNET CAMPAIGN 1471

© Hugh Bicheno

CHRONOLOGY OF THE 1471
BARNET CAMPAIGN

14–15 March	Edward lands at Ravenspur, Rivers at Paull. Local resistance under 'Martin de la Mare' melts away. Hull hostile, grudging acceptance by Percy affinity.
16–17 March	Edward marches through Beverley to York.
18 March	Edward enters York with retinue, persuades authorities to admit his army.
19 March	Departs York, overnight at Tadcaster. Exeter, Oxford and Beaumont at Bishop's Lynn.
20 March	Marches to his manor of Wakefield and Sandal Castle. Recruitment disappointing. Montagu afraid to emerge from Pontefract Castle.
23 March	Edward at Doncaster. First significant addition to his army led by William Sutton. Montagu leaves Pontefract, marches south behind and parallel to Edward.
25–26 March	Edward at Nottingham, joined by William Parr and James Harrington with 600 men. Marches towards Newark where Exeter, Oxford and Beaumont have arrived from East Anglia. They retreat north to join forces with Montagu.
28 March	Edward at Leicester, joined by William Stanley with 300 men and William Noreys leading Hastings's affinity of about 3,000.
29 March	Edward arrives at Coventry, where Warwick refuses to emerge.
1–2 April	Edward marches through Warwickshire.
3 April	Edward meets Clarence at Banbury, they reconcile and march together to Coventry.
4 April	Rearguard at Leicester faces down Montagu, Exeter, Oxford and Beaumont. Howard announces for Edward in Suffolk. Louis XI and Duke Charles sign truce.
5–7 April	Edward departs for London, from Daventry sends letters to London, as does Warwick from Coventry.

8 April	Palm Sunday. Archbishop Neville parades Henry VI through London. Somerset, Dorset and Devon depart for the West Country.
9 April	City authorities announce they will admit Edward's army.
10 April	Edward at St Albans receives letter from Archbishop Neville begging for grace.
11 April	Yorkists seize the Tower, release imprisoned lords. Elizabeth, her children and the Bishops of Ely, Bath and Rochester emerge from sanctuary.
12 April	Edward enters London, imprisons Lancastrian lords.
13 April	Good Friday. Warwick at St Albans.
14 April	Edward puts Elizabeth, their children and his mother in the Tower before setting out to intercept Warwick.
15 April	Easter Sunday. BATTLE OF BARNET.

the rest. Rivers eventually landed at Paull, a village near Hull, and Gloucester 8 miles further east; but Edward landed where he always intended, at Ravenspur, a village on the northern tip of the Humber estuary now lost to erosion. Why Ravenspur? Because there, in 1399, the future Henry IV landed from exile and announced he had come to reclaim his duchy of Lancaster, illegally taken from him by Richard II.

So also Edward, who proclaimed he had come to recover his duchy of York, professed loyalty to Henry VI and the Prince of Wales, and said that Warwick had forced him to claim the throne. One has to admire the breath-taking chutzpah. Edward also had two more convincing arguments – a war chest bulging with gold coins and a letter from Henry Percy to his affinity instructing them to let Edward pass. A combination of the two saw him through the challenge of several thousand local levies led by one Martin de la Mare.

Rivers reported that Hull was not well disposed and Edward marched to Beverley, and then through the Percy receivership of Leconfield to York. The civic authorities let him in with a few attendants and he rode into the city sporting the Prince of Wales's ostrich feather badge and crying out 'Long live King Henry'. After that gold coins worked their usual magic and the army marched in the next day.

Montagu, at Pontefract Castle, was wrong-footed. His experience with 'Robin of Holderness' in 1469 had given him a healthy respect for the fighting power of the Percy affinity, which he believed had rallied to Edward, and he needed strong reinforcement from the Neville affinity. He waited in vain because Scrope of Bolton never wished to fight against Edward, FitzHugh's feisty Neville wife could not, this time, goad him into action, and John Conyers had suffered irreparable personal loss at Edgcote.

Edward departed York on 19 March and marched down the Great North Road (Map 4) to begin a campaign that bears comparison with the greatest in history. For the first two weeks he had little more support than the men he brought with him and found no popular enthusiasm for his cause. The *Arrival* frankly admits that 'right few or almost none' welcomed him, and recruitment was disappointing even in ancestral Yorkist manors.

The first commented addition to his army was at Doncaster on the 23rd, where he was joined by 160 men-at-arms led by William, son of the 71-year-old West Midlands magnate John Sutton, Baron Dudley, who had fought and nearly died for Lancaster at Blore Heath in 1459.* Bypassed, Montagu emerged from Pontefract and shadowed Edward's army from a position well to the east of his line of march.

Meanwhile Exeter, Oxford and Beaumont marched out of East Anglia to confront Edward at Newark, only to find that he had left the Great North Road to gain the Western Spur at Nottingham, where 600 Lancashire men under William Parr, lord of Kendal, and James Harrington joined him. Edward then made a feint towards

---

*William Sutton's subsequent career in the Church was meteoric. Immediately made canon and then dean of the Chapel Royal at Windsor, Edward made him Bishop of Durham in 1476.

Newark and his enemies retreated to join forces with Montagu, putting themselves several days' march behind.

On 28 March Edward arrived at Leicester where he was joined by 300 men led by William Stanley, a signal that his weathervane brother Lord Stanley had deserted Warwick. The game-changer was the arrival of Hastings's east Midlands affinity, some 3,000 men led by William Noreys. Noreys had fought against Edward at Towton but was reconciled and made Sheriff of Buckinghamshire and Oxfordshire, and he also brought men of his own.

Numbers tell less than half the story, however. Even though Edward cannot have had more than 7,000 men by now, he had recovered his aura as a winner blessed by Lady Luck, and as an inspiring and dynamic military commander. Recruitment would have picked up markedly after Leicester and on 29 March Edward arrived at Coventry, where Warwick had shut himself up with 6–7,000 men,

Edward challenged him to personal combat but Warwick refused to emerge. He was waiting for Montagu and the others to close up behind Edward, but they were confronted by a strong rearguard left by Edward at Leicester, probably Hastings's men. It follows that Edward must have been posturing outside Coventry with considerably less men than Warwick had inside. It was a measure of Edward's reputation that Warwick preferred to be seen to play the coward than to risk a sortie.

The first three weeks of the campaign had seen a contrast between Edward's aggressive, direct English way of war and the continental style favoured by Warwick – of manoeuvre and of never risking battle unless the odds were stacked in your favour. The great heavyweight champion Jack Dempsey once defined the difference perfectly: 'All the time he's boxing, he's thinking, and all the time he was thinking, I was hitting him'.

EPIC OF ARMS

WHEN EDWARD LEFT COVENTRY AND MARCHED through Warwickshire on 2 April, it was a non-destructive *chevauchée* to show that the earl could not protect the heart of his Midlands power, whose military-age men were closed up with him in Coventry. But it was also a move dictated by the approach of Clarence from the West Country with about 4,000 men. He had sent messages to his father-in-law urging him to avoid combat until he arrived.

In fact Clarence had been intending to turn his coat again ever since Margaret lent Edward and Richard the money to return to England. She and their mother had been urging him to take stock of his precarious situation since Louis XI brokered the alliance between Warwick and Marguerite at Angers. He did, but needed their assurance that Edward would not punish his treachery and would permit him to claim his wife's Neville inheritance. No doubt Margaret required a solemn undertaking from Edward as the precondition for the loan.

It cannot be coincidence that Edward met him at Banbury, 6 miles from Edgcote, where Clarence's treachery had cost him Herbert and his Welsh supporters. That he took his army with him indicates how little faith he put in Margaret's assurances that her favourite brother would, for once, keep his word. There was no chance Clarence would face Edward in battle and he duly grovelled.

Edward embraced him, but kept him by his side for the rest of the campaign and dispersed his men among the rest of the army.

We should spare a thought for Clarence's followers. His retainers would be resigned to sharing their lord's fortunes, but for the levies, recruited under commissions of array issued by Warwick in the name of Henry VI, profound relief after the royal brothers embraced at Banbury would have been followed by bewilderment. Many would have considered their terms of service fulfilled and returned to their homes in Somerset, Wiltshire and Gloucestershire.

Clarence brought more than dubiously dependable men with him. He had been Warwick's liaison with John Talbot, Earl of Shrewsbury, and was able to assure Edward that Talbot had no intention of getting involved in the latest round of fighting. William of Worcester wrote that Shrewsbury was 'more devoted to literature and the muses than to politics and arms', and he may not have been physically robust – he was only 24 years old when he died in 1473.

On 4 April the reunited brothers were back before the walls of Coventry, where Clarence attempted to persuade Warwick to surrender. The Kingmaker's rage can readily be imagined. Clarence's defection also meant that Warwick's allied lords chose not to fight Edward's rearguard at Leicester. Meanwhile Lord Howard declared for Edward in Suffolk. Oxford and Beaumont had drawn away all those ready to fight for Lancaster and, like Hastings's affinity in the east Midlands, the East Anglian Yorkists were now free to show their colours.

News that Louis XI and Duke Charles had agreed a truce on 4 April would have taken time to percolate, and it must have been a bitter blow to Warwick. He had spent much of his political capital to deliver the Anglo–French treaty and to prepare for a war that might see him become lord of Holland and Zeeland, all now for nothing. We may fairly doubt Louis ever intended to deliver on his promise, but now whatever chance there had been was gone.*

---

*Louis must also have recalled the mercenaries he had lent Warwick at this time, in accordance with the terms of the truce.

Edward recalled Hastings's men and on 5 April set out for London. The fastest route was along Watling Street, but he detoured through Daventry and Northampton, perhaps to punish them for supporting the 1469 rebellion. From Daventry on 7 April he sent a letter to the mayor and aldermen of London demanding they welcome him as their king. The same day Warwick also wrote to the authorities and to his brother Archbishop Neville, ordering them to hold the city long enough for him to close up behind Edward.

A few days earlier Mayor Stockton had developed a diplomatic illness and left Alderman Thomas Cooke in charge. There was probably no more fanatical Lancastrian in all England. Cooke had been cruelly victimized by Edward and Elizabeth, and his hopes for reparation rested entirely with Warwick's regime. However, he was no fool, and once Edward's and Warwick's letters arrived he loaded his worldly goods and sailed to France.

On 8 April, Palm Sunday, Archbishop Neville summoned all Lancastrian men-at-arms to assemble at St Paul's in harness but only 600–700 responded. He rode holding Henry VI's hand from St Paul's through London, but it was a dismal parade. The king himself was shabbily dressed and only one secular lord, 70-year-old Ralph Boteler, Baron Sudeley, led the way, holding the king's sword. As the *Great Chronicle of London* elegantly put it, the spectacle 'pleased the citizens as a fire painted on the wall warmed the old woman'.

Notably not taking part in the parade were the Beaufort brothers. The restored Duke of Somerset, his brother the Marquess of Dorset and John Courtenay, Earl of Devon, departed together for the West Country on 8 April to meet Marguerite, who was expected to cross the Channel soon. They were armed with the king's appointment of Prince Edward, his son, as Lieutenant of England in replacement of Warwick.

On 9 April the city fathers sent Edward a reply saying they would welcome him, and on the 10th Archbishop Neville sent him a letter begging for grace. On the 11th Yorkist supporters peacefully took over the Tower, freeing the Duke of Suffolk, the Bourchiers, the Earl of Wiltshire, Baron Mountjoy and Henry Stafford. Elizabeth and her children remained at Westminster Abbey, but the Bishops of Ely, Bath and Rochester, Edward's office holders, emerged blinking from sanctuary at St Martin's Le Grand.

On 12 April Edward marched his army into the city, according to the *Great Chronicle* led by 'black and smoky sort of Flemish gunners'. He was greeted by Stockton and all those dignitaries who had not committed themselves too publicly to the Readeption. Sudeley, Archbishop Neville and the Lancastrian Bishops of Lichfield/ Coventry and Lincoln/Dorchester were sent to occupy the cells in the Tower so recently vacated by the Yorkist lords, but there was no purge of Lancastrian supporters. Even the mob prudently did not celebrate the occasion in the traditional manner.

Edward first gave thanks at St Paul's, and then went to the Bishop of London's palace to take possession of Henry VI. In a letter to her mother-in-law, Duchess Margaret said they shook hands and Henry greeted Edward with the words 'My cousin of York, you are very welcome. I know that in your hands my life will not be in danger'. It was a poignant remark, which also suggests he felt no such security with Warwick. He also went back to the Tower, perhaps to the old quarters from which he had been unwillingly plucked nineteen months earlier.

Finally Edward was free to be reunited with his family at the Abbey, and to hold his 5-month-old namesake son for the first time. There was little time to do more before he sent them, too, to the Tower – along with his mother. Whether Duchess Cecily was sent there for safekeeping or to make sure she did not try to deal herself a hand in the fluid situation we cannot know. Edward's meeting with his mother, no doubt accompanied by his brother Clarence, and her reaction to being forced to associate with Elizabeth are unfortunately not recorded, but no doubt all involved exercised a great deal of tight-lipped self-restraint.

Edward could spend no time on niceties because on Good Friday

Warwick arrived at St Albans with a large artillery train and an army that outnumbered his own. Edward was joined by contingents from the south-east led by Lord Saye and Humphrey Bourchier, Thomas FitzAlan and Anthony Grey, the heirs of Lord Berners and the Earls of Arundel and Kent. Lord Howard may also have arrived with men from Suffolk and Essex. The Duke of Norfolk, who had escaped from the Tower earlier, was still gathering his affinity.

Even allowing for wastage to ale and bawdy houses, and others who thought entering London was 'job done' and went home, the *Arrival* was propaganda and certainly understated Edward's numbers (9,000) while overstating Warwick's (20,000). More believable estimates emerge if we increase and decrease them proportionally, to give us 12,000 (the figure given in Duchess Margaret's previously cited letter) versus 15,000.

One can only guess where the others fought, but riding with Edward were Clarence, Duras and the Woodville brothers Anthony, Earl Rivers, and Edward, whom Anthony permitted to use his subsidiary title of Lord Scales. Richard of Gloucester led the vanguard with Lord Ferrers and William Blount, Lord Mountjoy's heir, and Hastings the rearguard with Henry Tudor's stepfather Henry Stafford, and another Humphrey Bourchier, Lord Cromwell.* Miserable Henry VI was with the baggage train – for what reason is hard to fathom.

Edward could expect Warwick to set up behind his artillery and wait to be attacked – it was what he had done at the Second Battle of St Albans, and what he had intended to do during the Edgcote campaign. The king might have contemplated marching around him, but by the time the foreriders of the two armies made contact his room for manoeuvre was severely limited. According to a very useful contemporary account by the well-connected Gerhard von Wesel, one of the Cologne Hansards' London representatives (my italics):

---

*Lord Cromwell was the son and Lord Berners the brother of Henry Bourchier, Earl of Essex.

42. BATTLE OF BARNET
15 April 1471

St Albans Road

Hatfield Road

WOODS

Deadman's Bottom

Warwick

Chantry ✠

Oxford   Montagu   Exeter

Richard

Edward

Hastings   Monken Mead Brook

Monument →

Warwick

Traditional

Oxford   Montagu

Ancient hedge

Exeter

Modern A.1061

Hadley Green

✠ Hadley church

Beech Hill →

Hadley Common

Richard

Edward

Hastings

N

Barnet church ✠

London →

Contours @ 15 feet intervals

© Hugh Bicheno

0   1/4   1/2

mile

On Easter Eve around seven o'clock in the evening, as King Edward marched away from here and came into the vicinity of Hornsey Park, six miles from London, Warwick's vanguard encountered him and they had a skirmish thereabouts and they chased each other in the dark as far as a village called Barnet, ten miles from London. Warwick and his lords and companions who had been in Coventry pitched their battle *a mile beyond the said village, just beside the highway to St Albans* on a broad green plot, and King Edward's people, not really knowing in the night where the opposing parties were, also in the night rode onto the same plot and set up their camp on the other side of the aforesaid highway, *just opposite Warwick, in a hollow and marsh*.

Even without the support of Wesel's report, topography argues that the northern site in Map 42, across the St Albans and Hatfield (Great North) Roads, was the logical place for Warwick to deploy. The traditional location further south was unconvincing even before archaeologists failed to find any battle debris at the site. The clinching argument is that Warwick's guns fired over the heads of Edward's troops through the night. They were, therefore, either in the featureless hollow south-east of Hadley, or else marched along the Beech Hill road before descending into the Monken Mead valley and forming up on the far side of the brook, as described by Wesel. There is no question which was the more likely.

Thanks to the earlier success of his fore-riders Edward knew where the enemy was deployed, while Warwick did not. He held nothing in reserve and in thick mist at dawn on Easter Sunday he launched his entire force in an oblique attack. The tactic, later made famous by Frederick the Great, involves crumpling the opposing line progressively from one flank. Ironically Edward learned the technique at Northampton, his first battle, where Warwick's uncle the veteran William Neville, Lord Fauconberg, employed it.

An oblique attack provides a unifying explanation for the known features of the battle. Warwick's guns were ineffective, which they would not have been had Edward made a frontal assault. Gloucester, on Edward's right, overlapped and drove in Warwick's left, under Exeter, and the main battle under Montagu could only wheel to face the oblique attack and to maintain contact with the retreating men. Warwick would have led the reserve to reinforce his left, which stabilized the fighting line roughly along the Hatfield (Great North) Road. The effect was to turn the line of battle through 45 degrees.

On Warwick's right Oxford and Beaumont did more than simply conform to Montagu's redeployment. They charged through their gun line to attack Hastings's approaching battle, which they out-flanked and drove back. It was probably here that Lord Cromwell was killed and Henry Stafford mortally wounded. If Oxford and Beaumont had managed to keep their men in hand they might have rolled up the outnumbered Yorkists, but they could not. The mist prevented the men from seeing that their success was not matched further north and they pursued Hastings's fleeing men as far as Barnet, where they found the Yorkist baggage train and fell to looting. They also found Henry VI, who was led away along the St Albans Road.

As so often in the Wars of the Roses, the outcome of the brutal struggle along the Great North Road was decided by a sudden collapse of morale. Oxford and Beaumont managed to rally about 800 men and marched back from Barnet. Prevented by the mist from seeing how far the battle lines had wheeled, they attacked what they believed was the rear of the Yorkist line. Unfortunately it was the flank of Montagu's battle, which had been holding its own against Edward's. The confusion was compounded by the similarity between the star with streams (rays) livery worn by Oxford's men and Edward's sun with streams.

Cries of 'treason' rippled through Warwick's army and it abruptly dissolved in flight. Local historian Brian Warren has identified the place where a chantry for the dead was built after the battle, which in our reconstruction would correspond to the place where Montagu and such of his men who did not flee made a last stand and were killed. Warwick, at the northern end of the line, rode away but was caught in the woods, killed and stripped of his armour. Severely wounded Exeter was also stripped and lay naked on the battlefield all day until his servants found him and bore him to sanctuary at Westminster Abbey.

Oxford, Beaumont and Oxford's brothers George and Richard Vere fled north, but the group escorting Henry VI abandoned him and he was recaptured and taken back to the Tower. Ten thousand arrows were said to have littered the field and about 3,000 men lay dead. A 3:1 ratio gives us a figure of 9,000 wounded for a staggering overall casualty rate. Wesel again:

> Those who went out with good horses and sound bodies brought home sorry nags and bandaged faces without noses etc. and wounded bodies, God have mercy on the miserable spectacle, but all men say that there was never in a hundred years a fiercer battle in England than this last Easter day as is aforewritten, may God henceforth grant us His eternal peace.

As well as Lord Cromwell and Henry Stafford, among the Yorkists Lord Berners's heir (the other Humphrey Bourchier), Lord Saye and William Blount were killed, while Richard of Gloucester and Earl Rivers were wounded, Rivers severely. Once again Edward, who would have been in the thick of the fighting, was unhurt. After a rest at Barnet he marched back to London, arriving in the evening at St Paul's, where the Archbishop of Canterbury and all the bishops not imprisoned in the Tower greeted him and a 'Te Deum' was sung.

The bodies of Warwick and Montagu were brought to St Paul's and exposed to public view for two days. Instead of quartering them and exposing their remains to further viewing around the kingdom, Edward permitted their burial alongside their parents at Bisham Abbey, the ancestral seat of the Earls of Salisbury in Berkshire. The once great Marcher and Midlands affinities of the Beauchamp,

Despenser and Montague earldoms would have no shrine to their lost leader.

Edward may have felt some regret it had come to this. Warwick had once been his admired mentor, and he had regarded Montagu as a friend. His greater regret, however, was for the sheer wastefulness of it all. The fruits of ten years of conciliation and moderate rule lay trampled into the blood-soaked earth north of Barnet. That the common people had favoured Warwick was something even the *Arrival* admitted and that, too, caused the iron to enter into his soul. He was a harder man and a more cynical monarch after Barnet.

With his battered army dispersed, and even as the corpses of Warwick and Montagu were on display at St Paul's, Edward learned that Queen Marguerite and her son Prince Edward had arrived from France at Weymouth in Dorset. It was no coincidence that they should have disembarked in the midst of the final showdown between Edward and Warwick – Marguerite and her supporters had been awaiting just such an opportunity.

CRUSH THE SEED

NCE IT IS ACCEPTED THAT THE EVENTS OF 1470–1 were a three-way struggle, the pieces of the jigsaw come together, as they never did in Warwick's mind. On 17 December he obtained £2,000 from the exchequer to cross the Channel 'with an army of ships and men' to bring Marguerite and her son to England, but she would not move from Rouen. Again, in late February 1471, he travelled to Dover to receive them, having sent John Fortescue and Lord Treasurer Langstrother ahead to reassure her, but she still refused to move.

At some point he also sent Lord Wenlock from Calais, presumably with warships, but when Marguerite and Prince Edward eventually left Rouen they went to Harfleur, opposite Honfleur in the Seine estuary. The Cotentin ports or Dieppe would have been the appropriate choices if her intention were to sail with the prevailing wind to the south-east of England, where Warwick expected them to land. Harfleur was, however, an ideal place from which to sail to the West Country with an easterly wind. We know Edward sailed with just such a wind from Flushing on 11 March, which poses the pregnant question why Marguerite did not.

There was, of course, a credible threat of interception at sea by the Burgundians or Bretons, and Marguerite presumably convinced Langstrother and Wenlock that this was the reason for her unwillingness to risk the crossing. But with adequate escorts on offer, as excuses go it was almost as thin as the unnecessary, and needlessly delayed papal dispensation for her son's marriage that served to explain the first three months of procrastination.

The final pieces dropped into place in late March and early April, after Warwick had left London to confront Edward. Henry VI disempowered him by declaring his son Lieutenant of England, and in response to Warwick's urgent request that London should be held as the anvil on which he would crush Edward, the Beaufort brothers and the Earl of Devon marched their retainers out of the city to meet Marguerite at Weymouth, next to the Purbeck peninsula, the ancestral domain of the Beauforts.

Once the royal party did set out across the Channel, the ship carrying Anne, Countess of Warwick, sailed separately to Portsmouth, 75 miles east of Weymouth. This was either because her ship's captain had instructions to separate her from her daughter, now Princess of Wales, or because the countess belatedly realized that the Lancastrians intended to stab her husband in the back. After she learned that Warwick was dead she made no effort to join Marguerite and sought sanctuary in nearby Beaulieu Abbey.

We have already reviewed the motives of Louis XI and Charles

43. THE CHANNEL, 1471

of Burgundy. Louis had no further use for Warwick once it became apparent he could not deliver the promised military support. Charles's simultaneous release of his Lancastrian pensioners and pressure on Edward to sail as soon as possible was flagrant pot-stirring. One can interpret their truce on 4 April as recognition that Louis's gamble had failed, and that they should await the outcome of events in England as spectators at a sideshow that now affected them very little.

In sum, there is no indication that Marguerite ever intended to make common cause with Warwick. The Beauforts and Devon could never be reconciled with the man who had killed their fathers and had been the mainstay of the regime that killed their brothers. Their plan was to recruit a new army under the banner of Prince Edward, which would then join up with Jasper Tudor's Welshmen and the Lancastrians of Cheshire and Lancashire before marching on London to put the prince on the throne, which his father would willingly abdicate.

Marguerite was supposed to have crossed earlier, before Barnet, but adverse winds kept her in port a crucial week too long. News of Warwick's defeat and death on the day of her arrival was certainly unwelcome. She had been counting on him to eliminate Edward, and then find himself challenged by her son at the head of an army of unsullied Lancastrians. However her supporters were undismayed – indeed delighted that one of their blood enemies was dead and the other's armed strength severely depleted.

Flanked by Somerset, Dorset and Devon, Prince Edward and his mother led a growing army to Exeter, where it was joined by Devon's affinity and by Hugh Courtenay of Bocconoc. The Courtenays of Powderham who, like Hugh, had crossed the Channel with Warwick, did not respond and later joined Edward's army. They had not forgotten their bitter feud with the senior branch of the family in 1459–61. Their Hungerford and Luttrell relatives did, however, join the Lancastrian army when it marched through Somerset.

They stayed too long at Exeter. They were there from 19 to 27

April, which compounded the royal party's delay in crossing the Channel and gave Edward too much time to prepare. He sent out urgent summons for a new army to assemble at Windsor, where he arrived on the 19th. Windsor was on the highway from Dorset to London but on the 24th, deciding that reports of a Lancastrian advance through Salisbury were probably a feint, he set out to prevent it joining forces with Jasper Tudor.

Edward marched with the hard core of the Barnet army and a large contingent brought by the Duke of Norfolk. Apart from his brothers and Hastings, the only other peer was John Brooke, Lord Cobham, following in his father's footsteps as the most doggedly loyal Yorkist baron. Other companies from all over England joined during the march. After Tewkesbury Edward honoured nine company commanders by making them knights banneret. They came from Suffolk, Norfolk, Cambridgeshire, Northamptonshire, Bedfordshire, Warwickshire, Staffordshire, Dorset and Devon (Powderham).

He covered only 36 miles in the first four days and spent 27–28 April at Abingdon, south of Oxford, gathering strength and waiting for his scouts to confirm that the enemy was indeed marching north, but ready to double back if necessary. Once sure, he covered the next 33 miles in a day, arriving at Cirencester on the 29th. Map 44 shows the strategic significance of the town, at the intersection of the main highway from south Wales, of Akeman Street to St Albans, and the Fosse Way between the West Country and the Midlands.

Meanwhile the Lancastrians arrived at Wells on the 28th, where, according to Edward's once and future Lord Chancellor Bishop Stillington, they sacked his palace and emptied the jails. He was not believed and later fined for not having ensured the secure custody of Lancastrian prisoners. The Lancastrians then returned to the Fosse Way to arrive at Bath on 30 April, where they learned that Edward was 31 miles away, across their line of march. A game of cat and mouse ensued, in which the Lancastrians initially had the better part.

First, they led Edward to believe they intended to continue along the Fosse Way, causing him to advance 12 miles to Malmesbury on 1 May. Instead they marched west to Bristol, where they reprovisioned, equipped their troops from the royal armoury, including field artillery, and were joined by the city militia led by City Recorder Nicholas Hervey. The next day they made a feint towards Sodbury, and Edward marched 14 miles overnight to arrive at the village in the morning of 2 May. He stayed there, without news of the enemy, until early the next day.

He had been sold a dummy, as the Lancastrians marched instead to Berkeley, 13 miles north of Sodbury. They had stolen a march and if they could have crossed the Severn by the causeway at Gloucester it might have changed the complexion of the campaign. Their hopes were dashed when they arrived at ten in the morning of 3 May, having marched the 37 miles from Bristol with only a brief pause at Berkeley.

The *Arrival* admits 'many of the inhabitants of [Gloucester] were greatly disposed towards them', but a loyal Yorkist forewarned by Edward held the town, and the Lancastrians found the gates barred and the wall guns manned against them: 'Of this demeaning they took right great displeasure, and made great menaces, and pretended as though they would have assaulted the town... but, as those that kept the town and [those] that so pretended knew well, the king with a mighty puissance was near to them.'

The footsore army could not stay and marched on towards the next Severn crossing at Lower Lode, a ferry crossing 10 miles away outside Tewkesbury. There was no question of trying to ferry the army across with Edward so close behind, and they rested for the night about half a mile from Tewkesbury, around some old earthworks today known as Queen Margaret's Camp. The queen herself is believed to have spent the night in nearby Gupshill Manor.

Edward's army was no less exhausted. On 3 May he drove it over the 31 miles from Sodbury to Cheltenham in twelve hours, arriving at 5 p.m. The town was 6 miles from Tewkesbury, but his scouts confirmed that the Lancastrians intended to make a stand:

> Upon the morrow following, Saturday the 4th day of May, [Edward] apparelled himself, and all his host set in good array; ordained three wards; displayed his banners; did blow up the trumpets; committed his cause and quarrel to Almighty God... and advanced directly upon his enemies; approaching to their field, which was strongly [placed] in a marvellously strong ground, full difficult to be assailed.

Assuming that neither the contours nor the courses of the river Swilgate and the Coln Brook have changed radically over the intervening centuries, the 'marvellously strong ground' lay across half a mile of undulating ground between the two streams, facing the Cheltenham road. From east to west the three battles were commanded by Devon, Wenlock and Somerset. A hill, now crowned by a cemetery, within the boundary of what was a cultivated area known as The Gastons, gave a commanding view of the area where the Yorkists deployed. The Lancastrian reserve, under Prince Edward, would have been stationed on its slopes.

**45. BATTLE OF TEWKESBURY
4 May 1471**

Contours @ 15 feet intervals

0   1/4   1/2

mile

Worcester road

Warwick road

Cross

Well Mill

Gander Lane bridge

River Swilgate

Abbey close

Fishponds

Holm bridge

Holm Hill

Severn

Bloody Meadow

Coln Brook

The Gastons

PoW

Devon

Wenlock

Hastings

Somerset

Norfolk

Lower Ferry Lode

Gloucester

King

Margaret's Camp

Gupshill Manor

WOODS

200 lances

Gloucester

Cheltenham

© Hugh Bicheno

The traditional deployment has Edward commanding the main battle, flanked on the left by Richard of Gloucester and on the right by Hastings. This cannot be correct. Norfolk was a royal duke, the hereditary Earl Marshal of England, and he had brought the largest contingent to join Edward's army. He was certainly in command of the main battle, while the king would no less certainly have commanded a reserve of hand-picked knights behind him. Edward also sent 200 'lances' to a wooded hill on his left flank.

A 'lance' was a unit of military accounting and usually meant a mounted man-at-arms *and his personal retinue*, so this was a force three or more times greater than 200. It was not a reconnaissance in force but a major tactical deployment with which Edward always intended to outflank the Lancastrian army. The absence of tactical details in the *Arrival* was quite deliberate – as before, with regard to the landing at Ravenspur, Edward did not want to advertise his skill.

It was a relatively small battle, with no more than 7–8,000 men on either side. The Lancastrian position was strong, with its flanks covered by the river Swilgate and Coln Brook, and could be attacked only over broken ground that would make it difficult to maintain formation, against an enemy partially concealed by vegetation. Unaware of the threat from the wooded hill, the *Arrival* describes how Somerset sought to use the terrain to deliver a flank attack of his own:

> In the front of their field were so evil lanes, and deep dykes, so many hedges, trees and bushes, that it was right hard to approach them near, and come to hands: but Edmund, called Duke of Somerset, having that day the vaward, whether it were for that he and his fellowship were sore annoyed in the place where they were, as well with guns-shot as with shot of arrows… or else of great heart and courage, knightly and manly advanced himself with his fellowship, somewhat aside-hand the king's vaward, and, by certain paths and ways before surveyed, and to the king's party unknown, he departed out of the field, passed a lane, and came into a fair place or close, and… from the hill that was in that close he set right fiercely upon the end of the king's [army].

Somerset's attack threw Gloucester's division into disorder, and if supported by Wenlock might have decided the battle. No such support came and 'the king, full manly, set forth even upon them, entered and won the dyke and hedge upon them, into the close, and with great violence, put them up towards the hill'. Somerset's men were also attacked from the rear by the cavalry Edward had sent to the wooded hill and they broke, fleeing towards Lower Lode, to be massacred in the area known today as Bloody Meadow.

Although the anecdote dates from an account written many years later, it is believable Somerset should have made his way back to

Wenlock and brained him with his poleaxe. Whether true or not, panic spread and Wenlock's division dissolved, followed by Devon's. The fleeing men ran towards the bridges over the Swilgate, their flight covered by knots of men-at-arms who stood their ground. Wenlock, Devon, the Prince of Wales, Dorset and twenty-one named knights were killed on the battlefield.

Somerset and no few others did not stand, and rode to seek sanctuary in Tewkesbury Abbey. It was not an authorized place of sanctuary and despite the protestations of the clergy they were dragged out the next day. Tried by Norfolk as Earl Marshal and Gloucester as Constable of England, they were beheaded on a scaffold erected at the crossroads in the middle of the town. The first two to die were Somerset and Langstrother, who feature in an illustrated Burgundian copy of a briefer, more immediately written version of the *Arrival*, which shows a simpering Edward in the last place one would choose to stand when witnessing a beheading.

The third, Humphrey Tuchet, personified the divided loyalties and rivalries that ran below the surface of the Wars of the Roses like a neural map. He was the brother of Lord Audley, Edward's close friend since 1460, uncle of Lord Cobham and married to one of the Powderham Courtenays, one of whom Edward made a knight banneret for his company's service during the Tewkesbury campaign.

Hugh Courtenay of Bocconoc was among the fifteen others beheaded. The nine lives of Thomas Tresham, the oft-pardoned Speaker of the 1459 'Parliament of Devils' who had so narrowly escaped execution in 1468, finally ran out. Foresworn Nicholas Hervey, Recorder of Bristol, and John Delves, High Sheriff of Staffordshire, followed, but several of the others were men who never compromised with the Yorkist regime and whose only crime had been to accompany Marguerite and her son through the long years of exile.

Edward was also liberal in reward. As well as the nine bannerets, he knighted forty-five men after the battle – one, James Crowner of Tunstall in Staffordshire, was knighted on the battlefield, an indication that he had saved the king's life or performed some other notable act of valour at his side. Another of those knighted was George, heir to Edward Neville, Baron Bergavenny. George's minority had given Warwick the opportunity to dispossess Edward, his own uncle, when he seized every inch of land he could claim as his wife's inheritance.*

On 7 May Edward set out towards Worcester to deal with reported disturbances in the North. En route he learned that Marguerite and her now widowed daughter-in-law Anne Neville had been found in a 'poor religious house', probably Little Malvern, 10 miles north-west of Tewkesbury. They may have observed the battle from the abbey tower and escaped across the footbridge over the weir at the nearby water mill. The queen had been a thorn in Edward's side for ten years, and the news was most gratifying.

Still better news came at Coventry on the 13th, when Henry Percy arrived to inform him that the reports from the North were false, and that Lancastrians and Warwick retainers alike sought only the king's grace. This was as well, because even as he hunted Marguerite's army Edward received disquieting reports that he had not severed all the heads of the Neville hydra.

Not the least of the smiles bestowed on Edward by Lady Luck was that the Bastard of Fauconberg, in command of Warwick's squadron at Calais, only crossed the Channel to arrive at Sandwich on 2 May, eighteen days after Barnet. With him were 300 of Warwick's Calais retainers led by Geoffrey Gates, deputy lieutenant since Wenlock's departure. Undeterred by Warwick's defeat and death, the men of Kent rose up once more and the Mayor of Canterbury, Nicholas Faunt, threw the resources of the city behind the insurgency.

Joined by contingents from Surrey and Essex, by 8 May Neville was at Sittingbourne, whence he sent a letter to the mayor and aldermen of London demanding free passage through the city so

*Unsurprisingly, Edward Neville was a loyal Yorkist throughout 1469–71. The title was George's by right of his mother, who died in 1448, but he respected his father's right to it by marriage until his death in 1476.

that he could fight 'the usurper'. The city worthies replied denying his request and asking if he was aware that Warwick and Montagu were dead. It was a good question, and the only logical explanation for the timing of the uprising is if Neville and Gates believed Edward had drawn all the fighting men out of London before marching west.

He had not. He had entrusted the defence of the city to the Earl of Essex and the recuperating Earl Rivers and their retainers, and veteran Lord Dudley had command of the well-garrisoned Tower. It was as well Edward did take these precautions, because Neville's squadron sailed up the Thames and during the week 12–18 May the city was subjected to combined assaults of unprecedented ferocity. Convalescent Earl Rivers himself had to lead a mounted charge to disperse an attack on Aldgate that came close to breaking through into the city.

Eventually the rebels fell back to Blackheath, where Neville, the Calais contingent and the ships deserted them. Gates and his men returned to Calais, but Neville stayed at Sandwich to trade the squadron for a pardon on 26 May. It bought him four months. Ordered to serve in Yorkshire, in late September Richard of Gloucester had him executed on trumped-up charges, and his head went to join the hideous collection spiked on Tower Bridge.

On 21 May Edward arrived in London with almost the entire peerage in his train, and with Marguerite paraded like a captive in a Roman triumph. Only her Valois blood saved her when Edward closed the book on the House of Lancaster. The *Arrival* disingenuously states that Henry VI died that night of 'pure displeasure and melancholy'. When his bones were examined in 1910 the skull was found to be shattered, with residual scalp and dried blood suggestive of a heavy blow to the back of the head. Edward probably ordered it done as mercifully as possible, and somebody hit him with a club as he knelt, head bowed in prayer.

GLOUCESTER

ITTLE MERCY WAS SHOWN TO THE MEN WHO HAD JOINED Thomas Neville when Edward followed Richard into Kent. Canterbury and the Cinque Ports were deprived of their civic rights and heavily fined. Mayor Faunt and one or two others were hanged, drawn and quartered, and many more were hanged, dispossessed or fined. 'Such as were rich were hanged by the purse, and the others that were needy were hanged by the necks', observed *The Great Chronicle*, 'by means whereof the country was greatly impoverished and the King's coffers some deal increased.'

The Earl of Essex was as harsh to the men of his namesake county. Men were hanged along the road from London to Stratford, and swingeing fines levelled on those rebels whom the Bourchiers chose to spare. Warkworth disapprovingly commented: 'Some men paid 200 marks, some 100 pounds, and some more and some less, so that it cost the poorest man 7 shillings which was not worth so much, but [forced them] to sell such clothing as they had, and borrowed the remnant, and laboured for it afterward.'

Added to which there was a virulent outbreak of the Black Death in August–October 1471, believed to have killed 10–15 per cent of the population, with East Anglia particularly hard hit. We cannot know whether this was seen as God's punishment for rebellion or for the murder of Henry VI; but a natural catastrophe of this magnitude must have had a chilling effect on political ardour.

The Calais garrison once more exploited its unique situation to obtain a pardon, and in July Hastings arrived with 1,500 men to reinforce its garrison and those of the outlying forts, dismissing the 500 men Warwick had sent in late 1470. Howard, Hastings's deputy, took over what had been Warwick's private navy. Geoffrey Gates and others who had played leading roles in the rebellions were, remarkably, left in place. Some months later Calais was attacked by Oxford and others who had escaped from Barnet, and the old garrison fought them off.

Jasper Tudor was still active in Wales and Edward commissioned Roger Vaughan of Tretower to deal with him. Instead, Jasper captured Roger and beheaded him at Chepstow in revenge for the execution of his father Owen after Mortimer's Cross in 1461. He then retreated with his nephew Henry to Pembroke Castle, where he was allegedly besieged by Morgan ap Thomas, who was in turn allegedly driven off by his brother David. The story was concocted by Morgan to discredit David, who was disputing his leadership of their locally powerful clan, and to conceal his own complicity in the unimpeded escape of the Tudors to Brittany.*

The most pressing political problem Edward had to resolve was not the South-East, Calais or Wales, but the perennial dilemma of what to do about the North. His solution brings 18-year-old Gloucester into the mainstream of our story, as he was entrusted with the delicate task of winning over the now leaderless Neville affinity. The purpose was to prevent both the resurgent Percy affinity and the untrustworthy Lord Stanley from filling the void of authority.

On 29 June Gloucester was given stewardship of Middleham, Sheriff Hutton and Penrith, and two weeks later Edward turned this into a grant of all the ex-Salisbury lands in Yorkshire and Cumberland entailed to male heirs. These should have passed to Montagu's 11-year-old son George, Duke of Bedford, but the king

*They were the sons of Thomas ap Gruffudd, killed fighting for Jasper at Mortimer's Cross. Edward did not believe Morgan's story and had him arrested.

and his brothers were to behave with total indifference to the property rights of the heirs, wives and mothers of the men they had lately defeated.

On 4 July Edward awarded Gloucester all the offices held by Warwick in the region. He became Warden of the West March, thus Constable of Carlisle Castle, Chief Steward of the duchy of Lancaster in the North – except for Knaresborough Castle, awarded to Henry Percy as complementary to his neighbouring lordship of Spofforth – and High Sheriff of Westmorland. The king also made him the Chief Steward of the duchy of York in the North and Constable of the family castles of Sandal and Conisbrough.

Warwick's retainers welcomed Gloucester. They had seen him grow up under Warwick's tutelage at Middleham from the age of 12 to 16, and appear to have liked him. It was their chance for redemption after many years of treasonous activity and they took it, serving him as faithfully as they had served Salisbury and Warwick. It was a warrior society, and his path was smoothed by his creditable performance at Barnet and Tewkesbury. To telescope the events of the following years, even as Gloucester was consolidating his new domain he set about extending it. The low-hanging fruit was picked first. The lands of Joan Fauconberg, widow of Warwick's uncle William Neville, Earl of Kent, were taken in exchange for an annuity. The Durham castles and manors of Raby and Brancepeth, held by the senior branch of the Neville family, were also ripe for plucking because Ralph Neville, 2nd Earl of Westmorland, had been incapacitated by dementia since the late 1450s.

The estates were managed by Westmorland's grandson and heir Ralph, Baron Neville, who was vulnerable for other reasons. His father had played a leading role in the ambush of Richard of York at Wakefield before being killed in turn, along with his cousin Thomas, Lord Clifford, at Dintingdale in 1461. Two more cousins, Humphrey and Charles Neville, had been executed for treason in 1469. All had been attainted.

Lord Ralph made a virtue of necessity and became not so much

**46. RICHARD'S NORTH
1471-5**

Based on maps in A. J. Pollard,
*North-Eastern England in the
Wars of the Roses* (Oxford 1990)

Castles held
by Richard

Penrith — Ex-Neville
lordships

Raby — Flashpoints

0   25   50
miles

© Hugh Bicheno

RICHARD'S PRINCIPAL RETAINERS AND THEIR MANORS

1	Ashton, Ralph (Salkeld)	16	Markenfield, Thomas (Markenfield)
2	Brackenbury, Robert (Selaby & Denton)	17	Metcalfe clan (Nappa)
3	Burgh, William (Brough)	18	Middleton clan (Belsay & Middleton)
4	Constable, Robert (Barnby)	19	Neville, Lord Ralph (Brancepeth Castle)
5	Conyers clan (Hornby, Sockburn & Winyard)	20	Percy, Robert (Scotton)
6	Dacre, Humphrey (Naworth Castle)	21	Pigot, Richard (Clotherhome)
7	Danby, Robert & James (Thorp Perrow)	22	Pilkington, John (Sowerby)
8	Fauconberg, Baroness Joan (Yarm)	23	Ratcliffe, Richard (Derwentwater)
9	FitzHugh, Lord Richard (Ravensworth Castle)	24	Redman, Richard (Harewood & The Levens)
10	Gower, Thomas (Sittenham)	25	Saville, John (steward Wakefield)
11	Greystoke, Lord Ralph (Henderskelfe Castle)	26	Scrope, Lord John (Bolton Castle)
12	Harrington clan (Farleton & Brierley)	27	Scrope, Lord Thomas (Masham Castle)
13	Huddleston, Richard (Millom)	28	Strangways, James (West Harlesey)
14	Lepton, John (Terrington)	29	Tunstall, Thomas (Thurland Castle)
15	Lumley, Lord Thomas (Lumley Castle)	30	Witham, Thomas (Cornburgh)

a retainer as a loyal and valued subject, and Gloucester was to use Raby Castle as though it were his own. No doubt this was deeply gratifying to Duchess Cecily, known as the 'Rose of Raby' in her youth, before the castle passed into the hands of the senior branch of the family. Gloucester also forced Edmund, heir to the attainted barony of Roos, to sell him the family seat of Helmsley Castle.

Edward had awarded the large lordship of Barnard Castle, long held by the Earls of Warwick but hotly disputed by the bishop's palatine of Durham, to Bishop Laurence Booth in 1470. Gloucester shared Warwick's view that possession was nine-tenths of the law and would not relinquish the lordship, and ignored subsequent injunctions to do so. After Booth was made Archbishop of York in 1476, his successor at Durham – the meteorically promoted William Sutton – all but handed over the governance of the palatinate to Gloucester.

Gloucester also calculated that Henry Percy would be inhibited by the same political fragility that emasculated Lord Neville. The first three earls of Northumberland had been killed backing the wrong side in civil wars, and the title twice attainted. With the erasure of the Nevilles, the main reason for Percy's restoration to the earldom in 1470 was gone. Percy had, however, delivered the crucial neutrality of his family's affinity in the struggle between Warwick and Edward, which won him considerable credit at court.

So, when Gloucester tried to undermine Percy's authority by challenging his stewardship of the castle and manor of Knaresborough, Edward summoned the two peers to appear before him at Nottingham in May 1473 and came down firmly on Percy's side. The king required his brother not to challenge or claim any office granted to Percy, and not to retain or accept into service any man previously retained by the earl. With their areas of authority now defined, Percy formally became Gloucester's retainer and accepted his overlordship in July 1474.

Gloucester's bullying tactics were not limited to the North. He had been awarded the Earl of Oxford's forfeited patrimony in 1471, but trustees for the dowager duchess held much of it. In response to her son's attacks on Calais, Edward put the lands in Gloucester's custody to prevent her sending any money to her son. In January 1473 Gloucester compelled the elderly lady to surrender her lands in exchange for an annuity. Six of her trustees, including the Bishop of Ely, refused to sign off on the agreement until compelled to do so by the king.*

Gloucester also clashed with Thomas, Lord Stanley, in Lancashire. Gloucester was the dominant lord of Lonsdale and Furness in the north of the county, in the centre lord of Clitheroe and Halton, and of the vast royal hunting grounds known as the 'forests' of Bowland, Amounderness and Blackburn. The feud he inherited between one of his new retainers and Lord Stanley over Hornby Castle and adjacent Farleton in Lonsdale, and of Brierley in the West Riding, was therefore a test of his local authority and good lordship.

The dispute began after Thomas Harrington and his eldest son John were killed fighting for the Yorkists at Wakefield. John left two daughters and after Edward assigned their wardship to others, their uncles James and Robert Harrington seized the girls and their lands, which they claimed were entailed in the male line. In 1468 Edward IV gave wardship of the girls to Lord Stanley, who married them to his sons, claimed the lands by right of primogeniture, and obtained a legal judgement against the Harringtons. Armed clashes, in which Richard may have been involved, followed in 1470.

The feud revived after Edward recovered the throne, with both parties believing they had earned royal favour. James Harrington had been among the first to join the king with a substantial following, but so had William, Lord Stanley's brother. Late in 1471 Edward made Lord Stanley steward of his household, and early in 1472 gave him permission to marry Margaret Beaufort, widowed for the second time when Henry Stafford was killed at Barnet. The balance of favours owed tipped towards the Harringtons.

*Richard assigned the stewardship of the Vere estates to John, Lord Howard, laying the basis for a strong working relationship between the two men.

In 1473 Edward paid it by appointing Gloucester to head a commission empowered to take possession of the castle and hand it over to the Stanleys. As he did in Durham, Gloucester simply ignored his brother's instructions and it was not until 1475 that the Privy Council agreed a compromise by which the Harringtons were granted Farleton and Brierley, and Hornby Castle was at last surrendered to the Stanleys.

The ex-Neville affinity would have been reassured to see their lord follow the principle of 'my retainer, right or wrong' in apparent defiance of his brother, but it was a charade. When Edward gave his brother an unequivocal order, he was obeyed – therefore he gave no such order. He probably felt he had done enough for Stanley, and the dubious value of his good will was not worth the certain cost of undermining Gloucester's good lordship.

Edward was inhibited from showing similar partiality when called upon to mediate between his brothers in their acrimonious dispute over the Warwick inheritance. In exchange for her loan he had promised Margaret that Clarence would be permitted to inherit Warwick's estate through his wife Isabel Neville. He had already reneged as much as he dared by awarding Gloucester lands in the North and in Wales dishonestly obtained by Warwick.

Blithely overlooking that Warwick would not have rebelled in 1469 without him, Clarence felt that Margaret's loan and his opportune coat-turning entitled him to as great or greater consideration than his younger brother. He was determined to take possession of the whole of the legitimate Warwick inheritance, to which end he claimed custody of Isabelle's 15-year-old sister Anne Neville, the other co-heiress and widow of the late Edward of Westminster.

Gloucester had grown up with Anne during his time at Middleham and liked her, but sentiment played no part in the tug-of-war that ensued when, not long after Tewkesbury, he obtained Edward's permission to marry her. In a repeat performance of the sordid squabble ninety years earlier between the sons of Edward III over the co-heiresses of the Bohun earldom of Hereford, Clarence planned to force Anne to become a nun and to renounce her inheritance, and in the meantime refused Gloucester access to her.

Gloucester returned from the North in the autumn of 1471 and allegedly spirited Anne away from the household where Clarence had tried to conceal her, and took her to sanctuary at St Martin's Le Grand. It is more likely that Anne escaped to sanctuary, perhaps in disguise, and then sought Gloucester's protection. The scandal became so notorious that Edward ordered his brothers to argue their case at a Council meeting. This they did, and impressed the councillors with their eloquence and legal sophistry.

All the eloquence in the world could not finesse the fact that Isabel and Anne were co-heiresses not so much of their Neville father as of their mother, Anne née Beauchamp, who was Countess of Warwick in her own right. She remained most inconveniently alive in sanctuary at Beaulieu Abbey, which she dared not leave because Edward refused to grant her safe conduct.

Gloucester went ahead and married Anne sometime in the spring of 1472, without waiting for the necessary papal dispensation to marry his cousin. Both brothers wanted to put their possession of ex-Warwick lands on a firmer legal footing than royal favour. Edward had made the original distribution in anticipation of an Act of Attainder, which would have put the whole Warwick inheritance in his hands, but his brothers were determined to pre-empt the issue.

With Burgundy such an uncertain ally Edward could not risk offending Margaret, who was Clarence's principal advocate – although we may depend on it that Duchess Cecily was also active in the background. At the same time Clarence could not be seen to have profited from his treachery, or permitted to achieve the regional dominance in the Midlands that adding the Warwick inheritance to his existing holdings would give him.

Edward's solution was to resume forty duchy of Lancaster and eight crown manors in the Midlands previously held by Clarence, including Tutbury Castle, the seat of what he had once imagined was his appanage. Although Clarence gained forty-four ex-Warwick estates in the Midlands and became the dominant lord in Warwickshire and Worcestershire, his lordship was eliminated from Derbyshire, Nottinghamshire and Staffordshire

In the final distribution Clarence got 105 ex-Warwick properties with revenues of about £3,450 [nearly £22 million], which was more than he had lost to resumption. The political price he paid was high, however, as the king could not have indicated his distrust more clearly. Adding to Clarence's uneasiness, when Edward had made him Earl of Warwick and of Salisbury in 1472 it had been as new creations and not by right of inheritance.

Gloucester made Edward's job easier in the matter of the Warwick inheritance by backing down from his original demand for parity, and was rewarded by being exempted from resumption. In addition to Barnard Castle, Glamorgan and Abergavenny, already in his possession, he settled for thirty-five properties scattered across sixteen counties. Not long afterwards he exchanged three of them for the castle and manor of Scarborough in Yorkshire, in a process of regional consolidation that also saw him exchange Chirk Castle (ex-Beaufort) in Denbigh for William Stanley's Skipton Castle (ex-Clifford) in the West Riding.

The final settlement, confirmed by Acts of Parliament in 1474–5, was shockingly cynical. Countess Anne was declared legally dead and her daughters' inheritances assigned to their husbands – *whether or not they were or remained legally married to them*. The legally dead countess was permitted to leave Beaulieu Abbey and was assigned to Gloucester's custody, which Clarence rightly saw as a threat: the settlement was a farce that could be unmade as easily as it was made. Should the countess's property rights be restored, Gloucester would be in a position to dictate the terms of their disposal.

To draw a line at 1475, Gloucester's achievements in the preceding four years paint a picture of a ruthless but sensible and charismatic young man. He had more than fulfilled Edward's hope that he would become the regime lock on the North, taming a region that had been a thorn in the side of every monarch since 1399. Although he was the beneficiary of a sea change among the northern lords and greater gentry, tired of being sacrificed to the national ambitions of the Nevilles, this alone does not explain how, in a relatively short period, he won the respect of a cohort of men as proud and hard-headed as any in England.

The discovery of Gloucester's bones has at least resolved one of the controversies that have swirled around him for so long. He did indeed carry one shoulder higher than the other as the result of a severe curvature of the spine (scoliosis), which may explain why contemporaries remarked on his habitual lip-chewing: he was probably in constant pain. The intense willpower required to overcome the handicap became his dominant character trait. As a result he was not greatly inhibited physically, proof of which was his performance as a commander and in battle during the Barnet and Tewkesbury campaigns.

Any king in history would have prayed to have such a sibling, and he was Constable of England and Lord Admiral for the duration of Edward's reign. As long as his elder brother drew breath Gloucester gave him no reason to doubt the sincerity of '*Loyaulte me lie*' (Loyalty binds me), the motto with which he signed every document.

ELIZABETH

THE GOOD THING/BAD THING SCHOOL OF HISTORY requires that Elizabeth should have exercised a malign influence over Edward, because otherwise the House of York was rotten to the core. That it undoubtedly was does not necessarily make her a 'good thing', although it should incline us to sympathy. All we really know about Elizabeth is that she was a conventional queen who administered her relatively modest estates competently, retained the affection of her philandering husband and gave him ten children in fourteen years.

There is no evidence that she tried to influence him to favour her family to the detriment of his authority, and it would have been foolish to try: he was not a biddable man, and with the sole exception of Jacquetta de Luxembourg he had little respect for women. He had slapped down his mother for presuming too much and would have done the same to his wife, his sisters or his mistresses. They could appeal for small favours in support of their own good ladyship, but it is highly unlikely any of them influenced him in matters of significance.

Warwick had struck at the Woodvilles to hurt Edward, but the spitefulness towards Jacquetta came from Duchess Cecily via Clarence. There can be no doubt about this: Clarence's will asked that compensation be made for the injuries and grievances he had inflicted on Earl Rivers and his parents, 'who had done him no harm'. The omission of Elizabeth is eloquent.

The queen did not name any of her daughters Jacquetta, but in addition to making the dowager duchess godmother to her own namesake firstborn, in 1469 she did name another daughter Cecily. This was the year Edward evicted his mother from Fotheringhay, and Elizabeth's gesture clearly did nothing to placate her mother-in-law. Hatred is often a projection onto another of deep personal unhappiness or even self-loathing, and Elizabeth had the misfortune to be the lightning rod for the sick relationship between Cecily and her eldest son.

Elizabeth's fourth daughter, born in 1472, was named for Edward's sister Margaret, and her third son, born in 1477, was named George in honour of Clarence.* It is difficult to see how this can be reconciled with the allegation by Mancini, repeated unquestioningly by later historians, that the queen nurtured deadly vengefulness towards Clarence. The king, who stood as godfather to Clarence's heir, Edward, born in 1475, would not have forced his wife to name the boy after a man she hated, least of all at a time when his own relationship with his brother had become frankly hostile.

The model for medieval queenship was set out in *The Treasure of the City of Ladies*, written in about 1405 by the Venetian-French Christine de Pisan. The book sought to buttress what she saw as an erosion of respect for the traditional role of women as mediators and peacemakers between their husbands and the rest of the world. Elizabeth's naming of her children should be seen as an attempt to build bridges between Edward and his family.

The worst that can be said of Elizabeth is that she did not win personal loyalty outside the circle of her own family, against which one can readily imagine what Edward's reaction would have been if her parents, her brothers or Elizabeth herself had tried to build a 'queen's party'. They were all totally dependent on the king's good will, as was almost everyone else in his court.

*Margaret died nine months later and George, a robust 2-year-old already made Duke of Bedford and Lord Lieutenant of Ireland, was carried off by the plague in 1479.

With regard to the alleged unpopularity of the queen and her kin, this was largely an artefact of Warwick's propaganda. We have seen the robust response of the City of London when he tried to get Jacquetta condemned for witchcraft, and she and her daughter won further admiration for their courage during their months in sanctuary during the Readeption, when Elizabeth gave birth to the long-awaited heir while enduring Spartan living conditions. They had also behaved courageously in the Tower during the Bastard of Fauconberg's desperate assault.

When the Commons were summoned in October 1472 the Speaker, William Alyngton, 'declared before the King and his noble and solemn Council the intent and desire of his Commons, especially in the commendation of the womanly behaviour and the great constancy of the Queen, he being beyond the sea'. Perhaps he would also have commended Jacquetta, but she had died five months earlier, aged 56. There is no record of her funeral, but we can be sure that it was befitting her high rank, and that her virtues were duly extolled.

Elizabeth and her mother had been exceptionally close, and Edward may have felt the loss of Jacquetta almost as keenly. Never a paragon of virtue, he became more dissolute after 1471 and it is not much of a stretch to speculate that the deaths of his respected parents-in-law released the brake on his self-indulgence. In this, as always, he was encouraged by Hastings, not simply because he had done so since Edward was a teenager, but also to undermine Elizabeth.

• ❧ •

Elizabeth's older brother Anthony, Earl Rivers, was poised to become a pillar of the regime in 1471 and spurned the opportunity. He had been a competent Keeper of the Seas for several years before Edward appointed him Lieutenant of Calais in 1470. Subsequently Rivers had organized the flight to Holland from Bishop's Lynn, where he had influence as lord of neighbouring Middleton, after which he played a leading role in assembling the invasion force and fought heroically at Barnet and against the Bastard of Fauconberg.

At the moment when he might have played a leading role in the post-war settlement, Rivers requested Edward's permission to go on a pilgrimage to fight the Moors in Portugal. In the preface to his 1477 translation of *The Dictes and Sayings of the Philosophers*, he wrote that during the recent turmoil he had sworn to devote his life to God's service.* Edward accused him of fleeing his obligations – although he had previously awarded the office of Constable of England, which should have been Anthony's in reversion from his father, to Gloucester. Now he did not reappoint him as Lieutenant of Calais and nominated Hastings instead.

Rivers went on pilgrimage in 1473 to Santiago de Compostela in Spain, and again in 1475 to Rome and other shrines in Italy, when the pope honoured him with the title of defender and director of papal causes in England. In Italy he travelled in sumptuous style, and was robbed of all his possessions when travelling in the Veneto. The notoriously tight-fisted Venetians made good his loss in deference to the English court, from which we can deduce that at least in 1475 Rivers was acting in an official capacity.

As well as being unusually cultured and learned, Rivers was an ascetic who wore a hair shirt next to his skin; but he was no better than the rest of his class with regard to worldly wealth. His father left him only three manors in Kent as well as Grafton in Northamptonshire, but he used legal chicanery to make himself the heir of his wife, whom he married not long after she became Baroness Scales in her own right in 1460. On her death in 1473 he retained fifteen manors in Norfolk and one in Cambridgeshire that should have reverted to the Scales family.

There was also something particularly unpleasant about the way Anthony extorted Maud Stanhope, dowager Lady Willoughby and

---

*Rivers was William Caxton's patron and the *Dictes* was the second book printed in England. Caxton also published Rivers's translation of the *Cordyal of the four last and final thinges* in 1479.

widow of Warwick's younger brother Thomas Neville, killed at Wakefield, into surrendering part of her Midlands inheritance to him in return for the pardon of Gervase Clifton, her third husband. This was a clear, if rare example of Anthony using his family's royal connection for personal profit. Clifton was to rebel again and was one of those beheaded after Tewkesbury.

After the death of Lady Scales Edward kept Anthony in reserve as a dynastic marriage counter for several years, but in 1480 granted him permission to marry Mary FitzLewis, granddaughter of Edmund Beaufort, the Duke of Somerset killed at St Albans in 1455. This was speculative, as although she was the sole heir of her recently deceased father, it was only a minor estate. However she was also the potential co-heiress of the attainted duchy of Beaufort, all legitimate male heirs being long dead. We may presume Rivers believed, and perhaps had been assured, that Edward would reverse the attainder so that he could inherit.

Edward's appreciation for his brother-in-law's talents preceded his marriage to Elizabeth. Anthony also won international renown for his skill in tournaments before he became the royal champion, and was elected to the Order of the Garter. Although exasperated by Anthony's unwillingness to play his part in the post-war settlement, on reflection he saw that Rivers's knightliness, erudition and lack of political ambition made him the ideal candidate to be entrusted with the education of the young Prince of Wales.

• ✌ •

The king lavished rewards on those who had looked after Elizabeth while she was in sanctuary and during her confinement. Thomas Myling, Abbot of Westminster, was made chancellor to baby Edward, and Elizabeth's midwife and doctor were given generous annuities. The boy was made Prince of Wales on 26 July 1471, and twelve days later the king appointed Elizabeth, Rivers, Clarence, Gloucester and the Archbishop of Canterbury to form his honorary Council,

The tomb effigy of Sir Ralph Fitzherbert in the Church of St Mary and St Barlok, Norbury, Derbyshire, *left,* is a fine example of a late fifteenth-century suit of armour, and has been used as the basis for a modern replica, *right.*

An illustration by the battle artist Richard Caton Woodville (1856–1927) of the slaughter at the Cock Beck following the Battle of Towton in 1461.

Middleham Castle, North Yorkshire, was a stronghold of the Neville family from the late thirteenth century.

Warwick Castle fell into the hands of Richard Neville when his wife Anne Beauchamp became 16th countess of Warwick in 1449.

Kenilworth Castle, Warwickshire, a key fortress in Marguerite d'Anjou's Midlands power base.

Ludlow Castle, Shropshire: the administrative centre of Richard of York's holdings in Wales and the Marches.

Edward IV and Queen Elizabeth, from life, as portrayed in the Royal Window
at Canterbury Cathedral.

A portrait of Edward IV, painted *c.* 1471.

A copy of the earliest known portrait of Elizabeth Woodville
at Queens' College, Cambridge.

King Louis XI of France
– 'the Universal Spider'.

Duke Charles 'the Bold'
of Burgundy.

Richard III: the portrait that launched the cult.

with day-to-day decisions taken by a cabinet run by the Queen.

So it remained until February 1473, when Edward decreed that the prince's household should move to the castle-palace of Ludlow in Shropshire. Along with Fotheringhay, Ludlow had been the principal administrative centre of the duchy of York, and the king had spent a carefree boyhood and adolescence there. This was not to be the prince's lot: the relocation was a political move of considerable significance designed to restore royal authority in Wales, and Edward intended it to be a working apprenticeship for his heir.

Gloucester was now fully taken up in the North, and Edward had no confidence in either of the two young magnates (both 18 years old in 1473) with large landholdings in Wales. William Herbert, Earl of Pembroke, had none of his father's ability. He was not allowed to enter his inheritance until 1475 and was to be deprived of it in 1479. Royal ward Henry Stafford, Duke of Buckingham, was allowed to enter his inheritance in June 1473, but he was another Clarence: a young man with an immense sense of entitlement unmatched by ability.

Edward made a progress through the north Midlands and the Welsh March, at the end of which Prince Edward and his Council were settled at Ludlow. The move diminished Elizabeth's role in her son's life, and while it was normal for aristocratic women to be separated from their sons, it was not usually done at such a young age. She remained at Ludlow until May and we know she accompanied Edward when he made his first progress with his son to deal with disorders in Shrewsbury, as that was where baby Richard was born on 17 August 1473.

The king's appointment of Earl Rivers as the Prince of Wales's guardian and head of his Council no doubt reassured Elizabeth that her son was in good hands, but the arrangement was misogynistic. He was to be brought up as far as possible without female influence, far away from his mother. To the degree that it recreated Edward's own childhood environment it may be taken as a sign of his vanity as well as his emotional immaturity.

• ᘒ •

At about this time Edward and Hastings added an unsavoury twist to their revels by welcoming 21-year-old Thomas Grey, heir to the Ferrers of Groby barony and Earl of Huntingdon since August 1471, to join them. Grey was Elizabeth's eldest son from her first marriage, thus the king's stepson, and also his nephew-in-law through marriage to Anne Holland, the namesake daughter of the king's older sister and heir to the imprisoned Duke of Exeter.

There are indications that Thomas had already fallen under Hastings's influence when he fought under his command at Tewkesbury. Any doubt about it was removed when Anne died childless early in 1474. With no claim to the Holland lands, Thomas was more than compensated by marriage to one of the richest heiresses in England, Hastings's 13-year-old stepdaughter and ward Cecily, Baroness Bonville and Harington in her own right.

In theory Elizabeth had paid 4,000 marks [£848,000] for Grey's marriage to Anne Holland and now paid 2,500 marks [£530,000] for the Bonville marriage, which took place on 5 September 1474. In reality Edward discounted the bridal prices from money owed him by Exeter and Hastings: in other words, he arranged them both. Exeter, who was in exile at the time, had no say in the matter, but it is inconceivable that Edward should have arranged the Bonville marriage against Hastings's will.

Grey was granted possession of Cecily's inheritance on 23 April 1475 and three weeks later he was knighted and created Marquess of Dorset, renouncing the earldom of Huntingdon. With the Courtenay lands divided up among Clarence and others, the Bonville/Harington estates were the largest cohesive block in the West Country, and Edward may have entertained the idea of making Grey his regime lock on the region. He may also have hoped the marriage would bring about a reconciliation between Hastings and Elizabeth, whose detestation of his best friend remained a mystery to him until the day he died.

Her hatred, of course, stemmed from Hastings's sordid exploitation of her appeal for his good lordship in her dispute with her first mother-in-law, Baroness Ferrers of Groby by right, over Thomas Grey's inheritance from his father. The arrangement between them, promptly rendered null by her marriage to the king, had included a provision that Thomas should marry a daughter of Hastings's family; and so, in the end, he did.

Hastings may have hoped that by favouring Thomas so extravagantly he would detach him from loyalty to his mother. If so he failed, as in due course the tension between Thomas and Hastings became as notorious as it was, to the king, incomprehensible. The most likely explanation is that Elizabeth, disgusted by Hastings extending his corrupting influence from her husband to her son, told Thomas the reason for her animosity.

· ∾ ·

Elizabeth's hatred of Hastings has been attributed to a competition for influence over the king, but there was no contest: Edward's attitude towards women precluded it. Hastings was the classic 'favourite' who normally served as a scapegoat for dissatisfaction with a medieval monarch. That neither at the time nor since does it seem to have occurred to anyone to blame him for Edward's policies is a tribute to Hastings's care to avoid incurring envy.

Elizabeth had no useful weapons to employ against such a man because she had no following at court, and the main reason appears to have been her personality. It is not unusual for mothers to resent their sons' wives. To overcome this requires a great deal of tact by the younger woman, and from the evidence of her poisonous relationships with both her mothers-in-law Elizabeth was lacking in that department. It cannot all be attributed to jealousy.

We may doubt that the Yorkists could ever have unequivocally accepted the daughter of a leading Lancastrian, or that the Lancastrians could ever forgive her family's outstandingly successful apostasy, or the Ferrers of Groby ever cease to hate her for marrying a man her first husband had died fighting against. But if she had exercised graciousness commensurate with her beauty she would have had no difficulty in winning devoted followers. Instead she invested all she had to offer in Edward, who would accept no less, and he was not worth it.

EDWARD

THE TASK CONFRONTING EDWARD AFTER TEWKESBURY was even more daunting than it had been ten years earlier. Then, he had been invested with the hope of a nation tired of factionalism and disorder, and ready to give him the benefit of the doubt as he learned how to be king. How thoroughly he had disappointed that hope became apparent in 1469–71. He was shocked to learn how unpopular he had become, and knew very well that he had succeeded in recovering the throne only because his opponents did not combine against him.

For several years afterwards the *Paston Letters*, a useful source for informed gossip, paint a picture of widespread surliness and rumours of sedition, often tendentiously linked to Clarence. Edward was aware of it and of the need to win back the good will of his people. Not long after the pacification of Kent he, Elizabeth and their children made a well-choreographed pilgrimage to Canterbury, and he was to show himself to his people in more ceremonial progresses over the next three years than he had made in the first half of his reign.

Few potential sources of sedition remained after Barnet and Tewkesbury, but one of them was Archbishop Neville. Edward had a score to settle with him and went about it like a cat with a mouse. For ten months he behaved graciously towards Neville, to the point that in April 1472 the archbishop was preparing to receive Edward for a hunting party at More Palace. The best tapestries were hung,

550 · THE WARS OF THE ROSES

the gold dinner service unpacked and no expense spared. Instead of the king, however, on the 25th royal Household Controller William Parr and Treasurer of the Chamber Thomas Vaughan* arrived, arrested the archbishop and looted his palace.

The given reason was allegedly treasonous communication between Neville and the exiled Earl of Oxford, his brother-in-law. No evidence was ever produced to support the charge and there is no reason to believe it. It was a highly personal act of vengeance, underlined when Edward had the archbishop's opulent mitre broken up to create a new crown for himself. The palace and its contents added £20,000 [£12.7 million] to the royal coffers and Edward also enjoyed the revenues of the archbishopric for several years. Neville himself was imprisoned at Hammes Castle in the pale of Calais until released at the petition of the pope in November 1474.

There is likewise no evidence linking Clarence to any plot against his brother after 1470. How much of the gossip stemmed from pot-stirring by Louis XI is hard to say, but on at least one occasion, in July 1473, the Milanese ambassador reported some typical disinformation. The Earl of Oxford, Louis said, had sent him twenty-four 'original seals of knights and lords and one duke' who were ready to rise up against Edward if Oxford could provide the spark. The duke in question could only be Clarence.

The remark came apropos a landing by Oxford at St Osyth in Essex on 28 May 1473. Ten days earlier John Paston reported the confession of a captured courier that £1,000 had been sent to Oxford from England, and that 'a hundred gentlemen in Norfolk and Suffolk have agreed to assist the said earl at his coming thither... within eight days after St Dunstan [21 May]'. In fact Oxford found no response from his old affinity, and with the Earl of Essex and others on their way to crush him he quickly re-embarked.

After several months cruising off the English coast, permitted to resupply and sell pirated goods and ships in Scotland, on 30

*Of Monmouth: distantly if at all related to the Welsh Marcher Vaughans.

September Oxford, his brothers and Beaumont occupied St Michael's Mount, a rocky tidal island in the far west of Cornwall. It was a pointless operation that should have been dealt with by local levies, but was not. Finally Edward sent 600 men with cannon and ships commanded by his esquire of the body John Fortescue, a Hertfordshire knight, who blockaded the rock from 23 December 1472.

Fortescue was also empowered to offer pardons to all except Oxford and Beaumont, and with his followers deserting Oxford surrendered on 15 February 1473. He and Beaumont spent the next decade imprisoned at Hammes, where John Blount, the castle captain, was paid £50 [£31,800] per annum for their maintenance. This does not mean they were kept in luxury – the generous payment simply gave Blount a keen interest in making sure they did not escape.

In sum, tangible threats to Edward's throne were insignificant or imaginary, but the general malaise reported by John Paston was real. To counter it, Edward's big idea was to unite the kingdom behind him by invading France. Bishop John Alcock of Rochester, Chancellor Stillington's deputy and president of the Prince of Wales's Council, announced the king's intention when Parliament assembled on 6 October 1472. It was to remain in session until March 1475, by far the longest of Edward's six parliaments.

Unabashed by the fact that he was repeating Stillington's opening words to the 1467 Parliament almost word for word, Alcock spoke of the dastardliness of Louis XI, 'the principal ground, root and provoker of the King's let and trouble'. He needed to be punished, and how better than reasserting in arms Edward's rightful claim to the throne of France? Such an enterprise would channel the energies of the more unruly elements of society. Give war a chance was the message – it had worked for the most revered of England's kings.

More practically, Alcock continued, control of the Channel and Atlantic coasts of France would boost trade, reduce losses to French piracy and provide lands for the younger sons of noble and gentry families. The king had spent £100,000 [£63.6 million] to bring about alliances with Burgundy and Brittany, and other princes would join a league against Louis XI. Therefore, the message concluded, Edward looked to his loyal subjects to provide him with the means to carry his enterprise through to a glorious conclusion.

Edward had not brought about the boasted triple alliance against France, not least because £100,000 was wildly beyond his ability to pay. The exchequer was bare and, even trading at a steep discount, the accumulation of royal 'tallies' and other liabilities was unsustainable. Today's central bankers would applaud Edward's intuitive understanding of his situation: had such a device existed at the time, he might have compared kingship to riding a bicycle – the choice was between maintaining forward momentum or falling off.

The only alliance Edward had achieved at the time of his boast was with Brittany. In March 1472 Fransez had appealed for 6,000 archers to help him resist an imminent French attack. Edward sent Rivers and his brother Edward Woodville with 1,000 archers, and by August the French had withdrawn. A further 2,000 archers under Duras followed in September, and Rivers negotiated a treaty by which, in return for continuing English protection, Fransez would permit an English army to invade Normandy or Guyenne through his territory.

When the lord of Gruuthuse crossed to England in October 1472 he was lavishly entertained and made Earl of Winchester with £200 [£1.27 million] a year from the customs of Southampton for the indispensable services he had provided during Edward's exile. He also brought with him Duke Charles's arrogant conditions for an alliance. These were that if Edward became king of France, Charles was to have, by hereditary right, the duchies of Champagne and Bar, the counties of Picardy, Nevers, Rethel and Guise, the prince-bishopric of Tournai and also Louis of Luxembourg's lands of Saint-Pol, Brienne and Ligny.*

---

*A glance back at Map 31 will explain the rationale for this shopping list – it would have united the two halves of Burgundy and would have brought the recreation of Lotharingia a giant step closer.

Edward used Gruuthuse's presence to convince Parliament that he had achieved a triple alliance, but by the time they voted him money for the war even Brittany had dropped out. In return for an annual subsidy of 40,000 gold francs [£4.9 million], in October Frañsez agreed a truce with Louis XI and urged Charles and Edward to do likewise. In November Charles agreed a truce to end in April 1473, but before then Edward had agreed his own.

There were other obstacles to be overcome, chiefly a renewal of the naval war with the Hanseatic League provoked by Edward when he reneged on the promises made to the Hansards in return for their assistance in returning to England in 1471. He also renewed an exclusive arrangement with Cologne that had led to the city's expulsion from the League. The war was not only extremely damaging to English trade, but also made it a near certainty that the furious Hansards would make a full-scale attack on any invasion fleet.

After much toing and froing by delegations led by the king's private secretary William Hatcliffe, in February 1474 Edward signed a treaty conceding the Hansards' demands for the full reinstatement of their unilateral trading privileges, the return of their walled compounds with extra-territorial rights in London and Boston, and the grant of similar premises in Bishop's Lynn, all in perpetuity. He also agreed to pay an indemnity of £15,000 [£9.54 million] and repay a £484 forced loan extorted from their representatives in 1468.

It was a capitulation that did not endear Edward to his creditors in the City of London and the English merchant community. They were even required to submit their own exports to Hansard 'quality control' and consequently their trade with the Baltic and north Germany dwindled even as the League's trade with England boomed. As with other trade deals negotiated during Edward's reign, the terms were so one-sided that it is fair to suspect that Hatcliffe negotiated secret and lucrative exceptions for the king and his friends.

Another obstacle was Scotland, where Louis XI could be depended on to stir up trouble for England unless forestalled. The frontier remained as lawless as ever, and mutual recriminations about piracy continued to poison Anglo–Scots relations. Even so, the truce agreed in 1464 still held and in September 1473 Edward proposed a marriage alliance between James III's namesake heir, born in March, and his own 4-year-old daughter Cecily. On 26 October the formal betrothal took place and a treaty was signed, which included a forty-six-year truce. Edward was to pay a dowry of 20,000 crowns [£2.5 million] in instalments over seventeen years, and was delighted to have covered his back at so little cost.

His sister Margaret's dowry of 200,000 crowns, which should have been paid within three years of her marriage, was another matter. Still outstanding were 115,000 crowns, and although Charles agreed to annual payments of 10,000 crowns starting in 1475, Edward only ever paid 16,000. The entire sum was a bagatelle to Charles, who wore a diamond-encrusted mantle of about the same value to his meeting with Emperor Frederick III at Trier in September 1473; but it had serious implications for Margaret, as her Burgundian endowment was tied to the fulfilment of the marriage contract.

City of London merchants had underwritten the dowry, but took the view that since Edward owed them more and had failed to keep faith with them, their obligation was not binding. It would be hard to identify a better example of how honest dealing is not simply a question of morality. Edward's chicanery earned him the contempt of Duke Charles, Margaret's enmity, and the drying up of his principal domestic source of credit.

Charles no longer regarded war with France as a priority because his heart was set on becoming King of the Romans and successor to Frederick III, the first of the Habsburg emperors. He believed this was a reasonable quid pro quo should he agree to peace with the Holy Roman Empire and to lend military assistance against the Ottoman Empire, cemented by the marriage of Marie, his only child, to Archduke Maximilian of Austria, Frederick's heir.

The emperor did not agree. Faced with the duke's demand that his estates should be declared a kingdom to include the bishoprics of Liege, Utrecht, Toul and Verdun, and the duchies of Lorraine, Savoy and Cleves, after two months of fruitless negotiations Frederick fled from their summit meeting at Trier during the night of 24 November 1473. Charles's browbeating display of opulence and military might had spectacularly misfired.

Edward would have been informed about Charles's state of mind by Hatcliffe and Bishop John Russell of Rochester, his emissaries to the duke before the Trier summit, and subsequently by Dr John Morton and Duras, who tried to negotiate with him during the first half of 1474. Yet he went ahead with plans for a military expedition whose only hope for success depended on Charles turning away from what Edward knew was now his principal concern.

Edward was not stupid – but he was in too deep to abandon the expedition and now developed a fall-back plan, which was to cash out if Charles left him to face France alone. Getting to that point, however, took all his powers of persuasion because even – perhaps especially – those who knew him well suspected the expedition was a dishonest subterfuge. The money voted by the Commons and Lords at the end of 1472 came with the stipulation that he must have mustered his army before it was released to him.

In April 1473 the Lords yielded to Edward's request for funds to stockpile weapons and other equipment and released their supposed tenth. The sum collected was a derisory £2,461, even though the peers could look forward to recovering much more once they could claim indentures for their troops. The perfunctory amount in itself argues persuasively that the peers would believe it when they saw it, and not before.

Between 1472 and 1475 the Canterbury Convocation granted three and a half clerical tenths of about £13,000 each and the York Convocation two-tenths of about £1,400 each, for a total of about £48,000. The *Crowland Chronicle Continuations*, the only account of the period written by someone with first-hand knowledge, seldom states the author's opinion outright – save once. Writing many years later the Chronicler was still incandescent with rage over the way Edward had milked the clergy:

> [The king] did not hide his needs from the prelates, blandly demanding from them, in advance, the tenths which were shortly to be granted as if, once prelates and clergy had assembled in their Convocation, they were obliged to do whatever the king demanded. O what a servile and pernicious ruin for the Church!

When Morton and Duras returned from Luxembourg in mid-1474, only £31,411 of the income tax voted by the Commons in 1472 had been collected, and none at all of a further tenth and fifteenth granted in 1473. The king's blushes over the long delay in obtaining a treaty of 'perpetual amity and alliance' with Burgundy were spared by the Commons' embarrassment over their failure to keep their side of the bargain.

In principle the Commons had voted Edward more tax revenues than in all the preceding years of his reign. In practice he was caught in a chicken-and-egg situation where he lacked the means to pay the indentures for a muster, but unless he did so he could not draw on the Commons' money. He could have resorted to a forced loan, but that would simply have added to the mountain of unpaid tallies already outstanding. Instead he travelled the country to collect money himself, or through special commissioners, by means of 'benevolences'.

This was a nationwide arm-twisting exercise in which he summoned leading citizens to personal audiences, where they were persuaded to make voluntary contributions. He turned on the charm and the *Great Chronicle* reported an occasion when a wealthy Suffolk widow increased her donation from £10 to £20 [£12,700] in exchange for a royal kiss. Of course it would have been a brave man or woman who refused, but those who made the donations would have probably considered it money well spent to have their names recorded in a ledger prominently displayed in the audience chamber.

Records for benevolences raised in fifteen counties survive, totalling £21,656; a pro-rata calculation for the other eleven would bring the amount up to a figure sufficient to pay the first quarter of indentures at the end of January 1475, thereby fulfilling the condition for releasing the first Commons disbursement. When Parliament met for its seventh and last session on 23 January 1475, the situation with regard to the 1472 grant had hardly improved at all. The reasons were set out in remarkably forthright terms:

> Some of the collectors have not delivered the sums by them received to the place limited and appointed by the commissioners, but have converted it to their own use, and some that have received it and not so delivered it are now dead, and some of the said tenth part delivered to the place limited have been converted to their own use by the governors of said places, and some of the commissioners who have received a part of the said tenth will not deliver it to the king's duly appointed receiver… and some persons with strong hands have taken part of the tenth out of the places where it was put by the collectors.

To make up the deficit, on 14 March the Commons voted a traditional tenth and fifteenth payable in mid-April, and a further three-quarters on 11 November. The deadline for the expedition was reset for St John's Day (7 January) 1476, and the Commons voted to make good half the deficit by St John's Day 1475, and the other half by the following St Martin's Day (11 November).

Edward's great scheme to unite the country behind him had instead produced a vote of little or no confidence in his integrity. The cynicism and corruption that characterized the preparatory stage of the enterprise may not have been far beyond the norm for a government system in which all involved were expected to enrich themselves from the public purse – but it was more blatantly shameless than usual. As the old adage puts it, 'the fish rots from the head'.

DISHONOUR

B Y HOOK OR BY CROOK EDWARD HAD COLLECTED ABOUT £120,000 [£76.3 million] with the expectation of a further £50,000, although much of it was spent before the expedition set out. The largest disbursements were two quarterly payments of indentures of about £45,000 each, but other advance costs included the acquisition of siege and field artillery, hiring an invasion fleet and hundreds of wagons to carry 10,000 sheaves of arrows, hard rations for the troops, fodder for the horses, cooking pots, anvils, tools, tents, etc.

The expected revenues would barely cover another quarter's indentures, and we may firmly reject the suspicion expressed by Philippe Commynes and others that the enterprise was fraudulent from its inception. Practically the entire peerage had signed up, and with so much money spent a cancellation had become unthinkable, not least because the Commons would undoubtedly conclude that the king had, once more, acted in premeditated bad faith. If Edward was to achieve anything at all he could delay no longer.

We are much better informed about the composition of this army than for any during the Wars of the Roses because it had to be paid for and, at least with regard to the fighting 'teeth', itemized royal accounts survive, set out in Appendix I. Payments made elsewhere than Canterbury and for the militia contingents sent by cities and boroughs are not included, and there was no separate accounting for mounted archers and the hobilars (light cavalry) who commonly rode with them. Their daily rate was ninepence and they were present in large numbers, yet the archers counted by the king's tellers were only paid sixpence.

The most likely explanation is that, as explained previously with reference to the Battle of Tewkesbury and in accordance with contemporary contracts for military service in Italy and Burgundy, a 'lance' (used interchangeably with 'spear' in the documents) meant a man-at-arms *and his mounted retinue*. This may be the reason why the 'lances' were paid sixpence more a day than usual for men-at-arms, and why knights and above were paid an additional lance's fee for themselves. Commynes personally observed that the English had more than 1,500 men-at-arms with 'many followers on horseback', and the same number of mounted archers.

In sum, nearly 12,000 units of account is likely to have meant actual combatants greatly in excess of the numbers tallied, if not quite the 20,000 men Edward claimed. It was a very large force indeed, perhaps double the size of the army with which Henry V had conquered Normandy sixty years earlier. However, the French now had a large standing army and had learned to avoid charging into arrow storms. There would be no new Agincourt unless Edward could force Louis to face him in battle, and he needed to do this before the money ran out. What he had in mind was a fast-moving *chevauchée* to which Louis must respond.

It was a reasonable plan, but it required Brittany and Burgundy to disperse French strength. Even bolstered by 2,000 archers under Lord Audley and Duras, Edward knew Frañsez would attack only if Louis XI suffered a severe defeat. Burgundy, however, was already at war with France, and after Charles let their truce lapse in May 1475 Louis sent columns to burn Burgundian towns in Picardy, to raid destructively as far as Arras and Hesdin in Artois, and also invaded the duchy of Burgundy

There is little doubt that Charles encouraged Edward to launch his expedition to relieve French pressure on his western flank, and never intended to join him. His relentless aggression had brought about an alliance between the Swiss and Sigismund of Austria that saw Upper Alsace lost to Charles in 1474–5, and Duke René II of Lorraine had made common cause against him with the Rhine cities and Emperor Frederick III. Defeating Louis would do little to resolve the wider strategic dilemma Charles had created for himself.

It is not clear when this finally dawned on Edward, but it must have been well before he launched the expedition. Instead of landing in Normandy, as Charles wished him to do and where Louis was waiting for him, he went to Calais, arriving on 4 July. Duchess Margaret was there to greet him, but Charles did not arrive until the 14th, and then with only a small retinue.

This came as an unpleasant surprise to much of the English army, but by now Edward and his inner circle knew to expect nothing more. Charles announced that he had abandoned the siege of Neuss and had sent his army to invade Lorraine, from where – he said – it would attack into Champagne while Edward advanced from the north. A glance back at Map 31 will reveal how little credibility could be attached to this alleged plan of action.

Indeed and as usual in military matters, maps speak louder than words. Map 47 illustrates that at no point did Edward venture into French territory. His strategic objective was Reims, where he hoped to be crowned king of France. He had spent vast amounts of money on jewellery and sumptuous clothing for himself and his household so that they should not look shabby when they met their Burgundian peers, and was accompanied by a panoply of prelates and heraldic officials to make the coronation ceremony sufficiently grand.

However the expedition could not become a self-sustaining *chevauchée* until it reached enemy lands. Even the peaceful passage of such a large army was destructive and Charles insisted it should avoid marching through Artois as far as possible. The first leg was through Boulogne to Fauquemberges, where Charles and Margaret met them again, after which they marched through Louis of Luxembourg's county of Saint-Pol. Charles met them at Doullens

47. EDWARD IV'S EXPEDITION 1475

0   5   10   15   20   25
miles

Army returns
4-18 September

Calais
4-18 July

Guînes

Charles &
Margaret

Saint-Omer

FLANDERS

BOULOGNE

Fauquembergues
22-24 July

Agincourt
25-26 July

Blangy

Saint-Pol

Hesdin

ARTOIS

ARTOIS

Arras

Charles

Charles

CAMBRAI

Doullens
28 July

Edward IV

R. Somme

PONTHIEU

PICARDY

Charles
12-18 August

Écluster

Picquigny
29 August

Amiens
25-28 August

Péronne
6 August

11 August

EU

AMIENOIS

Lihons
15 August

Saint-Christ
12 August

Saint-Quentin

Reims
37 miles

VERMANDOIS

Roye
14 August

Beauvais
27 July

Louis XI

Compiègne
6 August

N O R M A N D Y

© Hugh Bicheno

in northern Picardy and again at Péronne, neither of which opened their gates to the English. Charles could not have made it more clear that Edward could not count on him even for logistical support.

Louis XI had been frankly terrified at the prospect of a combined Anglo–Burgundian offensive and had spent many times more than Edward could dream of collecting to maintain large armies in the field and a fleet of warships patrolling the Normandy coast. His subjects were restless under the weight of taxation and he knew that some of his nobles would seize the opportunity to rebel should he suffer a military defeat. The last thing in the world he wanted was to face the fearsome English archers in battle.

Thus it was manna from heaven when, before the English even departed Dover, John Smert, Garter King of Arms, arrived at Louis's camp in Normandy to present Edward's formal challenge, and showed himself amenable to bribery. Commynes, who was present, says that Louis gave Smert a private message for his master that showed an accurate appreciation of the situation Edward was in. Duke Charles had tricked him, Louis of Luxembourg's word was valueless and little was left of the campaigning season.

> [Louis] also personally gave the Herald three hundred crowns and promised him another thousand if peace was agreed upon... The Herald replied that he would do all in his power to achieve this peace and that he believed his master would willingly entertain the suggestion; but nothing more should be said until the king of England had crossed the sea. When he had done so another herald should be sent to ask for safe conducts so that ambassadors could come to meet him; they should apply to Lord Howard or Lord Stanley and also to himself to help guide the herald.

In due course Edward learned the truth of Louis's warnings, the crowning disappointment coming on 11 August, when his Vanguard was fired on and attacked when approaching Saint-Quentin, which

Saint-Pol had promised in writing to deliver to him.* Even Charles's arrogance could not put a brave face on this and he departed the next day for Brabant to raise troops for the conquest of Lorraine. The English suffered a number of losses but came away with one prisoner, a valet, who was to play a crucial role in the events that followed.

The man was released with a gold noble pressed into his hand, along with a message from Lords Howard and Stanley urging Louis, by now at Compiègne, to propose negotiations. Louis realized that Garter King of Arms had not misled him and, as he scorned the traditional trappings of warfare, had a suitable tabard made for another valet to pose as a herald. The message he bore was that Louis had acted against Edward in the past only because of his alliance with Burgundy and, now that Duke Charles had made it clear how little he valued Edward's friendship, perhaps the time had come to talk.

On 15 August ambassadors from both sides met at Lihons-en-Santerre, about equidistant from Edward at Saint-Christ on the Somme and Louis, now camped outside Roye. After a perfunctory assertion, and rejection, of Edward's territorial demands, the English ambassadors spelled out their king's price. He required an immediate payment of 75,000 crowns [£9.54 million] to return home, and further annual payments of 50,000 crowns, guaranteed by the Medici and the pope, for the duration of a truce to last until the end of August 1482, renewable thereafter on the same terms.

Further conditions were for free trade between the two countries and a permanent treaty of amity to be sealed by the marriage of 5-year-old Dauphin Charles and 9-year-old Princess Elizabeth when they reached marriageable age, Louis to provide her with an endowment worth 50,000 crowns per annum. Should Elizabeth die before the marriage, her 8-year-old sister Mary would take her place. Both monarchs would undertake not to form alliances against each other, and would support each other if either faced armed rebellion. In

*A promise presumably made to dissuade Edward from running a *chevauchée* through his county evidence of the good faith of the last stipulation Edward offered to provide Louis proof of traitors in his service.

When Louis's ambassadors returned with these terms, they were relieved to find their king delighted with them. It was similar to the offer Louis had made through Warwick in 1466, although the payments were about one-third greater and on the earlier occasion there had been no possibility of a dynastic marriage because the dauphin was not yet born. All Louis had ever wanted was that Edward should not combine with Burgundy against him. As Edward was now prepared to renounce the Burgundian alliance, Louis was not going to quibble over the price.

Duke Charles returned to Péronne on 18 August and visited Edward the next day, but by that time the deal was done. Although he later poured scorn on what his brother-in-law had done, he did not so express himself at this, their last meeting. Edward had served his purpose; the French had fallen back across the river Somme and a month later Charles obtained a truce with the return of Saint-Quentin and other towns he had lost in Picardy. At no expense to himself he had covered his back and could now concentrate on his enemies along the Rhine.

The ambassadors agreed that their armies should march to Amiens on either side of the Somme. Louis wanted the English to pass through an area laid waste by his men so that they should be in no doubt about the hardship that would have awaited them had they marched on Reims. At the same time he wanted his own men to appreciate what a formidable army they would not now have to confront. The parallel march served its purpose and the two armies reached Amiens in a festive mood.*

Louis kept his own soldiers away and turned over Amiens to the English, with whores, tuns of wine and cartloads of meat pies brought in from many miles around. An epic three-day orgy ensued until Edward, embarrassed by their behaviour, posted armed guards

---

* ousand English soldiers, probably archers, were hired away by Duke Charles.

on the gates and ordered his men to sleep it off. On 29 August he rode at the head of his army to Picquigny, where he met Louis for the first time on a bridge divided by a trellis. Commynes, who was present, observed that Edward had become fat since he last saw him after he had fled England in 1470, when he did 'not recall ever having seen such a fine-looking man':

> When he was within four or five feet of the barrier he raised his hat and bowed to within six inches of the ground. The King, who was already leaning on the barrier, returned his greeting with much politeness. They began to embrace each other through the holes and… the King said to him 'My lord, my cousin, you are very welcome. There is nobody in the world whom I would want to meet more than you. And God be praised that we are here for this good purpose'.

Apart from the exaggerated depth of the bow this is probably an accurate description; but then Commynes gilded the lily by claiming to have heard words that would have been spoken in private – possibly Louis confided in him after the event. The words are consistent with Louis's view that Edward was too fond of creature comforts to have really wished to make war:

> Our King, who was never at a loss for words, jokingly said that [Edward] should come to Paris, that he would dine him with the ladies and that he would give him my lord the Cardinal of Bourbon as confessor, since [Bourbon] would very willingly absolve him from sin should he have committed any, because he knew the cardinal was a very merry fellow.

Once the treaty was signed and sworn, with 55,000 crowns in his saddlebags and the remaining 20,000 to follow once his army was back in England, Edward left Lord Howard and Master of Horse John Cheyne as hostages and marched to Calais. Before he left he told Louis that he would regard an attack on Duke Frañsez as a deal-breaker, as 'in his moment of need he had never found such a good friend'. It seems to have been a rather pathetic face-saving gesture at the moment when Edward was consigning the Burgundian alliance, for which he had laboured so long and at such great cost, to the diplomatic rubbish heap.

Edward did, however, avenge the treachery of his uncle by marriage Louis de Luxembourg. He handed over the letters he had received from him and Louis immediately sent Saint-Pol a letter saying 'he had need of a head such as his' to deal with some pending problems, commenting to his aides that the body did not need to be attached. Saint-Pol fled, but Duke Charles captured and handed him over. He was executed in Paris in December.

Edward dealt no less ruthlessly with Henry Holland, Duke of Exeter, thrown overboard during the journey back across the Channel. He had been held at the Tower since 1471 and in 1472 Edward's sister Anne divorced him, freeing her to marry her lover Thomas St Leger. Exeter had no lands, money or followers, and can only have been released from the Tower to join the expedition because Edward intended to have him killed under cover of a battle. That he disposed of him anyway argues that he no longer cared what people thought.

The army sailed back to England between 4 and 18 September, but Edward did not return to London until the 28th. Where he was we do not know, but there is little doubt that he was waiting to see if riots would greet the news of the inglorious outcome of the expedition. He did not dare – for many years – reveal the terms of the treaty of amity and marriage, and he also renounced the Commons' three-quarters of a subsidy due on 11 November. The moment is captured in an irony-studded commentary by the Crowland Continuator (my italics):

The lord king returned to England with *honourable terms of peace: for they were so regarded by the upper ranks in the royal army though there is nothing so holy or proper that it cannot be distorted by ill report.* Some, indeed, at once began to blame this action, for which they paid penalties befitting their presumption; others, once home, reverted to theft and pillage in consequence of which no road was safe for merchants or pilgrims throughout England. The lord king himself, therefore, was compelled to traverse his kingdom with his justices sparing no one, even of his own household, from being hanged if they were caught stealing or killing. This rigorous justice was put into operation wherever it was called for and daylight robberies were then checked for a long time afterwards. For, had the *farsighted prince* not vigorously resisted such evils from the beginning, the number of people complaining about the bad management of the country's wealth (after so much treasure had been snatched from the coffers of them all, and so uselessly consumed) would have grown so much that no-one would know whose heads were safe among the counsellors, *especially those who, moved by the friendship or by the gifts of the French king, had been influential in making peace on the terms described.*

He was right about the gifts: Louis lavished them on Edward's entourage and paid his closest advisers pensions totalling 16,000 crowns [£2 million], in accordance with how influential he believed them to be. Hastings received much the most, but Howard, Dorset, Stanley, Bishop Rotherham (who became Lord Chancellor on return to England), Master of the Rolls Dr John Morton, John Cheyne, the diplomat Thomas Montgomery and Edward's brother-in-law Thomas St Leger were all on Louis's annual payroll for substantial amounts.

We may reason that Edward made the best of a bad situation, even though it was one largely of his own making; but to the medieval mind what he had done was shameful. Worse, in the mirror held up by his fellow princes he had seen himself as of little account. He had set out proudly to be crowned king of France and returned furtively with sacksful of the real king's gold. The enterprise over which he had laboured for so long in the hope that it would rally his people behind him had instead undermined his prestige.

Perhaps worst of all, although probably a thought too bitter to be entertained, Warwick had been proved right about Duke Charles. Edward was now Louis's pensioner, a status which, had he been prepared to accept it in 1466, would have prevented the breach with Warwick and the deaths of countless brave and valued men. He returned from the expedition diminished in the eyes of his subjects – but perhaps also in his own.

SEPTIC SIBLINGS

GLOUCESTER OPPOSED THE DEAL STRUCK WITH LOUIS, although he and Clarence were among those who paid their respects to him at Picquigny and came away with valuable gifts. Counting Northumberland's contingent the army contained enough northerners to have constituted a battle in their own right. They almost certainly formed the vanguard under Gloucester's command and suffered casualties at Saint-Quentin. They would have felt the disgrace of going home without a fight more keenly than anyone else.

Gloucester's disillusionment would have deepened in the years that followed as Edward devoted his attention to money-making at the expense of England's international standing, while spending freely to pose as a great king. I use the word 'pose' advisedly, as after 1475 cosmopolitan Englishmen knew their king was just a small fish in a big pond. Richard of York had believed passionately in England's greatness, and nobody in the country would have felt the humiliation of its diminished status more viscerally than his namesake youngest son.

Gloucester must also have been affected by the same guilty knowledge that convinced Clarence he was the legitimate king. Why, if not true, would their mother have diminished herself in their eyes by confessing that Edward was the product of her adultery? It goes to the heart of the tacit question posed by the Crowland Continuator:

> 'These three brothers, the king and the two dukes, were pos-
> sessed of such surpassing talents that, if they had been able to
> live without dissensions, such a threefold cord could never have
> been broken without the utmost difficulty.'

But it was broken, repeatedly and without great difficulty, because Edward was so evidently dissimilar in body and character to his brothers and their father. Until quite recently there was no debate about genetic determinism – all believed that 'blood will out'. Edward's siblings would have perceived the coarseness of his appetites, his commercial dealings and even his affable approachability as further proof that he could not be their father's son.

Gloucester was 8 years old when Richard of York was killed and would have remembered him as a distant, god-like figure. He would have grown up hearing how austere and noble he was, and the contrast between how he believed a son of York should behave and what he observed in Edward was stark. He did not keep away from court because of the Woodvilles, far less favoured and powerful than he, but for fear his mask would slip.

Gloucester may have regarded Edward's profit-seeking as ignoble, but in terms of affirming his authority at home it is hard to fault the king's decision to do everything in his power to 'live of his own' after 1475, 'his own' including the regularly sheared ecclesiastical sheep. No doubt Lord Treasurer and royal uncle Henry Bourchier, Earl of Essex, strongly urged him to pursue this course of action, and also ensured compliance by his weak-willed younger brother the Cardinal Archbishop of Canterbury.

It was therefore highly significant that Edward decided to make the reinterment of Richard of York into one of the major political ceremonies of his reign. On one hand no expense was spared, demonstrating that the monarchy was solvent and capable of grandeur; on the other it was an opportunity to draw the House of York together and to indulge Gloucester's father-worship by permitting him to make the ceremony as splendid as he could have wished.

The bodies of Richard and his second son Edmund, killed with him at Wakefield, had remained undisturbed where their enemies had buried them at Pontefract since April 1461, when they were reunited with their heads, previously adorning the Micklegate at York. On 24 July 1476 they were disinterred and laid in state in Pontefract church, Richard's remains in a coffin covered with cloth of gold, under a funerary image of him decked in ermine and purple velvet, surrounded by banners and by a life-sized silver angel holding a golden crown.

After a night's candlelit vigil the funerary procession set out for Fotheringhay, stopping for the night at churches in Doncaster, Blyth, Tuxford and the Yorkist boroughs of Grantham and Stamford. Laurence Booth, Archbishop of York, went ahead to ensure that the churches and clergy were appropriately prepared for the vigils, and funded so that everyone who came to pay their respects received a penny, and pregnant women twopence.

The funerary chariot, draped in black velvet embroidered with the royal arms of England and France, was preceded by a knight displaying the ducal arms and followed by Gloucester and the northern lords, with alms distributed to the crowds along the way. When the procession reached Fotheringhay on the 29th it was met by the king and queen, Clarence, Dorset, Rivers, Hastings, Ferrers and other lords. Edward embraced the effigy and made a show of weeping before the coffins were taken into the collegiate church, which he had refounded in 1461.*

Five thousand people received alms in the church, and many times more feasted afterwards in the castle and in tents around it. The catering was lavish in quality as well as quantity, with the bill for food and drink alone exceeding £300 [£191,000]. As public relations it was a complete success; but as an act of family solidarity it was marred by the conspicuous absence of Duchess Cecily. It may

---

*Gloucester was born at now destroyed Fotheringhay Castle, but the magnificent parish church built in Perpendicular style, the truncated remains of a far grander establishment, is a shrine for modern Ricardians.

be that widows were not normally included in such ceremonies, but had she wished to be present she would have been. On past form her boycott of the event was a barbed reminder to her other off-spring that Edward was not Richard's son.

It was also a nail in Clarence's coffin. He had not been punished in 1471 because Edward was beholden to Margaret and hoped for her support to persuade Duke Charles to join him against France. This she had failed to do, and deceived him to boot. The king had also yielded to the entreaties of their mother, and she should have been grateful. Clearly she was not, any more than was Clarence himself. As Edward presided over the climax of his magnificent act of filial piety, it surely crossed his mind that he owed no loyalty to those who showed him none.

Another nail was that despite the 1473 resumptions Clarence still drew more wealth from land than anyone other than the king, and after 1475 Edward set about resuming royal and attainted lands wholesale. The outstanding exception was the estates held at the king's pleasure by Clarence, who incautiously confided in his servants that he believed the king intended to foreclose on him as well. Talking about it to people he should have known included royal informants went some distance towards making it a self-fulfilling prophecy.

Hammering on, Clarence attended court only when summoned and refused to eat anything prepared by the royal kitchens. Given that the court was populated with those he had wronged, not least the Woodvilles, it is understandable that he made no effort to win friends and allies. But to indicate that he feared poisoning in the king's household bordered on treason.

The problem was that Clarence's offences in 1469–70 had been unforgivable, and he knew it. There is an almost exact parallel in Louis XI's experience with his treacherous younger brother, who continued to conspire against him despite having been treated with outstanding generosity. The term 'catastrophizing' describes the common phe-nomenon of individuals driven by guilt to make the worst of an already bad situation, and it is a tenable hypothesis that Clarence was subconsciously courting the punishment he knew he deserved.

Matters came to a head when Isabel Neville, Duchess of Clarence, never recovered from the birth of their fourth child and second son in early October 1476 and died on 22 December, followed by baby Richard ten days later. The double tragedy appears to have unhinged Clarence, who in the months that followed cast aside what little circumspection he had previously shown. Projecting his mother-nurtured hatred, he convinced himself that Isabel and the baby had died because of the evil designs of the queen.

In all probability the action he took on the basis of this belief would have been sufficient to bring about his downfall, but Edward did not learn of it until other, more portentous events had already worsened relations between the two brothers. The first came after Duke Charles, already defeated heavily by the Swiss at Grandson and Morat in March and June 1476, was routed and killed at Nancy on 5 January 1477 by an army led by the Duke of Lorraine.

The northern Burgundian estates mutinied and, as there was no male heir, Louis XI declared the duchy of Burgundy and the counties of Picardy and Artois reversionary to France and invaded them. He also proposed a marriage between the 6-year-old Dauphin and 20-year-old Duchess Marie to get his hands on Flanders and Hainault, which had come to the dukes of Burgundy in the female line. It fell to dowager Duchess Margaret to salvage what she could for her stepdaughter Marie, with whom she had formed an exceptionally strong bond.

In the years that followed Margaret acted exclusively in the Burgundian interest. Some historians believe that England might have played a significant role in the struggle had Edward been willing to give up his French pension, but Edward could not have launched another expedition so soon after 1475 even if he had wished to. Margaret knew the duchy's salvation lay with the Empire, and bent all her efforts to getting Maximilian of Austria to marry Marie.

When she suggested in early 1477 that Marie might marry Clarence, it was simply a stratagem to get Maximilian and the emperor, his chronically indecisive father, to commit to the marriage and to the defence of Marie's patrimony. It was not seen as such by Clarence, but Edward showed he understood his sister's motives by flatly rejecting the suggestion and proposing that Marie should marry Earl Rivers instead. The idea that the greatest heiress in Europe might marry a mere English earl was ludicrous, and the proposal clearly not serious.

Louis XI dripped a little extra poison into the situation by sending Edward a warning that Margaret's proposal was intended to strengthen Duchess Marie's claim to the English throne in the Lancastrian line by uniting it with Clarence's claim to be the true Yorkist heir. Edward should have been well enough acquainted with Louis's inveterate pot-stirring to have dismissed this as ill-intentioned disinformation, but the seed fell on fertile ground.

Clarence's inflated idea of his own importance made it impossible for him to see how unrealistic it was for him to aspire to the hand of Duchess Marie. Edward also rejected a proposal by the Scots that Clarence might marry James III's sister Margaret, on the specious grounds that 'no honourable man' could contemplate remarriage within a year of his bereavement. There was definitely an ironic sting in the tail of that sentiment.

The final straw for Clarence and Edward alike was the trial for treason in May 1477 of the Oxford clerks John Stacy and Thomas Blake, and of Thomas Burdet, a member of Clarence's household. Blake and Burdet had been implicated in Stacy's tortured confession of necromancy in seeking to 'imagine and compass' the deaths of Edward and the Prince of Wales, and of telling others that they would die soon. Burdet was further charged with disseminating treasonable 'bills, writings, rhymes and ballads'.

This was so obviously an incandescently hot political potato that Edward appointed an extraordinarily powerful commission of five earls, twelve barons and six justices to hear the case. On 19 May they found the accused guilty and Stacy and Burdet were hanged the next day. Blake, whose role had been minor, was pardoned at the intercession of the Bishop of Norwich. Before he was executed Burdet made a long speech proclaiming his innocence.

On the same day the king sent a writ of judicial review to establish the facts of another capital case that had been tried under Clarence's authority at Warwick a month earlier. In mid-April two of Clarence's former servants, Ankarette Twynho and John Thursby, the former seized from her home in Somerset, were put on trial for having poisoned Duchess Isabel and baby Richard. Roger Tocotes, a Wiltshire knight banneret and a close associate of the duke, was accused of complicity but evaded arrest.

Clarence's justices of the peace and the Warwick jury found them guilty, even though the supposed evidence presented by Clarence was not even internally coherent – for example, Twynho was alleged to have poisoned Isabel at Warwick on 10 October, when the duchess was at that time resident at Tewkesbury. They were hanged and Clarence's later indictment stated that the verdict was obtained by the jury's 'fear and great menace and doubt of loss of their lives and goods', and that he had behaved 'as though he had used a king's power'.

It was the combination of the two that did for him. Intimidation by local magnates was commonplace in civil suits, but trials of capital offences were held to a higher standard. Edward had caused muted outrage by using his presence to obtain the judicial murders of Courtenay and Hungerford in 1469, but that is why the second point was so important. The king's word was legally unquestionable, and had he accused Courtenay and Hungerford himself their execution would not have been regarded as a perversion of justice.

By acting as he did Clarence had usurped the king's prerogative, in itself treason, and a day or two after the execution of Stacy and Burdet he compounded his offence by entering the Council chamber at Westminster and having Burdet's declaration of innocence read into the record. The most likely reason why he chose to insult the lords who had presided over the trial and to impugn the king's justice is that he knew Edward intended to proceed against him in the matter of Twynho and Thursby. By declaring his belief that Burdet was innocent he was saying that Edward was no better than he, and therefore unfit to judge him.

Edward returned from Windsor and in late June, equipped with full details of the Twynho and Thursby trial, summoned Clarence to appear before him at Westminster in the presence of the mayor and aldermen of London. According to the Crowland Continuator, who was there, the king himself accused him 'of contempt of the law of the land and a great threat to the judges and jurors of the kingdom'. Clarence was sent to the Tower to await trial.

Six months passed until Edward summoned Parliament on 19 January 1478 to arraign Clarence on a charge of high treason. The king himself presented the bill of attainder, which was long and detailed. Clarence had abused the king's trust and his own fraternal obligations, despite being the beneficiary of exceptional royal forbearance. He had repaid it with 'much higher, much more malicious, more unnatural and loathly treason than at any time hath been compassed [planned], purposed and conspired'.

The itemized indictments were a summary of the points made earlier about Clarence's growing paranoia, culminating in a plan to smuggle his son to Burgundy for safekeeping. In addition he had never ceased alleging that Edward was a bastard, and kept a copy of an agreement signed by Henry VI designating Clarence as the legitimate successor should Henry's line die out. The Crowland Continuator cut the long story short:

> No one argued against the duke except the king; no one answered the king except the duke. Some persons, however, were introduced concerning whom many people wondered whether they performed the offices of accusers or witnesses. It is not really fitting that both offices should be held at the same time, by the same persons, in the same case. The duke swept aside all charges with a disclaimer offering, if it were acceptable, to uphold his case by personal combat.

Parliament condemned him to death, the sentence pronounced on 7 February by Henry, Duke of Buckingham, newly created steward of England for the occasion. The Woodvilles are supposed to have influenced the king to execute his own brother, but there is no evidence that they did. Clarence doomed himself by making it clear that he did not regard Edward as his legitimate king, and no one apart from his mother made any effort to save him.

Edward still hesitated until William Alyngton, Speaker of the Commons, came to the Lords' chamber to ask that sentence be carried out. On 18 February Clarence was drowned in a wine barrel used as a bath, and permitted honourable burial next to Isabel behind the altar at Tewkesbury Abbey, where the remains of Edward of Westminster had been mouldering since 1471. The king paid his brother's debts, permitted his young son to inherit the earldom of Warwick, and paid for attendants to care for him and his older sister.

Edward possibly regretted the necessity of putting him to death, but the idea that he suffered from remorse is an invention by Polydore Vergil, who only came to England in 1502 and wrote his *Anglica Historia* at the invitation of Henry VII. Likewise we need place no credence in the story that Gloucester mourned his brother and blamed the Woodvilles for his death. He showed no hesitation in obtaining the earldom of Salisbury for his own son, in taking possession of Clarence's northern estates and in recovering the office of Great Chamberlain.

The main beneficiary was Edward himself, who took almost all Clarence's lands into the royal estate. For let us not forget the aphorism that it is not paranoia if they really are out to get you. Clarence was guilty as charged, but there was one important item that did not feature in the list of indictments: he had been holding lands worth £3,500 [£2.23 million] per annum, and Edward had better uses for this than to leave it in the hands of a dangerously erratic fool.

MONEY MATTERS

THE FINAL FIVE YEARS OF EDWARD'S REIGN ARE THE least commented of the period because, after years of headline events, nothing outstandingly dramatic happened. Rulers have a limited time to bring about changes in the way a country is governed. A standard X–Y graph would show a declining axis of energy, vision and popular good will crossing a rising axis of 'friction' – institutional inertia, fiscal constraints and indifference merging into sullen hostility.

Edward had won a second chance in 1471, so his X–Y axes crossed twice. His outstanding talent was for leading men in battle, but his effort to govern through the promotion of his comrades in arms was destroyed by Warwick in 1469. Then, after his heavy bet on the 1475 expedition came to an inglorious end, he was out of big ideas to unite the kingdom behind him and settled for repairing fences and not importuning his subjects for any more money.

The principal novelty in the later years of Edward's reign, therefore, is that he paid serious attention to the royal finances. They were in a deplorable state, with borrowing to pay for civil war campaigns piled on top of liabilities dating back to the years of Henry VI's personal rule. Royal tallies, bills and letters patent littered the country, with no clear idea of the total amount outstanding.

In February 1474 all creditors with claims predating December 1470 were ordered to present proofs to the exchequer for verification, to be settled by regular payments over twenty years. It is a measure of how rapidly the royal finances improved that in July 1478 Edward authorized Master of the Rolls Dr John Morton and William Essex, chief accountant of the exchequer, to settle – outright – all the verified debts called in by the 1474 proclamation.

Edward deserves considerable credit for recognizing Morton's exceptional ability. He went from principal adviser to Henry VI during the Readeption to becoming Edward's Master of the Rolls (keeper of the chancery records) in less than a year, and his advancement thereafter was extremely rapid. Between 1474 and 1478 he was awarded a succession of ecclesiastical sinecures, culminating in his appointment as Bishop of Ely. In terms of disposable income Ely was the richest diocese in England, and often a springboard to the archbishopric of Canterbury.

Morton was that rare being in public service – a man of principle. He took a potentially career-ending stand against Edward that might also have cost him his life, and came to terms with him only after Henry VI and his son were killed and the issue of usurpation became moot. Under him the Court of Chancery grew rapidly in importance and, although his relentless pursuit of efficiency made him no friends, he was incorruptible – and well paid to keep him that way. At the peak of his power, under Henry VII, he devised 'Morton's Fork' to pluck the feathers of the nobility: if a man lived well he was obviously rich, and if frugally he must have savings.

Also in mid-1478 Edward settled with the City of London, much the greatest of his domestic creditors. Arrears of £12,924 [£8.2 million] were cleared by granting the City the right to appoint a wide range of officials supervising commercial activity, as well as the office of Coroner for greater London. Royal appointees had been so corrupt and extortionate that the City judged it worth writing off the huge sum to be rid of them.

Edward continued to pay off international obligations, such as the loan raised by Margaret from the Flemish cities in 1471, by awarding trading privileges; but the irritation this caused English merchants was muted because the long recession in northern European trade came to an end. Greatly boosted by the opening up of French markets after 1475, exports and imports more than trebled in value between the nadir of 1469–71 and the end of Edward's reign, and complaints about systemic inequities are few when everyone is making money.

The southern and western regions were the principal beneficiaries of the trade bonanza, which dangerously accentuated the long relative decline of the North, exacerbated by the unilateral trade privileges enjoyed by the Hanseatic League. It is unlikely Edward gave this a moment's thought, because the normal signals of popular unrest were contained by his brother's good lordship. Gloucester put little effort into collecting the money voted by the Commons for the 1475 expedition, and a decline in royal revenue from the duchy of Lancaster estates entrusted to him suggests he took the same view of royal rents.

No doubt strongly influenced by his uncle the Lord Treasurer, and by Morton, Edward also tried to bring royal household expenditure under control. Detailed ordinances were issued concerning payments to suppliers, and the rules for catering were defined in minute detail to end wholesale abuse of the traditional 'perks' enjoyed by kitchen and serving staff. Condign punishment was also prescribed for staff who abused purveyance, the right of the sovereign to pay a lower than market price for goods and services. Originally introduced to prevent profiteering in time of war, it had become a commonly abused practice in peacetime as well.

With regard to revenue, Morton found such chaos in the king's accounts that he persuaded him to undertake a systematic review and enforcement of royal rights. Morton's own role was indirectly described by the Crowland Continuator: '[The king] also searches the registers and rolls of Chancery and exacts heavy fines from those who were found to have intruded into inheritances without following the procedure required by law, [the fines based on] what they had received in the meantime'.

We have already noted the Crowland Continuator's outrage at the king's regular demand for ecclesiastical tenths, added to which, 'the fruits of vacant prelacies, which according to Magna Carta cannot be sold, he lets out of his hands for a sum fixed by himself and on no other terms'. The conclusion nonetheless veered reluctantly towards admiration:

> These and similar kinds of snare, more numerous than anyone without special experience could imagine, together with the annual tribute of £10,000 due from the French... made him, within a few years, a very wealthy prince; so much so that in the collection of gold and silver vessels, tapestries and highly precious ornaments, both regal and religious, in the building of castles, colleges and other notable places and in the acquisition of new lands and possessions not one of his ancestors could match his remarkable achievements.

The annual payment from Louis XI was important, and the down payment of 85,000 crowns [£10.8 million] obtained at Picquigny – including 10,000 of 50,000 crowns Louis agreed to pay to ransom Marguerite d'Anjou – permitted Edward to begin the process of retrenchment with a healthy balance. But the ecclesiastical tenths, Clarence's estate, Morton's stricter financial oversight, the king's profit from trade and from his growing fleet of personally owned merchant ships would have permitted him to live comfortably 'of his own' without the French pension – so long as he could avoid ruinously costly wars.

It follows that the sole aim of Edward's diplomacy following the death of Duke Charles was to conceal the fact that he had no intention of going to war, because he could only continue to profit from the Franco-Burgundian war while the contestants believed he might come in on one side or the other. Two factors he did not control set a time limit on his balancing act. The first was that neither side should prevail militarily over the other; the second, of course, was his own credibility, which eroded the longer he played hard to get.

Perhaps the most remarkable feature of the Anglo–French negotiations in 1477–82 was that although Edward acted throughout in the belief that Louis would renege on the Treaty of Picquigny at the first opportunity, it was he who broke the terms repeatedly. The two kings had undertaken to support each other against enemies foreign and domestic, yet Edward continued to negotiate with Burgundy and Brittany against Louis's interests.

In the absence of military intervention it is doubtful whether any amount of English diplomatic skill could have influenced the outcome of the Franco–Burgundian conflict. Commynes smugly observed that 'there has never been a set of negotiations between the French and the English where the intelligence and cleverness of the French has failed to outshine that of the English'. Another way of looking at it is that Edward's ambassadors played a weak hand rather well.

Edward was a man of instincts and, with the exception of the trap he set for Warwick and Clarence in 1470 and the 1475 expedition, one looks in vain for evidence of the *furbizia* that characterized successful Renaissance princes. However, it would have availed him little in his dealings with the Universal Spider, who was the supreme practitioner of the dark art and whose network of informers kept him abreast of his opponents' machinations. Furthermore, with regard to Edward, Louis had the ace of trumps up his sleeve.

Edward himself put it there when he stipulated that the treaty of amity clause agreed at Picquigny should be kept secret, for fear of a violently adverse popular reaction in England. Even though the treaty was signed on holy relics, Louis had reneged on a similarly solemn undertaking with Charles of Burgundy and, as Thomas Hobbes put it in *Leviathan*, 'covenants, without the sword, are but words'. Worse, the treaty of amity would remain secret only until it suited Louis to reveal the terms.

The seemingly complex three-way diplomatic negotiations that took place in 1477–82 reflect the fact, evident since the loss of

Normandy and Guyenne, that England could be a player only if France and Burgundy remained at war with each other. The imperative of preventing the emergence of a single dominant power in Europe set the pattern for English diplomacy in peace and war for the next 500 years – to such good effect that the French, themselves past masters of negotiating in bad faith, still refer to England as 'Perfide Albion'.

Edward's alarm at Louis's proposal that the Dauphin should marry Duchess Marie was muted: it was clearly a bargaining ploy, like Margaret's proposed marriage with Clarence and Edward's own counter-proposal. Of greater concern was that Louis had not obtained the promised guarantee of the annual pension by the Medici and the pope. The instalments of Marguerite's ransom were also at risk, as she was of no further interest to Louis once he had forced her to sign over her rights of inheritance in Anjou, Bar and Lorraine.

Edward sensibly chose Lord Howard and Morton to lead the English delegations to France, as they had a strong personal interest in keeping the pensions coming. They were successful. Louis did pay Marguerite's ransom, and the last instalment of Edward's pension, as agreed at Picquigny, was paid in August 1482. By then Edward had received 475,000 crowns [£60.4 million] and the other pensioners 112,000 [£14.25 million], of which Howard alone received gifts to a value of 24,000 crowns in the two years following Picquigny.

Despite Louis's decrees, French merchants and port officials found many ways of obstructing English trade, while mutual piracy remained endemic. The main benefit of the treaty was the leverage it gave Edward in renegotiating the previously lopsided commercial treaty with Burgundy to abolish the tariff barriers to English textiles. Dowager Duchess Margaret promised further concessions during a state visit to England in 1480.

Louis believed the military cost of a renewed Anglo–Burgundian alliance against him would be greater then continuing to pay the burdensome English pensions. His moment of greatest weakness came after Archduke Maximilian smashed a French army at Guinegatte in Artois in August 1479. Even then, although he agreed to a 100-year extension of the Anglo–French treaty of amity, Louis continued to reject Edward's further demand to start paying Princess Elizabeth's dower after she reached the marriageable age of 12 in 1478.

The diplomatic quadrille came to an end after Duchess Marie was killed in a riding accident on 27 March 1482, with the title passing to her 3-year-old son Philippe. Despite Margaret's best efforts the Burgundian Netherlands distrusted Maximilian and refused to accept his authority as regent. His hope that England might be persuaded to enter the war on his side if he agreed to make good Edward's loss of the French pension was dashed when Louis finally played his ace of trumps by sending him the signed and sealed renewal of the Anglo–French treaty of amity.

The Franco–Burgundian Treaty of Arras, signed on 23 December 1482, marked the end of Edward's effort to keep himself profitably in the middle. It recognized Louis's right to the reversion of the duchy of Burgundy and the counties of Boulogne and Picardy. In addition Maximilian's not-yet 2-year-old daughter, named Margaret after her step-grandmother, was handed over to the French and betrothed to the Dauphin Charles, now 12 years old, with the imperial county of Burgundy (Franche-Comté) and Artois as her dowry.

Commynes suggests that Edward's furious chagrin at this outcome contributed to his death a few months later, but he had obtained all he could realistically have hoped for. He must have known that Elizabeth's marriage to the Dauphin had been unlikely to take place, and his demand for pre-payment of her marriage portion was transparently intended to extend the duration of his pension by other means. His disappointment would have been offset by the consideration that he was nineteen years younger than Louis, who had suffered two strokes during 1481, and could look forward to further opportunities to extort money during the minority of Louis's heir.

The release of Elizabeth from the French betrothal put her back in the pool for the more distasteful activity to which Edward also devoted considerable diplomatic effort, namely marrying his children for as much money as he could get. Cecily (born March 1469) was the only one offered with a traditional (and modest) dowry when she had been betrothed to the future James IV of Scotland in 1474. Margaret died in 1472 and George in 1479, while Catherine (born August 1479) and Bridget (born November 1480) were too young.

This left Mary (born August 1467), the 'spare' for Elizabeth agreed at Picquigny, Edward (born November 1470), Richard (born August 1473) and Anne (born November 1475). Mary was betrothed to the future Frederick I of Denmark in 1481, but she died the following year. Anne became a counter in her father's attempt to obtain a guarantee from Maximilian that he would make good the French pension if Louis ceased to pay it. She was affianced to baby Philippe of Burgundy in August 1480, when Maximilian also agreed not to seek any other contracts of marriage for three years. The betrothal, like Elizabeth's, was a casualty of the Treaty of Arras.

Edward hawked his namesake heir around the courts of Europe, first to Spain and then to Milan, before reaching agreement with Frañsez of Brittany in May 1480 that young Edward would wed the duke's 4-year-old daughter and heir Anne when she became marriageable in eight years' time. Her dowry was to be 100,000 crowns [£12.7 million] if she were still the heir at the time of their marriage, and double that amount if a son were born to the duke before then, the son to marry one of Edward's daughters. In breach of the Treaty of Picquigny Edward also undertook to provide 3,000 archers at his own expense to defend Brittany against an attack by France, and Frañsez to provide a like number if Edward were to invade France.

The validity of any contract with Frañsez was always tenuous, and in this case it was tacitly repudiated almost immediately. The duke's negotiator provided Louis with copies of all the secret correspondence, but did not live to enjoy the large bribe thus earned once

Louis revealed his knowledge of the exact terms of the agreement. Frañsez had the man killed, but quailed when Louis ominously reminded him that he held Brittany as a vassal of the French crown, and that his dealings with Edward were treasonous.*

Young Richard was the only one successfully married in his father's lifetime. In January 1476 John, the last Mowbray Duke of Norfolk, died very suddenly, his only child 4-year-old Anne. The Mowbray estate was vast but encumbered by two dowager duchesses, the doughty and much married Katherine née Neville and Anne's mother Elizabeth née Talbot, whom Edward pressured into surrendering most of her dower lands in exchange for an annuity.

The male Mowbray line had been thin for so long that should Anne die without issue, the legal heirs would be John, Lord Howard and William, Lord Berkeley, descendants of her father's great-aunts. Edward prevailed on Berkeley to surrender his succession rights in exchange for the cancellation of bonds totalling £34,000 [£21.6 million] extorted by the Lisle branch of the Talbots when they kidnapped the entire Berkeley family in the 1430s. In 1481 Edward also made him Viscount of Catherlough in Ireland.

In January 1477 Edward married Anne to his 4-year-old second son Richard, Duke of York, in the second no-expense-spared ceremony of state during the second half of his reign. Papal dispensation for consanguinity had been obtained, also at great expense, and the two infants became the centrepiece of a magnificent display. Anthony, Earl Rivers, and John de la Pole, Earl of Lincoln, led the young bride to St Stephen's Chapel, and the Dukes of Gloucester and Buckingham escorted her to the wedding feast for the massed nobility of England.

The prominence given to the Woodvilles during and after the marriage was a further signal that Edward had the utmost confidence in them. Rivers played a leading role in the wedding and

*Frañsez did not produce a male heir before he died in 1488. Brittany was finally annexed by France after Duchess Anne was forced to marry Charles VIII in 1491 and Louis XII in 1499.

the following tournament, where other contestants included his nephews Thomas and Richard Grey, his brother Edward, and Richard Haute, the son of the queen's aunt Joan.

Anne Mowbray died in November 1481 but before then, as he had done with the Countess of Warwick, Edward had set aside Howard's rights by an Act of Parliament that gave his son Richard a life interest in the estate, after which it would revert to the crown. Howard was paid nothing, on the face of it base ingratitude to a loyal servant. Possibly Edward judged that Howard's vastly profitable role as lead ambassador to Louis XI was compensation enough.

THE MARCHES

THE LATER YEARS OF EDWARD'S REIGN WERE NOT SOLELY devoted to the shameless pursuit of money: he also tried to resolve the problem of endemic lawlessness in the Welsh and Scots Marches. The policy he pursued for the first was innovative, economical and was copied by his successors. His approach to the second was the opposite – brutally traditional, ruinously expensive and counter-productive.

We have seen how Edward began to develop an alternative to the regime lock on Wales lost with the elder William Herbert by moving the Prince of Wales's Council to Ludlow in early 1473. The king did not push the project at first, as he was fully taken up with preparing the invasion of France. Also, it was prudent not to invest too much political capital in Prince Edward until he had survived the dangerous early years.

From 1476 onwards the project rapidly gathered pace. The two greatest non-royal Welsh landowners, Herbert's 25-year-old namesake heir and 21-year-old Henry Stafford, Duke of Buckingham, had not shown the capacity and dependability Edward looked for, and were excluded. The Council became a Woodville-dominated enterprise, grist to the mill of historians anxious to attribute the sordid failure of the Yorkist dynasty to their evil influence.

The idea that Rivers, his brothers and his nephews worked to a plan concerted by Elizabeth to increase their power and influence is manifest nonsense. To the contrary and as we saw in the case of Calais, Rivers spurned opportunities to make himself a magnate. He was a highly intelligent and cultivated individual, and the presumption must be that he knew to do so would risk the good will of his royal brother-in-law. The Woodvilles knew they owed everything to the king and repaid him by loyally performing the tasks he delegated to them.

Chief among them was the project nearest to Edward's heart – the rearing of his heir and preparing him for kingship. It is not remotely likely that a medieval king would have entrusted such a sensitive responsibility to men who showed any sign of independent ambition. Perhaps even more to the point, is it also not the slightest bit remarkable that the queen should have wished for her sons to be in the care of men she trusted.

As befits any experiment in governance, Edward increased the power of the prince's Council incrementally. Between 1473 and 1476 he still hoped that it could work in coordination with the Marcher lords, but the division of judicial authority sabotaged efforts to bring wrongdoers to justice. Local courts would pre-emptively acquit men indicted by the Council, with the Herbert affinity in south Wales among the most prominent offenders.

In January 1476 Edward increased the Council's judicial powers and summoned the Marcher lords to a meeting with the Council at Ludlow on 24 March, but before then he had decided to abandon the established structure. On 16 March he granted the Council power to intervene in all Welsh and Marcher lordships, and in June the Council pointedly met at Buckingham's lordship of Newport. Seventy-three individuals, three Herbert bastards and two sons of the late Roger Vaughan among them, were required to post bonds of good behaviour.

In December Edward completed the process of delegating to the Council most of the judicial and executive powers of the ancestral Mortimer earldom of March in Herefordshire, Shropshire, Radnor, Brecknock and Monmouth. Towards the end of 1477 he persuaded

Richard of Gloucester to exchange his sparsely populated lordship of Elfael (about a third of Radnor) for the duchy of Lancaster estate around the port of Ogmore in Gloucester's lordship of Glamorgan. In December 1477 Prince Edward was granted possession of almost all the March earldom's castles, lordships and manors, to which Elfael was added in March 1478.

The writing was on the wall for the younger William Herbert from the time of the Council sessions at Newport. In 1479 he was forced to surrender the earldom of Pembroke and all the lands once controlled by his father except the lordship of Raglan, including Caerleon and Usk. He was fobbed off with the title of Earl of Huntingdon vacated by Thomas Grey when made Marquess of Dorset, and with duchy of Cornwall lands in Dorset and Somerset, which complemented his existing Somerset holdings as Baron Dunster.

Prince Edward was made Earl of Pembroke on 8 July 1479, and ten days later Earl of March. Usk and Caerleon were transferred to him in February 1483, leaving Herbert with his father's magnificent castle at Raglan and little else in Wales and the March. Herbert's uncle Walter Devereux, Lord Ferrers of Chartley, remained a Council member and lord of Weobley and of Richard's Castle in Herefordshire, but surrendered the ex-Talbot manors of Archenfield and Goodrich in the south of the county.

The Talbots had been the only serious rivals of the House of York on the English side of the middle March. They never recovered from the loss of the 1st Earl of Shrewsbury and his son, Viscount Lisle, at Castillon in 1453, and of the 2nd earl at Northampton in 1460. When the 3rd earl died in 1473, his heir George Talbot was only 5 years old. His remaining, mainly Shropshire lands were put in the custody of the queen and administered by the Council.

Clerical members of the Council were promoted to the bishoprics of Hereford (Thomas Myling, the prince's chancellor, in 1474), Worcester (John Alcock, ex-Lord Chancellor, co-tutor and co-president of the Council with Rivers, in 1476) and St David's (Richard

48. PRINCE EDWARD'S COUNCIL

0 10 20 30 40 50
miles

Lancashire

STANLEY

Anglesey

Caernarvon

DIOCESE OF BANGOR

Merioneth

Denbigh
Ruthyn

Flint

Denbigh

Palatinate of Chester

STANLEY

DIOCESE OF ST ASAPH

Chirk

Bromfield and Yale

Shrewsbury (Talbot)

Powys

Montgomery

Shropshire

DIOCESE

Elfael

Radnor

Cardigan

DIOCESE OF

ST DAVID'S

Brecknock

Carmarthen

Palatinate of Pembroke

Kidwelly

Brecon (Buckingham)

Abergavenny

OF

Ludlow
Richard's Castle (Ferrers)
Weobley

HEREFORD

Herefordshire

Archenfield

Goodrich

Raglan (Herbert)
Usk

Monmouth

Gloucestershire

Gower

GLAMORGAN

Ogmore

Caerleon

Newport (Buckingham)

Somerset

© Hugh Bicheno

Martin, in 1482). All had close links with the Woodvilles – as Abbot of Westminster Myling had given the queen sanctuary in 1470–1 and stood as godfather to the new-born prince, and Martin had served with Rivers in his embassy to Charles of Burgundy in 1475.

The Council exercised direct government over a far larger proportion of the region than the older William Herbert had enjoyed, and it was clearly Edward's intention that Wales and the March should be a training ground where his heir could learn the business of kingship. The queen's influence was further strengthened by the appointment of her sons Thomas, Marquess of Dorset, and Richard Grey to the Council. In April 1482 the king gave Richard Grey the duchy of Lancaster lordship of Kidwelly, and in February 1483 made him co-equal with Rivers and Alcock as supervisor of Prince Edward's deportment and finances.

The Council shared territorial control only in the north of the region. Lord Stanley's areas of influence in Chester and Flint were respected, as were William Stanley's lordships of Holt and Chirk. William was also steward of the duchy of York lordship of Denbigh and administered the lands of the minor John Grey in Montgomery and Shropshire on behalf of the Council until November 1482, when John entered into his inheritance as Baron Grey of Powys.

When young Richard, Duke of York, married Countess Anne Mowbray his estate included half the lordship of Bromfield and Yale on the border of Denbigh and Shropshire. The king purchased the other half from George Neville, Baron Abergavenny, and the lordship was administered by the Council: which, since Bromfield and Yale was adjacent to Chirk, probably means William Stanley was made responsible for it as well. He was made steward of the prince's household in 1481 and both his active involvement in the Council and the lands put under his administration were to have a considerable bearing on future events.

The Woodvilles established an excellent working relationship with the Stanleys. They were trustees of each other's properties elsewhere in England, and the queen made Lord Stanley steward of her dower lands in Cheshire. In return, Thomas married his heir George to the land-poor widow Joan, Baroness Strange of Knockyn and daughter of the queen's sister Jacquetta. He had been steward of Edward's household since 1471 and would have been a member of a 'queen's party' if Elizabeth had ever dared to form one.

Prince Edward's Council did not have time to resolve the chronic problems of governance in Wales and the March. However it is notable as the one major institutional innovation made by Edward, and the prototype of the councils with which the Tudors and early Stuarts sought to bring a semblance of order and justice to a once ungovernable region.

• ∽ •

The contrast between Edward's policy in Wales and his attempt to impose his authority on the Scots Marches could not have been more stark. Not only did it waste the financial surplus he had built up since 1475, it also tied up the military resources that were his principal bargaining chip with Louis XI and Maximilian. At great expense he recovered the border fortress of Berwick; but it was an entirely self-inflicted strategic debacle.

After defeat at Guinegatte in 1479 Louis XI needed to distract Edward, who gave him an opening by tearing up the truce signed with James III of Scotland in 1473. It would have been more logical if James had done so, as the truce and the betrothal of his heir to Edward's daughter Cecily was highly unpopular with the Scots nobility. Unfortunately contemporary sources are negligible when not also wildly fanciful, and a rational explanation for Edward's decision to kick over the table is hard to identify.

It is fair to assume that Richard of Gloucester had a great deal to do with it. Scots raids were a reproach to his good lordship, particularly in the West March, for which he was personally responsible, but also in the East March, where Henry Percy, Earl of Northumberland and his chief retainer, was briefly captured in a border skirmish. Gloucester may also have calculated that a war against their ancestral enemy would cement the northmen's loyalty to him as their tribal leader.

The proximate cause of the escalation was that James III's sister Margaret, betrothed to Earl Rivers in 1478, became pregnant by her lover William, Lord Crichton. When news of this reached London in January 1479, Edward declared that England's honour had been insulted and demanded repayment of the dowry instalments he had made for Princess Cecily's future marriage. He seized Scots property in London, and Scots residents in England began to petition for denizenship to protect their assets.

During 1479 the rancorous Scots royal family fell apart. This was believed to be the work of James's low-born favourites led by his physician William Sheves, made Archbishop of St Andrews in 1478 when his predecessor was deposed for corruption and insanity. James's sister Mary was already in prison consequent on the attainder of her husband Thomas Boyd, Earl of Arran; his brothers John, Earl of Mar, and Alexander, Duke of Albany, suffered forfeiture and imprisonment. Mar died in mysterious circumstances and James gave the earldom to Robert Cochrane, his architect. Albany escaped from prison and fled to France.

Edward then funded Gloucester and Northumberland to prepare for war before Easter of 1480. He also sent an embassy to tell the Scots that they must surrender Berwick, Coldingham and Roxburgh as reparation and hand over Prince James to ensure that he married Cecily in May 1481, or else face 'rigorous and cruel war'. In May Gloucester was appointed lieutenant-general in the North and commissions of array were issued for all the northern counties.

In September 1480 Archibald 'Bell-the-Cat' Douglas, Earl of Angus, raided Northumberland and burned the town supposedly guarded by Bamburgh Castle. Gloucester and Percy chased him back into Scotland, but he had achieved the objective of preventing the negotiated settlement sought by James III. Angus was a 'Red' Douglas and knew that Edward had demanded the reinstatement of

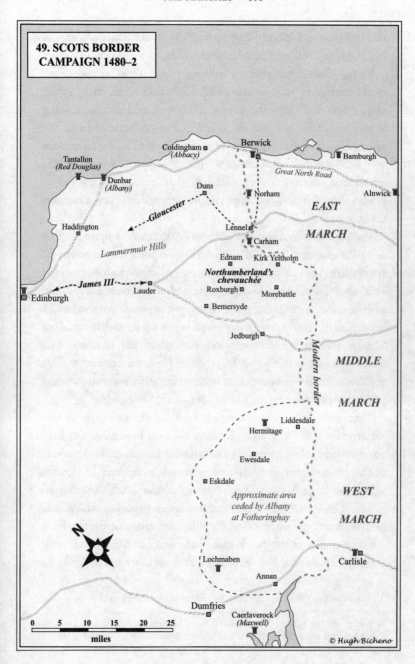

49. SCOTS BORDER CAMPAIGN 1480-2

Tantallon
(Red Douglas)

Coldingham
(Abbacy)

Berwick

Bamburgh

Dunbar
(Albany)

Duns

Norham

Great North Road

Haddington

Gloucester

Lennel

EAST

Alnwick

Lammermuir Hills

Carham

MARCH

Ednam

Kirk Yeltholm

**Northumberland's
chevauchée**

James III

Edinburgh

Lauder

Roxburgh

Morebattle

Bemersyde

Jedburgh

Modern border

MIDDLE

MARCH

Liddesdale

Hermitage

Ewesdale

Eskdale

*Approximate area
ceded by Albany
at Fotheringhay*

WEST

MARCH

N

Lochmaben

Carlisle

Annan

Dumfries

Caerlaverock
(Maxwell)

0   5   10   15   20   25

miles

© Hugh Bicheno

the attainted and exiled James, last of the 'Black' Earls of Douglas, who had been a Garter knight since 1463.

So far Edward had paid for military preparations entirely 'of his own', testimony to how successful he had been in transforming royal finances. During the winter of 1480–1, still loth to summon Parliament, he embarked on a new round of 'benevolences' and also claimed the three-quarters of a subsidy voted by the Commons in 1475, worth about £24,000 [£15.3 million], which he had renounced on return from France with his saddlebags full of Louis's gold. He also extracted another tenth from the Canterbury Convocation.

The York Convocation was not immediately called upon to make a similar contribution and the northern counties were exempted from the king's exactions in recognition of their payment in kind. This was burdensome: although there had been a poor harvest, supplies for the army were gathered by purveyance. Against which service in the forthcoming campaign was by paid indenture. Lord Stanley brought 3,000 archers from Lancashire, Rivers indented for 3,000 more from the Welsh March, and Dorset brought 600 from the West Country, but the main body of the army was naturally and profitably provided by the Gloucester and Percy affinities.

The plan for 1481 was for Lord Howard to make a naval *chevauchée* into the Firth of Forth while Edward led a land invasion. Only the naval assault, accompanied by a devastating attack on Scots trade by private ship-owners granted letters of marque, went ahead.* Howard seized the larger ships and burned the rest at Leith (Edinburgh's port), at Blackness, 17 miles further up the Firth of Forth, and at Kinghorn, opposite Leith on the northern side of the Firth.

Edward did not ride north to lead the army, and in a letter to the pope he explained this was because of unrest in England. We know

---

*The use of 'letters of marque and reprisal', traditionally issued to merchants who could not recover losses to pirates operating from foreign jurisdictions, became a scheme of licensed piracy in which the Crown took a share of the profits without necessarily risking a penny of investment. See my book *Elizabeth's Sea Dogs*.

nothing more, although it may have been prompted by the combination of a poor harvest and renewed demands for taxes. However it is also the case that Edward's continental diplomacy was at a particularly crucial stage that summer, and he would not have wanted to absent himself from London for long.

The situation changed in 1482 because Louis sent the Duke of Albany to England. Albany had been a strident opponent of the Anglo–Scots truce, but when he met Edward and Gloucester at Fotheringhay on 11 July he signed a treaty by which, if Edward made him king, he would surrender Berwick and, in the West March, cede Lochmaben and Hermitage Castles and the nests of border bandits in Annandale, Liddesdale, Eskdale and Ewesdale. Albany would also recognize that he held Scotland as Edward's vassal, would revoke the French alliance and, once extracted from a recent marriage arranged by Louis, he would marry Princess Cecily.

The treaty of Fotheringhay delayed and added a layer of political over-elaboration to what had been until then a straightforward campaign devised by Gloucester. In 1482 Edward had already spent, on indentures alone, about £4,300 [£2.7 million] on naval forces, £4,500 on English troops, and £2,200 on professional mercenaries. This was overkill against a penurious opponent who could command only feudal levies led by unruly lords who hated the court party. The intention was clearly to destroy Scots resistance utterly, but the two months' delay caused by Edward's dalliance with Albany ate up the campaigning season, supplies and money.

Gloucester and Albany rode north to join Northumberland and Stanley at Berwick. The town surrendered without a fight, but the fortress held out. Leaving Stanley to conduct the siege, Gloucester sent Northumberland to ravage the triangle between the Lennel and Jedburgh highways into England. Following with the main army, Gloucester waited until he knew the *chevauchée* had drawn the Scots army, then crossed the Tweed at Lennel and marched towards Duns before turning north-west. The aim was to go around the Lammermuir Hills and get between James's army and Edinburgh, trapping him against Northumberland's force and culminating in a battle of annihilation.

Oblivious to the fate Gloucester had planned for him and buoyed up a minor triumph in his first experience of battle in 1481, James marched at the head of a large feudal host towards Lauder, where the Jedburgh and Lennel highways divide. On 22 July his nobles, realizing that James was leading them to destruction, mutinied. They hanged Cochrane and other royal favourites from the bridge at Lauder and hustled James back to the capital, where they imprisoned him in Edinburgh Castle, an impregnable and well-supplied fortress.

With no one to fight and James out of reach, when Gloucester reached Edinburgh soon afterwards he found himself facing a strategic conundrum. He could not sack the city because of the commitment to Albany, and he could not besiege the castle because time and money were running out. The citizens of Edinburgh undertook to repay Edward's dowry payments if he did not want the marriage to take place, but that was the only return on investment Gloucester obtained before setting off back to England on 4 August.

Two days earlier he and Albany had signed an agreement with representatives of all the Scots noble factions that promised a pardon for Albany and the restoration of his lands and offices. When details of what Albany had agreed at Fotheringhay became known his situation became precarious once more, but he claimed that he had only signed to moderate the English plan to devastate the Lowlands. In his letter to the Pope Edward acknowledged that Albany did indeed save Scotland from severe consequences, which opens the door to suspicion that the Scot played him for a fool. The only English gain was Berwick Castle, which capitulated on 24 August. The Crowland Continuator was not impressed:

> This trifling, I really know not whether to call it 'gain' or 'loss' (for the safe keeping of Berwick each year swallows up ten thousand marks [£9.5 million]) at this period diminished the resources of

king and kingdom by more than a hundred thousand pounds [£63.6 million]. King Edward was vexed at this frivolous outlay of so much money, although the recovery of Berwick in some degree alleviated his sorrow.

Gloucester must have been consumed with rage that Edward had once more denied him the opportunity to win martial glory. Presumably aware of this, the king tried to appease him by making Gloucester's friend Lord Lovell a viscount, by declaring all his brother's offices in the West March hereditary, and by awarding him as an appanage the territory ceded in principle by Albany at Fotheringhay as well as any other he might conquer.

But nothing could conceal the fact that in 1481–2, as in 1475, the nation had provided Edward with a mighty sledgehammer to shatter his enemies, and he had just gone through the motions. When 1482 ended with the diplomatic humiliation of the Franco–Burgundian Treaty of Arras, the full extent of Edward's failure was revealed.

DAGGERS IN MEN'S SMILES*

T HE SIREN SONG OF 'AFTER WHICH THEREFORE BECAUSE of which' must be resisted during the last months of Edward's reign. We know he had little time to live – but *he* did not, although there are hints he had intimations of mortality before the fatal illness took him. He made a new will, but it was ignored and destroyed so we do not know what provisions it made for the succession. Not enough, certainly, but it is hardly surprising that he did not anticipate what was to come.

Despite his austere distaste for the king's morals and bitter condemnation of his regular shearing of the clerical sheep, our eye-witness the Crowland Continuator paints a glowing picture of the last great festivity of Edward's reign:

> King Edward kept the following feast of the Nativity at his palace
> of Westminster, frequently appearing clad in a great variety of
> most costly garments, of quite a different cut to those which
> had been usually seen hitherto in our kingdom… as to give
> that prince a new and distinguished air to beholders, he being a
> person of most elegant appearance, and remarkable beyond all
> others for the attractions of his person. You might have seen, in
> those days, the royal court presenting no other appearance than
> such as fully befits a most mighty kingdom, filled with riches

* 'There is daggers in men's smiles: the near in blood,/The nearer bloody': *Macbeth*, Act III, Scene 3.

and with people of almost all nations, and (a point in which it excelled all others) boasting of those most sweet and beautiful children, the issue of his marriage... with queen Elizabeth.

Edward's gargantuan appetites had barely moderated. According to the invaluable testimony of the Augustinian friar Dominic Mancini, who was in England during the crucial period as an envoy of the Archbishop of Vienne (Poitiers) and whose principal informant was the Italian-speaking John Argentine, one of the Prince of Wales's physicians, Edward had become 'fat in the loins'. The king remained 'most immoderate' in food and drink, and 'it was his habit... to take an emetic for the delight of gorging his stomach once more'.

However, it appears he had become less sexually promiscuous. For the last years of his life he had what the French would have called a *maîtresse en titre* in Elizabeth née Lambert, better known as Jane Shore, the name given to her by the dramatist Thomas Heywood in 1599, which I will use to avoid confusion with the queen. Jane had been married to a London merchant called Shore, but the marriage was annulled in 1476 on grounds of his impotence. Since her liaison with Edward began that year, it is fair to suspect that her husband preferred to accept the private stigma of impotence than to be a very public cuckold.

Thomas More knew Jane in old age and his *The History of Richard III* is our main source of information about her. From others More learned that in her prime, 'a proper wit had she, and could both read well and write, merry in company, ready and quick of answer, neither mute nor full of babble, sometimes taunting without displeasure, and not without playfulness'. In other words, a charming flirt. Nobody had a bad word to say about her because:

For many [Edward] had, but her he loved, whose favour, to speak truth, she never abused to any man's hurt, but to many a man's comfort and relief: where the King took displeasure, she would mitigate and appease his mind; where men were out of favour, she would bring them in his grace; for many who had highly offended, she obtained pardon; of great forfeitures she got men remission; and finally, in many weighty suits, she stood many men in great stead either for none or very small rewards, and those rather gay than rich – either because she was content with the deed itself well done, or because she delighted in being asked for favours and to show what she was able to do with the King.

Intriguingly, Jane told More that the king spoke of only three long-term lovers, 'in whom three diverse qualities differently excelled: one [Jane] the merriest; another the wiliest; the third the holiest harlot in his realm'. The other two 'were somewhat greater personages' but either Jane or More chose not to name them. The 'holiest harlot' may have been Lady Eleanor Boteler née Talbot, on whom more later. The 'wiliest' was probably Elizabeth Lucy née Wayte, Edward's mistress from the early 1460s, who bore the king two recognized bastards and may have died giving birth to the second in 1476.

There is every reason to believe More's suggestion that Jane and the queen were friends. Elizabeth was almost constantly pregnant during the marriage (the last of ten children, Bridget, was born in November 1480), and would have welcomed some relief from the corpulent king's attentions. Jane posed no threat, could serve as a conduit for favours the queen hesitated to ask for in person, and one can readily imagine them discreetly comparing notes and having a giggle about the man whose bed they shared.

Early 1483 was a time of heightened international tension for England. Smarting at having been outwitted by Louis XI, and believing the Scots had contributed to his humiliation, Edward went through the motions of preparing for war against both. He summoned Parliament, which assembled on 20 January, and before it adjourned a month later it had voted him the necessary funds.

Having failed to become the power behind the Scottish throne, the Duke of Albany sent ambassadors to London to meet Edward, Gloucester, Northumberland, Lord Scrope of Bolton and Lord Parr, and they signed another treasonous treaty on Albany's behalf.

After Parliament voted him the funds, on 20 February Edward offered Duke Fransez 4,000 archers for three months' service at Edward's expense, and to have them ready at Plymouth or Dartmouth within a month of the duke requesting them. On the same day Parliament voted Gloucester the hereditary grants described in the last chapter and adjourned. Gloucester departed London not long afterwards and never saw his brother again.

Giving Gloucester an appanage and an incentive to keep busy making war on Scotland is one indication that Edward's mind was turning to what might happen when he died. Another is that on 8 March Anthony Woodville sent his lawyer a copy of royal patents appointing him sole governor of the Prince of Wales, and empowering him to raise troops in the Welsh Marches. Taken together, the two measures are suggestive of a monarch seeking to ward off possible threats to his son's succession.

Some time between 25 March and 2 April Edward became ill and took to bed after a fishing trip on the Thames. It may have been malaria but pneumonia seems more likely, as he was lucid to the end. He had been blessed by good luck all his life, but there was none left for his posterity. The first and probably definitive domino to fall in the sequence that doomed his dynasty was that his uncle Henry Bourchier, Earl of Essex, Lord Treasurer and mainstay of the regime, died on 4 April, leaving no one else of his stature within the government.*

News of Bourchier's death appears to have become garbled with the king's illness and on 6 April a false report of Edward's death reached York, where a dirge was sung in the cathedral. On the 7th Edward summoned Elizabeth and their children, her son Dorset

---

*His interim replacement was under-treasurer John Wood, who had been responsible for the day-to-day running of the treasury since 1480.

and his old friend Hastings to his bedside. He begged them to sink their differences and work together to ensure his son's succession, and they tearfully assured him that they would. On the 9th he died.

Hastings immediately wrote to Gloucester at Middleham and possibly also to Buckingham at Brecon, telling them that the Woodvilles intended to seize power. It was 1469 all over again, and once more his fear of Elizabeth's vengeance for the wrong he had done her led him to put at risk the dynasty to which he owed everything. For all the fulsome posthumous praise of the chroniclers he had never been much more than chief panderer to the late king, and made the fatal error of believing he could continue to play a leading role.

The Woodvilles also owed their eminence entirely to the late king, and the idea that they might have thought they could impose their will on the Privy Council and on Gloucester is laughable. Although the Council in London proclaimed the Prince of Wales King Edward V on 11 April, and his coronation date set for 4 May, news of his father's death did not reach Ludlow until the 14th. If Rivers had been intent on seizing power he would have set out for London with the king at once; instead, he waited for orders from the Council.

The new king could easily have been in London in time for his father's funeral on 18–19 April. He was not because Hastings started the hare of a Woodville *coup d'état* by telling the Privy Council that if Rivers came to London with an army he would retreat to Calais. There is no indication that Rivers, although legally empowered to do so, had any such intention. Hastings prevailed on the Council to instruct Rivers to come with 'only' 2,000 men and to arrive in London on 1 May, and the royal party did not set out until 24 April.

In the evening of the 11th Hastings invited Lord Howard to dine. It is a safe assumption that Hastings was seeking to win him to an anti-Woodville alliance, and told him about his correspondence with Gloucester and Buckingham. It would have been prudent for Howard to have written to Gloucester immediately, both to confirm the truth of Hastings's assertions and to establish an independent line of communication to the most powerful man in the country.

On receipt of Hastings's and Howard's letters Gloucester wrote to Rivers, saying he wished to join the royal party before it entered London, to Elizabeth declaring his intention – according to the Crowland Continuator – 'to come and offer submission, fealty, and all that was due from him to his lord and King, Edward V', and to Hastings, Buckingham and Howard stating that he feared dire consequences from the Woodvilles having possession of the king.

Gloucester summoned his affinity to meet him at York and on 20 April set out from Middleham with 300 men-at-arms. On the 21st, at a heavily attended funeral service for his brother at York Minster, he led the northern nobility in swearing an oath of loyalty to Edward V. While in York, he received a reply from Buckingham, expressing a wish to rendezvous with him at Northampton.

During this time the Council met every day. The Crowland Continuator, who was present at these sessions, wrote of 'the most urgent desire of all present that the Prince should succeed his father in all his glory'. Discussions centred on the type of government to be established during the king's minority, but the emphasis was on how to counter foreign aggression aiming to exploit the interregnum. It was a given that Gloucester would become Protector, but the Council members do not appear to have doubted that the precedent of Henry VI's minority Council, in which no one lord predominated, would be followed. The Council also commissioned Edward Woodville to assemble a fleet to combat an expected surge of French and Breton piracy.

To avoid arousing suspicion Gloucester did not add to his retinue when set out from York on 23 April. The next day he stopped at Pontefract after receiving a reply from Rivers agreeing to meet at Northampton on the 29th. The town lay north of the royal party's itinerary along Watling Street, the high road from Ludlow to London. It was also where Gloucester had agreed to rendezvous with Buckingham, who had marched across country from Brecon with a likewise unremarkable retinue of 300 men-at-arms.

The trap was set and Rivers walked into it, accompanied only by his nephew Richard Grey, newly come from London. Men planning to seize power would not have left the security of the 2,000 men who remained with the new king at Stony Stratford, 15 miles south of Northampton, to put themselves at the mercy of the man they were allegedly conspiring against. After an apparently convivial dinner with Gloucester and Buckingham, they were put under arrest.

On the 30th Gloucester and Buckingham rode to Stony Stafford, dismissed the king's escort and arrested two members of the Prince of Wales's household: his chamberlain Thomas Vaughan and his household comptroller Richard Haute, son of Joan Woodville, Rivers's aunt. On the same day Gloucester sent a letter to the Council declaring that he had acted to pre-empt a Woodville *coup d'état*. The young king angrily rejected Gloucester's allegations but was powerless to influence events.

On 1 May Elizabeth, along with 9-year-old Richard, Duke of York, the five princesses, her son Dorset and brother Lionel, Bishop of Salisbury, fled to sanctuary at Westminster Abbey. In an act of panicked abdication the Lord Chancellor, Archbishop Rotherham of York, gave her the Great Seal. When the Council met to consider Gloucester's letter Hastings once again played a crucial role by assuring the councillors that Gloucester's loyalty to Edward V was unquestionable, that he would not make such allegations without substance, and that the arrested men would be granted the opportunity to defend themselves.

Giving the Woodvilles their day in court was the last thing either Hastings or Gloucester were going to permit. Instead of bringing them to London, Gloucester sent Rivers to Sheriff Hutton, Grey to Middleham and Vaughan to Pontefract. Haute did not share their fate, for reasons unknown. Gloucester also showed his hand by sending the Council an order he was not legally entitled to give, declaring that Rotherham had abdicated his responsibility, as indeed he had, but permitting him to remain a Council member. The royal party, now consisting entirely of men loyal to Gloucester and Buckingham, spent the night of 3 May at St Albans. Presumably this was where they were joined by Duchess Cecily from Berkhamsted, 10 miles away, as she was with them when they rode into London the next day.

There was an arms depot along the road and Gloucester had its contents loaded into wagons and sent ahead of the royal party, having it announced that this was proof of the Woodvilles' plan to seize power. Some people may have believed this, but every member of the royal party knew it to be false and presumably it failed to convince anyone else of substance, as no more was said about this supposed evidence.

The king was taken to the Bishop of London's palace and Gloucester went with Cecily to her palace of Baynard's Castle. We may be certain that she stilled whatever doubts Gloucester may still have entertained. She had waited nearly twenty years for revenge on Elizabeth and threw discretion to the wind when Gloucester summoned the late king's executors to Baynard's Castle sometime between 5 and 7 May.

Elizabeth had surrendered the Great Seal and Gloucester gave it to Cardinal Bourchier to bestow as he wished, in itself probably enough to win over a man whose vanity had been wounded by Edward IV's accurate assessment of his worth. The executors, Bourchier chief among them, then took the extraordinary step of agreeing that the late king's will should not be executed. The given excuse was that Edward's bequests to his children could not be honoured while they were in sanctuary.

The truth was that Cecily told the gathering that Edward had been conceived in adultery, and Bourchier and the others were convinced it must be true, because why would a distinguished lady admit to such a thing if it were not? This unsavoury fact has been glossed over to a remarkable degree, yet it was widely known at the time, and not forgotten for many years.

In a letter of 23 May 1535 to Emperor Charles V, his ambassador Eustace Chapuys reported a representation made to Thomas Cromwell, Henry VIII's chief minister, about Henry's having set aside Catherine, his first wife and the emperor's aunt, to marry Anne Boleyn. Chapuys was scornful of Cromwell's attempts to justify the king's action (my italics):

> The King ought not to attach so much weight in such a case to the judicial proceedings, or to the statutes of this realm, which only depended on the prince's wish, as might be seen by the Acts of King Richard, who, not content with having declared by sentence that the sons and daughters of King Edward were illegitimate, *caused King Edward himself to be declared a bastard, and, to prove it, called his own mother to bear witness to it, and caused it to be continually preached so. [Cromwell] confessed that was true of King Richard*; but the said King was a tyrant and a bad man, and he had paid for it accordingly.

Note the feline subtlety of Chapuys's thrust. If Edward was indeed a bastard and his children doubly so, then his eldest daughter Elizabeth, Henry VIII's mother, brought not the slightest legitimacy to the Tudor dynasty. Cromwell did not dispute the facts as stated by Chapuys and could only concur in the convenient fiction that her son forced 'proud Cis' to humiliate herself. Improbable, to put it mildly, especially in the light of a letter she sent Richard in 1474, imperiously summoning him to answer for a wrong done by his servants to one of hers.

Oceans of ink have been spilled debating when Gloucester decided to usurp the throne, the prevalent theory being that events inexorably forced him to do so. This is to dismiss abundant evidence of Cecily's deranged malice. Whether she lied about Edward's conception or not is immaterial: her other sons believed Edward was not the son of Richard of York, therefore Gloucester's decision was made as soon as he learned of his half-brother's death.

When Chapuys wrote 'caused it to be continually preached' he was referring to a sermon delivered on 22 June by Dr Ralph Shaw in the presence of Gloucester, Buckingham and many other lords at the open-air pulpit outside St Paul's Cathedral, and by others elsewhere in London. Shaw was the brother of Edmund, the Mayor of London, who was by now fully on board with the conspiracy. According to Mancini his topic was 'bastard slips should not take deep root', and he declared (my italics) that the 'progeny of King Edward *should be instantly eradicated*, for neither had he been a legitimate King, nor could his issue be so'.

Buckingham and others spoke in support of Shaw's assertions. They appear to have been oblivious to the discredit this brought on the entire House of York, but once it became apparent that the allegation reflected ill on him Gloucester changed tack, as he had with the wagons of arms. Even so, when in 1484 his tame Parliament passed *Titulus Regius*, the Act supposedly establishing his right to the throne (Appendix J), the words (my italics) 'Over this we consider how that ye be *the undoubted son and heir* of Richard late Duke of York' after a litany of accusations against Edward and Elizabeth.

'Over this' – that is to say *greater than* the preceding charges, which included 'sorcery and witchcraft' by Elizabeth and her mother, and Edward's 'sensuality and concupiscence' leading to recidivist bigamy. It is impossible to finesse this blunt statement by Gloucester himself that he believed his undoubted parentage was the principal plank of his right to the throne.

NAKED VILLAINY*

ETWEEN THAT FIRST SECRET MEETING AT BAYNARD'S Castle and the overt usurpation beginning on 22 June, Gloucester conducted a rolling *coup d'état* in which he deceived, divided and ultimately destroyed the minority Council. The Crowland Continuator judged that he enjoyed power 'just like another King', after the Council appointed him Protector on 10 May and gave him 'the tutelage and oversight of the King's most royal person', but in fact sovereignty was still vested in the Council. For the next month Gloucester showed friendly respect for Hastings, Stanley and Bishops Rotherham, Stillington and Morton, and even invited the young king's former tutor John Alcock, Bishop of Rochester, to join the Council.

With the Council's approval Edward V was moved to the royal apartments in the Tower and the neutral figures of Bishop John Russell, Rotherham's successor at Lincoln, and the cleric John Gunthorpe were made Lord Chancellor and Lord Privy Seal, both at Cardinal Bourchier's recommendation. These reassuring appointments were window-dressing: Bourchier became a co-conspirator from the moment he agreed not to implement or publish Edward IV's will and ordered the sequestration of the late king's goods, jewels and seals.

The Council concurred with Gloucester's condemnation of Edward

---

*'And thus I clothe my naked villainy/With odd old ends stol'n out of holy writ,/And seem a saint, when most I play the devil': *King Richard the Third*, Act I, Scene 3.

Woodville, who had sailed from Southampton on 29 April, having first robbed a vessel in port of £10,250 [£6.5 million] in gold coins. However the councillors rejected his attempt to extend the condemnation to Rivers, Grey and Vaughan, all supposedly part of the same treasonous plot. Since a charge of treason must mean they had planned the destruction of Edward V, it was a manifest absurdity. They also rebuked Gloucester for speaking disrespectfully of the dowager queen and on 13 May they rejected his request to declare that his Protectorate should last until Edward V's majority, saying this was a matter for Parliament to decide.

Irked by these legal niceties, Gloucester claimed that the queen, Dorset and Edward Woodville had looted the treasury. Records survive to prove this yet another false allegation. The Scottish campaign had depleted the hoard built up by Edward IV, but the loss was being made good by his enhanced revenue collection. Furthermore Richard was to spend lavishly in 1483–4 without recourse to taxation. The accusation stemmed from his fury when, although his agents persuaded the Genoese captains of most of the fleet to desert Woodville, he got away to Brittany with two ships and the looted money, leaving the crown liable for the loss.

Duke Frañsez publicly welcomed Woodville and gave him a pension. This was the first indication that opposition to Gloucester's rule might coalesce around the exiled Henry Tudor, another pensioner of the Breton court. Also, the withdrawal of the Channel fleet left English shipping defenceless against French and Breton pirates, and the new Protector was obliged to send the prominent London wool merchant Thomas Grafton to bribe the leading French raider, known to the English as 'Lord Cordes', for a truce.

Despite the Council's unwillingness to endorse his charge of treason against the Woodvilles, Gloucester never ceased to proclaim it and arbitrarily declared their lands forfeit. He did not again summon the whole Council but instead divided it into committees meeting separately, purportedly to plan different aspects of the coronation, now scheduled for 22 June. Meanwhile he appointed

Howard Chief Steward of the duchy of Lancaster, and Buckingham Constable of England and Chief Justice and Lord Chamberlain of Wales for life, also granting him the stewardship of all the lordships previously governed by the Prince of Wales's Council.

Hastings was allowed to continue as Lord Chamberlain and Governor of Calais, and was appointed Master of the Mint, but received no other reward for his treachery. He would have had to be a very dull man not to perceive that there was writing on the wall, but appears to have had no suspicion that it was his death sentence. He sent his lawyer William Catesby to attend the meetings of Gloucester's separate committee of co-conspirators, but Gloucester turned Catesby and used him to feed soothing disinformation to the loyalist councillors.

Catesby warned Gloucester of growing suspicion among Hastings, Stanley, Morton and Rotherham that he intended to seize the throne, but according to the Crowland Continuator this had not yet hardened into certainty before Gloucester moved against them. As Mancini observed, he would have done so anyway because he 'considered that his prospects were not sufficiently secure without the removal or imprisonment of those who had been the closest friends of his brother and were expected to be loyal to his brother's offspring'.

Realizing he had gained all he could by consent, on 10 June Gloucester wrote to the civic council of York requesting it to send as many men as possible 'to aid and assist us against the Queen, her blood adherents and affinity,' who of course by now posed no threat whatever. On the 11th, by hand of his retainer Richard Ratcliffe, he sent illegal warrants to the Earl of Northumberland and Ralph, Lord Neville, for the execution of Rivers, Grey and Vaughan.

On 12 June he summoned Buckingham, Howard, Hastings, Morton, Rotherham and Stanley to a full Council meeting at the Tower the next day. Howard's son Thomas played the role of Judas goat by ensuring that Hastings came to the meeting. Gloucester greeted them with smiles and then withdrew, only to return feigning a thunderous rage. Hastings was dragged out into the Tower yard and beheaded on a log, and Stanley was wounded in the scuffle.

With his own affinity marching south, Gloucester dared not risk an uprising by the powerful Stanley affinity in Lancashire and Cheshire, led by Stanley's capable brother William and his son George, Lord Strange. Accordingly Stanley was released, no doubt with apologies and a promise of compensation. Bishop Rotherham was committed to the Tower in the custody of Gloucester's knight of the body James Tyrell, and Bishop Morton was assigned to Buckingham, who eventually sent him under guard to his castle at Brecon. Even Gloucester did not dare murder princes of the Church.

A proclamation justifying Hastings's murder was read out to the people of London, details of which need not trouble us other than to observe the first appearance of a puritanical theme that appears to have been as sincerely felt as it was hypocritical from a man who had himself fathered two bastards. Gloucester ordered the imprisonment of Jane Shore, whom he believed had been acting as a conduit between the loyalist councillors and the queen, and she was condemned to a prostitute's public penance of being paraded through the streets in her underclothes 'for the life that she led with the said Lord Hastings and other great estates'.

The gambit backfired. Witnesses told Thomas More that 'she went in countenance and pace demure so womanly, and albeit she were out of all array save her kyrtle [petticoat] only yet went she so fair and lovely that her great shame won her much praise'.* We know from an undated letter written to Chancellor Russell by Gloucester after he had made himself king that Thomas Lynom, the royal solicitor, expressed a wish to marry Jane when she was still in Ludgate prison. The letter asked Russell to try to talk Lynom out of his infatuation, but failing that she was to be released. The two were married and Lynom prospered under Henry VII.

Vide the public shaming of Cersei Lannister in George R. R. Martin's *A Dance with Dragons*. A Freudian would argue that Richard's vindictiveness was a displacement activity for his ambivalent feelings about his mother.

Others now openly identified with the rolling coup, chief among them Gloucester's childhood friend Francis, Viscount Lovell, former Chancellor Bishop Stillington, and two magnates disesteemed by Edward IV: Gloucester's nephew John de la Pole, Duke of Suffolk, and William Herbert, Earl of Huntingdon. Richard later married his illegitimate daughter Katherine to Herbert, with an annuity of £600 [£381,600] as her dowry. So reduced were Herbert's circumstances that the annuity nearly doubled his income.

At about this time Dorset fled from Westminster Abbey, seemingly with the complicity of the abbot, and got away to join his uncle Edward with Henry Tudor in Brittany. Bishop Lionel Woodville was permitted to leave sanctuary to return to his diocese. He should have remained with his sister and her children, to stand with them against the baseness to come, but perhaps shared Elizabeth's belief that she would again be protected by the Church.

Instead, on 16 June Gloucester sent Cardinal Bourchier to prevail on her to give up Richard, her remaining son, failing which Howard and his son Thomas, who had surrounded the abbey with men-at-arms, were to seize him by force. Thomas More quotes Bourchier angrily telling her the Church would not protect her. Mancini wrote that 'when the Queen saw herself besieged and preparation for violence, she surrendered her son, trusting in the word of the Archbishop of Canterbury that the boy should be restored after the coronation'.

Not long after young Richard joined his brother in the Tower the young king's attendants were dismissed and later paid off for their services to 'Edward, bastard' and the boys were moved from the state apartments to close confinement within the fortress. Writs were issued cancelling the Parliament scheduled for 15 June and preparations for the coronation of Edward V halted. Gloucester ceased to wear mourning and rode through London dressed in purple with a large retinue of men-at-arms wearing royal livery.

A letter of 21 June in *The Stonor Letters and Papers* from Simon Stallworth, a servant of Bishop Russell, told William Stonor that he was lucky to be away from London, for there was 'much trouble, and every man doubts the other', precisely what Gloucester sought to achieve. Stallworth reported that Hastings's men had entered Buckingham's service and that Edward Grey, the dowager queen's brother-in-law from her first marriage, who had taken part in the arrest prior to murder of her father and brother Thomas in 1469, had come to curry favour with Gloucester. His reward was to be recognized as Viscount Lisle by marriage.

On 23 June Anthony Woodville, Earl Rivers, was told he was to be taken to Pontefract Castle for execution. The poem he wrote knowing he was soon to die has survived, set to music by Robert Fayrfax (1464–1521), to remind us what a shining exception Rivers was to the dull aristocratic norm:

> Somewhat musing/And more mourning
> In remembering/Th'unsteadfastness;
> This world being/Of such wheeling,
> Me contrarying,/What may I guess?
>
> I fear, doubtless,/Remediless
> Is now to seize/My woeful chance;
> For unkindness,/Withoutenless,*
> And no redress,/Me doth advance.
>
> With displeasure,/To my grievance,
> And no surance/Of remedy;
> Lo, in this trance,/Now in substance,
> Such is my dance,/Willing to die.
>
> Methinks truly/Bounden am I,
> And that greatly,/To be content;

*Withoutenless = to speak plainly

Seeing plainly/Fortune doth wry*
All contrary/From mine intent.

My life was lent/Me to one intent.
It is nigh spent./Welcome Fortune!
But I ne'er went†/Thus to be shent‡
But so she meant:/Such is her won.§

On 25 June Rivers, Richard Grey and Thomas Vaughan were beheaded in the presence of Northumberland, Neville, Ratcliffe and other members of Gloucester's northern affinity. They were not allowed to make final speeches and were buried in an unmarked common grave. Rous reported that Rivers was found to be wearing a hair shirt 'which was long after displayed in the church of the Carmelite friars in Doncaster as a holy object'. Vaughan was later reburied at Westminster Abbey, where his marble tomb survives in the Chapel of St John the Baptist.

Mancini and the Crowland Continuator concur that when Gloucester issued a new summons to the lords on 13 May, the day of Hastings's murder, Buckingham went to the key figures bearing a first draft of what was eventually to be published as *Titulus Regius*. Bishop Stillington had come up with an alternative to trumpeting Duchess Cecily's adultery and perjured himself by declaring that Edward IV, prior to his marriage with Elizabeth Woodville, had married Eleanor Boteler née Talbot. Therefore Edward's children by Elizabeth were illegitimate.

Because Edward was a notorious womanizer and his marriage to Elizabeth had been informal, the allegation that he might have made a habit of seducing women by going through a form of marriage was believable. However, the Boteler 'pre-contract' (which in the context means marriage, not betrothal) has been researched in great depth, without finding corroborative evidence. It was, anyway,

*Wry = turn aside; †Went = thought; ‡Shent = cut off; §Won[t] = custom.

a matter for the Church to decide, and no clerical ruling was sought. Even if Stillington's statement had been true both the princes in the Tower were born after Eleanor died in 1468, so they were free of the taint of bigamy. The claim did, however, shame the Talbots. Fifteen-year-old George, Earl of Shrewsbury, was a royal ward, but the Talbot Marcher affinity was led by his uncle Gilbert, who did not forget the insult.

On 25 June Gloucester's handpicked Parliament declared that Edward V was not the king although, as it had been summoned in his name, it had no legal standing to do so. The following day a delegation of tame lords led by Buckingham assembled at Baynard's Castle and petitioned Gloucester to take the throne, permitting Gloucester to claim that he had been ordained king 'by the concord assent of the Lords and Commons'.

He assumed the title of Richard III and confirmed Bishop Russell, John Gunthrope and John Wood, now also Speaker of the Commons, as Lord Chancellor, Lord Privy Seal and Lord Treasurer respectively. Lord Stanley was appointed to the honorary office of Steward of the Household, but real power was vested in the functional members, the new king's cabinet. Lovell took over Hastings's role as Lord Chamberlain, Hastings's betrayer William Catesby was made Chancellor of the Exchequer, Robert Percy of Scotton became Comptroller and John Kendall was appointed the king's private secretary.

Gloucester, Lovell and Percy had become friends as fatherless boys in the Kingmaker's household in the late 1460s, and Kendall had been Gloucester's private secretary during the years when he made himself lord of the North. Richard Ratcliffe, the other key figure in the regime, became hereditary Sheriff of Westmorland when his uncle Lord Parr of Kendal died in August 1483, but his informal power was far greater. The Prior of Durham commented on 'the great rule that [Ratcliffe] beareth under the king's grace in our country'.

On 28 June Buckingham was granted the ceremonial office of

Great Chamberlain of England and Lord Howard declared Duke of Norfolk and hereditary Earl Marshal of England, while his son Thomas was made Earl of Surrey. The Mowbray estates were divided between Howard and Lord Berkeley, who was made Earl of Nottingham. This reversed the award of the estates to Prince Richard by Acts of Parliament in 1478 and 1483, which were not formally repealed. By now Gloucester had shed any pretence of respect for the law.

In preparation for his coronation alongside his wife, Gloucester announced a curfew and prohibited the bearing of arms by anyone not in his livery. On 5 July all the nobles who had been summoned were required to join an imposing procession from the Tower to Westminster, with the route lined what by what Mancini estimated to be 6,000 of Richard's armed retainers.

Among the lords was William Hastings's younger brother Richard, Lord Welles. Edward IV had made him a contentious grant of the title and lands of the baronies of Welles and Willoughby by right of his wife, Joan Welles, after her father and brother were executed in 1470. The grant could be as easily erased by the new king, and Hastings could not afford to stand on principle. Like Gilbert Talbot, he was to eat the dish of revenge cold.

On the following day, 6 July, Richard III and Anne were crowned. There were two notable absentees. It is entirely understandable that Catherine Woodville, Duchess of Buckingham, should have refused to attend the coronation of her brother's murderer. It is, however, highly remarkable that Duchess Cecily was not present. Perhaps she was ashamed to show her face after being publicly branded an adulteress; but possibly it had dawned on her, much too late, that she had put her grandsons in mortal peril. The ostentatious piety of her later life suggests belated repentance for the great evil she had wrought, and when she died her will mentioned her husband and Edward IV, but not her youngest son.

Mancini left England in mid-July and reported that before his departure the princes had 'ceased to appear altogether', something corroborated by other sources. 'I have seen many men burst forth into tears and lamentations when mention was made of [Edward V] after his removal from men's sight, and already there was a suspicion that he had been done away with. Whether, however, he has been done away with and by what manner of death, so far I have not at all discovered'.

There is no reasonable doubt that Richard was responsible for the murder of his nephews: he had made them defenceless, and they were in the custody of his men. It would not diminish his culpability if, as some have suggested, either Buckingham or Norfolk pre-empted the issue, because he had created a situation where it was possible for them to do so. The sentence of death was pronounced when Dr Shaw declared in his approving presence that the progeny of King Edward must be eradicated.

Thomas More wrote that Richard ordered them killed after a failed attempt to spring them from the Tower in early August. When Robert Brackenbury, Constable of the Tower, refused to sully his hands with innocent blood, Richard sent his knight of the body, James Tyrell, previously Bishop Rotherham's jailer and so familiar with the Tower and its staff, to do the deed. The most minutely researched study of the question has identified 3 September, the day before Tyrell left London to re-join his master at York, as the most likely date.*

Tyrell certainly did something highly meritorious in Richard's eyes, as he subsequently received a cascade of rewards. Thomas More falsely accused Richard of earlier crimes, but he was in a position to verify that Tyrell confessed to murdering the princes during his trial for treason in 1502. As to why he should have admitted his guilt, he was doomed anyway and had nothing to lose, and men did not go to their deaths with mortal sins unconfessed. David Starkey has also uncovered evidence suggesting Henry VII and his queen, sister to the murdered boys, may have attended Tyrell's trial, which would have been a highly unusual occurrence.

---

* Alison Weir's admirable *The Princes in the Tower*, first published in 1992.

Wicked though the murder of the princes was, the greater crime was committed against the kingdom. Richard III trampled on the laws and the unwritten constitution of England, and in the process completed the destruction of the 300-year-old Plantagenet dynasty It may be argued that he was not a great deal more evil than some of his predecessors, but if so this would simply confirm that they were also psychopaths.

NEMESIS*

IT IS NOT SURPRISING THAT THERE WAS LITTLE OPPOSITION to the usurpation. The senior peerage had been hollowed out during Edward IV's reign and the simultaneous minorities of the three Bourchier lords – the Earl of Essex and Barons FitzWarin and Berners – disempowered the only clan that might have been able to restrain Richard. Once the nobles of the court party were neutralized the remaining magnates either supported the coup or kept their heads down. Those whose titles and lands depended on royal favour as usual rushed to jump on the bandwagon.

On 20 July 1483, a mere two weeks after his coronation, Richard embarked on a grand progress through the kingdom, initially accompanied by Buckingham and throughout by his 21-year-old nephew John de la Pole, Earl of Lincoln, leaving Howard in charge of the capital. This was a signal mark of trust in a man twice his age (Richard was thirty, Howard about sixty) who had been one of Edward IV's henchmen. Howard's enthusiastic participation in the usurpation testifies to how deeply betrayed he had felt when Edward cheated him of his right of succession to the dukedom of Norfolk.

At Reading Richard issued a posthumous pardon to William Hastings and granted his widow Katherine née Neville custody of

*'Nemesis, winged balancer of life,/dark-faced goddess, daughter of Justice.': Mesomedes of Crete.

his estates and the wardship and marriage of their son. He also thought it magnanimous to assure Rivers's widow that the lands she had brought into the marriage were safe, which should have been unquestionable. She received nothing from Rivers's estate, all of which went to Howard over the coming days, without a shred of legal justification.

The royal party was at Viscount Lovell's grand manor house at Minster Lovell when the fateful news arrived of the bungled plot to liberate the princes from the Tower. The next stop was Gloucester, where Buckingham departed for Brecon to assume his new role as Richard's regime lock on Wales. Even after being awarded the half of the historic Bohun estate stolen by Henry IV, Buckingham must have known that he lacked the personal following to make a success of the appointment. He was riding for a fall, and according to Thomas More he knew the king had ordered the murder of his nephews before they parted company.

Richard was joined by Queen Anne at Warwick, and by their sickly 9-year-old son Edward at Pontefract, where Richard's northern affinity gathered to honour the boy and to ride with their leader in a state entry to York at the end of August. This was the culmination of the progress, and Richard was to spend most of September in the city or in nearby Sheriff Hutton. On the 8th young Edward, already declared Earl of Salisbury, Duke of Cornwall and Lord Lieutenant of Ireland, was invested as Prince of Wales and Earl of Chester in a ceremony so grand that it was described as a second coronation.

Richard declared Sheriff Hutton a royal residence for his sister's son the Earl of Lincoln and for Clarence's 8-year-old son Edward, Earl of Warwick. They were the next in line to the throne should Richard's heir die before him, and it was probably an error to make such obvious preparation for the eventuality, however sensible it may have seemed to one obsessed with the purity of the York bloodline. It drew attention to the fact that the royal succession now rested with a single boy who could not even ride a horse for any great distance, instead of with Edward IV's robust 'heir and a spare'.

50. RICHARD III'S PROGRESS 1483

20 July	Windsor
22 July	Reading
24 July	Oxford
25 July	Woodstock
26-29 July	Minster Lovell
31 July	Gloucester
4 August	Tewkesbury
8-14 August	Warwick
15 August	Coventry
18 August	Leicester
22-23 August	Nottingham
25-27 August	Pontefract
30 August to late September	York and Sheriff Hutton
End September	Pontefract
10 October	Gainsborough
11 October	Lincoln
19-22 October	Grantham
23-25 October	Leicester
27-28 October	Oxford
29 October	Hungerford
30 October	Tidworth
31 October to 4 November	Salisbury
8-14 November	Exeter
25 November	London

© Hugh Bicheno

0   25   50   75   100
miles

There was a religious sub-plot to the progress. At Tewkesbury Richard made a donation to the abbey as atonement for Edward IV's breach of sanctuary, and at Pontefract he restored the landed endowment of the priory, rebuking his late brother for having taken it when it should have remained to support masses for the soul of Richard of York, buried there until 1476. He also ordered the construction of a chapel at Towton, where his father's death had been avenged.

Strangely uncommented until Michael Jones joined up the dots in *Bosworth 1485: Psychology of a Battle* (2002), Richard also undertook to fund a massive chantry of 100 priests at York Minster. Chantries were often established to pray for the souls of the founders, and the size of Richard's foundation meant that Masses for his soul would be conducted almost continuously. The coincidence of the foundation and the date of his nephews' murder suggests that Richard wished to reduce the amount of time his soul would be spending in Purgatory.

Not the least of Richard's early errors was to have sent a disrespectful reply on 18 August to a tentatively welcoming letter from King Louis XI. Louis died on the 30th, leaving the regency for his 13-year-old son Charles in the hands of his 22-year-old eldest daughter, Anne de Beaujeu. Richard's letter would have been among the first she read and confirmed in her mind her dying father's belief that Richard intended to reopen hostilities. In March 1484 she sent Bernard Stewart, Seigneur d'Aubigny and commander of the royal *Garde Écossaise*, to sign a treaty with the Scots renewing the 'Auld Alliance'.

According to the Rolls of Parliament the leaders of the October 1483 rebellion 'launched their enterprise' on 24 September, as this was the day Buckingham joined them by writing to Henry Tudor with regard to an invasion on 18 October. However Buckingham was in no way an initiator or leader of the revolt. He was a Johnny-come-lately to a conspiracy among former servants of Edward IV, including but not led by the surviving Woodvilles.

The crucial point is that the conspirators chose to make the exiled Tudor their candidate for the throne, although Edward IV had regarded him as a threat to his dynasty and had tried to eliminate him. The rebels therefore were certain that Richard III had murdered his nephews, which opened the door for Henry Tudor's mother Margaret Beaufort, Lady Stanley, to initiate contact with Elizabeth, and through her to a wider constituency united by hatred of the usurper.

While it is likely that Lady Margaret (through her confidential emissary Reginald Bray) and Buckingham's Woodville wife played some considerable part in persuading him to turn his coat, another agent was Bishop Morton, his prisoner at Brecon. Given that Morton was Thomas More's mentor, the subtly nuanced dialogue at the end of *The History of Richard III*, in which Morton turns Buckingham's head by suggesting he might claim the throne himself, probably came from the episcopal horse's mouth.

Of course this requires us to believe that Buckingham was a vain fool, a fair assumption in the light of his less than stellar career. Revulsion at the murder of the princes is not likely to have played any part in his decision to turn against the man whose willing accomplice he had been. More likely is that he belatedly realized that John Howard, not he, was going to be Richard's right-hand man, and was galled that once more he was not going to play the role corresponding to his royal blood, high rank and even higher opinion of himself.

The most regime-threatening part of the conspiracy was among the Yeomen of the Crown, royal household servants and a key component of the London garrison, led by George Brown, Sheriff of Kent and stepson of the lately murdered Thomas Vaughan, who had carried the flag of St George at Edward IV's funeral. Yeomen occupied a uniquely English place between esquires and commoners. The origin of the term may be 'yewmen', referring to the wood from which the longbow was made, and *Holinshed's Chronicles* (1577) described them as:

They that in times past made all France afraid, and albeit they
be not called Master, as gentlemen are, or Sir, as to Knights
apperteineth but onlie John and Thomas etc., yet have they
beene found to have done verie good service, and the Kings of
England in foughten battles were wont to remaine among them
(who were their footmen) as the French Kings did amongst their
horsemen, the Prince thereby showing where his cheefe strength
did consist.

Henry Tudor was to recognize a very particular debt to them and
in 1485 named them 'Yeomen of the Guard' with responsibility for
guarding the Tower of London, a duty they perform to this day. The
debt stemmed from their leading role in the1483 revolt, for which
Brown and five Yeomen of the Crown were put to death. The rest of
the rebels in the South-East, including John Fogge, Richard Haute,
the Earl of Essex's younger son Thomas Bourchier, and Thomas
Fiennes, grandson and heir to Joan, Baroness Dacre by right, either
fled to join Henry Tudor in Brittany or accepted an offer of pardon.

One of the yeomen, William Bracher, betrayed his comrades
to Howard and the ringleaders were rounded up on or about 10
October. Bracher also revealed that uprisings were planned in the
South-West and the West Country to coincide with Henry Tudor's
arrival on 18 October with an invasion force of 5,000 mercenaries,
replicating the Kingmaker's 1470 invasion and paid for by Edward
Woodville's loot and 10,000 crowns [£1.3 million] from Duke
Fransez. The bombshell was that Buckingham intended to lead an
army from Brecon to join them.

The astounding news reached Richard at Lincoln on the 11th,
and the following day he wrote to Chancellor Russell calling
Buckingham 'the most untrue creature living'. Although he summoned troops to join him at Leicester on 21 October, for the time
being Richard remained at Lincoln. On the 10th he had stayed with
Thomas Burgh at Gainsborough Hall, when his host warned him
there might by a local uprising.* The 1470 Lincolnshire rebellion

began with an assault on Burgh's manor, and he would have been alert to unrest among the Welles affinity. Richard would also have known that the broader Hastings affinity would move against him if the rebellion looked like succeeding.

As an experienced military commander Richard knew to remain in one place while intelligence reports came in, so his sojourn at Lincoln served a double purpose. Even after he set out, when he learned on the 20th that Lord Strange had departed Lathom in Lancashire at the head of a large force, he paused at Grantham until it was confirmed that Strange was not marching to join the rebels in the South-West. While he waited, nature took care of the rebellion for him.

On 15 October Richard proclaimed Buckingham a traitor and a prolonged storm of unusual violence struck south-western England. The storm kept Tudor's fleet in port during the crucial week he was supposed to have crossed the Channel and also caused the river Severn to flood, preventing Buckingham from using the lower river crossings, while Humphrey Stafford of Grafton destroyed the bridges across the upper river. Bombarded by rain, Buckingham's army, described by Polydore Vergil as Welshmen 'whom he, as a sore and hard dealing man, had brought to the field against their wills, and without any lust to fight for him', dissolved.

On 19 October Richard issued a further proclamation denouncing Dorset and Bishop Morton as traitors and putting a £1,000 [£636,000] price on Buckingham's head. Bizarrely, Richard issued another denunciation of Dorset a few days later, accusing him of immorality and adultery with 'Shore's wife', as though this would have meant anything to the general public. Richard obviously thought it would, although it is hard to imagine what constituency in bawdy England might have shared his obsessive prudery.

Buckingham marched his diminishing band to Weobley in

---

* There is no other obvious reason why Richard III made him a Garter knight later in 1483, in the select company of Lovell, Ratcliffe, Lord Stanley and John Howard's son Thomas, newly made Earl of Surrey.

Herefordshire in the hope of raising the Marches. Weobley belonged to Lord Ferrers of Chartley, and lay at the heart of the ancestral Yorkist domain that had turned out in force to defeat Jasper Tudor at Mortimer's Cross in 1461. Far from joining the rebellion, any doubts the Yorkist Marchers had about Richard were resolved. Led by Thomas Vaughan of Tretower, whose father had been beheaded by Jasper Tudor in 1470, they marched into Brecknock and captured Brecon Castle.

Buckingham went on to Shrewsbury, where he failed to enlist Gilbert Talbot, and then donned a disguise and rode north, perhaps hoping to find refuge with Lord Stanley in Lancashire. He stopped for the night at Wem, 10 miles north of Shrewsbury, at the home of his servant Ralph Banastre, who promptly betrayed him to Thomas Mytton, Sheriff of Shropshire.

The leaders of the rebellion in the South-West were Giles Daubeney and John Cheyne, later to be the only followers for whom Henry VII created new titles of nobility. Daubeney was a considerable landowner in Dorset and Somerset and was the first person in the area contacted by Reginald Bray, Lady Stanley's emissary. The giant (6ft 8ins) Cheyne held lands in Wiltshire and Hampshire. He had been Edward IV's Master of the Horse, and some of his men had been involved in the failed attempt to spring the princes from the Tower in early August.

Lionel Woodville, Bishop of Salisbury, was among those who fled to France when the rebellion collapsed, and Richard Woodville, who became Earl Rivers after Anthony's murder, was attainted. Given that the king would not have given any Woodville the benefit of the doubt, it is highly indicative of Richard Woodville's innocence that he did not flee and was later pardoned. Lionel's flight simply confirms that he was a coward, something already indicated when he needlessly joined Elizabeth in sanctuary and then abandoned her. He died the following year.

The Woodville influence made itself felt through the female line. Elizabeth's sisters were the mothers of the new Duke of Buckingham (aged 5 in 1483) and the future Earls of Essex (11), Kent (2) and Arundel (7). Finally, Lord Stanley's heir George was Lord Strange through marriage to the dowager queen's niece. Women could go where men dared not, and this was the network Lady Stanley tapped into when she made contact with Elizabeth in sanctuary and they agreed what became the unifying theme of opposition to Richard III: the marriage of her son Henry Tudor to Elizabeth's namesake eldest daughter.

The rebellion in the South-West collapsed and the main conspirators fled to France before Richard, at the head of a considerable army, marched into the region. He arrived at Salisbury on 31 October, but found nobody to execute except Buckingham, brought from Shropshire and beheaded on 2 November. Richard could not stand to see him, perhaps as well because the duke's heir later alleged that his father had a concealed dagger and meant to kill him.

It is not unusual for partners in crime to turn on each other, but Buckingham's motivation remains a tantalizing mystery. He appears to have been mourned by none, and one cannot dismiss the suspicion that Bishop Morton and Lady Stanley wound him up principally to refute Richard's claim that the 'old blood' of the English aristocracy supported his right to the throne.

There remained the rebellion in the West Country, whose principal movers were leading members of the Courtenay clan, notably Edward Courtenay of Bocconoc in Cornwall, heir to the attainted earldom of Devon, and Peter, Bishop of Exeter. Their allies the Luttrells of Somerset rose up on 2 November, the day that Henry Tudor arrived off Plymouth with two ships but found the port was in the hands of Richard's men. Thomas Grey, Marquess of Dorset, appears to have returned from exile to play some role, and Richard's brother-in-law Thomas St Leger was one of the few who did not flee opportunely. He was executed on 13 November.

There was a subtext to the West Country rebellion that must have concerned Richard deeply. Among the rebels now in exile were Thomas Arundel, his brother-in-law Richard Nanfan, Sheriff of Cornwall, and Robert Willoughby of Broke, Sheriff of Devon. In 1460–1 Nanfan and John, Lord Dynham, had been comrades-in-arms, Arundel was Dynham's brother-in-law, Willoughby his father-in-law – and Dynham himself was Lieutenant of Calais, whose garrison had all been members of murdered Lord Hastings's affinity.

As he rode back from Exeter to London, Richard had much to think about. He had needed a cathartic Towton, but circumstances had denied him the opportunity. Overly fixated on the nobility, he must have been shocked to discover how deeply he was loathed by the essential cogs in the machinery of government – royal servants and the sheriffs and commissioners of array of southern England, none of whom had suffered by his usurpation.

Perhaps most of all he would have been profoundly shaken to learn that men like Nicholas Latimer, who had once followed his brother Clarence and who by Richard's reckoning should have celebrated his overthrow of the bastard Edward's line, were now making common cause against him with the followers of Clarence's executioner, with unreconciled Lancastrians and even with the demonized Woodvilles. He had redeemed the House of York – how was it possible that so many once loyal Yorkists now supported Henry Tudor?

Psychopaths are polarizing individuals, mesmerizing to weak personalities but repulsive to those who can see them as they are. Richard commanded a loyalty from his northern retainers that went far beyond hope of gain, and clearly expected the same alchemy to work for him as king. It did not, and one of the reasons may have been that the personalities of his northern followers were pre-shaped by submission to the will of the no less psychopathic Kingmaker.

Nor should we overlook the fact that Richard was physically unimpressive, especially by comparison with his half-brother. Edward had also oozed charm – he was a seducer whose appeal was not limited to women, most clearly demonstrated by the manner in which he personally collected benevolences before the 1475 expedition. Richard had none of the easy self-confidence and common touch that had inclined people to be indulgent of Edward's many but very human failings.

Like the father whose memory he worshipped, Richard thought he could command by divine right; and so he could, but only among those persuaded he had right on his side. There can have been few who genuinely believed that God could possibly endorse a man who shamed his mother, terrorized a recently widowed queen and climbed to the throne over the murdered bodies of well-regarded lords and innocent children.

HEARTS AND MINDS

R ICHARD REALIZED IT HAD BEEN FOOLISHLY HUBRISTIC to embark on a grand progress so soon after his coronation. The rebellion had blind-sided him, and he spent the rest of his short reign ensuring that he would not again be caught unprepared. There is, however, an iron rule of political and military momentum: you do not get a second chance to make a first impression. Damaging civil strife had returned to England after twelve years of political stability and rising prosperity.

As soon as he returned to London Richard installed his knight of the body Marmaduke Constable at Buckingham's forfeited Penshurst palace in Kent and flooded the troublesome county with commissioners to administer an oath of allegiance. This was followed by a proclamation inviting any Kentishman with a grievance to submit a complaint for his personal attention, 'for his grace is utterly determined that all his subjects shall live in rest and quiet, and peaceably enjoy their lands, livelihoods and goods, according to the laws of this his land, which they were naturally born to inherit'.

With regard to the laws, Richard's sole Parliament assembled on 23 January 1484, with Catesby as Speaker of the Commons. Over the next five weeks eighteen private and fifteen public statutes were enacted and published. I cannot resist quoting a comment published online by a Yorkshire Ricardian: 'Richard's reforms, aimed at making England a more equal society, show him to have been a remarkably liberal King, with ideas on social justice that were far ahead of his time'. So there we have it: Richard III was 'progressive', and as we all know that means he must have been 'a good thing'.

Foremost of the private statutes was *Titulus Regius*, whose 'progressive' nature readers can judge for themselves. The rest showed Richard's commitment to social justice in acts of attainder against 104 rebels – which is to say declaring them guilty of treason without trial and legally non-persons, thus without right to life, titles of nobility or of property, thereby disinheriting their heirs. Irony aside, this was the normal consequence of failed rebellion and, as his brother had done, Richard pardoned those who stayed in England and petitioned for reversal of attainder, in the hope that they would be grateful.

The public statutes were another matter. They addressed chronic abuses of the legal system in considerable detail and were to be singled out for praise by generations of legal scholars. Three statutes condemned common fraudulent practices in property transfers and required those made in the Court of Common Pleas to be made public – what we call 'transparency', the most effective weapon in the unending struggle against government corruption. Other statutes condemned Edward IV's 'benevolences' and his abusive collection of ecclesiastical tenths.

Richard also attempted to pose as a restorer of legality. A statute prohibiting the confiscation of an accused's property before conviction harked back to Edward's theft from London Alderman Thomas Cooke in 1468. Another recalled Edward's (and Clarence's) intimidation of jurors by requiring that they should be men of independent means. This was cosmetic: the law already specified that they should be men of substance. The problem was that 'good lordship' trumped justice, and would continue to do so for centuries.

Five acts were in response to lobbying by the City of London and revoked some of the privileges corruptly awarded to foreign merchants by Edward IV – although notably not those enjoyed by the Hanseatic League. Richard was already at war with French and Breton raiders, and it would have been insane to antagonize the masters of the most powerful fleet in north European waters. There was one specific exception made to the new tariff barriers: printing presses and books were exempt. This was a spiteful attack on William Caxton, who had been printing books in England since 1476 thanks to the patronage of murdered Earl Rivers.

Thankful that the king had not asked for the usual tenth and fifteenth, before adjourning on 1 March Parliament voted Richard tunnage and poundage (customs revenues) for life. On the same day Richard brought an end to the shameful stand-off at Westminster Abbey, from which Elizabeth and her daughters refused to emerge without ironclad guarantees. Humiliating though it was, Richard accepted a document worked out with Elizabeth's legal advisors:

> I Richard by the grace of God King of England and of France, and lord of Ireland, in the presence of you my lords spiritual and temporal, of you aldermen and mayor of my city of London, promise and swear on my word as king and upon these Holy Evangiles of God by me personally touched, that if the daughters of Dame Elizabeth Gray, late calling herself Queen of England, that is to wit Elizabeth, Cecily, Anne, Katherine and Bridget, will come unto me out of the sanctuary of Westminster, and be guided, ruled and demeaned* after me, I shall see that they be in surety of their lives, and also not suffer any manner of hurt, by any manner of person or persons to them or any one of them in their bodies and persons to be done by way of ravishment or defouling contrary to their wills, nor any of them imprison within the Tower of London or other prison, but that I shall put them in honest places of good name and fame, and there honestly and courteously shall see to be found and treated, and to have all things requisite and necessary for their exhibition and finding as my kinswomen.

---

*Anglo-French *demener* = to lead or to conduct.

Other clauses undertook to provide modest dowries for the girls and an annuity for Elizabeth in three annual payments to be brought to her by one of Richard's esquires of the body, and a promise not to act against her or her daughters on the basis of any accusation against them without first hearing 'their legal defence and answer'.

There are some wicked barbs in this document, including the imputation of intent to rape, the fact that the princes were not mentioned and the pointed reference to the Tower of London where they had disappeared; but above all it impugned Richard's honour. Elizabeth could not have made it clearer that she did not trust him to behave decently or even respect the law unless bound by an exceptional and sacred oath, witnessed by the highest in the land.

Richard had to swallow the insult because nobody believed his siege of the abbey was anything other than unmanly bullying of a defenceless woman, who had made common cause with other dissidents out of desperation. Clearly he hoped that a show of magnanimity would persuade Elizabeth to abandon her agreement with Lady Margaret Stanley, but he was also playing to the gallery, as he continued to do for the rest of his reign.

The irreversible political fact was that Lady Margaret's initiative had made Elizabeth's namesake eldest daughter a political player, something confirmed when Henry Tudor declared himself betrothed to her at Rennes cathedral on Christmas Day 1483. Marguerite d'Anjou had died in August 1482, but the witnesses to Henry's declaration included veteran Lancastrians led by his uncle Jasper as well as the new Yorkist exiles.

Henry's Lancastrian credentials were thin: on his father's side he was the grandson of Henry V's French widow, and on his mother's the great-grandson of John of Gaunt, both through illegitimate lines. Having tried and failed to get Duke Fransez to hand him over, Edward IV had been negotiating an accommodation with Lady Margaret by which Henry would be restored as Earl of Richmond, his security guaranteed by marriage to one of Edward's daughters.

Even if Richard had been inclined to seek reconciliation with Henry, there was no credible guarantee a man who had murdered his nephews could offer. It was worse than a crime – it was a political blunder of the first order. Nothing less could have brought about the coalition that Lady Margaret formed against him with such astonishing rapidity. She had never ceased to lobby for her only child to be permitted to take his place in English society: Richard had created a situation where only one such place remained.

It is not clear where the dowager queen and her other daughters went after they left sanctuary, but Richard and Queen Anne welcomed 18-year-old Elizabeth into the royal household and treated her with honour and even affection. Tudor historians alleged that Richard intended to marry her to his heir, but to have done so would have called into question the bastardy of Edward's children. This said, it was thought highly suspicious that he married off her younger sister Cecily but not Elizabeth, when to do so would have annulled the Tudor betrothal.

Once Richard switched his propaganda effort to emphasizing his intention to rule justly and with respect for the law, it reassured those of his subjects who had not already made up their minds about him. The failure of the rebellion also invested him with the 'inevitability factor', the tendency of the undecided to support a winner, or at least conform to what they believe is a new status quo. If Richard could see off the Tudor challenge, he had a reasonable expectation of a relatively untroubled reign.

Accordingly and unsurprisingly, for the next eighteen months Richard devoted himself first to prevention and then to preparing for the inevitable invasion. Poignantly, one of his first acts of prevention was to require the rest of the nobility to swear the public oath of allegiance to his son that the northern lords had sworn at Pontefract in September 1483. When young Edward died on 9 April 1484, the Crowland Continuator permitted himself an uncharitable gloat about the vanity 'of a man who desires to establish his interests without the aid of God':

> This only son of his, in whom all the hopes of the royal succession, fortified with so many oaths, were centred, was seized with an illness of but short duration, and died at Middleham Castle. On hearing the news of this, at Nottingham, where they were then residing, you might have seen his father and mother in a state almost bordering on madness, by reason of their sudden grief.

Richard had continued to rule the North through his son's ducal council at Middleham. Now he buried the boy at Sheriff Hutton, which became the location of a new Council of the North akin to the one Edward IV had established for Wales at Ludlow ten years earlier. He appointed the Earl of Lincoln as president of the Council, which tacitly nominated him as his heir. The Council maintained the balance between the Percy, Neville and related affinities that had been Richard's greatest political achievement.

He was obliged to base the post-rebellion settlement on that achievement for lack of dependable supporters in the south, a measure of which was his appointment of the 67-year-old Earl of Arundel to replace Hastings as Warden of the Cinque Ports. Arundel was at best neutral, but he had collaborated with Marmaduke Constable in the relatively bloodless pacification of Kent and it was vitally important not to offend him.

The Bourchiers were a problem. At some point 14-year-old John, Baron Fitzwarin, crossed the Channel to join Henry Tudor, a defection made more ominous by the fact that his mother was the daughter and co-heir of Lord Dynham. The widowed mother of 12-year-old Henry, 2nd Earl of Essex, was Anne née Woodville, who had remarried George Grey, heir to the earldom of Kent, and had borne him a son. Against which the widowed mother of 17-year-old John Bourchier, 2nd Baron Berners, had remarried Howard's heir Thomas, now Earl of Surrey.

Cardinal Bourchier, the last of the older generation, had been conspicuous by his absence from Richard's coronation feast, and did not collaborate with him in the matter of the rebel Bishops of Ely, Salisbury and Exeter. Lionel Woodville's death in July 1484 permitted the king to appoint his man Thomas Langton to the see of Salisbury, but the Canterbury Convocation refused to deprive Morton (who had escaped to Flanders) and Courtenay (with Henry Tudor in Brittany) for rebellion. Furthermore both Pope Sixtus IV and his successor Innocent VIII openly received Bishop Morton as Henry Tudor's ambassador.

One does not look for genuine contrition in a psychopath, and Richard's most notable act of apparent atonement was yet another attempt to make himself look virtuous by contrast with his brother. This was the solemn transfer of the remains of Henry VI from Chertsey Abbey, where they had become an object of veneration, to a splendid new tomb in St George's Chapel, Windsor, Edward IV's magnificent creation. Henry was reburied on the other side of the altar from Edward's tomb, thus giving the last Lancastrian king parity of honour with his murderer.

Apart from the North, the regime was only really secure in East Anglia, thanks to Howard. Even there, however, there was residual sympathy for the imprisoned Earl of Oxford, and the rebellion and defection to Tudor of William Brandon, scion of a leading gentry family that achieved local prominence as Mowbray retainers, shows that acceptance of the new Duke of Norfolk was not universal. The only obvious reason was that his elevation was tainted by the murder of young Prince Richard, his predecessor and widower of the last direct Mowbray heir.

Richard was more worried by the Midlands than any other region. His frequent visits and the large sums spent to upgrade his castle-palace at Nottingham testify to his belief that it was an unexploded bomb. The Midlands had once been strongly Lancastrian, more recently Hastings had built up a strong affinity in the area, and Hastings's brother was the dominant lord in Lincolnshire. A layer below the Hastings affinity was the ancient barony of Roos and other Lancastrian lordships attainted after Towton.

Richard could count on John, Baron de la Zouche, a 25-year-old Northamptonshire lord, but he had more ambition than affinity.* Ferrers of Chartley had estates in Leicestershire and Shropshire as well as Herefordshire, but although he was rewarded for his actions against Buckingham he had been one of Edward V's councillors and did not wish for a role in the new regime. Richard's close friend Viscount Lovell had suffered the humiliation of learning that William Stonor, his chief Oxfordshire retainer, had been one of the leading rebels, and his extensive Midlands estates could not be regarded as an assured regime asset.

The 1484 attainders permitted Richard to redistribute the duchy of Buckingham estates, the most extensive after Lancaster and York, and to impose men he trusted across the South-West and the West Country. The Crowland Chronicler observed that the forfeited estates were 'distributed among his northern adherents whom he planted in every spot throughout his dominions, to the disgrace and lasting and loudly expressed sorrow of all the people in the south'. Perhaps, but that did not necessarily make them supporters of Henry Tudor.

In much of the country the strength of land-based affinities had been eroded by frequent changes of lordship. This was why propaganda became increasingly significant. The Kingmaker had been the first to appeal to the general public and Richard's effort to win hearts and minds drew on the accusations made against Edward in 1469–70, sometimes word for word. He controlled 'the media' – proclamations posted in public places, loyal addresses and sermons by roving preachers – but as many another dictator has discovered, rumour-mongering is a potent weapon of the opposition.

As maddened by subversive murmuring as Edward had been in 1468 when he judicially murdered Hungerford and Courtenay, in July 1484 Richard had William Collynsbourne, once one of his mother's servants but now a Tudor partisan, arrested, convicted of

*Zouche was, however, married to Lord Dynham's other daughter and co-heir, and Richard envisaged a leading role for him in an eventual settlement of the West Country.

treason, hanged, drawn and quartered for nailing a subversive couplet to the door of St Paul's Cathedral. Consequently the couplet became known across the country and survives to this day:

> The Cat, the Rat, and Lovell our Dog
> Ruleth all England under the Hogge.*

Another example was the canard spread by Richard's enemies when Queen Anne died following a long illness (probably tuberculosis) in March 1485. He was alleged to have poisoned her in order to marry young Elizabeth, and the rumour troubled his followers so greatly that Catesby and Ratcliffe warned him that the North would not stand for it. The outcome was that Richard found himself obliged to make a humiliating denial of any such intention at a gathering of notables in the great hall at St John's Hospital in London.

One of the strongest modern Ricardian arguments against the guilt of their hero is that Henry Tudor never specifically accused Richard of having murdered his nephews, even though he was widely believed to have done so. But that, surely, is the explanation: suspicion and rumour were already doing all the damage that could be hoped for, and an open accusation risked the possibility that Richard might produce the princes like a rabbit out of a hat. Later, having won the throne by conquest, Henry had nothing to gain by reopening the issue of legitimacy.

It is doubtful whether propaganda does more than reinforce opinions people already hold. The fact that Richard was a treacherous and murdering non-bastard was fully discounted by 1485. He had the advantage of incumbency, he was saying and doing the right things, there was rising prosperity and in such circumstances people are averse to change. The kingdom was his to lose.

---

*The cat being William Catesby and Richard Ratcliffe the rat. The hog referred to Richard's white boar badge.

OPENING MOVES

RICHARD WAS JUSTIFIABLY CONFIDENT OF HIS MILITARY skill. He was an experienced, competent and respected commander who had understudied Edward IV, one of the most successful generals in English history, and had led his half-brother's vanguard to victory at Barnet and Tewkesbury. During the 1475 expedition he had commanded the largest and most active contingent, and in 1480–2 he had occupied the Scots capital and recovered Berwick.

Soldiers do not care whether their leaders are good or bad men: their only criterion is whether they can deliver victory and the rewards that follow. The same consideration applies to political affiliation – stripped of the fig leaves of ideology with which they seek to camouflage their ambition, most people who enter politics do so in the hope of living well at public expense, and they will usually support whoever offers them the best chance of achieving their goal.

Henry Tudor was not an attractive leader under either heading. He had no combat experience, his Lancastrian uncle Jasper had been routed in every battle he had fought, as had the Earl of Oxford, who joined them in October 1484 under circumstances explained below. The Lancastrian cause died at Tewkesbury and the red and white rose narrative invented by Victorian historians caused them to cram events into a conceptual straightjacket from which they have been struggling to escape ever since. If it had been that simple, it is doubtful whether Henry could ever have mounted a believable challenge.

The whole of Henry's appeal was that he was not Richard III. Thanks to his remarkable mother he became the figurehead for those outraged by Richard's *coup d'état*, but the abject failure of the 1483 counter-coup exhausted the financial windfall brought by Edward Woodville and the subvention from deeply disappointed Duke Frañsez, while wasting key assets like the Yeomen of the Crown. Henry's standing should not have been able to recover from such a setback – and with regard to being able to inspire a broadly based rebellion, it did not.

The irreconcilable Edwardians who joined Henry in exile did not change his basic situation: he was totally dependent on support from England's enemies. Those still in England who hated Richard would join Henry if he could mount a credible invasion; but as in the case of the Kingmaker's invasion in 1470 and to a lesser degree Edward's in 1471, this would have to be provided by foreign money and troops. It was this consideration that made Richard's arrogant reply to Louis XI's last letter so profoundly unwise.

In fairness he had more pressing diplomatic problems. Among the offices he passed to Howard was that of Lord High Admiral, a role Howard had been performing as his nominal subordinate for many years and with considerable success, most recently in the Scots campaign. After the hiatus caused by Edward Woodville's defection Howard rapidly regrouped to wage a naval war against Brittany and Scotland – for trying to force Richard to do what he would have done unforced. It was all very Renaissance.

Contemporary princes laughed at the idea that the shortest route between two points might be a straight line. James III wanted Richard to resume the Anglo–Scots marriage alliance of 1473–80, which was opposed by his pro-French nobles, and Frañsez wanted an assurance of English support should he be attacked by France. Both thought the best way to achieve their objectives was to show

Richard how much trouble they could cause him. He wanted peace in the North and for Frañsez to stop supporting Henry Tudor, but could not afford to show weakness. So, after bloodying Scots and Breton noses, Richard gave them what they – and he – wanted.

James III, by renewing the 'auld alliance' with Anne of Beaujeu's emissary Bernard Stewart in March 1484 (and no doubt pocketing a financial inducement), and by besieging English-held Dunbar, appeased the nobles who had kidnapped him at Lauder, who were bitterly opposed to his pro-English policy. Thus when his brother the Duke of Albany and the long-exiled Earl of Douglas invaded in July, nobody rallied to them. Richard did not support them either, signalling his willingness to abandon Edward's aggressive policy.

The naval war and a display of force by land led by Richard himself served to discredit the pro-French faction and make it easier for James to sue for peace on his terms. The deal was done between 12 and 21 September 1484 at Nottingham Castle, where a Scottish delegation led by James's Chancellor the Earl of Argyll met with Richard. The proceedings began with a flowery oration by James's private secretary Archibald Whitelaw, Archdeacon of Lothian, who laid it on with a trowel:

> In you, most serene Prince, all the excellent qualities of a good king and great commander are happily united, such that to the perfection of your accomplishments nothing could be added by the highest rhetorical flights of a most consummate orator... I look for the first time upon your face [and see] a countenance worthy of the highest power and kingliness, illuminated by moral and heroic virtue... To you may not be unfitly applied what was said by the poet Statius of a most renowned Prince of the Thebans, that Nature never united to a small frame a greater soul or a more powerful mind.

Two treaties were signed on the 21st, a three-year truce and an agreement that James's namesake heir would marry Richard's niece,

Anne de la Pole, sister of his heir presumptive the Earl of Lincoln. Remarkably, both parties included Duke Frañsez among the foreign monarchs nominated to act as guarantors of the treaties, which shows that Richard was confident he had resolved his differences with Brittany.

In 1483 Duke Frañsez's chief minister Pierre Landais survived an effort by Breton nobles to overthrow him with support from France. Having facilitated Henry Tudor's expedition in the hope of putting an ally on the English throne, in September 1484 Landais offered to hand him and his uncle Jasper over to Richard in exchange for 4,000 archers on standby to combat a second incursion by French-backed rebels. Richard readily agreed and in early October Landais sent troops from Rennes to arrest the Tudors at Vannes, the port on the south-west coast of Brittany where they and about 300 exiles were now based.

Bishop Morton, at this stage still in Flanders, got wind of the negotiations and sent a warning that enabled Henry and Jasper to flee across the border into Anjou ahead of Landais's men. Frañsez denounced – but did not dismiss – Landais for his initiative and ordered the release from custody of other exiles arrested at Vannes. They were permitted to join Henry, now with the French court at Langeais in the Loire valley. Frañsez's aim, transparently, was to preserve Richard's military guarantee while hedging his bet with Henry, but for the time being Richard judged it politic to go along with the charade.

The French Regency Council required Henry and his followers to move to Montargis, 68 miles south of Paris, while they decided what to do with them. A trickle of voluntary exiles continued to arrive, as well as English residents in Paris including the cleric Richard Foxe, who was to become Henry's principal private secretary, Lord Privy Seal and successively Bishop of Exeter, Bath and Wells, Durham and Winchester.

Between October 1484 and January 1485 they were joined by part of the Calais garrison, England's only standing army. The back story was complex: Hastings had been Captain of Calais since 1471 and had appointed the entire garrison of the Pale, including John Blount, Baron Mountjoy, who was lieutenant of the fort at Hammes and well paid to keep the Earl of Oxford and Viscount Beaumont incarcerated. After Richard III murdered Hastings he appointed Lord Dynham as Lieutenant of Calais, promoted Mountjoy to Constable of the castle at Guînes, while Blount's younger brother James took over as Lieutenant of Hammes.

Mountjoy was ill and absent on 28 October when Richard ordered the return of Oxford and Beaumont to England. James Blount released them to Thomas Montgomery, Mountjoy's deputy at Guînes and once Edward's key diplomat in dealings with Louis XI; and Montgomery along with John Fortescue, to whom Oxford and Beaumont had surrendered in 1473, took them to join Henry Tudor, while Hammes held out against a half-hearted siege by Dynham.

In January 1485 Oxford and Montgomery returned at the head of a small French army, hoping the garrison at Guînes would defect. It is remarkable that any of the well-paid garrison in the Calais pale opted for the uncertainty of joining Tudor, but some did. Not enough to deliver Guînes, however, and Oxford could only relieve the desultory siege of Hammes and evacuate the garrison.

Convinced that Dynham had been complicit in Oxford's escape but anxious to avoid an open breach, Richard appointed his young bastard son John of Gloucester as Captain of Calais over Dynham's head, under the tutelage of his trusted assassin James Tyrell, whom he appointed Lieutenant of Guînes.* The defections permitted him to man Guînes and Hammes with his own men, but the main garrison remained as before. It was paid by the Company of the Staple, which had a long-established relationship with Hastings's men and

---

*The two pardons later issued to Tyrell by Henry VII have been grist to the mill of conspiracy theorists, but they were in keeping with pardons previously extorted by an ousted regime's officers – like Geoffrey Gates in 1471 – who could credibly threaten to sell Guînes or Hammes to the French or Burgundians.

did not want them replaced. This was a situation Richard had to live with for the time being.

There would have been many more defections and even greater success at Calais if the French had not imposed conditions on their support that came close to destroying Henry's credibility. In November the Council required him to claim the throne as the legitimate Lancastrian successor, supposedly as the younger son of Henry VI. It is not clear why they made this absurd stipulation and it may have been simply a requirement for a fig leaf of legality by the clerical members of the Council, with an eye to approval by the pope.

However it played in Paris and Rome, it went over like a lead balloon in England. Although he did not stress his alleged royal paternity, Henry sent letters to England claiming to be the legitimate Lancastrian successor, signed with the regnal initial H. He must have told the Yorkist exiles that he had been forced to do this by the French, as otherwise they would not have stayed. Richard alleged that Henry had bought French support by promising them Calais, and we cannot dismiss this as propaganda: Oxford's expedition into the Pale certainly lent itself to just such an interpretation.

When a copy of Henry's letter came into Richard's possession in early December he must have thought Christmas had come early. He promptly issued a proclamation published across the kingdom pouring scorn on Henry's double illegitimacy: the Beauforts were illegitimate offspring of John of Gaunt, specifically excluded from royal succession by Henry IV, and the Tudors were the product of dowager Queen Catherine de Valois's cohabitation with her majordomo Owen Tudor without benefit of clergy.

The proclamation was an own goal. Richard's father had claimed the throne by superior right of succession over the House of Lancaster, which made any claim by Henry Tudor immaterial. Richard himself had claimed the throne as the legitimate heir of his father, which undermined his argument that a Lancastrian restoration would undo the Yorkist settlement – because if Edward had not been the true heir, then the Yorkist settlement was legally questionable.

The contradictions finally compelled Richard to recognize what a pit he had dug for his own feet, and to seek reconciliation with Elizabeth Woodville. Historians of the greedy-and-grasping-parvenu Woodvilles persuasion have portrayed her coming to terms with her sons' murderer in the worst possible light, blithely ignoring her situation. She was at Richard's mercy, and what we now call the 'Stockholm syndrome' was a compelling survival strategy.

It may be that Henry Tudor's claim to the Lancastrian succession caused her to doubt that he would eventually deliver on his promise to marry her eldest daughter, but her more pressing concern was the likely result if she did not submit to Richard's will. The Crowland Continuator was a disapproving witness of the outcome during the Christmas celebrations at court:

> Oh God! why should we any longer dwell on this subject, multiplying our recital of things so distasteful, so numerous that they can hardly be reckoned, and so pernicious in their example, that we ought not so much as suggest them to the minds of the perfidious. So too, with many other things which are not written in this book, and of which I grieve to speak; although the fact ought not to be concealed that, during this feast of the Nativity, far too much attention was given to dancing and gaiety, and vain changes of apparel presented to queen Anne and the lady Elizabeth, the eldest daughter of the late king, being of similar colour and shape; a thing that caused the people to murmur and the nobles and prelates greatly to wonder thereat; while it was said by many that the king was bent, either on the anticipated death of the queen taking place, or else, by means of divorce, for which he supposed he had quite sufficient grounds, on contracting a marriage with the said Elizabeth. For it appeared that in no other way could his kingly power be established, or the hopes of his rival be put an end to.

Whether or not Richard had any such intention, well-informed people believed him capable of it. When news of the Christmas festivities reached Henry, Polydore Vergil says he felt 'pinched to his stomach' and the pain increased when in January 1485 Richard Woodville, and in February John Fogge, swore fealty to Richard and had their lands restored. In March even Richard Haute, who had somehow avoided being murdered in June 1483 along with the others arrested by Richard, also made submission and was pardoned.

It must have been at this time that Elizabeth's son Thomas Grey, Marquess of Dorset, tried to slip away from Henry's court, intending to return to England, but he was intercepted and brought back by John Cheyne's brother Humphrey. Presumably Dorset acted at the entreaty of his mother and with an assurance that Richard would reverse his attainder. Although Elizabeth's brother Edward remained steadfast, the final balance of Henry's claim to the Lancastrian succession was the loss of the extensive Woodville family network, minimally offset by the gain of the few Lancastrians who remained in England.

• ❧ •

To mix metaphors, the wild cards in the endgame were the Stanleys. Other peers, notably Arundel but by this time the great majority, survived the *Sturm und Drang* of the Wars of the Roses by masterly inaction. Lord Stanley alone had been an active player in every phase of the struggle, professing loyalty to whomever seemed to be winning at a given moment. Frequently demonstrating his ability to raise impressive numbers of troops at short notice, he displayed a no less impressive talent for arriving a little too late to take part in any fighting.

Stanley was supposed to be the hammer that smashed his father-in-law Richard Neville, Earl of Salisbury, against the anvil of Queen Marguerite's Cheshire army at Blore Heath in 1459, but his brother William rode with Salisbury and Thomas contrived not to arrive in time. Barely escaping attainder, he rode with Henry VI against Richard of York and the Nevilles during the subsequent Ludford Bridge campaign, but could not quite manage to join him at Northampton in 1460. Later that year he organized a civic reception for Richard of York at Chester when he returned from exile in Ireland, but refrained from further involvement while brother William joined Edward IV to fight at Towton.

Thomas joined his brother-in-law Warwick in the suppression of Lancastrian resistance in the North in the early 1460s and may have conspired with him prior to his 1469 rebellion. When Edward turned the tables on Warwick and Clarence in 1470 they marched to Manchester expecting Stanley to join them – in vain. When they returned later that year he marched at the head of a substantial body of retainers to greet them at Bristol, but having made it plain that he was best left alone he went home and took no part in the Readeption. Once again it was William who took the risk of openly joining Edward on his return.

Both Edward IV and Richard III made Lord Stanley steward of their households for the same reason: they wanted him at court, where they could keep an eye on him, and not back in Lancashire and Cheshire, where he could do as he pleased. He brought a force of retainers as large as Hastings's on the 1475 expedition and together they brokered the Treaty of Picquigny. It is unlikely that Stanley ever did anything without an ulterior motive, so when we read of him leading 3,000 archers to join Gloucester's Scottish campaign in 1480, we can be tolerably sure it was a show of force to remind the lord of the North why his remit ended in mid-Lancashire.

If Lord Stanley had been fatally wounded on 13 June 1483, Richard would not have become king. William Stanley and Thomas's heir Lord Strange would have marched south at the head of a combined affinity numbering many thousands, and would have been joined by Rivers's and Hastings's affinities. Without popular support Richard's northern retainers could not have stood against them. He never forgot that, and we have seen how he paused at Grantham to be sure that Strange was marching to join him at Leicester and not to join the 1483 rebellion.

Richard had no choice: he had to appease the Stanleys. Consequently he did not dare arrest Lady Stanley for organizing the rebellion, and although he declared her estate forfeit she was entrusted to the custody of her husband, who was to enjoy the income from her lands during her lifetime. Richard also felt obliged to reward the Stanleys for their military support, even though it had not been forthcoming until it was apparent the rebellion had failed, and made Lord Stanley a Garter knight.

Richard awarded the Stanley brothers additional offices in north Wales and the northern March, because they were the de facto rulers of the region anyway. He had every reason to believe that when Henry Tudor finally landed, Stanley would back the winning side. Having no doubt that it would be his, and since Stanley had made no move to support his stepson in 1483, Richard discounted the possibility that he might break the habit of a lifetime and commit to a risky adventure with no guarantee of success. It was to prove a fatal error of appreciation.

ENDGAME

ICHARD REMAINED AT NOTTINGHAM CASTLE UNTIL the end of the 1484 campaigning season and returned in late May or early June 1485, after spending a week with his mother at Berkhamsted. It is not difficult to imagine what passed between them. He had prepared thoroughly: beacons were built on headlands along the coast from East Anglia to south Wales, and he issued commissions of array to his supporters across the kingdom, requiring them to rehearse a general mobilization by mustering and drilling their men.

Richard's strategic deployment shows that while any landing near London was to be met with overwhelming force, elsewhere the role of his subordinates was to delay the invaders' advance to give him time to come up with the main royal army. There can be little doubt that he had in mind a battle of annihilation, as he had in Scotland. He wanted Henry to land far from London and to draw malcontents into the open – so that he could kill them all.

Howard was at Framlingham Castle in Suffolk, ready to counter a landing on the east coast or to march in support of Brackenbury's London garrison if it were made in the South-East. Lovell was at Southampton to supervise the fleet and to prepare the South-West to contain an invasion of the West Country. Should that occur, Lovell supposedly could count on support from the South March by Lord Ferrers and Thomas Vaughan, and by the Herberts of Raglan.

The Vaughans had a blood feud with the Tudors, but despite the marriage of Lord Herbert to Richard's bastard daughter, Henry made contact with Herbert's younger and more vigorous brother Walter after the Woodville affinity submitted to Richard. Henry mooted a possible marriage with one of the Herbert sisters, in the hope of also drawing in Henry Percy, who was married to the eldest. The matter was not pursued after Richard disavowed any intention of marrying Elizabeth of York, but the line of communication with Walter remained open.

In Wales, Richard's well-paid man on the spot was Rhys ap Thomas, head of a locally dominant Carmarthen clan that had fought for Lancaster and suffered for it, to whom Richard promised to restore offices held by his family before 1461. Rhys's father had died for Jasper Tudor at Mortimer's Cross in 1460 and his older brothers had played dangerous games in 1470–1, but Rhys had submitted to Edward IV to recover his lands, and supported Richard against Buckingham. Their reciprocal killings in 1460 and 1471, however, had left a legacy of latent blood feud between Rhys's clan and the Vaughans.

The brutal pacification of the Principality in 1468 had left deep scars, and Richard's obsession with blood right should have alerted him to the deep loyalty commanded by the Tudors, not only in Jasper's attainted earldom of Pembroke but also as descendants of one of Owain Glyn Dŵr's loyal nephews in the last Welsh rebellion. Henry enjoyed the unanimous support of the Welsh bards, who proclaimed the coming of *y mab darogan* (the man of destiny), and he was to march through Wales under the red dragon banner of Cadwaladr.*

Richard appointed his esquire of the body Richard Williams constable and steward for life of the castles and lordships of Pembroke, Tenby, and other fortified places, but Williams failed to win local support. In May 1485 he arrested John Savage, namesake son of

*A seventh-century king of Gwynedd made legendary as the last of the ancient kings of Britain in Geoffrey of Monmouth's twelfth-century *Historia Regum Britanniae*.

Lord Stanley's brother-in-law, who had come from France with messages for Jasper's supporters. Richard ordered him sent to London as a hostage for his father's good behaviour, but the young man escaped from Pembroke Castle dungeon with the connivance of the garrison.

Historians have generally accepted the Tudor narrative about how difficult it was to obtain significant support from the French court, and the supposedly low quality of the French troops who provided the bulk of Henry's invasion force. As to the first, supposedly Henry was required to leave Thomas Grey, Marquess of Dorset, and Thomas Bourchier, Lord FitzWarin, as surety for a loan of 20,000 *livres* [£3,000]. Nonsense. He received far more than that in cash and kind, and the 'hostages' were Yorkist lords he could do without. Dorset had already tried to desert and FitzWarin was too young to play a military role commensurate with his rank.

The French troops were professional soldiers, members of the standing army whose salaries were paid by the French court, and their commander was the Savoyard knight Philibert de Chandée, lord of Montfalcon and later a marshal of France. According to *The Ballad of Bosworth Field*, written by a participant and the only roll-call we have, Bernard Stewart, commander of the royal French *Garde Écossaise*, also took part in the expedition and would have led a contingent of his own men. There may have been only 2,000 of them, but that was four times as many as the English exiles, including the professionals from Calais.

The army that embarked at Harfleur, on ships also paid for by the French court, was therefore of far greater military weight than numbers suggest. Chandée and Stewart would have equipped and drilled the English to bring them nearer the standard of their own men. This would have included instruction in the combined use of the long pike and the shorter halberd in rectangular or wedge-shaped infantry formations, now the norm in continental warfare. The English still enjoyed the advantage of the deadly longbow, but about a fifth of the French and Scots would have been arquebusiers, with a smaller number of crossbowmen. They intended to conduct a fast-moving campaign over rough terrain, so brought only light field artillery.

The invasion fleet sailed on 1 August with a steady easterly wind and six days later made landfall at the mouth of Milford Haven, near the town of Dale. With no possibility of offering resistance Richard Williams fled Pembroke Castle to warn Rhys ap Thomas at Carmarthen. He then rode 200 miles to Nottingham to bring the news personally to Richard on the 11th.

Messengers were immediately dispatched across the country. A letter survives from the king to Henry Vernon of Haddon, Derbyshire, which demanded that he come at once with the men-at-arms he had promised, properly horsed and harnessed, on pain of forfeiture. Haddon had ignored a similar summons by the Kingmaker in 1471, and did so again.

John Howard summoned his men to rendezvous with him at Bury St Edmunds by the evening of 16 August. His letter to John Paston survives, requesting him to meet him with 'such a company of tall men as you can easily make up at my expense, as well as what you have promised the king'. Richard's reaction to the news from Wales was prompt and decisive, but it appears the machinery of general mobilization was not as well oiled as he had hoped.

Henry Percy had more ground to cover than Howard and could not have got from the far north to the rendezvous any faster than he did. On 19 August Richard moved from Nottingham to Leicester, a day's march nearer Howard and away from Percy, yet they arrived within twenty-four hours of each other. Richard's key retainers were already with him, but Percy had many lords and knights under his command who would have killed him at the slightest hint of trea-sonable intent, and it is absurd to suspect that he was laggard either in his response to the king's summons or during the battle.

The invading army blitzed up the west coast of Wales, bypassing the royal castle at Aberystwyth and turning inland at Machynlleth to avoid strongly garrisoned Harlech. Marching parallel to the

51. CONVERGING ARMIES

0   25   50
miles

Lathom
Tatton
York
Stanleys
Percy
Holt
Chirk
Stone
Nottingham
Harlech
Newport
Stafford
Richard
Henry
Lichfield
Leicester
Machynlleth
Welshpool
Shrewsbury
Tamworth
Sutton
Cheney
Aberystwyth
Atherton
Lanbadarn
Howard
Thomas
Herbert
Brackenbury
Cardigan
Haverford
Carmarthen
Raglan
Dale
Pembroke
Milford Haven
London
Bristol
© Hugh Bicheno

HENRY TUDOR'S INVASION, AUGUST 1485

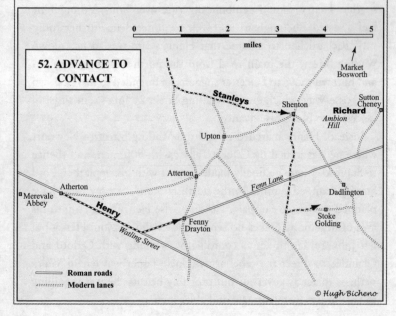

0   1   2   3   4   5
miles

52. ADVANCE TO CONTACT

Market
Bosworth
Stanleys
Shenton
Richard
Sutton
Cheney
Ambion
Hill
Upton
Atterton
Fenn Lane
Atherton
Dadlington
Merevale
Abbey
Henry
Fenny
Drayton
Stoke
Golding
Watling Street

——— Roman roads
········· Modern lanes

© Hugh Bicheno

invaders, Thomas and Herbert reported to Richard that they had prevented it from marching into England. In fact they had sent Richard Griffith and John Morgan to join Henry at Cardigan, bringing word that they had accepted his offer of the chamberlain-ship of south Wales for Thomas and immunity for his older brother for Herbert.

At Welshpool Henry was joined by fierce Rhys ap Maredudd from the Denbigh moors and other clan leaders from the hard uplands of Snowdonia. Thomas and Herbert finally joined him 6 miles east of Welshpool at Cefn Digoll (Long Mountain), which spans the border between Montgomery and Shropshire. The Welsh more than doubled the size of the army, but arguably as important was the food freely provided in its passage through Wales, which permitted Henry to dispense with foraging and to advance more rapidly than Richard expected.

Henry arrived outside Shrewsbury on 16 August, and the next day Thomas Mytton, the bailiff, opened the gates and lay down so that Henry should symbolically ride over him. Although he had arrested Buckingham in 1483, he suffered no further indig-nity. Richard had to assume that Henry's aim was to race down Watling Street, the main road from the north March to London, and his own move to Leicester suggests he intended to march down the Fosse Way, which crosses Watling Street 25 miles south-east of Leicester, to block his advance.

Instead, Henry marched away from Watling Street to Newport, where he was joined by Gilbert Talbot with 500 men, and thence to Stafford, where he finally made contact with his stepfather, Lord Stanley, camped 7 miles to the north at Stone. Stanley must have planned the whole campaign, as otherwise Henry's march into his area of hegemony makes no sense. Stanley did not join Henry but left John Savage to act as coordinator, working with Oxford and Chandée to direct the rebel army. Uncle Jasper was left in Wales, perhaps to act as governor but probably because he was unwilling to take orders from younger and abler men.

Some months before the invasion Richard had reluctantly permitted Thomas, Lord Stanley to leave the court, allegedly to attend to pressing business in Lancashire, but he had required him to leave his heir, Lord Strange, as a hostage. After failing to secure John Savage's heir he had instructed Brackenbury to arrest Thomas Bourchier, Walter Hungerford, John Fogge and others pardoned after the 1483 rebellion, and now ordered them brought to him. On the way, according to *The Great Chronicle of London*:

> Many gentlemen that held good countenance with master Brackenbury then lieutenant of the Tower, and had for many of them done right kindly, took their leave of him, in giving him thanks for his kindness before showed, and exhorted him to go with them, for they feared not to show him that they would go unto that other party, and so departed leaving him almost alone.*

Strange played a lonely and heroic part in his father's deception. Before departing for Leicester Richard had Strange 'put to the question' and extracted a confession that he, his uncle William and John Savage had indeed conspired against him. However, he insisted that his father remained loyal. Since he knew with absolute certainty that this was not the case, he resigned himself to death but had the wit to sustain the lie in letters to his father and wife.

With regard to the likely numbers who joined Henry, the *Ballad* roll-call must be handled with care. It is distorted by an over-representation of the exiles, who would have had small retinues and who may not have been joined by many from those of their affinity who had remained behind in England. It also grossly understates the numbers led by the Stanleys, perhaps because the author was a Stanley retainer and thought it unnecessary.

By sorting them into side-by-side columns arranged by region,

---

*Robert Brackenbury was a tragic character, torn between his tribal loyalty to Richard and the innate decency he showed in refusing to murder the princes or to deliver hostages for almost certain execution.

NAMED IN THE BALLAD OF *BOSWORTH FIELD* AND OTHER CREDIBLE SOURCES

(leading families in parentheses)

HENRY (122)		RICHARD (132)	
WEST COUNTRY / SOUTH-WEST (27)		THE NORTH (72)	
Devon (Courteney)	7	Yorkshire/Richmondshire*	40
Wiltshire (Hungerford, Cheyne)	6	Durham (Lord Lumley, Brackenbury)	8
Cornwall (Courtenay, Nanfan, Arundel)	5	Cumberland (Lords Dacre & Greystoke)	7
Somerset (Daubeney)	4	Northumberland (Earl of, Middleton)	7
Dorset (remnant Beaufort affinity)	3	Westmorland (Earl of, Radcliffe)	6
Gloucestershire (Berkeley)	2	Lancashire (Ashton, Harrington)	5
WALES (26)		MIDLANDS (23)	
Monmouth/Glamorgan (Herbert)	7	Derbyshire (Lord Audley)	5
Carmarthen (Thomas)	6	Warwickshire (Kendall)	3
Flint/Denbigh (Maredudd, Wm. Stanley)	6	Northamptonshire (Lord Zouche)	3
Pembroke/Cardigan (Jasper Tudor)	4	Worcestershire (Staffords of Grafton)	2
Caernarvon/Conwy (Eyri chieftains)	3	Staffordshire (Lord Ferrers)	2
HOME COUNTIES (23)		Oxfordshire (Lord Lovell)	2
Kent (Woodville, Fogge)	5	Leicestershire	2
Sussex	3	Rutland	1
Buckinghamshire	3	HOME COUNTIES (14)	
Essex (Vere)	3	London/Middlesex	3
Bedfordshire (Digby)	2	Essex (Howard)	3
Berkshire	2	Berkshire	3
Oxfordshire (Stonor, Harcourt)	2	Buckinghamshire	2
Surrey (Poynings, Bourchier)	2	Kent/Surrey	2
Hertfordshire (Fortescue)	1	Hertfordshire	1
MIDLANDS (22)		EAST ANGLIA (11)†	
Staffordshire (Blount)	7	Norfolk (Duke of)	6
Lincolnshire (Beaumont, Welles, Hastings)	3	Cambridgeshire	2

* Includes Lord Scrope of Bolton, the Conyers clan and most of Richard's other chief retainers.

† The small number of named individuals is misleading: this was the second largest regional contingent.

Northamptonshire (Hastings affinity)	3	Huntingdon	2
Warwickshire (Mountfort)	2	Suffolk (Duke of)	1
Gloucestershire (Berkeley)	2	WEST COUNTRY / SOUTH- WEST (7)	
Leicestershire (Hastings affinity)	2	Devon (Courtenays of Powderham)	4
Nottinghamshire, Rutland, Worcestershire	3	Cornwall (Bodrugan)	1
THE MARCHES (13)		Hampshire	1
Shropshire (Talbot)	9	Gloucestershire	1
Cheshire (Wm. Stanley/Savage)	4	THE MARCHES (5)	
THE NORTH (8)		Herefordshire (Lord Ferrers)	3
Lancashire (Lord Stanley)	5	Shropshire	2
Yorkshire	3		
EAST ANGLIA (3)			
Suffolk, Norfolk	2		
Cambridgeshire (Brandon)	1		

we can see that the great value of the *Ballad* roll-call lies in contrasting Henry's wide if shallow geographical support with the overwhelming preponderance (54 per cent of those named) of northerners in Richard's army. Also, while Richard's presence at Nottingham may have deterred a separate uprising in the east Midlands, it did not prevent the Welles brothers and members of the Hastings affinity from making their way to join Henry's army.

As one would expect, the main additions came along the line of march through Shropshire and Staffordshire, which contributed perhaps another 1,500 men. Contingents from elsewhere would have built up a total of about 8,000, not counting the Stanleys. Lord Stanley indented for 3,000 archers during the Scottish campaign and a full call-out of his Lancashire affinity plus levies under commissions of array could have doubled that number in 1485. Brother William and Savage may have assembled another 1,500 from north-east Wales and western Cheshire.

The Crowland Continuator believed Richard's was the largest army ever assembled in England, and a full turnout by the North cannot have produced much fewer than 10,000 men, pointing to a total in the region of 20,000. While it is unlikely to have been so tidy, a working hypothesis is that Howard's battle numbered about 10,000 and Percy's about 8,000, with the cream of the northerners forming a largely mounted reserve of 2,000 men under Richard's command. As we shall see, battlefield circumstances put most of the guns with Percy's battle.

Stanley repeated the tactic used by Thomas and Herbert. He marched parallel to Henry, reporting to Richard that he was blocking a rebel advance towards London but actually screening Henry's movements. Richard's scouts kept him well informed about the Stanleys' movements but do not appear to have been able to track Henry's. The invaders regained Watling Way at Tamworth and marched down it to Atherton, where Henry spent the night of 21 August at nearby Merevale Abbey.

Finally Stanley reported the startling intelligence that Henry's vanguard had turned along another Roman road called Fenn Lane running from Watling Street towards Leicester, and had camped at Fenny Drayton. There may have been a skirmish with Richard's scouts at Atterton, which would have given credence to Stanley's disinformation that the main enemy force was advancing north of Fenn Lane.

The aim of operational deception is to confuse the enemy commander with regard to where and in what strength the attack will come. Lord Stanley's performance before Bosworth marks him as one of the greatest but least recognized masters of medieval warfare. Richard was confused, and marched north of Fenn Lane to rendezvous with Stanley, who was camped at Shenton professing to be ready to form the right wing of the royal army.

Richard may have believed he held the trump card in Lord Strange, but he had to be ready for Stanley to jump either way. If loyal, the battle was a foregone conclusion. If not, Richard had to cover him at Shenton or risk being outflanked. Accordingly he advanced through Sutton Cheney, where Percy and the main artillery park remained, to Ambion Hill, which gave a commanding view of the broad valley in which Shenton nestles.

The outcome of Stanley's deception was that Richard gave battle at a location that neutralized his numerical advantage. Now we know where the battle was fought there can be no doubt that Chandée and Vere came forward on the 21st to confer with Stanley, to review the ground and to agree tactics. After seizing power Henry restored Vere as Earl of Oxford, richly endowed from Howard's forfeited estates, and also created and endowed Lord Stanley as Earl of Derby and Philibert de Chandée as Earl of Bath.

CHECKMATE

THANKS TO A MULTI-YEAR SURVEY OF THE SITE CON-
ducted by the Battlefields Trust and Leicestershire County
Council we now know where Bosworth was fought. Better
than that, the survey also established where there would have been
marshland in 1485, and among other significant battle debris found
more lead shot than in all other fifteenth- and sixteenth-century
European battlefields put together. The findings argue that highly
skilled battlefield tactics decided the battle.

The following is a wider interpretation than the authors of the
survey's findings permitted themselves, but rests entirely on their
admirable research.* In particular, the fall of shot points to a non-
treasonous explanation for Henry Percy's inaction. When John
Milton ended the sonnet 'On His Blindness' with the words 'They
also serve who only stand and wait' he had something else in mind
– but they apply with rare precision to the decisive role played by
Thomas, Lord Stanley.

The deception continued until the hour of battle. Early on 22
August Stanley marched from Shenton to Dadlington, located on
high ground overlooking Fenn Lane, almost certainly explaining
it as a response to learning that the rebel army was not, after all,
marching north of the road. Salazar, a Spanish professional soldier

---

*The new information is comprehensively set out in Glenn Foard and Anne Curry's
invaluable *Bosworth 1485: A Battlefield Rediscovered* (Oxford, 2013).

53. CLOSE APPROACH
Phase 1

Topography after Foss (1998)
Mere/marsh after Foard & Curry (2013)

⬚ Marsh
✝ Village church

Shenton

Howard

Richard

Percy

Sutton
Cheney

Guns

Fenn Lane

Vere

French

Henry

Lord Stanley

Dadlington

Stoke Golding

William

contours @ 50 foot intervals

0   1/4   1/2   3/4   1
mile

© Hugh Bicheno

BATTLE OF BOSWORTH, 22 AUGUST 1485

54. CLOSE APPROACH
Phase 2

Shenton

Ambion Hill
◼ Visitor
centre

Howard

Richard

Percy

Fowlismere

Tweed Brook

Guns

French

Vere

Henry

William

*Crown
Hill*

Dadlington

Lord Stanley

Stoke Golding

0   1/4   1/2   3/4   1
mile

© Hugh Bicheno

sent as an observer by Emperor Maximilian, later reported that 'my lord Tamerlant [Thomas would have been pronounced 'Tamas' by northerners] with King Richard's left wing left his position and passed in front of the king's vanguard'. Salazar incorrectly reported that 'Tamerlant' began to fight for Henry immediately, but he did not – and the move by itself did not reveal Stanley's intentions.

William Stanley probably concealed his battle behind the hill crowned by Stoke Golding. He had about 3,000 men under his command, so his brother must have lent him 1,500, to remain himself with about 4,500. Map 29 shows just how clever the deployment was. Lord Stanley appeared poised to form up on Richard's left, but equally he now held the high ground overlooking Fenn Lane, making any advance along it perilous. Since the heavy artillery must necessarily follow the road, Richard could only send his guns forward strongly escorted.

Richard formed his host in a long line overlooking the valley. The display was intended to intimidate Stanley and to dishearten Henry's army as it descended into the valley along Fenn Lane. Vergil wrote that it 'stretched forth a wondrous length, so full replenished both with footmen and horsemen that to the beholders afar off it gave a terror for the multitude, and in front were placed his archers, like a most strong trench and bulwark'.

Richard donned the crown of St Edward and rode the length of the battle line, drawing dutiful cheers as he went, and would have spoken some rousing words. The performance is unlikely to have been the boost to morale Richard intended. Soldiers have always taken an irreverent view of their commanders and what his men made of a tiny man on a big horse wearing a huge crown can readily be imagined. The state crown was returned to the camp at Ambion Hill, to be replaced by a gold circlet on his helmet.

The display precipitated a new manoeuvre by Stanley that could not be seen as anything other than a commitment to the rebel cause. He withdrew from Dadlington Hill and marched west to a new position in front of Stoke Golding, today known as Crown Hill, positioning himself as the flank guard for the approaching rebel army. At the same time William Stanley emerged from behind the hill and marched to join Henry on Fenn Lane. Furious, Richard ordered Strange beheaded, but his guards prudently opted to await the outcome of the battle.

At this point the position and extent of the marsh that used to be crossed by Fenn Lane in front of Crown Hill becomes extraordinarily important, and the key to understanding why Henry's forces suffered so few casualties. Richard had to divide his army, with Percy and the northerners marching down to Fenn Lane to escort the guns and to confront the Stanleys, while Howard's massive battle, formed deeper than usual because the terrain constricted his front, headed north of the marsh.

Without a doubt the marsh was the reason why the rebel leaders chose the location, knowing that Richard must attack. His authority rested on force of arms, and his army might not hold together if he backed down. Also, the trickle of volunteers joining Henry would have become a flood, and rebellions would have broken out in unguarded parts of the country. Salazar did not understand how fragile Richard's political situation was and advised him to pull back:

> Now when your little vassal, who was there in King Richard's service, saw the treason of the king's people, he approached him and said: 'Sire, take steps to put your person in safety, without expecting to have the victory today, owing to the manifest treason in your following'. But the king replied: 'Salazar, God forbid I yield one step. This day I shall die like a king or triumph'.

Chandée's vanguard peeled off from Fenn Lane to march behind the marsh along a ridge running between two brooks. After 500 years of cultivation, drainage and erosion, this is now an insignificant topographical feature, but there is a confused observation in the *Chroniques* of the Burgundian Jean Molinet that gives a hint why it was crucial in 1485: 'the French, knowing by the king's shot

55. ADVANCE TO CONTACT

Marsh

Ambion Hill

French

Ferrers

Savage

Howard

Richard

Tweed Brook

Vere

Talbot

Henry

Guns

Percy

William S

Dadlington

Lord Stanley

Crown Hill

Stoke Golding

contours @ 50 foot intervals

© Hugh Bicheno

1,000 yards

56. DEATH RIDE

French and
Scots

Savage

Ferrers

Richard

Vere

Howard

Talbot

Henry

William Stanley

M-A-R-S-H

0   250   500

yards

© Hugh Bicheno

the lie of the land and the order of his battle, resolved, in order to avoid the fire, to mass their troops against the flank rather than the front of the king's battle'.

Henry's commanders knew exactly what they were up against before a shot was fired. With their right flank secured by Stanley on Crown Hill and the centre protected by the marsh, the elite of the rebel army marched to secure the left at the confluence of two brooks. The best thing about the ridge between the brooks was that it permitted them to deploy out of sight, protected from artillery fire on the reverse slope. The Duke of Wellington employed the same tactic during his Iberian campaign in the early nineteenth century, and for the same reason: he too was usually outnumbered and outgunned.

Vere's battle followed the French, led by Savage's Cheshiremen and with Gilbert's Marchers bringing up the rear. They formed a curving line behind the ridgeline from Chandée's position back to a point opposite the start of the marsh. Henry was behind the marsh with a small entourage, and finally William Stanley's men formed up with the army's guns across Fenn Lane opposite the marsh crossing, a gravelled ford across the narrowest point.

The greatest concentration of shot discovered by the archaeological survey is well to the west of where the battle was fought, consistent with counter-battery fire to silence Stanley's guns on the ridge. The undershoots that must have pockmarked the ridge itself would have been dug up soon after the battle. Lead was valuable, and the cannon balls that lay undisturbed for 500 years were overshoots in distant places where scavengers did not think to look.

The hypothesis portrayed in Map 31 shows Percy's men formed in columns along Fenn Lane in the hope of being able to charge across the marsh bottleneck once the enemy guns were silenced, but also ready to repel an attack by Lord Stanley. The concentration of shot found by the survey beyond Crown Hill would have been overshoots from guns fired beyond effective range at Lord Stanley's men, perhaps hoping to provoke them to charge.

Unless they did, Percy's tactical situation was unenviable: he did not know how many men were waiting behind the ridge to his front, and if he attempted to charge across the marsh regardless, Lord Stanley could either march to support William or, more probably, attack Percy's battle in the flank. Nobody killed the Earl of Northumberland because all under his command could see they were stymied.

The curving configuration of the enemy line along the ridge caused Howard to dispose his battle with a strong right wing, angled back in a manoeuvre known as 'refusing the flank'. It is likely he entrusted this vital duty to his senior subordinate, Lord Ferrers, with his own and other Marchers and Midlanders.

Polydore Vergil's history was commissioned by Henry VII, who would have spoken to him about Bosworth. One section, the only detailed description of combat tactics in any account of the Wars of the Roses, reads like eyewitness testimony. The action portrayed on the north flank in Maps 31 and 32 is based on the following:

> The king, as soon he saw the enemy advance past the marsh, ordered his men to charge… the Earl of Oxford, afraid that in the fighting his men would be surrounded by the multitude, gave out the order… that no soldier should go more than ten feet from the standards. When in response to the command all the men massed together and drew back a little from the fray, their opponents, suspecting a trick, took fright and broke off from the fighting for a while… Then the Earl of Oxford in the one part, with tightly grouped units, attacked the enemy afresh, and the others in the other part pressing together in wedge formation renewed the battle.

I read this as Vere's men making a short charge downhill to check Howard's battle after it crossed the stream and then, outnumbered and under intense pressure, at an agreed signal falling back to regroup into defensive squares. There was a lull, but then it was

Howard's, not Vere's men who surged forward again.

Meanwhile the better drilled French and Scots formed attacking wedges and drove into Howard's refused right flank. Billmen facing this formation for the first time would not have stood for long, leaving their men-at-arms fighting for their lives. If my assumption is correct, this was where Ferrers and fourteen of the thirty-six royal Marchers and Midlanders named in the *Ballad* were killed.

Winston Churchill's aphorism that in war everything is going on all the time applies even more exactly to battlefield developments. By this stage Richard would have known that Percy and the northerners had not been able to achieve the breakthrough at the marsh crossing that would have split the enemy army; but it seems unlikely that the crumbling of his right wing had already begun, as otherwise he would have committed the reserve to shore it up. All he knew was that his battle plan was not producing the battle of annihilation he craved.

However, Howard's renewed push opened a gap at Vere's right wing, through which Richard caught a clear sight of Henry and his entourage, who may have moved to support Talbot. Richard's motives for what followed are not hard to deduce: mounting frustration and rage, the provocation of Henry's royal banners, confidence in his military judgement, perhaps a desire to prove the will of God in single combat with his rival. He assembled his household knights and launched the only all-out heavy cavalry charge of the Wars of the Roses.

The move achieved total tactical surprise. The brook emerging from the marsh and the slope beyond would have slowed its impetus, but when Talbot and some of his men tried to intercept the charge they were smashed aside, leaving Talbot himself severely wounded. Vergil's account again reads as though from Henry himself:

> In the first charge Richard killed several men, toppled Henry's standard along with the standard bearer William Brandon [actually Charles, the only notable fatality among Henry's followers],

contended with John Cheyne, a man of surpassing bravery who stood in his way, and thrust him to the ground with great force, and made a path for himself through the press of steel.

Tradition has it that Henry's Welsh bodyguard halted the charge, rallied by Rhys ap Maredudd, thereafter known as Rhys Fawr (Rhys the Mighty), who picked up Henry's red dragon banner and held it aloft for the remainder of the battle. 'Then, behold, William Stanley came in support with 3,000 men. Indeed it was at this point, with the rest of his men taking to their heels, Richard was killed fighting in the thickest of the press.' Molinet tells it differently:

> The king bore himself valiantly according to his destiny... but when he saw this discomfiture and found himself alone on the field he thought to run after the others. His horse leapt into the marsh from which it could not retrieve itself. One of the Welshmen then came after him and struck him dead with a halberd.

We cannot place much confidence in Molinet, whose estimates of the numbers involved are wildly exaggerated and whose account is a thinly disguised morality tale about Richard's deserved fate. However, examination of Richard's bones revealed that the death blow was indeed a skull-penetrating blow, probably by a halberd, to the back of his head. The remains eloquently confirm that once down he vanished under a hacking and stabbing mob.

There may have been a pause in the fighting, as the soldiers became spectators of the drama unfolding on the ridge at the centre of the battlefield. Once they saw Richard fall, Vere's men charged down the hill into Howard's demoralized men, the duke himself being killed and Surrey badly wounded, probably fighting to defend his fallen father. Vergil says 1,000 were killed, nearly all of them Richard's men, which seems about right.

The casualties deny the allegation that Richard was abandoned by his household: Robert Brackenbury, William Conyers, Ralph Danby, Alan Fulthorpe (Constable of Middleham), Thomas Gower, Thomas Markenfield, Robert Percy, Thomas Pilkington and Richard Ratcliffe all died with him.

The Crowland Continuator, who was not there, reported some words spoken by Richard on the morning of the battle that read like a textbook example of a psychopathic mirroring:

> 'He asserted that the issue of this day's battle, to whichever side the victory might be granted, would prove the utter destruction of the kingdom of England. He also declared that it was his intention, if he should prove the conqueror, to crush all the supporters of the opposite faction; while at the same time he predicted that his adversary would do the same towards well wishers to his own party, in case the victory should fall to his lot.'

Contrary to Richard's prediction the victors did not even indulge in the wholesale slaughter that almost invariably followed a medieval battle – the wounded Earl of Surrey was not killed though he refused quarter. It is likely the defeated men did not trigger the usual feral hunting response among their foes because instead of fleeing they dropped their weapons and surrendered in place; but Richard's death may well have been catharsis enough.

Nor did Henry indulge in a post-battle purge. The only executions were of William Bracher and his son for having betrayed their Yeomen of the Crown comrades, and of William Catesby for his treachery to Lord Hastings. Only twenty-eight men, ten of them killed at Bosworth, were attainted: five lords (Norfolk, Surrey, Lovell, Ferrers and de la Zouche), eight knights and fifteen others. Apart from Lovell and the Staffords of Grafton, who fled to sanctuary and remained adamant, the survivors made submission and most eventually recovered their family estates.

It was as though the spell cast over so many by the fierce will that had driven Richard in life had suddenly dissipated, and there was to be none of the lasting loyalty to the deposed king's cause that had bedevilled Edward IV and Richard himself. Once dead it was as though he had never been anything except Shakespeare's pantomime villain – until the emergence of a passionate fan club many centuries later.

SOMEWHAT MUSING

IT WOULD BE ANTICLIMACTIC TO EXTEND THE WARS OF the Roses narrative beyond Bosworth. There were several rebellions against the Tudor succession, including one by Thomas Vaughan in 1486, crushed with relish by Rhys ap Thomas, and two in 1487 and 1497 led by Yorkist impostors sponsored by Margaret of York, dowager Duchess of Burgundy. During the first John de la Pole, Earl of Lincoln and Richard III's heir presumptive, was killed.

Although Henry VII claimed the throne by right of conquest, he was finally provoked into crushing the Yorkist seed. He executed Clarence's feeble-minded and blameless son Edward, Earl of Warwick, in 1499. Emperor Maximilian surrendered John de la Pole's rebellious brother Edmund to Henry, under oath not to harm him. Previously demoted from duke to earl of Suffolk and then deprived of the earldom, Edmund was executed by Henry VIII in 1513. Richard de la Pole, the last Yorkist pretender, was killed in 1525 fighting for France in Italy.

Edward Gibbon observed that history is 'little more than the register of the crimes, follies, and misfortunes of mankind', hardly the stuff of comedy. Although the doings of our ancestors were often farcically inept, an awareness of our own on-going stupidities generally constrains our urge to laugh at them. Happily we need feel less inhibited when – to bowdlerize T. H. Huxley – a fanatically held belief is slain by an ugly fact.

Just such a moment occurred when, thanks to the persistence and brilliant deduction from sparse facts of Philippa Langley, a devoted Ricardian, the remains of Richard III were discovered and their identity confirmed by mitochondrial DNA. Unfortunately the bones revealed that he was, after all, the deformed individual portrayed by Shakespeare in *The Tragedy of King Richard the Third*.

The discovery undermines the defining purpose of the Richard III Foundation, which is 'to challenge the popular view of King Richard III by demonstrating through rigorous scholarship that the facts of Richard's life and reign are in stark contrast to the Shakespearian caricature'. It is going to be harder to defend that thesis now we know that the most salient characteristic of Shakespeare's Richard III was not, in fact, a caricature.

The modern Ricardian movement is the historiographical oak that sprang up from the acorn planted by Josephine Tey's 1951 detective story *The Daughter of Time* and a sixteenth-century portrait of Richard that portrays him as a sensitive soul. I could not have written these books without the vast amount of excellent scholarship the movement has generated. However the defining Ricardian dogma – that Richard III's black villainy was an invention of Tudor propagandists – was always skating on thin ice.

The key contemporary sources for the events of 1483, by which Richard III is rightly judged, are the Crowland Continuator and Mancini. The first was unknown to a wider audience until the end of the Tudor period, and the second not until 1934. As the editors of the *Crowland Chronicle Continuations* judiciously observe, this helps 'to explain why Tudor propaganda was so successful: like all good propaganda it offered an interpretation which even informed people, in independent possession of the facts, could accept'.

No serious historian doubts that Richard was directly responsible for the murder of his nephews, and that it was the defining act of his life and reign. Despite this, we saw the strength of the Ricardian cult in the veneration surrounding the reburial of his remains in March 2015. As Thomas Cromwell said to Ambassador

Chapuys, Richard was a bad man who met the end he deserved; that Cromwell's master Henry VIII was also loathsome does not alter the justice of that verdict. It is far more debatable whether Richard deserved a handsome tomb monument in Leicester Cathedral with '*Loyaulte me lie*' inscribed without irony on the plinth.

It was, however, perfectly expressive of the Zeitgeist. If a latter-day Richard III were put on trial today for murdering his nephews in order to steal their inheritance, well-paid apologists would be lining up to argue in mitigation not only that his intentions were good, but also that he was not responsible for his actions because of his congenital deformity and malignant upbringing. They would also, of course, assert that society, not he, was to blame.

It should go without saying that Richard's personality was shaped by his genetic endowment, his dysfunctional family and the violent social environment in which he grew up. But while such influences predispose to psychopathy, they are not predictive. He was also immensely privileged and raised in the Christian chivalric tradition, which did not constrain him in the slightest. Only his elevated social status differentiates him from common criminals.

If the Tudor 'big lie' turns out not to be so big after all, the same cannot be said for other black holes in the historiography of the Wars of the Roses. In Part I it was the demonization of Marguerite d'Anjou for having fought for her son's birthright, and in Part II it has been the greedy-and-grasping-parvenu Woodvilles trope. These influential interpretations have scant basis in fact and are little more than manifestations of the universal human tendency to 'blame the foreigner', of a startling amount of misogyny, and of petty bourgeois snobbery.

In Darwinian terms the final verdict on the Houses of York and Neville, who have dominated our narrative, is that even their mitochondrial DNA will be extinguished upon the death of the childless donor who provided the sample that permitted the identification of Richard's remains. By contrast, a fair proportion of the native English population, including the monarchy and much of the old aristocracy, carries the mitochondrial DNA of Jacquetta de Luxembourg, wife of murdered Richard Woodville, mother of Queen Elizabeth and of murdered Anthony and John, and grandmother of the little boys murdered in the Tower of London.

If, as Darwinian absolutists argue, human beings are simply DNA's means of reproduction, then the winner's rosette in the competition among the bloodlines of senior titles of aristocracy goes to John Howard. Despite vicissitudes including two subsequent attainders under Henry VIII and Elizabeth I and a genetic bottleneck in 1975, his linear descendant is Edward William Fitzalan-Howard, since 2002 not merely the 18th Duke of Norfolk and Earl Marshal of England, but also Earl of Arundel (with Jacquetta's DNA along for the ride), of Surrey and of Norfolk, and Baron Maltravers, Beaumont and Howard of Glossop.

Neck and neck with Howard in the DNA stakes is Charles Somerset, illegitimate son of Charles the Bold's heartthrob Henry Beaufort, 3rd Duke of Somerset. Charles married Elizabeth, daughter and sole heiress of the younger William Herbert and Margaret Woodville, and through her became Lord Herbert. From them descend the line of earls and marquesses of Worcester, finally made dukes of Beaufort in 1692. The current duke is the only member of the aristocracy descended in the male line from the Plantagenets.

This book was inspired by George R. R. Martin's *A Song of Ice and Fire* saga, for which he in turn drew inspiration from the Wars of the Roses. Martin's genius lies not only in his multi-layered and compelling narrative, but also in the interwoven motives of his vividly developed characters. Within the constraints of non-fiction I have tried to do the same.

Sadly, a lack of personally illuminating sources prevented me writing the story as the true-life sex'n'violence soap opera that it undoubtedly was, more akin to the florid 1980s American TV series *Dallas* and *Dynasty* than to the fastidious observation of aristocratic families not doing very much at which the BBC excels. I wonder, though, whether anyone would dare to broadcast a saga in which adultery, cuckoldry, homo-eroticism, incest and satyriasis punctuate a narrative of unchecked aristocratic greed and criminality, illuminated by savage blood feuds, spectacular battles, brutal beheadings and the ever-popular ritual disembowelments.

Alison Weir, Susan Higginbotham, Philippa Gregory and Sarah Gristwood have done sterling work in print and on TV to give a voice to the women of the Wars of the Roses, but all any of us can do is to reason that Catherine de Valois, Marguerite d'Anjou, Elizabeth Woodville, Jacquetta de Luxembourg, Cecily Neville, Margaret Beaufort and others filled many of the holes in the historical record. It is enormously frustrating that precisely how they did it is lost to us, because there was no other period in English history during which women were more influential. That it was also one of the bloodiest does not necessarily support the contention that the female of the species is more deadly than the male.

On a personal level, researching and writing these two books have brought to life so many of what Lawrence Durrell called 'spirits of place'. I live in a small market town that was once Richard of York's, not far from twice fought-over St Albans. My family lived near or in Cambridge for centuries but I was the first to attend the university, architecturally dominated by breathtaking King's College Chapel, Henry VI's foundation, and where several other famous colleges were founded by leading characters in this book.

By any measure of comfort and physical well-being we enjoy standards beyond the imagination of Renaissance princes, and if a cause and effect could be shown, the loss of the creative highs of the past would be considered a fair price to pay for the elimination of the squalid lows of endemic disease and violence. But it cannot, and therein lies the attraction of reading about a far less humane but more effervescent time, when some at least of the tax burden that rulers imposed on their subjects went to decorate the world with works of lasting beauty.

I have revisited with new eyes the tomb monuments in Westminster Abbey, St George's Chapel at Windsor and the spectacular Beauchamp sarcophagus at St Mary's, Warwick. But most of all I have been enormously privileged to walk the sites of the battles that provide the climaxes of the two books in the wake of meticulous archaeological research that at last permits an educated guess about how they were fought. For, like it or not, war has defined human history, and nothing better illustrates the definitive importance of *fortuna* – blind chance – than properly understood battles.

A hair's breadth of *fortuna* separated victory from defeat at Towton and Bosworth. Had either gone the other way the flow of history might have followed fundamentally divergent channels. Despite this, battles still tend to be presented in unnatural isolation from political and social history, I suspect largely because people do not want to be reminded of the irreducible element of often unmerited good or bad luck that governs human existence.

Readers will draw as much or as little deeper meaning from the events I have described as they choose, and it is not for me to say what it might be. I set out to tell a tale of families riven by ambition, greed, lust and folly and I hope to have done it justice. History is the mistress of life, and I have tried to make love to her as she deserves.

APPENDICES

ENGLISH PEERAGE
1440–62

By date of creation

KG = Knight of the Garter k. = killed in battle

DUKES

Date created	Name	Dates	Comments
York (1385)	Richard Plantagenet, KG, 3rd duke	1426–60	k. Wakefield
	Edward, Earl of March	1460–1	Merged with Crown
Norfolk (1397)[1]	John Mowbray, KG, 3rd duke	1432–61	
	John Mowbray, 4th duke	1461–76	
Gloucester (1414)	Humphrey of Lancaster, KG	1414–47	Extinct
Exeter (1416)	John Holland, KG, 2nd duke	1439–47	
	Henry Holland, 3rd duke	1447–61	Attainted
Somerset (1443)	John Beaufort, KG	1443–4	Extinct
Buckingham (1444)	Humphrey Stafford, KG	1444–60	k. Northampton
	Henry Stafford, 2nd duke	1460–83	
Warwick (1445)	Henry Beauchamp	1445–6	Extinct
Somerset (1448)	Edmund Beaufort, KG	1448–55	k. St Albans
	Henry Beaufort, 2nd duke	1455–61	Attainted
Suffolk (1448)	William de la Pole, KG	1448–50	Murdered, forfeit
Clarence (1461)	George Plantagenet	1461–78	
Gloucester (1461)	Richard Plantagenet	1461–83	

1. Also Earl of Nottingham, Baron Mowbray and Baron Segrave.

MARCHER LORDSHIP

Glamorgan (1439)	Henry Beauchamp	1439–46	*See Duke of Warwick*
Glamorgan (1449)	Richard Neville, KG	1449–71	*See Earl of Warwick*

MARQUESSES

Dorset (1442)	Edmund Beaufort, KG	1442–55	*See Duke of Somerset*
Suffolk (1444)	William de la Pole, KG	1444–50	*See Duke of Suffolk*

EARLS

Warwick (1088)	Richard Beauchamp, 13th earl	1401–39	
	Henry Beauchamp, 14th earl	1439–46	*See Duke of Warwick*
	Anne Beauchamp, 15th countess	1446–8	Daughter of duke
	Anne Beauchamp, 16th countess	1448–92	Sister of duke
	Richard Neville (son), KG, 16th earl	1449–71	
Arundel (1138)	William FitzAlan, 16th earl	1438–87	
Oxford (1142)	John Vere, 12th earl	1417–62	Executed
March (1328)	Richard Plantagenet, KG, 6th earl	1425–45	*See Duke of York*
	Edward Plantagenet, 7th earl	1445–61	Merged with Crown
Devon (1335)	Thomas Courtenay, 5th earl	1422–58	
	Thomas Courtenay, 6th earl	1458–61	Executed, attainted
Salisbury (1337)	Alice Montacute, 5th countess	1428–62	
	Richard Neville (father), KG, 5th earl	1442–60	k. Wakefield
	Richard Neville, KG, 6th earl	1461–71	
Stafford (1351)	Humphrey Stafford, KG, 6th earl	1403–44	*Eldest sons of the dukes of Buckingham*
	Humphrey Stafford, 7th earl	1444–58	
	Henry Stafford, 8th earl	1458–83	
Suffolk (1385)	William de la Pole, KG, 4th earl	1415–50	*See Duke of Suffolk*
	John de la Pole, KG, 5th earl	1450–92	
Rutland (1385)	Richard Plantagenet, KG, 2nd earl	1415–45	*See Duke of York*
	Edmund Pantagenet, 3rd earl	1445–60	k. Wakefield, extinct
Huntington (1387)	John Holland, 3rd earl	1417–47	*See Duke of Exeter*
	Henry Holland, 4th earl	1447–61	Attainted
Somerset (1387)	John Beaufort, KG, 3rd earl	1418–44	*See Duke of Somerset*

Westmorland (1397)	Ralph Neville, 1st earl	1397–1425	
	Ralph Neville, 2nd earl	1425–84	Dementia from *c*.1459
Pembroke (1414)	Humphrey, Duke of Gloucester	1414–47	Extinct
Northumberland (1416)	Henry Percy	1416–55	k. St Albans
	Henry Percy, 2nd earl	1455–61	k. Towton, attainted
Cambridge (1426)	Richard Plantagenet, KG, 2nd earl	1426–45	*See Duke of York*
	Edward Plantagenet, 3rd earl	1445–61	Merged with Crown
Dorset (1441)	Edmund Beaufort, KG	1442–55	*See Duke of Somerset*
	Henry Beaufort	1455–61	Attainted
Shrewsbury (1442)	John Talbot, KG	1442–53	k. Castillon
	John Talbot, KG, 2nd earl	1453–60	k. Northampton
	John Talbot, 3rd earl	1460–73	
Kendal (1443)	John Beaufort, KG	1443–4	*See Duke of Somerset*
Somerset (1444)	Edmund Beaufort	1444–55	*See Duke of Somerset*
Kendal (1446)	Jean de Foix, KG, Captal de Buch	1446–62	Resigned
Pembroke (1447)	William de la Pole, KG	1447–50	*See Duke of Suffolk*
Gloucester (1448)	William de la Pole, KG	1448–50	*See Duke of Suffolk*
Wiltshire (1449)	James Butler, KG, Earl of Ormonde	1446–61	Executed, attainted
Worcester (1449)	John Tiptoft, KG	1449–70	
Surrey (1451)	John Mowbray	1451–76	*See Duke of Norfolk*
Richmond (1452)	Edmund Tudor	1452–6	
	Henry Tudor, 2nd earl	1456–61	Forfeit
Pembroke (1452)	Jasper Tudor, KG	1452–61	Attainted
Essex (1461)	Henry Bourchier, KG	1461–83	
Kent (1461)	William Neville, KG	1461–3	
Pembroke (1461)	William Herbert, KG	1461–9	

VISCOUNTS

| Beaumont (1440) | John Beaumont, KG | 1440–60 | k. Northampton |
| | William Beaumont, 2nd viscount | 1460–1 | Attainted |

Bourchier (1446)	Henry Bourchier, KG	1446–72	*See Earl of Essex*
Lisle (1451)	John Talbot, KG	1451–3	k. Castillon
	Thomas Talbot, 2nd viscount	1453–70	

BARONS

Roos (1264)	Thomas Roos, 9th baron	1421–61	Attainted, executed 1464
Fauconberg (1295)	Joan Fauconberg, 6th baroness	1429–90	
	William Neville, KG, 6th baron	1421–63	*See Earl of Kent*
FitzWalter (1295)	Elizabeth FitzWalter, 8th baroness	1431–85	
	John Radcliffe, 8th baron (de jure)	1431–61	k. Ferrybridge
FitzWarine (1295)	Thomasine Hankeford, 9th baroness	1433–53	
	William Bourchier, 9th baron	1433–70	*See Viscount Bourchier*
Furnivall (1295)	Maud Neville, 6th baroness	1407–22	
	John Talbot, KG, 6th baron, et seq.	1407–53	*See Earl of Shrewsbury*
Grey of Wilton (1295)	Richard Grey, 6th baron	1396–1442	
	Reginald Grey, 7th baron	1442–93	
Morley (1295)	Robert Morley, 6th baron	1435–42	
	Alianore Morley, 7th baroness	1442–76	
	William Lovel, 7th baron	1442–76	By marriage
Neville of Raby (1295)	Ralph Neville, 5th baron	1425–84	*See Earl of Westmorland*
Clinton (1298)	John Clinton, 5th baron	1431–64	
Bardolf (1299)	Elizabeth Phelip, 6th baroness	1408–41	
	William Beaumont, 7th baron	1436–61	*See Viscount Beaumont*
Clifford (1299)	Thomas Clifford, 8th baron	1422–55	k. St Albans
	John Clifford, 9th baron	1455–61	k. Towton, attainted

Ferrers of Chartley (1299)	William Ferrers, 6th baron	1435–50	
	Anne Ferrers, 7th baroness	1450–68	
	Walter Devereux, 7th baron	1461–85	*De jure* from 1450
Ferrers of Groby (1299)	William Ferrers, 5th baron	1388–1445	
	Elizabeth Ferrers, 6th baroness	1445–83	
	Edward Grey, 6th baron [2]	1445–57	
	John Bourchier, 6th baron	1462–83	
Lovell (1299)[3]	William Lovell, 7th baron	1414–55	
	John Lovell, 8th baron	1455–65	
Scales (1299)	Thomas Scales, 7th baron	1419–60	Murdered
	Elizabeth Scales, 8th baroness	1460–73	
	Anthony Woodville, KG, 8th baron	1460–83	By marriage
Strange of Knockyn (1299)	Richard Strange, 7th baron	1397–1449	
	John Strange, 8th baron	1449–77	
de la Warr (1299)	Reginald West, 6th baron	1427–51	
	Richard West, 7th baron	1451–76	
Welles (1299)	Lionel Welles, KG, 6th baron	1421–61	k. Towton, attainted
Zouche (1308)	William Zouche, 5th baron	1415–63	
Beaumont (1309)	John Beaumont, KG, 6th baron	1417–60	*See Viscount Beaumont*
Audley (1313) *Also Tuchet*	James Tuchet, 5th baron	1408–59	k. Blore Heath
	John Tuchet, 6th baron	1459–90	
Cobham (1313)	Joan Brooke, 5th baroness	1434–42	
	Edward Brooke, 6th baron	1442–64	
Willoughby (1313)	Robert Willoughby, KG, 6th baron	1409–52	
	Joan Willoughby, 7th baroness	1452–62	
	Richard Welles, 7th baron	1452–70	
Dacre of Gilsland (1321)	Thomas Dacre, 6th baron	1398–1458	
	Joan Dacre, 7th baroness	1458–86	Granddaughter of Thomas
	Richard Fiennes, 7th baron	1458–83	By marriage

2. First father-in-law of Elizabeth Woodville, who married Edward IV in 1464.
3. Also Baron Holland, Deincort, Bedale and Grey of Rotherfield.

FitzHugh (1321)	William FitzHugh, 4th baron	1425–52	
	Henry FitzHugh, 5th baron	1452–72	
Greystoke (1321)	Ralph Greystoke, 5th baron	1436–87	
Grey of Ruthyn (1325)	Reginald Grey, 3rd baron	1388–1441	
	Edmund Grey, 4th baron	1441–90	
Harington (1326)	William Harington, 5th baron	1418–58	
	William Bonville, KG, 6th baron	1458–60	k. Wakefield
	Cecily Bonville, 7th baroness	1460–1530	*Combined with Bonville*
Burghersh (1330)	Henry Beauchamp, KG, 6th baron	1439–45	*See Duke of Warwick*
	Anne Beauchamp, 7th baroness	1445–9	Abeyant
Maltravers (1330)	William FitzAlan	1438–83	*See Earl of Arundel*
Talbot (1331)	John Talbot, KG, 7th baron	1421–53	*See Earl of Shrewsbury*
	John Talbot, KG, 8th baron	1453–60	
	John Talbot, 9th baron	1460–73	
Poynings (1337)[4]	Robert Poynings, 5th baron	1387–1446	
	Eleanor Poynings, 6th baroness	1446–82	
	Henry Percy, 6th baron by marriage	1446–61	*Earl of Northumberland*
Bourchier (1342)	Henry Bourchier, KG, 5th baron	1433–83	*See Earl of Essex*
Scrope of Masham (1350)	John Scrope, 4th baron	1426–55	
	Thomas Scrope, 5th baron	1455–75	
Botreaux (1368)	William Botreaux, 3rd baron	1392–1462	
	Margaret Botreaux, 4th baroness	1462–77	
Scrope of Bolton (1371)	Henry Scrope, 4th baron	1420–59	
	John Scrope, KG, 5th baron	1459–98	
Cromwell (1375)	Ralph Cromwell, 3rd baron	1417–55	Abeyant
Beauchamp of Bletsoe (1379)	Margaret Beauchamp, 4th baroness	1429–82	
	John Beaufort, KG, 4th baron	1441–4	*See Duke of Somerset*
	Lionel Welles, KG, 4th baron	1447–61	*See Welles*

4. Also baronies of FitzPayne and Brian.

Bergavenny (1392) *Dispute with 1450 creation*	Elizabeth Beauchamp, 3rd baroness	1421–47	
	Anne Beauchamp, 4th baroness	1447–92	Countess of Warwick
Grey of Codnor (1397)	Henry Grey, 3rd baron	1431–44	
	Henry Grey, 4th baron	1444–96	
Tuchet (1403) *Also Audley*	James Tuchet, 2nd baron	1408–59	k. Blore Heath
	John Tuchet, 6th baron	1459–90	
Berkeley (1421)	James Berkeley	1421–63	
Hungerford (1426)	Walter Hungerford, KG	1426–49	
	Robert Hungerford, 2nd baron	1449–59	
	Robert Hungerford, 3rd baron	1459–62	Attainted, executed 1464
Tiptoft (1426)	John Tiptoft	1426–43	
	John Tiptoft, KG, 2nd baron[5]	1443–70	*See Earl of Worcester*
Latimer (1432)	George Neville (disputed)	1425–69	Ruled incompetent 1447
	Richard Neville (custodian)	1447–69	*See Earl of Warwick*
Fanhope (1433)	John Cornwall, KG	1433–43	Also Milbroke, extinct
Dudley (1440)	John Sutton, KG	1440–87	
Sudeley (1299/1441)	Ralph Boteler, KG, 6th/1st baron	1441–73	
Milbroke (1442)	John Cornwall, KG	1442–3	Also Fanhope, extinct
Lisle (1444)	John Talbot, KG	1444–53	*See Viscount Lisle*
	Thomas Talbot, 2nd baron	1453–70	
Moleyns (1445)	Alianore Moleyns, 2nd baroness	1428–76	
	Robert Hungerford, 2nd baron	1449–64	*See Hungerford*
Beauchamp of Powick (1447)	John Beauchamp, KG	1447–75	
Hoo and Hastings (1447)	Thomas Hoo, KG	1447–55	Extinct
Saye and Sele (1447)	James Fiennes	1447–50	Murdered
	William Fiennes, 2nd baron	1450–71	
Rivers (1448)	Richard Woodville, KG	1448–69	

5. Shared the lordship and castle of Powys with Henry, de jure Baron Grey of Powys.

Stourton (1448)	John Stourton	1448–62	
	William Stourton, 2nd baron	1462–79	
Bonville (1449)	William Bonville, KG	1449–61	Executed St Albans
	Cecily Bonville, 2nd baroness	1461–1530	*Combined with Harington*
Egremont (1449)	Thomas Percy	1449–60	k. Northampton, extinct
Vescy (1449)	Henry Bromflete	1449–69	
Bergavenny (1450)	Edward Neville, 1st/3rd baron	1450–76	*Dispute with 1392 creation*
Rougement Grey (1450)	Thomas Grey	1450–61	Executed, extinct
Berners (1455)	John Bourchier, KG	1455–74	
Stanley (1456)	Thomas Stanley, KG	1456–9	
	Thomas Stanley, 2nd baron	1459–1504	
Dacre of the North (1459)	Randolph Dacre	1459–61	k. Towton, attainted
Montagu (1461)	John Neville, KG	1461–71	
Cromwell (1461)	Humphrey Bourchier	1461–71	
Hastings (1461)	William Hastings, KG	1461–83	
Lumley (1461)	Thomas Lumley	1461–85	
Herbert of Raglan (1461)	William Herbert, KG	1461–69	
Ogle (1461)	Robert Ogle	1461–69	
Wenlock (1461)	John Wenlock, KG	1461–71	

ENGLISH PEERAGE
1440–62
Alphabetical

KG = Knight of the Garter   k. = killed in battle

DUKES

Date created	Name	Dates	Comments
Buckingham (1444)	Humphrey Stafford, KG	1444–60	k. Northampton
	Henry Stafford, 2nd duke	1460–83	
Clarence (1461)	George Plantagenet	1461–78	
Exeter (1416)	John Holland, KG, 2nd duke	1439–47	
	Henry Holland, 3rd duke	1447–61	Attainted
Gloucester (1414)	Humphrey of Lancaster, KG	1414–47	Extinct
Gloucester (1461)	Richard Plantagenet	1461–83	
Norfolk (1397)[1]	John Mowbray, KG, 3rd duke	1432–61	
	John Mowbray, 4th duke	1461–76	
Somerset (1443)	John Beaufort, KG	1443–4	Extinct
Somerset (1448)	Edmund Beaufort, KG	1448–55	k. St Albans
	Henry Beaufort, 2nd duke	1455–61	Attainted
Suffolk (1448)	William de la Pole, KG	1448–50	Murdered, forfeit
Warwick (1445)	Henry Beauchamp	1445–6	Extinct
York (1385)	Richard Plantagenet, KG, 3rd duke	1426–60	k. Wakefield
	Edward, Earl of March	1460–1	Merged with crown

1. Also Earl of Nottingham, Baron Mowbray and Baron Segrave.

MARCHER LORDSHIP

Glamorgan (1439)	Henry Beauchamp	1439–46	*See Duke of Warwick*
Glamorgan (1449)	Richard Neville, KG	1449–71	*See Earl of Warwick*

MARQUESSES

Dorset (1442)	Edmund Beaufort, KG	1442–55	*See Duke of Somerset*
Suffolk (1444)	William de la Pole, KG	1444–50	*See Duke of Suffolk*

EARLS

Arundel (1138)	William FitzAlan, 16th earl	1438–87	
Cambridge (1426)	Richard Plantagenet, KG, 2nd earl	1426–45	*See Duke of York*
	Edward Plantagenet, 3rd earl	1445–61	Merged with crown
Devon (1335)	Thomas Courtenay, 13th earl	1422–58	
	Thomas Courtenay, 14th earl	1458–61	Executed, attainted
Dorset (1441)	Edmund Beaufort, KG	1442–55	*See Duke of Somerset*
	Henry Beaufort	1455–61	Attainted
Essex (1461)	Henry Bourchier, KG	1461–83	
Gloucester (1448)	William de la Pole, KG	1448–50	*See Duke of Suffolk*
Huntington (1387)	John Holland, 3rd earl	1417–47	*See Duke of Exeter*
	Henry Holland, 4th earl	1447–61	Attainted
Kendal (1443)	John Beaufort, KG	1443–4	*See Duke of Somerset*
Kendal (1446)	Jean de Foix, KG, Captal de Buch	1446–62	Resigned
Kent (1461)	William Neville, KG	1461–3	
March (1328)	Richard Plantagenet, KG, 6th earl	1425–45	See Duke of York
	Edward Plantagenet, 7th earl	1445–61	Merged with crown
Northumberland (1416)	Henry Percy	1416–55	k. St Albans
	Henry Percy, 2nd earl	1455–61	k. Towton, attainted
Oxford (1142)	John Vere, 12th earl	1417–62	
Pembroke (1414)	Humphrey, Duke of Gloucester	1414–47	Extinct

Pembroke (1447)	William de la Pole, KG	1447–50	*See Duke of Suffolk*
Pembroke (1452)	Jasper Tudor, KG	1452–61	Attainted
Pembroke (1461)	William Herbert, KG	1461–9	
Salisbury (1337)	Alice Montacute, 5th countess	1428–62	
	Richard Neville (father), KG, 5th earl	1442–60	k. Wakefield
	Richard Neville, KG, 6th earl	1461–71	
Stafford (1351)	Humphrey Stafford, KG, 6th earl	1403–44	*Eldest sons of the dukes of Buckingham*
	Humphrey Stafford, 7th earl	1444–58	
	Henry Stafford, 8th earl	1458–83	
Suffolk (1385)	William de la Pole, KG, 4th earl	1415–50	*See Duke of Suffolk*
	John de la Pole, KG, 5th earl	1450–92	
Richmond (1452)	Edmund Tudor	1452–6	
	Henry Tudor, 2nd earl	1456–61	Forfeit
Rutland (1385)	Richard Plantagenet, KG, 2nd earl	1415–45	*See Duke of York*
	Edmund Pantagenet, 3rd earl	1445–60	k. Wakefield, extinct
Shrewsbury (1442)	John Talbot, KG	1442–53	k. Castillon
	John Talbot, KG, 2nd earl	1453–60	k. Northampton
	John Talbot, 3rd earl	1460–73	
Somerset (1387)	John Beaufort, KG, 3rd earl	1418–44	*See Duke of Somerset*
Somerset (1444)	Edmund Beaufort	1444–55	*See Duke of Somerset*
Surrey (1451)	John Mowbray	1451–76	*See Duke of Norfolk*
Warwick (1088)	Richard Beauchamp, 13th earl	1401–39	
	Henry Beauchamp, 14th earl	1439–46	*See Duke of Warwick*
	Anne Beauchamp, 15th countess	1446–8	Daughter of duke
	Anne Beauchamp, 16th countess	1448–92	Sister of duke
	Richard Neville (son), KG, 16th earl	1449–71	
Westmorland (1397)	Ralph Neville, 1st earl	1397–1425	
	Ralph Neville, 2nd earl	1425–84	Dementia from *c.*1459
Wiltshire (1449)	James Butler, KG, Earl of Ormonde	1446–61	Executed, attainted
Worcester (1449)	John Tiptoft, KG	1449–70	

VISCOUNTS

Beaumont (1440)	John Beaumont, KG	1440–60	k. Northampton
	William Beaumont, 2nd viscount	1460–1	Attainted
Bourchier (1446)	Henry Bourchier, KG	1446–72	*See Earl of Essex*
Lisle (1451)	John Talbot, KG	1451–53	k. Castillon
	Thomas Talbot, 2nd viscount	1453–70	

BARONS

Audley (1313) *Also Tuchet*	James Tuchet, 5th baron	1408–59	k. Blore Heath
	John Tuchet, 6th baron	1459–90	
Bardolf (1299)	Elizabeth Phelip, 6th baroness	1408–41	
	William Beaumont, 7th baron	1436–61	*See Viscount Beaumont*
Beauchamp of Bletsoe (1379)	Margaret Beauchamp, 4th baroness	1429–82	
	John Beaufort, KG, 4th baron	1441–4	*See Duke of Somerset*
	Lionel Welles, KG, 4th baron	1447–61	*See Welles*
Beauchamp of Powick (1447)	John Beauchamp, KG	1447–75	
Beaumont (1309)	John Beaumont, KG, 6th baron	1417–60	*See Viscount Beaumont*
Bergavenny (1392) *Dispute with 1450 creation*	Elizabeth Beauchamp, 3rd baroness	1421–47	
	Anne Beauchamp, 4th baroness	1447–92	Countess of Warwick
Bergavenny (1450)	Edward Neville, 1st/ 3rd baron	1450–76	
Berkeley (1421)	James Berkeley	1421–63	
Berners (1455)	John Bourchier, KG	1455–74	
Bonville (1449)	William Bonville, KG	1449–61	Executed St Albans
	Cecily Bonville, 2nd baroness	1461–1530	Combined with Harington
Botreaux (1368)	William Botreaux, 3rd baron	1392–1462	
	Margaret Botreaux, 4th baroness	1462–77	
Bourchier (1342)	Henry Bourchier, KG, 5th baron	1433–83	*See Earl of Essex*

Burghersh (1330)	Henry Beauchamp, KG, 6th baron	1439–45	*See Duke of Warwick*
	Anne Beauchamp, 7th baroness	1445–9	Abeyant
Clifford (1299)	Thomas Clifford, 8th baron	1422–55	k. St Albans
	John Clifford, 9th baron	1455–61	k. Towton, attainted
Clinton (1298)	John Clinton, 5th baron	1431–64	
Cobham (1313)	Joan Brooke, 5th baroness	1434–42	
	Edward Brooke, 6th baron	1442–64	
Cromwell (1375)	Ralph Cromwell, 3rd baron	1417–55	Abeyant
Cromwell (1461)	Humphrey Bourchier	1461–71	
Dacre of Gilsland (1321)	Thomas Dacre, 6th baron	1398–1458	
	Joan Dacre, 7th baroness	1458–86	Granddaughter of Thomas
	Richard Fiennes, 7th baron	1458–83	By marriage
Dacre of the North (1459)	Randolph Dacre	1459–61	k. Towton, attainted
Dudley (1440)	John Sutton, KG	1440–87	
Egremont (1449)	Thomas Percy	1449–60	k. Northampton, extinct
Fanhope (1433)	John Cornwall, KG	1433–43	*Also Milbroke* Extinct
Fauconberg (1295)	Joan Fauconberg, 6th baroness	1429–90	
	William Neville, KG, 6th baron	1421–63	See Earl of Kent
Ferrers of Chartley (1299)	William Ferrers, 6th baron	1435–50	
	Anne Ferrers, 7th baroness	1450–68	
	Walter Devereux, 7th baron	1461–85	*De jure* from 1450
Ferrers of Groby (1299)	William Ferrers, 5th baron	1388–1445	
	Elizabeth Ferrers, 6th baroness	1445–83	
	Edward Grey, 6th baron[2]	1445–57	
	John Bourchier, 6th baron	1462–83	
FitzHugh (1321)	William FitzHugh, 4th baron	1425–52	
	Henry FitzHugh, 5th baron	1452–72	
FitzWalter (1295)	Elizabeth FitzWalter, 8th baroness	1431–85	
	John Radcliffe, 8th baron (de jure)	1431–61	k. Ferrybridge

2. First father-in-law of Elizabeth Woodville, who married Edward IV in 1464.

FitzWarine (1295)	Thomasine Hankeford, 9th baroness	1433–53	
	William Bourchier, 9th baron	1433–70	*See Viscount Bourchier*
Furnivall	Maud Neville, 6th baroness	1407–22	
	John Talbot, KG, 6th baron, et seq.	1407–53	*See Earl of Shrewsbury*
Grey of Codnor (1397)	Henry Grey, 3rd baron	1431–44	
	Henry Grey, 4th baron	1444–96	
Grey of Ruthyn (1325)	Reginald Grey, 3rd baron	1388–1441	
	Edmund Grey, 4th baron	1441–90	
Grey of Wilton (1295)	Richard Grey, 6th baron	1396–1442	
	Reginald Grey, 7th baron	1442–93	
Greystoke (1321)	Ralph Greystoke, 5th baron	1436–87	
Harington (1326)	William Harington, 5th baron	1418–58	
	William Bonville, KG, 6th baron	1458–60	k. Wakefield
	Cecily Bonville, 7th baroness	1460–1530	*Combined with Bonville*
Hastings (1461)	William Hastings, KG	1461–83	
Herbert of Raglan (1461)	William Herbert, KG	1461–9	
Hoo and Hastings (1447)	Thomas Hoo, KG	1447–55	Extinct
Hungerford (1426)	Walter Hungerford, KG	1426–49	
	Robert Hungerford, 2nd baron	1449–59	
	Robert Hungerford, 3rd baron	1459–61	Attainted, executed 1464
Latimer (1432)	George Neville (disputed)	1425–69	Ruled incompetent 1447
	Richard Neville (custodian)	c.1447–69	*See Earl of Warwick*
Lisle (1444)	John Talbot, KG	1444–53	*See Viscount Lisle*
	Thomas Talbot, 2nd baron	1453–70	
Lovell (1299)[3]	William Lovell, 7th baron	1414–55	
	John Lovell, 8th baron	1455–65	

3. Also Baron Holland, Deincort, Bedale and Grey of Rotherfield.

Lumley (1461)	Thomas Lumley	1461–85	
Maltravers (1330)	William FitzAlan	1438–83	*See Earl of Arundel*
Milbroke (1442)	John Cornwall, KG	1442–43	*Also Fanhope* Extinct
Moleyns (1445)	Alianore Moleyns, 2nd baroness	1428–76	
	Robert Hungerford, 2nd baron	1449–64	*See Hungerford*
Montagu (1461)	John Neville, KG	1461–71	
Morley (1295)	Robert Morley, 6th baron	1435–42	
	Alianore Morley, 7th baroness	1442–76	
	William Lovel, 7th baron	1442–76	By marriage
Neville of Raby (1295)	Ralph Neville, 5th baron	1425–84	*See Earl of Westmorland*
Ogle (1461)	Robert Ogle	1461–69	
Poynings (1337)[4]	Robert Poynings, 5th baron	1387–1446	
	Eleanor Poynings, 6th baroness	1446–82	
	Henry Percy, 6th baron by marriage	1446–61	*See Earl of Northumberland*
Rivers (1448)	Richard Woodville, KG	1448–69	
Roos (1264)	Thomas Roos, 9th baron	1421–61	Attainted, executed 1464
Rougement Grey (1450)	Thomas Grey	1450–61	Executed, extinct
Saye and Sele (1447)	James Fiennes	1447–50	Murdered
	William Fiennes, 2nd baron	1450–71	
Scales (1299)	Thomas Scales, 7th baron	1419–60	Murdered
	Elizabeth Scales, 8th baroness	1460–73	
	Anthony Woodville, KG, 8th baron	1460–83	By marriage
Scrope of Bolton (1371)	Henry Scrope, 4th baron	1420–59	
	John Scrope, KG, 5th baron	1459–98	
Scrope of Masham (1350)	John Scrope, 4th baron	1426–55	
	Thomas Scrope, 5th baron	1455–75	
Stanley (1456)	Thomas Stanley, KG	1456–9	
	Thomas Stanley, 2nd baron	1459–1504	

4. Also baronies of Fitzpayne and Brian.

Stourton (1448)	John Stourton	1448–62	
	William Stourton, 2nd baron	1462–79	
Strange of Knockyn (1299)	Richard Strange, 7th baron	1397–1449	
	John Strange, 8th baron	1449–77	
Sudeley (1299/1441)	Ralph Boteler, KG, 6th/1st baron	1441–73	
Talbot (1331)	John Talbot, KG, 7th baron	1421–53	
	John Talbot, KG, 8th baron	1453–60	*See Earl of Shrewsbury*
	John Talbot, 9th baron	1460–73	
Tiptoft (1426)	John Tiptoft	1426–43	
	John Tiptoft, KG, 2nd baron[5]	1443–70	*See Earl of Worcester*
Tuchet (1403) *Also Audley*	James Tuchet, 2nd baron	1408–59	k. Blore Heath
	John Tuchet, 6th baron	1459–90	
Vescy (1449)	Henry Bromflete	1449–69	
de la Warr (1299)	Reginald West, 6th baron	1427–51	
	Richard West, 7th baron	1451–76	
Welles (1299)	Lionel Welles, KG, 6th baron	1421–61	k. Towton, attainted
Wenlock (1461)	John Wenlock, KG	1461–71	
Willoughby (1313)	Robert Willoughby, KG, 6th baron	1409–52	
	Joan Willoughby, 7th baroness	1452–62	
	Richard Welles, 7th baron	1452–70	
Zouche (1308)	William Zouche, 5th baron	1415–63	

5. Shared the lordship and castle of Powys with Henry, de jure Baron Grey of Powys.

ENGLISH PEERAGE
1462–85
by Seniority

KG = Knight of the Garter   KIA = killed in battle; senior titles in italics

Under Edward IV the duchy of York and earldoms of March and Cambridge in England and Ulster in Ireland were added to the crown's existing merged titles, which included the Principality of Wales (conjoined with the earldom of Chester), the dukedoms of Cornwall, Lancaster and Hereford, the earldoms of Leicester, Lancaster, Derby and Northampton, and the barony of Halton.

Since 1422 the heir to the throne has been Prince of Wales, Duke of Cornwall and Earl of Chester.

DUKES

Date created	Name	Dates	Comments
Norfolk (1397)[1]	John Mowbray, KG, 4th duke	1461–76	Extinct in the male line
Exeter (1416)	Henry Holland, 3rd duke	1447–61	Attainted. Murdered 1475
Buckingham (1444)	Henry Stafford KG, 2nd duke	1460–83	Executed, attainted
	Edward Stafford, 3rd duke	1485–1521	Restored
Somerset (1448	Henry Beaufort, 2nd duke	1455–64	Attainted 1461–3, restored. Executed, attainted 1464
	Edmund Beaufort, 3rd duke	1470–1	KIA Tewkesbury, extinct
Suffolk (1448)	John de la Pole KG, 2nd duke	1463–91	Restored
Clarence (1461)	George Plantagenet KG	1461–78	Executed, attainted
Gloucester (1461)	Richard Plantagenet KG	1461–83	Merged to crown
Bedford (1470)	George Neville[2]	1470–8	Degraded for poverty
York (1474)	Richard (Edward IV's second son)	1474–83	Murdered
Norfolk (1477)	Richard (Edward IV's second son)	1477–83	Murdered
Bedford (1478)	George (Edward IV's third son)	1478–9	Died an infant
Norfolk (1483)	John Howard KG	1483–5	KIA Bosworth, forfeit
Bedford (1485)	Jasper Tudor KG	1485–95	Extinct

1. Also Earl of Nottingham, Earl Warenne, Baron Mowbray and Baron Segrave.
2. Son of John Neville, created Marquess Montagu in 1470, previously Earl of Northumberland.

MARQUESSES

Montague (1470)	John Neville KG	1470–1	KIA Barnet, forfeit
Dorset (1475)	Thomas Grey KG	1475–1501	

EARLS

Warwick (1088)	Anne Beauchamp, 16th countess	1448–92	
	Richard Neville KG, 16th earl	1449–71	KIA Barnet
	George Plantagenet KG	1472–8	*Duke of Clarence*
	Edward Plantagenet	1478–99	
Arundel (1138)	William FitzAlan KG, 16th earl	1438–87	
Devon (1141) (see 1469)	John Courtenay, 15th earl	1471	KIA Tewskesbury, attainted
	Edward Courtenay, 16th earl	1485–1509	Restored
Oxford (1142)	John Vere, 12th earl	1417–62	Executed
	John Vere KG, 13th earl	1462–75	Attainted, restored 1485
Salisbury (1337)	Richard Neville KG, 6th earl	1460–71	*Earl of Warwick*
Stafford (1351)	Henry Stafford, 7th earl	1460–77	*Duke of Buckingham*
	Edward Stafford, 8th earl	1477–1523	
Suffolk (1385)	John de la Pole, 5th earl	1463–92	*Duke of Suffolk*
Westmorland (1397)	Ralph Neville, 2nd earl	1425–84	Dementia from *c.* 1458
	Ralph Neville, 3rd earl	1484–99	Nephew
Northumberland (1416)	Henry Percy KG, 3rd earl	1470–89	Restored
Shrewsbury (1442)	John Talbot, 3rd earl	1465–73	Attainted 1461, restored
	George Talbot, 4th earl	1473–1538	
Worcester (1449)	John Tiptoft KG	1449–70	Executed
	Edward Tiptoft, 2nd earl	1470–85	Extinct
Surrey & Warenne (1451)	John Mowbray	1451–76	*Duke of Norfolk*
Richmond (1452)	Henry Tudor, 2nd earl (Henry VII)	1461	Attainted
		1485	Restored, merged to crown
Pembroke (1452)	Jasper Tudor KG	1452–61	Attainted
		1471	Restored, attainted
		1485–94	Restored

EARLS

Essex (1461)	Henry Bourchier KG	1461–83	
	Henry Bourchier, 2nd earl	1483–1540	
Kent (1461)	William Neville KG	1461–3	Extinct
Richmond (1461)	George Plantagenet KG	1461–78	*Duke of Clarence*
Northumberland (1465)	John Neville KG	1465–70	*Marquess Montagu*
Rivers (1465)	Richard Woodville KG	1465–9	Murdered
	Anthony Woodville KG, 2nd earl	1469–83	Murdered
	Richard Woodville, 3rd earl	1483–91	
Kent (1465)	Edmund Grey of Ruthyn	1465–98	
Lincoln (1467)	John de la Pole	1467–87	Son of Duke of Suffolk
Pembroke (1468)	William Herbert KG	1468–9	Executed
	William Herbert, 2nd earl	1469–79	Surrendered
Devon (1469) (see 1141)	Humphrey Stafford of Southwyck	1469	Murdered, extinct
Wiltshire (1470)	John Stafford KG	1470–3	
	Edward Stafford, 2nd earl	1473–99	
Huntingdon (1471)	Thomas Grey KG	1471–5	*Marquess of Dorset*
Winchester (1472)	Louis de Gruuthuse	1472–92	*Stadtholder of Holland*
Salisbury (1472)	George Plantagenet KG	1472–8	*Earl of Warwick*
Nottingham (1476)	Richard (Edward IV's second son)	1476–83	*Duke of York*
Surrey & Warenne (1477)	Richard (Edward IV's second son)	1477–83	*Duke of York*
Richmond (1478)	Richard Plantagenet	1478–83	*Duke of Gloucester*
Salisbury (1478)	Edward (Richard III's only son)	1478–84	Died, extinct
March (1479)	Edward (Richard III's only son)	1479–84	Died, merged to crown
Pembroke (1479)	Edward (Richard III's only son)	1479–84	Died, merged to crown
Huntingdon (1479)	William Herbert (son)	1479–91	
Nottingham (1483)	William Berkeley	1483–92	
Surrey & Warenne (1483)	Thomas Howard	1483–5	
Derby (1485)	Thomas Stanley KG	1485–1504	
Bath (1485)	Philibert de Chandée	Unknown	

VISCOUNTS

Beaumont (1440)	William Beaumont, 2nd viscount	1460–70	Attainted
		1470–1	Restored, attainted
		1484–1507	Restored
Bourchier (1446)	William Bourchier	1461–72	On promotion of his father
	Henry Bourchier, 2nd viscount	1472–1540	*Earl of Essex*
Lisle (1451)	Thomas Talbot, 2nd viscount	1453–70	KIA Nibley Green
Berkeley (1481)	William Berkeley	1481–92	*Earl of Nottingham*
Lisle (1483)	Edward Grey of Groby	1483–92	
Lovell (1483)	Francis Lovell KG	1483–7	Forfeit 1485

MARCHER LORDSHIPS

Glamorgan (1449)	Richard Neville KG	1449–71	*Earl of Warwick*
Crickhowell/Tretower (1463)	William Herbert KG	1463–9	*Earl of Pembroke*
	William Herbert (son)	1469–79	
Raglan/Caerleon/Usk (1465)	William Herbert KG	1465–9	
	William Herbert (son)	1469–79	

BARONS

Roos (1264)	Edmund Roos, 11th baron	1485–1508	Restored
Neville (1295)	Ralph Neville, 6th baron	1472–99	Restored
Fauconberg (1295)	Joan Fauconberg, 6th baroness	1429–90	Abeyant
	William Neville KG, 6th baron	1429–63	*Earl of Kent*
Fitzwalter (1295)	Elizabeth Radcliffe, 8th baroness	1431–85	
	John Radcliffe, 9th baron	1485–96	
FitzWarin (1295)	William Bourchier, 9th baron	1433–70	
	Fulk Bourchier, 10th baron	1470–9	
	John Bourchier, 11th baron	1479–1539	
Grey of Wilton (1295)	Reginald Grey, 7th baron	1442–93	
Clinton (1299)	John Clinton, 6th baron	1464–88	
de la Warr (1299)	Richard West, 7th baron	1451–75	
	Thomas West, 8th baron	1475–1525	

Ferrers of Chartley (1299)	Anne Ferrers, 7th baroness	1450–68	
	Walter Devereux KG, 7th baron[3]	1461–85	KIA Bosworth
Lovell (1299)[4]	John Lovell, 8th baron	1455–65	
	Francis Lovell, 9th baron	1465–87	*Viscount Lovell*
Fitzwalter (1295)	Elizabeth Radcliffe, 8th baroness	1431–85	
	John Radcliffe, 9th baron	1485–96	
FitzWarin (1295)	William Bourchier, 9th baron	1433–70	
	Fulk Bourchier, 10th baron	1470–9	
	John Bourchier, 11th baron	1479–1539	
Scales (1299)	Elizabeth Scales, 8th baroness	1460–73	
	Anthony Woodville KG, 8th baron	1460–83	By marriage. *Earl Rivers*
	Edward Woodville, 9th baron	1483–8	
Welles (1299)	Richard Welles, 7th baron	1468–70	Restored, executed[5]
	Joan Welles, 9th baroness	1470–5	Also Willoughby
	Richard Hastings, 9th baron[6]	1470–1503	Created again 1487
Clifford (1299)	Henry Clifford, 10th baron	1485–1523	Restored
Ferrers of Groby (1299) *Grandson of Lady Ferrers*	Elizabeth Ferrers, 6th baroness	1445–83	
	John Bourchier, 6th baron	1462–83	By marriage
	Thomas Grey, 7th baron	1483–1501	*Marquess of Dorset*
Morley (1299)	Alianore Morley, 7th baroness	1442–76	
	William Lovell, 7th baron[7]	1442–76	Son of Lord Lovell
	Henry Lovell, 8th baron	1476–89	
Strange of Knockyn (1299)	John Strange, 8th baron	1449–77	
	Joan Strange, 9th baroness	1477–1514	
	George Stanley KG, 9th baron	1477–1503	
Zouche (1308)	William Zouche, 6th baron	1462–8	
	John Zouche, 7th baron	1468–85	Attainted, restored 1495
Beaumont (1309)	John Beaumont, 6th baron	1417–69	*Viscount Beaumont*
	William Beaumont, 7th baron	1469–1507	
Audley (1313)	John Tuchet, 6th baron	1459–90	
Cobham (1313)	John Brooke, 7th baron	1464–1512	

3. By marriage, confirmed in his own right by Edward IV in 1461.
4. Also Baron Holland, Deincort, Bedale and Grey of Rotherfield.
5. His son Robert, 8th baron, executed a few days later.
6. Younger brother of Baron Hastings. The Welles/Willoughby succession is too complex to unravel here.
7. By marriage. Confirmed in his own right by Edward IV in 1461.

Willoughby (1313)	Richard Welles, 8th baron	1455–69	Also Welles. Executed
	Robert Welles (informally)	1469	Executed
	Joan Welles, 9th baroness	1470–5	Also Welles
	Richard Hastings, 9th baron	1470–1503	By marriage
Dacre (1321)	Joan Dacre, 7th baroness	1458–86	
	Richard Fiennes, 7th baron	1458– 83	
FitzHugh (1321)	Henry FitzHugh, 5th baron	1452–72	
	Richard FitzHugh, 6th baron	1472–87	
Greystoke (1321)	Ralph Greystoke, 5th baron	1436–87	
Grey of Ruthyn (1325)	Edmund Grey, 4th baron	1441–90	*Earl of Kent*
Harington (1326)	Cicely Bonville, 7th baroness	1460–1530	Also Bonville
	Thomas Grey, 7th baron	1474–1501	*Marquess of Dorset*
Maltravers (1330)	William FitzAlan KG, 3rd baron[8]	1417–61	*Earl of Arundel*
	Thomas FitzAlan KG, 4th baron	1461–1524	
Talbot (1331)	John Talbot, 9th baron	1460–73	*Earl of Shrewsbury*
	George Talbot, 10th baron	1473–1538	
Poynings (1337)	Eleanor Poynings, 6th baroness	1446–82	
	Henry Percy, 7th baron	1482–9	*Earl of Northumberland*
Bourchier (1342)	Henry Bourchier, 5th baron	1433–83	*Earl of Essex*
	Henry Bourchier, 6th baron	1483–1540	
Scrope of Masham (1350)	Thomas Scrope, 5th baron	1455–75	
	Thomas Scrope, 6th baron	1475–93	
Botreaux (1368)	Margaret Hungerford, 4th baroness	1462–77	
	Mary Hungerford, 5th baroness	1477–1529	Also Hungerford
Scrope of Bolton (1371)	John Scrope KG, 5th baron	1459–98	
Beauchamp of Bletsoe (1379)	Margaret Beauchamp, 4th baroness	1429–82	Grandmother of Henry VII
Lumley (1384/1461)	Thomas Lumley, 2nd baron[9]	1461–85	
Bergavenny (1392)	Edward Neville, 1st baron (de jure)	1450–76	By marriage 3rd baron
	Governed by Richard Neville KG	1450–71	*Earl of Warwick*
	George Neville, 2nd/4th baron	1476–92	
Grey of Codnor (1397)	Henry Grey, 4th baron	1444–96	
Berkeley (1421)	William Berkeley, 2nd baron	1463–92	*Earl of Nottingham*

8. Edward IV permitted Arundel's 11-year-old son Thomas to assume the Maltravers title in 1461.
9. First baron attainted in 1399. Attainder reversed for his grandson Thomas in 1461.

704 • THE WARS OF THE ROSES

Hungerford (1426)	Robert Hungerford, 3rd baron	1459–61	Attainted, executed 1464
	Mary Hungerford, 4th baroness	1485–7	Restored. Also Botreaux
Tiptoft (1426)	John Tiptoft KG, 2nd baron	1443–70	*Earl of Worcester*
	Edward Tiptoft, 3rd baron	1475–85	Extinct
Latimer (1432)	George Neville (disputed)	1432–69	Declared incompetent 1447
	Richard Neville, 2nd baron	1469–1530	
Dudley (1440)	John Sutton KG	1440–87	
Sudeley (1299/1441)	Ralph Boteler KG, 6th/1st baron	1441–73	Abeyant
Lisle (1444)	Thomas Talbot, 2nd baron	1453–70	*Viscount Lisle*
	Elizabeth Talbot, 3rd baroness	1475–87	
	Edward Grey of Groby, 3rd baron	1483–92	
Say and Sele (1447)	William Fiennes, 2nd baron	1450–71	KIA Barnet, dormant
Beauchamp of Powick (1447)	John Beauchamp	1447–75	
	Richard Beauchamp, 2nd baron	1475–1503	
Rivers (1448)	Richard Woodville KG	1448–69	*Earl Rivers*
	Anthony Woodville, 2nd baron	1469–83	As above. Also Scales
	Richard Woodville, 3rd baron	1483–91	As above
Stourton (1448)	William Stourton, 2nd baron	1462–79	
	John Stourton, 3rd baron	1479–85	
Bonville (1449)	Cicely Bonville, 2nd baroness	1461–1530	Also Harington
	Thomas Grey, 2nd baron	1474–1501	*Marquess of Dorset*
Vescy (1449)	Henry Bromflete	1449–69	
	Margaret Bromflete, 2nd baroness	1469–93	
Berners (1455)	John Bourchier KG	1455–74	
	John Bourchier, 2nd baron	1474–1533	
Stanley (1456)	Thomas Stanley KG, 2nd baron	1459–1504	*Earl of Derby*
Neville (1459)	Ralph Neville	1472–99	*Earl of Westmorland*
Montagu (1460)	John Neville KG	1460–71	*Marquess Montagu*
Cromwell (1461)	Humphrey Bourchier	1461–71	Extinct
Hastings (1461)	William Hastings KG	1461–83	Executed
	Edward Hastings, 2nd baron	1483–1506	See Botreaux, Hungerford
Ogle (1461)	Robert Ogle	1461–9	KIA Edgecote
	Owen Ogle, 2nd baron	1469–86	
Wenlock (1461)	John Wenlock KG	1461–71	KIA Tewkesbury, extinct

Herbert of Raglan (1461)	William Herbert	1461–9	*Earl of Pembroke*
	William Herbert, 2nd baron	1469–91	
Stafford of Southwyck (1461)	Humphrey Stafford	1461–9	*Earl of Devon*
Lumley (1461)	Thomas Lumley	1461–85	
Mountjoy (1465)	Walter Blount KG	1465–74	
	Edward Blount, 2nd baron	1474–5	
	John Blount, 3rd baron	1475–85	
Dunster (1466)	William Herbert (son)	1466–85[10]	*Earl of Pembroke*
Dynham (1467)	John Dynham	1467–1501	
Howard (1470)	John Howard KG	1470–85	*Duke of Norfolk*
Dacre of Gilsland (1473)	Humphrey Dacre	1473–85	
	Thomas Dacre, 2nd baron	1485–1525	
Parr of Kendal (1474)	William Parr KG	1474–83	
	Thomas Parr, 2nd baron	1483–1517	
Grey of Powys (1482)	John Grey	1482–97	
Daubeney (1486)	Giles Daubeney KG	1486–1508	
Cheyne (1487)	John Cheyne KG	1487–99	

10. Lands restored to the Luttrell family.

ARCHBISHOPS AND BISHOPS 1440–62

Diocese	Incumbent	Dates	Offices
CANTERBURY	John Stafford	1443–52	Lord Chancellor 1432–50
	Cardinal John Kemp	1452–4	Lord Chancellor 1426–32, 1450–4
	Cardinal Thomas Bourchier	1454–86	Lord Chancellor 1555–6
Bath and Wells	John Stafford	1424–43	Lord Treasurer 1422–6. *To Canterbury*
	Thomas Beckington	1443–65	Lord Privy Seal 1443–4
	Robert Stillington	1465–91	Lord Privy Seal 1460–67
Chichester	Richard Praty	1438–45	
	Adam Moleyns	1445–50	Lord Privy Seal 1444–50. Murdered
	Reginald Pecock	1450–59	*Deprived for heresy*
	John Arundel	1459–77	
Exeter	John Lacey	1420–55	
	George Neville	1455–65	Lord Chancellor 1460–7
Ely	Thomas Bourchier	1444–54	*To Canterbury*
	William Grey	1454–78	Papal Notary
Hereford	Thomas Spofford	1421–48	
	Richard Beauchamp	1448–50	To Salisbury
	Reginald Boulers	1450–53	King's secretary. *To Lichfield/Coventry*
	John Stanberry	1453–74	King's confessor. Carmelite monk
Lichfield/Coventry	William Heyworth	1420–47	
	William Booth	1447–52	Queen's Chancellor 1445–51. *To York*
	Reginald Boulers	1453–9	
	John Hales/Halse	1459–90	
Lincoln/Dorchester	William Alnwick	1436–50	
	Marmaduke Lumley	1450	
	John Chedworth	1452–71	
London	Robert Gilbert	1436–48	

	Thomas Kemp	1448–89	*Nephew of Archbishop John Kemp*
Norwich	Thomas Brunce	1436–45	
	Walter Lyhert	1446–72	Queen's Confessor
Rochester	William Wells	1437–44	
	John Lowe	1444–67	
Salisbury	William Ayscough	1438–50	King's Confessor. *Murdered*
	Richard Beauchamp	1450–81	
Winchester	Cardinal Henry Beaufort	1404–47	Lord Chancellor 1413–17, 1424–6
	William Wainflete	1447–86	Lord Chancellor 1456–60
Worcester	Thomas Bourchier	1434–43	To Ely
	John Carpenter	1443–76	
Bangor (Wales)	Thomas Cheriton	1436–48	Dominican monk
	John Stanberry	1448–53	Carmelite monk. *To Hereford*
	James Blakedon	1453–64	Dominican monk
Llandaff (Wales)	Nicholas Ashby	1440–58	
	John Hunden	1458–76	Resigned
St Asaph (Wales)	John Low	1433–44	Friar Eremite. *To Rochester*
	Reginald Pecock	1444–9	To Chichester
	Thomas Bird	1450–63	*Deprived for rebellion*
St David's (Wales)	Thomas Rodburn	1433–42	
	William Lyndwood	1442–6	Lord Privy Seal 1432–43
	John de la Bere	1447–60	*Absentee.** Resigned.
	Robert Tully	1460–81	Benedictine monk
YORK	John Kemp	1425–52	*To Canterbury*
	William Booth	1452–64	*Brother of Laurence*
Carlisle	Marmaduke Lumley	1429–49	Lord Treasurer 1446–9. *To Lincoln*
	Nicholas Close	1450–52	To Lichfield/Coventry
	William Percy	1452–62	*Brother of the Earl of Northumberland*
Durham	Robert Neville	1437–57	*Brother of the Earl of Salisbury*
	Laurence Booth	1457–76	Queen's Chancellor 1451–6, Lord Privy Seal 1456–60

* The temporalities were administered by Gruffudd ap Nicholas. The future Henry VII was conceived at the bishop's palace at Lamphey, outside Pembroke.

ARCHBISHOPS AND BISHOPS
1462–85

Diocese	Incumbent	Dates	Offices
CANTERBURY	Thomas Bourchier	1454–86	*Created cardinal 1467*
Bath and Wells	Thomas Beckington	1443–65	
	Robert Stillington	1465–91	Lord Privy Seal 1460–7 Lord Chancellor 1467–70, 1471–3
Chichester	John Arundel	1459–77	
	Edward Story	1478–1503	Queen Elizabeth's confessor
Exeter	George Neville	1455–65	Lord Chancellor 1460–67, 1471 *Translated to York*
	John Booth	1465–78	
	Peter Courtenay	1478–87	Fought at Bosworth
Ely	William Grey	1454–78	Lord Treasurer 1469
	John Morton	1479–86	*Translated to Canterbury*
Hereford	John Stanberry	1453–74	
	Thomas Myling	1474–92	*Previously Abbot of Westminster*
Lichfield/Coventry	John	1459–90	Lord Privy Seal 1470–1
Lincoln/Dorchester	John	1452–71	
	Thomas Rotherham	1472–80	Lord Privy Seal 1467–70,1471–4; Lord Chancellor 1475–83; *Translated to York*
	John Russell	1480–94	Lord Chancellor 1483–5
London	Thomas Kemp	1448–89	
Norwich	Walter	1446–72	
	James Goldwell	1472–99	
Rochester	John Lowe	1444–67	
	Thomas Rotherham	1468–72	*Translated to Lincoln*
	John Alcock	1472–6	Lord Chancellor 1475 *Translated to Worcester*
	John Russell	1476–80	Lord Privy Seal 1474 *Translated to Worcester*
	Edmund Audley	1480–92	

Salisbury	Richard Beauchamp	1450–81	
	Lionel Woodville	1482–4	*Brother of Queen Elizabeth*
	Thomas Langton	1485–93	
Winchester	William Wainflete	1447–86	
Worcester	John Carpenter	1443–76	
	John Alcock	1476–86	Lord Chancellor 1485 *Translated to Ely*
Bangor	James Blakedon	1453–64	*Dominican monk*
	Richard Edenham	1464–94	*Franciscan monk*
Llandaff	John Hunden	1458–76	*Resigned*
	John Smith	1476–8	
	John Marshall	1478–96	
St Asaph	Thomas Bird	1450–63	*Deprived for rebellion; see vacant*
	Richard Redman	1471–95	
St David's	Robert Tully	1460–81	*Benedictine monk*
	Richard Martin	1482–3	
	Thomas Langton	1483–5	Edward IV's chaplain *Translated to Salisbury*
YORK	William Booth	1452–64	*Half-brother of Laurence*
	George Neville	1465–76	
	Laurence Booth	1476–80	
	Thomas Rotherham	1480–1500	Lord Chancellor 1485
Carlisle	William Percy	1452–62	*Brother of the Earl of Northumberland*
	John Kingscote	1462–3	
	Richard Scroope	1464–8	
	Edward Story	1468–78	Queen Elizabeth's confessor *Translated to Chichester*
	Richard Bell	1478–95	
Durham	Laurence Booth	1457–76	Lord Chancellor 1473 *Translated to York*
	William Dudley	1476–83	
	John Sherwood	1484–94	

THE BEAUCHAMP INHERITANCE

k. = killed in battle   x. = executed

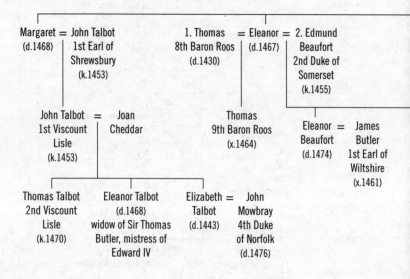

Margaret = John Talbot
(d.1468)   1st Earl of
Shrewsbury
(k.1453)

1. Thomas = Eleanor = 2. Edmund
8th Baron Roos   (d.1467)   Beaufort
(d.1430)   2nd Duke of
Somerset
(k.1455)

John Talbot = Joan
1st Viscount   Cheddar
Lisle
(k.1453)

Thomas
9th Baron Roos
(x.1464)

Eleanor = James
Beaufort   Butler
(d.1474)   1st Earl of
Wiltshire
(x.1461)

Thomas Talbot
2nd Viscount
Lisle
(k.1470)

Eleanor Talbot
(d.1468)
widow of Sir Thomas
Butler, mistress of
Edward IV

Elizabeth = John
Talbot   Mowbray
(d.1443)   4th Duke
of Norfolk
(d.1476)

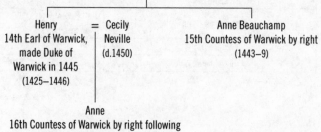

= 2. Isabel Despenser
(d.1439)
*Beauchamp entailed most of his own and part of the Berkeley
and Lisle inheritances to his children from this marriage.*

Henry = Cecily
14th Earl of Warwick,   Neville
made Duke of   (d.1450)
Warwick in 1445
(1425–1446)

Anne Beauchamp
15th Countess of Warwick by right
(1443–9)

Anne
16th Countess of Warwick by right following
the death of her namesake niece, and wife
of Richard 'the Kingmaker' Neville
(1426–92)

Richard Beauchamp = 1. Elizabeth Berkeley
13th Earl of Warwick   (d.1422)
(d.1439)   sole heir of Thomas,
Lord Berkeley (d.1417),
and Margaret, Baroness
Lisle by right (d.1422)

Elizabeth =   George Neville
(d.1480)   dubious Baron Latimer (d.1469)
declared incompetent 1447
with brother Richard, Earl of
Salisbury as guardian

Henry Beaufort   Edmund Beaufort   John Beaufort
3rd Duke of   styled Duke of Somerset   styled Earl of Dorset
Somerset   (k.1471)   (k.1471)
(x.1464)

Margaret = Humphrey   Anne = Sir William
Beaufort | Earl of Stafford   Beaufort | Paston
(d.1474) | (d.1458)   (d.1496) | (d.1496)

Henry Stafford
2nd Duke of Buckingham
(x.1483)

OTHER INHERITANCES

Isabel Despenser, Richard Beauchamp's second wife, was the sole heir of Thomas (k.1399), Earl of Gloucester, who was attainted for conspiring against Henry IV. Her mother was Constance of York, whose role in the 1415 conspiracy against Henry V is mentioned in Chapter 4. Isabel was also the sole heir of her older brother Richard, Baron Burghersh (d.1414). The only child of Isabel's first marriage to Richard's cousin (also Richard Beauchamp), 1st Earl of Worcester, was Elizabeth, Baroness Bergavenny by right (d.1448), who married Edward Neville (d.1476), uncle of the Kingmaker.

The Kingmaker claimed all the Beauchamp, Bergavenny, Burghersh and Despenser estates in the name of his wife. Various parts of this were strongly contested by the older two daughters of Richard Beauchamp's first marriage, supported by their husbands, John Talbot, Earl of Shrewsbury and Edmund Beaufort, Duke of Somerset.

There was a separate, deadly sub-dispute known as:

THE BERKELEY-LISLE FEUD

James Berkeley (d.1463) was heir to the title and property entailed in the male line of his uncle Thomas, 5th Baron Berkeley (see above). This was disputed by Thomas's daughter and named heir Elizabeth Berkeley, Richard Beauchamp's first wife. To finesse the dispute, in 1421 James was summoned to Parliament as the 1st, not the 6th Baron Berkeley.

Elizabeth held Berkeley Castle until her death in 1422, when James recovered it. In 1451 Elizabeth's grandson John Talbot, later Viscount Lisle, took it back. James retaliated by sacking the manor house at Wotton-under-Edge owned by Lisle's mother Margaret, wife of John Talbot, Earl of Shrewsbury. Lisle then kidnapped Isabel Mowbray, James's third wife, whom Margaret imprisoned in Gloucester Castle, where she died in 1452.

Following the deaths at Castillon of Margaret's husband and son, James Berkeley married Joan Talbot, Margaret's stepdaughter from her husband's first marriage, whom she had raised from infancy.* This achieved a cessation of hostilities – until the next generation. Isabel's and James's son William, 2nd Baron Berkeley, was the victor of the last private battle in English history at Nibley Green in 1470, where Thomas, 2nd Viscount Lisle was killed.

The lawsuit, one of the most protracted in English legal history, dragged on until 1609.

---

* John Talbot married first Maud Neville, Baroness Furnivall by right and sister of Ralph, Earl of Westmorland, who died in 1422 giving birth to Joan. Their son John (k.1460) became 2nd Earl of Shrewsbury.

CHIEF OFFICE HOLDERS
1460–85

Lords Treasurer	Lords Chancellor
EDWARD IV	
1460–2 Henry Bourchier, Earl of Essex	1460–7 George Neville, Bishop of Exeter Archbishop of York 1465
1462–3 John Tiptoft, Earl of Worcester	
1463–4 Edmund, Baron Grey of Ruthyn[1]	
1464–6 Walter Blount[2]	
1466–9 Richard Woodville, Earl Rivers	1467–70 Robert Stillington, Bishop of Bath
WARWICK	
1469 John Langstrother, Prior of St John	Stillington
EDWARD IV	
1469–70 William Grey, Bishop of Ely	Stillington
WARWICK	
1470–1 John Langstrother	1470–1 George Neville, Archbishop of York
EDWARD IV	
1471–83 Henry Bourchier, Earl of Essex	1471–3 Stillington
	1473–5 Laurence Booth, Bishop of Durham
	1475 John Alcock, Bishop of Rochester
	1475–83 Thomas Rotherham, Bishop of Lincoln[3]
RICHARD III	
1483–4 John Wood[4]	1483–5 John Russell, Bishop of Lincoln
1484–5 John Tuchet, Baron Audley	

1. Earl of Kent 1466.
2. Baron Mountjoy 1466.
3. Archbishop of York 1480.
4. Under-treasurer of the exchequer 1480–3 and Speaker of the Commons in 1483

TITLES, LANDS, HONOURS and OFFICES of RICHARD 'THE KINGMAKER' NEVILLE*

BY MARRIAGE TO ANNE BEAUCHAMP

1449 16th Earl of Warwick (senior earldom). The Beauchamp (including part Bergavenny) and Despenser (including barony of Burghersh) estates in Glamorgan, Powys, Warwickshire, Worcestershire, Gloucestershire, Staffordshire and Barnard Castle, Durham. *All disputed.*

ROYAL APPOINTMENT OR ASSENT (HENRY VI)

c. 1449 Marcher Lordship of Glamorgan, including the lands, and apparently with the consent of his uncle Edward Neville, Baron Bergavenny by marriage.

1450 Hereditary Chamberlain of the Exchequer. *Disputed.*

1452 Co-Warden of the West March (North) with his father.

1454 Rulings in his favour over the Beauchamp inheritance, including the Chamberlainship of the Exchequer.

Dec 1455 Captain of Calais.

1457 Keeper of the Seas, with the right to collect customs dues at all ports except Sandwich and Southampton.

c. 1458 Made custodian of his uncle George Neville (dementia), Baron Latimer in Buckinghamshire, with seat at Snape Castle in Richmondshire.

1459 Attainder and forfeiture of all titles and honours.

1460 Reversal of attainder.

BY INHERITANCE FROM HIS FATHER AND MOTHER

1460–2 6th Earl of Salisbury and 7th Baron Montacute. Heads of Lordship at Penrith (Cumberland), Sheriff Hutton (Yorkshire),

Middleham (Richmondshire), with seat at Bisham (Berkshire).
Estates in Dorset, Wiltshire, Somerset, Hampshire, Norfolk and
Nottinghamshire.

ROYAL APPOINTMENT (EDWARD IV)

1461   Lands of the barony of Bergavenny legally transferred to Warwick
        and all disputes relating to the Despenser inheritance resolved in
        his favour.

1461   Brother George, Bishop of Exeter, made Lord Chancellor.

1461–2 Great Chamberlain of England, Master of the King's Mews,
        Warden of the Cinque Ports and Constable of Dover Castle and
        Carlisle, all for life. Captaincy of Calais renewed and made Admiral
        of England for five years. Wardenship of the East March added to
        his wardenship of the West March. Steward of the entire duchy of
        Lancaster. Awarded Newport Pagnell (Bucks) from the attainted
        Earl of Wiltshire's estates.

1463–4 Awarded some of the Percy and all the Clifford estates in Yorkshire
        and, for two years, the temporalities of the Bishop of Durham,
        whose claim to Barnard Castle was dismissed in Warwick's favour.

1463   Wardenship of the East March transferred to brother John, Baron
        Montagu.

1464   Montagu made Earl of Northumberland, endowed with the Percy
        estates not previously awarded to Warwick or Clarence, the king's
        brother.

1465   Warwick awarded Percy and Clifford estates in Cumberland and
        Westmorland, and the shrievalty of Westmorland.

1465   Brother George, Lord Chancellor, made Archbishop of York.

MARRIAGE

1469   Eldest daughter Isabel married George, Duke of Clarence, heir
        presumptive to the throne, defying Edward IV's prohibition.

ROYAL APPOINTMENT (HENRY VI)

1470   Lieutenant of England.

ACQUISITIONS

1461–70 Many – notably around Little Snoring in Norfolk, Collyweston in
        Northamptonshire and Erdington in Warwickshire.

1475 EXPEDITION: INDENTURES

Duke – 13s. 8d. | Marquis – 10s. | Earl – 6s. 8d. | Baron/Banneret – 4s.
Knight – 2s. | Lance (man-at-arms) – 1s. 6d. | Archer – 6d.

Principals	Lances	Per diem	Archers	Per diem
Relatives and Household				
11 Peers & heirs	516	£38 14s. 0d.	4,080	£102 10s. 0d.
7 Bannerets	69	£5 3s. 6d.	720	£18 0s. 0d.
5 Knights	39	£2 18s. 6d.	370	£9 5s. 0d.
28 Esquires	107	£8 0s. 6d.	910	£22 15s. 0d.
3 Gentlemen (a)	45	£3 7s. 6d.	323	£8 1s. 6d.
9 Officials	29	£2 3s. 6d.	134	£3 7s. 0d.
7 Others	10	15s. 0d.	80	£2 0s. 0d.
King's archers			184	£4 12s. 0d.
Sub-total	**815**	**£61 2s. 6d.**	**6,801**	**£170 10s. 6d.**
Non-Household				
12 Peers & heirs	231	£17 6s. 6d.	1,619	£40 9s. 6d.
2 Scots Peers	8	12s. 0d.	60	£1 10s. 0d.
5 Bannerets	32	£2 8s. 0d.	272	£6 16s. 0d.
13 Knights	52	£3 18s. 0d.	449	£11 4s. 6d.
52 Esquires	91	£6 16s. 6d.	672	£16 16s. 0d.
6 Gentlemen	5	7s. 6d.	32	16s. 0d.
32 Others	40	£3 0s. 0d.	268	£6 14s. 0d.
Sub-total	**463**	**£34 8s. 6d.**	**3,372**	**£84 6s. 0d.**
Specialists (b)			387	£9 13s. 6d.
TOTAL	**1,278**	**£95 11s. 0d.**	**10,560**	**£264 10s. 0d.**

The cost of combat troops alone for the main expedition was therefore no less than **£32,760** per quarter.
There were also 2,000 archers (£50 p.d.) deployed to Brittany under Lords Audley and Duras, and 3,000
men (£75 p.d.) serving on Lord Dinham's fleet, a minimum additional quarterly cost of **£11,375**.

NOTES: Roll taken in Canterbury by Teller of the King's Money John FitzHerbert in June 1475.
From Jack Lander, 'The Hundred Years War and Edward IV's Campaign in France', in Arthur Slavin
(ed.), *Tudor Men and Institutions* (Louisiana State University, 1972).
The per diems are my calculations. The quarterly calculation is per diems x 91.
(a) Includes 43 'Gentlemen of the House of the Lord King' under Sir John Elrington.
(b) Non-combatant but essential support personnel such as armourers, blacksmiths, coopers,
farriers, fletchers, saddlers, sawyers, plumbers, turners, wheelwrights, etc.

PARTIAL LIST OF JUNE 1475 INDENTURES

KG = Garter Knight

Principals	Knights	Lances	Archers
5 DUKES			
Clarence KG	10	100	1000
Gloucester KG (a)	10	100	1000
Buckingham KG (b)	4	40	400
Norfolk KG	2	40	300
Suffolk KG	2	40	300
Sub-total	28	320	3000
1 MARQUESS			
Dorset	*Not listed – separately reported to have brought 600 archers*		
5 EARLS			
Northumberland KG	10	40	200
Rivers KG	2	40	200
Pembroke		40	200
Douglas KG (Scots)		4	40
Ormond (Irish)		2	16
Sub-total	12	126	656
11 BARONS			
Hastings KG		40	300
Stanley		40	300
Scrope of Bolton KG		20	200
Howard KG		20	200
Ferrers of Chartley KG		20	200
Grey of Codnor		10	155
Grey of Ruthyn (c)		10	140
FitzWarine		10	50
Lisle		7	50
Cobham		5	50
Boyd (Scots)		2	20
Clinton	*Not listed*		
Sub-total		184	1665

11 KNIGHTS BANNERET			
William Parr KG		16	140
Thomas Burgh		16	140?
Thomas Montgomery		10	100
Humphrey Talbot (d)		10	100
Richard Tunstall		10	100
Ralph Hastings (e)		8	100
Robert Tailboys		12	80
John Grey (f)		8	80
John Ratcliffe		6	70
Thomas Howard (g)		6	40
John Fiennes (h)		4	40
William Stanley (i)		2	20
John FitzAlan (j)		2	20
John Astley KG		2	12
Sub-total		**112**	**942**
15 KNIGHTS			
James Harington		12	100
Robert Chamberlain		12	100
William Norris		12	100
Laurence Rainford		12	60
Nicholas Langford		8	60
William Trussell		6	60
John Croker		6	60?
John Harlewin		3	50
John Mauleverer		3	30
John Savage		3	30
Richard Corbet		3	30?
John Ferrers		2	15
James Radcliffe		1	12
Richard Brandon		1	12?
Simon Mountfort		1	12?
Sub-total		85	731
TOTAL (k)	**74**	**827**	**6994**

NOTES: From Francis Barnard (ed.), *Edward IV's French Expedition of 1475* (1925), facsimile of a manuscript in the College of Arms by John Sorell and John FitzHerbert, Tellers of the King's Money, of indentures submitted by those entitled to heraldic arms. An additional list of mainly non-combattant and non-armigerous royal officials omitted here. Question marks indicate extrapolations for missing entries.

(a) Gloucester was paid an extra £666 13s. 4d. for the next quarter because he took a larger-than-indented-for retinue to France. This was probably because some of his knightly retainers (Parr, Burgh, Tunstall, Harington, Mauleverer and Mountfort) subsumed their indentures to his.

(b) The manuscript notes that Buckingham 'went home' before embarkation.

(c) Lord Grey of Ruthyn was heir to the Earl of Kent.

(d) Humphrey Talbot was the uncle of the Earl of Shrewsbury.

(e) Ralph Hastings was the younger brother of Lord Hastings.

(f) John Grey was heir to Lord Grey of Wilton.

(g) Thomas Howard was heir to Lord Howard.

(h) John Fiennes was heir to Lord Dacre of the South.

(i) William Stanley was the younger brother of Lord Stanley.

(j) John FitzAlan was a younger son of the Earl of Arundel.

(k) The total financial disbursement differed from the first list by only £265, despite considerable divergence in the numbers tallied. Creative accounting, perhaps?

TITULUS REGIUS

Key passages italicized

To the High and Mighty Prince Richard, Duke of Gloucester

Please it your Noble Grace to understand the consideration, election, and petition of us the lords spiritual and temporal and commons of this realm of England, and thereunto agreeably to give your assent, to the common and public weal of this land, to the comforts and gladness of all the people of the same.

First, we consider how that heretofore in time passed this land many years stood in great prosperity, honour, and tranquillity, which was caused, forasmuch as the kings then reigning used and followed the advice and counsel of certain lords spiritual and temporal, and other persons of approved wisdom, prudence, policy, and experience, dreading God, and having tender zeal and affection to indifferent ministration of justice, and to the common and politic weal of the land; then our Lord God was feared, loved, and honoured; then within the land was peace and tranquillity, and among neighbours concord and charity; then the malice of outward enemies was mightily repressed and resisted, and the land honourably defended with many great and glorious victories; then the intercourse of merchandises was largely used and exercised; by which things above remembered, the land was greatly enriched so that as well the merchants and artificers as other poor people, labouring for their living in diverse occupations, had competent gain to the sustenance of them and their households, living without miserable and intolerable poverty.

But afterward, when that such as had the rule and governance of this land, delighting in adulation and flattery and *led by sensuality and concupiscence*, followed the council of persons insolent, vicious, and of inordinate avarice, despising the council of good, virtuous, and prudent persons such as above be remembered, the prosperity of this land daily decreased so that felicity was turned into misery, and prosperity into adversity, and the order of policy, and of the law of God and man, confounded; whereby it is likely this realm to fall into extreme misery and desolation – which God defend – without due provision of convenable remedy be had in this behalf in all godly haste.

Over this, amongst other things, more specifically we consider how that the time of the reign of King Edward IV, late deceased, *after the ungracious pretence of marriage, as all England hath cause to say, made between the said King Edward IV and Elizabeth, sometime wife to Sir John Grey, Knight, late naming herself and many years heretofore Queen of England,* the order of all politic rule was perverted, the laws of God and of God's church, and also the laws of nature, and of England, and also the laudable customs and liberties of the same, wherein every Englishman is inheritor, broken, subverted, and slighted, against all reason and justice, so that this land was ruled by self-will and pleasure, fear and dread, all manner of equity and laws laid apart and despised, whereof ensued many inconveniences and mischiefs, as murders, extortions, and oppressions, namely of poor and impotent people, so that no man was sure of his life, land, nor livelihood, nor of his wife, daughter, no servant, every good maiden and woman standing in dread to be ravished and befouled.

And besides this, what discords, inward battles, effusion of Christian men's blood, and namely, by the destruction of the noble blood of this land, was had and committed within the same, it is evident and notorious through all this realm unto the great sorrow and heaviness of all true Englishmen. *And here also we consider how the said pretended marriage, between the above named King Edward and Elizabeth Grey, was made of great presumption, without the knowing or assent of the lords of this land, and also by sorcery and witchcraft, committed by the said Elizabeth and her mother, Jacquetta Duchess of Bedford, as the common opinion of the people and the public voice and fame is through all this land*; and hereafter, if and as the case shall require, shall be proved sufficiently in time and place convenient. And here also we consider how that the said pretended marriage was made privately and secretly, with edition of banns, in a private chamber, a profane place, and not openly in the face of the church, after the laws of God's church, but contrary thereunto, and the laudable custom of the Church of England.

And how also, that at the time of the contract of the same pretended marriage, and before and long time after, the said King Edward was and stood married and troth plighted to one Dame Eleanor Butler, daughter of the old Earl of Shrewsbury, with whom the said King Edward had made a precontract of matrimony, long time before he made the said pretended marriage with the said Elizabeth Grey in manner and form aforesaid. Which premises being true, as in very truth they are true, it appears and follows evidently, that the said King Edward during his life and the said Elizabeth lived together sinfully and damnably in adultery, against the law of God and his church; and therefore no marvel that the sovereign lord and head of this land, being of such ungodly disposition, and provoking the ire and indignation of our Lord God, such heinous mischiefs and inconveniences as is above remembered, were used and committed in the realm amongst the subjects. *Also it appears evidently and follows that all the issue and children of the said king are bastards, and unable to inherit or to claim anything by inheritance, by the law and custom of England.*

Moreover we consider how that afterward, by the estates of this realm assembled in a Parliament held at Westminster the 17th year of the reign of the said King Edward IV, he then being in possession of the crown and royal estate, by an act made in the same Parliament, George Duke of Clarence, brother to the said King Edward now deceased, was convicted and attainted of high treason; as in the same act is contained more at large. *Because and by reason whereof all the issue of the said George was and is disabled and barred of all right and claim that in any wise they might have or challenge by inheritance to the crown and royal dignity of this realm, by the ancient law and custom of this same realm.*

Over this we consider how that ye be the undoubted son and heir of Richard late Duke of York very inheritor to the said crown and royal dignity as in right King of England by way to inheritance and that at this time the premises duly considered there is no other person living but ye only, that by right may claim the said crown and royal dignity, by way of inheritance, and how that ye be born within this land, by reason whereof, as we deem in our minds, ye be more naturally inclined to the prosperity and common weal of the same: and all the three estates of the land have, and may have more certain knowledge of your birth and filiation above said. We consider also, the great wit, prudence, justice, princely courage, and the memorable and laudable acts in diverse battles which we by experience know ye heretofore have done for the salvation and defence of this same realm, and also the great nobleness and excellence of your birth and blood as of him that is descended of the three most royal houses in Christendom, that is to say, England, France, and Spain.

Wherefore these premises by us diligently considered, we desiring affectuously the peace, tranquillity and public weal of this land, and the reduction of the same to the ancient honourable estate, and prosperity, and having in your great prudence, justice, princely courage and excellent virtue, singular confidence, have chosen in all that is in us nd by this our writing choose you, high and mighty Prince unto our King and sovereign lord &c., to whom we know for certain it appertains of inheritance so to be chosen. And hereupon we humbly desire, pray, and require your said noble grace, that according to this election of us the three estates of this land, as by your true inheritance ye will accept and take upon you the said crown and royal dignity with all things thereunto annexed and appertaining as to you of right belonging as well by inheritance as by lawful election, and in case ye do so we promise to serve and to assist your highness, as true and faithful subjects and liegemen and to live and die with you in this matter and every other just quarrel.

For certainly we are determined rather to adventure and commit us to the peril of our lives and jeopardy of death, than to live in such thraldom and bondage as we have lived long time heretofore, oppressed and injured by new extortions and impositions, against the laws of God and man, and the liberty, old policy and laws of this realm wherein every Englishman is inherited. Our Lord God King of all Kings by whose infinite goodness and eternal providence all things have been principally governed in this world lighten your soul, and grant you grace to do, as well in this matter as in all other, all that may be according to his will and pleasure, and to the common and public weal of this land, so that after great clouds, troubles, storms, and tempests, the son of justice and of grace may shine upon us, to the comfort and gladness of all true Englishmen.

Albeit that the right, title, and estate, which our sovereign lord the King Richard III hath to and in the crown and royal dignity of this realm of England, with all things thereunto annexed and appertaining, have been just and lawful, as grounded upon the laws of God and of nature and also upon the ancient laws and laudable customs of this said realm, and so taken and reputed by all such persons as are learned in the above-said laws and customs. Yet, nevertheless, forasmuch as it is considered that the most parte of the people of this land is not sufficiently learned in the above said laws and customs whereby the truth and right in this behalf of likelihood may be hid, and not clearly known to all the people and thereupon put in doubt and question: And over this how that the court of Parliament is of such authority, and the people of this land of such nature and disposition, as experience teaches that manifestation and declaration of any truth or right made by the three estates of this realm assembled in Parliament, and by authority of the same makes before all other thing, most faith and certainty; and quieting men's minds, removes the occasion of all doubts and seditious language:

Therefore at the request, and by the assent of the three estates of this realm, that is to say, the lords spiritual and temporal and commons of this land, assembled in this present Parliament by authority of the same, be it pronounced, decreed and declared, that our said sovereign lord the king was and is very and undoubted king of this realm of England; with all things thereunto within this same realm, and without it annexed unite and appertaining, as well by right of consanguinity and inheritance as by lawful election, consecration and coronation. And over this, that at the request, and by the assent and authority above said be it ordained, enacted and established that the said crown and royal dignity of this realm, and the inheritance of the same, and other things thereunto within the same realm or without it annexed, unite, and now appertaining, rest and abide in the person of our said sovereign lord the king during his life, and after his decease in his heirs of his body begotten. And especially, at the request and by the assent and authority above said, be it ordained, enacted, established, pronounced, decreed and declared that the high and excellent Prince Edward, son of our said sovereign lord the King, be heir apparent of our said sovereign lord the king, to succeed him in the above said crown and royal dignity, with all things as is aforesaid thereunto unite annexed and appertaining, to have them after the decease of our said sovereign lord the king to him and to his heirs of his body lawfully begotten.

WORKS CONSULTED

Place of Publication London unless otherwise stated.

If you read only one other book, make it *The Politics of Fifteenth-Century England: John Vale's Book* (Stroud, 1995) by Margaret Kekewich, Colin Richmond, Anne Sutton, Livia Visser-Fuchs and John Watts. It is an exemplary presentation of selections from a unique treasure trove of primary sources, accompanied by brilliant analytical essays. See also Simon Payling's invaluable articles listed separately at the end of this bibliography.

Most of the printed works listed are only available in research libraries. However, anyone can access the first section below by searching for the titles online. There may well be more, but these are the ones I consulted. Also, the learned articles I consulted are listed separately and by journal for the benefit of those with access to JSTOR.

ONLINE SOURCES (PRIMARY AND SECONDARY)

Anon., *The Edward IV Roll* (1461?).

Anon., *The Talbot Shrewsbury Book* (1445).

Anon., *A Chronicle of London from 1089 to 1483* (1828).

Bain, John (ed.), *Calendar of Documents Relating to Scotland 1357–1509* (1988).

Brooke, Richard, *Visits to the Fields of Battle in England of the Fifteenth Century* (1857).

Brown, Horatio (ed.), *Calendar of state papers and manuscripts relating to English affairs, existing in the archives and collections of Venice, and in other libraries of northern Italy* (1864).

Burley, Peter, Michael Elliott and Harvey Watson, *The Battles of St Albans* (Barnsley, 2007).

Carpenter, Christine, *Locality and polity: a study of Warwickshire landed society, 1401–1499* (1992).

Castor, Helen, *The King, the Crown and the Duchy of Lancaster* (Oxford, 2000).

Commynes, Philippe de (trans. Michael Jones), *Memoirs: the reign of Louis XI, 1461–83* (1972).

Coward, Barry, *The Stanleys, Lords Stanley and Earls of Derby* (Manchester, 1983).

Curry, Anne, *The Hundred Years' War* (2003).

Davey, John, 'The Battle of Towton 1461 – A Re-Assessment' (2003).

Davies, John (ed.), *An English Chronicle of the reigns of Richard II, Henry IV, Henry V, and Henry VI written before the year 1471* (1856).

Dictionary of National Biography (Oxford, 2004–).

Dillon, Viscount and W. Hope (eds.), *Pageant of the birth, life and death of Richard Beauchamp, Earl of Warwick* (1914).

Dockray, Keith, 'The Battle of Wakefield and the Wars of the Roses', *The Ricardian* (June 1992).

Du Boulay, Francis (ed.), *Documents Illustrative of Medieval Kentish Society* (Ashford, 1964).

Ellis, Henry, *Hall's Chronicle* (1809, reprinted 1965).

English Heritage, *Battlefield Reports: Blore Heath, Northampton, Towton* (1995).

Flenley, Ralph (ed.), *Six Town Chronicles of England* (1911).

Fortescue, Sir John (ed. Shelley Lockwood), *On the Laws and Governance of England* (1997).

Gairdner, James (ed.), *The Historical Collections of a Citizen of London* (1876) (mainly a history of London from 1189 to 1469 known as *Gregory's Chronicle*).

Gairdner, James (ed.), *Three Fifteenth-Century Chronicles* (1880).

Gairdner, James (ed.), *The Paston Letters, 1422–1509* (1904).

Giles, John (ed.), *The Chronicles of the White Rose of York* (1845) (includes 'Hearne's Fragment', the 'Warkworth Chronicle' (q.v.) and the 'Historie of the Arrivall' (*q.v.*).

Given-Wilson, Chris (ed.), *Parliament Rolls of Medieval England 1275–1504*, vols. 10–16 (Woodbridge, 2005).

'Gregory's Chronicle' – see Gairdner, James (ed.), *The Historical Collections of a Citizen of London.*

Haliwell, James (ed.), *Warkworth's Chronicle* (1839).

'Hearne's Fragment' – see Giles, John (ed.), *The Chronicles of the White Rose of York.*

Hinds, Allen (ed.), *Calendar of State Papers and Manuscripts in the Archives and Collections of Milan – 1385–1618* (1912).

'Historie of the Arrivall' – see Giles, John (ed.), *The Chronicles of the White Rose of York.*

Kingsford, Charles (ed.), *Chronicles of London* (Oxford, 1905).

Knowles, R., 'The Battle of Wakefield: the Topography', *The Ricardian* (June 1992).

Michael Drayton, 'The Miseries of Queen Margaret' in Samuel Johnson (ed. Alexander Chalmers) *The works of the English poets, from Chaucer to Cowper* (1810).

New Advent, *The Catholic Encyclopedia* (1917).

Nichols, John (ed.), *Chronicle of the Rebellion of Lincolnshire 1470* (1847).

Oxford Dictionary of National Biography (2004–).

Pollard, A., 'Percies, Nevilles and the Wars of the Roses', *History Today* (1993).

Power, Eileen, *The Wool Trade in English Medieval History* (1941).

Richmond, C., 'Propaganda in the Wars of the Roses', *History Today* (1992).

Riley, Henry (ed.), *Registra quorundam abbatum monasterii S. Albani*, 2 vols. (1872–3).

Rosenthal, Joel, 'Other victims: peeresses as war widows, 1450–1500', *History*, 72 (1987).

Rous, John, *The Warwick Roll* (1483).

Site of the Battle of Northampton, 1460: Conservation Management Plan (Northampton, 2013).

Stevenson, Joseph (ed.), *Letters and Papers Illustrative of the Wars of the English in France during the reign of Henry the Sixth* (1861) (contains William Worcester's 'Annales Rerum Anglicarum').

Sutherland, Tim, 'Killing time: challenging the common perceptions of three medieval conflicts – Ferrybridge, Dintingdale and Towton', *Journal of Conflict Archaeology*, 5:1 (2010).

Thomson, Thomas (ed.), *The Auchinleck Chronicle: Ane Schort Memoriale of the Scottis Corniklis for Addicioun* (1819).

The Towton Battlefield Archaeological Survey Project, *Unknown soldiers: the discovery of war graves from the battle of Towton*.

UK Battlefields Resource Centre.

Vergil, Polydore (ed. Dana Sutton), *Anglica Historia* (1555) (critical edition, 2005).

Vigiles du roi Charles VII (1487) – illustrations only.

Walker, John, *Fourmilab Calendar Converter* (2009).

'Warkworth Chronicle' – see Giles, John (ed.), *The Chronicles of the White Rose of York*.

Wavrin, Jehan de (trans. William and Edward Hardy), *Collection of the chronicles and ancient histories of Great Britain* (1864).

Worcester, William, 'Annales Rerum Anglicarum' – see Stevenson, Joseph
(ed.), *Letters and Papers Illustrative of the Wars of the English in France
during the reign of Henry the Sixth.*

PRINTED PRIMARY SOURCES

'Benet's Chronicle' – see Harriss, G. and M. (eds.), *John Benet's Chronicle for
the Years 1400 to 1462.*

'Crowland Chronicle Continuations' – see Pronay, Nicholas and John Cox
(eds.), *The Crowland Chronicle Continuations, 1459–86.*

Dockray, Keith, *Henry VI, Margaret of Anjou and the Wars of the Roses: a
Source Book* (Stroud, 2000).

Fiorato, Veronica, Anthea Boylston and Christopher Knüsel (eds.), *Blood
Red Roses: The Archaeology of a Mass Grave from the Battle of Towton*
(Oxford, 2000).

Hallam, Elizabeth (ed.), *The Wars of the Roses: From Richard II to Bosworth
Field as seen through the eyes of contemporaries* (1998).

Harriss, G. and M. (eds.), *John Benet's Chronicle for the Years 1400 to 1462*,
Camden Miscellany, Vol. XXIV, 4:9 (1972).

Myers, Alec (ed.), *English Historical Documents: Volume 4, 1327–1485* (1995).

Pisan, Christine de (trans. Sarah Lawson), *The Treasure of the City of Ladies,
or, The Book of the Three Virtues* (2003).

Pius II, Pope (ed. and trans. Margaret Meserve and Macello Simonetta),
Commentaries (2003).

Pronay, Nicholas and John Cox (eds.), *The Crowland Chronicle
Continuations, 1459–86* (1986) (though there is a nineteenth-century
version online, this one is superior).

'Somnium Vigilantis' – see article in *Historical Research* by Margaret
Kekewich.

'The Stow Relation' – see Kekewich et al., *John Vale's Book.*

Sutherland, Tim and Simon Richardson, 'Arrows point to mass graves:
finding the dead from the Battle of Towton', in Scott, Babits and
Haeker (eds.), *Fields of Conflict: Battlefield Archaeology from the Roman
Empire to the Korean War* (2007).

SECONDARY SOURCES

BOOKS

Adams, Max, *The King in the North* (2013).

Allmand, Christopher, *Lancastrian Normandy, 1415–1450* (Oxford, 1983).

Ambühl, Rémy, *Prisoners of War in the Hundred Years War: Ransom Culture in the Late Middle Ages* (Cambridge, 2013).

Archer, Rowena and Simon Walker (eds.), *Rulers and ruled in late medieval England* (1995).

Baldwin, David, *Elizabeth Woodville* (Stroud, 2012).

Barber, Richard (ed.), *The Pastons: A Family in the Wars of the Roses* (Woodbridge, 1993).

Barker, Juliet, *Conquest: The English Kingdom of France in the Hundred Years War* (2009).

Bean, John, *The Estates of the Percy Family* (Oxford, 1958).

Bell, Adrian, Anne Curry, Andy King and David Simpkin (eds.), *The Soldier in Later Medieval England* (Oxford, 2013).

Bicheno, Hugh, *Vendetta: High Art and Low Cunning at the Birth of the Renaissance* (2007).

Boardman, Andrew, *The Medieval Soldier in the Wars of the Roses* (Stroud, 1998).

Boardman, Andrew, *The Battle of Towton* (Stroud, 2000).

Boardman, Andrew, *The First Battle of St Albans* (Stroud, 2006).

Bramley, Peter, *A Companion & Guide to the Wars of the Roses* (Stroud, 2011).

Brenan, Gerald, *A History of the House of Percy*, Vol. I (1902).

Carpenter, Christine, *The Wars of the Roses: Politics and the Constitution of England, 1437–1509* (Cambridge, 1997).

Cheetham, Anthony, *The Wars of the Roses* (2000).

Chrimes, Stanley, Charles Ross and Ralph Griffiths (eds.), *Fifteenth-century England, 1399–1509: Studies in Politics and Society* (Manchester, 1972).

Clark, Linda and Christine Carpenter (eds.), *Political Culture in Late Medieval Britain* (Woodbridge, 2004).

Contamine, Philippe (trans. Michael Jones), *War in the Middle Ages* (1984).

Cox, Helen, *The Battle of Wakefield Revisited* (York, 2010).

Dockray, Keith, *William Shakespeare: The Wars of the Roses and the Historians* (Stroud, 2002).

Duggan, Anne (ed.), *Queens and Queenship in Medieval Europe* (Woodbridge, 1997).

Evans, Howell, *Wales and the Wars of the Roses* (1995).

Goodman, Anthony, *The Wars of the Roses: Military Activity and English Society* (Stroud, 2004).

Goodman, Anthony, *The Wars of the Roses: the Soldiers' Experience* (Stroud, 2005).

Goodwin, George, *Fatal Colours: Towton 1461* (2011).

Gregory, Philippa, David Baldwin and Michael Jones, *The Women of the Cousins' War* (2013).

Griffith, Paddy (ed.), *The Battle of Blore Heath, 1459* (Nuneaton, 1995).

Griffiths, Ralph (ed.), *Patronage, the Crown and the Provinces* (Gloucester, 1981).

Griffiths, Ralph, *King and Country: England and Wales in the Fifteenth Century* (1991).

Griffiths, Ralph, *The Reign of King Henry VI* (Stroud, 1998).

Haigh, Philip, *The Battle of Wakefield* (Stroud, 1996).

Harriss, Gerald, *Cardinal Beaufort* (Oxford, 1988).

Harriss, Gerald, *Shaping the Nation: England 1360–1461* (Oxford, 2005).

Harvey, Isobel, *Jack Cade's rebellion of 1450* (Oxford, 1991).

Hicks, Michael, *Warwick the Kingmaker* (Oxford, 1998).

Hicks, Michael, *The Wars of the Roses* (2010).

Hilton, Lisa, *Queen's Consort: England's Medieval Queens* (2008).

Hodges, Geoffrey, *Ludford Bridge & Mortimer's Cross: the Wars of the Roses in Herefordshire and the Welsh Marches* (Little Logaston, 2001).

Johnson, P. A., *Duke Richard of York, 1411–1460* (1988).

Karsten, Peter, *The Military-State-Society Symbiosis* (1999).

Kendall, Paul, *Warwick the Kingmaker* (2002).

Lander, Jack, *Conflict and Stability in Fifteenth-Century England* (1969).

Lander, Jack, *Crown and Nobility 1450–1509* (Montreal, 1976).

Lander, Jack, *The Limitations of English Monarchy in the Later Middle Ages* (Toronto, 1989).

Laslett, Peter, Karla Oosterveen and Richard Smith (eds.), *Bastardy and its Comparative History* (1980).

Loades, Mike, *The Longbow* (Oxford, 2013).

MacFarlane, Alan, *The Origins of English Individualism* (Oxford, 1978).

McFarlane, Kenneth, *England in the Fifteenth Century* (1981).

Maurer, Helen, *Margaret of Anjou* (Woodbridge, 2003).

Nicholson, Ranald, *Scotland: the Later Middle Ages* (Edinburgh, 1974).

Payling, Simon, *Political Society in Lancastrian England: The Greater Gentry of Nottinghamshire* (Oxford, 1991) – see list of articles by author.

Pollard, Anthony, *North-eastern England during the Wars of the Roses* (Oxford, 1990).

Pollard, Anthony (ed.), *The Wars of the Roses* (Basingstoke, 1995).

Pollard, Anthony, *Warwick the Kingmaker* (2007).

Rawcliffe, Carol, *The Staffords, 1394–1512* (Cambridge, 1978).

Reid, Peter, *A Brief History of Medieval Warfare: The Rise and Fall of English Supremacy at Arms: 1344–1485* (2008).

Rodger, Nicholas, *The Safeguard of the Sea: A Naval History of Britain, 660–1640* (1997).

Rose, Susan, *Calais: An English Town in France, 1347–1558* (Woodbridge, 2008).

Rosenthal, Joel and Colin Richmond (eds.), *People, Politics and Community in the Later Middle Ages* (Gloucester, 1987).

Ross, Charles, *The Wars of the Roses* (1976).

Ross, Charles (ed.), *Patronage, Pedigree and Power in Later Medieval England* (Gloucester, 1979).

Sadler, John, *Towton: the Battle of Palm Sunday Field 1461* (Barnsley, 2011).

Santiuste, David, *Edward IV and the Wars of the Roses* (Barnsley, 2013).

Scofield, Cora, *The Life and Reign of Edward the Fourth*, Vol. I (New York, 1967).

Starkey, David, *Crown and Country: a History of England through the Monarchy* (2011).

Storey, R. L., *The End of the House of Lancaster* (Gloucester, 1999).

Spufford, Peter and Wendy Wilkinson, *Handbook of Medieval Exchange* (1986).

Tuck, Anthony, *Crown and Nobility: England 1272–1461* (Oxford, 1999).

Vale, Malcolm, *Charles VII* (1974).

Vale, Malcolm, *War and Chivalry: Warfare and Aristocratic Culture in England, France and Burgundy at the End of the Middle Ages* (1981).

Wagner, John, *Encyclopedia of the Wars of the Roses* (Santa Barbara, 2011).

Watts, John, *Henry VI and the Politics of Kingship* (Cambridge, 1996).

Weir, Alison, *Lancaster and York* (1995).

Wolffe, Bertram, *Henry VI* (Yale, 2001).

ARTICLES

(alphabetical by journal and chronological)

Archaeologia

 Madden, F., 'Political poems of the reigns of Henry VI and Edward IV', 29 (1842).

Archivum Historiae Pontificiae

 Head, C., 'Pius II and the Wars of the Roses', 8 (1970).

Bulletin of the Institute of Historical Research

McFarlane, K., 'Bastard feudalism', 20 (1943–45).

Armstrong, C., 'Politics and the Battle of St Albans, 1455', 33 (1960).

Hicks, M., 'Descent, partition and extinction: the Warwick inheritance', 52 (1979)

Hicks, M., 'The Beauchamp Trust, 1439–87', 54 (1981).

Kekewich, M., 'The attainder of the Yorkists in 1459: two contemporary accounts', 55 (1982).

Bulletin of the John Rylands Library

Myers, A. (ed.), 'The household of Queen Margaret of Anjou, 1452–3', 50 (1957–8).

Virgoe, R., 'The death of William de la Pole, duke of Suffolk', 47 (1964–5).

Virgoe, R., 'William Tailboys and Lord Cromwell: crime and politics in Lancastrian England', 55 (1972–3).

English Historical Review

Ransome, C., 'The Battle of Towton', 4 (1889).

Gilson, J., 'A Defence of the proscription of the Yorkists in 1459', 26 (1911).

Baskerville, G., 'A London chronicle of 1460', 28 (1913).

Kingsford, C., 'An historical collection of the fifteenth century', 29 (1914).

Kingsford, C., 'The Earl of Warwick at Calais in 1460', 37 (1922).

Gray, H., 'Incomes from land in England in 1436', 49 (1934).

Storey, R., 'The wardens of the marches of England towards Scotland 1377–1489', 72 (1957).

Harriss, G., 'The struggle for Calais: an aspect of the rivalry between Lancaster and York', 75 (1960).

Jones, M., 'Somerset, York and the Wars of the Roses', 104 (1989).

Historical Research

Kekewich, M. 'The Attainder of the Yorkists in 1459: Two Contemporary Accounts', 55 (1982) – contains text of *Somnium Vigilantis*.

Rawcliffe, C., 'Richard, Duke of York, the king's "Obesiant Leigeman": a new source for the protectorates of 1454 and 1455', 60 (1987).

Pugh, T., 'Richard, Duke of York, and the rebellion of Henry Holland, Duke of Exeter, in May 1454', 63 (1990).

Journal of Medieval History

Cron, B., 'The Duke of Suffolk, the Angevin marriage, and the ceding of Maine, 1445', 20 (1994).

Medieval History

    Hicks, M., 'Warwick: the reluctant Kingmaker', 1:2 (1991).

Medieval Warfare

    Ingram, M., 'War in Writing', 5:3 (June 2015).

Northern History

    Hicks, M., 'The Duke of Somerset and Lancastrian localism in the North', 20 (1986).

Nottingham Medieval Studies

    Richmond, C., 'The nobility and the Wars of the Roses 1459–61', 21 (1977).

Royal Historical Society Studies in History

    Pollard, A., 'John Talbot and the War in France, 1427–1453', 35 (1983).

Speculum

    Bennett, J., 'The Medieval Loveday', 33 (1958).

    Griffiths, R., 'Local rivalries and national politics: the Percies, the Nevilles, and the Duke of Exeter', 43 (1968).

The Ricardian (not all are online)

    Cron, B., 'Margaret of Anjou and the Lancastrian march on London'(December 1999).

Transactions of the Royal Historical Society

    Armstrong, C., 'The inauguration ceremonies of the Yorkist kings, and their title to the throne', 4:30 (1948).

University of Birmingham Historical Journal

    Kenecht, R., 'The Episcopate and the Wars of the Roses', 6 (1957).

Yorkshire Archaeological Society

    Leadman, A., 'The Battle of Towton', 10 (1889).

    Markham, C., 'The Battle of Towton', 10 (1889).

ARTICLES BY SIMON PAYLING

'The Ampthill dispute: a study in aristocratic lawlesness and the breakdown of Lancastrian Government', *English Historical Review*, 104 (1989).

'Social mobility, demographic change, and landed society in late-medieval England', *Economic History Review*, 45 (1992).

'A Disputed Mortgage: Ralph, Lord Cromwell, Sir John Gra. and the Manor of Multon Hall', in R. Archer and S. Walker (eds.), *Rulers and Ruled in late Medieval England: Essays Presented to Gerald Harriss* (1995).

'The Politics of Family: Late Medieval Marriage Contracts', in R.H. Britnell and A.J. Pollard (eds.), *The McFarlane Legacy* (Stroud, 1995).

'The Later Middle Ages', in R. Smith and J.S. Moore (eds.), *The House of Commons* (1996).

'Murder, motive and punishment in fifteenth-century England: two gentry case-studies', *English Historical Review*, 113 (1998).

'County parliamentary elections in fifteenth-century England', *Parliamentary History*, 17 (1999).

'The economics of marriage in late medieval England: The marriage of heiresses', *Economic History Review*, 54 (2001).

'The Rise of Lawyers in the Lower House, 1395–1536', in L. Clark (ed.), *Parchment and People: Parliament in the Middle Ages* (Edinburgh, 2004).

'Identifiable Motives for Election to Parliament in the Reign of Henry VI: the Operation of Public and Private Factors', in L. Clark (ed.), *The Fifteenth Century, VI: Identity and Insurgency in the Late Middle Ages* (Woodbridge, 2006).

'War and Peace: Military and Administrative Service amongst the English Gentry in the Reign of Henry VI', in P. Coss and C. Tyerman (eds.), *Soldiers, Nobles and Gentlemen: Essays in Honour of Maurice Keen* (Woodbridge, 2009).

'The House of Commons, 1307–1529', in C. Jones (ed.), *A Short History of Parliament* (Woodbridge, 2009).

FURTHER READING

Dates are of the most recent, usually paperback editions
Published in London unless otherwise specified

As it appears I did not make it clear enough the last time, this is not an academic bibliography. It is a guide for readers who may wish to pursue their own investigations online, or by daisy-chaining citations in hard copy. I have cited one or two particularly valuable sources in the text, and recommend below, by category, only other books and articles I found informative or stimulating, rather than make an undifferentiated list of all the works consulted.

Nearly all the primary sources are online, along with an enormous amount of genealogical research. Fascinating nuggets can appear if you simply input a name and date. Wikipedia is often useful, but should be cross-checked where possible against the online *Oxford Dictionary of National Biography*, available to anyone with a public library card, or failing that on sites like *Tudor Place* and *Geni*. The *Dictionary of Welsh Biography* is open access.

The Ricardian is partially online, with more back catalogue being added, and is a cornucopia for the period covered in Part II. An online index identifies earlier articles that can be downloaded as PDFs. Some articles in other journals are also open access, the rest can be accessed via JSTOR. Those I found useful are listed below.

Second-hand books are easy to find online and I have got into the habit of buying those I need for regular reference that cost less than the price of a round trip to the Cambridge University Library, my home from home. Definitely not in that category is Cora Scofield's two-volume biography of Edward IV published in 1923, an ex-library copy of the 1967 edition of which was wincingly expensive but worth every penny for her unrivalled international research.

More recent biographies of Edward IV, Richard III, Clarence and Warwick the Kingmaker are listed below, also valiant efforts to weave the stories of Elizabeth Woodville and Margaret Beaufort from barely adequate facts. Sources beyond the dreams of historians writing about contemporary English subjects illuminate the standard biographies of Louis XI, Charles the Bold and his father Philippe, and Margaret of York.

Robert Stansfield's prohibitively priced study of the South-West and the West Country fills a gaping hole in the historiography of English regional trouble-spots. Howell Thomas Evans's classic account of Wales has aged well thanks to his bardic sources, but is best checked against Ralph Griffiths's more recent study. The North has been well served by Anthony Pollard and others. No specifically regional studies have been written about the Midlands, East Anglia, the Home Counties or the South-East, but some partial accounts are listed below.

ONLINE PRIMARY SOURCES (search by title)

Anglica Historia (Polydore Vergil).
Battlefields Resource Centre (Battlefields Trust).
Bosworth Contemporary and Tudor Accounts (by permission of Michael Bennett *q.v.*).
Calendar of documents relating to Scotland 1357–1509.
Calendar of Patent Rolls (1461–67; 1467–77; 1476–85).
Calendar of state papers and manuscripts in the archives and collections of Milan.
Calendar of state papers and manuscripts relating to English affairs, existing in the archives and collections of Venice, and in other libraries of northern Italy.
Cely Letters 1472–88.
Chronicle of the Rebellion in Lincolnshire.
Chronicles of London.
Chronicles of the White Rose of York, contains:
 Hearne's Fragment of an Old Chronicle from 1460 to 1470.
 Doctor John Warkworth's Chronicle of the first thirteen years of King Edward the Fourth.
 History of the Arrivall of Edward IV in England and the final recovery of his kingdoms from Henry VI A.D. 1471.
 The Manner and Guiding of the Earl of Warwick at Angiers.

Chroniques (Jean Molinet).

Collection of the chronicles and ancient histories of Great Britain (Jehan de Wavrin).

Complete peerage of England, Scotland, Ireland, Great Britain, and the United Kingdom (lead editor George Cockayne).

Crowland Chronicle Continuations (the hard copy 1986 edition by Nicholas Pronay and John Cox is better).

Excerpta Historica (contains confession of Robert Welles).

Fabyan's 'The new chronicles of England and France', in two parts.

Gerhard von Wesel's Newsletter from England, 17 April 1471 (Hannes Kleineke).

Gregory's Chronicle.

Hall's Chronicle.

History of King Richard the Third (Thomas More).

Letters and Papers, Foreign and Domestic, Henry VIII, Vol. 8, January–July 1535 (contains Chapuys-Cromwell conversation).

Memoirs (Philippe de Commynes).

Oeuvres de Georges Chastellain.

Parliament Rolls of Medieval England 1275–1504.

Paston Letters.

Stonor Letters and Papers 1290–1483.

Usurpation of Richard the Third (Dominic Mancini).

Warwick Roll (John Rous).

SECONDARY SOURCES

BOOKS

BIOGRAPHICAL

Armstrong, Charles, 'The Piety of Cecily Duchess of York', in Douglas Woodruff (ed.), *For Hilaire Belloc: Essays in Honour of his 72nd Birthday* (1942).

Baldwin, David, *Elizabeth Woodville: Mother of the Princes in the Tower* (2012).

Breverton, Terry, *Jasper Tudor: Dynasty Maker* (2014).

Castor, Helen, *Blood & Roses: the Paston Family and the Wars of the Roses* (2005).

Dockray, Keith, *William Shakespeare: The Wars of the Roses and the Historians* (Stroud, 2002).

Dockray, Keith, *Richard III: from Contemporary Chronicles, Letters and Records* (2013).

Dockray, Keith, *Edward IV: from Contemporary Chronicles, Letters and Records* (2015).

Field, Peter, *The Life and Times of Sir Thomas Malory* (1993).

Gregory, Philippa, David Baldwin & Michael Jones, *The Women of the Cousins' War* (2013).

Gristwood, Sarah, *Blood Sisters: The Women behind the Wars of the Roses* (2013).

Hicks, Michael, *False, Fleeting, Perjur'd Clarence: George, Duke of Clarence* (1992).

Hicks, Michael, *Warwick the Kingmaker* (2002).

Horrox, Rosemary, *Richard III: A Study of Service* (2010).

Jones, Michael & Malcolm Underwood, *The King's Mother: Lady Margaret Beaufort* (1993).

Kendall, Paul, *Louis XI* (1974).

Kendall, Paul, *Warwick the Kingmaker* (2002).

Mitchell, Rosamund, *John Tiptoft 1427–1470* (1938).

Rawcliffe, Carol, *The Staffords 1394–1512* (Cambridge, 1978).

Ross, Charles, *Edward IV* (1997).

Scofield, Cora, *The Life and Reign of Edward the Fourth, King of England and of France and Lord of Ireland*, 2 vols. (New York, 1967).

Vaughan, Richard, *Charles the Bold: The Last Valois Duke of Burgundy* (2014).

Vaughan, Richard, *Philip the Good: The Apogee of Burgundy* (2014).

Weightman, Christine, *Margaret of York, the Diabolical Duchess* (Stroud, 2012).

Weir, Alison, *The Princes in the Tower* (2011).

REGIONAL

Carpenter, Christine, *Locality and Polity: a Study of Warwickshire Landed Society* (1992).

Evans, Howell Thomas, *Wales and the Wars of the Roses* (1998 – 1915 edition online).

Griffiths, Ralph (ed.), *Patronage, the Crown and the Provinces in Later Medieval England* (Stroud, 1981).

Griffiths, Ralph, *King and Country: England and Wales in the Fifteenth Century* (1991).

Horrox, Rosemary (ed.), *Richard III and the North* (Hull, 1986).

Pollard, Anthony, *North-Eastern England during the Wars of the Roses* (Oxford, 1990).

Pugh, Thomas (ed.), *The Marcher Lordships of South Wales 1415–1536* (1963).

Stansfield, Robert, *Political Elites in South-West England, 1450–1500: Politics, Governance, and the Wars of the Roses* (2009).

MILITARY

Barnard, Francis (ed.), *Edward IV's French expedition of 1475: the Leaders and their Badges* (1975).

Bell, Adrian, Anne Curry, Andy King & David Simpkin (eds.), *The Soldier in later Medieval England* (2013).

Bicheno, Hugh, *Vendetta: High Art and Low Cunning at the Birth of the Renaissance* (2008).

Bicheno, Hugh, *Elizabeth's Sea Dogs: How the English became the Scourge of the Seas* (2012).

Clark, David, *Barnet 1471: Death of a Kingmaker* (2007).

Cunningham, Sean, 'The Yorkists at War: Military Leadership in the English War with Scotland 1480–82', in Kleineke, Hannes & Christian Slater (eds.), *The Yorkist Age* (2014).

Foard, Glenn & Anne Curry, *Bosworth 1485: a Battlefield Rediscovered* (Oxford, 2013).

Foss, Peter, *The Field of Redemore: the Battle of Bosworth* (1998).

Gill, Louise, *Richard III and Buckingham's Rebellion* (1999).

Goodchild, Steven, *Tewkesbury: Eclipse of the House of Lancaster 1471* (2005).

Goodman, Anthony, *The Wars of the Roses: the Soldiers' Experience* (2005).

Haigh, Philip, '…Where both the hosts fought…': the Rebellions of 1469–70 and the Battles of Edgecote and Lose-Cote Field* (1997).

Hammond, Peter, *The Battles of Barnet and Tewkesbury* (Stroud, 1990).

Ingram, Mike, *Bosworth 1485* (2012).

Jones, Michael, *Bosworth 1485: Psychology of a Battle* (2002).

Lander, Jack, 'The Hundred Years War and Edward IV's Campaign in France', in Arthur Slavin (ed.), *Tudor Men and Institutions* (Louisiana State University, 1972)

Matthews, Rupert, *The Battle of Losecoat Field 1470* (2013).

Rodger, Nicholas, *The Safeguard of the Sea: a Naval History of Britain 660–1649* (2004).

GENERAL

Bellamy, John, *Crime and Public Order in England during the later Middle Ages* (1973).

Bramley, Peter, *A Companion and Guide to the Wars of the Roses* (2011).

Kekewich, Margaret, Colin Richmond, Anne Sutton, Livia Visser-Fuchs & John Watts (eds.), *The Politics of Fifteenth-Century England: John Vale's Book* (1995).

Lander, Jack, *The Limitations of English Monarchy in the Later Middle Ages* (1989).

Pisan, Christine de (trans. Sarah Lawson), *The Treasure of the City of Ladies, or, The Book of the Three Virtues* (2003).

Power, Eileen, *The Wool Trade in English Medieval History* (1941) – online.

Ross, Charles (ed.), *Patronage, Pedigree, and Power in Later Medieval England* (1979).

Wagner, John, *Encyclopedia of the Wars of the Roses* (2011).

ARTICLES

(alphabetical by journal and chronological)

Archaeologia Aeliana

Charlesworth, D., 'Northumberland in the early years of Edward IV' (1952).

Bulletin of the Board of Celtic Studies

Lowe, D., 'The Council of the Prince of Wales and the decline of the Herbert family during the second reign of Edward IV' (1976–78).

Lowe, D., 'Patronage and Politics: Edward IV, the Wydevilles and the Council of the Prince of Wales' (1981).

Bulletin of the Institute of Historical Research

Peake, M., 'London and the Wars of the Roses' (1926–7).

Lander, J., 'Council, administration and councillors' (1959).

Lander, J., 'Marriage and politics in the fifteenth century: the Nevills and the Wydevills' (1963).

Hicks, M., 'Descent, partition and extinction: the Warwick inheritance' (1979).

Hicks, M., 'The Beauchamp Trust, 1439–87' (1981).

Orme, N., 'The education of Edward V' (1984).

Allan, A., 'Royal propaganda and the proclamations of Edward IV' (1986).

Bulletin of the John Rylands Library

Myers, A., 'The household of Queen Elizabeth Woodville 1466–7' (1967–8).

Economic History Review

Payling, S., 'Social mobility, demographic change, and landed society in late-medieval England' (1992).

Payling, S., 'The economics of marriage in late medieval England: the marriage of heiresses' (2001).

English Historical Review

Storey, R., 'The wardens of the marches of England towards Scotland 1377–1489' (1957).

Lander, J., 'The Yorkist council and administration' (1968).
Richmond, C., 'Fauconberg's Kentish rising of May 1471' (1970).
Holland, P., 'The Lincolnshire rebellion of March 1470' (1988).
Virgoe, R., 'The benevolence of 1481' (1989).

Historical Journal
Lander, J., 'Attainder and forfeiture 1453–1509' (1961).

History
Richmond, C., 'English naval power in the fifteenth century' (1967).
Rosenthal, Joel, 'Other victims: peeresses as war widows, 1450–1500' (1987).

Journal of Medieval Military History
Curry, A. & A. Bell, 'Soldiers, weapons & armies in the fifteenth century' (2011).

Nottingham Medieval Studies
Ballard, M., 'An expedition of English archers to Liège in 1467 and the Anglo-Burgundian marriage alliance' (1990).

Northern History
Hicks, M., 'The Duke of Somerset and Lancastrian localism in the North' (1986).

Parliamentary History
Jurkowski, M., 'Parliamentary and prerogative taxation in the reign of Edward IV' (1999).

The Ricardian
Hillier, K., 'The Rebellion of 1483: Part 1', PDF (September 1982).
Hillier, K., 'The Rebellion of 1483: Part 2', PDF (March 1983).
Dockray, K., 'The Yorkshire Rebellions of 1469' PDF (December 1983).
Visser-Fuchs, L., 'The Casualty List of the Battle of Barnet', PDF (March 1988).

Transactions of the Royal Historical Society
Armstrong, C., 'The Inauguration ceremonies of Yorkist Kings and their title to the throne' (1948).
Brown, A., 'The King's councillors in fifteenth-century England' (1969).
Morgan, D., 'The King's affinity in the polity of Yorkist England' (1973).

University of Birmingham Historical Journal
Knecht, R., 'The Episcopate and the Wars of the Roses' (1957).

ACKNOWLEDGEMENTS

To George R. R. Martin for the inspiration and for creating a compelling parallel world.

In particular I want to thank:
Ian Drury, agent extraordinaire, who encouraged me to develop the idea of writing 'The Real Game of Thrones';
Dr Tobias Capwell FSA, Curator of Arms and Armour at the Wallace Collection, for sharing his unique expertise on medieval warfare;
My sister Lyn McMeekin for patiently beta-reading the manuscript;
Richard Milbank, non-fiction publisher at Head of Zeus, for comprehensive editing;
Annabel Warren of Whitefox, only the second copy editor ever to add value to my books.

Many others – you know who you are – have helped me in many ways and I thank you all.

IMAGE CREDITS

Ludlow Castle (Wikimedia Commons)

Stained glass window of Edward IV and Elizabeth Woodville (Topham / Woodmanstern)

King Edward IV (Royal Collection Trust © Her Majesty Queen Elizabeth II, 2016 / Bridgeman Images)

Elizabeth Woodville (Queen's College, Cambridge)

Louis XI of France (Wikimedia Commons)

Charles the Bold, Duke of Burgundy (Wikimedia Commons)

King Richard III (Wikimedia Commons)

INDEX